Outdoors
Canada

Published by The Reader's Digest Association (Canada) Ltd.,
in conjunction with the Canadian Automobile Association

Reader's Digest

Outdoors Canada

Acknowledgments The publisher acknowledges with thanks the contributions of Terence M. Shortt and of Claude Adams, Fred Bruemmer, Joseph MacSween, Boris Miskew, Russell Peden, Norman N. Powe, Susan Purcell, James Stewart, Ian Walker and Adrian Waller, and of Judith Buckner, Georgia Clarke, Sonia Day, Peter Madely and Brendan Walsh.

Thanks is expressed also to the Department of Energy, Mines and Resources (particularly the Secretariat, Canadian Permanent Committee on Geographical Names), Parks Canada and the staffs of the national parks (of the Department of Indian and Northern Affairs), the Department of Fisheries and the Environment (particularly the Canadian Wildlife Service, the Atmospheric Environment Service, the Arctic Biological Station and the Canadian Forestry Service);

To provincial parks administrations and park wildlife services and information services; to provincial and regional tourist associations, tourist bureaus and chambers of commerce, and to the following individuals, organizations and associations:

Alberta Whitewater Association
Canadian Youth Hostels Association
Dr. Francis R. Cook
Dr. C. G. van Zyll de Jong
Fédération de Canotage du Québec
Dr. M. B. Fenton
Dr. John M. Gillett
Dr. W. Earl Godfrey
Dr. Jules Lévesque
McGill University Herbarium
McGill University Libraries
The Mountain Hut
National Herbarium
National Museum of Natural Sciences
Northwest Voyageurs
Elizabeth M. Parnis
A. L. Ringlet
Royal Ontario Museum
Scouts Canada
Dr. Dorothy E. Swales
C. E. Van Wagner
Waskahegan Trail Association
Westmount Library
Dr. D. W. Woodland

EDITOR: Douglas R. Long
ART DIRECTOR AND DESIGNER: Brian E. Priest
ASSOCIATE DESIGNER: Pierre Léveillé
ASSISTANT EDITORS: Keith Bellows (map section), Mary Ricard, and H. Victor Mayhew, Michael Shelton
DESIGN ASSISTANTS: Bob Pucci, Adela Yerushalmi
EDITORIAL RESEARCHERS: Eileen McKee (research editor), Alice Lévesque (map section), Deena Anne Soicher (plants), Horst D. Dornbusch, David L. Dunbar, Roslyn Farmer, John R. F. Gillis, Janet Holmes, Karin Judkins, Lynda Leonard, Susan Marcovitz
PHOTO RESEARCHERS: Penelope Cowie (chief), Lyne Young, Guylaine Mongeau and France Gillespie
COPY PREPARATION: Gilles Humbert (chief), Lynne Abell, Margot Weinreich
ILLUSTRATORS: Anker Odum (The Animals), Elayne Sears (How to Cope, Just for Fun, Camp Cookery, map section), Peter Van Gulik (black-and-white illustrations, except in map section), Diane Desrosiers (Food From the Wild), George Buctel (The Weather)
CARTOGRAPHY: K. G. Campbell Corporation Ltd., Ottawa, and Mary Ashley
INDEXER: Carolyn McConnell
PRODUCTION: Holger Lorenzen, Mark Recher

BOOK DEPARTMENT
DIRECTOR: Louis Hamel
MANAGING EDITOR: George Ronald
MANAGING ART DIRECTOR: James Hayes
ADMINISTRATOR: Denise Hyde-Clarke

SBN: 0-88850-052-1
Printed in Canada 7 8 9 80/5 4 3 2 1

Foreword

Paul Gélinas

H Smith Johannsen

Herman Smith-Johannsen
"Chief Jack Rabbit"

Piedmont, Que.
January 1977

An avid cross-country skier, Johannsen often went into distant Indian country. The Crees, admiring his nimbleness on skis, honored him with the title of *Okumakun Wapoos*—Chief Jack Rabbit. The name stuck, and most Canadians know him today as Jack Rabbit Johannsen. Still an enthusiastic outdoorsman, he skis regularly near his home in the Laurentians.

This book is for everyone who wishes to explore the Canadian wilderness, to observe wildlife at close range, and to find joy and health and happiness through vigorous outdoor experience. It will help the novice to live with the elements and to adapt, as the pioneers did, to difficult conditions. It will encourage the youthful enthusiast to find exhilaration in overcoming obstacles through his own efforts. It will give the armchair explorer a vicarious sense of adventure.

I have spent a great part of my 101 years in the Canadian wilderness. What I know about it I have learned the hard way—I still have much to learn—but I am richer for having endured hardships in the outdoors.

I am thankful that my boyhood in my native Norway prepared me so well for outdoor life in Canada, this vast land bordered by three oceans, a land whose forests, plains, mountains, lakes and rivers offer such abundant variety. Canada's climate and geography provide superb opportunities for fishing, hiking, canoeing, skiing, climbing and countless other outdoor activities.

Hundreds of thousands of Canadians are turning their backs on the cities and are flocking to the out-of-doors. Many formerly inaccessible places can be reached in a matter of hours, in contrast to the months of struggle experienced by the voyageurs. Nevertheless, every wilderness traveler should be well equipped, and ready for the unexpected. In an emergency, he may be forced to rely on his wits to survive. This book will fortify him with sound advice.

But a word of caution. While insight, wisdom and innumerable facts fill these delightful pages, this information should be seen as complementary to practical experience, not a substitute for it. It appears simple in print, but merely reading how to swing an ax does not produce a woodsman. The most vulnerable person in the wilderness is one who thinks he knows it all. Though long on theory, he is short on practice. Overconfidence may lure him into a false sense of security. Only when his book knowledge is tempered by experience and common sense will he be fully able to appreciate the great outdoors.

May all who read this book be inspired to enjoy and protect the wilderness. May we realize that our presence can be in harmony with the wild—or mar it forever.

When we leave the beaten path, our own survival and the survival of the wilderness are at stake. The results are up to us. We must accept the challenge.

Contents

Outdoors: The Challenge

Wild flowers like a patchwork quilt at the foot of a mountain; shadowed forests and sun-sprinkled woodlands; a loon's eerie yodel across a lake; an alpine brook gurgling nature's melody as it leaps and dances from boulder to boulder; the crunch of caribou hooves on crusty arctic snow; morning ghosts of mist haunting a reedy marsh . . . outdoors Canada is all of these, and more. It is the thunder of breakers against a rocky headland on Cape Breton Island, the bellow of a bull moose in northern Ontario, a lonely coyote howl shattering a prairie stillness, the pungence of pines and sea air on the Pacific coast. It is unclimbed mountains, grasslands stretching beyond the horizon, steep-sided gorges where mighty rivers rage, soft green hills that seem to flow in harmony with quiet

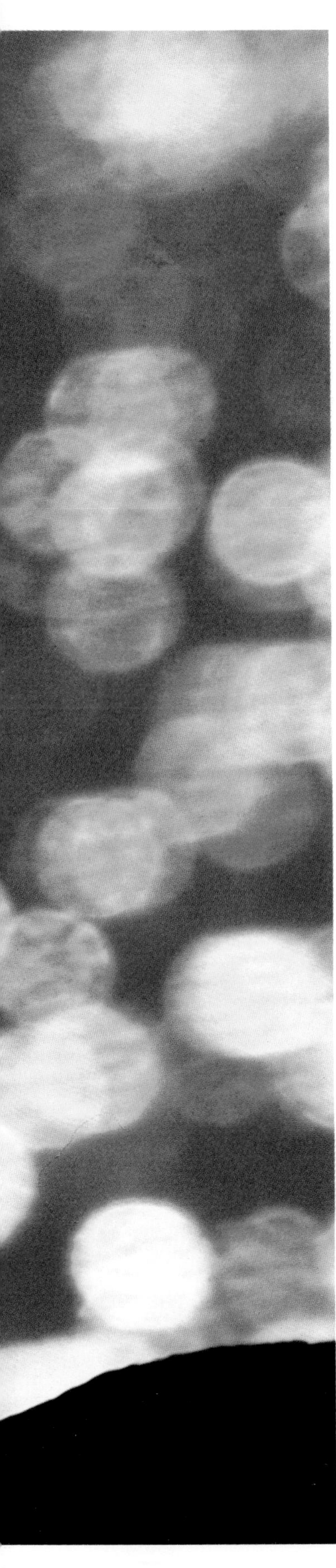

meandering streams, the hum and buzz of a placid pond. It is miles and miles of untrampled wilderness where even weeds are flowers.

The wilderness, changeless but ever changing, preserves a way of life whose pace is the pace of the sun and the seasons. It is a refuge for wildlife—and a refuge for man. It is a cathedral that enshrines man's ancestry, uplifts his spirit and fills him with a sense of his oneness with all living things. It is among our most valuable—and vulnerable—natural resources.

Impressive abundance greeted the people who explored and settled this land. Millions of bison and pronghorn roamed the prairie grasslands. Migrating flocks of passenger pigeons and Eskimo curlews darkened the skies. In 1818 the explorer John Ross saw "vast numbers" of whales and narwhal in Baffin Bay. In 1893 J. W. Tyrrel of the Canadian Geographical Survey saw so many caribou on the tundra that "they could only be reckoned in acres or square miles."

But no longer do great herds of bison and pronghorn raise the prairie dust. The passenger pigeon is extinct, the Eskimo curlew nearly so. Most great whales are endangered species. Caribou, three million strong a century ago, now number about 600,000. Naturalists have called the last half of the 19th century "The Age of Extermination."

For centuries man has faced the wilderness as an adversary to be subdued, a challenge to be overcome, a

resource to be exploited. Almost unchecked he has trapped its animals, felled its trees, dammed its rivers, polluted its lakes, scarred its face with roads and railways, and gouged gaping wounds to extract its minerals.

The pioneers had little incentive to practice conservation. Always, just over the next hill, there were more furs, more trees, more fish, more minerals. Today few natural stands of giant Sitka spruce or Douglas fir remain. Many fur-bearing mammals are near extinction. Fish populations have suffered seriously from pollution and overfishing. Spectacular mineral finds now are rare. There are not many "next hills," no more new frontiers.

Fortunately, although the wilderness suffered in silence, farsighted persons cried out in its defense. In 1887, 260 square miles were set aside for Rocky Mountains (now

Banff) Park, Canada's first national park. Today it preserves and protects 2,564 square miles of spectacular scenery along 150 miles of the eastern slope of the Continental Divide. Here, amid towering peaks, crystal lakes, color-splashed meadows and massive glaciers, visitors can hike more than 700 miles of trails, choose from among 2,500 campsites, raft down the churning Bow River, swim, fish, ski, climb a mountain—do anything the outdoors has to offer.

Since Rocky Mountains Park was created, 27 other national parks and hundreds of provincial parks, wildlife sanctuaries, nature preserves, wilderness regions, forest reserves and recreation areas have been established. From

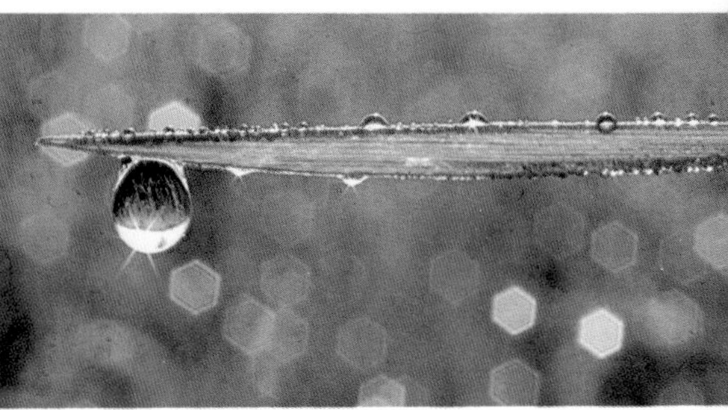

semitropical Point Pelee to cold and remote Auyuittuq on Baffin Island, from the 1,000 acres of St. Lawrence Islands Park (Canada's smallest national park) to the 17,300 square miles of Wood Buffalo (the largest national park in the world), Canada is a wonderland of wilderness. It is picturesque provincial parks within an hour's drive of

major cities—and huge natural areas accessible only by aircraft. It is western Canada's mountain parks (seven in all) sprawling over an area larger than Lake Ontario. These include 4,200-square-mile Jasper National Park (one of Canada's largest mountain parks) and Yoho National Park where spectacular Takakkaw Falls plunges 1,248 feet over the rim of the Yoho Valley.

Although much of Canada is a paradise for the camper, fisherman, canoeist, backpacker and winter sportsman,

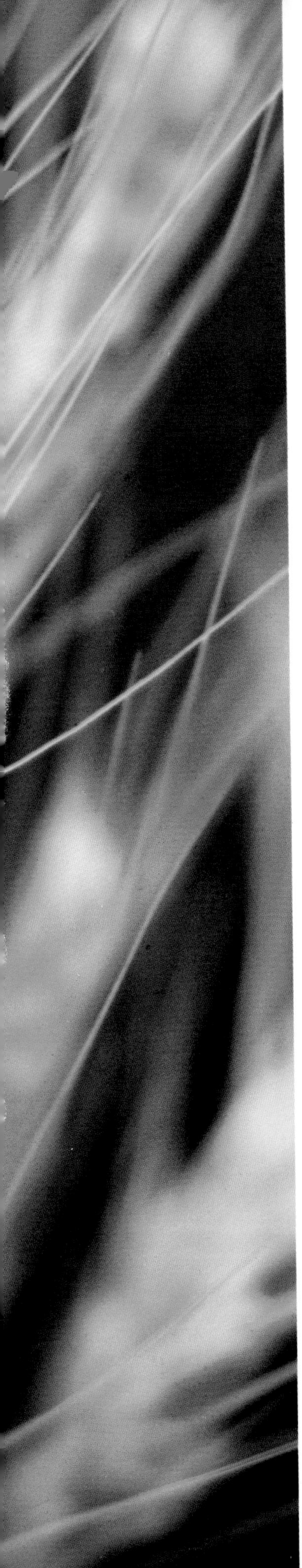

few Canadians really know the variety of their immense land. Most are familiar with Niagara Falls, the Cabot Trail, the principal cities and the most popular scenic attractions. But few appreciate the compelling beauty of the Canadian outdoors as Susanna Moodie did when, in 1853, she wrote: "Beautiful—most beautiful in her rugged grandeur is this vast country. How awful is the sublime solitude of her pathless woods! What eloquent thoughts flow out of the deep silence that broods over them! We feel as if we stood alone in the presence of God, and nature lay at His feet in speechless adoration."

Our cities, our towns, our homes provide every conceivable comfort. But they spawn pollution and traffic and noise and ever-growing ugliness. When we tire of concrete and steel, we need to experience the natural world. When we grow weary of daily routines and hectic living, we must tune into the ancient rhythms of the sea,

the sun, the seasons. We need to close our eyes and listen to the singing of birds, to sniff the delicate fragrance of a forest after rain, to lie on the ground and dream at the sky through the spreading branches of a century-old oak, to kneel in the grass and examine the minute perfection of nature.

Civilization and wilderness make poor neighbors but Canadians are fortunate that our wilderness is so close we can be refreshed by it. All you need to begin a lasting relationship with the outdoors are sturdy legs, observant eyes and a sense of adventure. Naturalist John Muir, who hiked and paddled through thousands of miles of wilderness in Canada and the United States, carried no gun, no tent, no sleeping bag. Tea, stale bread and the bounty of the wild sustained him. He relied upon nature as a friend and learned that she was the finest friend a man could have.

Whether you seek such a rugged life or choose the

comforts of a modern tent, a trailer, a motor home or a cottage, you will be most rewarded when you become intimate with the countryside. You will get closer to the wild and to its wildlife if you trade your outboard motor for a paddle, your trail bike for hiking boots, your snowmobile for cross-country skis.

Explore the outdoors in summer, fall, winter and spring and you will be spellbound by the striking displays and changeability of the seasons. Perhaps you will be inspired as painter A. Y. Jackson was when he said of a Canadian landscape: "In summer it was green, raw greens all in a tangle; in autumn it flamed with red and gold; in winter it was wrapped in a blanket of dazzling snow, and in the springtime it roared with running waters and surged with new life . . . ."

Teach yourself to see more than the sweeping scenic views. Look for the little things. Listen for the quiet sounds. Walk in the rain. Watch the sunset. Count the stars. Enjoy the perfume of a mountain meadow. Look closely at the intricate structure of a wild flower. Be silent. Savor the solitude of a woodland clearing. Be still and the wilderness will talk to you, will share its secrets, will stir your soul.

"Climb the mountains and get their good tidings," John Muir exhorted. "Nature's peace will flow into you as sunshine flows into trees. The winds will blow their freshness into you, while cares drop off you like autumn leaves."

To enjoy, to appreciate, to want to protect the Canadian outdoors you must spend time in it. But never forget that the wilderness is fragile, with only limited ability to accommodate man. We must respect this vulnerability in order to preserve and to protect our wild country. Nature writer Fred Bodsworth warns: "If we go on as we are, we will destroy in the next 50 years everything that poets have been singing about for the past two thousand."

Those who love the wilderness enter it humbly. They take from it only photographs and memories, leaving behind nothing but footprints. Instead of littering, they carry out what they carried in. They understand that modern man can be no more than a visitor to the wild. If he visits too often or too carelessly there will one day be no wilderness.

Outdoors: The Animals

Every living thing is either an animal or a plant. An animal moves and it feeds on plants or other animals. A plant does not move and it usually manufactures its own food. The more than a million species of animals in the world include about 30,000 of bony fishes, 3,000 of amphibians, 5,000 of reptiles, 8,700 of birds and 4,500 of mammals. The rest of the animal kingdom is made up of invertebrates (animals without backbones), including 750,000 species of insects, 26,000 of crustaceans and some 175,000 single- and multi-celled creatures.

To survive, often in harsh physical and climatic conditions, animals must obtain food, secure shelter, escape predators, resist parasites and reproduce. Most animals in Canada are well equipped to survive Canadian winters. Many escape the cold by migrating south in the fall or combat it by growing a winter coat of fur or feathers. Some animals store food for winter; others hibernate, living off body fat.

Animal life varies dramatically from region to region.

• Little vegetation and few species of land animals are found in the Arctic but its waters support a great number and variety of seals, whales, fishes and seabirds.

• In the coniferous forests of northern Canada, winters are long and cold, summers short and warm. The bark, buds and seeds of coniferous trees provide year-round nourishment for hares, squirrels and birds. In winter, animals such as moose trample snow to feed on exposed brushwood. Birds, such as warblers, flycatchers and thrushes, flock to northern forests to feed on the numerous insects found there in summer. Birds of prey, such as owls and hawks, and plant eaters, such as crossbills and grouse, are year-round residents.

• In mixed and deciduous forests farther south, fallen leaves harbor a multitude of insects. Insect-eating mammals, such as shrews, and birds, such as tree swallows, thrive there in summer. In winter, the insect-eating birds migrate; the insect-eating mammals feed on plants.

• Grasslands support plant eaters, such as mule deer and partridges, and their predators. Many animals of the grasslands shelter in burrows to escape extremes of hot and cold.

• Canada's coastal and inland waters teem with animal life, such as fishes, amphibians and marine mammals, all of it ultimately dependent on floating colonies of microscopic plankton.

Silhouetted at sunset, a solitary caribou grazes on an arctic hillside.

Mammals

The Great Blue Whale...the Pygmy Shrew

Mammals are animals that nourish their young with milk from mammary glands. All such creatures—and birds—are thought to have evolved from reptiles. Mammals have inhabited the earth for more than 65 million years. The scientific class *Mammalia* includes 19 living orders of mammals.

Of the 3,200 species of land mammals, 163 are found in Canada. Thirty-three of the world's 85 species of whales frequent Canadian waters—including the 150-ton blue whale, the largest creature known to man. The pygmy shrew, weighing only a tenth of an ounce, is Canada's smallest mammal.

All mammals breathe air through lungs. They have internal skeletons. Backbones are flexible (unlike the partially fused backbones of birds) and there are two sets of teeth—infant teeth are replaced by adult teeth.

Unlike reptiles but like birds, mammals are warm-blooded and maintain a constant body temperature. While reptiles have simple conical teeth, mammals have specialized teeth—chisel-like incisors for gnawing, sharp canines for tearing, flat molars and premolars for chewing. Mammals have body hair; reptiles have scales or bony plates.

Mammals can be classified as *monotremes* (such as the duck-billed platypus and the spiny anteater), whose young are hatched from eggs; *marsupials* (such as the opossum and the kangaroo), whose young are nurtured within the mother's pouch following a brief period in her womb, and *placentals* (which include most mammals in Canada), whose young are incubated in a womb and born at an advanced stage of development.

Man, the most intelligent mammal, has destroyed the habitat of many animals and has hunted, trapped and poisoned species to extinction. Extinct Canadian species include the Great Plains wolf, Dawson caribou and sea mink. Others are endangered: the grizzly bear, black-tailed prairie dog and black-footed ferret.

But strict hunting regulations and the establishment of wildlife parks and sanctuaries are reversing the effect of past overkill.

When attacked by predators, such as wolves, musk-oxen form a circle, facing outward. The young are protected within the circle.

Sharp-rimmed hooves enable musk-oxen to climb ice and rocks with surprising speed.

Umingmak Gives the World's Finest Wool

The musk-ox braves arctic cold, as it survived the Ice Age, in a dense coat of the world's finest wool, overlaid by long, coarse guard hairs. The dark brown wool is qiviut, "the Golden Fleece of the Arctic." Its fibers are twice as long as those of cashmere—the wool of the Kashmir goat—and stronger. A mature musk-ox yields about six pounds of qiviut when it molts in June or July.

The musk-ox's scientific name *(Ovibos moschatus)* means "musky sheep-cow"—but the short-legged, humped animal is neither musky nor a sheep nor a cow nor even an ox. The odor of its urine and droppings has been mistaken for musk. Its closest relative is probably the takin, a goatlike antelope found in the highlands of central Asia. Inuit call the musk-ox *umingmak* (bearded one).

The musk-ox prefers arctic willow but also eats grasses, sedges and flowers. In winter it paws through snow to feed, so survives best in regions of light snowfall. Its thick fleshy lips are well suited to arctic grazing because they can withstand extreme cold and are not easily cut by crusty snow.

At the height of the mating season, in mid-August, long violent fights occur between bulls six years and older. In an average-sized herd there are about five bulls that take part in the rut. Two at a time, they charge head-on from 100 yards or more; the bull that survives all the charges wins the opportunity to mate with the mature cows in the herd.

Musk-oxen are slow to reproduce. A cow usually bears a single calf every second year in the spring. Within a week the newborn nibbles grass. It is usually weaned by the end of its first summer although it may suckle for a year. Bulls reach adult size at age six, cows at four or five. Bulls stand 4½ feet at the shoulder and weigh up to 700 pounds. Cows are smaller and weigh about 500 pounds.

Although fossil evidence suggests that musk-oxen have survived in North America since crossing from Asia 90,000 years ago, their continued existence is precarious. So many musk-oxen were killed by explorers, traders and whalers that by 1917 fewer than a thousand of the shaggy animals were thought to exist in Canada. That year the federal government prohibited musk-ox hunting on the mainland. Musk-oxen on arctic islands were protected by law in 1926. By 1976 there were about 10,000 musk-oxen in Canada. Of those, about 8,500 inhabited arctic islands, 1,500 lived on the northern mainland.

Magnificent Loner of the Woods

Bull-moose rivals clash head-on in a mating-season ritual.

The ungainly yet majestic moose is the largest and least sociable member of the deer family. Its long, lumpy head has a drooping snout and its massive body is covered with cocoa-brown hair. Some full-grown bulls tower over a horse, weigh up to 1,800 pounds and carry magnificent shovel-shaped antlers, which begin as insignificant buttons every April and sometimes attain a remarkable six-foot spread by September. Females are smaller than males and usually have no antlers.

Despite its size, the **moose** *(Alces alces)* moves nimbly and swims strongly. It has been known to swim 12 miles and remain underwater for 30 seconds while searching for water-lily roots, a summer treat it relishes.

Unlike other deer, the moose dislikes company. For most of the year it meanders alone, or occasionally in groups of two or three, on wooded hillsides and along riverbanks, munching small branches of willow and other trees. An adult eats about 50 pounds of twigs a day—moose comes from an Algonkian Indian word meaning twig eater.

Normally shy, bull moose become belligerent in the September-October mating season and rivals may fight ferociously. Sometimes two bulls lock antlers, are unable to get free, and both die of exhaustion and starvation.

The mating season is heralded by the shedding of the soft velvet that covers the growing antlers through spring and summer. Once the velvet has been stripped from the shiny bone, the bull is ready for battle. The antlers drop off in winter.

Cows attract bulls with a pleading bawl, a sound mimicked by a hunter's moose call. Calves are born in May or early June in shrubbery near a lake or river. Within a few days they can outrun a human. Considered to be Canada's fastest growing big-game animals, they gain up to two pounds a day for the first month and up to five pounds daily thereafter until autumn. This rapid growth slows in winter and resumes in spring. Moose are fully grown at about age five.

Once common in Canada, moose populations had declined sharply in their

Shreds of velvet cling to the antlers of a wapiti basking in a late summer sun.

eastern range by the early 1800s because of excessive hunting. The introduction of moose to certain areas since 1930 has helped increase the population to an estimated 1,000,000 in 1976. They are found in all provinces except Prince Edward Island and are especially numerous in northern regions of British Columbia, Alberta, Ontario and Quebec.

Caribou *(Rangifer tarandus)*, the last great migratory mammals in North America, are of the same species as the wild reindeer of Eurasia. Aided by hooves that act as snowshoes, these restless nomads of the North move constantly in orderly herds, sometimes 50,000 to 100,000 strong. Between spring and fall, caribou that inhabit the tundra of northern Quebec, the Yukon and Northwest Territories and Alaska may trek 800 miles from one feeding ground to another, over vast mountain ranges, flat, frozen wastes and icy rivers. Following the mating season, entire herds retrace their steps.

Caribou of the woodlands, larger and darker than those of the tundra, may migrate only several miles in herds of fewer than 200 animals. They inhabit northern boreal forests from British Columbia and the southern Yukon to Newfoundland. Small populations of pale, mostly white caribou remain on Arctic islands all year.

Smaller than moose, caribou are stocky and rarely grow taller than four feet at the shoulder. Lopsided antlers, one often bigger than the other, are usually borne by both sexes. Males wear antlers from May to midwinter but the antlers of females appear in June and drop off during calving the following April. Caribou sometimes chew on calcium-rich discarded antlers.

Wolves sometimes attack caribou herds but usually kill only weak, sick or old animals. Hunting by man is the main reason for the reduction of caribou populations from several million at the turn of the century to an estimated 600,000 in 1972.

Until recently, caribou were the lifeblood of northern native peoples. Caribou meat fed families and dogs; pelts were used for clothing, bedding and tepees; bones and sinews became tools and thread, fat a source of heat and light.

The **wapiti,** or **American elk** *(Cervus elaphus)*, the most vocal deer in Canada, bleats when young, barks when scared and roars, grunts and bugles in the mating season. The high, clear bugling sound of wapiti bulls challenging one another carries a mile or more.

Second in size to the moose in the deer family, the wapiti is an impressive creature. Bulls are big and bulky. Their heavy, 12-pointed antlers mature into a rich polished brown, tipped with ivory. An early fashion of turning antler tips into cutlery handles wiped out many of the species, as did the demand for the wapiti's large, rounded teeth. Elk teeth, tokens of a fraternal order, once fetched up to $75 a pair.

The summer coat of a bull wapiti is sleek and tawny brown with a large, paler patch around the rump and tail. (Wapiti is an Indian word meaning white rump.) Females have darker flanks than males and seldom have antlers.

Primarily grazers, wapiti migrate to alpine meadows in warm weather and to sheltered hills and lakeshores in winter. They paw at light snow to reach the grass beneath. When food is scarce, they may strip bark from trees.

In summer, bulls browse in bachelor bands and females and calves forage together. As the autumn mating season nears, a bull gathers a harem of cows and is truculent toward rivals. During the rest of the year, large mixed herds move peacefully, generally headed by an elderly female.

Besides humans, the wapiti's enemies are cougars, wolves, grizzly bears, lynx and coyotes. Three subspecies linger on in the Rockies and in national parks in British Columbia, Alberta and Manitoba.

Nomads of the North, caribou travel up to 32 miles a day during migration.

Our Vanished Wildlife

Never abundant, the **Dawson caribou** *(Rangifer tarandus dawsoni)* was gunned out of existence by hunters. Extinct since the early 1900s, it was darker and smaller than the Barren Grounds caribou of the mainland. Females, unlike those of other caribou, had no antlers.

The **eastern elk** *(Cervus elaphus canadensis)*, a subspecies of wapiti, disappeared from its range in southern Quebec and Ontario early in the 19th century. It was unable to withstand the hunting pressures that still threaten other wapiti.

Gentle, Graceful Big-Game Animals

Alert to danger, a whitetail buck stands motionless in a woodland clearing.

Canada's most familiar game animal faces harsh winters, natural enemies such as wolves, coyotes, wild dogs, cougars and bobcats, and destruction of its habitat by man. Yet the gentle, graceful **white-tailed deer** *(Odocoileus virginianus)* thrives across southern Canada from Cape Breton Island to southeastern British Columbia.

The whitetail survives because it is well adapted to a habitat of forests and swamp edges and wooded riverbanks. Its innate caution and alertness, its sensitive hearing and acute sense of smell, all help forewarn it of approaching enemies—wolves, cougars, coyotes and bobcats.

Unless in immediate danger, whitetails move stealthily and silently—they can walk through brushwood or brittle leaves without a rustle—or they remain motionless, depending on their camouflage to hide them. When they must flee, they do so with three or four quick bounds, then a high leap, the tail wagging or held high to reveal the white hairs on the buttocks and on the underside of the tail. They can gallop at 30 miles an hour through rugged woodland.

Whitetails are handsomest in early autumn. Their bodies are rounded by fat stored for the lean months of winter, and a thick, gray-brown coat has replaced their thin, chestnut-red summer coat. The winter coat of stiff, air-filled hairs and a soft undercoat insulates so effectively that deer can sleep warmly in the snow without melting it.

Tiny knobs that sprout from the male's forehead in spring are proud, pointed antlers by late summer. A soft covering of blood-rich velvet nourishes the antlers until they are fully grown and bone hard. Then the velvet is shed. In winter, the antlers drop off.

In August and September, males spar in preparation for real battles to come. During the October-to-December rut, bucks fight fiercely for the opportunity to mate. Sometimes a buck is wounded or killed but usually the weaker deer quits the fight uninjured. Bucks occasionally lock antlers and both die of starvation or are killed by predators.

Does, which usually give birth to twins, are doting mothers. They hide each newborn fawn separately, choosing a place where its red coat, broken by hundreds of white spots, is camouflaged on the forest floor. For about a week after birth, fawns have no odor. The mother watches them from a distance so that her scent does not betray them to predators. She returns only to nurse them.

When food is plentiful, whitetails eat 10 to 15 pounds of twigs, leaves, plants and sometimes grasses each day. Second-growth shrubs, saplings and other plants that grow in areas cleared by loggers provide excellent food for deer.

The drastic reduction of wolves and cougars in some areas of Canada has harmed rather than helped the white-tailed deer. When less threatened by natural enemies, deer populations grow so rapidly that many deer die of starvation during severe winters. Those that survive to spring are gaunt shadows of the sleek, sturdy animals of autumn.

The **pronghorn antelope** *(Antilocapra americana)* is an orphan among Canadian game animals—sole survivor of the North American family *Antilocapridae.* Though not closely related to the antelopes of Africa and Asia, it shares their reputation for speed, agility and the ability to withstand the heat of the noonday sun.

It is smaller than most Canadian deer and both sexes have thick, curved, black horns. A tan and white coat of long, brittle hairs and a thin undercoat cover its chunky body in winter. The neck is short and thick, but the legs are slender and graceful. The summer coat is grayish brown.

Pronghorn are energetic, curious and sociable. They congregate in herds, often mingling with cattle, sheep and deer, on the plains of southern Alberta and

Fleet pronghorn raise clouds of prairie dust. Their habitat provides little cover, so pronghorn rely on speed to escape enemies.

Saskatchewan and in the foothills of southeastern Alberta. They have exceptional vision. Pronghorn rely on speed to escape enemies. When frightened, they dart away at speeds up to 60 miles an hour with the rosette of white hairs on the rump raised to alert other pronghorn.

Weeds and twigs make up most of their diet although in spring they eat prairie grasses. In winter, when they must paw through snow to feed, they move to sheltered valleys or windswept hillsides where the snow is not deep. Pronghorn once migrated great distances in search of winter food. Roads, railways and fences now hinder their movement across the prairies. Unlike deer, they refuse to jump barriers, so even a low wire fence can interfere with their migration.

A buck puts on a curious show during the rutting season of August and September. He postures, hangs and waves his head and quickly jumps from one side to the other. He bristles his mane and rosette hairs, often causing ripples to pass through his rump. A buck gathers 2 to 15 does during the mating season and defends his harem against rival males.

Pronghorn kids, normally twins, are dappled gray with cream-colored rumps. They stand on wobbly legs within an hour of birth, run awkwardly the second day and can outrun a man by the fourth. Eagles and ravens sometimes attack kids but bobcats, coyotes and wild dogs are the pronghorn's chief enemies.

An estimated 45 million pronghorn once roamed North America. Hunting, severe winters and the spread of civilization reduced them to 1,400 in Canada by 1924. But hunting restrictions, mild winters and the development of sanctuaries helped the pronghorn population rebound. By 1976, western Canada had more than 20,000—in parks and sanctuaries and on the open plains. The survival of this amiable speedster seemed assured.

Large mulelike ears, a short, black-tipped tail, and a stiff-legged, bouncing gait distinguish the ***mule deer*** (Odocoileus hemionus) *from the whitetail.*

Mountain Sheep: As Rugged as the Rockies

Of the world's six species of wild sheep, two are found in western Canada—the bighorns of southern regions and the thinhorns of the North.

The presence of two subspecies of each main type gives British Columbia the widest variety of wild sheep in Canada. However, bighorns also dwell in Alberta and thinhorns are most populous in the Yukon and the Northwest Territories west of the Mackenzie River.

Two bighorn subspecies—the **Rocky Mountain bighorn** *(Ovis canadensis canadensis)* and the **California bighorn** *(Ovis canadensis californiana)*—are similar in appearance and possess speed, agility and strength.

Powerfully built with stocky bodies and long slender legs, bighorns have a smooth pelage or coat—rich brown in summer and fall but fading to grayish brown by late winter. The rump, except for a short dark tail, is white as are the backs of the legs, the belly and the muzzle.

A typical adult ram stands more than 40 inches high at the shoulder and may weigh between 280 and 340 pounds. Ewes, considerably smaller, measure about 32 inches high at the shoulder and weigh about 150 pounds. The California bighorn tends to be smaller than the Rocky Mountain subspecies and thinhorns are smaller still.

Dall's sheep *(Ovis dalli)*, a thinhorn variety, are creamy white. The most northerly race of sheep in North America, they are apparently related to Siberia's **snow sheep** *(Ovis nivicola)*. The more southerly **Stone's sheep** *(Ovis dalli stonei)* are mostly dark except for white on the face, belly, insides of the legs and rump patch.

The Stone's thinhorn tends to be about 20 pounds heavier than the Dall's, a Stone's ram weighing about 220 pounds.

Wild sheep of both sexes and of all ages engage in butting jousts. These become most vigorous among rams during the rutting season, when horn tips are frequently broken or "broomed." The same horns continue to grow throughout the life of a wild sheep, though growth stops for a period each autumn, resulting in annual horn rings from which the minimum age of the animal can be read.

Stylized butting bouts between evenly matched rams with massive horns provide one of nature's fantastic spectacles. In an elaborate ritual during the October-to-December breeding season, rams inspect each other, then amble apart with apparent unconcern, only to wheel suddenly and charge at a combined speed of up to 70 miles an hour. They survive repeated charges—each with an impact force of more than a ton—thanks to a double layer of bone that protects their foreheads. By fighting and scuffling, males establish a hierarchy of dominance in breeding.

After a gestation period of about 180 days, lambs—occasionally twins—are born in late May or early June. Bighorns, unlike thinhorn sheep, cache their young for about a week.

Ewes, lambs and young rams congregate in bands of 10 or so and stay together all year. Rams over age three spend the summer in bachelor bands, then generally join the ewes, who lead a migration to winter ranges. Winter bands may number 100. In summer, wild sheep are found at elevations between 6,000 and 8,500 feet, in winter at 2,000 to 5,000 feet.

Wild sheep graze on alpine meadows, grassy mountain slopes and in foothill country—always keeping close to rocky cliffs where they can take refuge from natural enemies. Their main food is grass.

Wild sheep are generally much quieter than the domestic variety. Rams snort loudly during the rut. Male and female adults sometimes make throaty rumbles or "blow" when frightened. The keen gaze of their golden eyes is their greatest protection against such predators as cougars, wolves, coyotes, bears, bobcats

When threatened by predators, mountain goats usually retreat to high ledges where their enemies cannot follow.

A male bighorn, with massive curved horns characteristic of the species, toboggans down a hillside. The horns of some older males complete a full circle.

The Stone's ram (above) is similar to the Dall's ram (below), but the Dall's is the most northerly sheep in Canada and the only white wild sheep in the world.

and lynx. The lighter, speedier thinhorns are also preyed upon by wolverines.

Hundreds of thousands of wild sheep once roamed the West. The introduction of domestic livestock by man meant disaster for those wild herds. They were squeezed out of their grassland ranges and ravaged by the diseases of domestic sheep. The populations also suffered from indiscriminate hunting. In 1976 the North American population of bighorns was estimated at 100,000, of which about 53,000 were in Canada.

The **mountain goat** *(Oreamnos americanus)*, found in the mountainous regions of western Canada, inhabits rugged terrain above the alpine tree line where it feeds on grasses, sedges and shrubs. When threatened by cougars or wolves, it scrambles to safety up sheer rocky bluffs and crags.

Mountain goats remain high in the mountains despite snow, although very deep snow sometimes forces them to lower altitudes. Although skidproof pads on their black hooves provide grip and traction, many of the animals die every year when they slip on ice-covered rocks, tumble down steep slopes or fall from precarious ledges. Avalanches sometimes wipe out several members of a herd.

Mountain goats stand up to 45 inches at the shoulder and weigh 150 to 300 pounds—somewhat larger and heavier than domestic goats. Their slender, black horns, which are not shed, develop annual growth rings. The female (nanny) is smaller than the male (billy) and only the tips of her horns are curved.

During the November-December rut, mature males fight and occasionally inflict fatal wounds with their horns. In May or June, the nanny seeks a secluded, sheltered place in a cave or beneath a rock overhang to give birth—usually to one kid. The mother nurses the kid until it can follow her to the herd.

From 60 Million to Fewer Than 27,000

Stampeding bison thunder across the prairie. When bison panic, slow animals in the herd are often trampled.

Until less than two centuries ago some 40 to 60 million **bison** *(Bison bison)* roamed North America from Great Slave Lake to the Rio Grande, from the Rockies to Pennsylvania. Today there are fewer than 27,000 bison—about 12,000 in Canada. The largest herd is the estimated 8,000 in 17,300-square-mile Wood Buffalo National Park on the Alberta/Northwest Territories border.

In 1801, while wintering 60 miles south of Winnipeg on the Red River, Alexander Henry of the North West Company described "incredible" numbers of bison—calling them buffalo, a term that properly refers to African or Asian species. "The ground was covered at every point of the compass," Henry wrote, "as far as the eye could reach, and every animal was in motion."

Even today a herd of a few thousand bison is an impressive spectacle; more common, however, is a band of 4 to 20, traveling in single file. Despite their size —11 feet from head to tail—these creatures with their peculiar pitching gallop cover short distances over rough terrain at more than 30 miles an hour. They have great endurance over long distances and are fresh after as much as 10 miles. Bison communicate within the herd by grunting, but when danger threatens they snort noisily. They swim strongly with their heads and much of their shoulders exposed.

Most bison are bigger than domestic cattle. Males weigh 1,700 to 2,000 pounds, females 1,400 to 1,600. Bulls reach adult size at age six, some standing six feet at the shoulder. Some bison live 40 years but the average is 20 to 25 years. Both sexes have horns, but the cow's are shorter.

In spring and early summer, the bison's winter coat hangs from its body in tattered masses. During this transition period, before the lighter and shorter summer coat is fully grown, they are plagued by insects. To get relief from stinging and itching bites and to shed the remainder of their winter coats, they spend much of their time taking mud and dust baths and rubbing against boulders and trees.

The bellow of a bull in rut can be heard for miles. The breeding season is from July to September, although matings do occur at other times. Cows normally give birth twice in three years—usually to one 50-pound calf each time. The long-legged calves have orange-brown, crinkled coats, and lack their parents' hump. Within half an hour of birth they are on their feet.

Bison are active by day, though they sometimes feed by the light of a full

Slaughter on the Prairie

The Pemmican War of 1814-17, between the fur traders of the North West Company and the Red River settlers, was fought over bison meat. Pemmican, a staple of the West, was made from dried, pounded bison meat, marrow, fat and dried berries. Both sides fear that the other would drive away the bison or reduce their numbers—thus no more pemmican—led to the conflict. Between 1820 and 1874 the annual Red River Hunt—one of history's greatest slaughters, by Métis and Indians ranging west out of Manitoba—further reduced bison populations: on the hunt of 1840 alone more than a million pounds of bison meat were taken. By 1885 the bison was all but extinct in Western Canada.

The animals were gone but their bones remained. A bone collecting industry sprang up in 1890 and soon bison bones were a major export, being sold for $3 to $6 a ton for use in fertilizer and refining sugar. By 1893, the bones were gone.

A bison takes a dust bath to relieve the sting and itch of insect bites and to help remove its winter coat.

moon. They eat mostly grass and ration themselves when food is scarce. Their eyesight is poor but they can scent an intruder that is a mile away. Their only enemies are grizzly bears, cougars, wolves—and men.

Plains Indians depended on bison. Horns were used for drinking vessels, hooves for glue, fat for hair grease and gall for yellow paint. Indians also ate bison meat, made clothes and tents from hides, and used bones for sled runners and toys. But the Indians made only necessary demands on the bison; the white man upset the age-old population balance by commercially marketing hides, meat and bones.

Although bison are as large as domestic cattle and eat only a third as much, their unpredictable temperament makes them difficult to domesticate.

The bison was first protected by Canadian law in 1893. In 1922 the federal government established Wood Buffalo National Park to protect the last remaining herd of **wood bison** *(Bison bison athabascae)*—some 1,500 animals. Later, 6,700 **plains bison** *(Bison bison bison)* were introduced to the area from Wainwright, Alta., and the two species have interbred.

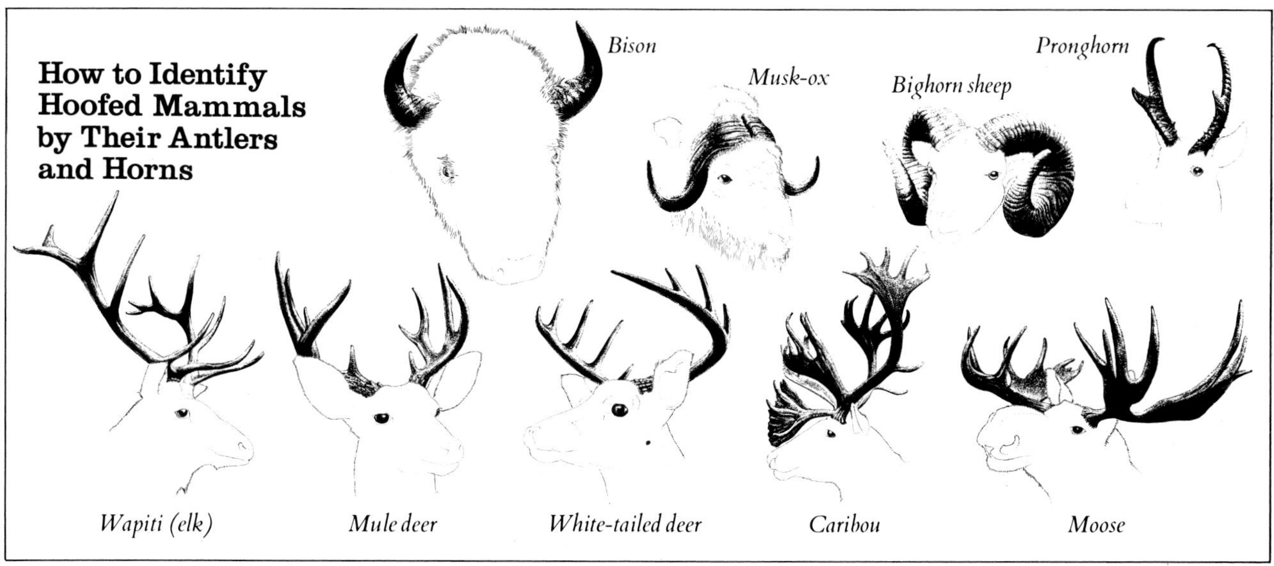

The Masked Bandit Wins a Test of Wits

The raccoon often outwits larger, faster enemies. This raccoon escaped a German shepherd by leading it across the thin ice of a lake.

The hound was gaining, baying excitement into the night as it scented blood. Normally it would have stood no chance against an adult raccoon, but this tired female was heavy with pregnancy. She wanted to bear her young, not waste her own life and that of her unborn kits. There wasn't time to climb a tree so she scurried with rolling gait through lacerating undergrowth to her other element, the lake. The dog followed, dodging thick bushes. Two diving splashes showed how close they were. But the odds were changing fast.

The dog splashed clumsily in the dark direction of his prey. Suddenly he felt sharp claws on his hindquarters. The raccoon climbed up, grabbed the dog's ears, took a breath and put her 20-pound weight on his head. A few bubbled yelps and it was over. The hound's owner would call his name in vain next morning. Later he would see the body floating in the lake, and speculate sourly as to who had done it and why. A neighbor annoyed by the barking? A gang of sadistic youths? Maybe. A raccoon? Impossible!

But scientists have established that the raccoon is remarkably intelligent. It seems to use reason, as a naturalist observed during another chase.

It was early winter, with ice well formed around the edges of the lake but treacherously thin toward the middle. The naturalist's dog barked as it picked up a scent. A round, furry raccoon raced from cover and across the ice. As it neared the middle of the lake, it turned to size up the loping hunter, much faster than itself. There seemed no escape. Then the raccoon lay down and rolled toward the other shore. The thin ice bowed and creaked but held the animal's well-distributed weight. The dog followed until the ice gave way, plunging him into the icy water. . . .

The raccoon's black mask and fondness for bird and turtle eggs has earned it the nickname masked bandit.

Little wonder, with such intelligence, that the **raccoon** *(Procyon lotor)* has survived centuries of hunting by arrow, snare, trap, bullet and dog.

A creature of twilight and darkness, the raccoon deserves its burglar's mask of black fur. It is a glutton and will eat almost anything, stuffing its belly, belching, napping and eating again when food is plentiful. It is a common evening visitor to campsites where food or garbage is available. Fish, frogs, mice, fruit, vegetables, insects and birds are all on its diet. Sweet corn is a favorite and the raccoon relishes crayfish, which it catches by dabbling sensitive paws under streambed boulders. A liking for chickens and their eggs, and raids on garbage cans often make the raccoon unwelcome.

If kindness is shown to a raccoon it responds with affection, charm and endearing good manners. It is easily tamed, but authorities advise against keeping it as a pet. It has been known to bite its human friends without warning. An adult raccoon will fight bravely against great odds. Alone, a fit young raccoon can beat off two or three dogs. A mother will defend her offspring to the death.

About 33 inches long and averaging 19 pounds in weight, the raccoon resembles a fat cat, the result of the excess body fat it stores in preparation for a long winter's sleep. Its stout body is clothed in a long thick coat, generally of grizzled gray, and it is easily recognized by the black mask across cheeks, eyes and nose, which gives it a mischievous appearance. It has four to six prominent black rings around its short bushy tail.

Its pointed face is framed by a ruff of gray hairs behind the cheeks and alert, white-tipped ears. Its legs are short. Its narrow paws, which it uses with amazing dexterity, have five toes each tipped with strong curved claws. The raccoon can open hen-house latches, climb metal posts, snatch insects in flight, even unscrew the lids of jars.

Adult males usually forage alone. When they meet, males often engage in good-natured tussling. The young are extremely playful and quick to imitate the devoted mother's lessons on hunting for food. Contrary to popular belief, raccoons in the wild do not wash or fondle their food. They do so only in captivity—perhaps because they are unable to pursue aquatic prey, perhaps because they are nervous.

Two families normally occupy a square mile of good habitat. Riverbanks are their usual haunts. They prefer forested terrain and are not found in arid regions.

In winter, several raccoons den together in a sheltered leaf-lined nest. During this period of semi-hibernation the animals live mainly on stored body fat.

Mating takes place between late January and March. The male raccoon takes several wives in a season and the females show no jealousy, although they are fastidious about choosing a mate.

The young, born from mid-April to mid-May, spend a year learning from their mother. They are well furred when born, but their eyes remain closed for three weeks. When their eyes open, they go on their first short outing and learn how to hunt insects. They soon start the characteristic churring noise of raccoons, growling in imitation of the mother.

Because of their excellent climbing and swimming abilities, the raccoon has few natural enemies, although bobcats, foxes, coyotes, and great horned owls sometimes capture the young.

Raccoons are hunted by men with dogs. The flesh is good to eat, but the main attraction is the long dense fur. In Canada, 74,442 pelts were taken in 1973-74. During their fashion heyday raccoons were bred on ranches.

The raccoon inhabits all of southern Canada except Newfoundland, Cape Breton Island, the Gaspé Peninsula and the Rockies. On the Prairies it is found as far north as Lake Athabasca. It has been introduced to Prince Edward Island.

Where Raccoons Den

Raccoons prefer to den more than 10 feet above the ground in tree hollows, particularly in elms, maples and basswoods. They also occupy caves, burrows and culverts, lining them with leaves and wood chips for insulation against severely cold weather.

Glare, Hiss, Stamp, Aim . . . Fire!

The glossy black-and-white coat warns most animals away. One evening at dusk it attracted the attention of a bear cub. Innocent or desperately hungry? What other sort of creature would dare disturb a skunk on its evening forage for food?

The cub was innocent—and curious. Intrigued, it approached the slow-moving skunk and tried to entice it to play. Annoyed, the skunk turned its hind end toward the cub, glared over its shoulder with beady black eyes and raised its black-and-white-tipped tail like a plume over its head. Then the skunk hissed, stamped its forefeet, aimed for the cub's face, and fired. Two thin yellow streams of musky fluid shot out from the skunk's scent glands, met and atomized into a dense choking spray.

For its efforts to be friendly, the bear was rewarded with a stench that would cling to its fur for days—and a lesson it would never forget: leave skunks alone. Only one skunk, the western spotted skunk, does not rely solely on a stench defense. It also climbs trees.

Skunks, the size of large house cats, have plump, squat bodies. Their legs are short, their tails long and bushy.

The **striped skunk** *(Mephitis mephitis)* and the **western spotted skunk** *(Spilogale gracilis)* are easily distinguished. The striped skunk has a white line on its forehead and a white patch on the neck. From the neck patch, two stripes run along the back. The spotted skunk has short, silky black fur with six white stripes broken into spots extending down its back, flanks and rump. There are white spots between its eyes and in front of its ears. The striped skunk is larger but less agile than the western spotted skunk.

Although skunks are naked at birth, their coats are dense and full within three weeks. The striped skunk is found across Canada except in Newfoundland and in northern areas. The spotted skunk inhabits southwestern coastal British Columbia. The striped skunk sometimes frequents forests and river valleys but is most common in agricultural lands. The western spotted prefers rocky canyons and scrublands.

Skunks inhabit community dens. The western spotted skunk may live in warm, dry tree hollows. A family of seven or eight skunks usually shares a nest.

Skunks occasionally usurp other animals' burrows instead of digging their own. But when a badger or a weasel refuses to leave—and the skunk cannot kill it with a bite to the neck—they share the den.

One male, several females and their young hibernate together in winter. Skunks become very fat in the autumn and may lose 10 to 30 percent of their weight by spring. Their winter sleep is sometimes interrupted by mild temperatures, physical movement or noise and males sometimes leave the den during mild spells to search for food.

Why Animals Hibernate

Animals hibernate to escape winter food shortages and cold temperatures. Many small animals, whose bodies lose heat rapidly, are true hibernators. Large animals, such as bears, go into torpor—a sluggish "half sleep" that is not true hibernation.

As an animal's body temperature drops, so do its metabolism, heartbeat and respiration—to a fraction of normal. The animal appears to sleep but the "sleep" is seldom continuous. If the temperature in the hibernating den dips below freezing, the animal is awakened by a fit of shivering which raises its body temperature.

Chipmunks and some mice awaken two or three times a day to feed on stored food; others, such as ground squirrels, live off body fat.

A striped skunk raises its hindquarters and sprays foul-smelling musk at a bear cub. The musk can cause temporary blindness and nausea.

Males wander during the breeding season in February and March and each mates with several females. Striped skunks bear 4 to 10 young per litter after a gestation period of about 62 days. Western spotted skunks bear 2 to 6 young after 120 days.

Fully weaned and able to defend themselves by emitting musk at six to eight weeks, young skunks venture from the den with their mother after dusk. They remain with their mother until the next mating season. Skunks are sexually mature at 11 months.

The **American badger** *(Taxidea taxus)* is powerful and aggressive and fears only man. Its large jaws, strong teeth and powerful claws are effective for defense and hunting. This large member of the weasel family fights ferociously when attacked and, like the skunk, the badger can defend itself by emitting a foul-smelling musk from its anal glands.

The badger uses burrows for shelter and to escape its enemies. Sometimes it digs into a ground squirrel's burrow and overtakes the rodent in a blind tunnel.

The badger's burrow can be 30 feet long and 10 deep. The animal builds a bulky nest of grasses in an enlarged chamber at the end of the burrow. Sometimes it takes over and enlarges the burrow of a prairie dog or ground squirrel. The entrances of badger burrows are marked by large mounds of excavated earth.

Through winter it sleeps in the burrow and lives on body fat accumulated from a diet of rodents, ground-nesting birds and insects. This is not true hibernation because the badger's body processes and temperature are not substantially reduced.

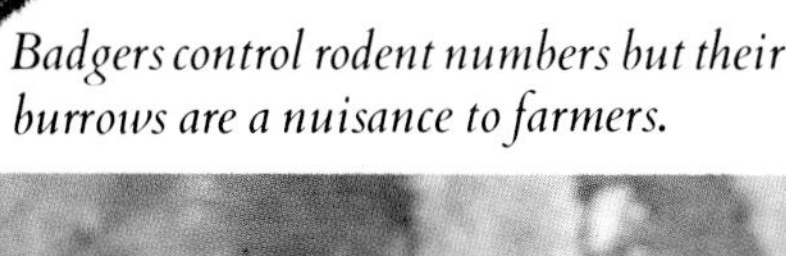

Badgers control rodent numbers but their burrows are a nuisance to farmers.

The badger is a solitary animal except during the mating season, which occurs in August and September. Implantation of the embryo is delayed until about mid-February. A litter of four or five is born in April or mid-May and the young remain with their mother until September. The young are weaned when half-grown but the mother brings them food until they are almost full-grown.

Occasionally called the prairie badger, it inhabits the Prairies, the mountain valleys of British Columbia and the farmlands of southwestern Ontario. It does not frequent forests.

A white stripe from its nose to its shoulders and black patches on the face, chin and throat identify the American badger. Its small head is broad between the ears and tapers to a snout. Short legs with large feet, a stubby tail and long hair, grizzled in gray or brown, contribute to its low, stocky profile. Males weigh up to 25 pounds.

Although primarily nocturnal, the badger sometimes lies near its burrow in the morning sun of early summer. It is not an agile animal. It usually waddles leisurely; when frightened it trots with a rolling gait.

The Shy, Misunderstood Bear

Although a polar bear is little more than a pound at birth, an adult male may weigh more than 1,000 pounds, a female about 700.

The familiar bear is a much misunderstood creature. It seems awkward and ungainly—but can sprint at 35 miles an hour. It is considered ferocious—but this shy scavenger seldom attacks unless provoked. It is thought to hibernate all winter—but does not hibernate at all.

The commonest and smallest species in North America is the **black bear** *(Ursus americanus)*. It is not always black. Many specimens range from dark brown to pale cinnamon, often with a white patch on the chest.

A scavenger, the black bear is seen most often in wooded areas, frequently striking its familiar erect pose to sniff the wind for odors. The bear compensates for poor eyesight with a remarkable sense of smell and good hearing. Its compact build makes it look heavier than it is. Adult males weigh 300 to 400 pounds and are up to three feet high at the shoulder; females weigh about 150 pounds.

A constant feeder, it devours nuts, roots, plants, berries, fish, small animals and carrion. Near civilization, it forages through garbage dumps and can be dangerous to interfering humans. It does most of its traveling between dusk and dawn, within a well-defined area of 1 to 80 square miles.

By autumn, the bear is fat and wears a sleek coat of fur. It finds a rocky den or hollow in which to sleep away the winter months. This is not true hibernation, since its body temperature drops only a few degrees. This state is sometimes called torpor. Late in winter, the she-bear gives birth to two or three cubs. (Mating takes place every second year, in June or July.)

The **grizzly bear** *(Ursus arctos horribilis)* ranks with the shark as an object of terror for man. But in fact the nomadic grizzly avoids man. Attacks usually result from sudden meetings at close range, sometimes at a garbage dump.

The grizzly is a magnificent, heavy-limbed animal ranging from off-white or yellow to black. After seven or eight years a male weighs 600 to 800 pounds.

A Polar Bear Den

Polar bears do not hibernate but the female retires to a winter den to bear her young. The den is often dug down to the permafrost.

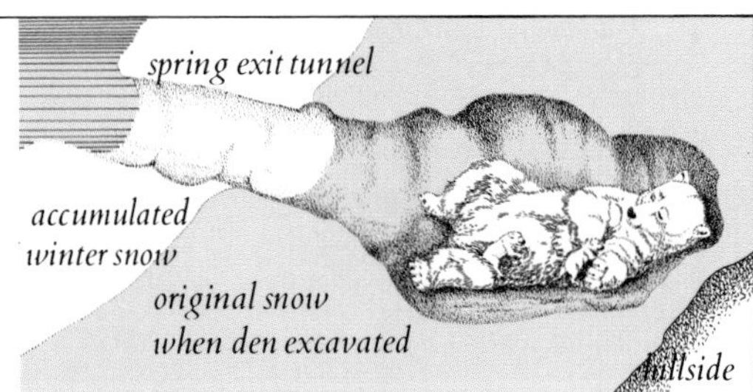

A grizzly bear (left) sniffs the air for danger. Black bears are not always black. They vary from black or brown to cinnamon (above) or creamy white.

The sleek hide is prized as a hunting trophy. But an even greater threat to the grizzly's survival is the erosion of its habitat by man.

Once numerous as far south as California and Mexico, it now is restricted to northwestern North America—in Montana, western Alberta, British Columbia, the Yukon, the Northwest Territories and Alaska.

In spite of its reputation as a ferocious cattle killer, the grizzly usually eats fish, rodents, insects, roots and berries. It occasionally kills a large animal that is sick or crippled, and sometimes a newborn elk or deer.

The grizzly, like the black bear, passes the winter in a semiconscious state resembling hibernation. In midwinter every second year, a female produces cubs—usually two. They remain with the mother until June of their second year.

Another garbage grubber is the **polar bear** *(Ursus maritimus)*. By nature a seal hunter, the polar bear has acquired a taste for anything from cheese and tea leaves to rope and cardboard. Away from settlements where dumps sustain the bears, they rely on grasses, seaweed, berries, duck and goose eggs and birds in summer, and on seals in winter.

Polar bears roam vast areas of land, sea and ice in northern Canada, the Soviet Union and the coast of Greenland. They are seen occasionally around Hudson Bay and James Bay, along the Newfoundland coast and in the Gulf of St. Lawrence. About 1,300 polar bears are killed each year, leaving 12,000—an estimated 6,000 of them in the Canadian Arctic.

A powerful beast with a streamlined body, the polar bear is protected from cold by a thick pelt of waterproof fur. Thick hair on its paws provide insulation and give sure footing on ice. Its huge paws make it a strong swimmer.

Mating takes place in April. Cubs, usually twins, are born the third winter after a previous birth.

Man is a great threat to the survival of the great white bear. He methodically hunts seals, the main prey of polar bears, and—often aided by airplanes and snowmobiles—hunts the dwindling population of bears, although kills are restricted by international agreement. Eskimos sell polar bear hides or use them to make sled robes, blankets and rugs. Bears are sometimes killed to protect personnel in oil camps and weather stations.

A treeful of bears. When danger threatens, an adult black bear often chases its young up a tree. A mother cares for her cubs until they are at least a year old.

They Stalk, Crouch, Rush . . . Kill

The bobcat dens in rock crevices, hollow logs, thickets or under tree stumps. It makes its bed from dry leaves or moss.

No other wild cat in Canada has the strength and the kill efficiency of the lithe, muscular cougar. With a sudden leap onto the shoulders, this big cat can slay a moose or an elk three times its size. Yet the **cougar** *(Felis concolor)*, most populous in rough, rocky regions of western Canada, seldom attacks man.

The cougar, also called the mountain lion and the puma, is by far the most impressive hunter among Canadian cats, which include the smaller lynx and bobcat. All are solitary, secretive predators with keen eyesight and unique stalking tactics.

An adult cougar, which may be nine feet long and weigh more than 200 pounds, is an inveterate loner. It socializes only for mating. The male establishes scent posts to attract a mate. When breeding—which is normally not restricted to any special season—the female forsakes her characteristic silence and emits loud blood-curdling screams. One to five cubs are born after a gestation period of about 96 days and the young remain with the mother until age two.

Like all cats, cougars hunt by sight and hearing. They stalk to within 30 or 40 feet of their prey, then charge in two or three great, lightning-fast leaps. This blitz ends on the shoulders of the prey. The cougar bites into the back of the neck, near the base of the skull.

If the prey escapes the initial charge, the cougar rarely follows. Instead it stalks another animal. Its favorite victims are mule deer and white-tailed deer. It also feeds on moose, wild sheep and goats, small mammals and birds. Even the painfully sharp quills of a porcupine will not deter a hungry cougar. The cougar leaves high regions in winter and follows deer to lower elevations. When wild game is scarce, a cougar will sometimes prowl near barnyards and chicken coops. It jealously guards its hunting territory against other cougars.

The cougar was once plentiful wherever there were deer. Today it is restricted largely to parts of Alberta and British Columbia. A remnant population of the eastern subspecies exists in unsettled parts of New Brunswick.

The cougar's short, coarse fur varies from tawny to grayish brown. The throat and chest are white. The tip of the tail is black. The fur, brighter in summer, darker and longer in winter, is replaced throughout the year.

A cougar snarls defiantly, its tail twitching and its ears lowered. Although they have few enemies, cougars are sometimes treed by wolves or hunting dogs.

The **lynx** *(Lynx canadensis)* lacks the graceful appearance of the cougar and is much smaller. But it too can strike powerful blows with its paws and is an efficient predator. A mature lynx is about three feet long and weighs from 15 to 40 pounds. It is distinguished by long, tufted ears, cheek fur and a bobbed, black tail. Its rump is higher than its shoulders, giving it an awkward appearance.

The lynx is found throughout Canada, mainly in coniferous forests. It is a night stalker, rising shortly before sunset to search for hares, waterfowl and the carcasses of large mammals. Its hunting technique is similar to the cougar's: the careful stalk, the crouch, the rush, the kill. The lynx normally ranges over six to eight square miles but it will go long distances when food is scarce.

Lynx populations peak about every 10 years, following peak populations of the snowshoe hare. A lynx devours as many as 200 hares a year.

Although excellent climbers, lynx live and hunt mainly on the ground. In the open they gallop clumsily but make long leaps. They are sometimes treed by dogs and wolves and preyed upon by cougars.

A pair of lynx remain together during the mating season, and the young spend their first winter with the mother. Lynx young are born in early summer after a gestation period of about 60 days.

The **bobcat** *(Lynx rufus),* smaller than the lynx, resembles a big house cat with most of its tail cut off. But it makes up for its diminutive size with ferocity. Bobcats, also called wildcats, prefer nighttime hunting. Each covers a territory of four to five square miles, following well-traveled trails and leaving scent markings. They sharpen their claws on tree trunks and, like the cougar and lynx, have a variety of calls ranging from a purr to a raucous caterwauling.

Bobcats are adept climbers and tireless walkers but are capable of only short bursts at high speeds. They inhabit swamps, deserts, rocky hillsides and young forests, and adapt better to changing environments than lynx do. Bobcats occasionally attack deer for food, but they are generally too small to take on deer effectively. They exist largely on small mammals.

Bobcat kittens are born in late spring, after a gestation period of 60 to 70 days. The mother drives off her mate when the one to seven kittens are born but allows him to return when the young are weaned, at about two months. Young bobcats remain with the mother for about nine months.

The lynx stalks small mammals at night and often ambushes its prey.

Doting Relatives That Hunt in Packs

The **wolf** *(Canis lupus)* fears and avoids man. It sometimes raids domestic livestock but more often hunts moose, deer, caribou and mountain sheep, especially animals that are weak, sick or old. It also eats small mammals, birds, fishes, berries—even insects. Wolves generally hunt and forage in packs.

The wolf is a doting relative. If a mother is killed when she returns to the hunt after weaning, an aunt takes over her role. All pack members take turns at protecting and educating the pups, submitting themselves to ever rougher play as the pups grow.

After weaning at about nine weeks, the pups are taken to a rendezvous site where they are left alone for the first time. By early November they get their first lesson in how to hunt.

A female wolf matures in two years and a male in three. The biggest wolves are found in northwestern Canada and the smallest in the Arctic islands. A large male is six feet long from nose to tail-tip, three feet high at the shoulder and weighs 95 to 100 pounds. Females are smaller and weigh 80 to 85 pounds.

The wily **coyote** *(Canis latrans)* is more successful than the wolf at living on the fringes of civilization. Hunted, trapped and poisoned since the early 1800s, when it began to prey on western livestock, it has learned to evade man and has extended its range far beyond its original habitat.

It is now established in Canada as far north as the Mackenzie Delta, from the west coast to the St. Lawrence Valley, and it may soon invade the Maritimes. But the coyote will always be associated with the prairies, where its melancholy howling at dusk and dawn pierces the vast emptiness.

Coyotes usually hunt in family packs or in pairs. Although they prey on livestock, they are great scavengers, cleaning up carcasses that might otherwise rot and spread disease. They also eat small mammals, rodents, birds, insects and vegetation.

Coyotes often pair for life. Mating takes place between late January and late March. Eight weeks later the blind and helpless pups are born—six on average. By fall the pups are big enough to establish their own ranges but often stay together through the winter. Coyotes live about eight years in the wild.

Adults are 38 to 52 inches long, including the tail. Males average 28 to 30 pounds, females 24 to 26 pounds. The coyote's color is usually buff, but some are grayish or blackish. The bushy tail is generally darker toward the tip and is carried low when running. Wolves and most dogs run with their tails held high.

Like the coyote, the **red fox** *(Vulpes vulpes)* has thrived on the settlement of North America. Its hunting is made easier by open farmland, and it has adapted readily to a varied animal and vegetable diet.

The red fox has migrated in this century to Baffin, Cornwallis and Ellesmere islands, where it now competes for territory with the arctic fox. The red fox

Most big-game animals (such as moose and caribou) are fleeter than wolves; but wolves have greater stamina. So a pack wears down a victim by pursuing it over long distances—up to 25 miles a day.

At about six months, red fox kits leave their den and fend for themselves. A loner, the arctic fox (below) leaves its den about three months after birth.

Our Vanished Wildlife

The **Great Plains wolf** *(Canis lupus nubilus)*, often called the buffalo wolf, once preyed on the great herds of bison that roamed the prairies. As the plains were settled, and the bison was slaughtered, the wolf began to attack livestock. Bounties encouraged hunting, trapping and poisoning of the buffalo wolf and by the 1930s it was extinct.

Like other subspecies of wolf, the **Newfoundland wolf** *(Canis lupus beothucus)* had a price on its head when it turned to prey on settlers' cattle. The last Newfoundland wolf was killed about 1913 and the extinction of this large, white subspecies was recognized in the 1930s. This wolf was white with pale yellow tinges on its head and limbs. Some black individuals may have existed.

A lone coyote howls. The coyote's scientific name (Canis latrans) *means barking dog.*

shuns deep forest and is rare on the southern plains of Alberta and Saskatchewan.

Although it kills poultry and game birds, it prefers small rodents and is a valuable predator. The red fox has keen senses of sight, hearing and smell.

Its enemies, apart from man, are the wolf, coyote, lynx and bobcat, though its speed and narrow burrow make it difficult to catch.

Disease and competition for territory claim many in the first year or two of the natural three-year lifespan, and man traps the red fox for its long, silky fur.

Most red foxes have reddish brown cheeks, back, rump and tail, with a creamy underside and black on the backs of legs and ears. But more than 20 percent—called cross foxes—are gray-brown with a cross of black hairs on the shoulders. About 10 percent are silver foxes, their black hair tipped with silver.

Male and female are thought to mate for life, ranging over a square mile or so of territory. They breed between December and March and seek out a den, often a hollow tree, shallow cave or the abandoned burrow of a groundhog or skunk, which the vixen enlarges and lines with dry grass and leaves. A litter of up to 10 kits is born about two months after conception. The kits are weaned at one month. By autumn they leave the den to fend for themselves.

The long, bushy winter coat of the **arctic fox** *(Alopex lagopus)* is white and covers even the soles of the feet. The summer coat is short and brown.

The arctic fox is found from Labrador through the Northwest Territories. Its main food is the lemming, which it can scent under the snow. It eats small mammals, birds, fish and shellfish and will trail a wolf pack or a polar bear in the hope of cleaning up a caribou or seal carcass.

Arctic foxes may mate as early as February and up to 25 kits are born about 8 weeks later. Litters are large when food is plentiful, small when it is scarce. The velvety brown newborn are blind, deaf and toothless but emerge weaned from their den at two to four weeks. By mid-August the kits are able to fend for themselves.

Fearless, Ferocious Furbearers

A loner, like most of the weasel family, the **American mink** *(Mustela vison)* restlessly patrols riverbanks, lakeshores, marshes and tidal flats. Ferocious when attacking prey or enemies, this luxuriously furred flesh eater has few natural enemies. Even large predators seldom attack it although it sometimes falls prey to a swooping owl.

The mink feeds on small mammals, fish, birds, frogs and salamanders. It attacks muskrats but avoids pursuing them into their dens—cornered muskrats are formidable opponents. The mink prefers freshly killed meat, but kills whether or not it is hungry. Carcasses are hoarded in its several dens and often remain uneaten. Dens are made under tree roots, in beaver and muskrat lodges, hollow logs and riverbanks.

Its slender body and partially webbed feet make the mink a fine swimmer. It can stay underwater for up to three minutes.

The gestation period varies between 39 and 76 days because of delayed implantation of the embryo after mating. The 4 to 10 kits in a litter are born blind in April or May. They are weaned at five weeks and can fend for themselves at two months.

The American mink, found throughout mainland Canada south of the tree line, has been introduced to Newfoundland.

Despite its name, the **fisher** *(Martes pennanti)* rarely goes fishing—although it swims well and occasionally eats fish.

It is, however, one of the few animals that successfully attack porcupines. Fast and agile, the fisher flips a porcupine on its back and attacks the soft belly, which is unprotected by quills.

Except during the breeding season, the adult fisher lives alone. It establishes hunting circuits, as wolves do, and hunts along set routes up to 60 miles long within an area of 10 square miles. It eats small mammals, birds, carrion and berries. When attacked, it fights ferociously and secretes a strong-smelling musk.

The fisher inhabits forests throughout Canada and dens in hollow trees, rock crevices or under brush piles. It is considered to be rare in Canada, mainly because trapping has reduced its numbers.

Long brown guard hairs cover the fisher's gray, buff-tipped underfur. The rump, tail, feet and belly are chocolate brown to black.

Mating occurs in March and April but implantation of the embryo is delayed until January or February. One to four kits are born, on average 352 days after mating—an unusually long gestation period for a small mammal. Kits are blind until seven weeks old. They stay with the mother for about six months.

The curiosity of the **marten** *(Martes americana)* makes it an easy furbearer to trap. Once it inhabited coniferous forests across North America. Trapping and destruction of its habitat have confined it to small areas in Canada's forests.

Its soft fur is dark brown to almost black. The undercoat is a paler brown. The male hunts in an area of about one square mile. A third of a square mile will support the smaller female. Squirrels and mice are the marten's main food, but it also eats snowshoe hares, grouse, fish, insects, berries and carrion. Its swiftness and its ability to swim underwater enable it to elude its few enemies—lynx, coyotes, great horned owls and golden eagles.

One to four kits are born in March or April in a hollow lined with leaves or moss. Deaf and blind at birth, they hear at 26 days and see at 39. They are weaned at 6 weeks and are fully grown at 3½ months.

Canada has three species of weasels, all prized for their white winter coats. They are the ermine, the long-tailed weasel and the least weasel.

The **ermine** *(Mustela erminea)*, called the stoat in its brown summer coat, inhabits all of Canada except southern Alberta and southern Saskatchewan.

The fisher sometimes nests in tree hollows and often leaps from tree to tree.

Our Vanished Wildlife

The **sea mink** *(Mustela macrodon)*, a large mink that inhabited the rocky Atlantic coast, was exterminated even before scientists recognized it as a distinct species in 1903. Its extinction was probably the work of trappers and hunters in the early 19th century. Premium prices were paid for large pelts—adult males

The **pine marten** (Martes americana atrata) *is an endangered subspecies.*

Though only about 14 inches from nose to tail tip and weighing about 10 ounces when fully grown, it kills hares and rats by hanging with its sharp teeth to the victim's neck. The ermine also feeds on mice, squirrels and chipmunks. Its slender body allows it to enter the holes and burrows of its prey. These burrows are often taken over by the ermine and lined with grass and sometimes with the fur of its victims.

Mating may take place in early summer. Implantation is delayed until a month before birth and four to nine young are born in April or May. The chocolate-brown summer coat grows within three weeks and soon after, the kits hunt with the mother. Male kits are as big as the mother at seven weeks but she still carries them in her mouth when danger threatens and defends them courageously against such predators as coyotes, badgers and foxes.

The **long-tailed weasel** *(Mustela frenata),* about 20 inches long including its five-to-six-inch tail, is the longest of Canada's weasels. It is confined to southern Canada except in the West where it reaches central Alberta and British Columbia. Open parkland is its favorite habitat, though it also lives on mountains to the 10,000-foot level. It feeds on rabbits, hares and poultry. It is preyed upon by the fox, coyote, wolf, domestic cat and dog.

The mink usually hunts alone. In winter it eats rabbits and other small animals.

The long-tailed weasel's winter coat conceals it from predators and prey.

were almost four feet long, about twice the size of the common American mink. The only Canadian record of the sea mink's existence is a specimen taken from Campobello Island, N.B.

The last known **black-footed ferret** *(Mustela nigripes)* in Canada was caught in 1937 at Climax, Sask. Its annihilation is an example of the chain reaction set off when man interferes with natural processes. Its main food is the prairie dog; with programs to eradicate the prairie dog, the ferret's food supply was seriously reduced.

The long-tailed weasel's summer coat is cinnamon brown with ocher underfur. This weasel mates in July or August and three to nine young, with unusually large heads and long necks, are born about nine months later. Within a week fuzzy white coats cover their pink skins and by two weeks the fur is sleek. The kits are weaned at 25 days, 12 days before their eyes open.

Scarcely larger than the mice on which it preys, the **least weasel** *(Mustela nivalis rixosa)* is Canada's smallest carnivore. An adult is seldom larger than eight inches overall. It has a seemingly insatiable appetite for mice and voles and often takes over the nests of its victims. Predators of the least weasel are the long-tailed weasel, owl and house cat.

Unlike the larger weasels, the least weasel does not have a black tail tip to its white winter coat. In summer this weasel is walnut brown with a white belly.

Too Tough, Too Tenacious to Trap

The Eskimo glared at the blood-stained snow. This trap was gone. At the first trap he had found only the torn fur of a marten. The second had still been set, but the bait had been cleverly stolen. The third time the thief had been less lucky. The trapper identified the blurred tracks leading from the scene. The thief—a **wolverine** *(Gulo gulo)*—was bleeding, and no wonder. It still had the trap gripping one foot. Was it worth chasing? Trap or no trap, it might be miles away. It might even have sacrificed a few toes to get rid of the trap.

The Eskimo abandoned the hunt, aware that he would be unlikely to catch the determined and cunning wolverine. So tenacious is this creature—only the size of a spaniel—it will chase a grizzly bear away from a kill. Because of its size, strength and temperament the wolverine has few natural enemies.

Eskimos prize the wolverine's pelt for parka trim because, alone among animal fur, it will not frost up from the moisture of a person's breath.

Originally the wolverine ranged from the Arctic Ocean to New Mexico, but now it is being crowded out by the spread of civilization and is confined to the Rockies and the Arctic tundra. Occasionally it falls prey to wolves.

Primarily a scavenger, cleaning up the kills of wolves and bears, the wolverine is capable of killing a moose. It also eats roots, berries, birds' eggs and fish.

It is a strong climber and swimmer, and gallops tirelessly on its flat, bearlike paws. It can run down a rabbit by sheer endurance rather than speed.

An adult wolverine weighs 30 to 50 pounds and stands 14 to 18 inches high on its long, strong legs. It may live for 15 years in the wild.

The two to five pups in a litter are born in March or April. They are suckled for eight to nine weeks before the mother brings them solid food. They stay with her for their first winter, learning to hunt, and mature in a year.

The **sea otter** *(Enhydra lutris)*, a playful amphibious mammal, was discovered in 1741 by a Russian crew shipwrecked in the North Pacific. The crew marveled at its sleek black fur, tipped with silvery gold. Warmer than sable and more durable than mink, it was to become the most valuable fur in the world. Trade in the fur flourished. And the sea otter soon faced extinction.

Between 1790 and 1820, the Russians hauled 200,000 sea otter hides back from the North Pacific. Other countries joined the hunt. The otters were easy prey. Herds were encircled by men in small boats and the animals were clubbed or shot as they came up for air.

The ***river otter*** (Lutra canadensis), *prized for its fur, is at home on land and in water. It feeds on fish, frogs, shellfish and small mammals.*

The fierce and fearless wolverine: Indians call it the invulnerable beast.

By 1900 the sea otter was thought to be extinct in Canadian waters. Only in 1911 was the killing made illegal by international treaty. By then hunting of sea otters was no longer profitable because of declining numbers. Since the treaty, the sea otter's comeback has been slow. The present population is estimated at between 25,000 and 40,000, concentrated mainly in the Aleutian Islands.

An attempt to reintroduce it to Canada's Pacific coast was made in 1969, when about 30 sea otters were shipped from Alaska to the northwestern coast of Vancouver Island. Occasional sightings have since been made but the colony is jeopardized by boats harvesting abalone, a main food of the otter.

Before the slaughter, the sea otter thrived along rocky coastlines, taking refuge in kelp beds from killer whales and sharks.

It feeds mainly on shellfish and sea urchins. A voracious eater, it consumes 20 to 35 percent of its body weight of about 80 pounds every day. Full-grown adults, four to five feet long, can dive as deep as 25 fathoms (150 feet) with the help of webbed hind feet, a streamlined body and a powerful tail.

Although the sea otter mates at any time of the year, it is not a prolific breeder. Herds average one junior to 12 adults. Twins are rare and pups take three years, of an average eight-year life span, to mature.

The pups, weighing about four pounds, are born with eyes open and teeth cut. Their fur is reddish brown. They are weaned at two months but are fed tidbits placed on the mother's chest until they learn to swim and forage.

Floating on its back, the sea otter hammers shellfish against a stone on its chest until the shells break. The chest then serves as a dining table for itself or a pup.

Feller of Trees, Builder of Dams

No animal has contributed more to Canada than the **beaver** *(Castor canadensis)*. Its luxurious fur enticed men into the wilderness, thus pushing back the frontiers of settlement; its dams have helped restore a land scraped bare during the Ice Age. Vast areas of soil and pasture have been built up through the industry of this humpbacked, flat-tailed animal.

Beaver dams on major rivers stabilize water flow, reduce erosion and provide a habitat for many forms of wildlife. Insects lay eggs in beaver ponds and trout feed on the aquatic larvae. Waterfowl nest in the marshy shallows. Water lilies and weeds flourish in rich muck that accumulates on the bottom of the ponds.

When it has felled and stripped nearby trees, or when its pond fills with silt, the beaver moves on to build another dam. The abandoned dam soon disintegrates. Grasses sprout in fertile soil behind it, forming a "beaver meadow" that attracts white-tailed deer and a host of other creatures. But the beaver is not invariably regarded as a friend of man. Its dams often flood roads, fields and orchards.

The young beaver takes a mate and starts building its first dam after being driven from its parents' colony at about two years of age. Branches are laid on the stream bed—along the direction of flow so that they dig into the bed and anchor the dam. These branches are then weighted and solidified with stones and mud carried in the beaver's front paws. As the water level rises, layers of branches, sod and mud are piled on and leaks are sealed.

Some dams are 100 yards long and 18 feet high, though the average is 50 yards long and 6 feet high. Subsidiary dams are sometimes built downstream. Then the lodge—a home for a new colony—is built in the main pond. The outside of the lodge is plastered with mud, except at the top, where the tangled wood serves as an air vent. The mud freezes hard in winter, frustrating predators.

The beaver also digs burrows in the banks of streams and excavates canals. The water level in the canals is sometimes regulated by small dams or locks. The beaver is nervous far from water. Burrows with underwater entrances provide refuge in case of attack or if the lodge is flooded; canals enable it to go farther inland in search of food and building materials.

The beaver stands on its short hind legs and, using its broad tail for support, grasps the trunk of a tree with its front paws and cuts two deep horizontal grooves about three inches apart. The wood between is chipped out. The procedure is repeated on the other side of the trunk until the tree falls. Contrary to folklore, the beaver cannot judge the direction of the fall. Often a falling tree catches in neighboring branches. Sometimes it maims or kills a beaver.

Trembling aspen is the beaver's favorite food, but it also thrives on poplar, willow, white birch and pond vegetation. Leaf-bearing branches are stripped from felled trees, cut into manageable lengths and dragged to water along well-

An adult beaver normally fells 200-300 thin trees each year. It can gnaw through a three-inch willow tree in five minutes.

How Beavers Build

A beaver lodge and dam are built of sticks cemented with mud. The lodge rises about 4 feet out of the water and is up to 20 feet in diameter, although the living chamber is only about 2 feet high and 5 feet in diameter. A winter food pile is submerged near one of several underwater entrances. Crisscrossed sticks in the air vent keep out predators.

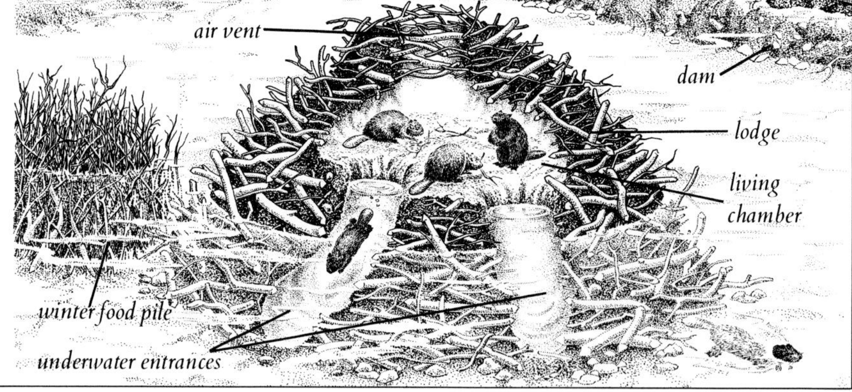

How a Beaver Gnaws

A beaver's front cutting teeth (incisors) grow continuously, but constant gnawing keeps them sharp—and the proper length. The teeth, harder in front than in back, wear more quickly at the back, leaving a chisel-like cutting edge. When a beaver gnaws, its lips close behind the incisors to keep wood chips and water out of its mouth.

defined "logging trails." Piled branches eventually sink under their own weight, providing the beaver colony with a food supply close to the lodge.

Valves close the beaver's ears and nostrils when it swims underwater, propelled by its webbed hind feet and steered by its tail. It is able to close its large furry lips behind its incisors to permit underwater woodcutting.

The beaver's dark beady eyes are weak, but this is compensated for by acute senses of smell and hearing. When alarmed, it warns other beavers with a loud slap of its tail on the water before diving.

In water the beaver's chief enemy is the otter, which can get into the lodge through the underwater entrances. On land the beaver is hunted by wolves, wolverines and lynxes. Beaver kits are sometimes killed by minks, hawks and owls.

North America's largest rodent, the beaver attains an average weight of 50 pounds although a beaver that survives 12 years may exceed four feet in length and weigh 100 pounds. The beaver's prehistoric ancestors were nine-foot-long giants that weighed up to 800 pounds.

The pelt, of long guard hairs and thick underfur, grows during summer, molts in late autumn, is most lustrous at the onset of winter and molts again at the approach of spring. Trapping had reduced the beaver population drastically by the 1930s. Now the animal is again abundant in Canada.

In summer a beaver strips and eats the green bark of trees and saplings. In winter it feeds on branches it has piled underwater near its lodge.

Like the beaver, the **muskrat** *(Ondatra zibethicus)* is an amphibious rodent with valuable fur, a scaly tail and long sharp incisors. The muskrat lives in marshes, streams and lakes throughout Canada, either in riverbank burrows or in houses made of twigs, roots, leaves and mud. The houses may stand four feet high and measure six feet across. The walls are up to a foot thick.

Each family unit has a system of feeding platforms, canals and tunnels. Muskrats prefer water plants, though in hard times they eat whatever they can, even dead muskrats and their own house walls.

Winter is a time of high mortality. Most muskrats do not survive more than a year and few live more than three years. Starvation and overcrowding lead to quarrels and fatal feuding.

Trapping claims up to four million pelts a year, but muskrats produce two or three litters each year, with four to seven kits in each litter. The young, weighing about three-quarters of an ounce, are naked, blind and helpless at birth but are active and furred by five days, can see at two weeks, are weaned by the 28th day and are independent at one month. They mature as yearlings.

A wary muskrat pokes its head from the entrance of a riverbank burrow.

Quills That Can Kill

Its thousands of quills make the **American porcupine** *(Erethizon dorsatum)* a prickly enemy but, contrary to widespread belief, it cannot "shoot" its quills.

This generally sluggish rodent erects its quills when it is disturbed or threatened. They detach easily and their barbs dig painfully, sometimes fatally, into the flesh of an attacker. Animals as large as bears have been killed by porcupine quills. The porcupine also implants quills with a flicker-fast slash of its tail.

Among Canada's rodents, the black-to-chestnut-colored porcupine is second in size only to the beaver. An adult, about three feet long, may weigh 25 pounds or more. It inhabits all Canadian provinces and territories south of the tree line, except Newfoundland and Prince Edward Island.

The porcupine carries as many as 30,000 quills on its short-legged, thick body. Lost quills begin to be replaced within a few days. Broken quills are replaced during the annual molt, between spring and summer.

The porcupine is active mainly at night. When startled, it waddles away clumsily. A good climber, it is often seen by day resting high in a tree. On the ground it sleeps on its stomach with its legs splayed out and soles turned upward.

By late autumn the porcupine has built up a store of fat that helps it remain active and well nourished through winter. It seeks protection from the weather in such ready-made shelters as caves, hollow logs and road culverts. It often tunnels through snow to its den.

Porcupines apparently live nearly nine years in the wild, despite the depredations of wolverine, fisher and bobcat—which flip the prickly rodent onto its back and attack its unprotected belly.

November-December is mating time for procupines. After a gestation period of approximately seven months, unusually long in the rodent family, a single birth occurs—or, rarely, a twin birth.

The mating ritual of porcupines is noisy and robust. Squealing and grunting they rise to their hind feet and move about as if dancing. They may rub noses and exchange affectionate clouts on the head. A female may mate with several males and come into heat again in midwinter or spring if the initial mating has been unsuccessful.

Their bark-eating habits, which damage and destroy timber, sometimes benefits forests by thinning out trees but, generally, foresters see porcupines as pests.

The **woodchuck** *(Marmota monax),* best known of North American mar-

The usually slow moving woodchuck puts on bursts of speed when frightened. It can leap a narrow stream—or swim a wide one—and can climb trees.

The ***hoary marmot*** (Marmota caligata), *the largest marmot in North America, is limited to remote mountain regions of the West and the Yukon.*

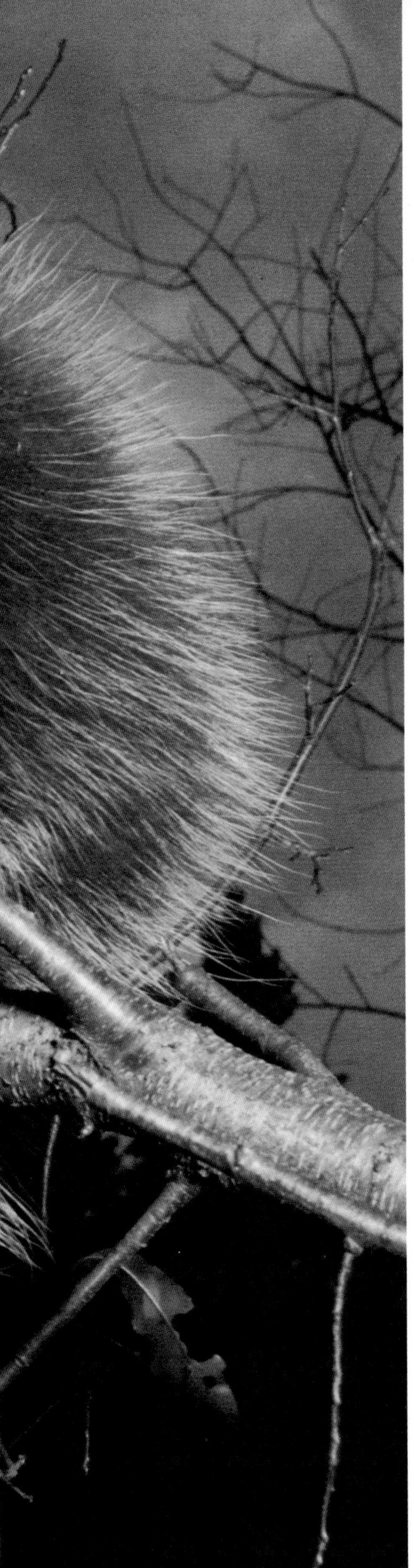

mots, is better known in Canada as the groundhog. It is wrongly cast as a weather prophet and harbinger of spring. The story goes that the groundhog, stirring from hibernation, emerges from its winter burrow on February 2, Candlemas Day. If skies are sunny, it sees its shadow and, frightened, retreats below ground—thus forecasting another 40 days of winter. If skies are cloudy, it becomes active—heralding an early spring. So goes the story. In fact, the woodchuck or groundhog rarely leaves its burrow as early as February 2 unless the weather of late winter is exceptionally mild.

The woodchuck has a short body, neck and tail typical of marmots, a family of large ground-dwelling squirrels. It inhabits all Canadian provinces and territories except Prince Edward Island. One of the few wild mammals whose numbers increased as civilization spread, it finds acceptable living conditions in a landscape largely ordered by man. That is why this brownish gray, bushy-tailed rodent is familiar in mixed woodlots, pastures and fence rows. It marks its territory with musk secreted from three anal glands—seldom roaming more than 100 yards from its den. When frightened, it dives for cover and gives a short, shrill whistle.

The woodchuck, active by day, is slow-moving and solitary. Although it spends most of its time sunning or foraging in fields, it can also swim, climb trees and perch sentinellike on fence posts. An adult is about 22 inches long and weighs up to 14 pounds.

Instead of storing food in the autumn as squirrels and chipmunks do, the woodchuck accumulates body fat. It vanishes into hibernation in late October.

Mating occurs after females emerge from hibernation in April. At the end of a gestation period of about 32 days, from one to eight young are born. Mother and young may nest together during the next winter. The life span is 6 years in the wild, 10 in captivity.

A summer home excavated by woodchucks may comprise 40 feet of 10-inch-wide tunnels with up to five entrances. The foot-wide main entrance is betrayed by excavated dirt but a nearby "plunge hole" is small and well hidden, with a vertical drop of about two feet. Hibernating chambers are rarely found. It is known that the animal seals itself in its den, rolls into a ball, sinks into a deep torpor, and loses about 30 percent of its weight during the winter.

Primarily a grazing animal, the woodchuck eats bark and twigs in early spring. As soon as the season permits, it turns to green vegetation. When feeding, it keeps a wary eye peeled for the fox, its most dangerous predator.

The porcupine is a climber that sleeps by day—high in a tree—and feeds by night, in trees or on the ground.

An Impudent Campsite Visitor

The chipmunk is an impudent but welcome invader of gardens, farms and campsites. A beguiling way of clasping its hand-like paws to its chest and gazing alertly at humans often wins handouts.

A member of the squirrel family, it has distinctive light and dark stripes on its narrow face, black stripes banded with white on its reddish or grayish brown body, and pale underparts.

It crams nuts, seeds, berries, insects and sometimes birds' eggs into large pouches inside each cheek and can carry 30 or more beechnuts at a time. To unload the cheeks it pushes the food out with its forepaws.

When digging its burrow the chipmunk either hides the dirt in nearby vegetation or simply piles it outside the opening. An entrance which might be easy for enemies to find is blocked; another is dug under a rock or clump of bush. In its burrow the chipmunk is safe from hawks, foxes, coyotes and dogs and cats but still may fall prey to the ermine or the long-tailed weasel.

The burrow, as deep as three feet, is reached by a tunnel two inches in diameter. A chipmunk may live alone in the same burrow for its lifetime, building new storage tunnels and chambers each year. (Chipmunks rarely survive in the wild for more than three years but may live up to eight years in captivity.) The main chamber is 6 to 12 inches in diameter. As much as a half bushel of food may be stored in the burrow. Chipmunks remain in their burrows from about November to March. They sleep for long periods but awaken at intervals to nibble on stashed food and may even venture outdoors on warm days.

As do most squirrels in Canada, chipmunks mate in spring. A female carries three to six young for about a month.

The **eastern chipmunk** *(Tamias striatus)* is found from the Gulf of Mexico to James Bay, and from the Maritimes to Ontario and southern Manitoba, overlapping the range of the chipmunks of western Canada, which are smaller, slimmer and have proportionately longer tails and grayer fur than the eastern varieties. The **least chipmunk** *(Eutamias minimus)*, smallest of all, may weigh as little as one ounce. It is found throughout the West and Northwest, and as far east as Quebec.

The **red squirrel** *(Tamiasciurus hudsonicus)*, weighing seven or eight ounces and measuring seven or eight inches long, is among the most active of small mammals. Its furry tail, almost as long as its body, helps it to maintain balance as it leaps from branch to branch—sometimes as far as ten feet. When a hawk passes overhead the red squirrel hides by either flattening itself against a tree trunk or crouching low on a branch.

There are fifteen subspecies of red squirrel across Canada. The great variety of food this species eats enables it to survive in many habitats. Like the western chipmunk, it enjoys the seeds of coniferous trees; like the eastern chipmunk, it can live on hardwood nuts. Its diet also includes buds, flowers, fleshy fruits, mushrooms, tender inner bark, insects, birds' eggs and fledglings. Red squirrels, like most squirrels, are preyed upon by owls, hawks and flesh-eating mammals.

These versatile animals adapt to a variety of homes. In the south they live in leafy nests, tree cavities and woodpecker holes. In the north they build their nests beneath trees or stumps. They store food—up to 10 bushels of pinecones—in a labyrinth of tunnels as large as 13 feet across and three feet deep. Red squirrels do not hibernate, although they remain inactive during extremely cold weather.

They mate in February, March or April and one to eight young are born about six weeks later. Red squirrels have lived 10 years in captivity.

The **gray** or **black squirrel** *(Sciurus carolinensis)* is seen in many parks in eastern Canadian cities, but is less widely spread than the red squirrel is. Most often it is a grizzled gray but black individuals are often found in southeastern

Though awkward on the ground, a flying squirrel soars gracefully.

Chipmunks often forage in trees but live in underground burrows.

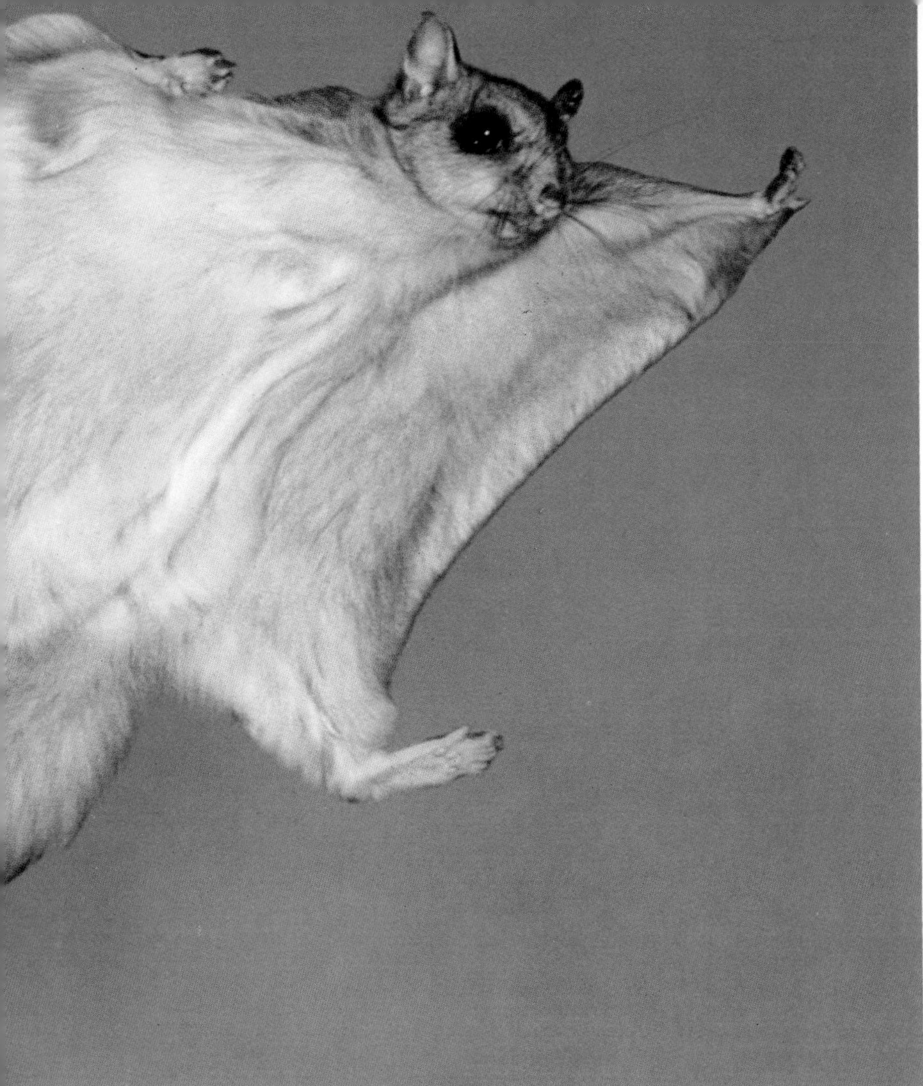

How a Flying Squirrel Flies

Although it appears to fly, a flying squirrel actually glides—as far as 50 yards. It climbs to a high branch, crouches, then springs into the air with its legs and tail extended. Membranes connecting its front and hind legs form an airfoil. Its tail serves as a rudder. When landing the flying squirrel tilts its body to check its speed and uses its legs as shock absorbers. The flying squirrel glides only at night.

Neither the gray squirrel (above) nor the red squirrel (below) hibernates. But on cold or stormy days they stay in their nests and eat stored food.

Canada. It is about 20 inches long, its bushy tail making up nearly half of this, and weighs up to 1½ pounds.

A sociable animal, unlike its red relative, the gray squirrel seems to care little about territorial rights. Each local population forms its social hierarchy by means of what passes for fighting in the squirrel world—sham battles or pushing encounters. Gray squirrels do not hibernate but, like red squirrels, remain in their nests on cold and stormy days. They sometimes starve if the previous autumn's yield of food from forest trees has been poor.

Flying squirrels, Canada's only nocturnal squirrels, are clumsy on the ground, but are marvels of grace and accuracy in the air. They inhabit vast regions of coniferous and deciduous forests but are seldom seen by humans. Sociable animals, they may feed together and keep close for warmth in winter. Nine or more may nest together in a tree cavity. Though they do not hibernate in winter, they remain inside their homes during extreme cold, probably subsisting on great stores of nuts. The young, usually three or four to a litter, are born in April, May or June, or in July or August if a second mating occurs.

Of the two species found in North America, the **northern flying squirrel** *(Glaucomys sabrinus)*, including its 14 subspecies in Canada, is the larger. It is widely distributed from Alaska to Labrador. The range of the **southern flying squirrel** *(Glaucomys volans)* reaches up to the Great Lakes, southern Ontario and Quebec and southwestern Nova Scotia.

Adults sometimes measure up to 18 inches in length, half of that being tail, and weigh up to six ounces. Their thick soft fur is grayish brown tending to reddish on top. Flying squirrels have the characteristic dark, bulging eyes of many nocturnal animals and their diet is similar to that of larger tree squirrels.

Gopher Homes Honeycomb the West

Ground squirrels are among the great tunnelers of the Canadian West, digging labyrinthine passageways leading to chambers where they nest, store food and pass the winter in hibernation. They inhabit prairie grainfields, the mountainous regions of British Columbia and Alberta, and the North, where the arctic ground squirrel burrows as deep as the permafrost line.

One of the most familiar mammals of the Prairies is **Richardson's ground squirrel** *(Spermophilus richardsonii)*, better known as the gopher. Gopher comes from the French *gaufre*, honeycomb, a word that describes the animal's complex tunnel system. Its burrow, as long as 50 feet and with an average of eight entrances, consists of several chambers and many blind passageways. A mound of earth at the main entrance is used as an observation post.

Richardson's ground squirrels are about 12 inches long and have short legs and long, slightly curved claws. The short fur is buffy gray on top and yellowish on the thighs, flanks, shoulders and cheeks. Living in loose communities in southern parts of the Prairie Provinces, they collect seeds of wheat, oats and wild buckwheat in late summer and store them in underground chambers. The stored seeds are eaten when food is scarce. This species also preys on grasshoppers and other insects. They are the victims of hawks, falcons, badgers, coyotes, foxes, weasels and snakes.

A 13-lined ground squirrel dashes to its burrow to escape a red fox.

Richardson's ground squirrels have been known to be carriers of such diseases as bubonic plague, Rocky Mountain spotted fever and tularemia, a type of blood poisoning transmitted by insect bites.

They mate just after emerging from hibernation in late March or early April. The gestation period averages 27 days and the litter varies from 5 to 11. At six weeks, the young appear at burrow entrances in late June. They are full-grown by September.

This ground squirrel comes out on warm, sunny days and remains underground when it is very hot or raining. Its short, shrill whistle is accompanied by a sharp jerk of its tail. When alarmed, it chatters shrilly and runs to its burrow.

The **golden-mantled ground squirrel** *(Spermophilus lateralis)*, found mainly in the mountainous regions of British Columbia and Alberta, is one of the most attractive small mammals in Canada. It has two distinctive black-bordered whitish stripes from shoulder to rump and is sometimes called the big chipmunk.

A ground dweller which occasionally climbs low shrubs and can swim small

A Richardson's ground squirrel chatters its alarm call to warn of an intruder.

A Columbian ground squirrel eats 17 percent of its weight in food each day.

An arctic ground squirrel keeps a watchful eye for predators.

The golden-mantled ground squirrel is often mistaken for a chipmunk.

brooks, this ground squirrel is often seen standing erect and alert. In that posture, it looks like a tiny tree stump. It has good eyesight and hearing. Reacting quickly to danger, it lets out an explosive hissing note of alarm or a buzzing chatter. Its burrows are short and the entrances—under rocks, stumps or brush—have no telltale piles of earth nearby. The burrow, about four feet long, leads to a chamber with a nest of shredded leaves, grass and pine needles.

Golden-mantled ground squirrels store seeds in late summer after growing excessively fat, and begin hibernating early in September.

The **13-lined ground squirrel** *(Spermophilus tridecemlineatus)* found in the Prairie Provinces is quicker, more elusive and more of a loner than its related species. It digs simple burrows by scratching the dirt out with its long clawed forefeet. The forehead is used to pack the roof of the burrow and the hind feet spray loose dirt outside the entrance, leaving no sign of the newly dug earth. It inhabits abandoned, overgrown fields and shrubby areas rather than open grasslands, a favorite of other ground squirrels.

Mating occurs during a two- or three-week period in late April or early May and litters of 3 to 13 are born after a gestation period of 28 days. Females have been known to eat some of their young soon after birth.

The **Columbian ground squirrel** *(Spermophilus columbianus)* lives in colonies along the eastern flank of the Rocky Mountains, from the United States border to near Grande Prairie, Alta., and in parts of British Columbia. It eats roots, bulbs, leaves, flowers, seeds, grain, and some vegetables.

The Columbian ground squirrel warns its neighbors of danger and dashes for the nearest hole when frightened. Its clear chirp can be heard several hundred yards away.

The gestation period is 24 days and litters vary from two to seven. The young, born blind, begin to see about three weeks after birth. They are almost fully grown by hibernation time in the autumn.

Franklin's ground squirrel *(Spermophilus franklinii)* is secretive and lives alone or in small family groups. It is active in summer from dawn to dusk but may not venture from its burrow on rainy or windy days. It climbs better than other ground squirrels do, is a strong swimmer and has a clear musical whistle.

This species is found from the Rainy River region of western Ontario to the Edmonton area of Alberta. It does not inhabit the shortgrass prairie. The three-week breeding period follows the emergence of the females from hibernation in late April or early May. The young are born by the beginning of June, the litter varying from 4 to 11.

Franklin's ground squirrels eat beetles, grasshoppers, crickets and ant eggs, as well as roots, cherry stones and dandelions. They like such domestic grains as oats, wheat and corn.

The **arctic ground squirrel** *(Spermophilus parryi),* also known as the sik-sik, is found in the northern Yukon and along the lower Mackenzie River in the Northwest Territories. It also inhabits the continental tundra of the Mackenzie and Keewatin districts.

The young are born after a 25-day gestation period. Mortality is high during their first winter because the young often select sites for their burrows that become flooded or enveloped in permafrost. The arctic ground squirrel digs an extensive maze of tunnels, usually less than three feet deep. Permafrost prevents deeper burrows.

Individual tunnels, as long as 60 feet, may have 50 and more entrances in an area of 50 square yards. This squirrel spends about seven months in hibernation, in a den connected to the main tunnel. Seeds and leaves are stored in the den in late summer, to be eaten in the spring before new vegetation grows.

Artful Burrowers, the Last of Millions

Before the West was settled and cattle ranching became a major industry, millions of **black-tailed prairie dogs** *(Cynomys ludovicianus)* populated the grasslands from southern Canada to Mexico. Their enormous "dog towns"—one in Texas occupied 25,000 square miles—were among the wonders of nature. But man decimated these sociable, artful burrowers, seeing them as a threat to ranching. Today there are only an estimated 6,000, restricted to about 1,600 acres in southern Saskatchewan. A colony of black-tailed prairie dogs on 160 acres east of Val Marie is under the protection of the Saskatchewan Natural History Society.

Prairie dogs were so named because of their distinctive, high-pitched *yap-yap* that serves to warn of danger. They are closely related to ground squirrels, but are larger, have shorter tails, weigh up to three pounds and measure as much as 16 inches. The short ears are often hidden in the pale cinnamon buff fur.

Prairie dogs have many enemies. Eagles, hawks, coyotes and foxes attack them above ground; rattlesnakes and badgers invade their burrows.

No two burrows are alike, although key construction principles are similar. Soil excavated from a burrow is heaped around the entrance and the result looks like a crater. The mound keeps the burrows dry and serves as a sentry post. A main tunnel drops vertically for about 8 feet, then continues horizontally for as much as 40 feet. Off the tunnel are nesting and toilet chambers.

The animals come out of their burrows about 15 minutes after sunrise. They groom, stretch in the sun and visit neighbors on warm days. They feed cautiously, crawling for 5 to 10 seconds, then sitting on their haunches for 3 or 4 seconds to make sure they are not in danger. They eat leaves, grasses, weeds, grasshoppers, beetles and bugs.

The black-tailed prairie dog is not a true hibernator and has been seen outdoors on fine winter days. The litter, believed to be born in May, varies from two to eight. The young are weaned in about seven weeks.

Deliberate poisoning by man nearly wiped out the black-tailed prairie dog.

Prairie dogs have a strong sense of territory, forming homes or coteries sometimes consisting of several neighboring burrows. Coteries are occupied by one or two males, several females and their offspring. When two prairie dogs meet on open ground, they exchange a "kiss" or embrace that is believed to be a form of identification. They stand upright when alarmed and bark to warn other prairie dogs. Strangers are quickly routed from the feeding area.

A Norway rat peers from a half-eaten turnip. Most rats eat almost anything.

Pocket gophers sometimes burrow as deep as nine feet.

The **northern pocket gopher** *(Thomomys talpoides)* is a rat-sized, short-tailed rodent about nine inches long, with fur-lined external cheek pouches. Its pelage is soft and dense. The back is usually pale brown, the belly is pale buffy gray and the flanks are gray. Its mounds in Alberta, Saskatchewan and Manitoba are sometimes wrongly credited to moles.

Pocket gophers can inflict serious wounds with their chisellike incisor teeth. Their sense of smell is keen but their eyesight is poor. They generally are silent but squeal and grind their teeth in captivity.

Northern pocket gophers are common across the prairies from southwestern Manitoba to the Rockies. They also inhabit valleys in south-central British Columbia. They are active from August to October, tunneling and collecting roots for winter storage. They clean out their tunnels in the spring. In summer they eat the green parts of plants, obtaining food during brief nocturnal forays above ground.

Pocket gophers live on grasslands, in cultivated fields and along riverbanks. Their tunneling and foraging destroy gardens and grain fields, so farmers consider them as pests. They seldom leave their burrows in the daytime. The deeper tunnels are between three and nine feet below the surface and have nesting and food-storage chambers.

These are solitary animals except during the mating season, in April and early May. The gestation period is about 19 days. The young, born blind and naked, leave their home burrows in August and usually move a short distance away to dig their own burrows. They are adult size at five or six months.

The **Norway rat** *(Rattus norvegicus),* a hardy, adaptable rodent, is despised by man. Heavily built, with a grizzled coat and thick, brown tail, a male Norway rat weighs as much as a pound and measures nine inches from snout to rump. Also known as the brown rat, it is found in settled parts of Canada, except in most of British Columbia, Alberta and northern Canada.

It consumes grain, meat, vegetables, fruit, butter and cheese. A vicious fighter, it kills chickens, ducks and even small lambs. In cities it is a garbage scavenger and disease carrier. It can gnaw through wood and most building materials—even aluminum. Its chisel-sharp teeth grow at the astounding rate of five inches a year so the rat gnaws constantly to file them down. The Norway rat is prolific. Breeding may occur throughout the year and an average of nine young are born after a gestation period of about 21 days.

Pocket-Size and Plentiful

Some 76 species and subspecies of mice scurry through meadows and forests, cities and suburbs the length and breadth of Canada. Of these, the **deer mouse** *(Peromyscus maniculatus)*, found throughout most of Canada, has one of the widest ranges. Its brown and white coat resembles that of a deer—hence the name—deer mouse. Difficult to detect because of its color, small size and nocturnal nature, it often crouches well hidden among leaves and grasses, mainly in rural areas. It has beady black eyes, alert ears and a slender body with well-developed hind legs. It hops quickly on all four legs, climbs well and walks.

Deer mice are tolerant and sociable, particularly during winter when as many as 13 have been known to huddle together to conserve heat. These groups usually consist of family units but may include other species such as the harvest and jumping mouse.

In autumn, deer mice store food for the winter, transporting seeds in their cheek pouches. They eat acorns and apple, cherry, conifer and weed seeds.

Deer mice spend their lives in an area of about two acres. Shortly before the young are born, between April and October, the female expels the male from the nest, but welcomes him back later. She alone defends her territory in this interval. When the male returns, he helps maintain the nest and takes the young out to seek food. The brood consists of from one to nine mice.

The tail of the deer mouse is about half the length of the body in some subspecies and longer than the body in others. Those with long tails use them for balancing, especially when climbing. Long-tailed subspecies tend to live in the woods; those with short tails inhabit plains or fields and seldom climb.

The deer mouse has three distinct coats during its lifetime. As young mice mature, their gray and white coats turn brownish. Adults wear rufous brown.

The **northern grasshopper mouse** *(Onychomys leucogaster)* was discovered along the Missouri River in the United States in 1833. Compared with the deer mouse, it has a stouter body, shorter tail and legs, smaller ears, and slightly larger forefeet, with longer claws. The upper parts of the body are brownish and tawny; the cheeks, feet and underparts are grayish white. The nose is pink. Like the deer mouse, it has three pelage changes in its lifetime.

Found from the Gulf of Mexico to the Canadian Prairies, the northern grasshopper mouse occurs sparingly in southern regions of Manitoba, Saskatchewan and Alberta.

The northern grasshopper mouse is primarily carnivorous, preying on insects (mainly grasshoppers) and on other mice. It often corners its prey, then seizes it, biting through the base of the victim's skull with sharp incisors.

The northern grasshopper mouse is mainly nocturnal. Insects are about 90 percent of its diet in summer.

Mice are meticulously clean. Here a ***white-footed mouse*** (Peromyscus leucopus) *grooms its paws, tail and fur—even behind its ears.*

When the young are 10 days old, and for about 6 days thereafter, the mother teaches them to hunt by leaving dead insects for her offspring to find and eat.

Like other mice, the young are born pink, naked and blind. They have incisor teeth and silky, dark gray fur by the 12th day. Their eyes open between 15 and 20 days of age. They must fend for themselves when they are weaned and evicted from their nest 24 days after birth.

This little rodent usually takes over the burrows of other small animals rather than do its own digging. It is alert and active and largely nocturnal. It utters a variety of calls, including a shrill, insectlike whistle. It does not hibernate but lives through the winter on its body fat and stored seeds.

The **house mouse** *(Mus musculus)*, a familiar species, is a small rodent with large ears and a pointed head. The long, scaly tail is paler than the brown and gray coat. Albino house mice (white mice) are used in laboratory experiments and are also sold in pet shops.

House mice can be found in human settlements throughout southern Canada and as far north as the Mackenzie Delta in the Northwest Territories. The species found in Canada had its origins in Russian Turkestan, and reached North America from Europe in baggage of early explorers and settlers.

It is frequently found in barns and outbuildings where it feeds on grain, fruit, vegetables and refuse. It often falls prey to cats, dogs, weasels, owls and hawks. The house mouse breeds throughout the year if conditions are ideal. Several litters of four to eight mice are born each year.

The **meadow jumping mouse** *(Zapus hudsonius)* has the widest North American distribution of all jumping mice. It inhabits a broad area from the Atlantic to the Pacific and as far north as the Arctic tree line.

It is small, with long hind legs and an unusually long, wiry tail. A broad olive-brown band stretches along the back from the nose to the rump. The flanks are lined with black hairs and the underparts are a buffy white.

The young squeak; adults make a rasping sound, chatter their teeth or beat the ground with their tails. They usually move by a series of short hops. When frightened, they take off in a series of erratic leaps, each leap about a yard long. They crouch after a few leaps, hoping to escape notice. Meadow jumping mice can dive and they swim strongly—sometimes underwater—with their hind legs.

In summer, they nest in grass and leaves. They eat seeds, berries and insects and are preyed upon by owls, weasels, snakes and large frogs. They begin hibernation in late September or early October, usually in burrows dug by other mammals, and live on stored body fat.

The meadow jumping mouse sometimes swims to escape its enemies.

The house mouse is found near human habitation.

There are more than 30 subspecies of deer mice in Canada.

In Theory, a Family of a Million in One Year

Voles and lemmings can be distinguished from mice by their small ears and eyes, comparatively stout bodies and, in many cases, shorter tails. There are 18 species of voles in Canada and five species of lemmings.

In one species, the **meadow vole** *(Microtus pennsylvanicus)*, a female can give birth to her first litter at six weeks of age and produce as many as 11 offspring every three weeks. Theoretically, if all the progeny of one pair of meadow voles lived and bred, they would be more than a million after one year. In the wild, however, few meadow voles produce more than three litters a year. The mating season is from April to October. The gestation period is about 20 days, and the litter averages six young. The meadow vole's life span—seldom longer than a year—is believed the shortest of all mammals.

Voles are meticulously clean, spending much of their time washing their faces and combing their flanks. Each colony uses a communal toilet some distance from the nesting area. Voles use well-traveled pathways to and from their short, shallow burrows. They build globular nests of woven grass about six inches in diameter and also nest under boards, rocks and shrubs, inside hollow logs and in abandoned chipmunk and squirrel burrows. They eat grasses, leaves and flowers.

The meadow vole is found from Newfoundland to British Columbia, with the exception of Vancouver Island and the Queen Charlotte Islands. Its coat consists of a dense gray underfur with orange-yellow bands the length of the body and black-tipped guard hairs. The winter fur is long and silky. Meadow voles are from six to eight inches long.

The **heather vole** *(Phenacomys intermedius)* so closely resembles the meadow vole that until 1889 the two were thought to be the same species. It has small eyes and short, rounded ears that extend just beyond the fur. It has a plump body, a short, thin tail and white or silvery gray feet. The top fur is mostly an ocher brown among eastern Canadian subspecies and a grayish brown in western Canada. Its range is similar to that of the meadow vole.

Smaller than the meadow vole, the heather vole is docile and does not try to bite when captured. It is a solitary rodent in summer—except during the breeding season when males fight viciously—but families nest together in winter. The communal nest is a hollow sphere of heather, twigs and lichens.

The **Gapper's red-backed vole** *(Clethrionomys gapperi)* is found in forested and brush-covered areas across Canada, with the exception of Newfoundland, Anticosti Island, Vancouver Island, the Queen Charlotte Islands, part of southern Ontario, southern Alberta and southwestern Saskatchewan.

This vole has small eyes, prominent ears, a relatively slender body and a short, slim tail. It has a bright chestnut stripe along its back from the forehead to the base of the tail. The underparts and feet are a pale gray. It is most active from sunset to sunrise, remains active all winter and seldom wanders far from springs or streams.

Four subspecies of the **brown lemming** *(Lemmus sibiricus)* are found in Canada, mostly in the North from Hudson Bay to the Yukon—except in the Mackenzie Delta and the southern part of the Northwest Territories. Some brown lemmings inhabit the northern part of British Columbia.

Lemmings are gregarious and will not back away from a fight. When threatened, they bunch together and squeal at their assailant. They swim and can float high in the water because of their dense fur. Lemming populations fluctuate widely, reaching peaks every four or five years.

The brown lemming digs tunnels, from 2 to 12 inches below the surface of the ground, that lead to two or three adjoining chambers some 6 inches in diameter. Winter nests, of dried grass and lined with lemming fur, are on the surface. A series of nests is used in winter; each is abandoned when it becomes soiled.

The meadow vole (field mouse) is preyed upon by birds, mammals and snakes. Since it can swim, it is also eaten by fish. Below: a Gapper's red-backed vole. It may faint or die if handled.

The Ups and Downs of the Lemming

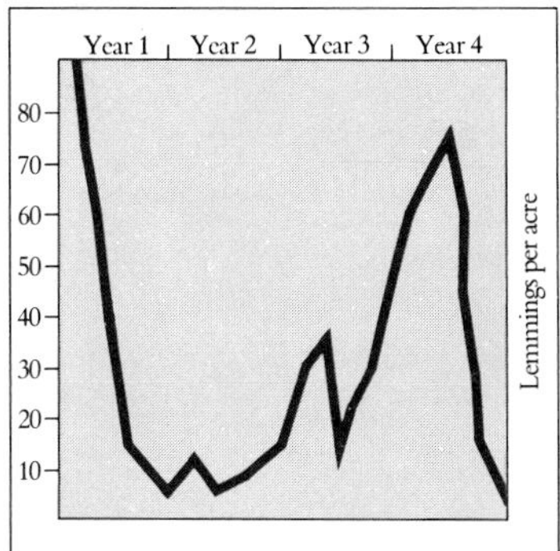

The lemming population peaks every four years, then declines sharply. When lemmings are plentiful, so are their predators—snowy owls, short-eared owls, jaegers, weasels and arctic foxes. When the lemming population declines, so does the number of predators.

Overcrowding leads lemmings to migrate by the thousands to new territory. Contrary to popular belief, they do not make a suicidal rush to the sea.

Scientists have not yet discovered why the lemming population fluctuates in four-year cycles. Recent studies suggest that overpopulation may inhibit reproduction.

The density of brown lemming populations varies from 20 to 130 an acre. Lemmings have been known to live as long as 14 months, surviving on tender grass shoots and leaves. They also like bark and twigs of willows and dwarf birch. They do not store food for winter.

The **collared lemming** *(Dicrostonyx torquatus)* is the only rodent that turns white in winter. It looks very much like the brown lemming in its summer coat but begins changing to white after the first autumn snow. Two of the claws on this rodent's forefeet grow long in winter, enabling it to tunnel into snowbanks.

It is most concentrated in the northern tip of Greenland but is found also in the Yukon and Northwest Territories, the Ungava region of northern Quebec and in Alaska. There are seven subspecies in northern Canada.

About six inches long, the collared lemming has a chubby body and moderately large eyes. Its ears are hidden in the fur and the tail is a mere stub. The feet are broader than those of the brown lemming and have more fur on the soles. The fur is dense and silky. Collared lemmings live less frequently in colonies than brown lemmings do but family bonds are strong and both male and female care for the young. Only a few collared lemmings live more than a year.

The **northern bog lemming** *(Synaptomys borealis)* inhabits northern areas of Quebec, Ontario and the Prairie Provinces and is found throughout British Columbia, the Yukon and western regions of the Northwest Territories. Similar to the **southern bog lemming** *(Synaptomys cooperi)*, it can be identified with certainty only by its teeth. The distribution of the two species overlaps only in southeastern Manitoba and Quebec and in northern New Brunswick. They are small and plump with short tails and small feet.

The coat of the northern bog lemming varies from a grayish brown to chestnut brown in the various subspecies. These rodents are about five inches long. They dig short underground burrows and use runways through vegetation. Globular nests of grass are built underground in summer and on the surface in winter. They eat grass and sedge.

Lemmings seek refuge on an ice floe far from land. These tiny rodents are good swimmers but often drown when they try to swim large bodies of water.

Symbols of Spring, Renewal and Fertility

Since ancient times, rabbits have been symbols of spring, renewal and fertility. They have thrived in the popular literature and legend of many cultures and are among the best-known and best-loved of all animals.

Rabbits and hares deserve their reputation for fecundity. They live in constant peril from disease and predation but their high birthrate helps to guarantee survival of the species. Rabbits and hares are a favorite of hawks, eagles, foxes, coyotes and other predators, including man.

The **eastern cottontail rabbit** *(Sylvilagus floridanus)*, which ranges from southern Canada to South America, gets its name from its white, powderpuff tail. Upper body fur is gray to reddish-brown, usually streaked with black. The underparts are white or light buff. There is little change of color during winter. The overall body length is 12 to 18 inches, average weight about three pounds. The cottontail, like other rabbits and hares, has acute senses of hearing and smell.

Because of their many enemies, few cottontails live longer than a year.

Between mid-March and September, after 28-day gestation periods, the female has 4 or more litters, each with 2 to 8 young. She often breeds again within 24 hours of giving birth.

The young are raised in fur-and-grass-lined nests or shallow depressions in fields or brush. They are nursed and cared for by the mother until, at about two weeks, they begin leaving the nest to feed on green plants. A few days later they leave the nest permanently. They reach adult size about eight weeks later.

Cottontails are most active at night, with peak feeding around dusk and dawn. They eat almost any plant in their range, showing a preference for grasses, clover, alfalfa and, of course, garden vegetables. In winter they eat the bark of trees and shrubs. A mixture of grassland, cropland and brushland is ideal habitat, but cottontails adapt well to many types of cover, including old buildings and junk heaps. They avoid tracts of mature forest.

With a top speed of about 20 miles an hour, cottontails are not as quick as their zig-zag motion leads one to believe. In fast motion, their forefeet come down first, then the hind feet land in front of the forefeet. Persons unaware of this sometimes track rabbits (or hares, which make a similar track) in the wrong direction.

The pika, or rock rabbit (Ochotona princeps), *is related to rabbits and hares but looks more like a guinea pig.*

The **white-tailed jack rabbit** *(Lepus townsendii)* is really a hare. Early settlers on the plains spotted its jackass-like ears and dubbed it jackass rabbit.

These are prairie hares, long-legged and built for speed. They can clear obstacles five feet high, leap 15 feet at a single bound, and reach speeds of 35 miles an hour in short bursts. The species inhabits prairie areas of Manitoba, Saskatchewan and Alberta. A small number are found in the Okanagan Valley of British Columbia.

How to Tell Hares From Rabbits

Hares are larger than rabbits and have longer ears and legs and wider hind feet. Unlike rabbits, hares have black-tipped ears and their coats turn white in winter. Hares nest on the ground, rabbits in burrows. At birth, hares are fully furred and their eyes are open. Rabbits are born naked and blind. When threatened by predators, hares flee, rabbits hole up.

Strong claws and long incisors enable the arctic hare to forage in snow.

Seeing Wildlife in Parks

Visitors who hurry through Canada's national and provincial parks looking for wildlife are usually disappointed. But take off on a side road early or late in the day—feeding time—and you may have better luck.

Bighorn sheep and mountain goats can sometimes be seen near main highways and at natural salt licks in British Columbia.

Look for moose, beaver, muskrat, wildfowl and reptiles and amphibians in and around small lakes, ponds and marshy valleys.

Bears often visit garbage dumps. If you spot a bear, stay in your car—all wild animals are dangerous and bears are particularly unpredictable.

Loud, unexpected noises and sudden hurried movements will frighten away most animals. Field glasses and quiet patience will help you observe an abundance of wildlife missed by the hurried traveler.

This jack rabbit's summer coat is grayish-brown. The tail and underparts are white and the ears have black tips. Its winter coat is white with black ear tips.

Like most hares, the white-tailed jack rabbit is nocturnal, solitary and usually silent. When wounded, it screams shrilly. When caught, it may defend itself, and can inflict deep scratches with its hind claws.

By day, the hare crouches with flattened ears in its form, a slight depression scratched in ground or snow. At dusk it forages and feeds on grass, clover, cultivated grain, alfalfa and vegetable greens. In winter, it eats hay and the bark of shrubs and trees. Its overall length is about 22 inches, ear length 4 to 5 inches, and average weight 6 to 9 pounds.

The white-tailed jack rabbit mates in spring and the young, born in June or early July in litters of three to six, are nursed in the nest for five or six weeks.

A white-tailed jack rabbit can leap from birth. Below: a snowshoe hare. It has shed most of its brown summer coat. By midwinter, it will be completely white.

The **snowshoe hare** *(Lepus americanus)*, often called the varying hare, is found in most parts of Canada, most abundantly in woodlands and forest regions that are snow-covered all winter. Large, well-furred paws, for footing on ice and snow, give it its name.

The snowshoe is smaller than the white-tailed jack rabbit. Its length is 16 to 21 inches, ear length 2 to 3 inches, and average weight about four pounds. Gray-brown in summer, it turns white in winter. Long, stiff hairs grow on its hind feet, almost doubling the foot size and permitting quick and easy passage over soft snow in which predators might flounder. It rests in forms during the day, feeding and foraging at night.

Breeding is normally in early spring. Two or three litters of 2 to 6 young are born during the summer after gestation periods of 36 to 40 days. The young begin eating grass in their second week and cease nursing after about four weeks.

The **arctic hare** *(Lepus arcticus)* of northern Canada, like the snowshoe hare, has widespread toes and stiff, bristled hair on its feet to support it on snow and ice. About the size of a house cat, it is the smallest animal in Canada with fur thick enough to protect it against an arctic winter. Smaller animals must take refuge in burrows under the snow. In the high arctic islands its coat remains white year round. In more southerly parts of the Northwest Territories it wears a brown coat in summer.

The **European hare** *(Lepus europaeus)*, or common hare of Europe, is not native to Canada. It was introduced from Germany to southern Ontario, where it thrives and is often called a jack rabbit. Heavily built and long-eared, its average length is 27 inches.

The European hare lives mainly in open country. Its summer coat is rusty brown with grayish flanks and a white underbelly. Ears are black-tipped, the tail black on top and white underneath. Its coat does not turn white in winter, but merely becomes somewhat paler and grayer.

Tiniest of Nature's Fierce Fighters

Among the smallest of mammals, the shrew is in many ways one of the most vicious. Weighing less than an ounce, this tiny fighter is constantly hungry, burning energy so fast that it will starve to death in less than a day if deprived of food. Like the mole, the shrew spends virtually all its life searching for food. Though classified as an insectivore (insect eater), it can kill and devour creatures twice its size, gobbling them in spasms of excitement.

The shrew's fierce spirit is out of all proportion to its size and appearance. With its long, pointed snout, velvety fur, black beady eyes and short legs, it fits easily into the palm of a hand. Cursed by poor eyesight, it relies on its senses of smell, touch and hearing to locate prey, or simply blunders upon it.

Unlike moles, which are accomplished burrowers, shrews often take over the abandoned burrows of other animals. Shrews rarely live beyond 16 months.

One of the most common shrews in Canada is the **masked shrew** *(Sorex cinereus),* which scampers among decayed logs, leaves and stumps. About four inches long, with dull sepia fur that gets longer and darker in winter, it is found as far north as the Ungava region of Quebec. The masked shrew was introduced into Newfoundland in 1958 to counteract the destructive larch sawfly.

Like most shrews, it is most active after dusk and during the early morning. It eats insects and occasionally salamanders, mice and worms. In winter it burrows under the snow in search of dormant insects, hibernating mice and the carcasses of small mammals and birds. It is preyed upon by larger shrews, weasels, hawks, owls and snakes. Other predators are driven away by its musky odor.

The **short-tailed shrew** *(Blarina brevicauda),* of eastern Canada, has musk glands and a venom similar to cobra poison. The venom, secreted by the shrew's salivary glands, causes paralysis in animals it attacks. The poison causes only local swelling and pain in humans.

The short-tailed shrew is about five inches long. Its body is dark and robust with tough skin, a blunt nose and small pinkish feet. Its eyes are weak but its hearing, smell and tactile senses are keen. This shrew nests in tunnels dug about a foot underground in forest loam and leaf litter. It prefers the dampness and loose humus of eastern hardwood forests from the Gulf of Mexico to the Gaspé Peninsula. It is sometimes found as far west as Saskatchewan.

Moles have thick midsections that taper to the head and tail, front limbs attached near the base of the skull, and pinprick eyes hidden under facial fur. These burrowing insectivores are admirably suited to life in damp, dark earth.

Not so the **star-nosed mole** *(Condylura cristata).* A poor digger, it forages above ground in woods, meadows, marshes and along lakes and streams.

The hairy-tailed mole (above) is awkward above ground. The star-nosed mole (below) often forages on the surface.

Like most moles, the coast mole feeds mainly on earthworms.

A short-tailed shrew attacks a meadow vole, paralyzing it with venom, similar to cobra poison, from its salivary glands.

This eight-inch-long mole makes up for poor eyesight with a snout that expands into a naked, pink disc supporting 22 extremely sensitive feelers that give the animal tactile information about its surroundings. When it tunnels it folds the tentacles over its nostrils to keep out dirt, then pushes earth away from its nose with its forefeet. It twists its body and spreads its hind limbs as it digs.

It eats mainly water insects, worms, crustacea and mollusks and hunts throughout winter. Mating probably takes place in late February. The one litter, usually born in April, consists of two to seven young.

Star-nosed moles, the northernmost moles in Canada, are found from Hamilton Inlet in Labrador to the east coast of Hudson Bay and westward to Lake Manitoba. A dark-colored subspecies has been sighted in Nova Scotia.

The **coast mole** *(Scapanus orarius)* rarely ventures above ground. Found from northern California to southern British Columbia, where it inhabits the lower Fraser Valley, this mole prefers forests and thickets on meadow edges.

It is about 6½ inches long. Its coat, dark slate on its back and paler on its belly, has a silvery sheen. After mating in late January, the female gives birth to about four young in late March or early April.

Tunnels of the coast mole, often three or more feet deep, can ruin gardens and lawns. A positive contribution to gardens is the mole's appetite for white grubs and cutworms, though its main food is earthworms and fly larvae.

The **hairy-tailed mole** *(Parascalops breweri)* is a loner that usually digs a permanent tunnel system 10 to 18 inches deep. As its name suggests, its short tail is covered with black stiff hairs. It is about six inches long. Its dusky black fur has a copper sheen and its feet and snout are flesh-colored. The forefeet are broad with long, flat nails.

Found from southwestern New Brunswick and central Ontario southward to North Carolina, the hairy-tailed mole inhabits eastern hardwood forests and pastureland where the soil is loose.

This hungry creature consumes considerable quantities of worms, though its main foods are beetles, ants and larvae. Like other insectivores, it can eat more than its body weight in earthworms in a 24-hour period. During nightly forages, the hairy-tailed mole may be attacked by foxes, owls and large snakes.

Mating usually takes place in late March when a light brownish secretion stains the abdominal fur of both sexes and probably helps in locating mates. The gestation period lasts four to six weeks and an average of four young are born. Hairy-tailed moles may live as long as four years, a ripe old age for an insect-eating mammal.

*The **eastern mole*** (Scalopus aquaticus) *has well-developed front legs for digging. Only about four ounces, it can push a load of earth 20 times its own weight.*

*The **pygmy shrew*** (Microsorex hoyi) *is the smallest and one of the rarest mammals in North America. An adult weighs only a tenth of an ounce.*

The masked shrew consumes its own weight in insects each day.

The Only Mammals That Fly Like Birds

Largely because of their appearance and nocturnal habits—and man's vivid imagination—bats for centuries have been fantasized about and feared. Myth says these winged mammals are the embodiment of evil, feeding on the blood of humans, living a vampire existence. But, in fact, most bats are beneficial to man because they eat as much as 50 percent of their own body weight in insects every day. Furthermore, their mastery of echolocation intrigues scientists the world over.

Bats are the only mammals to have mastered true flight. No other animal has wings like the bat's—thin tough membranes that stretch from the sides and rear of the body and are supported by the arms, legs and tail. Using the wing membranes as nets, or using their mouths, bats catch insects on the fly or pick them off the ground and from vegetation.

Dependence on insects threatens the survival of many bat species, since insecticides enter the bats' systems and build up to lethal levels. Several species have declined drastically in recent years as a result of this poisoning.

Among mammals, bats rank only behind rodents in number—perhaps tens of billions—and diversity of species, some 900. By far the greatest number live in the tropics. Canada has about a dozen species of bats, all of which feed on insects. Some bats live in caves where they spend the winter in hibernation. Others, tree bats that generally roost in shrubs and trees, may migrate to warmer climates when the cold approaches. When resting, bats hang upside down by their tiny clawed hind feet.

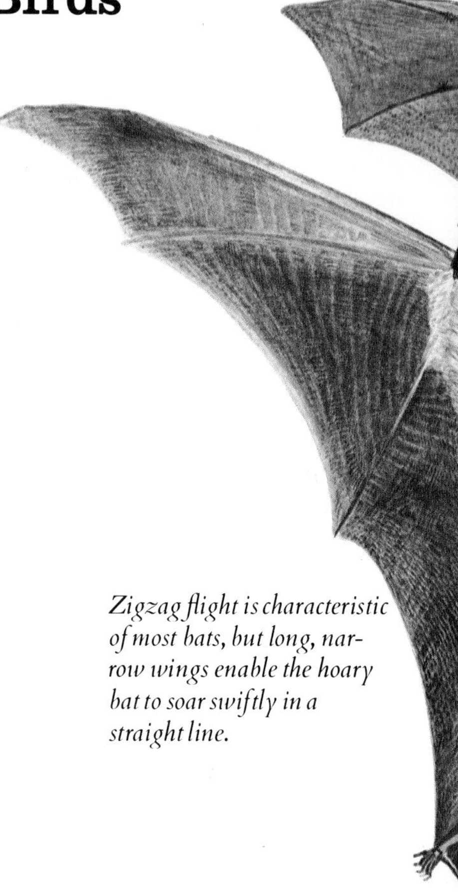

Zigzag flight is characteristic of most bats, but long, narrow wings enable the hoary bat to soar swiftly in a straight line.

The **little brown bat** *(Myotis lucifugus)*, the commonest species in Canada, zigzags over water, meadows and tree-lined roadsides in search of insects. Active mainly at dusk and dawn, it is found across North America from Georgia to Labrador in the east and from California to Alaska in the west.

The little brown bat has a 10-inch wingspread and weighs a mere third of an ounce. Its long, silky brown hair is tipped on its back with a copper sheen.

In summer, hundreds of females and their young form nursery colonies in warm dark attics and similarly enclosed places. Males, either alone or in small groups, seek cooler shelter under bark and behind shutters. By late fall, little brown bats have gathered by the hundreds of thousands in cool damp caves where they hang from dark draftless ceilings. They are thought to subsist all winter on body fat. When they emerge in April or May the males and females go separate ways.

Mating may occur in late autumn or when the bats awaken during the dormant months. Although females do not ovulate until April or May, sperm remains viable in the uterus for long periods during hibernation. Usually only one egg matures at a time so only one young is born in June or July. For the first few days of its life, the newborn clings to its mother's breast—even when she makes brief flights from one roosting spot to another. At three weeks, the young bat can fly. Some little brown bats live as long as 24 years. A few fall prey to hawks, raccoons, weasels and even to house cats.

The big brown bat withstands winter weather better than most bats and goes into hibernation as late as December. It is usually the first bat to emerge, in April.

The **big brown bat** *(Eptesicus fuscus)* is found across most of southern Canada and north to northern Alberta. Despite its name, this bat measures only 5 inches, with a wingspread of about 13 inches. It increases its body weight by as much as a third before going into hibernation in November—then loses the extra weight during winter. As many as four young may be born but since the female has only two teats for nursing, no more than two of the young survive.

One cave-dwelling bat that keeps its distance from humans is the **western big-eared bat** *(Plecotus townsendii)*, found from central Mexico to central British Columbia in mine shafts, caves and abandoned buildings. It prefers cultivated valleys bordered by brush or open forests. Easily identified by erect ears,

Female big brown bats sometimes fly short distances with their young clinging to their breasts.

A little brown bat captures a woolly bear moth.

At night, the western big-eared bat (above) frequently roosts in buildings.

In summer, the ***silver-haired bat*** (Lasionycteris noctivagans) *lives in hollow trees, under loose bark, or in abandoned bird nests.*

longer than an inch, this species of bat is only 4 inches long with an 11-inch wingspread. Western big-eared bats form clusters as do little brown bats. By late July a single young is born—pink, naked and blind, with floppy ears and spiderlike fingers and toes.

The **red bat** *(Lasiurus borealis)* has narrow pointed wings spreading about 11 inches and long silky fur. The male is brick red. In the East the female is paler, more yellowish red.

Found in southern Canada from Nova Scotia to Alberta, the red bat also occurs southward to Central America. In early September the northern populations migrate to areas from Washington, D.C., to the Gulf states. They return north in April and May. Red bats mate in August and September, sometimes in the air. The female usually bears two or three young in May or June.

One rare species is the **hoary bat** *(Lasiurus cinereus)*, Canada's largest bat. It has a wingspan of 15 inches or more although it weighs only 1½ ounces. Its dense brown coat is tipped with silver, giving it a frosted look. Its range is enormous—from the Northwest Territories to Argentina, the West Indies to Hawaii—though in Canada it is far from abundant. Migration southward is in August or September. The return north is from March to June. The hoary bat, a forest dweller, roosts on leafy branches in the day and hunts in late evening. It flies swiftly and powerfully.

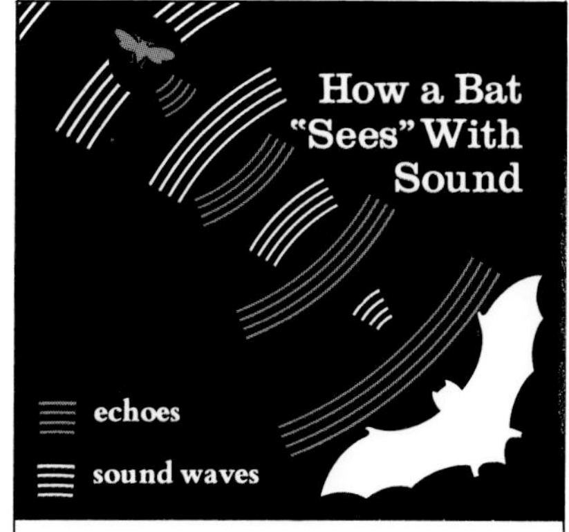

A bat is not blind but its eyes are weak. To detect obstacles or insect prey, it emits high-frequency sounds and picks up the echoes. It varies the frequency and rate of the sounds to determine the position, distance, size and movement of objects.

Nine-Ton Wolves of the Sea

Killer whales, with powerful jaws and 10 to 14 pairs of large, sharp teeth, are the wolves of the sea. Killer whales are curious and highly intelligent but they are not, as is popularly believed, savage vicious animals that kill indiscriminately. Prowling in packs of 3 to 40, they feed mainly on fish. Sometimes they attack marine mammals—including the biggest baleen whales—but usually take only the weak or the sick.

A pack may encircle a school of dolphins. Because young dolphins respond to danger by bunching together, they are easy prey. One killer at a time swims into the school to feed while the others continue circling.

When hunting the immense blue whale—the world's largest known creature—an entire pack of killers attacks at once. Several killers tear flesh from the blue whale's lower jaw, others attack the pectoral fins, immobilizing the prey. Killer whales usually feed on the soft body parts, tongue, lips and parts of the jaws. The carcass is eaten by seabirds, fish and other marine mammals.

Found in most oceans and seas, including those off Canada's northern islands, the **killer whale** *(Orcinus orca)* is the largest, fleetest, most powerful member of the dolphin family. It grows to 31 feet in length and nine tons in weight. Its streamlined body enables it to slice through water at 10 knots. Although the species is feared by man, there is no authenticated record of a killer whale having attacked a human. A killer in captivity is easily trained and will leap 40 feet to snatch food from a trainer's hand. Many scientists have reported that, like most dolphins and porpoises, killer whales in the wild are docile toward humans.

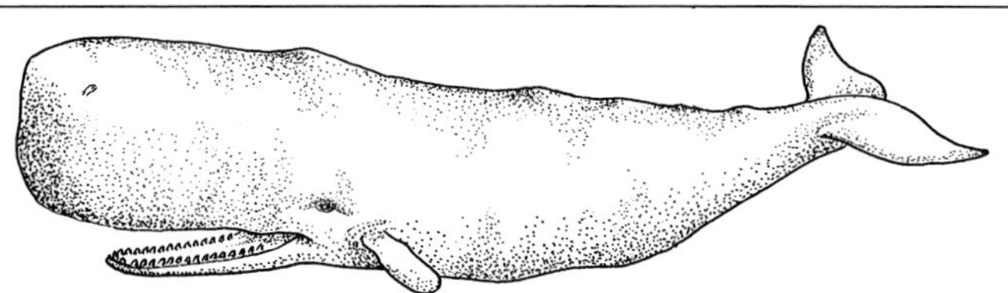

Toothed Whales

Some whales have teeth. Others—baleen whales—have whalebone instead. Toothed whales, generally smaller than baleen whales, include dolphins and porpoises. The teeth are used to seize fish, squid, other marine mammals—even seals. Teeth range in number from two (in the narwhal) to 300 (in some porpoises). Toothed whales have only one blowhole.

A killer whale can leap 8 feet out of the water, its nose 40 feet in the air.

The **sperm whale** *(Physeter catodon)* is the largest toothed whale. It can be twice as long as the killer and can weigh 50 tons. Its head, a third of its body length, contains approximately a ton of spermaceti—an oily wax used today to make candles, ointments and cosmetics. Early whalers mistook this fluid for sperm—hence the name of sperm whale.

Scientists speculate that the fluid may enable the slow-swimming sperm whale to dive deeper than any other sea mammal—to more than 3,000 feet, where the pressure is nearly 100 times greater than at sea level. The sperm whale can stay submerged for more than an hour. During long dives, its heart beats only 10 times a minute, pumping five gallons of blood with each contraction.

Generally slate gray, sperm whales are found off both Canadian coasts. One of these creatures consumes a ton of food every 24 hours. Strong, conical eight-inch teeth along its lower jaw fit into sockets in the upper jaw, enabling it to seize and hold a 300-pound squid. The sperm whale was immortalized in Herman Melville's *Moby Dick or The Whale.*

Rapid pursuit of prey often leads the **Atlantic pilot whale** *(Globicephala melaena)* close to shore—where it becomes stranded at ebb tide. Because pilot whales travel in groups and tend to follow a leader, entire gams of stranded or

The sperm whale feeds mainly on giant squid.

Little is known about mating and reproduction in killer whales and attempts to breed them in captivity have been unsuccessful.

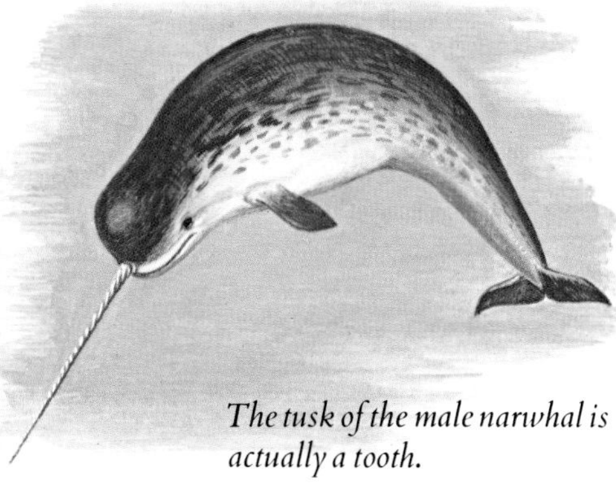

The tusk of the male narwhal is actually a tooth.

The Atlantic pilot whale (above) is a type of dolphin. The white or beluga whale (below) is related to the narwhal.

dead pilot whales have been found along the Atlantic coast of North America.

The pilot whale—Newfoundlanders call it the pothead—has a bulging, melon-shaped snout and what looks like a fixed, fatuous smile. The bulging forehead may help the whale to hear and to dive. In the mating ritual, male and female pilot whales crash head-on then rise out of the water, chests together, in a cumbersome union.

A pilot whale can live more than 20 years if it manages to stay afloat, evades killer whales and steers clear of commercial fishermen.

The **white** or **beluga whale** *(Delphinapterus leucas)*, a small whale related to dolphins and porpoises, is normally seen in Canadian arctic waters. It has also been sighted in the Bay of Fundy and in the Gulf of St. Lawrence.

White whale hunting, once a successful industry, is now restricted to arctic residents. Eskimos boil white whale skin to prepare *muktuk*—a delicacy. The skin is also used for boots and laces. The oil—a large white whale yields about 30 gallons—provides fuel for lamps and a base for margarine.

The **narwhal** *(Monodon monoceros)*, a porpoise-like whale, has a long, twisted horn. In medieval times the narwhal was thought to be a descendant of the mythical unicorn. The horn, which sometimes grows to nine feet, is actually a tooth that spirals from the upper jaw. Its function is not known but it may be used in courtship rituals. Only the male has a horn.

Favorite haunts of the narwhal are deep fjords along the coast of Baffin, Ellesmere, Devon and Southampton islands and off Greenland. When trapped by ice, the narwhal sometimes uses its hard forehead—not its horn—to butt its way to freedom. It frequently lies motionless on the surface.

Eskimos shoot narwhals at breathing holes or harpoon them from kayaks. Narwhal oil is considered superior to other whale oil and the skin and flesh are prized. Valuable carvings are made from the ivory horns. During the Middle Ages, narwhal tusks were worth their weight in gold to Europeans. Today, the narwhal is of little value to commercial whalers.

Biggest of All Creatures, Yet Shy and Placid

The biggest creature known to man, the **blue whale** *(Balaenoptera musculus)*, grows to more than 100 feet in length and 150 tons in weight. Nearly two thousand gallons of blood pulse through its immense heart. It can down 20 barrels of food in a single gulp.

The blue whale weighs two tons at birth and gains 200 pounds a week during its seven-month weaning period. Yet, despite its staggering proportions, it is a shy, placid creature that feeds only on krill—minute crustaceans and larvae.

Blue whales that inhabit the North Atlantic enter the Gulf of St. Lawrence in April and remain in Newfoundland waters until July, when they return north. Blue whales usually swim at 12 knots but can reach 20; they dive to nearly 1,200 feet and can remain underwater for 50 minutes.

The oil of the blue whale (each produces 90 to 300 gallons) is used in the manufacture of soap, candles and synthetic resins.

Between 1913 and 1931 the blue whale comprised about 90 percent of the world's total whale catch. Fewer and fewer blue whales were caught as overhunting pushed the species to the brink of extinction. Blue whale hunting was prohibited in the north Atlantic in 1965, yet in 1971 only 3,000 of the creatures were thought to exist. Their numbers now are slowly increasing.

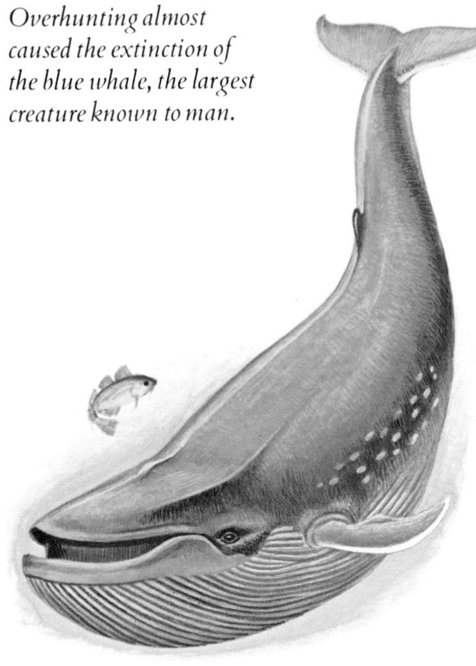

Overhunting almost caused the extinction of the blue whale, the largest creature known to man.

The **fin whale** or **common rorqual** *(Balaenoptera physalus)* and the **sei whale** *(Balaenoptera borealis)* generally inhabit the same regions of the Atlantic as the blue whale. They migrate in small groups and sometimes feed in large herds, or gams. Like other large whales, they are preyed on by killer whales.

Because of its speed and its long sleek body—averaging 65 feet—the fin whale is sometimes called the greyhound of the sea. In short bursts, fin whales achieve 20 knots. Sei whales, smaller (about 60 feet) but swifter, can swim short distances at up to 35 knots. Fin whales consume about a ton of food daily; seis eat half a ton. Both species feed on krill, herring and capelin.

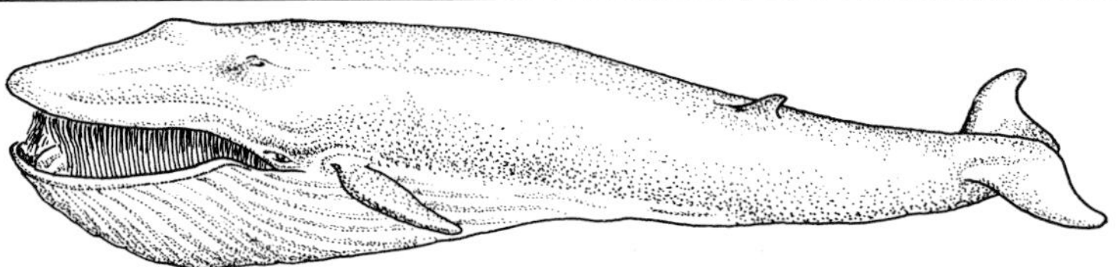

Baleen Whales

These whales are born toothless. In place of teeth, they have layers of baleen—or whalebone. The 130 to 400 baleen plates on the upper jaws act like sieves to separate food from water inside the whale's mouth. Among the largest creatures on earth, baleen whales feed on the smallest life forms in the sea—microscopic zooplankton, tiny crustaceans and larvae, collectively called krill, and small fish. Baleen whales have two blowholes.

The fin whale (above) can swim at 20 knots. The gray whale (below) usually cruises at a leisurely two to four knots. Its top speed is 10 knots.

During early whaling days both species were relatively safe because of their speed and small size—six sei whales yielded the same amount of oil as one blue whale. Sei and fin whales also sank when killed, which made them difficult to capture. But with the advent of faster whaling vessels they could be successfully pursued, hauled alongside and pumped full of air before they sank. After World War II, fin whales comprised half the world catch and were almost rendered extinct. Recently, sei whales have been intensively hunted because of the scarcity of blue and fin whales.

One whale recovering from near extinction is the **bowhead** *(Balaena mysticetus)*, which has been protected from commercial hunting since 1937. The bowhead (or Greenland) whale grows to about 60 feet and is thought to weigh up to 110 tons. Its massive head accounts for a third of its body. Its mouth may be 20

The sei whale often swims long distances just under the surface, where it feeds on colonies of microscopic zooplankton and on schools of small fish.

feet wide, its lips 6 feet thick and its narrow, flexible baleen plates 15 feet long.

This species was one of the first arctic resources exploited by Europeans. After the whale population declined about Spitsbergen in the early 18th century, Europeans began hunting in the western Atlantic, to supply corset manufacturers with whalebone. By the 1860s American whalers were also hunting in Canadian arctic waters. At the end of the 19th century bowheads were virtually extinct.

Today the International Whaling Commission permits the hunting of bowheads only if they are to be used by native peoples. Eskimos still hunt them with harpoons and rifles in umiaks—small open boats covered with hides. Eskimos use whale oil for fuel, bones for implements, and meat to feed their dogs.

Gregarious and migratory, bowheads travel north in spring, and return south before early winter—although they never migrate far from the arctic pack ice. They swim at two to four knots and stay underwater for up to 30 minutes. Surfacing, they exhale a blast of moist air 10 to 20 feet high.

The 30-ton **humpback whale** (Megaptera novaeangliae) *is the clown of the sea. When playing it somersaults and leaps backward from the water.*

A bowhead whale surfaces and its massive head sends spray flying.

The **gray whale** *(Eschrichtius robustus)* is seen off Vancouver Island and the Queen Charlotte Islands during spring and fall migrations. Like the bowhead, it sometimes swims close to shore when pursued.

While 40 to 50 feet long and weighing 35 tons, the gray (or scrag) whale has a relatively small head with a wide mouth. Whiskers on its jaws make it one of the hairiest of all whales. It feeds for only six months of the year (usually through summer) by scooping crabs and other shellfish from the ocean floor. It travels at a leisurely 2 to 4 knots, sometimes accelerating to 10 knots when alarmed.

The gray whale's migratory habits, slow speed and fondness for shallow waters have made it easy prey for whalers. The North Atlantic population of gray whales was killed off by the early 1700s and the Pacific breed seemed destined for the same fate until 1937 when international whaling controls banned the capture of the remaining gray whales.

A Hairy Ton of Blubber With Flippers for Legs

Equipped with powerful flippers and protected by hairy coats and thick blubber, most seals and sea lions thrive in polar waters or in the cold currents of temperate seas, diving for the fish, squid and crustaceans on which they feed. They are mammals, with lungs and milk glands, and they return annually to where they were born, there to give birth and to mate. In some species embryo development is delayed for months: the pup is born a full year after the mating, but at a time and place that virtually ensure its survival.

The **northern sea lion** *(Eumetopias jubata)*, which inhabits the North Pacific, easily outranks in size all land-bound carnivores, even polar and grizzly bears. The adult male, with huge forequarters and a swollen neck, is about 12 feet long and weighs up to a ton, nearly twice the weight of the female. These buff or brown animals with thin manes and short pointed ears use their large flippers for support on land and to fan themselves on hot days.

Besides man, only killer whales and large sharks threaten sea lions, which have been known to survive 17 years in the wild. Their range extends from Japan to the Soviet Union's Commander Islands, to the Pribilof Islands off Alaska and down the coast to southern California. In British Columbia coastal waters, the main rookeries are among the Scott Islands off the north end of Vancouver Island and at Cape St. James in the Queen Charlotte Islands.

The older and bigger bulls—termed harem masters—reserve mating privileges to themselves, "hauling out" of the sea at breeding colonies in mid-May after females have arrived. Establishing harems of 10 to 30 cows, the pugnacious bulls try hard to control the more agile, straying females. Bulls defend their breeding area in the rookery until early August, fasting all the while. The densely-packed rookeries are marked by the constant din of roaring bulls, barking cows and whining pups.

The **northern fur seal** *(Callorhinus ursinus)*, smaller than its sea lion relatives, occurs in great numbers both sides of the North Pacific, frequenting British Columbia waters in winter and during spring and fall migrations.

By the early 1900s, commercial hunting had greatly reduced the numbers of fur seals. Conservationists worried about the survival of fur seals and about the future of other species—harp seal, for instance—point to the success of the North Pacific Fur Seal Convention of 1911 that banned sealing in the open ocean.

The United States manages the herds that breed on the Pribilof Islands and the Soviet Union manages those on the Commander Islands. The two nations harvest a controlled number of pelts from bachelor seals—sexually immature males. Profits from the harvest are divided among the United States, the Soviet Union, Canada and Japan.

Adult male fur seals average 427 pounds. The finely-proportioned cows average less than 100 pounds but have been known to live 21 years in the wild, compared with a known life span of 14 years for the mighty males. The species hunts mostly at night for fish and squid.

One of nature's great spectaculars unfolds when 1.5 million northern fur seals congregate for their reproduction ritual. The vast majority converges on the Pribilof Islands. Breeding bulls—apparently all 10 years or older—haul out in late May or early June. They bellow and battle in what seems utter confusion but a fundamental territorial pattern emerges.

According to their physical power and beach strategy, the bulls collect harems of 10 to 100 females. The harem sizes vary greatly, however, as fickle females wander and are kidnapped by rival bulls.

Within two or three days of arrival in the breeding grounds, females give birth to the pups conceived the previous year. A week later, mating takes place. The closeness of birth and mating is possible because the cow seal's V-shaped

Within days of birth the harbor seal's white coat becomes spotted.

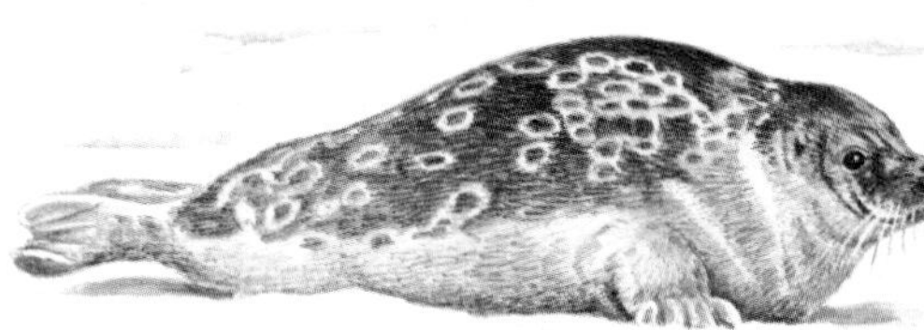

Ringed seals, smallest of all seals, seldom weigh more than 200 pounds.

A ***walrus*** *uses its tusks to open breathing holes, fight enemies and haul itself onto ice floes. Its Latin name,* Odobenus, *means tooth walker.*

Northern sea lions are extremely cautious and fight only with one another. When threatened by predators, adults abandon their young.

A breeding colony of northern fur seals is a bedlam of bellowing as bulls fight to control their harems.

womb has two branches that are alternately impregnated from year to year. This permits her to give birth from one branch and become impregnated in the other—all within a brief period.

Unlike most mammal young, a fur seal pup feeds as infrequently as once every six days during the four-month nursing period—the mother forages at sea for six days or so at a time. Nonetheless the pup grows from 11 pounds to 50. Because the mother heads southward in November, leaving the pup to follow as it can, mortality is high among the young.

The **harbor seal** *(Phoca vitulina)* is perhaps the most far-flung species in the family of true or earless seals, which have relatively short flippers and use their hind limbs alone for propulsion in the water.

This playful creature inhabits the northern seafronts of North America, Asia and Europe and different subspecies are native to Canada's Atlantic and Pacific coasts. One subspecies of harbor seal in Canada *(Phoca vitulina mellonae)* is land-locked, inhabiting two lakes in Quebec's Ungava Peninsula.

Generally buff brown on top and white on the underparts, harbor seals average five feet in length. Males average 300 pounds, females slightly less. Harbor seals herd together loosely on land but forage singly in the water.

The **ringed seal** *(Phoca hispida),* abundant in arctic and subarctic waters, is the smallest of all seals and sea lions. This species gets its common name from a coat with irregular white rings and dark centers. A mainstay of the coastal Eskimo economy, it yields meat for man and dog, skins for clothing, boots and dog harnesses and blubber for fuel. Tools were once fashioned from its bones.

The harvest of pelts is expected to remain an important source of cash for Eskimos, though the price for prized young "silver jar" pelts slipped after a boom in the early 1960s.

With Canadian Eskimos now grouped into villages, there have been reports of overexploitation of seals. At first glance, the ringed seal would seem safe in its vast habitat so sparsely settled by man, but experts point out that this might change with improved hunting equipment and increased demand for skins.

With a short, thick body like that of the harbor seal, this species averages 4½ feet in length. Males weigh roughly 200 pounds, slightly larger than females.

Half the World's Harps Are in Canadian Waters

More than half the world's two million harp seals live in Canadian Arctic waters. Each year in November and December they travel 3,000 miles south to breed on pack ice in the Gulf of St. Lawrence and off the east coast of Labrador.

The adult **harp seal** *(Pagophilus groenlandicus)* is about 6 feet long and weighs up to 300 pounds. Its common name and one of its several nicknames—saddleback—derive from a dark harp-shaped band that loops around its dark-spotted, brownish gray body.

Harp pups, brown-eyed and 25 pounds, are born on the pack ice after almost a year's gestation. The female suckles her pup for about two weeks until it weighs about 100 pounds. Then she abandons it and the pup begins to starve. It also begins to shed its creamy white, fluffy fur, for which it is often called a whitecoat.

Within a month the pup wears a gray coat flecked with dark spots. By this time it is a proficient swimmer. It is also 35 pounds lighter. It reaches maturity at between five and nine years.

The young seal's life is perilous. Many young seals are crushed to death when fierce storms toss and tilt the ice floes on which they take refuge. Those that survive to adulthood often live as long as 30 years.

The harp seal spends most of its life in herds in the open seas. Males and females remain together all year.

Harp seals can dive as deep as 100 fathoms (600 feet) and stay underwater for 20 minutes. They surface to breathe at a natural opening in the ice. As many as 60 seals may share the same breathing hole.

Seals are noisy. A pup's cry is a wail like that of a tomcat fighting. A group of adult females sounds like thousands of rusty, screeching door hinges—and the sound carries long distances in crisp wintry air. Females defend their territory during whelping time and harshly reject other pups. But harp seals are generally timid and flee danger, making little or no effort to save their pups when hunters attack.

Seals are harvested in March for fur, leather and oil. The largest haul ever recorded was in 1831 in Canadian waters off the coast of Newfoundland. It totaled 687,000 seals—mostly harps. The hunt involved 300 ships and 10,000 sealers from Nova Scotia, Newfoundland, Norway and Scotland. Now, in the Gulf of St. Lawrence, the Canadian government limits the annual harvest to 150,000 seals and prohibits the use of aircraft and large sealing ships.

The **bearded seal** *(Erignathus barbatus)* is a large, robust, solitary animal with a curly mustache. It ranges along Canada's northern shores and as far south

Bearded seals use their whiskers to feel for food on the ocean floor.

Awkward on land, the elephant seal humps along like a monstrous inchworm.

A hooded seal inflates its nasal sac to intimidate a rival.

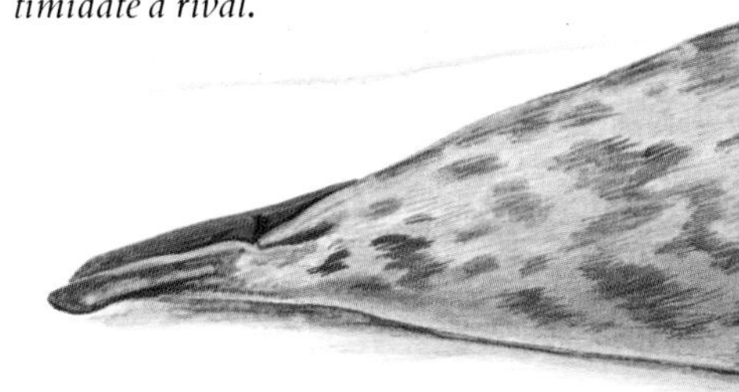

How to Tell Sea Lions From Seals

Sea lions, unlike seals, have ears. They are generally smaller than seals and manage a waddling walk on land; seals, with small forelimbs, drag themselves in a slow crawl. Sea lions swim with their forelimbs and flippers. Seals swim by wriggling their bodies and sculling with the hind flippers. Sea lions have a single coat of hairs; seals have underfur covered by long guard hairs.

Gray seals begin to molt three weeks after birth and are then abandoned by their mothers. Alone on the ice, the pups are easy prey for hunters.

Female harp seals recognize their young by odor and reject all other pups.

as Hamilton Inlet, Labrador. Both sexes of this square-flippered species are about 5½ feet long and weigh up to 750 pounds. Eskimos use the tough hide of bearded seals for boot soles, tents and kayaks, and their meat for dog food.

The **gray seal** *(Halichoerus gryphus)* is found along the Atlantic coasts as far south as Nova Scotia and in the Gulf of St. Lawrence, where it angers fishermen by feeding on salmon. Herds of gray seals sometimes damage fishnets and traps. About 15,000 of the world's 50,000 gray seals are found in Canada—in temperate waters along exposed, rocky coasts and on remote islands. They mate on ice floes or rocky islets during January and February.

Bulls are about 8 feet long and weigh up to 600 pounds. Cows are about 7 feet and weigh 550. Flexible forelimbs with long, slender claws enable gray seals to move easily on ice. Because of their long, broad, straight snouts, gray seals are often called horse face.

The **hooded seal** *(Cystophora cristata)* breeds at the same time as the harp, but farther north. Adults have elastic nasal sacs but only the male's can be inflated to form a football-like "hood" from nostrils to forehead. Males grow as long as 7½ feet—larger than females—and pups are called bluebacks because of their lustrous deep-blue fur. Hooded seals form family groups during breeding and the female is uncommonly aggressive in defense of her pups.

The hooded seal belongs to the same family as the **northern elephant seal** *(Mirounga angustirostris)*, among the largest of all mammals. Adult elephant seals may be 16 feet long and weigh 2½ tons. Bulls have a foot-long, bulbous nose which hangs over the mouth like a short trunk. The world population of elephant seals is about 15,000, found mostly off southern California. Occasionally an elephant seal is spotted off British Columbia.

Birds

The Rare Whooper . . . the Clever Crow

People often speak of "birds and animals" but birds *are* animals—feathered animals.

All birds—and *only* birds—have feathers. Like mammals, they are believed descended from reptiles: their feathers are derived from reptilian scales, their wings from reptilian forelimbs.

The earliest bird probably appeared about 140 million years ago. Today the scientific class *Aves* includes about 27 orders of birds and some 8,600 species. Of these, approximately 520 species have been recorded in Canada.

Birds' streamlined bodies offer minimum air resistance and most species can fly. Their bones are light and generally hollow and the lower vertebrae of their backbones are fused, making bird skeletons among the most rigid in the animal world. The backbone, breastbone and ribs form a sturdy cage. Well-developed pectoral muscles—often accounting for more than a quarter of a bird's weight—provide power to the wings.

Another characteristic of birds is large eyes, each with two sets of eyelids and a transparent membrane that acts like a windshield wiper when the creature is in flight. Birds have no teeth although some species, such as ducks, have tooth-like ridges on their bills. All birds reproduce by laying and incubating hard-shelled eggs.

A bird expends enormous energy in flight so it consumes as much as twice its own weight in food each day. An infant robin eats as much as 14 feet of earthworms in a day. An adult nighthawk may eat 500 mosquitoes in a single meal.

Most bird societies are highly organized and governed by complex instinctive behavior. Birdsongs define territorial limits. Spectacular displays of plumage help to attract mates.

Some birds migrate astounding distances. The champion migrant is the arctic tern. It summers in the Arctic and winters in Antarctica—making an annual round trip of about 22,000 miles. One of the swiftest birds, the peregrine falcon, can dive faster than 200 miles an hour. Canada's smallest bird, the calliope hummingbird of western Canada, weighs a mere tenth of an ounce.

Neck outstretched and wings flapping, a common loon may patter across the water for up to a quarter of a mile before becoming airborne.

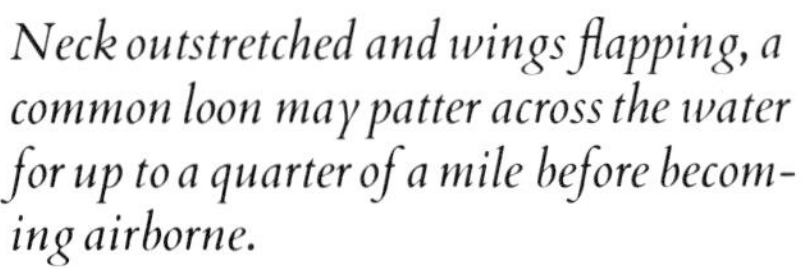

The Loon's Lonely Wail: True Cry of the Wild

Like most waterfowl, the horned grebe swims and dives expertly.

The cry of the loon—a lonely wail, a frenzied laugh or an eerie yodel—is a true call of the wild, as distinctive as the howl of a wolf and, like it, associated with desolation and the primitive.

The **common loon** *(Gavia immer)* is found in most Canadian provinces and its cry is often heard by cottagers, campers and canoeists. Its range is from the northern mainland United States to northern Alaska and east to Newfoundland.

Loons are noted for swimming and diving and seldom go ashore except to nest. They catch fish by underwater pursuit, propelling themselves with their webbed feet. Because their legs are far to the rear of their bodies, they are awkward on land, floundering with their breasts on the ground. A loon's flight is swift and direct but most species cannot launch into the air from land; even from water their take-off appears labored.

Like other diving birds, loons remain underwater for long periods. They have been seen to submerge then surface three minutes later half a mile away.

The common loon, about three feet long, has a straight, pointed bill and hard glossy plumage. Its bright greenish black head and neck turns grayish in winter. A white, striped collar and a black and white back make it easily visible.

Only one pair of loons inhabits a lake, although larger lakes may have two or more pairs. Usually two eggs are laid and they are incubated by both sexes until they hatch in about 28 days. The nest, built at the water's edge in a clump of vegetation, is abandoned soon after the chicks hatch. Until the young can fly, at about 10 weeks, they are cared for by both parents. Both adults and young winter at sea coasts and on large lakes where water does not freeze.

How to Tell a Loon From a Duck

Loons have larger and longer bodies than ducks. Loons' bills are sharply pointed; ducks' are round-tipped and flat. There's no confusing the sounds: ducks quack; the loon's long, lonely cry is something else again.

The grebe, a smaller, shorter bird with a straighter neck than the loon and an insignificant tail, swims and dives well. Unlike the loon, it can stand upright on land. Most grebes have crests or ruffs during the breeding season and when in flight a patch of white can be observed on each wing.

The grebe has a strange habit of swallowing its own feathers. These wrap around fish bones and act as a filter to the gizzard, keeping bones in the stomach until they are soft enough to pass safely.

The **horned grebe** *(Podiceps auritus)* is a small bird with a short, straight bill. Male and female look alike with buffy ear tufts against a black head and a chestnut neck as summer attire. This bird spends summer in freshwater ponds and shallow bays, and winters in salt water and large, open lakes.

Both parents incubate the four to five eggs. The family spends the summer feeding on aquatic insects and preening, dozing or just floating. As with other grebes, the young often ride on the adults' backs.

The horned grebe's summer habitat extends from the northern Yukon and adjoining parts of the Northwest Territories, south through British Columbia and the Prairie Provinces and parts of Ontario and Quebec. Winter is spent in southern Canada or farther south.

The V Formations That Signal the Seasons

Wild geese are sentinels of the Canadian seasons. When flocks fly south, winter is near. The flap of wings in March and April heralds spring.

Though geese, swans and ducks are all members of the same family, geese are smaller than swans and bigger than ducks. Unlike most ducks, geese of both sexes have the same plumage. Because they are better walkers, they feed more often on land. Geese have three long toes joined by a membrane; the small hind toe is slightly elevated and free.

The **Canada goose** *(Branta canadensis)* is perhaps best known for the familiar V formation of a flock in flight. The name Canada goose applies to about 20 widely varying subspecies that range from 2½ to 18 pounds and in wingspread from 3 to 6½ feet. While subspecies vary in color, all Canada geese have a long black neck, black head and large white cheek patches. Their habitat includes treeless prairies, arctic coastal plains, mountains and, occasionally, northerly regions of Quebec and Ontario. Canada geese have been known to live 30 years in captivity but average 3 years in the wild. Perhaps because of a constant threat by man, they are remarkably wary. They are regular in their feeding habits and return day after day to the same grounds, usually at midmorning or just before sunset. During feeding, two or more black necks are stretched upward—on the lookout for danger.

Goslings eat tender grasses and other green herbage. During fall and spring migration, the geese eat green shoots of grasses, wheat, barley and other cultivated grains. Canada geese sometimes group, especially in parts of the West where lakes are scarce. But in the North where lakes are numerous each pair reserves a lake or bay to itself.

Family ties appear strong. A pair usually mates until the death of one. Nests are generally built on the ground near water or on beds of waterlogged plants in marshes or on muskrat and beaver lodges. The four to six eggs are incubated by the female while the male stands guard, often several hundred yards from the nest. In summer, as goslings grow flight feathers, adults molt and regrow theirs.

The family moves together, the adult female leading the way, followed by the goslings, and the gander brings up the rear. When another family ventures too close and appears to be invading the feeding area, battle formation is assumed with the male moving to the head of a V-like phalanx. Even an imagined territorial infringement may flare into a battle. Strength of numbers rather than individual size seems to win in these encounters.

Canada geese range over most of the interior of North America. They winter in the southern United States and Mexico but small numbers remain in coastal British Columbia, southern Ontario, and Prince Edward Island, Nova Scotia and Newfoundland.

Threatened by heavy hunting in the early 1900s, the **greater snow goose** *(Chen caerulescens atlantica)* has returned to the Arctic in record numbers. Its white plumage is set off by a sizable section of black at the tip of its broad wings. Its facial expression features a black "grinning patch" on each side of the bill.

The **lesser snow goose** *(Chen caerulescens caerulescens)* is the smallest of the two subspecies of snow geese in Canada. It is also known as the wavy, from the Cree word *wawa* which means wild goose. The blue goose is simply a lesser snow goose with bluish gray plumage. Both the blue and white varieties mix freely and crossbreed.

From June to September snow geese live in colonies on the low, flat tundra where the goslings are hatched and raised. If a crane or other predator raids the nest during incubation and damages the eggs, the female snow goose may eat the yolks of her own eggs, either for nourishment or to keep predators from getting them. Usually four eggs are laid. They hatch near the end of June. Goslings feed

Canada geese breed as far north as southern Baffin Island.

Gregarious brant geese gather in colonies even when nesting.

The ***trumpeter swan*** (Olor buccinator) *is found mainly in Alberta and Saskatchewan. Lesser snow geese (below) nest in the High Arctic.*

and swim with their parents by the end of their first day. Sometimes one gosling hatches later than the others. If it is too weak to follow the flock, it may fall prey to herring gulls cruising above the colony.

The lesser snow goose, found throughout the Arctic, flies south across the Prairies and down the Mississippi Valley or the Pacific coast. The greater snow goose, found only in the eastern Arctic, migrates across the Ungava Peninsula and down the Atlantic coast.

The world population of greater snow geese is not difficult to assess. Every fall and spring most stop at the Cap Tourmente National Wildlife Area, 30 miles east of Quebec City, where they are counted. A count in 1906 revealed only 3,000 geese but hunting controls helped get the population to 150,000 by 1976.

A long wavering line of small geese or a formless flock may signal the passing of the **brant** *(Branta bernicla)*. At home in arctic maritime areas during the summer, the brant winters along the Pacific coast from the Queen Charlotte Islands to Baja California. An eastern subspecies of **brant** *(Branta bernicla brota)* winters along the Atlantic coast from Massachusetts to North Carolina.

Like the Canada goose, the brant has a black head and neck but has no white cheek patches. The adult brant has a black chest and a narrow white crescent on each side of the neck. The eastern subspecies' brownish gray belly contrasts with its dark chest.

A sociable goose, the brant sometimes nests in loose colonies. The nest may be a mere hollow in the ground or a mound of mosses and lichens, but it is always well lined with down for the five or more goslings. The brant calls with a hoarse honk and chatters when feeding.

The northward migration of the brant in spring is late. In the Maritimes, brant tend to linger at feeding places as late as the first week of June. On the wintering grounds and during migration, brant feed mainly on eelgrass uncovered by the ebb tide. They also feed by going tail-up in shallow water like ducks.

A Flapping, Quacking Vertical Takeoff

The common, colorful mallard: yellow, green, white, chestnut, blue.

The wildly flapping takeoff of puddle ducks—amid a chorus of urgent quacking—is a familiar sight on Canadian rivers and marshlands, especially in the West. The takeoff is almost vertical. That and iridescent wing patches distinguish puddle ducks from diving ducks. Puddlers feed on aquatic plants and small aquatic animals and go surefootedly on land in search of grain.

The **mallard** *(Anas platyrhynchos)* is one of the largest and most common ducks in North America. The drake is 20 to 28 inches long. Its breeding plumage includes a glossy green head and neck, a white collar, a chestnut breast and metallic blue wing patches bordered by white bars. The eclipse plumage of summer and fall resembles the female's: mottled brown with greenish wing patches bordered by white bars.

The mallard cruises at about 30 miles an hour. A wary bird, it feels at ease only when darkness covers its feeding ground and makes its flight less conspicuous. It is found throughout the Yukon and Northwest Territories, from British Columbia to Manitoba, and in parts of Ontario and southwestern Quebec.

Mallards winter south as far as Mexico. Mating is in spring after the migratory flight north. A nest, usually on the ground, is built of grasses, reeds, leaves and down, and the female lays and incubates about 10 dull green or gray-buff eggs. Newly hatched chicks are fully feathered in yellow and black and begin flying at eight weeks. Drakes ignore the family after the eggs are laid and gather in small flocks by themselves.

Mallards frequent wet areas of all kinds but can also survive where there is little water. Most of their food consists of sedges, grasses, pond weeds and bulrush seeds. Mallards sometimes damage grain fields but they also devour large

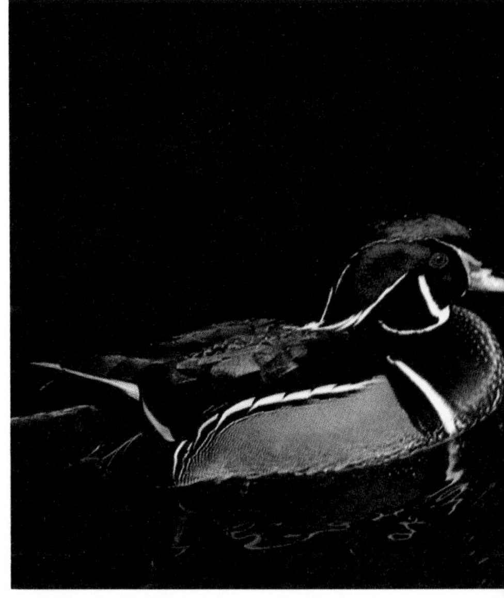

More colorful than the mallard: the beautiful, tree-climbing wood duck.

The **pintail** (Anas acuta) *reaches speeds of up to 65 miles an hour.*

amounts of mosquito larvae. They swim underwater to escape danger but rarely to collect food.

The **wood duck** *(Aix sponsa)*—so called because it prefers ponds, lakes and streams in wooded areas—frequently lives in a hollow tree, as much as 50 feet above the ground. The 8 to 15 downy ducks hatched each year have sharp claws and a hook at the tip of their bills. They use these to climb to the nest entrance, then drop to the ground; because they are so light and resilient they are not injured by the fall.

The drake, one of the most beautiful ducks in North America, is identifiable by its gracefully crested iridescent head of green, bronze, blue and purple interspersed with white stripes. Its back and rump are bronze green. The less colorful female is a mixture of gray, brown and green with a smaller crest.

Wood ducks often perch in trees and fly easily through dense bush in search of acorns and berries. The species is found in southern parts of British Columbia, Manitoba, Ontario, Quebec and New Brunswick. A few winter in southwestern British Columbia and around Lake Erie.

The bill of the **shoveler** *(Spatula clypeata)* is large, flat and long and widens

The shoveler's "shovel"—a long, flat bill—digs food from ponds.

A Burst of Power and It's Airborne

Powerful wings, large in relation to weight and body size, enable a puddle duck (a surface feeder such as the mallard, pintail, wood duck and teal) to launch itself almost directly upward from water or land. Legs well forward on the body provide balance.

toward the end. Both sexes use their bills to shovel pond water, mud and vegetable matter. Food particles are sifted out through comblike teeth. The drake has a white breast, green head, and chestnut belly and sides. The female is a mottled brown. Both have a large blue patch on each wing. Shovelers gather near lakes, rivers, marshes and potholes. They eat seeds, insects, small fish, mollusks and crustaceans. The female builds the nest and incubates 8 to 10 pale green eggs.

In summer shovelers inhabit the interior of British Columbia and southern Alberta and Saskatchewan. In winter they are the most common duck along the coast of southern British Columbia.

Among the smallest duck species in Canada are the **blue-winged teal** *(Anas discors)* and the **green-winged teal** *(Anas carolinensis)*. Like other puddle ducks, they prefer shallow freshwater ponds and marshes, but the blue-winged variety may also be found on the weedy margins of sluggish rivers. The green-winged teal frequents shallow salt water during migration and winter. Both build nests on the ground, generally near water, and usually lay 9 to 12 eggs.

The green-winged teal is often seen in winter in shallow salt water.

A large white crescent in front of the eye and a conspicuous white patch on each side of the tail base distinguish the male blue-winged teal from teals with similar wing markings. The female is a mottled brown with a blue patch on the fore part of each wing. Small, compact flocks of blue-winged teals fly low over marshes, twisting and dodging around trees and bushes.

The green-winged teal breeds from Alaska and northwestern and central Canada to California, and winters in the United States. The blue-winged species breeds southward from southern Canada and winters from the southern United States to Brazil and Ecuador.

Deep Water and Seafood Attract Divers

Most ducks prefer freshwater lakes and rivers and feed mainly on vegetable matter on or near the surface. But some species, the so-called diving ducks, are attracted to wild coastal areas where their food consists chiefly of small marine animals. Their favorites are mollusks and crustaceans, for which they often dive to great depths. They also eat small fish, aquatic insects and some seaweeds. These ducks are rarely hunted as game birds, for their heavy intake of seafood gives their flesh a strong, fishy flavor.

Histrionicus histrionicus, the scientific name for the **harlequin duck,** comes from the Latin for little actor—and although the drake's behavior is not dramatic, its appearance is. This bird, mainly metallic blue, sports a vivid white crescent at the base of its bill, oval white ear patches, a circular white mark behind each eye, a chestnut stripe on each side of its head and a white collar. Its back is slate blue. The female's plumage is brown, gradually whitening toward the abdomen. She has three circular white marks on each side of the head.

The harlequin leaves the Pacific and Atlantic seaboards to breed throughout British Columbia and southwestern Alberta and from southeast Baffin Island to the Gaspé Peninsula. It winters as far south as California and Massachusetts.

The harlequin builds its nest in a clump of bushes or between rocks along a swift-flowing river or stream. The female incubates six or seven buff eggs for about 30 days.

The **oldsquaw** *(Clangula hyemalis)* is one of the few ducks whose plumage changes only twice a year. In spring and summer the drake is brownish black with a white abdomen, a patch of buff at the base of the bill and a white blotch around each eye. The back and chest are brownish black in winter but the rest of the plumage is a mixture of gray and white.

The oldsquaw breeds throughout the Arctic, along the coast of Hudson Bay, in northern Quebec and along the coast of Labrador. It winters along both seacoasts and on the open water of the Great Lakes. The nest is a depression in the ground, often near water. Six to eight olive to yellowish buff eggs are incubated by the female for about 24 days.

A plumper, darker and homelier coastal duck is the **surf scoter** *(Melanitta perspicillata).* The drake, sometimes called skunkhead, is black with a white triangle on the forehead and another on the back of the neck. It has a black patch margined on top by orange and below by white on each side of the bill. The dark brown female has two whitish areas on each cheek and on the back of the head.

The surf scoter prefers saltwater coasts but is sometimes found on lakes and large rivers. Like the harlequin, it rarely goes on land except to breed—in northern Canada. It nests near fresh water in shrubby tangles and woodland, often on an island. Its down-and-feather-lined nest is built in a small hole in the ground and concealed by shrubbery. Five to seven pinkish or buffy white eggs are incubated by the female.

The surf scoter summers in the Yukon and western Northwest Territories, in northern Alberta, Saskatchewan and Manitoba, and in interior Labrador and northeastern Quebec.

Similar to the surf scoter, but without white head markings, is the **common scoter** *(Oidemia nigra).* The drake is black except for the gray undersurface of its flight feathers. Its black bill has a swollen, orange-yellow base. The female is brown and lacks the beak swelling.

Most scoters are silent but the male of this species has a pleasant, whistling call. It is often seen flying restlessly over oyster and scallop beds in search of food.

The common scoter breeds in northern continental Canada. Its nest is a grass-lined depression in the ground, near water. Six to 10 pinkish buff eggs are incubated by the female. The common scoter summers along the British Colum-

The common scoter shuns land except to breed.

Our Vanished Wildlife

Not more than 45 specimens in museums and scientific collections are all that remains of the **Labrador duck** *(Camptorhynchus labradorius).*

It probably shared breeding grounds on the Labrador coast with eiders and other sea ducks that were hunted for their feathers. The Labrador duck was apparently unable to survive this exploitation.

In 1871, in New Brunswick, a lone Labrador duck was shot. The last recorded sighting of this black and white waterfowl was in 1878 at Elmira, N.Y. The Labrador duck had a long, broad bill and probably ate mussels and small clams.

The male surf scoter (right) is called skunkhead for the white markings on its head. The female (above) is smaller and brownish.

Masked face, variegated costume—a duck with the look of Harlequin.

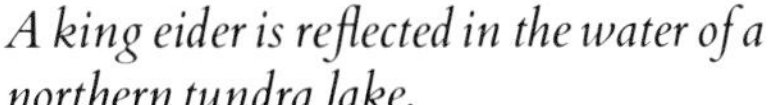

A king eider is reflected in the water of a northern tundra lake.

The oldsquaw ("hell's chicken") dives to depths of 180 feet.

bia coast, the coasts of Hudson Bay, James Bay, Ungava Bay and the south coast of Hudson Strait, in Newfoundland and on the Gulf of St. Lawrence. In winter common scoters flock to the British Columbia coast and to the Atlantic coast from Newfoundland south.

The Arctic is the breeding ground of the **king eider** *(Somateria spectabilis)*, one of Canada's largest and hardiest ducks. An excellent diver and a strong swimmer, the king eider is a whitish bird with black markings. The drake's head, neck and breast are white with a large black V on the throat. Much of its sides, tail and wings are black. Its knoblike bill broadens into a yellow frontal shield margined by black. In full plumage the king eider has a pearl-gray crown.

The king eider builds its down-lined nest beside tundra freshwater lakes and streams, where it is sheltered by rocks and vegetation. Sometimes it nests on flat tundra some distance from water. The female incubates four to seven eggs for about 22 days.

The king eider breeds from the High Arctic to the coasts of the Yukon and Northwest Territories, and along Hudson Bay. It winters on open water off Labrador and Newfoundland and in the Gulf of St. Lawrence and the Bering Sea.

They Seem to Walk on Water Before Liftoff

Diving ducks prefer deep open water to small lakes and marshes. When danger threatens, they swim great distances underwater, only occasionally breaking the surface with heads or bill tips to breathe, then dive again. They dive deep in search of fishes, mollusks and aquatic plants. Diving ducks rely on large webbed feet to patter over the water before taking off.

The wings of diving ducks are smaller in proportion to weight and body size than those of puddle ducks. Divers compensate with a quicker wing beat. And diving ducks have less brilliant wing patches.

The **canvasback** *(Aythya valisinera),* one of the best divers, often plunges to 20 or 30 feet in search of food. A long dark bill and a sloping forehead give it a unique profile.

The drake is a large white-bodied duck with a long rusty neck and head and black hindquarters. The female is slightly smaller with reddish brown head, neck and breast. Drakes are generally silent except during courtship when they utter a series of guttural croaks.

The canvasback is found in western Canada and in the Yukon and the western Northwest Territories. On the Prairies, where once the species was plentiful, its numbers have been reduced by drought, hunting and tampering with water levels in the potholes where it breeds. The nest, built in shallows and sometimes on dry land, is made from marsh vegetation on a bed of cattails or rushes. The 10 eggs are incubated by the female.

Neither a diver nor a puddler, the common merganser nests in trees.

Canvasbacks are great divers (down to 30 feet) and fast, powerful fliers (70 miles an hour, altitudes of up to 11,000 feet).

Canvasbacks are powerful fliers that can reach 70 miles an hour in the air. They migrate as far as Mexico in large wedge-shaped flocks, usually flying at under 3,000 feet although they have been seen as high as 11,000.

Similar in coloring but not in head profile is the **redhead** *(Aythya americana)*. Its forehead rises abruptly and its bill is slightly concave. The male's chestnut head has a slight purplish gloss and its back is more gray than white. The wing patch is gray.

Redheads like freshwater lakes and nest near the shallow edges or on dry land. They tend to gather in large numbers in deep water, coming closer to shore morning and evening to feed. Even near the sea they seek fresh or brackish water.

Redheads breed in British Columbia and the Prairie Provinces. In the fall,

The male redhead's head is not really red but purplish chestnut.

There's a whistling sound in the beat of the common goldeneye's wings.

large flocks traveling in V formation migrate to the United States and Mexico.

The loud whistle of its wings in flight has earned the **common goldeneye** *(Bucephala clangula)* the nickname whistler. A medium-sized, chunky duck with large areas of white in its wings, the goldeneye nests around woodland lakes and muskeg ponds. It breeds throughout Canada.

The male's blackish head, with green and purple iridescence, contrasts sharply with the large white spot on each cheek. Its back, rump and tail are dark. The female's head is brown and its sides and flanks gray with white-tipped feathers. The white on its wings is less extensive than on the male.

Goldeneyes nest from 5 to 60 feet above the ground in natural cavities in trees and rocks, large woodpecker holes and occasionally chimneys. At other times they gather near freshwater lakes and rivers, on the sea coast and in tidal estuaries. In the fall, most goldeneyes fly south, notably to Chesapeake Bay, but some winter on open rivers in southern Canada. Goldeneyes are strong fliers. They move in small loose flocks high in the air, often rising in rapid spirals. They are extremely wary.

Although named for its faint chestnut collar, the **ring-necked duck** *(Aythya collaris)* is distinguishable from other species of ducks by its dark, glossy triangular head. Its bill is slate-colored with a bluish white band near the tip and a thin white margin at the base and edges. This duck has a black back with a spur of white in front of its folded wings. The male is usually silent, but in breeding season has a low, hissing whistle. The female makes a series of growls.

A Flapping of Wings, a Pattering of Feet . . .

A diving duck takes off into the wind. Wings flapping rapidly and paddlelike webbed feet pattering over the water, the duck eventually gains momentum to become airborne or to be tossed up by an oncoming wave.

The ring-necked duck generally inhabits shallow freshwater marshes and bogs and, occasionally, tidal estuaries and bays. Unlike most diving ducks, it is rarely found on large expanses of open water. In migration it is found on rivers and lakes, particularly those with marshy edges.

Ranging across southern Canada, except southern Alberta and Saskatchewan and coastal British Columbia, the ring-necked duck nests in low vegetation at the edge of a bog, pond or slough. It lays 6 to 14 olive-gray, olive-brown or buffy eggs in a nest of marsh vegetation lined with down. The eggs hatch in 25 to 29 days.

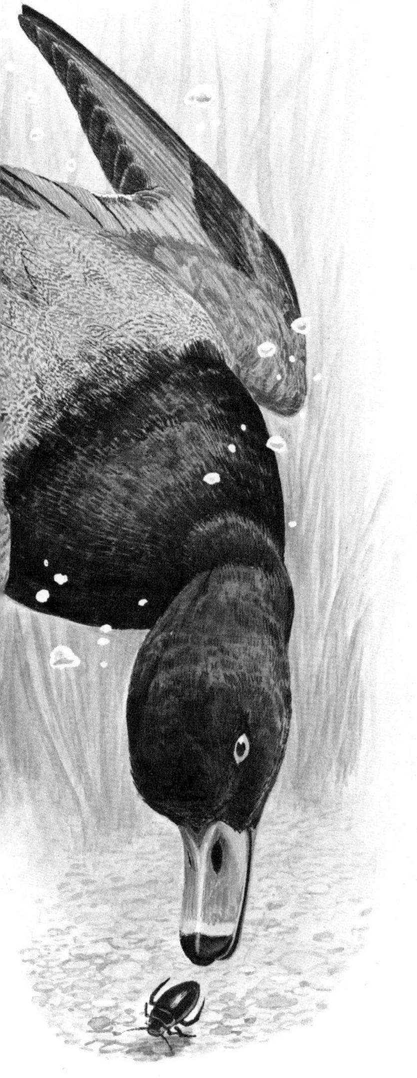

Holes in trees are a favorite nesting place for the **common merganser** *(Mergus merganser)*, a large freshwater duck belonging neither to the diving ducks nor the puddle ducks. It is found on lakes and rivers throughout Canada. Nests are also built in holes in riverbanks, in rock piles and on the ground among bushes. They winter as far south as Mexico.

Mergansers have long slender bills. Toothlike serrations on the back of the tongue and on the upper and lower jaws enable them to catch and to hold fish.

The drake's head and neck are black with a greenish tinge and the upper back and wing tips are black. Its body is whitish. The female's head is brown with a noticeable crest. Mergansers often fly low over the water in single file.

The Perilous Life on a Cliff Top

Almost from birth in its cliff-top nest the **double-crested cormorant** *(Phalacrocorax auritus)* faces a hazardous existence. Many birds, failing in their first attempt to fly—at about six weeks—fall to their deaths. Others leave the nest before their fishing instinct has developed, and so starve.

The young double-crested cormorant is sooty brown with dark-margined wings. The adult is a shiny greenish black and the feathers of the upper back are bronze edged in black. The throat patch and the area around the eyes are yellowish orange. The 2½-inch bill is slender and hooked. In spring the mature bird sprouts a small double crest of feathers on each side of the head.

Cormorants nest in colonies. Male and female incubate the three or four pale blue eggs for 25 to 29 days. At about three weeks the young cormorant first ventures from its nest of twigs, weed stalks and seaweed.

Avid hunters, cormorants dive quickly and easily for food. Their feathers, unlike those of most other web-footed birds, are not waterproof and cormorants must frequently come ashore to dry. Thus they rarely fly far out to sea, preferring freshwater lakes and rivers, estuaries and coastal salt water.

In spring and summer cormorants range from eastern Alberta to the Atlantic and are common along the coast of southern British Columbia.

Cormorants usually nest on cliffs. These have colonized a pier piling.

The **gannet** *(Morus bassanus)* is a graceful aerialist—its six-foot wingspan can take it to 6,000 feet. On land it is awkward. With wings partially outstretched, it waddles and hops between nests, jostling both eggs and young.

The gannet usually lays a single bluish white egg in its nest atop a cliff. Male and female take turns incubating the egg by holding it in their webbed feet. The young bird is slate brown, spotted with white. It matures to a dazzling white with black wing tips and buffy yellow neck and head.

The gannet has binocular vision (the ability to see an object with both eyes and get one image) and can spot a fish 100 feet below. To fish, it dives almost vertically into the water, catches its prey, swallows it and surfaces seconds later. From spring until autumn this bird is common along the Atlantic coast.

Three species of storm-petrel are frequently sighted in Canada. The commonest is the **Leach's storm-petrel** *(Oceanodroma leucorhoa)*. The **fork-tailed storm-petrel** *(Oceanodroma furcata plumbea)* is common off the B.C. coast. The **Wilson's storm-petrel** *(Oceanites oceanicus)* is a summer visitor to the Atlantic coast and, at 7 to 7½ inches long, is the world's smallest seabird.

Only the Leach's storm-petrel and the fork-tailed storm-petrel nest in Canada—in densely populated colonies on coastal islands (the Leach's on both coasts, the fork-tailed along the B.C. coast). The nest is a shallow burrow. Male and female take turns incubating the single egg for about 41 days. The eggs of storm-petrels are similar—dull white, sometimes with a faint wreath of lilac dots around the larger end. The Wilson's storm-petrel nests in Antarctica.

Nesting storm-petrels travel to and from their burrows only at night. During daylight the incubating parents remain hidden and silent while their mates forage far at sea. The colony bustles into life when the foragers return at dusk and their mates fly out to the hunt. Soon the colony again appears deserted. Storm-petrels are harmless and gentle but have many enemies. They are preyed upon by dogs, cats, rats, crows and gulls.

The **great blue heron** *(Ardea herodias)*, once hunted for its long slender head plumes, is now protected by law. It breeds along the B.C. coast as far north as the Queen Charlotte Islands and in southern Canada from Alberta to the Atlantic. In summer it is found in the southern Yukon, the southeastern Northwest Territories, northern Ontario and Quebec and the Maritimes. It winters from southern British Columbia to South America.

Gannets have long, slender tails, tapered black-tipped wings and sharp downward-pointing bills.

The four-foot-high great blue feeds in shallow fresh or salt water. Besides

A gangly young great blue heron tries its wings. Herons were once hunted mercilessly but federal law now prohibits killing them.

The Leach's storm-petrel, like all storm-petrels, seeks land only to nest.

An alarmed American bittern hugs its feathers close and points its bill skyward.

fishes, frogs and salamanders, it eats water snakes, large insects and small rodents.

To attract a mate, the male starts repairing an old nest or building a new one of sticks, high in a tree or on the ground. Once paired off, the male leaves construction of the nest to the female. Four pale greenish blue eggs are incubated by the parents for about 28 days. Immature herons are a more subdued color than their parents and have no plumes.

Herons are usually silent but under stress they squawk, croak and honk. In flight they are sometimes mistaken for cranes—but cranes fly with their necks extended; herons double theirs back against the shoulders.

The deep hollow call of the **American bittern** *(Botaurus lentiginosus)* so resembles machinery that the bird has been nicknamed thunder pump. The bittern has a yellow-and-buff-streaked breast and yellow-brown back feathers.

This bird lives in marshes, swamps, moist meadows and, on rare occasions, dry fields. It eats fishes, eels, frogs, crustaceans and insects. The nest is a platform of reeds and rushes. Four to six olive-brown or olive-buff eggs are laid.

The bittern breeds as far north as Great Slave Lake. In summer it is found throughout Canada except in the Yukon and Northwest Territories, and northern British Columbia, Quebec and Labrador. It winters in Canada only in southwest British Columbia and very rarely in southern Ontario.

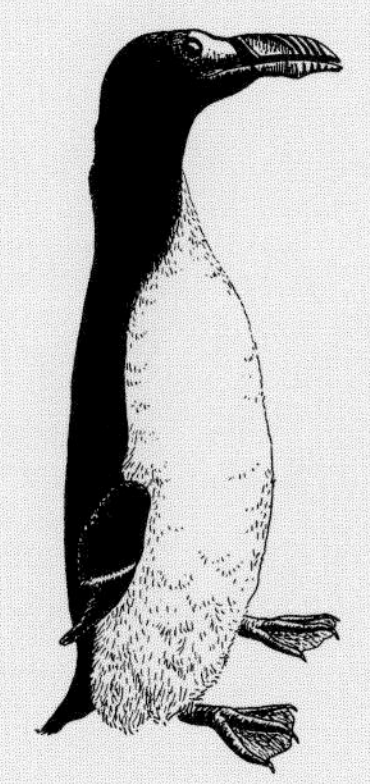

Our Vanished Wildlife

The **great auk** *(Pinguinus impennis),* a penguin-like bird that once flourished on coasts and rocky islands of the North Atlantic, has been extinct since 1844.

In 1534 Jacques Cartier described seeing huge colonies of these slow, flightless birds, valued for their flesh, fat and eggs. By the early 1800s only 50 great auks remained.

The great auk was finally wiped out in the name of science. Museum directors offered large sums for a complete skin, skeleton or egg. On June 4, 1844, three fishermen hired by an Icelandic bird collector landed on Eldey Island, near Iceland, and slaughtered the last of the great auks.

This Master Migrant Flies 22,000 Miles a Year

The **arctic tern** *(Sterna paradisaea)* has one of the longest migratory paths of any bird. Each year it travels from the Arctic to the Antarctic and back—a round trip of about 22,000 miles. It sees more daylight than any other animal, summering in the North in total light and wintering in the South in more light than darkness.

The arctic tern, about the size of a pigeon, breeds in colonies throughout the North and the Maritimes. Breeding grounds are sometimes shared with other tern species. Occasionally a pair will nest alone.

The nest is scratched in soil, sand and gravel or moss and is often unlined. Two or three eggs are laid. They are pale buff, olive or brown with spots and blotches in darker browns and purplish gray. Both parents incubate the eggs, which hatch in about 21 days. At the end of August the adults and newly fledged chicks begin the long flight to Antarctica.

A formidable adversary, the male arctic tern defends the nest against intruders: other terns, gulls, crows and humans. With a high-pitched scream it swoops down and attacks repeatedly with its sharp bill. A persistent intruder will be blitzed by a flock of terns. Rival terns grasp each other's beaks and beat each other with their wings. The tern's cry at other times is more subdued.

Other tern species have coloration and breeding habits similar to the arctic tern but they seldom migrate as far. Generally, the farther north a tern flies in summer, the farther south it ranges in winter.

Another arctic and subarctic inhabitant is the jaeger, which feeds on small birds and mammals, particularly lemmings. Three species are common in Canada: the **pomarine jaeger** *(Stercorarius pomarinus)*, the **parasitic jaeger** *(Stercorarius parasiticus)* and the **long-tailed jaeger** *(Stercorarius longicaudus)*. They nest in colonies or pairs near lakes, pools and sluggish streams, usually on coastal plains. The sparsely lined nest is scraped in the ground.

Jaegers usually lay two eggs which are incubated by both parents for about 23 days. The eggs of the pomarine jaeger are brownish olive, spotted with darker brown. The eggs of the long-tailed jaeger are smaller than those of the parasitic jaeger, but those of both species are either green or brown, spotted and blotched with dark brown.

Of the 33 gull species in Canada, the **herring gull** *(Larus argentatus)* is the

The herring gull scavenges at sea, often following fishing boats. Below: a glaucous gull chick's instinctive pecking at the red spot on its parent's bill is a signal for the adult to regurgitate food.

Graceful in flight, arctic terns are the swallows of the far north.

one usually called "sea gull." White with black-tipped gray wings and gray mantle, the adult measures about two feet from bill to tail. Its bill is yellow with a red spot on the lower tip. Young herring gulls are darker, with brown backs and darker brown tails.

The herring gull is a natural scavenger. It eats garbage, refuse from fish processing plants—even the eggs and chicks of its own species. It forages along the Atlantic and Pacific coasts and inland as well.

Herring gulls usually nest on the ground in colonies that they establish almost anywhere—on broken rocks, driftwood, grassy knolls or sand dunes. After a courtship ritual during which male and female toss their heads and circle round each other, the male utters a hoarse, rhythmic call and mating occurs. By mid-May nests usually contain three eggs of widely varying colors. As soon as a chick hatches, the broken eggshells are removed because they attract predators.

The **glaucous gull** *(Larus hyperboreus)*, a large bird with a four-foot wingspan, thrives along seacoasts, in harbors and occasionally offshore. The adult has a heavy bill and yellowish eye rings. A pale gray cloak of feathers along the neck is tinged with brown in winter. Its body and wings are white.

The glaucous gull breeds along the Arctic coast and islands and along the northeast coast of Hudson Bay. Colonies are found on cliff tops and sometimes single pairs nest on islands. The nest is a small platform of grass, seaweed and debris which may be added to yearly. Both parents take turns incubating the three buff to olive-brown eggs. The glaucous gull migrates along both coasts, often reaching southern California.

Two extra long feathers extend from the tail of the long-tailed jaeger. Below: kittiwake neighbors incubate eggs. These birds nest in densely populated cliff-side colonies.

The **black-legged kittiwake** *(Rissa tridactyla)* is a gull which roams the Arctic over oceans and seas for much of the year. It follows ships and schools of fish, going on land only to breed. Its *kitt-ee-wake* cry is heard during courtship.

The kittiwake nests in large colonies on Arctic islands and Canada's east coast. Its nest, a well-cupped structure of seaweed, grass, moss and other vegetation, is anchored by mud to narrow cliff ledges, the ledges of piers and even windowsills of seaside houses. The kittiwake's claws are long and sharp, giving it a secure footing on the most hazardous ledge. One to three eggs are laid, varying from buff to green or blue, spotted and blotched with brown and gray. Male and female take turns incubating the eggs for about 23 days.

A Comic That "Flies" Underwater

The puffin seems to try to show off as a solemn, dignified creature—and fails comically. With blue, yellow and red beak held high, it waddles along on tiptoe, inquisitively swaying its head from side to side. The puffin has difficulty becoming airborne, often flapping frantically for hundreds of yards before gaining enough momentum for lift-off. But in water it is graceful and deadly. It swims rapidly, using short wings and webbed feet to "fly" under water; it can carry some 10 fish in its beak.

The **common puffin** *(Fratercula arctica)* of east coast Canada and the **tufted puffin** *(Lunda cirrhata)* are related to the now extinct great auk which was a flightless bird.

Puffins swarm on rocky islands and coastal cliffs in spring. After mating, each pair chooses a crevice or rocky hollow for a nest, or excavates a burrow two to five feet long. The bills are used for defense, mating identification and digging.

One egg is laid, usually a dull white but sometimes spotted with browns and lilac. The task of caring for it falls mostly to the female. The parent on duty leans awkwardly against the egg, tucking it under a wing. The fluffy black and white chick hatches in about 40 days.

After six weeks, the parents depart for the open sea. Within a week, the chick instinctively leaves its nest or burrow, totters to the water and takes its first plunge. It soon learns to swim, dive, fly and hunt, then it flies south to join the older birds.

In late summer the puffin sheds the outer plates of its beak, which then appears

Murres do not build nests. Eggs are laid directly on rock ledges.

Puffins carry fish crosswise in colorful beaks. After the breeding season the outer layers of the beak are shed, leaving it a somber black.

The black guillemot forages along the Atlantic and eastern Arctic coasts.

The dovekie is a chubby arctic seabird about the size of a starling.

The razorbill, a duck-sized diving bird, has a deeply grooved bill.

Murres nest in crowded cliffside colonies along the Atlantic and Pacific coasts.

faded. Unwary and curious, it falls easy prey to cats, rats, dogs and foxes.

The puffin often shares breeding grounds with a noisy, blustering neighbor, the **common murre** *(Uria aalge)*. It is about the size of a small duck and has a long, slender, pointed, all-black beak. In winter it forages in Atlantic and Pacific coastal waters. Murres cluster on ledges, screaming and jostling in excited groups. A sudden alarm sends thousands hurtling into the air. In the commotion hundreds of eggs, laid in rocky hollows, are swept off the ledges and splatter on the rocks below.

Each pair of murres produces a single egg, pale green to bluish and spotted and blotched with browns or black. The egg is well designed for its precarious existence because it is pear-shaped and therefore unlikely to roll off cliff ledges when moved gently. Murres warm the eggs with the naked brooding patches on their abdomens.

Chicks hatch after about 30 days and 18 to 25 days later take their first plunge into the ocean. Encouraged by the parents, they soon swim and dive expertly.

The **thick-billed murre** *(Uria lomvia)* is distinguished from the common murre by its heavier bill. In Canada it breeds in the eastern Arctic regions and along the east coast of Newfoundland.

The **razorbill** *(Alca torda)* is similar to the murre but has a deeper bill grooved with a white line across it. Colonies breed among puffins and murres on the Atlantic coast, and winter offshore from Newfoundland south.

The razorbill nests in crevices and holes or under rocks or overhangs. One pear-shaped egg is laid, buff to greenish white, spotted and blotched with browns and black. The chick is hatched after about 33 days.

Immense flocks of the diminutive **dovekie** *(Plautus alle)* arrive off the Canadian east coast each spring. These birds have black backs and white underparts. Though dovekies do not breed south of the High Arctic and Greenland, they swarm along the Atlantic coast as far as southeastern Quebec and the Maritimes to forage for small shrimps and insects. Flocks cover massive rock faces when the birds land to rest from the hunt. For its small size—seldom longer than nine inches—the dovekie lays a large egg, nearly two inches long. (According to Eskimo superstition, a dovekie foot tied to a newborn girl will enable her as a woman to have large babies.)

Another common visitor to Canada's east coast is the **black guillemot** *(Cepphus grylle)*, recognizable by its slender, pointed bill and the large white patch on each wing. It breeds and forages in the eastern Arctic and along the Atlantic coast as far south as the Gaspé Peninsula and Nova Scotia.

The **pigeon guillemot** *(Cepphus columba)*, a larger version of the black guillemot, inhabits Canada's west coast. Its nesting habits are similar to those of the black guillemot, although it sometimes excavates a burrow.

The Comeback of the Whooping Crane

The magnificent **whooping crane** *(Grus americana)*, North America's rarest bird, probably has never existed in great numbers. About a century ago there were an estimated 1,500 whoopers but by 1941, because of man's encroachment on the birds' habitat, only 15 remained. Now, with legislation protecting the whoopers, and a Canadian-American breeding program, there are about 80.

Each pair of whooping cranes ranges over 400 acres (two-thirds of a square mile) of low-lying marshes and sloughs. This provides the safety, vegetation and abundant supply of insects, fishes and other water life the birds require.

The whooping crane, standing erect, is about five feet tall with a wingspan of more than six feet. Its black beak, wing tips and legs contrast with its glistening white satiny plumage. It has a loud, clear buglelike call.

Cranes are thought to mate for life. The eggs are laid after the spring flight to Wood Buffalo National Park from the winter range in the Aransas National Wildlife Refuge on the Texas coast. The nest, built of rushes, reeds and grass in more than a foot of water, contains two buff, brown-blotched eggs. The parents take turns incubating them for about 34 days and keep constant vigil for marauders. Charges by the male often deter foxes, coyotes and eagles.

The **common gallinule** *(Gallinula chloropus)* is recognizable by the pumping motion of its neck as it swims. It is a gray-black bird with white-streaked flanks and its bill and unwebbed feet resemble those of a chicken. It cannot take flight quickly from water and skims awkwardly across the surface when frightened. Its cry is a strident note repeated in groups of three.

The common gallinule lives in freshwater marshes and along lakes, ponds and sluggish rivers. It breeds in southern Ontario and southwestern Quebec. Its nest is a platform of marsh vegetation at water level. Nine to 12 buff eggs with reddish brown spots are incubated for 21 days by both parents.

The **spotted sandpiper** *(Actitis macularia)*, with its teetering walk, is a familiar sight along rivers, lakes, ponds and at the seashore. It breeds throughout Canada as far north as the tree line.

The common snipe, shy except when courting: then he's a noisy, flamboyant aerialist.

The little bird called the sandpiper, a common sight at the seashore.

The whooping crane, a big and beautiful bird only recently snatched from the brink of extinction, walks sedately on long, strong (if spindly) legs.

How a Bird Flies

A bird flies by flapping its wings or by gliding with its outstretched wings used as airfoils. In the powerful downstroke of flapping flight, the wings move down and forward to lift the bird; the wing feathers are closed flat to meet maximum air resistance. In the rapid recovery of the upstroke, the wings describe an arc and the feathers are twisted open, allowing air to pass between them.

Structure of a Flight Feather

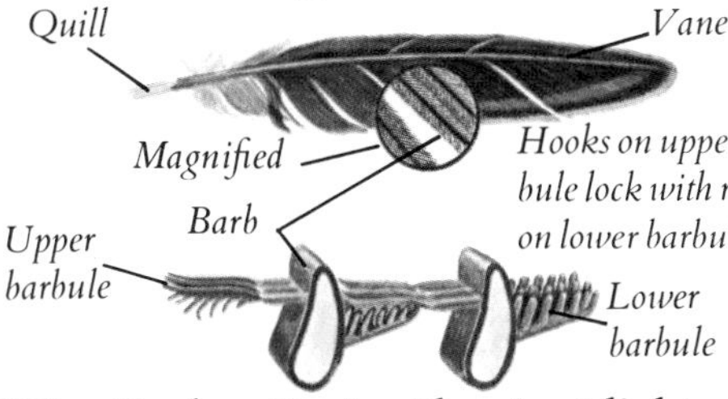

Quill

Vane

Magnified

Barb

Hooks on upper barbule lock with ridges on lower barbule

Upper barbule

Lower barbule

Wing Feathers During Flapping Flight

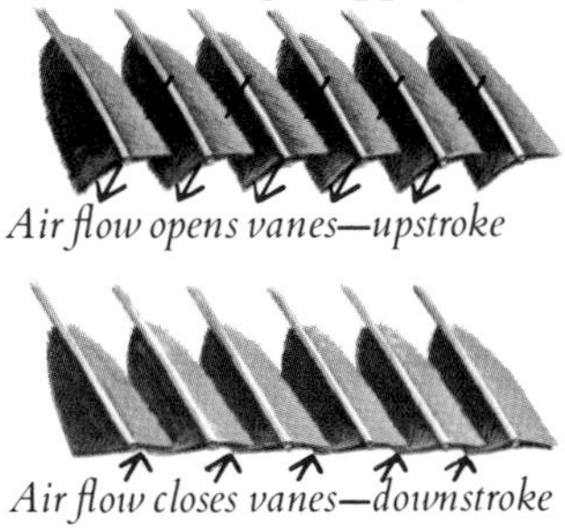

Air flow opens vanes—upstroke

Air flow closes vanes—downstroke

Honeycombed Bone

Many bones of birds, such as those of the upper arm, are hollow for lightness and crisscrossed with struts for strength

A Sandpiper's Skeleton and Flight Feathers

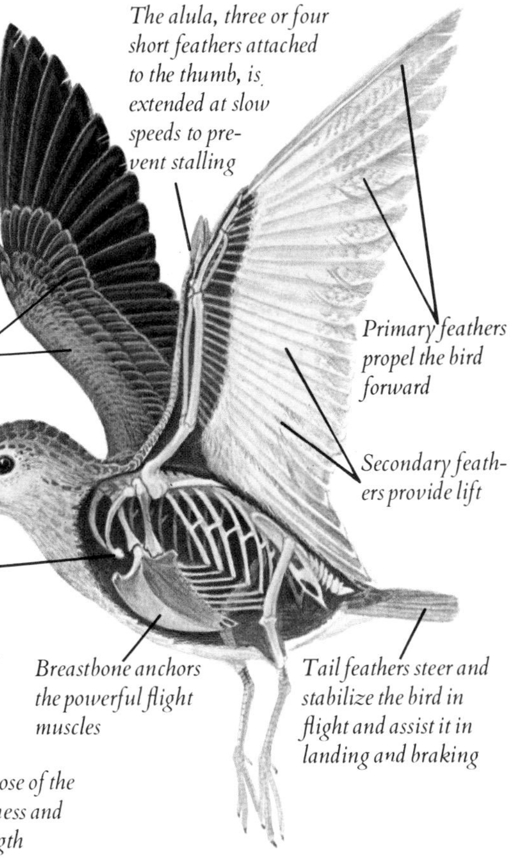

The alula, three or four short feathers attached to the thumb, is extended at slow speeds to prevent stalling

Coverts, small feathers, make the flight surface smooth

Primary feathers propel the bird forward

Secondary feathers provide lift

Wishbone, the fused collarbones, helps to support the wings in flight

Breastbone anchors the powerful flight muscles

Tail feathers steer and stabilize the bird in flight and assist it in landing and braking

The marsh-dwelling common gallinule has a yellow-tipped red bill.

A long, slender bill helps the woodcock probe for earthworms.

This sandpiper is about eight inches long. Its white breast has brownish black spots which disappear in the fall. It flies with quick strokes of its down-curved wings and glides frequently. The spotted sandpiper eats insects, worms, spiders and small crustaceans. Its cry is a loud whistle.

Its nest is a grass-lined depression in gravel or sand, near water. Its four eggs are buff with black, brown and lavender spots. Incubation lasts about 20 days.

The **common snipe** *(Capella gallinago)* is a shy shorebird fond of meadows and freshwater swamps. It breeds throughout Canada south of the tree line. It winters in southern British Columbia and sometimes in southern Ontario, New Brunswick, Nova Scotia and Newfoundland.

This snipe is 10 to 12 inches long, including a sharp 3-inch bill. It is a dumpy-bodied bird with pointed wings and a mixture of buff, brown and black on its back. It has a light brown breast, white underparts, black-brown bars on its flanks and a spot of red on its stubby tail. Its flight is zigzag.

The common snipe's nest is near water, in a depression in the ground lined with grass. Its three or four eggs are olive to greenish brown with brown spots. The parents incubate the eggs for about 20 days. Its mating cry is a harsh *kak-kak.*

The **American woodcock** *(Philohela minor)* breeds from Manitoba to the Atlantic coast. About the size of a quail, it has a short neck and tail, broad wings and a sharp three-inch bill.

It is shy and elusive and in dense moist woods relies for camouflage on the mottled brown dead-leaf pattern of its back and wings. Its underparts are cinnamon and it has light and dark bands across the back of its head. Four buff eggs with small brown spots are incubated by the female.

The Turnstone: Transient With a Prying Beak

The **ruddy turnstone** *(Arenaria interpres)* is named for its coloring and its habit of prying up stones and shells with its beak as it forages along the seashore for mollusks and crustaceans. It also eats larvae—which it picks from the fur of dead seals—and, in the breeding season, the eggs of other seabirds.

The ruddy turnstone sports a bright, patchwork plumage. Its back is russet and black, its abdomen is white and its breast is black edged with white. In fall and winter this plumage is duller with a less pronounced breast pattern. The turnstone has a tapered bill, a short neck and short orange legs.

A spring and summer transient in southern Canada, it is most often sighted on migratory routes along both coasts and near the Great Lakes. It breeds throughout the Arctic. Its nest, a depression in the ground, is lined with arctic plants. Male and female take turns incubating the four brown-blotched olive eggs.

Long, bright yellow legs make the **greater yellowlegs** *(Totanus melanoleucus)* one of Canada's most conspicuous shorebirds. Its upperparts are mottled black and gray, its underparts are whitish and its tail is white barred and mottled gray. Its two-inch bill is slightly upturned. The greater yellowlegs' call is a series of three or four ringing, whistled notes on a descending scale.

Noisy and talkative, the greater yellowlegs is called the tattler.

This 14-inch bird breeds throughout the wooded muskeg areas of central Canada. The nest, a depression in the ground or in moss, is built on a sparsely wooded ridge or in an area of muskeg. Four buff eggs with brown blotches are laid and both parents care for the young.

The greater yellowlegs migrates along the Pacific and Atlantic coasts and through central Canada. It rests on salt marshes and tidal flats and on the shores of lakes and streams. It feeds on small fishes, crustaceans, worms and insects. It winters from the southern United States to South America.

Almost identical to the greater yellowlegs, but smaller and with a straight bill, is the **lesser yellowlegs** *(Totanus flavipes)*. Often seen in the company of the greater yellowlegs, it breeds throughout the Yukon and in northern British Columbia, Alberta, Manitoba and Ontario. Its nesting and migratory habits are similar to those of the greater yellowlegs.

Other ringed plovers have one breast band; the killdeer has two bands.

Plovers are a family of small- to medium-sized shorebirds with plump bodies, large eyes and rich plumages. Plovers are found in open meadows and uncultivated fields and along the shores of lakes, ponds and rivers. They walk easily on land and are strong fliers.

The **killdeer** *(Charadrius vociferus)* is a noisy but handsome member of the plover family. It favors open interior uplands and is identifiable by two black bands across its white breast and by its cinnamon-colored rump. It was named for its shrill, vociferous cry of *kill-dee, kill-dee, kill-dee.* This 9-to-11-inch bird is one of the first birds to appear in spring, arriving just as the snow begins to melt. It is found throughout southern Canada west of the Maritimes.

The killdeer inhabits pastures, plowed fields, golf courses and ditches. Its nest, a shallow depression in the ground, is lined with weeds and pebbles. Four eggs, buff with dark blotches, are incubated by both parents. If its nest is threatened, the killdeer—like all plovers—feigns a broken wing and lures the aggressor away.

The feet of the **semipalmated plover** *(Charadrius semipalmatus)* are partially webbed. It is a short-billed, brown-backed bird with a conspicuous black band across its white breast. It is smaller than the killdeer and inhabits both freshwater and salt mud flats, beaches, and the shores of lakes and rivers. Its call is a clear, plaintive, two-note whistle with the second syllable the high note.

The semipalmated plover nests in sparsely vegetated gravel patches. Its nest is a depression in sand, gravel or moss. Its three or four eggs are buff, spotted with blackish browns.

The turnstone pushes and overturns sizable objects with its stout bill.

When foraging, the semipalmated plover—like all plovers—runs for several

A single black band across the breast, a short, dark-tipped bill and yellow legs distinguish semipalmated plovers.

seconds, then freezes. Its color and motionless stance make it difficult to spot on the wet sand where it forages. It eats shellfish, crabs, worms, seeds, grasshoppers and other insects.

This plover breeds in the Yukon and the Northwest Territories, along the coasts of Hudson Bay, James Bay and Ungava Bay, the south coast of Hudson Strait and the coast of Labrador, and in Newfoundland and Nova Scotia.

The godwits are a family of large shorebirds with long legs and long slender bills. The **marbled godwit** *(Limosa fedoa),* about 18 inches high, is Canada's largest godwit. It is a buffy brown bird with cinnamon on the undersides of its wings. It breeds in the grasslands of central and southern Alberta, southern Saskatchewan and southern Manitoba and around James Bay, and winters as far south as Guatemala. An extremely noisy bird, it repeats its ratchety call in couplets or triplets.

The marbled godwit nests usually in a depression in damp grassland, although sometimes on dry land far from water. It lays four buff, brown-blotched eggs in a nest sparsely lined with grass.

The **Hudsonian godwit** *(Limosa haemastica)* is about 15 inches high and has a slender, slightly upturned bill and a white- or gray-tipped black tail. Its upperparts are dark brown and black and its rump patch and wing stripe are white. This godwit builds its unlined nest among tufts of grass in wet sedge or on grassy tundra. It lays four olive-buff, brown-blotched eggs.

In fall, from its breeding grounds in the western subarctic, it makes a 3,000-mile non-stop migratory flight to South America.

The **American avocet** *(Recurvirostra americana)* is a tall, showy shorebird with long, slender legs and webbed feet. It is sometimes called the cobbler's bird because its upcurved bill is shaped like a cobbler's awl. It forages along lakeshores and mud flats, skimming mollusks and small crustaceans from the surface of the water and filtering them through its bill.

The American avocet has a pinkish buff head, neck and breast. Its legs are pale blue and each of its dark wings has a white bar. In winter the head, neck and breast are dirty white. Its cry of alarm is a loud, fretful *kleep-kleep.*

This gregarious bird nests in colonies near water. Its nest is a depression in the ground, lined with grass and weeds. The three to five olive-brown eggs, with dark-brown and some lavender spots, hatch in about 24 days.

The American avocet breeds in central and southern Alberta, southern Saskatchewan and southeastern Manitoba. It winters as far south as Guatemala.

A lone Hudsonian godwit. Only in the Arctic are godwits seen in large flocks.

A Short Flight, an Audible Snap...

The **eastern kingbird** *(Tyrannus tyrannus)*, like all kingbirds, is a flycatcher: it feeds on insects taken on the wing. A short flight, an audible snap of its broad, slightly hooked bill and the kingbird picks off an insect in midair.

The bird, about 8½ inches long, has a dark slate back, white undersides and a white-tipped black tail. Its cry is a solitary note or a long shrill twitter.

In summer the eastern kingbird is found throughout most of southern Canada. It inhabits open fields, wooded pastures and orchards. It nests in a tree or a bush or occasionally on a fence post or a tree stump. Its nest is a bulky structure of grass and twigs lined with roots, animal hair and plant fiber. The eastern kingbird's three or four white eggs, spotted with browns or grays, hatch in 12 days.

The **western kingbird** *(Tyrannus verticalis)* ranges mainly across southern Canada from British Columbia to Manitoba. In summer it inhabits sparsely treed areas in both mountainous and prairie regions. Its head, neck and breast are pale gray and it has faint dusky patches on each side of its head. Its abdomen is yellow and its tail is black with a white stripe down each side. Its cry ranges from a series of high squeaks and twitters to one or more hoarse notes.

The western kingbird nests in the fork of a large tree or shrub or on a telephone pole. Its nest and its three to five eggs are similar to those of the eastern kingbird.

The horned lark is the only species of lark native to North America.

About the size of a bluebird, the **eastern phoebe** *(Sayornis phoebe)*—another flycatcher—has a grayish olive back and white, yellow-tinged underparts. Its head and the back of its neck are blackish brown and its call is a thin *fee-be*.

The eastern phoebe breeds from northeastern British Columbia and the southwestern Northwest Territories to New Brunswick but not in northern Manitoba, Ontario or Quebec. It is found near lakes and streams and, away from water, around buildings. Its hemispheric nest of mud and plant material is built on rock and building ledges, under bridges and in culverts. The phoebe's five white, occasionally brown-spotted, eggs hatch in 13 to 20 days.

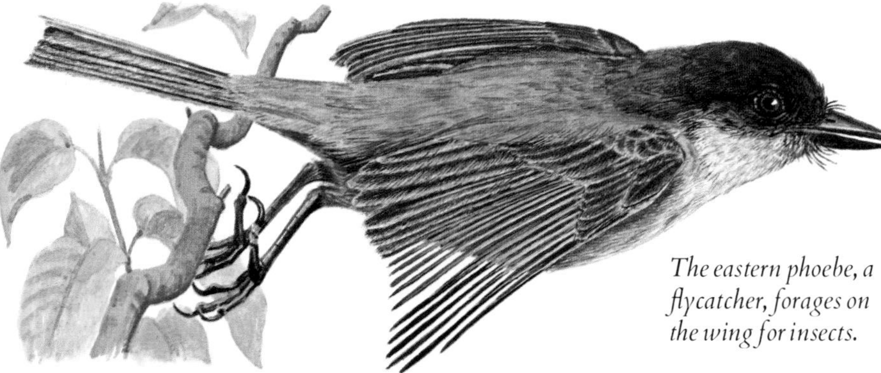

The eastern phoebe, a flycatcher, forages on the wing for insects.

The **great crested flycatcher** *(Myiarchus crinitus)* is an aggressive bird about the size of the eastern kingbird. It has a yellow abdomen, gray throat and breast, and reddish tinges in its tail and wings. It has two white bars on each wing. Its cry is a loud whistle followed by a number of harsh notes.

Ranging across southern Canada from eastern Saskatchewan to Nova Scotia, the great crested flycatcher inhabits mature woodlands, groves and orchards. It perches high in a tree, watching for insects.

The flycatcher's nest of leaves, pine needles, moss, animal hair, feathers and litter, such as cellophane, is in a natural tree cavity or a hole cut by a woodpecker. Often a piece of cast-off snake skin is used in the lining. The bird's four to six white or buff eggs are blotched and streaked with browns and occasionally lavender. The eggs hatch in about two weeks.

The great crested flycatcher eats insects as well as berries.

A least flycatcher stands guard over four ravenous nestlings.

The **least flycatcher** *(Empidonax minimus)*, Canada's smallest flycatcher, is a pale grayish bird with yellow-white underparts. It has a broad bill, whitish wing bars and a slightly forked tail. The young are similar but with buff wing bars and more brownish upperparts.

This bird resembles several other species of flycatchers and is best identified by its voice—a distinctive, oft-repeated strident note. A voracious insect eater, the least flycatcher inhabits mixed or deciduous woodlands, forest edges and clearings, orchards, gardens and parks. It nests in alder thickets and other tall shrubbery. Its nest, a thin-walled cup, is built in the fork of a branch 5 to 25 feet above ground. The three to six creamy white eggs hatch after 12 days.

The least flycatcher breeds throughout southern Canada excluding eastern British Columbia. It winters in Mexico and Panama.

The "horns" of the **horned lark** *(Eremophila alpestris)* are really small dark feathers on the back of its head. Larger than a sparrow, it has a slender pointed bill, a narrow black patch below each eye, a black patch on its upper breast. Its hind toenail is elongated and its black tail is bordered on the sides with white. A dark band across the male's crown distinguishes it from the female. Its call is a shrill hiss often repeated.

On the ground, the horned lark walks or runs instead of hopping. It searches for food in cultivated fields, in prairie and coastal areas and on the Arctic tundra. Although it also feeds on insects, its main diet is weed seeds and grain.

The horned lark nests in a hollow in the ground. Its nest of grass and other vegetation is lined with feathers, animal hair and plant down. Its three or four grayish eggs are speckled with brown.

The eastern kingbird is combative and ruthlessly defends the nesting area against trespassers. It will attack birds as large as herons.

A western kingbird darts after an insect.

The Braking, Rolling, Soaring, Gliding Swallow

The extravagantly beautiful **barn swallow** *(Hirundo rustica)* is a metallic blue bird with cinnamon underparts and a chestnut breast. Like most swallows it has a forked tail (hence "swallow-tailed"), long tapered wings, and slotted wing tips which enable it to brake, roll, soar and glide with mercurial agility—to outwit even the tiniest insect.

Bright, happy chattering, sometimes punctuated by a slight trill, signals the barn swallow's presence as it forages over water, marshes and open land. Its diet of insects makes it a favorite of farmers and gardeners throughout most of southern Canada. Like all swallows it winters in South America.

The barn swallow often perches on telephone wires. It nests in a building, cave or other sheltered location. This sparrow-sized bird lays four to six white, brown-spotted eggs in a nest of mud and grass lined with feathers.

The purple martin, 7½ to 8½ inches long, is Canada's largest swallow.

The **cliff swallow** *(Petrochelidon pyrrhonota)* is similar to the barn swallow but stockier, with a shorter tail. It has a buff patch on its rump and a white patch on its forehead. Its call is squeakier than that of other swallows.

In summer, throughout most of southern Canada, the cliff swallow eats insects taken on the wing over open terrain and water. Its nest is a roofed-over structure of mud pellets plastered to the side of a cliff or a canyon. A slanting entrance leads down to a grass-and-feather-lined nesting chamber. Four or five creamy, brown-spotted eggs hatch in about two weeks.

The cliff swallow often has its nest occupied and its eggs destroyed by house sparrows.

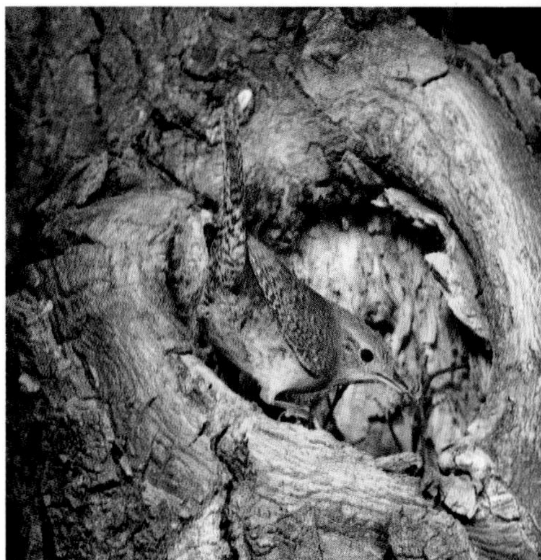

The house wren's small size and nondescript color make it difficult to spot.

The wings of the **rough-winged swallow** *(Stelgidopteryx ruficollis)* are edged with a fine row of tiny hooks. This swallow has a brown back, a gray throat and brown-gray flanks. It ranges from British Columbia to eastern Quebec. Like other swallows, it consumes large numbers of insects.

The rough-winged swallow builds its nest of grasses, roots and leaves in a burrow excavated in a bank of clay, gravel or sand. It also nests in a culvert, a hole in a wall or the abandoned burrow of a kingfisher, or under a bridge. Six or seven white eggs hatch in about 16 days.

The **purple martin** *(Progne subis)* is named for the male's iridescent bluish purple plumage. The female, like the young, has a gray throat and breast and a white abdomen. Male and female have forked tails and slightly hooked beaks.

The purple martin has a loud pleasant voice and is often seen gliding over waterways, marshlands and open areas in search of insects. Easily attracted to nesting boxes in gardens and on farms, it is also found in woodlands and burned-over areas where it nests in natural cavities in trees, in woodpecker holes and holes in cliffs. The purple martin ranges from British Columbia to Nova Scotia.

The diminutive winter wren forages in the undergrowth of mature woodlands.

Lively and inquisitive, the **house wren** *(Troglodytes aedon)* has no distinctive markings. It is a tiny dark bird with a stubby, perky tail. Its pleasant off-key song is heard throughout the day.

The house wren usually nests in a birdhouse or a hole in a tree. The nest, an accumulation of twigs and rubbish such as nails, tacks and wire, is lined with grass, horsehair and feathers. Six to eight pink-white eggs, heavily dotted with reddish brown, hatch in about 14 days.

The house wren, like all wrens, is an insect eater. It forages over shrubbery and thickets in mountainous, wooded and open areas throughout southern Canada.

Smaller than the house wren and with a shorter, perky tail is the **winter wren** *(Troglodytes troglodytes)*. It is reddish brown above with pale barred underparts and heavily barred flanks. Its voice is a succession of varied notes with an occasional warble.

The winter wren is frequently seen bobbing and dipping over tangled undergrowth in forest regions across southern Canada. During the mating season it is found near lakes and streams. It nests in the cavity of a fallen tree or beneath a stump or in brushwood or on mossy banks. Its nest, a bulky roofed-over structure of twigs, moss and grass, is lined with feathers and fur and has a side entrance. The five or six white eggs are lightly dotted with reddish brown.

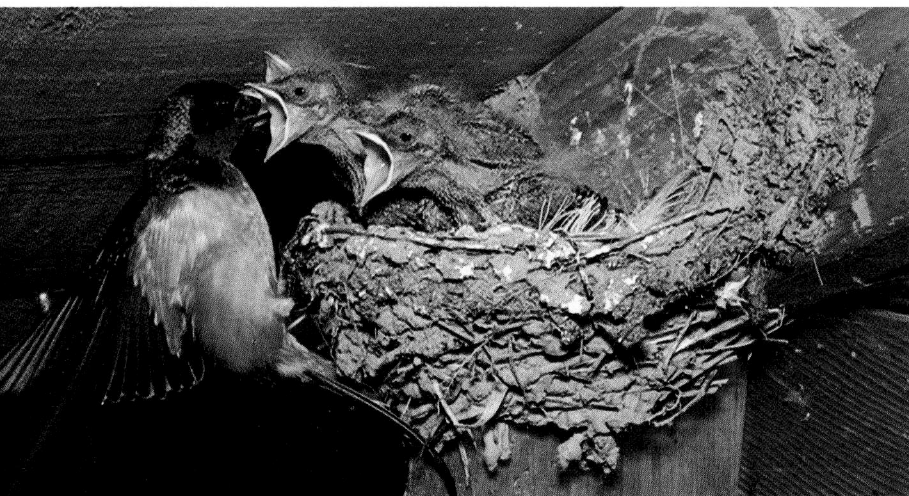

Voracious barn swallow chicks need no encouragement to eat. Nestlings of all bird species have seemingly insatiable appetites.

The **long-billed marsh wren** *(Telmatodytes palustris)* is a brownish bird with conspicuous white eyebrows, a dark white-streaked triangular patch on its back and a brown-barred tail. Its sides and flanks are buff. Its song is a lively, low-pitched staccato.

The long-billed marsh wren inhabits cattail marshes from British Columbia to Quebec. Its nest, a large ball of coarse marsh vegetation with a side entrance, is lined with cattail down and feathers. In addition to the main nest, the male builds several incomplete nests—the function of which is unknown. The long-bill's five or six dull brown eggs, finely spotted with darker browns, hatch in about 13 days.

The **short-billed marsh wren** *(Cistothorus platensis)* is similar to its long-billed cousin, but without a stripe over each eye. Its voice is coarser—a dry, tuneless chirp. This perky bird inhabits moist grass and sedge marshes—often bordered by willows or alders—from southeastern Saskatchewan to eastern New Brunswick. Four to eight white eggs hatch in about 13 days.

As if standing on stilts, a long-billed marsh wren perches on reed stalks.

The Cunning Crow Lives by Its Wits

The **common crow** *(Corvus brachyrhynchos)* is an omnivorous bird: it forages on field crops, garbage, large numbers of insect pests and the eggs and young of other birds. Crows' instinct for detecting danger enables them to dodge most attempts to slaughter them—a system of variously pitched *caws* warns other crows of peril.

This cunning bird is large and black with a long black bill. Its back, wings and tail have a greenish blue or violet iridescence. The young are a dull brownish black with glossy wings and tail.

The common crow ranges across southern Canada except the west coast. Adaptable to a variety of environments, it is found in marshes and densely forested areas, along coasts and waterways and near cities and towns—especially around garbage dumps. Flocks congregate in winter along the east coast.

This crow nests in a tree or occasionally in a low bush or on the ground. Its nest of sticks is lined with grass, moss and other soft material. Four to six brown-spotted greenish eggs hatch in about 19 days.

The **northwestern crow** *(Corvus caurinus)* is similar to the common crow but smaller with a more rapid wing beat, and its voice is a flat, nasal *caw*. This bird's range is restricted to the coast and islands of British Columbia where it forages along beaches and on tidal flats.

It builds a grass-lined nest of sticks in a tree or on the ground under a bush or large rock. Its four or five eggs are similar to the common crow's but smaller.

The **common raven** *(Corvus corax)* is occasionally confused with the common crow. The raven is a bigger bird with a larger, heavier bill and a wedge-shaped tail. Its all-black plumage has a faint purple or violet iridescence and its throat feathers are long and pointed. Young ravens are brownish black and their throat feathers are not long or pointed.

The raven's flight is more spectacular than the crow's. It soars, glides and occasionally executes barrel rolls, tumbles and dives. Its cry is a harsh, wooden croak or a resonant bell-like call.

The common raven ranges across Canada except southern and central Alberta, Saskatchewan and southwestern Manitoba. It inhabits mountainous, hilly and coastal terrain in the Arctic and in forested areas. It nests on a cliff ledge or high in the fork of a tree. Hair, seaweed, moss and grass line its nest of sticks. Four to six brown-spotted blue or green eggs hatch in about 20 days.

The **black-billed magpie** *(Pica pica)* is notorious for its thievery. Attracted by brightly colored or shiny objects, it often invades human habitations to

The magpie is a scavenger that eats almost anything, including (above) carrion—but it sometimes destroys the eggs and young of other birds.

The common raven, primarily a scavenger, often forages in garbage dumps.

The Steller's jay is a year-round resident of British Columbia.

The gray jay, bold and curious, is a frequent campsite visitor.

The blue jay is unmistakable in its blue, gray-white and black plumage.

An exclusive trio. Crows are gregarious and customarily roost in large flocks.

"steal" articles which catch its eye, then hoards the booty in its nest. This magpie is about 20 inches long and is black except for its white abdomen, sides and flanks. In flight it is recognizable by white patches on its wing tips and by its long tail. Its voice is a quick series of harsh notes but it can be taught to imitate words and phrases.

The black-billed magpie is a year-round resident of western Canada. Its habitat is thickets, scattered trees and shrubbery in canyons and along streams and woodland openings.

The magpie nests in a tree or tall bush. Its nest is a domed structure of sticks with one or more entrances leading to an inside cup of mud lined with hair, roots and fine grass. The female incubates the seven greenish gray, brown-spotted eggs for about 16 days.

A saucy, inquisitive bird, the **gray jay** *(Perisoreus canadensis)* has fluffy gray feathers, a long tail and a short dark bill. Its white head has a small dark cap which extends to the nape of the neck. The young are dark gray with brownish white tips on wings and tail feathers. The gray jay mimics the calls of other birds but its most common call is a weak complaining note.

The gray jay—also called Canada jay and whiskey jack—ranges year round across Canada as far north as the tree line. It inhabits forested areas, forest openings and bogs. The gray jay's bulky nest of twigs, bark and moss is lined with hair, feathers and pine needles. Its two to six grayish eggs, dotted with olive buff, hatch in about 17 days.

The **blue jay** *(Cyanocitta cristata)* is found in mixed and deciduous woodlands, especially in beech and oak. It is a wily bird and announces the presence of hunters with boisterous calls. It eats fruits, insects, grains, acorns, chestnuts, beechnuts, hazelnuts and occasionally the eggs and young of other birds.

Is It a Raven? Is It a Crow?

They are look-alikes but . . . a raven is larger than a crow and has a stouter bill and a wedge-shaped tail (a crow's is squarish). A raven's throat feathers are long and ragged, a crow's are smooth. To become airborne a raven first takes two or three hops; a crow launches itself directly. A raven's commonest call is a harsh croak—a crow usually emits a soft caw.

The blue jay, a handsome, crested bird, has blue upperparts and grayish white undersides. It has a black necklace and white spots on its wings and tail. Its voice ranges from a loud *jay jay* or a scream to a tinny whistle.

This jay ranges year round across southern Canada from Alberta to the east coast. Its nest, a bulky structure of sticks, moss and lichens lined with grass and feathers, is 8 to 20 feet high in a coniferous tree. Four to six buff to greenish blue eggs, splotched with brown, hatch in about 18 days.

The **Steller's jay** *(Cyanocitta stelleri)* is British Columbia's counterpart of the blue jay. It is a deep blue bird with a blackish crest, head, upper back and upper breast. Its cry is harsh and strident.

The Steller's jay inhabits coniferous and mixed forests, orchards and gardens. Its bulky nest of sticks and mud is in a coniferous tree, often a Douglas fir. Its three to five greenish or bluish eggs are spotted with brown or olive.

The **Clark's nutcracker** (Nucifraga columbiana).

The Red, Red Robin, Cheerful Symbol of Spring

The **American robin** *(Turdus migratorius)* is Robin Redbreast, the red, red robin that comes bob-bob-bobbin' along in spring with a happy call to the winter-weary to *cheer up, cheer up, cheer up.*

The male's sides, flanks and upper abdomen are the same brick red. It has a white lower abdomen and gray back; the wings, tail and head are black—with small white areas around the eyes. The female's plumage is similar but duller.

The robin forages in spring and summer for fruit and berries in woodlots, thickets and open fields across Canada. In residential areas it searches in shrubbery for insects and on lawns for earthworms.

The female robin builds a nest of grass and twigs mixed with mud in a tree, bush or nook in a building. She incubates three or four blue eggs for about 12 days. During the hatchlings' two-week stay in the nest, each consumes about three pounds of earthworms.

Smaller than the robin is the **red-breasted nuthatch** *(Sitta canadensis)*, a tree-climbing bird with a compact body, a large head and short legs and tail. It has reddish underparts, bluish gray upperparts, white-tipped tail feathers and a black head with a white eyebrow stripe. It feeds on nuts and, using long toes and claws to climb, it forages up and down tree trunks for insects and snails.

The brown creeper is the only species of creeper in North America.

Chickadees—cheerful and lively even on the coldest of winter days—are easily attracted to backyard feeders.

A brown thrasher hatchling leaves no doubt that it wants to be fed.

It nests in an abandoned woodpecker hole, in a cavity excavated in soft wood or in a decaying post, stump or tree. Four to seven white eggs, dotted with reddish brown, are incubated for 12 days by the female.

This nuthatch is a year-round resident throughout Canada except in southern Saskatchewan, Manitoba and Ontario. Its call is a repeated nasal note.

The **black-capped chickadee** *(Parus atricapillus)*, a fluffy, gregarious little bird, is found throughout Canada. It has a dark cap and bib contrasting with the white on the sides of its head. It has an olive-gray back, and dark, slate-colored wings and tail. Its underparts are white, its sides and flanks buff-tinged.

Its lively twitters are heard most often in late winter and spring as it forages in tall alder and willow thickets, in deciduous or mixed woodlands and in ornamental shrubbery around houses. Like nuthatches, the chickadee nests in abandoned woodpecker holes or other excavated cavities. Nesting areas vary with the size of the individual, and the oldest and strongest males claim the largest territory. It lays six to eight dull white eggs, spotted with reddish brown; they hatch in about 13 days.

The **common bushtit** *(Psaltriparus minimus)*, a brownish gray bird, is a member of the chickadee family. It is a permanent resident of southwestern British Columbia and Vancouver Island. Its nest, a baglike structure with a side en-

A male American robin, familiar to all, proudly puffs out its red breast.

A red-breasted nuthatch returns to the nest with an insect for its chicks. The nesting cavity is lined with shredded bark, grasses and roots.

A bushtit often hangs upside down from a branch to forage for insects.

trance near the top, is woven with mosses, lichens and plant down. Five to seven dull white eggs are incubated for about 13 days. The hatchlings are fed insect larvae 8 to 12 times an hour.

The **brown creeper** *(Certhia familiaris)* is named for its habit of spiraling up tree trunks in its search for insects. This bird has dark brown upperparts streaked with grayish white, and white underparts with buff-tinged flanks. It has whitish eyebrows and a buff patch on each wing.

The brown creeper's crescent-shaped nest of twigs, bark, moss and feathers, is located under a piece of loose bark or in an abandoned woodpecker hole. Four to eight white eggs, sparsely dotted with reddish brown, hatch in about 12 days.

The **brown thrasher** *(Toxostoma rufum)* is slightly larger than a robin. Its upperparts are reddish brown and its wings are barred with white. It has buff-white underparts and its breast, sides and flanks are heavily streaked with dark brown. The brown thrasher's song is a long, musical series of phrases and pauses.

This bird forages for insects in deciduous thickets and woodland edges. Its nest of twigs, sticks and strips of bark is located in a thorny thicket, in a shrub or on the ground. The brown thrasher's four or five eggs are pale blue, spotted with brown; they are incubated by the parents for 11 to 14 days.

The brown thrasher is found in southern Canada from the Rockies to Quebec. It winters in the southern United States.

There's Usually a Message in the Melody

The songs of birds—which can bring joy to the hardest heart—are seldom sung simply for the beauty of their melody. Most birds sing for practical reasons—to emphasize their claim to certain territory or to advertise for mates.

One of the world's most lyrical songbirds is the **hermit thrush** *(Hylocichla guttata)*. Its clear, flutelike song is a long pure note followed by a cluster of notes. The hermit thrush usually sings deep in the forest.

It feeds on the forest floor where insects, wild fruits and seeds are plentiful. Even its nest of twigs, bark and ferns is built on the ground. Its eggs, usually three or four, are greenish blue. The hermit thrush, about seven inches long, has an olive-brown mantle and a darkly spotted breast.

In summer it inhabits the southern Yukon, the Prairie Provinces, Ontario, Quebec and the Maritimes. It winters in Canada in southern British Columbia and occasionally southern Ontario.

The **varied thrush** *(Ixoreus naevius)* is a familiar sight in the Yukon and western Northwest Territories and in British Columbia and southwestern Alberta. Nine to 10 inches long, similar in size and shape to the robin, the varied thrush, a gray-backed bird, sports a distinctive orange-brown stripe over each eye, two orange-brown wing bars and a black band (gray in the female) across its rust breast.

The ruby-crowned kinglet, 3½ to 4½ inches long, often searches for food with other woodland birds such as woodpeckers and nuthatches.

When perched on a branch a hermit thrush slowly raises and lowers its tail.

A creature of the forest floor, the varied thrush favors shady, damp areas. Its call is a long, haunting quaver followed, after a pause, by a lower or a higher note.

The varied thrush nests in a tree and—like all thrushes—cleans its nest regularly. Some varied thrushes winter in western and southern British Columbia.

The **veery** *(Hylocichla fuscescens)* is a summer resident throughout southern Canada. Its faintly spotted breast and tawny upperparts distinguish it from the hermit thrush. Its song—a rolling whistle on a descending scale—is unlike that of other thrushes. The veery is found near lakes and streams in the low, leafy shrubbery of open woodlands.

Bluebirds are bold attractive members of the thrush family. One familiar species found in Canadian woodlands and farmlands is the **eastern bluebird** *(Sialia sialis)*. This 6½-to-7-inch bird has an indigo mantle, reddish brown underparts and a white belly. It inhabits settled areas.

The eastern bluebird's song is a series of low, short warbles. In spring and summer it is heard in southern Canada from Saskatchewan to Nova Scotia.

The **mountain bluebird** *(Sialia currucoides)*, about the size of the eastern bluebird, has indigo upperparts and a blue breast. The mountain bluebird's song is a clear, short warble, higher pitched than the eastern bluebird's.

A loud chorus of hungry cheeping greets a veery parent. The veery usually lays four eggs in a nest built on or near the ground.

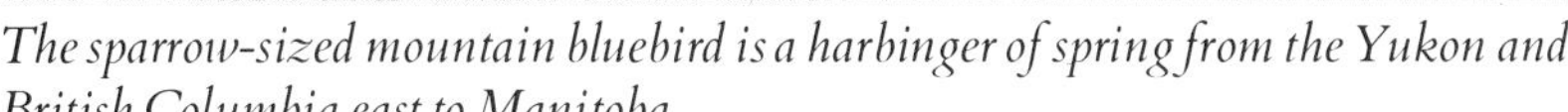

The sparrow-sized mountain bluebird is a harbinger of spring from the Yukon and British Columbia east to Manitoba.

The eastern bluebird is often seen perched on a tree stump.

The varied thrush is about the size of a robin.

Kinglets, tiny olive-green and gray birds about half the size of sparrows, are the smallest songbirds in Canada. Two species are native to this country: the **golden-crowned kinglet** *(Regulus satrapa)* and the **ruby-crowned kinglet** *(Regulus calendula)*.

Short-tailed and chunky, kinglets often flick their wings excitedly as they dart about on tree branches. During the spring and summer nesting season, both species occupy coniferous forests and mixed woodlands in most provinces.

In spring and summer they are seen near buildings—in shrubbery and at outdoor feeding stations. Insects and insect eggs form the bulk of their diet.

The golden-crowned kinglet ranges year round across southern Canada except Saskatchewan and southern Ontario. The ruby-crowned kinglet ranges in spring and summer south of the tree line, except the southern prairies and southern Ontario; it winters from southern British Columbia to Central America.

Kinglets suspend their spherical nests from twigs high in coniferous trees. They lay eight or nine brown-spotted creamy-colored eggs.

The yellow crown of the male golden-crowned kinglet is bordered with black. This bird's song is a rapid, high-pitched twitter that ends in a series of unharmonious warbles. The reddish crown of the male ruby-crowned kinglet is usually visible only when the bird raises it in anger. This kinglet trills several high, flutelike notes followed by several low melodious tones.

The Year-Round Resident of Almost Everywhere

Sleek, silky, not a feather out of place. Berries and wild fruit are the main diet of the bohemian waxwing, although it sometimes eats insects taken on the wing.

The aggressive little roughneck known as the **house sparrow** *(Passer domesticus)* was introduced to North America from England in 1850 to help control cankerworms in Brooklyn, N.Y. Flourishing beyond all expectation, it has established itself as a year-round resident virtually everywhere.

This buffy brown and chestnut bird is sometimes confused with native sparrows. The male is distinguishable by a gray crown and a black throat or bib. The female has an unstreaked crown and a broad buff line over each eye. This robust six-inch bird has a strong bill well adapted for cracking seeds.

The house sparrow, sometimes called the English sparrow, nests in almost any kind of cavity, filling the hole with straw, feathers and trash. Its three to seven dingy white eggs, speckled with darker brown, hatch in 12 to 14 days.

Waxwings—named for the waxlike drops of color on their wing tips—have short, curved beaks and silky plumages. Two species are in Canada: the **cedar waxwing** *(Bombycilla cedrorum)* and the **bohemian waxwing** *(Bombycilla garrulus)*. Both have crests, red-tipped wings and dark, masked eyes.

The cedar waxwing, slightly larger than a sparrow, is a cinnamon-colored bird with a yellow-tipped tail and pale, yellowish green underparts. It is usually seen in flocks in fruit trees and bushes in open woodlands, orchards and gardens. It feeds on grapes, berries and insects. Its call is a repeated, high-pitched whistle.

The cedar waxwing's nest is a bulky mass of twigs, grass and plant fibers in a tree. Its three to five dark-spotted, gray-blue eggs hatch after about 12 days. This waxwing ranges throughout most of Canada and winters in southern British Columbia, Ontario and Quebec and in the Maritimes. Its cousin the bohemian waxwing is similar in appearance but larger and grayer, with white or yellow wing patches. Four to six black-dotted, pale blue eggs hatch in 12 to 15 days.

The bohemian waxwing breeds in the Yukon, interior British Columbia, northern and western Alberta and northern Saskatchewan and Manitoba. It

The house sparrow is a common sight throughout most of Canada.

Nests for the Nestlings

Birds' nests vary from a simple scrape in the ground to a hole in a tree, from a tunnel in a sandbank to a mud-and-grass hideaway attached to a wall. Some nesting examples: loon—anchored to reeds near shore; cliff swallow—on a factory wall; woodpecker—deep in a tree trunk; magpie—high in a tree; marsh wren—suspended in reeds; bank swallow—dug deep in a sandy cliff.

A loggerhead shrike eats an insect it has impaled on a thorn.

An insect-eater, the starling is beneficial to farmers.

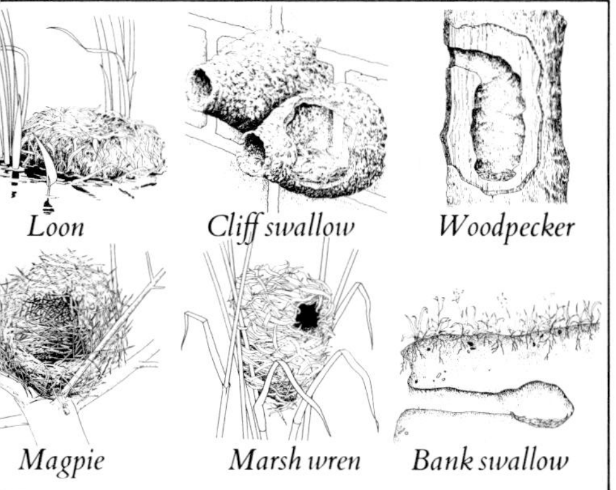

winters through much of this area and occasionally as far east as Nova Scotia.

Although shrikes are songbirds, they are also birds of prey. They belong to the group known as butcher birds—birds which impale their kill on a thorn or sharp branch to hold it steady for eating or to store it for later use. Both species of North American shrike are found in Canada: the **loggerhead shrike** *(Lanius ludovicianus)* and the **northern shrike** *(Lanius excubitor)*.

The loggerhead shrike, also called the migrant shrike, is light gray with brownish black wings and tail, white underparts and black-masked eyes. Its strong black bill is slightly hooked for tearing the flesh of its prey—small mammals, birds and large insects. Its song is a pleasing warble mixed with harsh notes.

This shrike nests 10 to 20 feet up in a tree or in a thorny shrub. Its bulky nest of twigs is lined with plant fibers, feathers, rags and paper. Four to six white eggs with gray and brown spots hatch in about 15 days.

The loggerhead shrike is found in central and southern Alberta and Saskatchewan, and in southern Manitoba, Ontario, Quebec and New Brunswick. It winters in the central United States and south of that.

The northern shrike is similar to the loggerhead but larger, with fine barring on its breast and a light-colored lower bill. Its song is a mixture of warbles, harsh notes, whistles and imitations of other birds' songs.

The northern shrike's nest of twigs is built in a tree or bush and lined with roots, lichens, hair and feathers. Its four to seven grayish brown eggs, spotted with olive and brown, hatch in 14 to 16 days.

In summer the northern shrike is found in open woods, bogs and thickets above the tree line. It winters in southern Canada.

The **starling** *(Sturnus vulgaris)* was introduced to North America from Europe at the turn of the century. On March 16, 1890, a group of Americans, who planned to introduce into the United States all the birds mentioned by Shakespeare, released 60 starlings in Central Park in New York City. The following year another 40 were released. The birds adapted and multiplied so well that now there are millions of starlings throughout North America.

The starling is a plump, short-tailed bird with black, glossy plumage and buff-edged wings and tail. In spring and summer it is the only black bird in Canada with a yellow bill. In winter the bill darkens and the starling's plumage is heavily speckled with light dots.

This avid insect eater forages in pastures, orchards, gardens and garbage dumps. Although it destroys many tree and crop parasites, it also damages orchards and uses nesting cavities of birds such as the red-headed woodpecker and the bluebird. Its four to six pale blue or green eggs hatch in 11 to 14 days.

Starlings travel in flocks of thousands and roost on buildings or in trees. Their presence is announced by a continuous chattering chorus. They also emit a rambling series of whistles, chirps, squeaks and warbles and can mimic other birds' cries. Some starlings migrate south in winter but many remain in Canada.

In North America the **crested myna** *(Acridotheres cristatellus)* is found only in the Vancouver area and southern part of Vancouver Island. It was introduced from Asia in the 1890s. Unlike the starling's, its range has not spread significantly and its numbers are estimated at only two to three thousand.

This black, chunky, short-tailed bird is about the size of a robin. It has a white patch on each wing and an unruly crest at the base of its yellow bill.

The crested myna forages in fields, orchards, gardens and garbage dumps. It roosts in flocks on city buildings and in trees. For nesting, it seeks out holes in trees and buildings and, occasionally, bird boxes. The nesting cavity is filled with grass, weeds, feathers, cast-off snake skins and trash. The crested myna's four to seven greenish blue eggs hatch in about 14 days.

If It Warbles, It's No Warbler

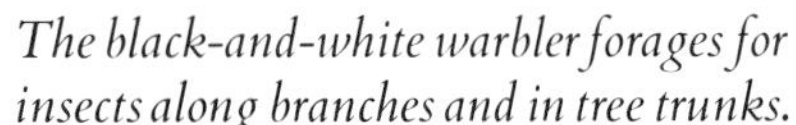

The black-and-white warbler forages for insects along branches and in tree trunks.

A yellow warbler plays foster parent to cowbird fledglings. Cowbirds (p. 124) avoid the chore of rearing their young by laying eggs in other birds' nests.

Warblers do not warble. They buzz, chip, tweet and trill. These frequently brightly colored birds forage in leafy treetops and in bushes, snatching insects out of the air with their sharp slender beaks. They also forage on the ground.

The **yellow warbler** *(Dendroica petechia)*, probably Canada's most familiar warbler, is often found in ornamental shrubbery. It has yellowish olive upperparts with large yellow patches on its tail. Its breast, sides and flanks are a rich yellow, striped with chestnut, and its dark yellowish olive wings are edged with yellow. Its varied song is sprightly and unmelodious.

In the wild, the yellow warbler nests in shrubbery or in alder and willow thickets on the edge of a stream, lake or marsh. Its nest, a bulky cup of plant fibers, grasses and shredded bark, is in the fork of a branch. The female incubates four or five brown-and-magenta-spotted white eggs for about 11 days.

The yellow warbler is found throughout Canada south of the tree line and winters from Mexico to South America.

The **myrtle warbler** *(Dendroica coronata)* is the most prolific warbler in Canada. It has a bright yellow crown, a yellow rump patch and a yellow patch on each side of its breast. Its upperparts are bluish gray, streaked with black, and its underparts and throat are white, heavily streaked with black on the breast, sides and flanks. Its call is a trill with rising and falling inflections.

The myrtle warbler nests 10 to 15 feet above ground in a coniferous tree. Its nest is a bulky structure of twigs, grass and moss. The female incubates four to five white eggs, blotched with brown, for about 13 days.

This warbler ranges throughout the Yukon and western Northwest Territories and most of southern Canada. It winters in the northern United States.

The population of the **Cape May warbler** *(Dendroica tigrina)* rises and falls with the availability of its main food, the spruce budworm. This warbler has chestnut cheeks and yellow patches on each side of its neck. Its back is yellowish green, spotted or streaked with black, and its tail is black with large white patches on the outer feathers. Its yellow underparts, fading to white on the lower

The ***black-throated blue warbler*** (Dendroica caerulescens) *is found from southern Ontario to the Maritimes.*

A Wilson's warbler darts after insects.

A Cape May warbler perched among springtime blossoms. The male is identifiable by bright yellow cheek patches and a white stripe on each wing.

part of its abdomen, are streaked with black on the breast, sides and flanks.

The Cape May warbler inhabits coniferous and mixed woodlands in the southwestern Northwest Territories, northern Alberta and Saskatchewan, central Manitoba and Ontario, southern Quebec, and the Maritimes. It nests as high as 60 feet in a loose mass of twigs, moss and grass. The female incubates four to nine white eggs with reddish brown spots for about 12 days.

The **Wilson's warbler** *(Wilsonia pusilla)* traps insects in stiff bristlelike feathers around its mouth. When perched it twitches its tail nervously. The male has a black cap and a bright yellow stripe over each eye, an olive-green back and tail and yellow underparts. The female, a plain olive, has no special markings although it may have a smaller, paler cap. This warbler's song is a series of rapid, staccato *chips* dropping in pitch near the end.

The Wilson's warbler is found in shrubbery near swamps or streams, on mountainsides and in valleys and alpine meadows. Its bulky nest of grass, small leaves and moss is at the base of a shrub or small tree. Five white eggs, finely speckled with reddish brown, are incubated by the female for about 12 days.

This five-inch-long bird ranges throughout most of Canada south of the tree line. It winters from southern Texas to Central America.

The **black-and-white warbler** *(Mniotilta varia),* one of the first warblers to arrive in spring, is a black-and-white-striped bird with a white abdomen and a broad white stripe on its crown. Its song is a rolling high-pitched series of double syllable tweets. Unlike other warblers, it has long claws and short, stout legs which enable it to creep up tree trunks and along branches to forage for insects in the bark.

The black-and-white warbler inhabits moist deciduous and mixed woodlands from northern Alberta through central and southern Canada to Newfoundland. It winters from southern Texas to South America.

This warbler's nest, a hair-lined depression often at the base of a tree or shrub, is made from grass, bark strips, leaves and moss. The female incubates four or five white eggs, speckled with reddish brown, for 13 days.

A Warbler Look-Alike

Because of its size, coloration and occasionally its song—usually short phrases that sometimes run together into a rich warble—the little vireo is often mistaken for a warbler. Vireo, from the Latin for green, describes the olive-gray back and wings of this white- or yellow-breasted bird. Four to six inches long, the vireo is difficult to observe because it spends most of its time foraging for insects in the tops of tall trees and shrubs.

The **solitary vireo** *(Vireo solitarius)*, sometimes called the blue-headed vireo, is identifiable by its "spectacles": white rings around the eyes joined by a white bar. The bird has a black tail with olive edging, two white or yellow bars on each wing and a white throat and underparts.

The solitary vireo builds its cup-shaped nest of leaves, bark and moss in a coniferous tree. Its four brown-spotted white eggs hatch in about 10 days.

The cover of an ovenbird's nest resembles a Dutch oven—hence the name.

Red-eyed vireo fledglings hungrily gobble berries. All vireos are insect-eaters, but the red-eyed vireo also feeds on fruit.

A male American redstart feeds a female incubating her eggs.

The solitary vireo is found from British Columbia to Newfoundland but not in southern Alberta, Saskatchewan and Ontario. It winters from the southern United States to Central America.

The **red-eyed vireo** *(Vireo olivaceus)* is the only vireo in Canada with red eyes. It is a white-breasted bird about 6½ inches long, with a gray crown, a broad gray stripe over each eye and dusky gray, yellow-edged wings and tail. Its robin-like song, delivered tirelessly during the breeding season, consists of short, rising phrases and abrupt pauses. This vireo eats berries as well as insects.

The red-eyed vireo's nest of bark, paper from wasp nests, plant fibers and leaves is suspended from the fork of a tree branch. Three or four dull white eggs with dark brown spots are incubated for 12 to 14 days by the female. This vireo is found in most of Canada including the southwestern Northwest Territories.

Except for its brown eyes, the **Philadelphia vireo** *(Vireo philadelphicus)* has a head similar to that of the red-eyed vireo. Its breast and sides are pale yellow, fading to white on the throat and abdomen, and its wings and tail are gray brown edged in olive. Its song is similar to the red-eyed vireo's.

The Philadelphia vireo nests in deciduous or mixed woodlands and in tall shrubbery. Its nest is a grass-lined cup of bark strips, plant down and lichens. The parents incubate three to five brown-spotted white eggs for about 14 days.

The Philadelphia vireo is found in northern and central Alberta, most of Saskatchewan, central Manitoba and Ontario, and southern Quebec and New Brunswick. It winters in Central and South America.

The male **American redstart** *(Setophaga ruticilla)* has colorful orange

Mysteries of Migration

Why some birds migrate (about one-third of all species) and others do not is a mystery. Nor is it known precisely what triggers the migratory urge—but some factors undoubtedly are food supply, length of day and changes in a bird's sexual chemistry.

Before their semiannual flights, most birds exhibit restlessness and a tendency to flock. Some species, such as sea gulls and ducks, molt. All accumulate body fat, some nearly doubling their weight. Some birds, for example chickadees and juncos, migrate only a few miles. Others, such as the arctic tern and the ruby-throated hummingbird, migrate thousands of miles.

The ***common grackle*** (Quiscalus quiscula) *is Canada's largest blackbird. It is found near marshes and in damp alder thickets throughout most of southern Canada.*

The Philadelphia vireo suspends its nest 10 to 45 feet up in a shrub or tree.

The solitary vireo inhabits coniferous and deciduous woodlands in southern Canada.

patches on each side of its tail and on each wing. Its upperparts are black, its underparts white with orange on each side of its breast. The male often drops its long pointed wings and fans its tail. The female has olive upperparts, grayish white underparts and yellow in place of the male's orange markings. This bird's song is a lisping, high-pitched monosyllable slurring downward at the end.

The American redstart inhabits open areas of deciduous and mixed woodlands and often nests in the crotch of upright branches. Its nest of grass and bark is lined with feathers, animal hair and fine grasses. The female incubates four brown-and-magenta-speckled white eggs for about 12 days.

The American redstart is found in the southwestern Northwest Territories, in British Columbia and Alberta, central Saskatchewan and southern Manitoba, in Ontario, southern Quebec and the Maritimes. It winters as far south as Ecuador and northern Brazil.

The **ovenbird** *(Seiurus aurocapillus)* is also called the teacherbird because of its song—*teacher* repeated 5 to 15 times. This warbler has olive upperparts, two black stripes on its orange crown, a black line on each side of its throat and a white ring around each eye. Its underparts are white, spotted and streaked with black on the breast and sides.

Most warblers hop on the ground but the ovenbird walks through leaf litter in its search for insects. Its dome-shaped nest of grass, leaves and moss is on the ground. Three to six white eggs, spotted with reddish browns, are incubated for 12 days by the female. The ovenbird is found in northern British Columbia and across southern and central Canada to the Maritimes.

The Loud, Melodious, "Upside-Down" Bobolink

Sharp, conical beaks and flattish profiles are features common to birds of the family Icteridae, which includes the bobolink, meadowlark, blackbird and oriole. The **bobolink** *(Dolichonyx oryzivorus)*, about the size of a sparrow, has still another distinguishing feature: while most birds have light undersides and darker mantles, its markings are "upside-down": black below and white above.

The bobolink's loud and melodious song is *bob-o-link, bob-o-link.* The bird is seen in spring and summer from southeastern British Columbia to Nova Scotia; it feeds primarily on insects and weed seeds. In autumn millions of bobolinks fly about 7,000 miles to the rice fields of central South America.

A bobolink nest, flimsily built of grass and weeds, is usually hidden on the ground in a field of tall grass, alfalfa or clover. The five or six grayish brown eggs hatch in 10 to 13 days.

As fall approaches, the male bobolink discards its handsome plumage for the dull, sparrowlike markings of the female.

The meadowlark is not a lark but a blackbird. The two species in Canada—the **eastern meadowlark** *(Sturnella magna)* and the **western meadowlark** *(Sturnella neglecta)*—are almost identical in appearance but dissimilar in vocal performance. About the size of robins, both have short, white-trimmed tails and a black crescent on their bright yellow breasts. The western meadowlark is slightly paler with more yellow on each side of its throat. The eastern meadowlark has a thin, reedy whistle—less aesthetic than the rich, jubilant song of its western cousin.

A male Baltimore oriole searches for insects. These birds winter from Mexico to Colombia and Venezuela, returning to Canada in early May.

Both species fly with rapid beats of their short wings, punctuated by brief, periodic glides. They inhabit open grassy fields and conceal their nests in grass, often covering them with a dome-shaped roof. The female meadowlark incubates three to seven white eggs, speckled and blotched with brown and gray, for about 14 days.

Meadowlarks guard territory jealously. They require as much as seven acres per bird for their food needs; other songbirds, such as the robin, require less than half an acre. The meadowlark feeds on insects, grain, weed seeds and occasionally berries.

The eastern meadowlark is found in summer from southern Ontario to New Brunswick; it winters in the United States. The western meadowlark ranges year round in Canada from southern Ontario to British Columbia.

Marshes are still icebound when the male **red-winged blackbird** *(Agelaius phoeniceus)* appears in spring. An attractive bird with vivid red epaulets, it flits

Perched atop a fence post, a western meadowlark sings its heart out.

Male yellow-headed blackbirds are 8½ to 11 inches long; females are shorter.

from perch to perch singing its bubbling *kon-ker-ee* song. The female, a dark-streaked brown bird without the bright markings of the male, arrives later. Between the arrival of the first redwing and the last, there may be an interval of up to three months.

The red-winged blackbird is found from the Yukon and British Columbia to Newfoundland. It forages in fields and open areas and nests in marshes. It lays three to five blue-green eggs, blotched with brown, black, gray and purple, in a loose, cup-shaped nest often supported by reed stalks. It spends the summer hunting insects and earthworms. Each day the parents make several hundred feeding flights to satisfy the blind and scrawny nestlings. Throughout fall, winter and spring, redwings gather in flocks—some as large as a million birds capable of wreaking havoc on grain crops.

The male redwing's red shoulder patch is often concealed when the bird is perched (only the buffy white or yellow border patch is visible). However, the male puffs out its red epaulets to threaten a rival.

The male **yellow-headed blackbird** *(Xanthocephalus xanthocephalus)* has a rich orange-yellow head, neck and breast. It has a white patch on each wing and the rest of its plumage is black. The female is a dusky brown with a faded yellow head, neck and breast. She lacks the white wing patch of the male.

The male red-winged blackbird displays bright red epaulets.

The female red-winged blackbird's plumage is unlike the male's.

The male bobolink's striking plumage makes it an easy bird to identify.

The song of the yellow-headed blackbird is a discordant yodel; its call a low *chuck*. It can often be heard in marshes and along lakes where it nests, and in grainfields and barnyards and on freshly plowed ground where it forages. Its nest is a basketlike structure of dead, wet vegetation. Its three to five white eggs are speckled with gray and brown and incubated by the female for 12 to 13 days.

This blackbird ranges from central interior British Columbia to western Ontario. It winters from California east to southern Louisiana and south as far as central Mexico.

The **Baltimore oriole** *(Icterus galbula)* weaves a baglike nest of plant fibers, horsehair and twine. The nest, usually six or more inches deep, is suspended from the tip of a high branch where it may remain intact for several years. The oriole's five or six grayish white eggs are streaked and blotched with brown and black.

The male has fiery orange and black markings. The female is a duller, dusky orange with two pale bars on each wing. Found mainly in open deciduous woodland, particularly in tall trees, the Baltimore oriole ranges from central Alberta to central Nova Scotia. Its loud, piping whistle is heard as it searches for caterpillars and other insects.

Four fledgling Baltimore orioles survey the world around them.

Every Cowbird Has a Foster Parent

A brightly plumed male scarlet tanager perches on a branch.

The **brown-headed cowbird** *(Molothrus ater)*, a small blackbird that feeds mainly on insects, forages over pastures and grainfields. It is often seen near cattle and horses, where insects are plentiful—hence the name cowbird.

The male has a brown head and an iridescent black body. Its bill is short and sparrowlike. The female is brownish gray with a pale throat. The cowbird's song is a series of gurgles and high-pitched squeaks.

The cowbird lays its four to six brown-blotched whitish eggs in the nests of other birds, such as warblers, finches, flycatchers and thrushes, but lays only one egg in any one nest. Occasionally, the nesting bird throws out the cowbird's egg or covers it with grass and twigs and refuses to incubate it. Usually, however, the young cowbird is raised by the foster parent.

The brown-headed cowbird breeds in central and southern British Columbia and Saskatchewan, all of Alberta, and southern regions from Manitoba to Newfoundland. It winters in southern Mexico.

Of the three tanager species in Canada, the **western tanager** *(Piranga ludoviciana)* is the most widely distributed. This small, brilliantly colored bird—easily distinguished from other tanagers by its bright yellow breast—normally inhabits open coniferous and mixed woodlands. It is found in most of British Columbia and Alberta and in central Saskatchewan. It winters from central Mexico south.

In the mating season the male's head is red, its tail, back and wings are black, and its underparts are bright yellow. In autumn its head darkens to olive and only a faint tinge of red is visible. Females and young western tanagers have dull greenish gray upperparts, yellowish underparts and two white or yellow bars on each wing.

With its short, thick bill, the western tanager feeds mainly on insects, occasionally on fruit. It builds a loose nest of twigs, roots and grasses—usually in a coniferous tree. The nest, lined with hair and fine roots, holds three to five eggs. The pale blue eggs, speckled with browns, hatch in about 13 days.

In breeding plumage, the **scarlet tanager** *(Piranga olivacea)* is a bright scarlet bird with black wings and tail. Its autumn plumage is dull red, molting into greenish yellow. The female and the young have olive upperparts and grayish brown wings fringed with olive. Underparts are dull yellow and tail coverts are bright yellow. The scarlet tanager's voice, like the western tanager's, is similar to the robin's but coarser.

The brown-headed cowbird forages on insects, including many harmful ones.

Fond of thistle seeds, the American goldfinch is also called the thistle bird.

A bedraggled male western tanager washes his breeding plumage.

The conical beak of the purple finch is heavy—good for crushing seeds.

Bird Bills and How They Are Used

Curved The sharp, hooked beaks of hawks, ospreys and shrikes are used to tear flesh.

Chisel Woodpeckers use strong, pointed beaks to bore through wood.

Nutcracker The stout bills of sparrows, finches and crows are used to crack seeds, pine cones and nuts.

Probe Snipes and sandpipers probe in mud with long, flexible bills.

Spear Long-legged wading birds such as herons have slender, pointed bills for spearing fish.

Flycatcher Swallows have small bills for catching insects in the air.

Duck bill Some of the broad, flat bills of ducks and geese have plates or "teeth" to strain food from mud and water.

Can opener Oyster catchers use flat-sided bills to pry shells open.

The scarlet tanager prefers to nest in mature deciduous woodlands, on branches 10 to 30 feet above ground. Its shallow nest of twigs, roots and grasses holds three to five blue-green eggs dotted and speckled with browns.

In summer this insect-eating songbird is found across southern Canada, from New Brunswick to southeastern Manitoba. It winters in South America.

The **purple finch** *(Carpodacus purpureus)*, a lively bird about the size of a house sparrow, has a short heavy bill and a slightly forked tail. The male is predominantly red, with a reddish purple crown and a pink rump. Its wings and tail are dark brown with pale fringes. The female, like the young, is olive and heavily streaked with white and dark brown.

The purple finch inhabits open forests and woodland, farm woodlots and orchards. In winter it seeks out trees and tall shrubs in parks and gardens where its song—a happy warble—is often heard. In spring the purple finch usually nests 5 to 60 feet above ground in a coniferous tree. The nest of twigs, grass and roots is lined with fine grass and hair. The four to six eggs, which hatch in about 13 days, are blue, with fine black or brown speckles at the large end.

The purple finch breeds throughout all of British Columbia and Alberta and in central Saskatchewan, Manitoba, Ontario and Quebec. It winters in southern Canada except Alberta and Saskatchewan.

Sometimes called the wild canary, the **American goldfinch** *(Spinus tristis)* is a bright yellow bird with a distinctive, undulating flight. Its song is a long melodious series of continuous trills and twitters.

In summer the male's bright yellow body contrasts vividly with its black cap, wings and tail. Its dark-tipped yellowish orange bill is short and blunt. In winter the male's cap is brownish olive with a suggestion of yellow and its wings take on buffy white markings. The female goldfinch, duller than the male, has brownish olive upperparts, olive-yellow underparts and dark brown wings.

The American goldfinch's diet is mainly seeds. Goldfinches are normally seen in flocks in weedy fields and cultivated areas and along roadsides.

The American goldfinch nests in shrubbery or open deciduous woods. Its cup-shaped nest, as high as 20 feet above ground, is made of shredded bark, plant stems and grass, and usually lined with thistledown. Four to six pale blue eggs, incubated by the female, hatch in 12 to 14 days. The goldfinch is found through most of southern Canada.

Spirited Songster of Parks and Gardens

A chipping sparrow returns to the nest with a worm for its hungry hatchlings. This species nests 3 to 10 feet above ground in a tree, vine or bush.

The white-crowned sparrow is found throughout most of southern Canada.

The lively and vocal **song sparrow** *(Melospiza melodia)* makes its presence known with a spirited three-syllable call accompanied by warbles and shorter notes. It is a brown-backed bird with black and gray streaks on the top of its head, a long rounded tail, a streaked olive-brown rump, white underparts heavily streaked with brown and a dark brown spot on its breast.

The song sparrow forages for weed seeds in parks and gardens. In the wild it is found in thickets and pastures and in shrubbery along lakes, streams and ponds. The song sparrow ranges most of central and southern Canada.

Its nest of grass, weeds, bark and leaves, lined with roots and animal hair, is on the ground or in a bush or small tree. Three to five bluish green eggs, speckled and mottled with brown, hatch in about 12 days.

The **white-crowned sparrow** *(Zonotrichia leucophrys)*, about seven inches long, is larger than most sparrows. It has a gray, black-and-white-striped head, a gray, brown-streaked back, a white throat patch and two white bars on each wing. Its underparts are gray and its tail is dark brown.

This sparrow is found in the Yukon and Northwest Territories, northern Quebec, Labrador, most of British Columbia and northern Alberta, Saskatchewan, Manitoba and Ontario. It inhabits thickets and shrubbery in open areas, dwarf birch and willow patches on the tundra, and windswept coasts and mountainsides.

The white-crowned sparrow nests on the ground or in a bush or scrub tree. Its nest is a bulky structure of grass, bark and often lichens and moss. It is lined with grass, roots and sometimes hair. Four or five gray-white to green-blue eggs, mottled and dotted with reddish browns, hatch in about 12 days.

A thin black stripe over each eye, highlighted by a broad white eyebrow, gives the **chipping sparrow** *(Spizella passerina)* an inquisitive look. The chestnut-crowned male has gray flanks and a gray breast. The female is similar but duller, with a black-streaked head. In fall the male's plumage darkens and its crown is obscured by buff feather tips. Its call is a long monotonous chipping trill.

The chipping sparrow is found in open and wooded areas across central and southern Canada. It nests 3 to 10 feet above ground in a tree, bush or vine. Its cup-shaped nest of grass, stems and weeds is lined with horsehair, fur and roots. Three to five blue eggs, spotted with brown, black, red and lavender around the larger end, hatch in about 11 days.

The voice of the **swamp sparrow** *(Melospiza georgiana)* is similar to that of

A swamp sparrow's nest, hidden in marsh grass, is safe from predators.

The snow bunting is seen in winter along roadsides and in fields.

the chipping sparrow but louder, more articulate and more melodious. In the mating season, this sparrow has a chestnut crown, a gray breast and a brown tail. Its back is reddish brown with black and white streaks. In autumn and winter it is more buff-colored and its head has distinct black markings.

In the breeding season, the swamp sparrow is often seen near lakes, ponds, streams, freshwater swamps with dense vegetation, and patches of willow and alder. In migration it is found in weedy fields near water and, occasionally, in dry woodland thickets.

The swamp sparrow builds its grass nest in a cluster of marsh vegetation or low in a bush. Four or five pale bluish green eggs, mottled and dotted with browns, hatch in about 13 days.

This sparrow is found in the western Northwest Territories and throughout central and southern Canada, except British Columbia and southern Alberta and Saskatchewan.

Every autumn, as though to forewarn of winter, the **tree sparrow** *(Spizella arborea)* arrives in southern Canada from its breeding grounds in the North. Its pleasant two-syllable call, ending in a warble, fills the air as it forages for weed seeds in sparse shrubbery in fields and gardens. Although similar to the chipping sparrow, this bird has a conspicuous brown spot in the middle of its breast.

The ***savannah sparrow*** (Passericulus sandwichensis) *eats seeds and insects.*

It's a harbinger of winter when the sprightly little tree sparrow returns to southern Canada from its northern breeding grounds.

The tree sparrow breeds from the Yukon to Labrador and as far south as northwestern British Columbia and northern Saskatchewan, Manitoba and Ontario. It is found along streams and bogs and in open wooded regions.

The tree sparrow nests under a woody shrub or, occasionally, in a low tree. Its cup-shaped nest of grass, weed stalks, lichens and strips of bark is lined with feathers, horsehair and moss. Four to six bluish green eggs hatch in 12 to 13 days.

The arrival of the **snow bunting** *(Plectrophenax nivalis)* in southern Canada also signals the onset of winter. In late autumn flocks forage for seeds in weedy fields. In summer they range above the Arctic Circle and in the northeastern Northwest Territories where they nest among rocks or in a crevice.

The snow bunting is predominantly white with a black back, black patches along the top of its wings and a black streak on its tail. It is an impressive sight as its black and white markings flash against the winter sky. Its voice in flight is a brief musical twitter with a pronounced ending.

The nest of moss and grass is lined with grass, feathers and animal hair. Four to seven pale grayish blue eggs, mottled and speckled with browns, hatch in about 12 days.

The song sparrow is one of the earliest birds of spring in Canada.

Social and Agile, the "Red Cap" of the North

One of the most easily identified Canadian songbirds is a lively creature distinguished by its forehead cap of bright red feathers and its black chin. These are markings of the **common redpoll** *(Acanthis flammea)*, a small finch 4½ to 6 inches long. Its stubby, conical beak is equipped with tweezer-like tips for plucking seeds from pine cones and tearing the seeds off ground plants. The crushing power of the finch's beak has been estimated at more than 150 pounds per square inch.

The redpoll is a gray-brown bird with dark streaks on the sides. In spring, the male has a rosy blush of pink on the cheeks, breast and sides. It breeds in arctic and subarctic regions between Newfoundland and the northern Yukon and winters in southern Canada. Its song is a sweet lilting trill accompanied by a twitter. Its flight call is a double-noted *zit-zit.* Feeding flocks keep up a constant commotion of metallic notes.

The redpoll is an agile bird, capable of clinging to the hanging cones of coniferous trees, perching on thin twigs and even running up the slender stalks of weeds and wild flowers.

A social bird, the redpoll usually nests in small colonies on or near the ground, in rock crevices or dwarf trees and shrubs. Nests are made of grass and twigs, cozily lined with plant down, feathers and sometimes fur or hair. Five or six blue eggs, spotted with reddish brown, hatch in 10 to 11 days.

A ***pine siskin*** (Spinus pinus) *on a showy Vancouver Island camellia.*

The **slate-colored junco** *(Junco hyemalis)*, another bird of coniferous woodlands, is a finchlike bird about six inches long with uniform dark gray plumage except for a clear white abdomen and outer tail feathers. Its white underside is conspicuous in flight. In its first year, the female's sides and back are often brownish.

Some slate-colored juncos winter in southern Canada, braving the cold and snow. Others winter as far south as Mexico.

The junco is usually seen on the ground where it feeds on the seeds of such weeds as crabgrass and ragweed. Occasionally it eats insects.

Its song is a trill, similar to the chipping sparrow's, or a soft combination of twitters, warbles and *chips.* A sharp metallic *chip* signals danger.

The junco breeds in most of the forested areas of Canada, from the northern Yukon to Labrador and Newfoundland. During the nesting season it can be found at wood edges, in clearings and in burned-over areas. During migration, flocks are often seen in weedy patches of fields, roadsides and gardens, usually close to the protective cover of trees or bushes. A few juncos winter in southern Canada but most migrate to the southern United States and Mexico.

The common redpoll's bright red summer cap is paler in winter.

The rufous-sided towhee is also known as the red-eyed towhee.

Enormous mouths dwarf the bodies of chestnut-collared longspur chicks.

The junco's cup-shaped nest is built on or near the ground in fallen trees and upturned roots, under vegetation or in a hollow in a steep slope. The nest of grass, moss and rootlets is lined with fine grasses, hairs, moss stems and sometimes porcupine quills. Four or five pale bluish white eggs with brown spots are incubated by the parents for about 11 days. Two broods are raised annually.

The easily recognized **rufous-sided towhee** *(Pipilo erythrophthalmus)* ranges in southern Canada from British Columbia to southwestern Quebec.

The male, about eight inches long, has a black head, back and tail, a white waistcoat, striking reddish brown side patches and bright red eyes. The smaller female has brown coloration instead of black.

The towhee, a ground bird, is often seen scratching industriously for insects in dead leaves. Its favorite places are bushy areas with an accumulation of leaves on the ground—in brushy fields, willow or alder patches, woodland edges and clearings. The towhee's common call is *to-whee,* with the second note higher.

A nest of bark and twigs, dead leaves, weed stalks and grass is usually built on the ground, or in low bushes, and is lined with fine grasses and rootlets.

The towhee lays four to six white or pinkish eggs, with specks of reddish brown and lavender at the large end. They hatch in 12 to 13 days.

The **chestnut-collared longspur** *(Calcarius ornatus),* about six inches in length, inhabits the fields and plains of southern Alberta, Saskatchewan and Manitoba. As it forages on shortgrass plains, it walks or runs, seldom hops. Its call sounds like *til-lip,* with the accent on the first note.

The male in breeding plumage has solid black underparts, a white or buff-colored face and throat, a black stripe behind the eye, a black cap and a distinctive patch of deep chestnut on the back of the neck.

The grayish buff, sparrowlike female has a faintly streaked breast and a large amount of white on the sides of the tail.

The chestnut-collared longspur nests in a hollow, under shrubs or concealed in grass. The nest is made of grass and weed stems and is lined with fine grasses, sometimes with hair. The bird lays four to six eggs, grayish white to greenish white or pale buff, speckled with browns and lavender. Only the female sits on the eggs which hatch in about 12 days.

Big, Heavy Beaks for a Diet of Seeds and Buds

Grosbeaks are tree-dwelling songbirds that brighten Canada's forests with colorful plumage and sweet warbling. As their name implies (grosbeak means large beak), they are distinguished by heavy, conical beaks, well suited to their main diet of seeds and buds.

Seldom seen on the ground, except when feeding on fallen seeds, grosbeaks choose tree branches for their shallow, loosely made nests, which resemble platforms rather than cups. They lay two to five light-colored eggs, usually bluish or greenish, spotted with brown.

A male rose-breasted grosbeak in its striking breeding plumage.

The **pine grosbeak** *(Pinicola enucleator)* and **evening grosbeak** *(Hesperiphona vespertina)* are hardy year-round residents of Canada. The **rose-breasted grosbeak** *(Pheucticus ludovicianus)* winters in Central and South America and heads north in March.

The pine grosbeak is almost the size of a robin. The striking male is rosy red on the head, breast and back. Its wings are black with two white bars and its tail is black and forked. The male can be identified easily by its large size, rosy color and wing bars.

The female grosbeak usually nests in open coniferous forest, up to 30 feet off the ground. Its nest of twigs, grass and moss is lined with grass and hair. This grosbeak lays four or five greenish blue eggs spotted with brown and purplish gray. In its natural habitat it is usually tame, calm and deliberate in its motions.

The pine grosbeak sometimes gets conifer seeds by using its powerful neck and thick blackish bill to batter cones apart. It also feeds on conifer buds, berries and the seeds of birch, sumac and willow.

Its song is a melodious warble and its call note a clear, three-syllable whistle on a descending scale.

The pine grosbeak ranges across the open coniferous forests of northern and central Canada from the northern Yukon to Newfoundland. It has no migratory pattern and its winter movements are irregular. It seems to travel, in flocks of up to 100 birds, only when food supplies in an area are exhausted.

The gregarious evening grosbeak, originally a western bird, has pushed its breeding range east to the Atlantic.

It has a shorter tail and chunkier proportions than the pine grosbeak, and a pale yellowish green bill. The male has dusky or dull yellow plumage, a yellow stripe over each eye, a black cap and tail, and black wings with large white patches that can be seen at a great distance in flight. The female's plumage is mostly gray or olive.

The evening grosbeak nests in coniferous or mixed woodlands, 15 to 60 feet off the ground, and lives mainly on seeds. It has a special liking for seeds of the Manitoba maple and box elder, and is readily attracted to backyard feeding stations where its first choice is sunflower seeds.

In winter, when food is scarce, evening grosbeaks will fight fiercely among themselves, even male against female, for feeding station tidbits.

The song of the evening grosbeak is a short, uneven warble and its call a clear, ringing note, louder and more strident than the cheep of a house sparrow.

The evening grosbeak breeds mainly in a narrow strip across southern Canada. In winter it is a common sight in towns and cities.

The male rose-breasted grosbeak, black and white with a deep rose patch on its breast, is easily recognized. Seven to 8½ inches long, it has a black head, neck and back, white-spotted black wings, pink wing linings, white underparts and a whitish beak. The female is a mottled yellow brown and white, like an overgrown sparrow, but with two white or buff wing bars and yellow wing linings. She has no pink on her breast.

The song of the rose-breasted grosbeak is similar to the robin's but is richer,

Seeds form a large part of an evening grosbeak's diet.

The common yellowthroat is often sighted in marshes.

The pine grosbeak, a hardy bird, remains year round in Canada.

more energetic and more rapidly delivered. Its alarm note is a high-pitched *tick.*

After reaching its northern breeding grounds in May, the rose-breasted grosbeak chooses a nesting site in a woodland area, usually near a river or marsh but sometimes in a park or garden. Its nest is a bulky structure of twigs, grass and plant fibers. Three to five pale green or bluish eggs, lightly spotted with brown, hatch in about 12 days.

It breeds across Canada from northeastern British Columbia to Nova Scotia, covering nearly all of Alberta and the Maritime provinces, central and southern Saskatchewan and southern areas of the other provinces.

It is a rarity among small forest birds in that the male usually incubates the eggs and takes part in nest-building and the rearing of the young. Nestlings are fed mainly caterpillars and insect larvae, making the rose-breasted grosbeak an important destroyer of harmful insects.

The **common yellowthroat** *(Geothlypis trichas)* is a lover of swamps, streambeds and marshes.

The male is easy to recognize by its bright yellow throat and jet-black mask. The rest of its upperparts, wings and tail are olive green. Its belly is whitish. In autumn, the black mask feathers are tipped with gray.

Females and immature birds are grayish olive or olive brown, usually with some yellow on the throat and a buff-yellow breast. Their whitish bellies distinguish them from other similar warblers, which are solid yellow below.

The yellowthroat, wrenlike in size and energy, seeks out tangles of vegetation, usually in a marshy area, for its nest. It builds a deep cup of leaves, grass and plant fibers on or near the ground and lines it with fine grasses and hair. The female lays three to five creamy white eggs which are speckled with brown and black.

Intruders upon the yellowthroat's nesting domain are fussed about and scolded with a repeated, husky *chip* of disapproval. The yellowthroat's song is unmistakable: a rapid, well-enunciated *witchety-witchety-witchety-witch.*

It lives on caterpillars and insects, and breeds across southern and central Canada from Vancouver Island to Newfoundland. It ranges as far north as the southern Yukon and James Bay, and winters from the southern United States to Panama and Puerto Rico.

On Target, On Time

Birds navigate with uncanny accuracy and punctuality, following four principal North American flyways (shown here) and hundreds of lesser ones. Guided by the sun and the landscape, the moon and the stars, they often fly over the same locality on the same date year after year. Migratory flight, faster than normal flight, ranges from 20 to 45 miles an hour. Flight altitudes vary with species and weather conditions—from 200 to 20,000 feet—but apparently most birds fly at about 3,000 feet.

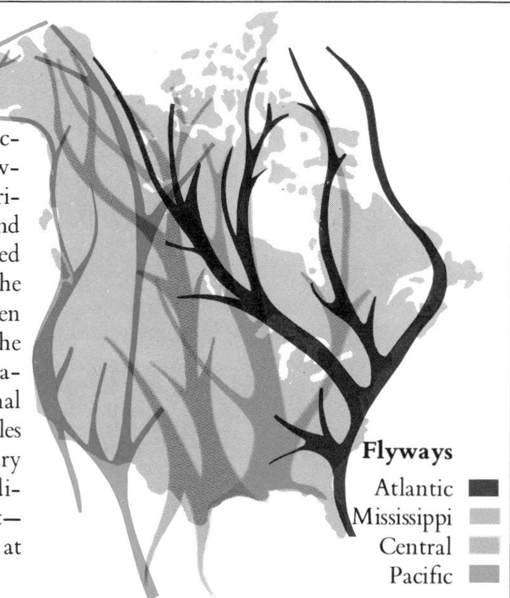

Silent, Sharp-Eyed, Savage

A great horned owl wings silently from its nest—probably abandoned by a hawk, crow or squirrel—in search of food for hungry fledglings.

As darkness envelops the forest, hunger stirs the nocturnal **great horned owl** *(Bubo virginianus)*. Sharp eyes pierce the night and sensitive ears pinpoint the sound of scurrying animals. On soft, silent wings this savage hunter swoops to kill rats, mice, shrews, squirrels and rabbits—even animals as large as porcupines. Small rodents and birds it eats whole. As do all owls, it regurgitates indigestible bones, feathers and fur as pellets.

Prominent earlike tufts of feathers hide the highly sensitive ears of the great horned owl. It is about 23 inches long—Canada's largest tufted owl—and ranges from the Maritimes to British Columbia and north as far as the tree line. Its call is a series of soft, deep hoots—or a scream.

In early spring the great horned owl lays two or three round, white eggs in the abandoned nest of a crow, hawk or squirrel, in a natural tree cavity or on a cliff ledge. These hatch in about 30 days.

The **great gray owl** *(Strix nebulosa)*, the largest of Canada's 15 owl species, is up to 30 inches from head to tail. Its back is grayish brown and mottled gray; the pale gray underparts are lightly streaked with brown. This owl ranges across the northern coniferous belt and winters in smaller numbers in southern and eastern Canada. It usually forages at dusk and at night but also hunts during the day over open fields, using fence posts and shrubs as lookouts. Its slow, gliding flight resembles that of a hawk or falcon and gives this owl good maneuverability—an advantage in its search for prey. The great gray owl's call is a perfectly spaced hoot repeated several times. Its two to five dull white eggs are more oval than the eggs of most owls.

A slender body and a long, tapering tail give the **hawk owl** *(Surnia ulula)* a hawkish appearance. Its dark brown back contrasts with its gray chest and abdomen, barred with brown. Its grayish white face has a black border.

The hawk owl, found across Canada, inhabits open coniferous and mixed

The great gray owl has a wingspan of up to 5 feet but weighs only about 2½ pounds.

Noted for its strength, the snowy owl hunts birds as large as ducks.

woodland, muskeg and burned areas with standing stumps. It usually nests in a hole in a tree or in another bird's abandoned nest. Its three to seven oval, white eggs hatch in about four weeks.

A densely feathered coat enables the **snowy owl** *(Nyctea scandiaca)* to live as far north as Baffin and Ellesmere islands. When it roams southward, the snowy owl spurns forest protection, relying for warmth and camouflage on its feathers, which cover all but its searching yellow eyes. Males are almost entirely white; females and young are spotted and barred with brown. This large bird has no earlike tufts of feathers.

In the Arctic, the snowy owl depends mainly on lemmings for food. When the lemming population declines—usually every four years—the snowy owl travels to southern Canada in search of food. It nests on the ground and its five to seven oval, white eggs hatch in about 32 days.

Two owls widely distributed in Canada are the **long-eared owl** *(Asio otus)* and the **short-eared owl** *(Asio flammeus)*. The long-eared owl, about the size of a crow, has conspicuous ear tufts near the center of its head. Another distinguishing feature is its boldly striped abdomen. It dozes during the day in dense brush and is seldom seen. Its three to seven eggs hatch in about 28 days. The short-eared owl has barely discernible earlike tufts of feathers, buff plumage and brown-barred wing and tail feathers. It ranges to the Arctic Ocean, winters mainly in southern British Columbia and southern Ontario, and hunts throughout the day, particularly at dusk, near marshes and meadows. It nests on the ground and lays four to nine oval, white eggs which hatch in about 26 days.

A long-eared owl peers quizzically from its perch on a tree branch.

The **barred owl** *(Strix varia)*, a brown and white bird without ear tufts, is found near marshes and in woodlands across southeastern Canada, the northern Prairies and the Rockies. Its barred breast, black eyes and smaller size distinguish it from the great gray owl. Its call is a distinctive *who cooks for yo-all.* It lays two or three oval, white eggs in a tree hollow or the deserted nest of a hawk or crow.

The smallest Canadian owls are the **pygmy** *(Glaucidium gnoma)* and the **saw-whet** *(Aegolius acadicus)*. About the size of a bluebird, the pygmy is found in British Columbia and western Alberta. A black and white band on the back of the neck is its most distinctive mark. Its call is a series of low, hollow *ook* notes. Slightly larger than the pygmy, the saw-whet ranges across southern Canada. Its name comes from one of its calls which sounds like the filing of a saw.

The **burrowing owl** *(Speotyto cunicularia)* inhabits dry, treeless grasslands in southern Alberta, Saskatchewan and Manitoba where it hunts during the day and at night, but particularly at dusk. Its mottled sandy plumage blends with prairie vegetation.

This owl is usually seen on the ground or on low fence posts. It nests in the abandoned burrow of a ground squirrel. In spring it lays 6 to 10 white eggs which hatch in about 30 days.

The saw-whet owl, 7½ to 8 inches long, remains year round in Canada.

How an Owl Sees All Round

Birds with eyes on the sides of the head can see almost 360°. Front-facing eyes give owls a narrower field of vision but a greater area of binocular sight (the ability to see an object with both eyes and get one image). An owl can turn its head through most of a circle and even upside down for all-round vision.

A Lazy Hunter That Would Rather Steal Food

The **bald eagle** *(Haliaeetus leucocephalus alascanus)* ranges over most of Canada. The bird stands 2½ to 3 feet tall and has a wingspan of up to 7½ feet. It is more often a scavenger than a predator and feeds on cast-up fish both inland and along seacoasts. A lazy bird, it eats carrion or steals the prey of other birds although it will prey on all manner of birds and small animals.

The bald eagle's plumage is brown for one year; during the next four years its head, neck and tail feathers gradually lighten to their characteristic pure white.

The nests of bald eagles are built of sticks and weeds and lined with pine needles, corn stalks, leaves and grass. They are usually in tall trees, occasionally on cliff ledges. Most are used and added to year after year. In spring a female bald eagle lays one to three small off-white eggs which hatch in about 35 days.

A bald eagle—a frequent scavenger—seizes a fish with its talons.

The **golden eagle** *(Aquila chrysaëtos)* is a large, dark brown bird with a golden nape and a less massive bill than the bald eagle's. Its legs are feathered; the bald eagle's are not.

About three feet tall, the golden eagle has a wingspan of up to eight feet. It breeds and winters throughout Canada, inhabiting mountainous areas, foothills and grassy plains. Its taloned feet—powerful enough to pierce a human hand—measure about six inches across and grow to full size in the bird's first 10 weeks.

The golden eagle nests on cliff tops, cliff faces and occasionally in trees. The nest is constructed of sticks and twigs and lined with grass and leaves. Like the bald eagle's, it is often added to over the years; it may weigh up to a ton. The eagle's two eggs, white or buff and spotted with brown, hatch in about 43 days.

The golden eagle feeds on a variety of animals, from foxes, marmots and rabbits to snakes and mice. It surprises its prey, then swoops. The victim may be killed on the ground or in the air—in the iron grip of the talons.

The **marsh hawk** *(Circus cyaneus)* is a slender-bodied bird with a wingspan of about four feet. It glides low over fields and marshes. During the mating season it wheels, somersaults and drops in spectacular fashion. It has a long dusky-banded gray tail and a distinctive white rump patch. The male's plumage is bluish gray; the female is reddish brown with brown-streaked buffy white undersides. The hawk's nest of weeds, sticks and grasses is on the ground, usually in

Legs outstretched and wings and tail feathers fully spread to break its flight, an osprey lands with its prey gripped in one powerful talon.

The peregrine falcon can dive at faster than 200 miles an hour.

a wet meadow or marsh. In early April the female lays four to six white eggs.

The marsh hawk breeds from the Yukon to the Maritimes. Some winter in southern British Columbia, in Alberta and southern Ontario and in Nova Scotia and others travel south as far as Colombia and the West Indies.

The **osprey** *(Pandion haliaetus)* is a brown-bodied bird with a white head and a speckled breast. A broad brown stripe runs along each side of its neck. A young osprey is the same color as its parents except its head is more heavily streaked with brown and its feathers have whitish tips. A fully grown bird is about two feet high with a wingspan of six feet.

A hooked beak, long sharp talons and bony spikes on its feet well equip the osprey for fishing. It cruises high in the air, spots its prey, dives—often plunging into the water—and impales the fish on its talons. But the bony spikes fix so firmly into its prey that the osprey is sometimes dragged under by its victim and drowned.

The osprey's nest, a large structure of sticks, is built in an isolated tree or occasionally on man-made structures such as a telephone pole. The female lays two to four brown-spotted buff-white eggs and incubates them for about 35 days.

The osprey breeds throughout Canada near lakes and coastal bays. It winters from the southern United States to the West Indies and South America.

The **peregrine falcon** *(Falco peregrinus)*—about 15 inches tall for the female, less for the male—is probably one of the swiftest birds of prey. Despite its speed and power—distinct advantages in nature—the peregrine population has been declining due to pesticides, pollution and nest destruction. Only on the Queen Charlotte Islands is the peregrine falcon still holding its own.

Like other falcons, the peregrine has a toothed upper bill. It has a large, black-capped head, a sturdy slate-barred ash-blue body, brown-barred buffy white underparts and a wingspan of up to 46 inches.

The peregrine returns to breed on the same coastal and inland cliffs year after year. It has little or no nest; its cream eggs, marked with rich reddish browns, are usually laid on ledges.

The peregrine migrates through all of southern Canada. Those on the Queen Charlotte Islands winter along the British Columbia coast and in the interior.

A marsh hawk returns to its nest with a catch; mice and rats are its main diet. Below: a golden eagle and its prey, a yellow-bellied marmot.

This fluffy ***red-tailed hawk*** *hatchling* (Buteo jamaicensis) *will grow to about 22 inches and have a wingspan of 3 feet.*

Tiny, Aggressive, They'll Battle a Hawk

Hummingbirds, the smallest and most aerobatic birds in the world, are named for the sound of tiny wings that beat up to 100 times a second. These birds hover almost motionless in midair, rise vertically, dart sideways, fly backward—even upside down. When they hover, their wing tips move at 20 miles per hour. They are about three inches long and weigh scarcely an ounce but their size is misleading. Hummingbirds are aggressive; quite capable of attacking birds as big as hawks. At night they lapse into deep sleep and can be mistaken for dead.

Of the four species of hummingbirds in Canada, the most widely distributed is the lively **ruby-throated hummingbird** *(Archilochus colubris)*. This resplendent three-inch bird inhabits gardens, orchards and woodland fringes across southern Canada from eastern Alberta to Nova Scotia. With a long, extensible tongue, it sips nectar and feeds on the tiny insects it finds in flowers. On the wing, it plucks insects from the air. The male has a vivid red throat patch and a luminous metallic green back. Its sides are grayish brown and white with a green luster, its breast and abdomen are grayish white and the feathers of its forked tail are tapered toward the ends. The female lacks a red throat patch, her tail is not forked and her tail feathers are rounded and the outer ones are white-tipped.

The rubythroat nests in trees. Its cup-shaped nest, less than two inches in diameter, is made of plant down and lichens bound with spider silk. The female incubates two white eggs for about two weeks. When hatched, the young are about the size of bees.

The rubythroat makes the longest of all hummingbird migrations. It fuels up by accumulating an additional 50 percent of its normal weight in body fat, then travels about 2,000 miles to winter in the southern United States and Mexico.

Hummingbirds belong to the same order as swifts: both have long narrow wings, and small feet. The **chimney swift** *(Chaetura pelagica)*, about five inches long, is a sooty bird with a short tail, long wings and a short broad bill. It flies high and fast in a jerky, zigzag motion with short, intermittent glides.

By day the swift rarely lands. It feeds in the air on insects and swoops over lakes and rivers and scoops water with its bill. The swift usually nests in an old building or a chimney and with saliva fastens its nest of twigs to a wall. Sometimes it nests in a hollow tree or on a cliff face. The parents incubate four or five white eggs for about 20 days. The swift sleeps by clinging to a vertical surface.

A thick skull enables a woodpecker to withstand the pounding of its hard straight bill as it bores holes in trees, fence posts and utility poles. Sharp curved

How a Hummingbird Hovers

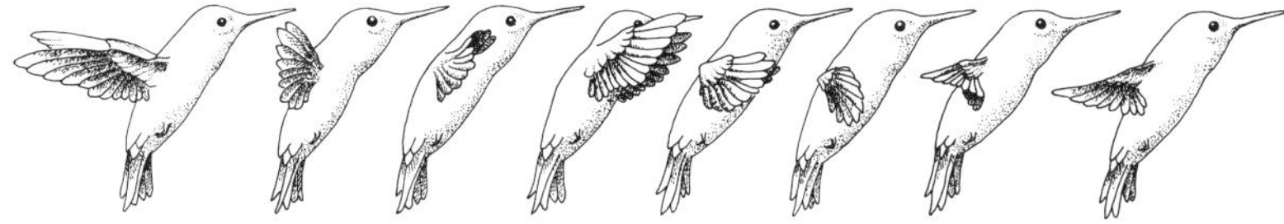

The tiny hummingbird beats its wings 55 to 100 times a second—the tips move at as much as 20 miles an hour—using powerful muscles that account for more than 25 percent of its weight. Unlike the wings of most birds, the hummingbird's rotate on swivel joints at the shoulders. On the down (forward) stroke the wings move conventionally, providing lift but no forward movement. On the up (back) stroke the wings swivel 180 degrees and again there is lift without acceleration. In this way the hummingbird remains aloft and—seemingly—motionless. To maintain energy it feeds on nectar.

The downy woodpecker remains year round in Canada.

Hovering as if motionless, a hummingbird probes for nectar.

The chimney swift nests in a hollow tree or a chimney.

The yellow-bellied sapsucker, mainly an insect-eater, occasionally feasts on berries.

claws help it climb; a stiff tail braces the bird when it drills. With a long, thorny-tipped tongue it impales and withdraws insect larvae from deep in the holes.

The **downy woodpecker** *(Dendrocopos pubescens)*, Canada's smallest woodpecker, is a black and white bird slightly larger than a song sparrow. It is common throughout southern Canada in wilderness areas, parks, orchards and woodlots. It ventures closer to humans than do most woodpeckers. It nests in a hole drilled 15 to 70 feet above ground, usually in a dead tree. The parents incubate four to five white eggs for about 12 days.

Most woodpeckers have four toes. Exceptions are the **black-backed three-toed woodpecker** *(Picoides arcticus)* and the **northern three-toed woodpecker** *(Picoides tridactylus)*. The male black-backed is bluish black with a yellow crown and white spots on its flight feathers. The male northern is similar but smaller, with white bars across its back. Both range throughout Canada.

How a Woodpecker Extends Its Tongue

A woodpecker can extend its long, sometimes barb-tipped or sticky tongue several inches.

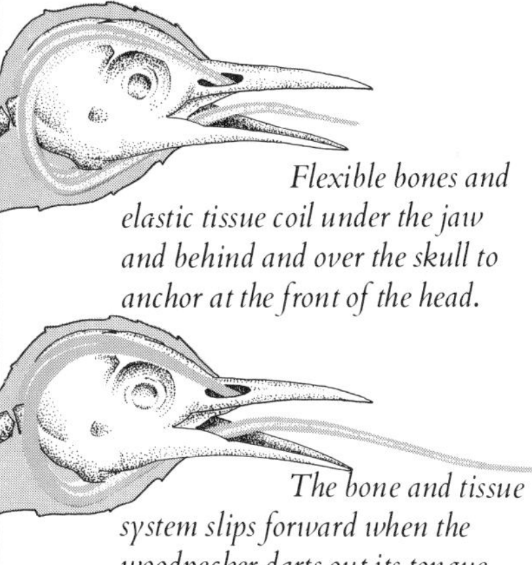

The black-backed three-toed woodpecker usually nests in a coniferous tree.

Two flickers are found in Canada: the **yellow-shafted** *(Colaptes auratus)* and the **red-shafted** *(Colaptes cafer)*. The yellow-shafted, the smaller, has yellow wing linings; the red-shafted has red linings. The cries of both birds sound like a repetition of the word flicker. The yellow-shafted ranges throughout most of Canada; the red-shafted is confined to the southern half of British Columbia.

In summer they both forage for insects on the ground and in trees. Their nesting habits are similar to those of the downy woodpecker. The parents incubate six to nine white eggs for about 12 days.

The **yellow-bellied sapsucker** *(Sphyrapicus varius)* breeds throughout most of Canada and winters along the coast of British Columbia. The three subspecies of yellow-bellied sapsucker in Canada have yellowish white bellies and white wing patches. East of the Rockies the male has a red crown and throat, the female, a red crown and white throat; both have a black patch across the breast. In southwestern Alberta and southeastern British Columbia the female's throat is red, and in the central interior of British Columbia and along the coast both sexes have red heads and throats but no throat patch.

The yellow-bellied sapsucker lays four to seven white eggs in a hole excavated in a tree. Male and female take turns incubating the eggs.

The yellow-shafted flicker is a woodpecker that feeds voraciously on ants.

A Woodland Ritual: the Drumming of the Grouse

Many of Canada's game birds are fowl-like scratchers that live, hunt and feed on the ground: grouse, partridge, ptarmigan, pheasant and quail.

The **ruffed grouse** *(Bonasa umbellus)* forages year round in woodlands for berries, buds, catkins and twigs. Its plumage is reddish brown or grayish brown with a darkly barred tail; a reddish brown or black ruff distinguishes it from other grouse.

The ruffed grouse is found throughout most of wooded Canada; in central Canada the gray color phase is more common, while in southwestern British Columbia the red predominates. The bird grows 16 to 19 inches long and weighs up to 1½ pounds.

The male's courting ritual is impressive. Standing on a log, it beats its wings, slowly at first, the tempo rapidly increasing. This drumming, heard at regular intervals usually at dawn and sunset, sounds like a car engine at a distance. Then, the male struts with its tail held erect, its neck ruff raised and its tail feathers spread like a fan.

The ruffed grouse population peaks mysteriously about every 10 years, declines sharply, then recovers gradually. Up to 14 chicks are hatched by each hen each year. Many young, however, do not survive their first year, despite the mother's attempts to distract aggressors by hissing, clucking and feigning a broken wing. In the fall, when the family breaks up, chicks that have not fallen prey to great horned owls, goshawks and foxes disperse over the countryside.

Snowy white in winter, mottled brown (below) in summer, the ptarmigan's protective coloration hides it year round from predators.

The **gray partridge** *(Perdix perdix)*, a fast, wily and unpredictable bird, has a short tail, a brown body with a gray breast and chestnut-brown bars on its flanks. About 12 inches long, it inhabits fertile open areas, particularly cultivated fields where other game birds are not as abundant.

The gray partridge feeds on weed seeds that native grouse do not eat, and survives winter nights by roosting in tight coveys. When snow is deep, it shelters near farms and suburbs. Its voice is a raspy two-syllable cry.

Although heavy snows and predators kill many gray partridge, the species maintains its population with prolific reproduction. Up to 20 olive-brown eggs hatch in 23 to 25 days. The nest, a hollow scraped in the ground, is lined with dead leaves or grass and usually sheltered by low shrubs. The gray partridge breeds in southern Canada.

Ptarmigan are small arctic or alpine grouse. Their superb camouflage is mottled brown in summer, pure white in winter. Feathers on legs and feet provide insulation against the cold and make walking on soft snow possible. In winter they sleep in snow hollows. Although sheltered, they are vulnerable to one of their main enemies, the arctic fox.

The **willow ptarmigan** *(Lagopus lagopus)* is found throughout most of northern Canada and in Newfoundland and most of British Columbia wherever vegetation is abundant. In June it nests on the tundra. Its nest is on the ground usually sheltered by shrubbery. The female incubates 7 to 10 yellowish, dark-spotted eggs for about 22 days. The parents are diligent guardians and distract intruders while the chicks hide in surrounding vegetation.

In late September the willow ptarmigan migrates to the southern part of its breeding range and sometimes farther south. It does not make its journey in one long flight as some migrating birds do, but in a series of short journeys with much feeding and walking along the way.

The willow ptarmigan shares part of its breeding range with the **rock ptarmigan** *(Lagopus mutus)*, which ventures almost as far as the North Pole. The **white-tailed ptarmigan** *(Lagopus leucurus)* is confined mainly to higher elevations in the Rocky and Cascade mountains.

The male **ring-necked pheasant** *(Phasianus colchicus)*, with its green head

A male ruffed grouse drums atop its courting post, a fallen log.

In Canada the bobwhite is found mainly in southern Ontario.

and copper-brown plumage, is one of Canada's most colorful game birds. It was introduced to North America from Asia in the late 1800s. It ranges across most of southern Canada, particularly Alberta and Saskatchewan and is much sought by hunters.

The male has a white neck ring, a red patch across the eyes, grayish green wings and rump and a 16-to-18-inch tapered tail. The female, a mottled buff-brown bird without a neck ring, resembles a domestic hen. Males are about 35 inches long and weigh about three pounds; females about 20 inches and two pounds.

Deep snow, severe winters and cold springs keep pheasants from over-populating the croplands, marsh edges and bushy pastures they inhabit. They feed on seeds, fruit, grain, insects, leaves and grass.

The female scratches a nest in the ground or uses a natural depression and lines it with vegetation. Eight to 15 olive-brown eggs hatch after about 23 days. The chicks feed mostly on insects for the first few weeks.

The **bobwhite** *(Colinus virginianus)*, a North American quail, is a permanent resident in southern Ontario. Its cry is an unmistakable *bobwhite.*

The bobwhite is also prized as a game bird. About 10 inches long, it is smaller than a grouse and is distinguishable from other quail by its white face markings and ruddy upperparts. It feeds mostly on seeds and insects.

The bobwhite can often be seen in grain and cornfields and around abandoned farms. Its nest—a hollow in the ground, lined with dead grass—is usually concealed in an arch made from the surrounding vegetation. The female and occasionally the male incubate 14 to 16 white eggs for about 23 days.

Despite bright markings, the ring-necked pheasant is adept at concealing itself.

Our Vanished Wildlife

The **greater prairie chicken** *(Tympanuchus cupido pinnatus)*, a medium-sized grouse, is thought to be extinct, although mixed breeds are known to exist. Its decline is attributed to man's destruction of its brushland habitat.

Like other prairie chickens, it roosts on the ground and only rarely flies up into trees or bushes.

In the early 1900s this brownish bird with a short rounded tail was common in southern Manitoba, Saskatchewan and Alberta and parts of southern Ontario. A small population on Manitoulin Island in Lake Huron may already have been lost through crossbreeding with the sharp-tailed grouse.

That Pesky Pigeon May Be a Mourning Dove

A belted kingfisher flies to its burrow with food for its hungry brood. Its main diet is small fishes of little economic importance.

Pigeons and doves are similar in appearance and behavior. They have small heads, short legs and full-breasted bodies and drink by sucking water through round horny-tipped bills. They feed their young predigested food from their crops and build flimsy nests of twigs or straw. Town and city pigeons depend on humans for food handouts and are extremely hardy.

Although pigeons and doves generally migrate south in winter, common city pigeons remain in the urban environment, living mostly under the eaves of buildings and frequently weakening walls by feeding on mortar. The common pigeon is sometimes a carrier of parasites and of diseases such as typhus.

The **mourning dove** *(Zenaidura macroura)* is named for its slow, mournful cry. This slender, brown bird has a long, pointed tail and—in flight—much white in its outer tail feathers. It feeds almost entirely on weed seeds.

The mourning dove is found in towns and cities and in wooded areas. It nests 12 to 25 feet up in a tree, sometimes building in the nest of another bird. Where there are no trees, it nests on the ground or in a bush. The female lays two white eggs, usually twice a year. In summer the mourning dove ranges across southern Canada; in winter it flies south.

The **rock dove** *(Columba livia)* is a familiar permanent resident throughout southern Canada—especially in towns and cities. It has a square tail, two dark wing bars, a white rump patch and a dark bill. It nests in buildings and forages in streets, garbage dumps and railway yards. It usually avoids forested areas and occasionally perches in trees.

The rock dove breeds two or three times a year to compensate for the smallness of its brood. The female lays only two eggs. They hatch in about 18 days.

While most cuckoos lay eggs in the nests of other birds whose eggs are the

Because of its hearty appetite for insects, the whip-poor-will is valuable to farmers.

The mourning dove each year raises two families of two chicks each.

The common nighthawk's wings create a booming sound when it pulls out of a dive.

same color as their own, the two species in Canada usually do not. The **yellow-billed cuckoo** *(Coccyzus americanus)* and the **black-billed cuckoo** *(Coccyzus erythropthalmus)* both build a flimsy nest about six feet above ground in bushes. Four bluish green eggs are incubated by the parents.

Both the yellow-billed cuckoo and the black-billed cuckoo have slender bodies typical of the cuckoo family. They both emit similar wooden clucks and forage for insects over open woodland, particularly willow and alder thickets. The yellow-bill has brown upperparts, grayish white underparts and a long, slender black tail with large white spots. The black-bill, longer than a robin, has brown upperparts, white underparts, a red eye-ring and a long, white-tipped tail.

While the black-bill breeds throughout most of southern Canada, the yellow-bill is found in only a few areas of British Columbia and central Canada.

The **whip-poor-will** *(Caprimulgus vociferus)* is named for its haunting, far-carrying call—heard in spring and early summer at dusk and after nightfall. A close relative of the owl, the whip-poor-will can see at night. The colors of its soft plumage are variable—generally browns and grays mottled with black. It has a small beak, a large mouth and a black-streaked head.

The whip-poor-will builds no nest. It lays two white, gray-spotted eggs on the ground or in a pile of leaves in woodlands from Saskatchewan to Nova Scotia.

Despite its name, the **common nighthawk** *(Chordeiles minor)* is not a member of the hawk family. It has long wings, a slightly forked tail, a small soft beak and a large mouth. White spots on its long slender wings make it easily identifiable—and it is often seen throughout Canada wheeling high in the sky on summer evenings. The nighthawk consumes vast numbers of insects as it forages in the air over cities and woodlands. It winters in South America.

Mouths agape, black-billed cuckoo chicks wait to be fed.

Our Vanished Wildlife

A century and a half ago, no North American bird was more abundant than the **passenger pigeon** *(Ectopistes migratorius)*: passing flocks once darkened the sky. But this graceful, slate-blue bird was gunned, trapped and clubbed to extinction. Its habit of gathering in huge flocks made it easy prey.

Passenger pigeons were shipped by the boxcar and sold for a dollar a dozen. The breast meat was eaten, the wings and feathers were used to fill potholes in roads.

In 1902, the last recorded wild specimen was shot near Penetanguishene, Ont. The only remaining flock, caged in a Cincinnati zoo, dwindled to a single pair of 24-year-old birds. They mated. The egg did not hatch. Before the male died, ornithologists offered thousands of dollars for a live bird. Not one was found.

On September 1, 1914, the last passenger pigeon in the world—Martha, she was called by zoo employees—died. The passenger pigeon was extinct.

The nighthawk usually spends the daylight hours perched on a branch or on a flat rooftop. It has a nasal, single-note call. Like the whip-poor-will—which it resembles—it builds no nest and lays its two creamy white eggs on the ground.

The **belted kingfisher** *(Megaceryle alcyon)*, a blackish blue bird with a large, crested head and loud rattling call, is larger than a robin but smaller than a crow. It fishes in both salt water and fresh water. Perched motionless on a rock above clear water, it watches for prey, then dives and catches small fish in its long, pointed bill. Occasionally it feeds on grasshoppers and frogs.

The kingfisher excavates a burrow three to seven feet long in a bank of earth, often beside a highway or a gravel pit, for its five to eight white eggs.

In summer the kingfisher ranges across Canada. It winters in British Columbia and southern Ontario.

The rock dove is the familiar pigeon of towns and cities.

Amphibians and Reptiles

The Harmless Mudpuppy... the Deadly Rattler

Amphibians and reptiles are the ancients of the kingdom of land animals. Amphibians appeared some 380 million years ago. The oldest known reptile fossil is an animal called *Hylonomus,* found in coal deposits laid down about 300 million years ago in Nova Scotia. In the evolutionary process, amphibians and reptiles are the bridge between aquatic creatures and birds and mammals. Reptiles are thought to have evolved from amphibians just as amphibians are thought to have evolved from fishes. Probably there were many intermediate forms of life—neither totally reptile, amphibian or fish.

Unlike mammals and birds, reptiles and amphibians cannot regulate their body temperatures internally. They maintain a fairly constant temperature by moving between warm and cool surroundings.

One hundred and ten species and subspecies of amphibians and reptiles have been identified in Canada—24 kinds of frogs, tree frogs and toads, 26 of salamanders, 16 of turtles, 38 of snakes and 6 of lizards.

Most amphibians and reptiles are harmless to man. The greatest number is found along the Canada-United States border. Twenty-nine species and subspecies are rare or endangered. The main threat to the survival of reptiles and amphibians is the destruction of their habitat.

The word amphibian, meaning double life, refers to the fact that many of these animals are at home both in water and on land. Amphibians are thought to be the first vertebrates to adapt to life out of the water. They are able to breathe through gills, lungs, skin, or a combination of these. Unlike reptiles, they have smooth, moist skin and their eggs are usually laid and fertilized in water and need no tough shell. Most of their young pass through a gill-breathing stage. There are three living orders of amphibians. Their closest living relatives are reptiles, scaly-skinned lung-breathers that generally exist out of water and whose eggs are fertilized inside their bodies.

Reptiles—turtles, snakes and lizards—likely evolved from lung-breathing amphibians and their forebears include the dinosaur.

A bullfrog (above) eats any creatures it can get into its mouth: salamanders, snakes, mice, birds, turtles—and other frogs. The leopard frog (below) is common in meadows and near water.

They Help Make the Music of Springtime

A male Canadian toad, its vocal sac inflated, adds its voice to the spring chorus.

The tiny spring peeper, a good climber, is often seen in trees and low bushes.

The music of springtime in forests, meadows and swamps and along rivers and streams includes the croaking and the whistling of Canada's 24 species and subspecies of frogs and toads. This spring song is almost exclusively male: the male of each species and subspecies has a distinctive mating call; the female, whose voice is quieter and occasionally altogether absent, listens.

Most frogs and toads mate in water and the eggs are usually fertilized as soon as they are expelled by the female. Often numbering in the thousands, the eggs are contained in a jellylike substance and are attached to water plants or deposited in shallow water. The eggs hatch into tadpoles, completely aquatic creatures with eyes, mouths, gills and long, flat tails. They eat algae, water plants and tiny animals floating on the water. As a tadpole matures, it loses its tail, grows legs and develops lungs for a life on land.

Many frogs and toads are land dwellers but some live in trees or in the water, and others burrow beneath the earth. They have large heads, wide mouths and short bodies. Females are generally larger than males. Frogs and toads eat almost any small animal that moves—including other frogs and toads. Their enormous appetite for insects makes them valuable to farmers and gardeners.

The **leopard frog** *(Rana pipiens),* also known as the meadow frog, often wanders far from water to feed on crop-damaging insects. This species, up to four inches long, has light-bordered irregular dark spots along its green or brown back. One of Canada's most widely distributed frog species, it ranges from the Maritimes to eastern British Columbia and as far north as Great Slave Lake.

How to Tell a Frog From a Toad

A frog is slender, has moist smooth skin and leaps on long hind legs. A toad is stocky, has dry rough skin and hops on short hind legs. A frog lives in or near water. A toad is often found far from water.

The **bullfrog** *(Rana catesbeiana)* with its booming bass call is North America's largest frog—its body grows to eight inches long. Highly aquatic, with webbed toes and fairly smooth green or brown skin on top, it lives in or near water. It feeds on small frogs, fish, snakes, birds, mice and insects. Its leap is a blur to the human eye, but high-speed cameras have shown that it controls its direction in flight by twisting its webbed hind feet. The bullfrog is native to southern parts of the Maritimes, Quebec and Ontario and has been introduced into British Columbia.

The evening chorus of the **spring peeper** *(Hyla crucifer)* is a marvel of sound. With its mouth closed, this inch-long frog produces high-pitched whistles that are amplified by a balloonlike sac on its throat. The spring peeper is brownish with an X-shaped mark on its back. It inhabits woodlands and marshes from the Maritimes to Manitoba. In winter it hibernates under moss or dead leaves or in a shallow burrow.

Toads are fewer in kind and number than frogs. One common toad species in Canada is the **Canadian toad** *(Bufo hemiophrys).* About three inches long, it is found near water throughout the Prairies. It is brownish or greenish on top with reddish wartlike bumps, a whitish stripe on its back and a brown band along each side.

The Abundant, Bashful Lizards

Lizards are the world's most abundant reptiles, outnumbering even snakes, but only 5 of some 3,000 known species have been identified in Canada. All but one of the species in Canada are restricted to extreme southern parts of the West. These scaly cold-blooded creatures survive freezing temperatures by burrowing beneath the frost line and hibernating.

Lizards are among the most primitive of animals; some fossils are an estimated 200 million years old. Except for certain extinct ocean-dwelling species, the lizards of prehistory apparently were much like today's. Despite their appearance, lizards are not aggressive to man unless cornered. Most are bashful.

Unlike snakes, lizards have a skeletal support for the front limbs, ear openings and movable eyelids. Lizards are sometimes confused with salamanders, although salamanders are amphibians and have smooth skins.

The few lizard species and subspecies in Canada fall into strikingly different groups: horned lizards, skinks and alligator lizards.

The spiny "horns" of the eastern short-horned lizard are enlarged scales.

To frighten a predator, a pygmy horned lizard, such as this, squirts blood from the inside corners of its eyes.

Horned lizards, sometimes called horned toads, are the **eastern short-horned lizard** *(Phrynosoma douglassi brevirostre)* of Saskatchewan and Alberta and the rare **pygmy horned lizard** *(Phrynosoma douglassi douglassi)* of British Columbia. Flat-headed and squat but with prominent pyramid-shaped spines over much of their bodies, both subspecies look like crawling cacti. All horned lizards, when excited or angered, squirt blood from the corners of the eyes, to a distance of several feet.

While most lizards lay eggs, eastern short-horned lizards give live birth in late summer to as many as 36 young, each slightly over an inch long. They grow to about four inches.

Eastern short-horned lizards inhabit dry regions of the short-grass prairie and are often active in the hottest part of the day. When threatened, they sometimes puff themselves up, open their mouths, hiss and charge.

Skinks are alert, smooth-scaled creatures with tails that break off easily, making capture difficult. They are brightly marked with brown and silver stripes above and with cream and blue gray on their undersides. The tails of young skinks are a brilliant blue.

If a predator grasps the tail of a skink, the tail comes off and continues to twitch, distracting the attacker while the skink escapes. The tail breaks along a fracture plane near the middle of a vertebra; muscles pinch the blood vessels to prevent excessive bleeding. The skink then grows another, shorter tail.

One subspecies, the profusely striped **northern prairie skink** *(Eumeces septentrionalis septentrionalis)*, is found only in a forest reserve east of Brandon, Man.

An elegantly patterned five-lined skink clings to a decaying log.

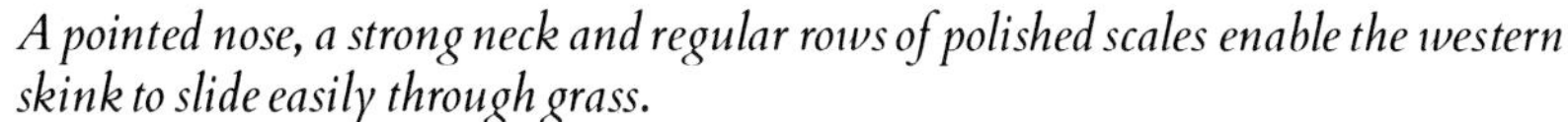

A pointed nose, a strong neck and regular rows of polished scales enable the western skink to slide easily through grass.

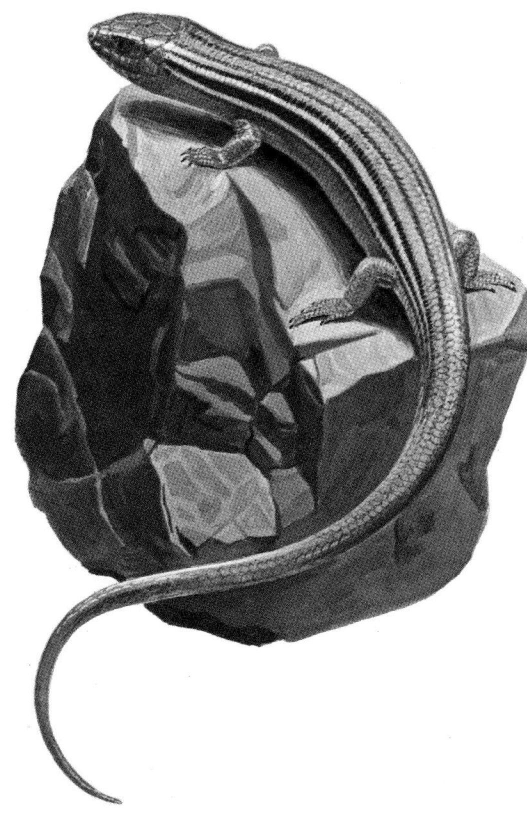

The northern prairie skink is seen nowhere but in southern Manitoba.

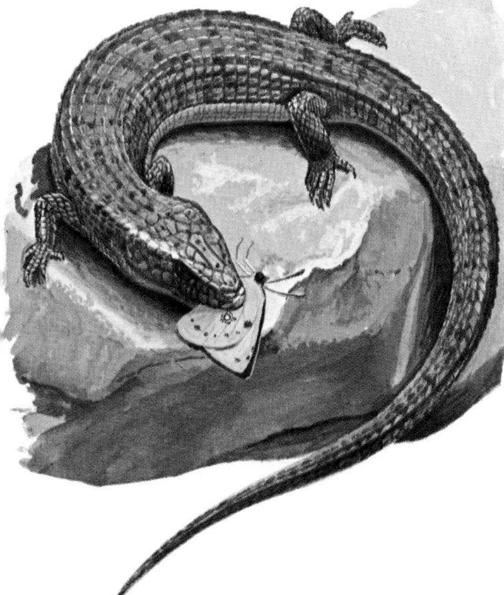

The northern alligator lizard feeds on snakes, spiders and millipedes.

It is seldom seen in the open, preferring the shallow excavations it digs in soft, loose soil. The Manitoba skinks are believed to be a colony separated from the continuous range of the species, which extends from Minnesota to Texas.

The northern prairie skink, which grows to a maximum of eight inches, lays up to a dozen eggs in late spring or early summer. Deposited in holes dug out beneath stones or logs, they hatch in 40 to 52 days. This skink hibernates in burrows dug in sandy soil to a depth of 4½ feet.

The slightly smaller **five-lined skink** *(Eumeces fasciatus)*, found in parts of Ontario, favors a damp environment—rotting stumps or logs and decaying debris in or near wooded areas. It is essentially a terrestrial animal but sometimes climbs trees in search of dead and decaying "snags" where insects collect. It derives its name from the five white or yellowish stripes along its back.

The **western skink** *(Eumeces skiltonianus)* is found in Canada only in southern British Columbia, particularly the southern Okanagan and Kootenay regions. It frequents forest clearings, rocky riverbanks and dry hillsides. The smallest of Canadian skinks, it measures five or six inches at maturity. The female lays three or four eggs and attends them until they hatch.

The king of Canadian lizards, at least in size, is the **northern alligator lizard** *(Gerrhonotus coeruleus principis)* which looks like a scaled-down alligator. Up to nine inches long, it is easily identified by a deep, flexible groove along each side of the body. The northern alligator lizard inhabits dry rocky areas throughout southern British Columbia. Like the skink, it is a tail-shedder. The female gives live birth to 2 to 15 young.

Only the Rattlers Are Dangerous

Most snakes in Canada are harmless to humans. Nonetheless, many people loathe and fear all snakes and often needlessly kill those that pose no danger whatsoever. The only snakes really to be feared in Canada are rattlesnakes, found only in the interior dry belt of southern British Columbia and in parts of southern Alberta, Saskatchewan and Ontario.

There are three groups of snakes:

- Constrictors wrap themselves around victims and kill by compression.
- Poisonous snakes paralyze or kill with venom injected through fangs.
- Nonpoisonous snakes (such as garter and water snakes) seize prey and swallow it alive.

All snakes are carnivores, preying on earthworms, insects, fish, small mammals and birds. Limbless and unable to tear food apart, they must swallow it whole, even though it is sometimes larger in circumference than they are. But a snake's two-piece lower jaw is attached to its skull with muscles that stretch and permit wide dislocation. The two pieces of the jaw are joined by an elastic ligament. Skin between the scales is elastic. Ribs are not connected to the breastbone.

The Lake Erie water snake beats a hasty retreat at the first sign of trouble.

The snake that Canadians see most often (but not in Newfoundland, which has no native snakes) is the **common garter snake** *(Thamnophis sirtalis)*. Three stripes that run the length of the body help distinguish it from other snakes. The stripes, against a background of dark brown or black, vary from nearly white to yellow, orange or green. These snakes normally grow to about 30 inches. They may bite in self-defense—the bite is not poisonous—or emit a foul-smelling fluid to discourage attackers.

Slender and fast, the ***western yellow-bellied racer*** (Coluber constrictor mormon) *crawls with its head held high and occasionally moves it from side to side.*

The rubber boa (above) is blunt at both ends. Its head and tail look alike. Below: The ***eastern garter snake*** (Thamnophis sirtalis sirtalis) *is found in southeastern Canada.*

The **western plains garter snake** *(Thamnophis radix haydeni)*, common in southern Alberta, Saskatchewan and Manitoba, usually has a vivid orange stripe against a black, brown or greenish background.

The **Maritime garter snake** *(Thamnophis sirtalis pallidula)* is found in Prince Edward Island, Nova Scotia, New Brunswick and parts of Quebec.

All garter snakes give birth to live young rather than hatching them from eggs, as some other snakes do. Newborn garter snakes—10 to 40 in a litter and about six inches long—are given no parental care. They live in woods, fields, farmlands and marshes and along lakes and streams. They eat earthworms, frogs, minnows, and mice.

Water snakes are found in and near lakes, rivers, streams and marshes. The

A western plains garter snake about to eat a mouse. Snakes have no limbs and are unable to tear prey apart so swallow their victims whole.

A poisonous eastern Massasauga rattlesnake sheds its skin.

If threatened, a hognose snake, such as this ***western hognose*** (Heterodon nasicus nasicus)*, may shudder convulsively, roll over and play dead.*

Lake Erie water snake *(Natrix sipedon insularum)* is found on Pelee Island and on a few other islands in western Lake Erie. It suns on branches of shrubs and is an excellent diver and swimmer. It is timid and feeds on fish, frogs, salamanders and small snakes and mice.

The rattlesnake's legendary forked tongue, like that of all snakes, is harmless; it serves as an organ of smell. Two temperature-awareness organs in pits between the eyes and the nostrils enable a rattlesnake to detect the presence of warm-blooded prey. The venom-conducting fangs, resembling a hypodermic needle, are in the upper jaw in front of the mouth. A rattlesnake is born with fangs and venom, but no rattle. When it molts (about three times a year) it retains a single spherical scale at the end of its tail. This scale and the unshed scales of previous molts harden into a loosely jointed chain or rattle—hence the name rattlesnake. The rattler's warning signal can be heard nearly 100 feet away.

The **eastern Massasauga rattlesnake** *(Sistrurus catenatus catenatus)* is also known as the swamp rattlesnake and the little gray rattlesnake. These snakes are born between late July and early September, seven or eight to a litter. This species is found along the shore of Georgian Bay—and up to 20 miles inland in some places—and on islands in the bay and on the Bruce Peninsula. It also occurs along some parts of the Lake Huron and Lake Erie shores.

The Massasauga's stout body grows to about 2½ feet long. Nine large symmetrical scales on top of the broad head are similar to those of nonpoisonous snakes; other rattlers have many small scales on the head. The snout is blunt.

This snake is gray or brownish with dark blotches patterned along the middle of the back. The belly is mostly black, the throat and chin gray and white. The Massasauga is sluggish and mild-tempered. It likes swamps and bogs and swims better than other rattlers. Frogs and mice are its favorite food.

Canada's only boa, the **rubber boa** *(Charina bottae)* feeds mainly on mice and other small animals. It is known as the two-headed snake because its tail is almost as blunt as its head. It rolls into a ball when threatened, hiding its head and making the tail appear to be the head.

This short, stout snake, usually between 18 and 24 inches long, has vestigial hind limbs or spurs and the scales are smooth and overlapping. The color varies from pale tan, to grayish or dark brown. The belly is a light yellow or cream.

The Slithery Salamander

The tiny spotted salamander hides by day in the litter of moist leaves on the forest floor. It emerges at night to forage for earthworms and other invertebrates.

In a pond or a stream, beneath a rock or under the litter of the forest floor, the tiny salamander lives safe from the sun's dehydrating rays. Like toads and frogs, salamanders are amphibians but, although a few species are strictly aquatic, most are land dwellers and enter the water only to breed.

Most salamanders have two four-toed front feet, two five-toed hind feet. Their bodies are elongated and cylindrical, their skins smooth and slippery. They walk with the slithery movements of snakes.

All salamanders have tails; in land forms they are long and rounded; in aquatic forms, laterally compressed. All species have teeth. They drink by absorbing water through the pores of their skin.

Salamanders have three breathing systems, which they use singly or together. Like fish, from which they have evolved, they extract oxygen from water. They also absorb oxygen through the skin. Most salamanders, however, develop lungs for a life on land. Salamanders in captivity have been known to live for 30 years; in the wild, due to predators, they live only a few months. Many salamanders resist predators by exuding a toxic secretion from the skin. Like a skink, if a salamander's tail is gripped by an enemy, it sheds the tail, then grows a new one. Land-dwelling salamanders are preyed upon by skunks; aquatic forms are prey to otters, snapping turtles, muskrats and snakes.

Lacking vocal chords, salamanders have no mating call; mates are found through scent. For most of the year male and female look alike, but during courtship the males of some species take on vivid colors. Jellylike clusters of eggs are laid and hatched in water, occasionally on land.

Northern two-lined salamander
(Eurycea bislineata bislineata).

During its land stage (above) the red-spotted newt is known as a red eft.

Salamanders are found almost entirely in woodlands of northern temperate regions. In North America there are 135 species.

The **spotted salamander** *(Ambystoma maculatum)* is found in eastern North America. About seven inches long, it is a stout, blunt-nosed creature with a slate-gray belly and dark upperparts. Its back is marked with irregular rows of yellow spots.

When the spring rains come, swarms of spotted salamanders, like most salamanders, head for ponds to breed. They pair off and the male deposits sperm on the pond bed. The female draws the sperm into her body, then lays up to 250 eggs, attaching them to an underwater branch. They hatch from three to eight weeks later.

The **gray tiger salamander** *(Ambystoma tigrinum diaboli)* may grow to 11 inches. It has a wide, flat head and dark-blotched olive upperparts. Its underparts

The mudpuppy, sometimes called waterdog, lives in permanent bodies of fresh water. This salamander grows to be 8 to 13 inches long; the largest on record is 17 inches.

The gray salamander breeds in shallow ponds and woodland pools.

A ***red-backed salamander*** (Plethodon cinereus cinereus).

are marked with brown. This salamander is found in southern Manitoba and southern Saskatchewan.

The **common mudpuppy** *(Necturus maculosus)* is found in lakes, ponds and rivers in Manitoba and eastern Canada. It spends its entire life in water and although it does not develop beyond the larval stage—a phenomenon known as neotony—it is sexually mature and can reproduce. Though essentially nocturnal, it sometimes swims by day in muddy and weed-choked waters.

This salamander takes its name from the mistaken belief that mudpuppies emit sharp, doglike barks. Gray or rust brown, it has blue-black spots along its back and orange-red tail fins. It retains its gills throughout its life. A mature mudpuppy's gills resemble maroon-colored ostrich plumes.

Newts—sometimes called water salamanders—are similar to salamanders but have rougher skins. They are essentially aquatic but often have a land stage.

The **red-spotted newt** *(Diemictylus viridescens viridescens)* breeds in spring. The female attaches fertilized eggs singly to water plants and in about a month a greenish yellow larva with feathery gills hatches. In two to three months, the larva metamorphoses into a red eft—an orange-red land animal with feet and lungs. The adolescent remains on land for one to three years. Upon returning to the water, it develops into a three-to-four-inch olive-green aquatic adult—a newt.

Few predators feed on newts, for their skin secretions are toxic—or at least offensive. Newts feed on insects, leeches, worms, tiny mollusks, young amphibians and frogs' eggs.

A "Living Fossil" That Predates the Dinosaur

An eastern spiny softshell turtle, its long snakelike neck extended, grips a crayfish in razor-sharp teeth. About two-thirds of this turtle's diet is crayfish.

A snapping turtle uses powerful hind legs to cover her eggs with soil.

Few animals have endured as long as the turtle. This "living fossil" that witnessed the rise and fall of the mighty dinosaur has survived almost unchanged for more than 200 million years.

Canada has about a dozen species of turtles. Most are found in or near ponds, lakes and streams. Man's destruction of their habitat, through road building and urban development, poses the greatest threat to the turtle's survival.

One Canadian subspecies is the **common snapping turtle** *(Chelydra serpentina serpentina)*, a large, formidable reptile with a short temper. It weighs 10 to 35 pounds, although one has been fattened to 86 pounds in captivity. A snapper's horny beak can inflict a painful bite. Even the young are vicious and will attack larger creatures if provoked. Unlike most turtles, the snapper is unable to protect itself by withdrawing its head and legs beneath its carapace (upper shell).

Snapping turtles are found from Nova Scotia to the Rockies. They rarely leave the water except to dig nests and lay eggs. Mating usually occurs in early spring. The female carries the eggs for several weeks, and then lays between 10 and 20 in a hole scraped out above high-water level. The female crawls back and forth over the filled-in nest to hide any trace of digging. The eggs are a favorite of skunks, raccoons, rats and other predators.

The eggs usually hatch in early fall. The young dig their way out of the sandy nest, and instinctively head for water where they burrow into the mud bottom and hibernate for the winter. Occasionally, in northern regions, snapper eggs remain through winter and hatch in early spring.

Snappers are mud-brown in color. They have large heads, long studded tails

The ***wood turtle*** (Clemmys insculpta), *although at home in water, spends the summer in meadows, fields and woods.*

The ***Blanding's turtle*** (Emydoidea blandingi), *found mainly in southern Ontario, is an endangered species.*

Piled three deep, map turtles bask peacefully on a log.

and shells up to 18 inches long. Another identifying feature is their plastron, or under shell, which is narrower than that of most turtles. Snapping turtles eat small invertebrates, frogs, fish, birds, mammals and aquatic plants.

The **midland painted turtle** *(Chrysemys picta marginata)*, found in southern Quebec and southern Ontario, has a smooth, rounded, patterned shell. The female's shell, larger than the male's, grows up to 5½ inches long.

A compulsive sunbather, this turtle will bask for hours on logs, stones or banks near shallow, quiet pools or backwater. It sometimes eats vegetable matter, but prefers earthworms, crayfish and frogs.

The **map turtle** *(Malaclemys geographica)* is sluggish and unusually shy and prefers large bodies of water. It derives its name from the intricate pattern of its shell. The pattern is more distinctive on the young of both sexes and on the male than it is on the adult female. This turtle is found in Ontario and Quebec.

Map turtles often lie on rock ledges or mud banks—sometimes piled two or three deep with their legs stretched out. If disturbed, they scurry away and plunge into deep water. They can crush the shells of clams and snails with their broad sharp-edged jaws. They also eat crayfish and water insects.

Most turtles have rigid shells that serve as tough armor. The one exception in Canada is the **eastern spiny softshell turtle** *(Trionyx spiniferus spiniferus)*. It is covered with a leathery carapace that is pliable along the edges. Females sometimes grow to a shell length of 17 inches.

It is sometimes called the "flapjack turtle" because of its unusually flat carapace. This rare species has been seen in southwestern Ontario and in Quebec. Its survival is said to be threatened by pollution.

The eastern spiny softshell ranks with the snapping turtle in ferocity; its razor-sharp claws and teeth can inflict serious injuries on anyone handling it. It often lies under the mud of shallow water, with only its long, snakelike neck protruding. It can stay submerged for hours by extracting oxygen from water through a lining in the throat. The eastern spiny softshell feeds on fish, frogs and mollusks.

The midland painted turtle is a sun lover. Its body temperature, like that of all cold-blooded creatures, is regulated by the environment.

Invertebrates

The Pesky Mosquito...the Bizarre Giant Squid

Ninety-five percent of all animal species are invertebrates—animals without backbones. Ranging from primitive single-celled Protozoa to 65-foot giant squids, they include such diverse forms as wasps, octopuses, shellfish and spiders—in four major groups: insects, arachnids, mollusks, crustaceans. Some invertebrates feed on such organic matter as plant juices, bark, leather and sugar; others devour weaker invertebrates or thrive on the blood of birds and mammals. All have simple nervous systems composed of ganglia (nerve tissues).

More than 800,000 known insect types and probably that many more not yet identified are found from the polar regions to the tropics. At least 40,000 species have been recorded in Canada. An insect has six legs and three main body sections: a head with antennae, a chest (thorax) and a tail section (abdomen). It breathes air through porelike openings called spiracles. An insect is usually unable to see clearly for more than a few feet. It depends on touch, taste and smell to identify food. Most adult insects have wings and are surprisingly strong: a bee can pull 300 times its weight.

Arachnids—such as spiders, ticks and mites—normally live on land and breathe with book lungs, organs that resemble gills. An arachnid has two main body segments and four pairs of legs. Of the world's 50,000 species of arachnids, at least 10,000 are found in Canada.

A mollusk has a rough-edged tongue for grinding food, and a soft unsegmented body composed of a fleshy mantle and a muscular foot. Generally slow-moving, mollusks live on land and in fresh and salt water. The 55,000 known species—some 1,200 are found in Canada—include oysters, limpets, slugs and snails.

A crustacean—from the Latin *crusta* (shell)—has a segmented, armored body, two pairs of antennae, and several pairs of legs adapted for walking and swimming. Most of the 35,000 species (more than 800 in Canada) live in water and breathe with gills. They include shrimps, crayfish, crabs and lobsters.

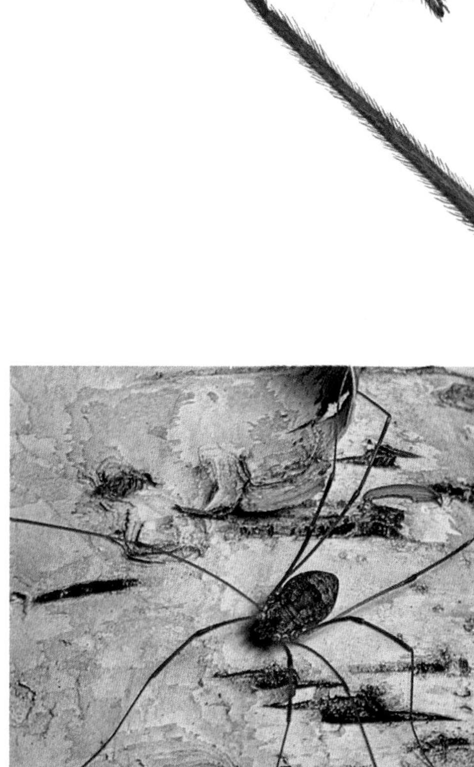

At twilight, the spindly legged harvestman emerges from under rocks or logs to forage for insects, fruits and vegetables.

When the centipede walks, only one leg in eight is on the ground at any one time.

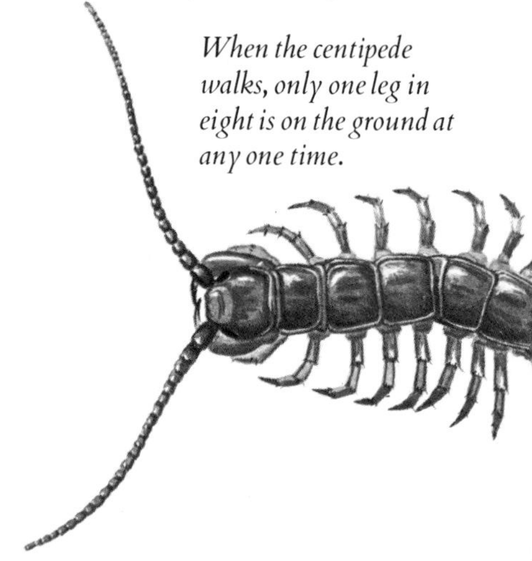

A Centipede May Have 30 Legs—or up to 342

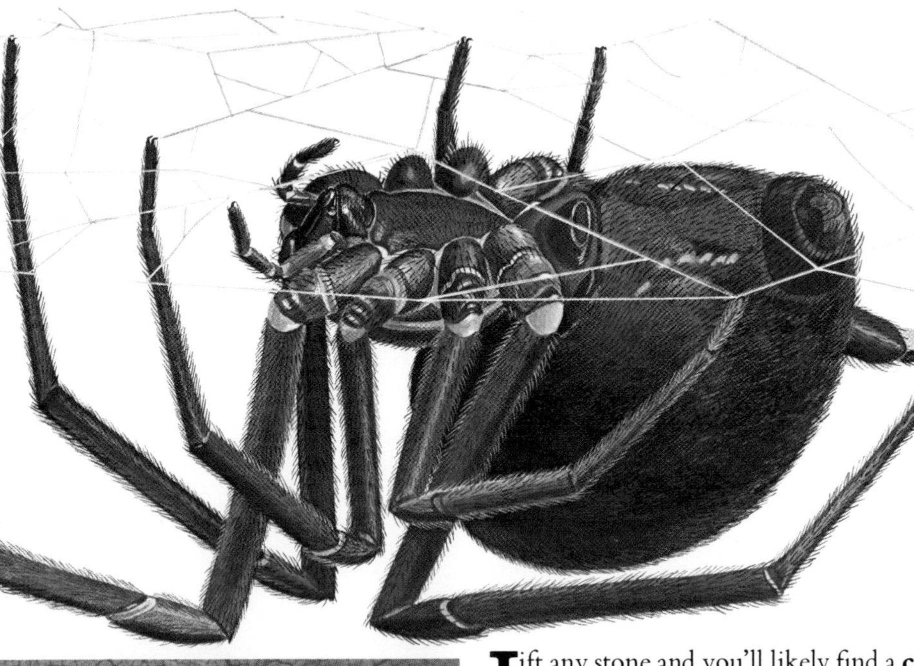

A blowfly has blundered into the web of a female black widow spider hanging upside down on her web.

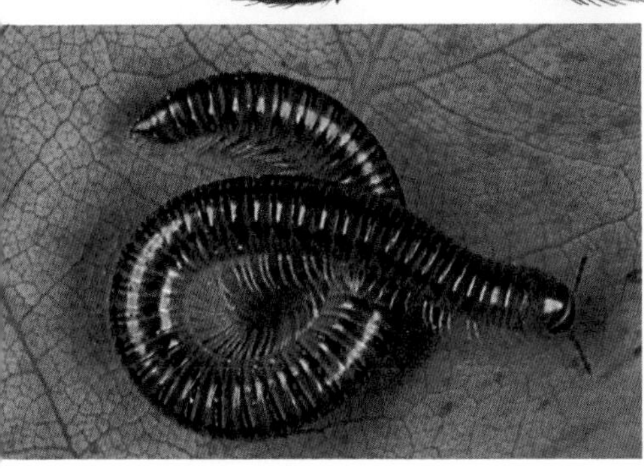

A millipede (above) has two pairs of legs on each segment of its body. The red spider mite (below) often causes extensive damage to fruit trees.

Lift any stone and you'll likely find a **centipede** *(Chilopoda)*—which, despite its name (hundred-footed), may have as few as 15 pairs of walking legs or as many as 171, the number always being uneven. The average is 15 to 31. Centipedes have a single pair of multijointed antennae and the front pair of feet in many species is modified into poisonous jaws for paralyzing insects and worms; the poison of some larger species may affect humans. Flat and usually fast-moving, centipedes live in the soil under stones and bark or in crevices. In Canada the biggest reach a length of two to three inches.

Millipedes *(Diplopoda)*—the common name means thousand-footed—are slower than centipedes but similar in appearance. Most have slender, multijointed bodies and up to 240 pairs of legs. They defend themselves by emitting repulsive or toxic secretions from pores on the sides of their bodies. Most millipedes are harmless scavengers that feed on decaying animal and plant material but a few are garden parasites.

The **black widow spider** *(Latrodectus hesperus)* is named for its color and because the female sometimes kills and devours her partner after mating. This spider is smooth and glossy and the female is distinguishable by a red mark on her abdomen. When disturbed, the female often attacks humans and her venomous bite can be fatal.

The black widow spins an irregular web of coarse silk in a dark, protected location on or near the ground, usually near human dwellings or in cultivated areas. In summer an egg sac containing several hundred pearl-like eggs is suspended from the web. The eggs hatch 14 to 30 days later. Black widows live about a year and a half.

The **daddy longlegs** or **harvestman** *(Phalangium opilio)*—not a true spider—has a tiny gray or brown body and eyes that protrude sideways. Its eight widespread spindly legs are usually bent to keep the body close to the ground while searching for prey. If a leg is seized by a predator, it is simply dropped off.

The daddy longlegs has no silk glands and spins no web. It lays eggs in autumn on the ground, under stones or in crevices in wood. The eggs hatch the following spring and the young change from white to their adult coloring as soon as they reach daylight. In fall adults are often seen in large numbers in fields, trees and farm buildings. Few survive the winter.

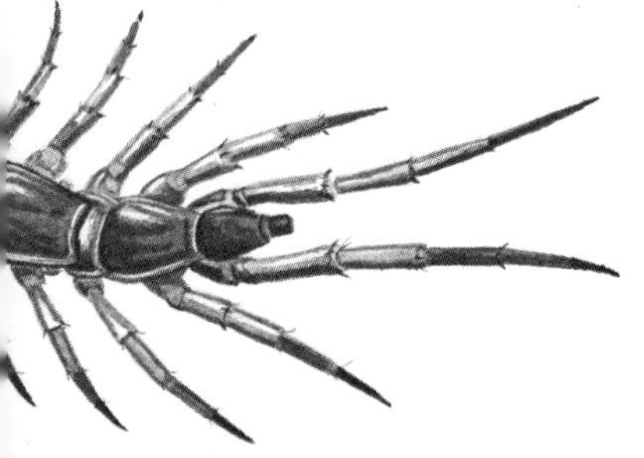

Killer With Superb Camouflage

The **praying mantis** *(Mantis religiosa)* is named for its prayerlike posture: it sits motionless on a blade of grass with spiky forelegs raised and held together as though in supplication. But quick as a flash this three-inch creature lashes out with its front legs and grasps a victim in a powerful death grip. The mantis' green color, giving it a grasslike appearance, provides superb camouflage; bulging compound eyes help it to detect prey—mainly insects but occasionally small birds, lizards and frogs. Male and female mantises are cannibalistic; the female often devours a partner during or immediately after mating.

The blackfly, especially the **white-stockinged blackfly** *(Simulium venustum)*, so named because of its white-banded legs, is the scourge of man and beast throughout much of Canada in spring and early summer. Hairy, humpbacked and usually blackish gray, these troublesome insects, only an eighth of an inch long, are the most widely distributed blackfly species in North America. They are found most frequently in forested areas and near fast-flowing rivers.

A few blackflies prey on birds rather than on animals but some attack both. However, of the more than 125 blackfly species in Canada only 11 suck blood: of those 6 attack humans and livestock and 5 livestock only.

Only female blackflies bite (they extract protein from blood to nourish their eggs). Males feed on nectar and plant juices as do females of many nonbiting species. Blackflies, unlike mosquitoes, feed only during daylight. They are most active in the morning and evening on warm humid days and seldom venture forth when it is raining or windy.

Blackflies develop in four stages: clusters of eggs (laid beside rocks or plants along rivers and streams and in ponds) hatch into larvae which grow to at least a quarter of an inch within two or three weeks. Following the pupal stage, which

lasts only a few days, adult blackflies emerge and congregate in dense mating swarms. Two or three generations are produced each year.

Ponds and swamps are the breeding grounds of nearly 60 species of **mosquitoes** *(Culicidae)* found in Canada. These prolific blood-sucking flies are carriers of disease—particularly to animals. One disease, a form of sleeping sickness that affects horses, is sometimes passed on to humans by these insects. Only the female mosquito bites.

Most Canadian species lay eggs in autumn, near water. Spring flooding activates the eggs and within one to three weeks they pass through the larval and pupal stage and develop into adults. Each year millions of adult mosquitoes provide food for birds, bats, snakes, dragonflies and spiders. In the aquatic stages (egg, larva and pupa), they are devoured by water beetles, toads and minnows.

Aside from hampering humans' outside activities, mosquitoes cost farmers untold millions each year: they cause cows to give less milk, beef cattle to gain less weight and chickens to lay fewer eggs.

In its moth stage—in late summer or autumn—the **eastern tent caterpillar** *(Malacosoma americana)* builds up huge populations over large areas of Canada

Poised for attack, a praying mantis awaits a victim.

A pupa (below)—originally a caterpillar—cracks open after about two weeks and slowly (right) releases a monarch butterfly.

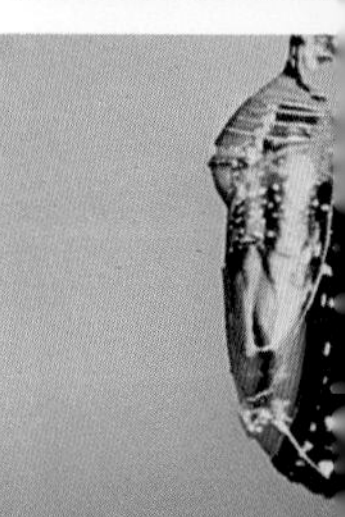

The luna moth's delicate pale green and its long, tapering hind wings make it one of Canada's most exquisite moths.

by laying masses of eggs around branches and twigs. In spring the eggs hatch into caterpillars with black velvety heads and a white stripe down the middle of the back. Newly hatched caterpillars remain together and, to house their community of several hundred, spin a silvery white "tent" which stretches from branch to branch. When mature, caterpillars are about three inches long. Tent caterpillars feed on tender new leaves and shoots—usually at night. They spin a strand of silk wherever they go and follow it back to the tent after feeding.

Tent life lasts four to eight weeks—until the family breaks up. The mature caterpillar, after a week of wandering, selects a suitable place—perhaps a shed or barn—for enclosing itself in a cocoon. If the cocoon is not attacked by parasites, a moth will emerge three weeks later.

The eastern tent caterpillar is found across southern Canada east of the Rockies. It is most common in the orchards of southern Ontario. The **forest tent caterpillar** *(Malacosoma disstria)*, another common species and one that does not make a tent, is found throughout Canada. Its eggs are laid in the folded blades or under the leaf sheaths of grass and grain in wet or sheltered areas.

The **luna** or **moon moth** *(Actias luna)* passes from egg to caterpillar to cocoon and emerges as an exquisite winged creature whose destiny is solely to mate and die. Like other giant, night-flying moths, the luna has no mouth and takes no food during the few days of its adult life. Often the female mates, lays its eggs and dies within inches of the discarded cocoon. The male's plumelike antennae, sensitive to odor, can locate a female from a distance of several miles.

Tent caterpillars do incalculable damage to Canadian orchards and forests.

How to Tell Butterflies From Moths

Most butterflies fly in the day; most moths fly at night. The antennae of butterflies end in knobs; those of moths end in points. At rest, most butterflies close their wings vertically or hold them open at an angle. Moths usually rest with their wings flat. Most butterflies have thin bodies; moths have thick bodies.

The **monarch** *(Danaus plexippus)* is perhaps Canada's most familiar butterfly. It begins life as a striped, milkweed-eating caterpillar with 16 legs. Later, it sheds its skin and is metamorphosed into a legless, immobile creature. Soon there emerges a butterfly with bright, orange-brown wings and six legs. In summer the monarch ranges from the Atlantic to the Pacific. In fall, it migrates 2,000 miles or more to Florida, California or Mexico.

Cicadas *(Cicadidae)* are grasshopperlike insects with transparent wings and strong legs for digging. Depending on the species, they range in color from green to buff, to gold, to dark brown. Cicadas grow up to 1½ inches long. Females are silent but males are more likely to be heard than seen. On hot summer days they call from trees—a shrill sound caused by two muscular drumlike structures beneath the body.

Ichneumon flies *(Ichneumonidae)* are four-winged wasplike insects. Many species have a dark spot on each fore wing. Usually half an inch long, they may grow to two inches. These insects lay their eggs on the larvae of other insects. The grubs devour the host and are thus important in controlling many insect populations.

Shy, Intriguing Devilfish of the Deep

Squids and octopuses, among the sea's most bizarre creatures, have long been objects of fascination and fear. Giant squids have been known to attack anchors, boat hooks—almost anything. They have rammed boats and mauled the occupants, they have pulled sailors from the decks of ships. But such hair-raising aggression is rare. Most squids attack humans only when provoked. Similarly, octopuses—the devilfish of fishermen's tales—are shy, retiring creatures although they may attack when threatened.

These mollusks are cephalopods—or head-footed—a term that suggests how their sucker-studded tentacles (8 for the octopus, 10 for the squid) extend from their heads. Two of the squid's tentacles, longer than its other arms, are used to grasp prey and pull it toward the squid's parrotlike beak. The largest octopuses have tentacles that spread about 12 feet, although the average is about a foot. The largest squid ever measured was 72 feet long but how large squids actually grow is unknown. Most are shorter than 8 inches.

A giant squid uses its two long sucker-studded tentacles to snare prey.

Octopuses, the most intelligent invertebrates, have rounded saclike bodies, usually without fins. Normally, they crawl on their tentacles. When frightened they propel themselves backward by squirting water through a nozzlelike siphon. Squids use this method of propulsion even more effectively and are capable of speeds up to 20 miles an hour. On each side of their streamlined bodies are two fins which enable squids to hover, swim backward or forward, or turn sharply.

A chemical reaction similar to that in the firefly enables squids and octopuses to change color. When threatened by a predator, they can turn a pale watery color, become mottled like the ocean bottom, or turn dark green to blend with seaweed. If camouflage fails, they emit a cloud of thick, black fluid which conceals them as they escape.

Squids and octopuses are carnivores that feed on crabs and other crustaceans. Octopuses stalk alone, usually on the bottom and at night. Squids hunt in packs. Scientists speculate that false bottom readings from sonar equipment may be caused by millions of squids floating above the ocean floor.

The **giant squid** *(Architeuthis princeps)*, the largest known invertebrate, is a true sea monster that rarely leaves the ocean depths. Most sightings are of injured squids floating on the surface or washed up on beaches. Sperm whales feed on these creatures and often bear circular scars, up to five inches across, caused by the suction cups of giant squid tentacles.

The common **Pacific octopus** *(Octopus hongkongensis)*, ranging from six inches to six feet in length, is found along the Pacific coast from Alaska to California. Its skin is wrinkled and pimply.

Above: The ***horseshoe crab*** (Limulus polyphemus) *is not a crab but a relative of scorpions and spiders. Below: Some octopuses paralyze prey with a poison secreted by glands near the beak.*

Squids and octopuses are not the only unusual creatures in the sea. Close to shore, where they are often exposed at ebb tide, are fascinating varieties of mollusks and crustaceans.

Abalones or sea-ears, common along the Pacific coast from Alaska to California, are small, flattish snails that cling to seaweed-covered rocks and feed on marine algae. Abalones breathe through a row of holes along the shell. Unlike most mollusks, abalones are nearly blind. They distinguish light and dark with eye spots along the edges of their fleshy mantles. The **Japanese abalone** *(Haliotis kamtschatkana)*, four to six inches long, has a corrugated shell. A few specimens have faint, spiraling ridges on the shell.

The **ten-ridged neptune whelk** *(Neptunea deceomcostata)*, a relative of the abalone, grows to four inches and has a heavy, grayish white shell. It lives on rocky bottoms, particularly in the Bay of Fundy. Using its tubular snout, the ten-ridged neptune whelk makes a hole in the shell of a dead oyster or clam and feeds on bits of flesh with its sharp teeth.

Abalones cling to submerged rocks and feed on sea lettuce, kelp and algae.

The chiton is a common mollusk that clings to rocks by a suction cup on its oval foot. It is also called the sea cradle because, when detached from a surface, it curls into a ball and rocks gently in the water. The **sea boot** or **gumboot** *(Cryptochiton stelleri)*, the largest chiton, browses for algae on the Pacific coast. It is about 13 inches long and 6 across.

The **tortoiseshell limpet** *(Acmala testudinalis)*, like most limpets, can cling to a rock more tightly than other mollusks can. When this limpet is alarmed, its suction strength can be as great as 70 pounds a square inch. Its sturdy, streamlined shell resists the force of waves and, when closed, protects the limpet's soft body. The limpet eats marine algae.

Unlike mollusks, crustaceans have segmented bodies and a pair of appendages on each segment. The **American lobster** *(Homarus americanus)*, a hard-shelled, ten-legged creature with two powerful claws and two pairs of antennae, is a crustacean. This bottom dweller lives under rocks and in small caves and crannies in rocky regions of the Atlantic coast. It rarely leaves its den except to forage for small crabs, fishes and dead animals. It uses its largest claw to crush shells, the other to pick at and scrape away flesh.

During early life, lobsters shed and regrow their shells several times a year. Fully grown lobsters, which weigh about 2 pounds but may reach 35, replace their shells every two years.

The **crayfish**, which looks like a tiny lobster, is found in inland waters. This spiny, snapping, slow-walking, fast-swimming, six-inch crustacean is the largest freshwater invertebrate in Canada. It has a tough, armored body with a pair of fierce-looking claws for catching prey, a fanlike tail for swimming, and four legs that it can move forward, backward or sideways. The crayfish (also called the mudbug and crawdad) eats almost anything—insects, tadpoles and plants.

The **purple starfish** (Asterias vulgaris) *inhabits tidal pools.*

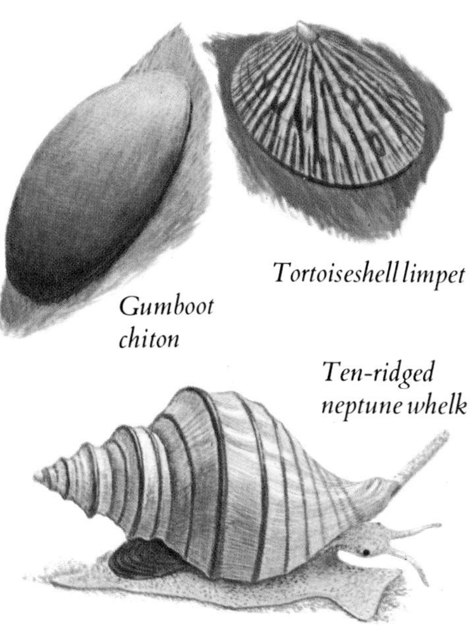

Tortoiseshell limpet

Gumboot chiton

Ten-ridged neptune whelk

Protected by tough, spiny armor, a crayfish grasps a ribbon snake in powerful claws. There are nine crayfish species in eastern Canada and at least five in the West. Oronectes virilis *is an eastern species,* Astacus trowbridgei *a western one.*

Outdoors: The Plants

Plants, from the algae in a pond to trees as tall as the Douglas fir, are among the most numerous and widespread of all living things. Algae and bacteria, the smallest and most primitive, are almost everywhere—in fresh and salt water, in soil and snow, on animals and other plants, in deserts and on mountaintops. Mushrooms and other fungi are plants that lack chlorophyll, the matter that enables plants to utilize sunlight to manufacture food. They live on other plants and decaying vegetation and can grow in total darkness. Flowering plants, the most highly evolved, account for more than half of the 375,000 plant species in the world.

Born of the sea hundreds of millions of years ago, plants gradually adapted to life on land. Fossils show that it took millions of years for them to develop even simple roots, stalks and leaves.

Coniferous (cone-bearing) trees have changed little since they appeared 300 million years ago. The oldest trees, the bristlecone pines of eastern California, are conifers that live more than 4,500 years. Canada's tallest tree species is the Douglas fir, a conifer that often exceeds 200 feet. Other conifers—the white spruce, jack pine and alpine fir—survive farther north and higher up mountain slopes than any other tree species.

Deciduous trees, which shed their leaves in the fall and do not bear seed cones, evolved from coniferous trees. The sap of deciduous trees circulates better than the sap of conifers does, enabling the leaves of deciduous trees to manufacture food quickly—the large, efficient leaves produce enough food in the spring and summer to sustain a deciduous tree throughout the winter. The less efficient foliage of a conifer remains on the tree throughout the year.

Canada has vegetation of startling contrasts, from the almost tropical wild flowers of Point Pelee to the treeless arctic tundra, from the brilliantly colored fall foliage of the mixed forest to the lush evergreen of the Pacific rain forest. More than 800 million acres (nearly a third of Canada) is forested. Canada has more than 165 million acres of grasslands and more than 700 million acres of tundra and exposed rock.

Trees, the greatest of plants, are among Canada's richest natural resources. But they are more than pulpwood and timber. Forests feed and shelter wildlife, cleanse and enrich the air we breathe, regulate the quality and quantity of our water supply, and provide recreational opportunities and places of beauty and peace.

Black-eyed Susans, near Carberry, Man.

Forests and Woodlands

From earliest times man has relied on forests for shelter and sustenance. The first settlers came to Canada in wooden ships. They cleared forests to create farmlands and homesites. They used wood to make implements, to build houses and barns and entire communities.

Our forests beckoned the fur trader, the logger, the lumber merchant—all of whom helped mold the image of this country long before it was formally

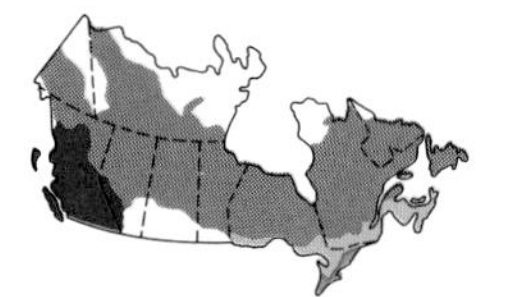

■ Boreal Forest
■ Coastal Forest
■ Deciduous Forest
■ Mixed Forest

called Canada. Despite much clearing of land, Canada's forests are still a rich and renewable—though not inexhaustible—natural resource.

About a third of Canada's land area is forest. The boreal (northern) forest is composed primarily of coniferous (cone-bearing or evergreen) trees. Deciduous trees (which shed their leaves in the fall and do not bear seed cones) and mixed forests of deciduous and coniferous trees are found from the Great Lakes to the East Coast. The West Coast is our densest tall timber region.

Only 31 of the 140 species of trees in Canada are conifers—yet conifers greatly outnumber deciduous trees. Native conifers include the pine, spruce, larch, fir, hemlock, cedar, juniper and one species of yew.

In recent decades, with the depletion of our richest stands of timber, Canadians have realized the urgent need for conservation and reforestation. Forests must be treated with concern and reverence if their wealth and beauty are to be inherited by future generations.

White spruce (Picea glauca), *shown at right, and* ***black spruce*** (Picea mariana), *not shown, dominate Canada's boreal forest and account for about 65 percent of the country's pulpwood. White spruce may grow to 120 feet. Black spruce seldom exceeds 50 feet. White spruce prefers well-drained land; black spruce thrives in wet areas but also grows well in drier soil. Both range to the timberline and reproduce by seed. Black spruce also reproduces by layering—live lower branches touch fertile ground, take root and develop into new trees. Layering is most noticeable in the North. Lumbermen chew spruce resin like gum.*

Mosses grow abundantly in damp, shady forests and about 1,750 species of these primitive green plants thrive in Canada. Mosses reproduce by spores instead of by seeds as flowering plants do. Tufts of erect, brush-like ***broom moss*** (Dicranum scoparium) *grow in soil or on rocks and decaying logs. The pale or golden green leaves all point in one direction, giving the plant a windblown look.*

Pipsissewa (Chimaphila umbellata), *a small evergreen plant of dry, shady woods, spreads by means of creeping rootstocks. In summer, clusters of fragrant blossoms bloom.*

Indian pipe (Monotropa uniflora), *a waxy white or pinkish plant, contains no green chlorophyll and so cannot utilize sunlight to make its own food. Instead, it lives on decaying vegetation. The Indian pipe's thick scaly stems often emerge in a clump from a tangle of tiny roots. An oblong flower, which hangs from the tip of each stem, turns upright as it matures. Indian pipe becomes black with age.*

An Evergreen Arch From Coast to Coast

One of the greatest expanses of forest in the world is the nearly one million square miles of Canada's boreal (northern) forest. This almost unbroken arch of green, bordered in the north by tundra and in the south by grasslands and the Great Lakes, is Canada's richest source of pulpwood.

The dainty evergreen ***twinflower*** (Linnaea borealis) *often carpets vast areas of the forest floor. Between June and August, slender stalks grow from wiry, creeping stems that are up to three feet long. A pair of sweet-scented, pink flowers, resembling tiny nodding bells, blooms at the top of each stalk. The twinflower is found in all Canadian provinces and territories but does not grow north of the timberline.*

The exquisite little ***fairy slipper*** (Calypso bulbosa), *a wild orchid, hides deep in the shade of cool coniferous forests throughout Canada. In the wilderness it is sometimes found in large groups among mosses, evergreen needles and mats of twinflowers. It is scarce near settled areas. If the single flower is picked, the bulblike base of the stem usually breaks off and the plant dies. Like many orchids, the fairy slipper's flower is showy and fragrant to attract insects.*

Balsam fir (Abies balsamea) *is a familiar Christmas tree, distinguished by upright seed-bearing cones. In autumn the cones break apart, scattering the seeds. The tree's resin, known as Canada balsam, is used to cement lenses in optical instruments.*

Most ferns flourish in damp, shady forests. Known for their large, green, often lacy leaves, these flowerless plants are related to primitive plants that grew millions of years ago. Fossilized ferns are commonly found in sandstone and shale. Like their prehistoric ancestors, ferns reproduce by minute cells called spores. Among Canada's commonest woodland species are the ***lady fern*** (Athyrium filix-femina), *above, and the* ***shield fern*** *or* ***wood fern*** (Dryopteris spinulosa), *not shown. Both have feathery fronds (leaves) which grow in fountainlike clusters. The lady fern has horseshoe-shaped spore sacs on the underside of mature fronds. The shield fern has round sacs.*

The Gnarled, Stunted World Along the Tree Line

A lichen is two primitive plants in one—an alga and a fungus which combine to form a complex thallus (body). The fungus absorbs moisture and shields the alga from drying winds and sunlight. The chlorophyll-rich alga makes food for itself and for the fungus. The ***British soldier*** *or* ***red jacket*** (Cladonia cristatella) *is a common shrubby lichen that grows from Labrador to Alberta. Found on the ground or on decaying stumps, it bears red, caplike fruits on hollow stalks.*

Trees grow sparsely and only the hardiest of fungi, lichens and wild flowers survive in the northern reaches of Canada's boreal forest. The tamarack, spruce and pine along the tree line are gnarled and stunted by the harsh climate and poor soil. A 100-year-old tree may stand only five feet.

The ***bush honeysuckle*** (Diervilla lonicera) *is a short shrub that grows at forest edges and in clearings and dry rocky woods from the Maritimes to Manitoba. It was named after Dièreville, a surgeon who in 1700 took to France several specimens he had collected in Acadia. Bush honeysuckle blooms in early summer, its narrow, funnel-shaped flowers a pale yellow; later they deepen to reddish yellow.*

The ***common club moss*** *or* ***running pine*** (Lycopodium clavatum), *which looks like a miniature pine tree, is a dwarf descendant of treelike plants that dominated the earth 300 million years ago. Club mosses formed much of the world's great coal deposits. Common club moss is also called staghorn moss because its branches resemble deer antlers.*

From Labrador to Alaska, the ***bunchberry*** (Cornus canadensis) *thrives in open woods, shady forests and bogs. Like some other dogwoods it has bracts, modified leaves that resemble white petals. Most dogwoods are shrubs or small trees but the bunchberry is an herb that grows to only about 5 inches. It bears tiny red fruits in the fall.*

Lichens cling to rocks, trees and logs, growing where other vegetation can not grow. They require little sunlight or moisture or minerals, and no soil; they are found from the polar regions to the tropics. Lichens thrive on the tundra and form thick carpets near the tree line. Yet they grow and reproduce so slowly that a patch several inches across may be older than 100 years. They become inactive—but do not die—when the climate is too cold, too hot or too dry. Caribou feed on many species of lichens, including ***beard lichens*** (Usnea) *which resemble tangled masses of green or gray threads. Beard lichens hang from trees in strands up to 10 feet long.*

Larches are the only cone-bearing trees in Canada that shed their needlelike leaves in the fall. The ***tamarack*** *or* ***eastern larch*** (Larix laricina) *is the commonest larch in North America, although it was practically wiped out by a sawfly epidemic in the 1920s. Like the black spruce, the tamarack thrives in cold, poorly drained areas and is stunted near the tree line. In moist, well-drained soil it grows with balsam fir, white birch and trembling aspen.*

The ***edible boletus*** (Boletus edulis), *like all mushrooms, lacks chlorophyll, the vital food-making material of green plants. So it lives as a parasite on living or decaying vegetation. Its smooth, fleshy cap grows to about six inches in diameter and varies from pale buff to reddish brown. Its tapering stem, up to eight inches long, is marked with a network of tiny ridges. This mushroom has a sweet, nutty flavor but is often infested with insect larvae.*

Early settlers regarded the ***jack pine*** (Pinus banksiana) *as a bad omen, probably because it grows abundantly in poor soil where crops usually fail. Jack pine, the most widespread pine tree in Canada, is found as far north as the tree line. It flourishes in dry, sandy soil and is often one of the first seedlings to take root in cleared or burned areas. It seldom grows higher than 60 feet. Its yellowish green needles, no longer than two inches, are shorter than those of any other pine. With age, the jack pine's thin, reddish brown bark darkens and becomes scaly.*

Food From the Wild

Baked-apple berry *(Rubus chamaemorus)* grows throughout the boreal forest in bogs and among lichens and on acidic rocks. Its large, juicy, amber berries, which ripen in August, can be eaten raw or used in jelly and pie.

Sometimes called the lady of the forest, the ***white birch*** *or* ***paper birch*** (Betula papyrifera) *has smooth, white bark that peels in thin papery sheets. Traditional Indian canoes are made from this bark. The white birch, often found near lakes and streams, reaches 80 feet. Its dull green leaves, oval or triangular, have pale undersides. It is prized for its beauty and its wood. Bark from a dead white birch makes good kindling even when wet.*

The Tall Timber of the Pacific Rain Forest

Mnium, *which takes its name from the Greek for moss, forms soft, green carpets along shady stream edges, on moist, rotting logs and in cool, wet woodlands. It grows to one or two inches and has large, translucent green leaves. Of the more than 30 species of mnium in North America, about 25 grow in Canada.*

The tart red or yellow fruit of the ***salmonberry*** (Rubus spectabilis) *looks like a raspberry. This prickly shrub grows to 15 feet in woods and swamps and on mountain slopes.*

Canada's tallest trees, among them the Douglas fir and Sitka spruce, grow in dense stands along the lower slopes of mountains facing the Pacific Ocean. Here the growing season is long and precipitation is more abundant (up to 262 inches annually) than elsewhere in Canada. At higher elevations such subalpine species as alpine fir grow.

The ***chanterelle*** (Cantharellus cibarius), *above, is a golden, edible mushroom with a pleasant odor. But it is easily confused with the poisonous* ***jack-o'-lantern*** (Clitocybe illudens), *not shown. Chanterelle has a broad, fleshy cap and grows beneath trees.*

Since early times the ***western red cedar*** (Thuja plicata) *has helped support man on the West Coast. Indians used its light, soft, decay-resistant wood for totem poles, lodges and huge seagoing war canoes; and they made coarse yarn from its soft, inner bark. Today its wood is used in boat building and for shingles, exterior siding and posts. Western red cedar, a massive tree with a tapering trunk and a thick fluted base, grows to 200 feet. Its distinctive stringy bark is reddish brown. The bark of old trees is deeply furrowed. Its branches spread, droop and turn up at the tips. Its tiny, scalelike, yellowish green leaves overlap along the flat twigs. Western red cedar reproduces prolifically by seed and occasionally lives to 800 years. Its seed cones, about a half-inch long, ripen by late summer. After the double-winged seeds are released, the open cones remain on the tree until spring.*

The ***Pacific dogwood*** (Cornus nuttallii), *one of Canada's showiest ornamental trees, is the floral emblem of British Columbia. Its white, petal-like bracts brighten gardens and the edges of streams and forests. Its fruits look like small, red plums. Its dull purple flowers are inconspicuous.*

The flowers, leaves and stems of the ***western spring beauty*** (Claytonia lanceolata) *make a delicious salad. Its small, starchy corm (underground stem) is also edible. This white or pink wild flower grows at woodland edges and in mountain foothills.*

Most plants of the heath family are evergreen, but the ***white-flowered rhododendron*** (Rhododendron albiflorum) *sheds its pale green leaves in the fall. In the summer its bell-shaped flowers, each about an inch across, appear in small clusters near the ends of the branches. The wilted remains of the blossoms often cling to the branches until the next spring. This two-to-six-foot shrub of the Rocky Mountains grows alongside streams and forms tangled thickets in moist mountain clearings.*

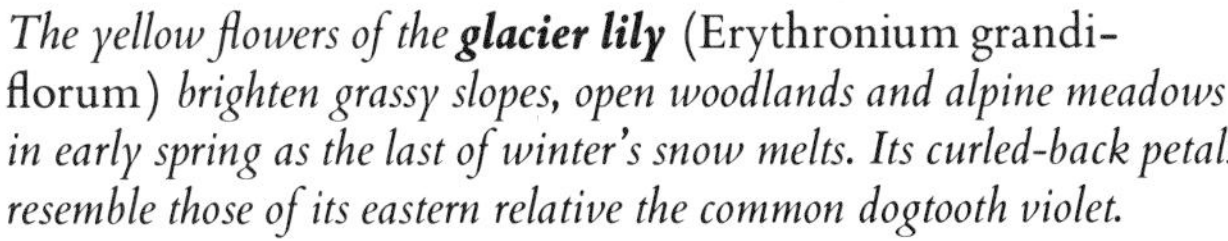

The yellow flowers of the ***glacier lily*** (Erythronium grandiflorum) *brighten grassy slopes, open woodlands and alpine meadows in early spring as the last of winter's snow melts. Its curled-back petals resemble those of its eastern relative the common dogtooth violet.*

The towering ***Douglas fir*** (Pseudotsuga menziesii), *the tallest tree in Canada, is an important source of lumber. Its durable softwood is used in almost every form of carpentry—from house building to furniture making. The Douglas fir grows to 200 feet high and 9 feet in diameter in moist, well-drained soil along the Pacific coast. A shorter, stockier form, with bluish green foliage, grows in the interior where rainfall is light. Near the tips of its needle-clad branchlets are reddish brown buds which develop into three-inch cones. After pollination, the cones hang down, as do those of the spruce and hemlock. The smooth, ashy brown bark of the Douglas fir darkens and becomes rutted with age. (Some of these trees are an estimated 1,200 years old.)*

One of Canada's most striking wild orchids, the ***striped coral-root*** (Corallorhiza striata) *lacks chlorophyll and so lives on decaying vegetation as most mushrooms and fungi do. Its knobby roots resemble lumps of branching coral. Its thick stems are practically leafless.*

Food From the Wild

Salal *(Gaultheria shallon)* is an evergreen, oval-leaved shrub that flourishes on rocky cliffs and in damp forest thickets of the West Coast. Its fuzzy, aromatic, black berries, which ripen in midsummer, can be eaten raw. Indians make syrup and dried cakes from salal berries.

Parklands in the Shelter of Western Mountains

Black bears feast in late summer on the small, red fruit of the ***bearberry*** (Arctostaphylos uva-ursi), *a creeping evergreen shrub found in open woodlands and on hillsides and sandy bluffs across Canada. Its tiny, white or pink urn-shaped flowers grow in clusters among thick, leathery leaves. Indians boiled the plant for tea. The bearberry is also called kinnikinnick—from the Algonkian word for that which is mixed—because Indians used a mixture of dried bearberry, sumac or willow leaves and the inner bark of the dogwood as a tobacco substitute. Bearberries are safe for human consumption. The dry mealy berries, tasteless when raw, are good when cooked or used in jelly.*

In the lee of British Columbia's Coast Mountains rainfall may be as light as seven inches a year. The blue Douglas fir, smaller than the giant species of the coast, grows here, along with the lodgepole pine and drought-resistant plants. In the north are mixed forests. The driest sections are parklands—mosaics of meadows and thinly wooded slopes.

In the fall squirrels tear apart the mature cones of the ***alpine fir*** (Abies lasiocarpa) *to feast on the ripe seeds. This 65-to-100-foot tree commonly grows among larches, spruces and pines on well-drained, subalpine slopes. Its smooth bark is ash-gray, its spirelike crown dense. The drooping branches are short, the stout, brownish twigs hairy, the evergreen foliage grayish green to pale bluish green. The soft, odorless wood of the alpine fir, light in color and weight, is used for low-grade lumber and for pulp.*

The ***russet buffalo berry*** (Shepherdia canadensis) *is called soapberry because the juice of its fruit has a soapy texture. The red or golden yellow berries of this sprawling deciduous shrub are safe to eat but barely palatable. Its tiny, yellowish green flowers bloom from April to June. Russet buffalo berry grows to eight feet and is common in sandy and rocky woods.*

Bear grass (Xerophyllum tenax), *a favorite of bears, wapiti and rodents, grows in dense stands on dry slopes and in subalpine meadows. In spring and summer its stalk, which rises to five feet, is topped with a large cluster of small, creamy white flowers. Long, narrow, rough leaves which surround the base of the stalk were used by Indians to weave baskets and clothing. Bear grass, of the lily family, is also called squaw grass and elk grass. Its stout, smooth, light green stem grows from a thick, woody rootstock.*

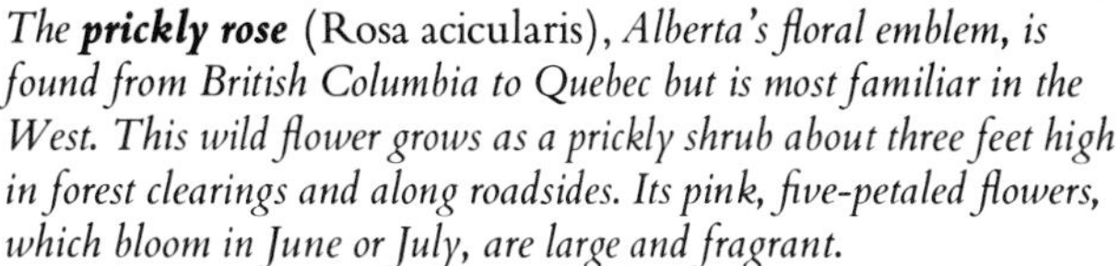

The ***prickly rose*** (Rosa acicularis), *Alberta's floral emblem, is found from British Columbia to Quebec but is most familiar in the West. This wild flower grows as a prickly shrub about three feet high in forest clearings and along roadsides. Its pink, five-petaled flowers, which bloom in June or July, are large and fragrant.*

The ***lodgepole pine*** (Pinus contorta) *is the commonest tree in the Rocky Mountains and the foothills. On the B.C. coast, it grows to 50 feet and is often scrubby and crooked; inland, it grows straighter and up to 100 feet. The coastal tree has dark, yellowish green needles and thick, furrowed, reddish brown bark. The inland variety has brighter foliage and its thinner, paler bark is finely scaled. When fire destroys a stand of lodgepole pine, the heat opens the dense hard cones and their seeds are released. Indians made wigwam poles from lodgepole pine and boiled its soft, inner bark for food. Today the coastal tree is used locally for firewood. The moderately hard wood of the inland tree is used for railway ties, mine timbers and pulp.*

The ***low larkspur*** (Delphinium bicolor), *of the buttercup family, is named for its spurlike, blue-and-white blossoms. This 6-to-24-inch plant is poisonous, particularly to livestock. Low larkspur blooms in the spring along roadsides and woodland edges and on hillsides. Its leaves are borne on long stalks.*

Food From the Wild

The reddish seed pods or hips of the **wild rose** *(Rosa)* make a refreshing tea. Steep a teaspoonful of hips in a cup of boiling water for 10 minutes.

The ***three-flowered avens*** (Geum triflorum) *of the rose family is called prairie smoke or old man's whiskers because its seed heads have long, feathery plumes. In the spring, this long-stemmed plant bears three yellowish flowers, each surrounded by red, pink or purple sepals (modified leaves). Its roots can be boiled to make a tea that tastes somewhat like sassafras.*

The aromatic, bluish black berry-like cones of the ***Rocky Mountain juniper*** (Juniperus scopulorum) *can be used to flavor gin. This coniferous tree, the largest of the Canadian junipers, stands about 20 feet and commonly grows in rocky or sandy areas. It has a shaggy, conical silhouette, reddish or grayish brown bark and yellowish green foliage. Its wood is used in pencils.*

The Rich, Exotic Forest of the Great Lakes

*The **white trillium*** (Trillium grandiflorum), *floral emblem of Ontario, grows in breathtaking profusion in the humus-rich soil of moist deciduous woods. This large three-petaled wild flower is also called large-flowered trillium or wake-robin. It blooms white in spring and turns pink with age. Its stout, flowering stem rises to 18 inches and near the top is a whorl of three broad, oval leaves. If this flower is picked, its roots are usually disturbed so that it fails to bloom again for seven or eight years.*

The deciduous forest—Canada's smallest, most varied and most exotic forest—occurs in a 7,000-square-mile area bounded by lakes Ontario, Erie and Huron where the climate is mild, the soil rich. Many trees here grow nowhere else in Canada: the wild crab apple and the black walnut are examples.

*The root of **ginseng*** (Panax quinquefolius), *right, is reputed to have medicinal and aphrodisiacal qualities. Rare in Canada, this herb grows in moist, shady woodlands. Between May and August its single stalk bears a cluster of tiny yellowish green flowers which later develop red berries. Ginseng has three leaves, each with five leaflets. **Dwarf ginseng** or **groundnut*** (Panax trifolius), *not shown, has white flowers and yellow berries.*

Bladdernut (Staphylea trifolia), *a 3-to-12-foot shrub, grows in moist thickets and on hillsides and at stream edges. Between April and June its white, bell-shaped flowers form drooping clusters. Its fruit, which resembles a tiny inflated paper bag, matures between August and October and splits open releasing the three to five loose seeds. The bladdernut's dark green leaves are composed of three leaflets.*

*One of the largest hardwood trees in eastern Canada, the **sycamore*** (Platanus occidentalis) *can be identified by its massive, twisted branches and by its flaky, brown-and-white-mottled bark. Scattered among other hardwoods, the sycamore reaches 150 feet and 8 feet in diameter but is usually less than half that size. Its wide, bright green coarsely toothed leaves resemble a maple's. The leaves are shed in the fall. The sycamore is also called the buttonball for its spherical clusters of fruit, which remain on the branches through the winter. In the spring the clusters break apart and the one-seeded fruits are scattered by the wind. Sycamore wood, hard and nearly impossible to split, is used to make butchers' blocks.*

*Of some 80 species of oak in North America, 10 grow in Canada. The **white oak*** (Quercus alba), *one of Canada's largest and most valuable hardwood trees, grows to 100 feet. It provides strong, high-quality lumber which is used for doors, furniture and flooring. Its massive, spreading branches, which may extend 50 feet and more, make the white oak a favorite shade tree. Its edible acorns contain little of the bitter tannin present in the acorns of many oaks; they can be ground into meal for making bread. Acorns are an important source of food for animals. The white oak is named for its whitish gray bark. In its Canadian range (southern Ontario and southwestern Quebec) it grows best in deep, moist, well-drained soil.*

*Deer and rabbits browse on the twigs of **sassafras*** (Sassafras albidum). *Bark from its roots makes a refreshing tea; oil from the roots flavors root beer.*

Food From the Wild

Gather the creeping rootstocks of **wild ginger** *(Asarum canadense)* in the spring or summer. Scrubbed and sliced, or dried and ground, they can be used as a spice. They can also be boiled in a sugar syrup to make candy. Wild ginger grows from the Maritimes to Manitoba. Its two broad, green leaves are heart-shaped.

*The **wild crab apple*** (Malus coronaria) *grows to 30 feet. Its small, green, sour apples make delicious jelly. It commonly grows in the shade of large deciduous trees.*

*The large, sweet berry of **mayapple*** (Podophyllum peltatum) *may cause illness if eaten raw in large quantities. The rootstocks, stems and leaves of the plant are poisonous. Mayapple grows in meadows and rich deciduous woods. Its waxy white flower blooms in the spring.*

Shagbark hickory (Carya ovata), *named for its shaggy, gray bark, grows to 100 feet in the rich, moist soil of valleys, hillsides and swamp edges. Its exceptionally strong wood is used for ax handles. Hickory nuts are sweet and edible.*

Canada's Second Largest Forest Region

The mixed forest, Canada's second largest forest region, is a transitional zone between our smallest forest region, the deciduous, and our largest, the boreal. Southern areas of the mixed forest resemble the deciduous forest but contain more conifers and fewer species of deciduous trees.

Jack-in-the-pulpit (Arisaema atrorubens), *also called Indian turnip, was used as a test of Indian manhood: braves were required to eat the raw, bitter, bulblike corm without flinching. Boiled, the corm is quite palatable. Named for the pulpitlike enclosure around its flower spike, this familiar spring plant is abundant in moist woods and thickets. It grows to several feet high. Its one to three long-stalked leaves, each made up of three leaflets, resemble poison ivy. Its cluster of bright red berries appears in late summer.*

Bloodroot (Sanguinaria canadensis), *an attractive but poisonous member of the poppy family, is named for the bright red sap of its rootstock. The sap, once used by Indians as a dye, is used in medicine as a stimulant. This six-to-eight-inch plant has a brilliant white, cup-shaped flower that blooms in early spring. Its fruit is a slender, pointed capsule.*

The ***oyster mushroom*** (Pleurotus sapidus), *named for its shell-shaped cap, grows on fallen logs and the trunks of such deciduous trees as elm, willow and maple. Young specimens of this white-to-brownish mushroom are edible. Mature oyster mushrooms tend to be tasteless.*

The ***honey mushroom*** (Armillaria mellea), *a parasite that damages trees, grows in clusters at the base of living and dead trees and on buried logs. This edible species, with a honey-yellow-to-rusty-orange cap, is common in late summer. Its two-to-six-inch stem is brownish.*

A row of delicate, pinkish white blossoms, strung like miniature, upside-down pantaloons, gives ***Dutchman's breeches*** (Dicentra cucullaria) *its common name. This dainty woodland plant, also called whitehearts, grows well in shady gardens and woods.*

The berries of ***red baneberry*** (Actaea rubra) *and of* ***white baneberry*** (Actaea pachypoda) *are poisonous. These wild flowers bear spikes of white blossoms in the spring. In the fall, their green berries turn to distinguishing red or white.*

The leaf of the ***sugar maple*** (Acer saccharum) *appears on the Canadian flag, coat of arms and penny. The sugar maple, a tree of great beauty and economic value, sometimes grows to 130 feet. In autumn it paints the Canadian landscape, from Nova Scotia to western Ontario, with yellow, gold, orange, red and purple. Indians were the first to use the tree's sap to make syrup and sugar. Settlers used its wood for furniture and fuel and its ashes to obtain potash used in soapmaking. Sugar maple, one of Canada's most abundant and valuable hardwoods, is used for flooring, furniture, veneer, toys and sporting goods. Waste wood is processed to produce charcoal and wood tar for fuel, creosote oil for protecting wood from decay, methyl alcohol for antifreeze, acetone and acetic acid for use in industry. The sugar maple's sap provides syrup, sugar and taffy. The tree's seeds and inner bark are good emergency foods—the seeds are tastiest when roasted and salted.*

With its straight trunk, its rutted grayish brown bark and its large umbrella-shaped crown, the ***white elm*** *or* ***American elm*** (Ulmus americana) *is one of Canada's most stately deciduous trees. It sometimes reaches 125 feet and 7 feet across. Often planted along roadsides and in parks, it grows best in moist, well-drained soil. White elm has crooked twigs and gracefully arching branches. Its tiny, pointed leaf buds are reddish brown. Its wide, lopsided leaves are dark green above, pale below. White elm wood, tough and hard to split, is used for boats, barrels, kitchen chopping blocks and paneling. Elms are unfortunately susceptible to Dutch elm disease, a blight that surfaced in Canada in 1944. This fungous disease is carried by a beetle that burrows into the bark of trees.*

Food From the Wild

Fiddleheads, unopened fronds of the **ostrich fern** *(Matteuccia struthiopteris)*, are a springtime delicacy. They grow in wet woods and along riverbanks. In early spring, pick fiddleheads that are curled tightly and covered by rusty scales. Simmer them for 10 minutes in salted water.

The ***wild lily of the valley*** (Maianthemum canadense) *blooms in late spring in moist woods across Canada. Its slender stems grow from thick underground rootstocks. Each stem bears several heart-shaped leaves and a cluster of tiny, white flowers. These develop into speckled, pale red berries.*

A Varied and Verdant Vacationland

The red and yellow flowers of the ***wild columbine*** (Aquilegia canadensis) *bring a blaze of color to cliffs, rocky woodlands and gardens. In a breeze its drooping, bell-shaped flowers sway and dance on tall, slender stems. Wild columbine is of the buttercup family.*

Rolling hills, sheltered valleys, fertile lowlands and rugged, windswept highlands where trees are twisted and stunted, characterize the mixed forest. Despite the effects of logging, agriculture and frequent fires, this is one of Canada's most splendid recreational and wildlife areas.

Wintergreen (Gaultheria procumbens), *found from Newfoundland to Manitoba, has more than 10 common names including mountain tea, ground holly and spiceberry. A tangy tea can be brewed from its aromatic leaves and stems. Its red, berry-like fruit makes delicious pies. Pungent wintergreen oil is used to flavor candy and chewing gum. This short, evergreen shrub grows in sandy woods and on wooded mountain slopes. Its leaves and fruits are winter food for birds and deer.*

The deadly ***fly agaric*** (Amanita muscaria)—*an orange, yellow, scarlet or white mushroom—was once used as a poison for flypaper. Beneath its sticky cap, usually covered with warts, is a conspicuous ring. There are several scaly rings above the base of its bulbous stem.*

The beautiful but deadly ***destroying angel*** (Amanita virosa) *is so poisonous that it should not even be touched. If you accidentally touch one, wash your hands immediately. Destroying angel grows from July to October in woods and on lawns. Its stem, spores and cap are usually pure white although the cap is sometimes discolored slightly. A collarlike sac at the base of the stem is often hidden in the soil. A skirtlike membrane encircles the stem just below the two-to-six-inch cap.*

The ***bracken*** (Pteridium aquilinum), *Canada's commonest fern, spreads so rapidly that other plants have little chance to grow. This fern of open woods and hillsides also thrives in recently burned areas. The bracken is also called the eagle fern because its unopened fronds, covered with silver-gray hairs, resemble eagle claws.*

The edible ***giant puffball*** (Calvatia gigantea) *is white, round or oval, smooth-skinned and 20 inches or more in diameter. Only those puffballs with clear white interiors should be eaten.*

The ***eastern white pine*** (Pinus strobus) *is the monarch of eastern North American forests. It commonly grows to 100 feet and sometimes reaches 175. It is used for cabinets, paneling and framework. It thrives in sandy or loamy soil and may live 450 years. It can be distinguished from other eastern pines by its long, flexible, bluish green needles in bunches of five. Its grayish green bark darkens and becomes rutted with age. The inner bark has been used in cough medicines. Its twigs, green and downy, turn orangish brown with age. Its seed cones, up to eight inches long, mature in autumn and drop off in winter. They are food for squirrels, chipmunks and birds.*

Weather prophets claim that when the ***American mountain ash*** (Sorbus americana) *is heavy with fruit, a mild winter is ahead. This small, bushy tree of swamp edges and rocky hillsides bears flat-topped clusters of white blossoms. Its bitter but edible red fruit ripens in August.*

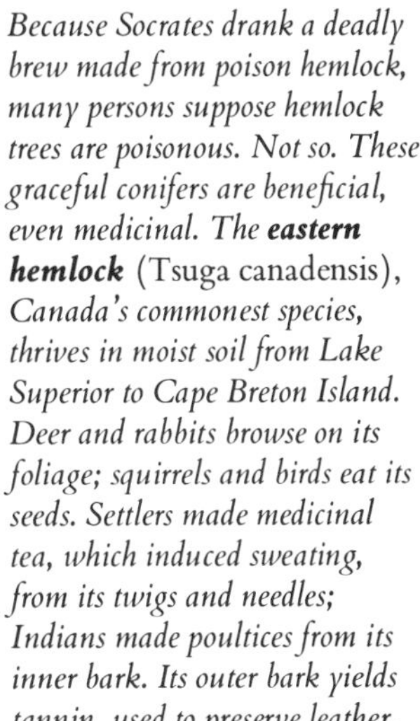

Because Socrates drank a deadly brew made from poison hemlock, many persons suppose hemlock trees are poisonous. Not so. These graceful conifers are beneficial, even medicinal. The ***eastern hemlock*** (Tsuga canadensis), *Canada's commonest species, thrives in moist soil from Lake Superior to Cape Breton Island. Deer and rabbits browse on its foliage; squirrels and birds eat its seeds. Settlers made medicinal tea, which induced sweating, from its twigs and needles; Indians made poultices from its inner bark. Its outer bark yields tannin, used to preserve leather.*

A refreshing beverage can be made with the tiny, scarlet fruit of the ***staghorn sumac*** (Rhus typhina). *Indians blended the leaves of this shrubby tree with tobacco. Named for its velvety, antlerlike branches, staghorn sumac grows to 15 feet in sandy or rocky clearings.*

Orchids, one of the largest families of plants, include the ***pink lady's-slipper*** *or* ***moccasin flower*** (Cypripedium acaule)*—the floral emblem of Prince Edward Island. Named for its slipper-shaped lower petal, this native orchid grows from Newfoundland to northern Alberta. It takes 12 years or more to reach flowering size and is difficult to grow. In the wild it grows best in bogs, moist woodlands and dry, open sandy areas. It blooms in June and July.*

Food From the Wild

Morel *(Morchella esculenta)*, far right, is edible; **false morel** *(Gyromitra esculenta)*, right, is poisonous. In the wild, it is often difficult to distinguish an edible mushroom from a similar, but poisonous, one. Unless you have made a positive identification of a mushroom, do not eat it.

Wetlands

Most of the 300,000 square miles of wetlands in Canada occur in the boreal forest. Vegetation is abundant, but less so than in moist, well-drained areas. Nearly all wetland plants are "invaders"—land species that can also survive in a watery environment. A few species, such as pondweeds, are true aquatic plants: their long flexible stems are anchored to underwater roots.

Wetlands can be broadly classified as bogs, marshes and swamps.

• Bogs are round soggy patches of land, carpeted with mosses. The soil is peaty and saturated with water. Most bogs, found in the tundra and northern areas of the boreal forest, support sedges, grasses and wild flowers, such as orchids and pitcher plants.

• Marshes are treeless areas with standing water. They occur at the mouths of rivers and near seashores and support sedges, grasses, rushes and such wild flowers as marsh marigolds. Floating plants, such as water lilies, rarely grow in marshes. Muskrats, otters and other fur-bearing animals inhabit inland marshes. Salt marshes serve as breakwaters and are breeding grounds for fishes and waterfowl, and feeding grounds for a variety of wildlife.

• Swamps resemble marshes but support trees—usually cedars, maples and willows—as well as sedges, grasses, rushes and wild flowers.

The white, bell-shaped flowers of the ***leatherleaf*** (Cassandra calyculata) *bloom in early spring in drooping, leafy clusters. This evergreen shrub grows to four feet in wetlands. Its dark green leaves turn reddish brown in winter. Its seeds are borne in small, dry pods.*

Grass pink (Calopogon pulchellus), *found in bogs, swamps and wet meadows in eastern North America, bears several purplish pink or magenta flowers along its smooth, wiry stem. Unlike most orchids, its liplike petal forms the uppermost part of the flower. A dense tuft of knobby yellow hairs on the lip resemble stamens and so attract pollinating insects. Grass pink has a single, grasslike leaf.*

As its name suggests, ***Labrador tea*** (Ledum groenlandicum) *can be used to make a vitamin-C-rich brew. The thick, leathery leaves should be steeped—not boiled—or a harmful alkaloid will be released.*

The ***round-leaved sundew*** (Drosera rotundifolia) *feeds on insects. Its leaves are armed with hundreds of tiny, sticky, red hairs that entangle insects. Then the leaf slowly closes, suffocating its victims.*

Water-filled Depressions Formed by Glacial Ice

Grassy bogs, called muskeg, are common in Canada's heavily glaciated northland where huge blocks of ice melted thousands of years ago, leaving stagnant water-filled depressions. Tamarack and black spruce often grow along the edges of muskeg. Bogs are usually treeless.

*The **pitcher plant*** (Sarracenia purpurea), *the floral emblem of Newfoundland, attracts and traps insects with its hooded, pitcher-shaped leaves. When an insect crawls inside the leaf, tiny downpointed bristles prevent its escape and it drowns in liquid at the bottom of the pitcher. The liquid, a mixture of rainwater and enzyme-rich secretions from the plant, extracts nutrients from the insect's body.*

Despite its name, ***cotton grass*** (Eriophorum) *is not a grass but a sedge—a grasslike plant with solid stems. Its leaves are narrow; its white flowers resemble balls of cotton.*

During World War I, ***sphagnum*** *or* ***peat moss*** (Sphagnum) *was used as a surgical dressing because it is naturally sterile and twice as absorbent as cotton—sphagnum can absorb up to 20 times its weight in water. In forests, it contributes to the death of trees by drowning their roots. Dried peat moss is commonly mixed with garden soil to inhibit the growth of fungi.*

Bog laurel (Kalmia polifolia) *is a low evergreen shrub of cold bogs. Narrow, leathery leaves grow on smooth, slender branchlets. From May to July, purplish, saucer-shaped flowers appear in clusters of six or seven. The 10 pollen-bearing stamens in each blossom spring outward when the center of the flower is touched by an insect.*

*The **Canadian rhododendron*** *or* ***rhodora*** (Rhododendron canadense), *a deciduous shrub with clusters of rose-purple flowers, blossoms on heathlands and rocky slopes and in bogs and damp thickets. Its oval or oblong leaves are dull green with pale undersides. Its twigs are usually hairless. Its small fruits are capsule-shaped.*

Wetland Feeding Grounds for Wildlife

Swamps (wetlands with trees) and marshes (which are treeless) are found throughout Canada. Swamp trees include willows, alders and maples. Grasses, sedges and rushes, which thrive in the mineral-rich soil, make swamps and marshes important feeding grounds for wildlife.

The ***spotted water-hemlock*** (Cicuta maculata), *left, is deadly poisonous. Its roots, where the poison is concentrated, resemble small sweet potatoes and smell like parsnips. It has sharply toothed leaflets and clusters of small white flowers. A similar poisonous species,* ***bulbous water-hemlock*** (Cicuta bulbifera) *has small bulbs in the axils of its upper leaves.*

Spring sunshine brings the golden ***marsh marigold*** *or* ***cowslip*** (Caltha palustris) *into bloom. Its brilliant yellow flowers and broad, glossy leaves brighten swamps, marshes and wet meadows. This plant, of the buttercup family, produces a sweet nectar that attracts insects.*

One of Canada's foulest-smelling plants is the ***skunk cabbage*** (Symplocarpus foetidus). *When bruised or broken, it emits a skunklike odor. In spring the skunk cabbage pushes up through the frozen soil of wet meadows and swampy woodlands. Its pointed, hood-shaped leaves—called spathes—vary from reddish brown to yellowish green and are spotted and streaked with purple. Inside each spathe is a cylindrical cluster of tiny flowers.*

Marsh reed grass (Calamagrostis canadensis) *is common in swamps, marshes, moist woodlands and meadows. This tall grass has a pyramid-shaped cluster of flowering spikelets on its two-to-three-foot stalk. Each tiny spike bears a single flower.*

The iris family, named after the Greek goddess of the rainbow, includes about 1,500 species. The multicolored **blue flag** (Iris versicolor), *with violet-blue flowers tinted with yellows, greens and whites, often forms breathtaking stands in marshes, thickets and wet meadows.*

The **purple violet** (Viola cucullata) *is the floral emblem of New Brunswick, and, like all violets, it has five petals. The lowermost petal provides a landing strip for insects and has a nectar-secreting spur. Stalks up to seven inches suspend the blossoms above heart-shaped leaves. This wild flower grows in wet places from Newfoundland to northwestern Ontario.*

The **buckbean** *or* **bogbean** (Menyanthes trifoliata), *a marsh plant with thick, creeping underground stems, grows to about 12 inches and supports a long-stalked cluster of 10 to 20 white or purplish flowers. Its fruit is a seed-filled capsule.*

The **fragrant water lily** (Nymphaea odorata), *one of Canada's sweetest-smelling flowers, floats on ponds and slow-moving streams. Its blossoms, anchored to underwater rootstocks by long, flexible stems, open early in the morning and close shortly after noon. Its pinkish or white petals are arranged spirally in a cup shape three to five inches across. Each petal is broadest near the middle. Its leaves, rounded with a V notch at the base, usually have purplish undersides. Its fruit, a leathery, seed-filled berry, ripens underwater. Fish and mammals eat its leaves and protein-rich seeds. The fragrant water lily, also called the pond lily or toad lily, blooms from June to September. It is found from Newfoundland to Manitoba.*

Despite their coarse appearance, bulrushes are a year-round source of food. Crisp white sprouts and the tender parts inside the base of young stalks are delicious raw or cooked. When washed and scraped, the rootstocks (underground stems) can be roasted in campfire coals or dried and ground into flour. The ripe seeds make a hearty gruel; the pollen can be used in muffins and bread. The **hardstem** *or* **pointed bulrush** (Scirpus acutus), *a common North American species (there are about 200 species of bulrush in the world), grows in marshes and at the edges of streams and lakes.*

Food From the Wild

Practically every part of the familiar **cattail** *(Typha)* is edible. The young spring shoots are delicious. In all seasons the starchy rootstocks can be eaten raw, baked, roasted or boiled.

The reddish purple flowers of the **elephant's head** (Pedicularis groenlandica) *look like tiny elephant heads. This plant blooms in summer in northern swamps, bogs and wet meadows and alongside lakes and rivers.*

Bottomlands Where Plants and Animals Abound

Vegetation is lush in the moist, fertile bottomlands along rivers, streams and lakeshores. Wild flowers, grasses, shrubs and trees provide shelter and food for wild animals. Mosses often carpet shady banks. Rocky shores are usually slippery with algae. Rushes and reeds grow in shallows.

At least 500 species of ***sedge*** (Carex) *grow in North America. Unlike the grasses and rushes they resemble, most sedges have solid stems. Although characteristic of wet places, many sedges thrive in extreme dryness.*

Heralding the warm breezes of spring the ***Canada anemone*** *or* ***windflower*** (Anemone canadensis) *blooms across Canada in damp woodlands and thickets, and in low, moist areas.*

Of the 75 species of willow in North America, most can be found in Canada. One of the commonest, the ***pussy willow*** (Salix discolor), *grows in swampy areas and alongside streams. This shrub has purplish red branchlets and slim, oval leaves with white undersides. The fuzzy male catkins, regarded as harbingers of spring, appear before the leaves. Deer and moose eat the bark and twigs of this shrub, grouse and ptarmigan the buds and leaves.*

From July to September, the ***cardinal flower*** (Lobelia cardinalis) *highlights moist meadows, swamps and stream edges with its brilliant red blossoms. So attractive is this perennial plant that it is often cultivated in gardens. Hummingbirds frequently sip nectar from the flowers but their deep, narrow tubes make their nectar inaccessible to bees. The flowers grow in long, dense clusters, the toothed leaves are oblong, the stout stem grows to about four feet.*

Food From the Wild

The hard, small tubers of **broad-leaved arrowhead** *(Sagittaria latifolia)*, which resemble new potatoes, grow in shallow water at the tips of long roots. Harvest the tubers in the fall and winter. They are easy to peel after they have been boiled for 30 minutes in salted water, or cooked for an hour in hot coals.

Red-osier dogwood (Cornus stolonifera), *a deciduous shrub, grows to nine feet in moist or swampy areas across Canada. Its whitish flowers bloom in flat clusters from May to July. Its round white berrylike fruits, which ripen by late summer, are eaten voraciously by birds. Red-osier dogwood, with oval green leaves and red branches, is often planted as an ornamental shrub.*

When touched, the ripe pods of the ***spotted jewelweed*** (Impatiens capensis) *burst open and scatter their seeds. This plant, also called the spotted touch-me-not, grows in moist woodlands and alongside rivers and lakes. Its orange blossoms are dotted with purples and reddish browns.*

Early settlers planted the ***balsam poplar*** (Populus balsamifera) *as a windbreak around their homes and barns where its descendants can still be seen today. This 60-to-80-foot tree lives as long as 200 years and is found across Canada. Its smooth, greenish brown bark darkens and becomes rutted with age; its stout twigs are reddish brown; its egg-shaped leaves are dark green above and paler below. In spring, long catkins (flower and seed stalks) hang from its branches. The balsam poplar's clear, fragrant resin has been used in ointments and cough medicines. Its wood is used for pulp and for low-grade lumber.*

Silverweed (Potentilla anserina), *a short herb with bright yellow flowers and an edible root, is common in low, wet places.*

The ***mayflower*** (Epigaea repens), *a creeping evergreen with pinkish blossoms, is the floral emblem of Nova Scotia.*

The ***hedge bindweed*** *or* ***wild morning glory*** (Convolvulus sepium) *can be a farmer's nightmare. Its roots grow so deep and its stems spread so rapidly that this plant is almost impossible to eradicate. Common in moderately moist areas, the hedge bindweed climbs and entwines shrubs, bushes and fences. Its stems grow to 10 feet long. Its pink or white flowers are trumpet-shaped.*

Hair cap moss (Polytrichum commune) *grows six inches or higher in large beds along the shores of lakes and streams. Its small leaves are reddish brown or dark green with whitish, sheathed bases. Its spore-bearing capsules are covered by pale brown, hairy hoods.*

A Kaleidoscope of Rock, Sand, Mud and Surf

Cordgrass (Spartina alterniflora) *flourishes at the midtide level in east coast salt marshes. Its underground stems and sturdy roots trap silt, causing the shoreline to build up.*

The ***sea-milkwort*** (Glaux maritima), *a ground-hugging herb with thick, fleshy leaves, grows in coastal meadows and damp saline areas of the western provinces. It is often found among grasses. Its flowers have pinkish or purplish, petal-like sepals but no petals.*

Canada's 115,000 miles of seacoast are a kaleidoscope of rugged cliffs, shifting sand dunes, muddy tidal flats, rocky inlets and sandy surf-swept beaches. Seaweed clings to wave-battered rocks. Grasses and reeds cover tide-washed flats. Farther from shore, vegetation is more varied and abundant.

The edible ***beach pea*** (Lathyrus japonicus) *is thought to be the wild pea referred to by Jacques Cartier and other early explorers. It sprawls along gravelly and sandy seacoasts and the shores of the Great Lakes and Lake of the Woods. Its long, creeping underground stems help to anchor shifting sand. Its purple or bluish flowers, which blossom in clusters all summer long, are followed by a hairy seed pod.*

An unpleasant odor and broad leaves divided into three leaflets distinguish the ***cow parsnip*** (Heracleum lanatum) *from the deadly water hemlock. This sturdy seaside plant is common on both coasts and also inland, in moist meadows and open woodlands. The scientific name* Heracleum *refers to Heracles—a Greek god of great size and strength. The cow parsnip grows to 8 feet and its stout, hairy stem is often several inches across at the base. Small, white flowers grow in large, umbrellalike clusters.*

American dune-grass (Elymus mollis) *thrives on dunes and sandy or gravelly salt-water beaches. This stout, robust plant spreads rapidly by means of long, tough, underground stems. In humid or rainy weather the tall, narrow leaf blades open flat; in dry, windy weather they curl up lengthwise to prevent the plant from losing too much moisture by evaporation.*

In some places, ***beach grass*** *or* ***marram grass*** (Ammophila) *is protected by law because it prevents sand dunes from shifting. Shallow, spreading rootstocks sprout fibrous roots and new shoots along their length. As windblown sand piles up around the shoots, new roots develop higher up, holding the accumulated sand.*

Greasewood (Sarcobatus vermiculatus), *a spiny shrub with narrow pale green foliage, grows to 10 feet in saline and alkaline soils of western North America. Its white, smooth bark darkens with age. Male blossoms usually occur in small spikes at the ends of the twigs; female flowers grow singly in the leaf axils. Livestock may become ill from eating large amounts of greasewood.*

Foxtail barley (Hordeum jubatum), *a weedy grass of seashores, salt marshes, fields and roadsides, is especially common west of the Great Lakes. Its nodding seed heads, covered with long, slender awns or bristles, grow at the tops of its smooth, one-to-two-foot stems. The awns, which turn glossy cream as they mature, sometimes pierce the mouths, noses, skin and eyes of grazing animals—causing sores and even blindness. When ripe, the seed heads break apart, scattering the seeds.*

Food From the Wild

Orach *(Atriplex patula)*, right, grows on coastal beaches and salt marshes. It is often confused with **lamb's-quarters** *(Chenopodium album)*, far right, a common weed of cultivated land. The young leaves of both plants make good substitutes for spinach. The tiny seeds can be ground for flour or boiled to make porridge.

Grasslands

Canada's 239,000 square miles of prairie grasslands include some of the world's richest agricultural land. This open, mainly flat region is the northern extension of the great western plains of the United States. Pockets of grassland also occur in low-lying parts of British Columbia's dry interior.

The grasslands are mostly covered with mixed grasses, ranging from six inches to four feet. Tallgrasses, up to eight feet, grow on the moist prairies of southern Manitoba. Shortgrasses, some only a few inches high, grow sparsely in the dry regions of southwestern Saskatchewan and southeastern Alberta.

Light rainfall, drying winds, extremely cold winters, fierce snowstorms in late spring, and drought in summer inhibit the growth of trees. Scattered stands of poplars and willows are found in sheltered places and moist lowlands and alongside rivers.

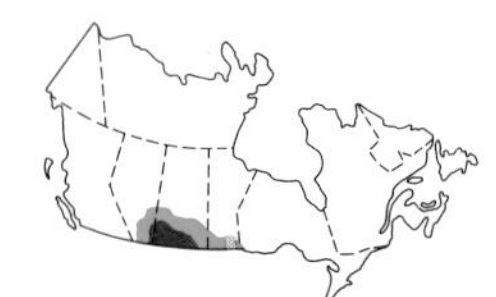

Plant growth on the Prairies is affected more by variations in rainfall from year to year and season to season than by the total annual rainfall.

Grasses are well-suited to the prairie climate. Their abundant roots, which form dense tangles in the rich soil, readily absorb moisture and nutrients. Their narrow leaves help conserve moisture. Their slender, flexible stalks bend with the wind. Because grasses grow from the bases of their leaves and stalks, they continue sprouting after the tips of their shoots have been burned, cut or nibbled by grazing cattle.

The ***many-flowered aster*** *or* ***tufted white prairie aster*** (Aster pansus), *of the composite family, is common on open prairies and along roadsides. It has a thick, tufted rootstock and a long, hairy stem. Its many leaves are narrow and hairy. In late summer or early fall, the many-flowered aster bears numerous white or pinkish blossoms. Most of the flower heads face the same direction.*

Despite its delicate appearance, the ***prairie crocus*** (Anemone patens), *Manitoba's floral emblem, is poisonous to sheep. Indians used the leaves to ease the pain of rheumatism. The prairie crocus is also called the pasqueflower because it blossoms around Paschal, or Easter. Often as early as April, its downy bud pushes up through the melting snow. Before the leaves unfold, the lavender flower blooms.*

Although its leaves are grasslike, ***blue-eyed grass*** (Sisyrinchium angustifolium) *is not a grass but a miniature member of the Iris family. This 3-to-12-inch plant grows in moist meadows and along stream edges. Its small, clustered, blue-violet flowers bloom from May to July. The flowers, composed of six petal-like segments, are star-shaped with yellow centers and sharply pointed tips.*

The True Prairie Where Giant Grasses Grow

Grasses as tall as eight feet once covered about 2,500 square miles in southern Manitoba. Remnants of these grasses still grow along roadsides and railroads. This tallgrass or true prairie region, moist and low-lying, has deep layers of black humus-rich topsoil. In most of Canada's grasslands rainfall is light and grasses grow to about four feet.

Early in May, the delicate yellow blossoms of the ***prairie buttercup*** (Ranunculus rhomboideus) *highlight open prairies. It grows to about eight inches. Oval or rounded leaves grow on long stalks at the base of its hairy stem; its upper leaves are stalkless and deeply cleft.*

The ***golden alexander*** (Zizia aurea) *stands one to two feet high in meadows and wet woodlands from New Brunswick to Saskatchewan. In spring small, golden-yellow blossoms grow in clusters at the end of its stalk.*

Wild bergamot *or* ***horsemint*** (Monarda fistulosa) *is sometimes used to scent closets and linen chests. Indians used it to treat skin and intestinal ailments, and modern medicine uses it as an antiseptic. This two-to-three-foot, square-stemmed plant blooms in July and August. Its flowers vary from pink to lilac; its gray-green, aromatic leaves are oval. Wild bergamot is common in thickets, clearings and on hillsides. It grows mainly in Manitoba and eastern Saskatchewan.*

The Plains Indians boiled the roots of the ***northern bedstraw*** (Galium boreale) *and mixed them with cranberry and strawberry juices to make a red dye. This perennial herb of the madder family flourishes in woodlands, clearings and moist prairie meadows and along roadsides and railway grades. It grows, sometimes to two feet, from slender brown rootstocks. Its long, narrow leaves grow in whorls of four around the stout, square stems; its tiny, fragrant, white blossoms bloom in midsummer in dense clusters. The ripe fruits of the northern bedstraw are bristly, paired burrs that spread by catching on clothing and the fur of animals.*

The ***big bluestem*** (Andropogon gerardii), *also called the turkey-foot because of the shape of its seed heads, is common on the tallgrass prairies. This bluish green plant, an excellent forage grass, grows to about six feet. It turns red or purple after the first frost. Its scaly rhizomes send up new shoots.*

The poisonous ***white camas*** (Zygadenus elegans), *a one-to-two-foot plant with a bulbous, onionlike root, is easily mistaken for the prairie onion. The white camas, a lily, has greenish flowers that bloom in midsummer. Its leaves are grasslike.*

Sun-scorched, Wind-parched Plains

The shortgrass prairies of semiarid southwestern Saskatchewan and southeastern Alberta are dominated by short grasses and sages—their shallow, spreading roots readily absorb the little rainfall. Small leaves help conserve moisture despite the scorching sun and drying wind.

Like patches of snow, the tiny five-petaled white blossoms of the ***moss phlox*** (Phlox hoodii) *can be seen on prairies and hillsides in April and May.*

Needlelike spikes on the seed stalks of the ***needle-and-thread*** (Stipa comata) *often injure livestock. When the spikes drop off this grass is good forage.*

The ***early yellow locoweed*** (Oxytropis macounii), *which takes its name from the Spanish word* loco, *meaning crazy, is said to cause madness in horses.*

The ***gaillardia*** (Gaillardia aristata) *grows to 24 inches on prairies and on sunny foothill slopes. Its flower head has a brownish purple disc surrounded by yellow rays.*

Oil from the edible seeds of the ***sunflower*** (Helianthus annuus) *is used in candy, margarine and soap. The seeds are a favorite of birds. Resembling an overgrown daisy, this coarse, stout-stemmed plant grows to six feet along roadsides and on prairies. Its orangish rays surround a large, brown or dark purple disc. The sunflower grows well in heavy, claylike soil.*

Sage was the Indian's panacea—a cure-all for fever, influenza, indigestion, rheumatism, numbness, body sores, and numerous other ailments. It was also used as shampoo—to make hair grow—and as yellow dye. It was even used as fuel. About 12 species of sage, or wormwood, are found in Canada. One of the most attractive, aromatic species, ***pasture sage*** (Artemisia frigida), *is a small, soft, hairy herb with silver-gray foliage. It grows from 6 to 20 inches in dry prairie regions and on sun-scorched hills and mountains. Its yellow, nodding flower heads bloom in July and August. Because this species is seldom eaten by cattle it is abundant on overgrazed rangeland.*

Golden-yellow rays and a long purplish or brown cylinder of florets make the ***prairie coneflower*** *or* ***long-headed coneflower*** (Ratibida columnifera) *a striking wild flower. Its petals droop, as though peeled away from the cylinder. This one-to-two-foot high plant of the composite family blooms in July and August. Its broad leaves are deeply divided into narrow segments; its stems are rough and bristly. Indians made tea from the leaves and conelike centers of this aromatic plant.*

Food From the Wild

The **prairie onion** *(Allium textile)*, like the domestic onion, has edible underground bulbs. Its leaves are grasslike; its pink or white flowers bloom in umbrella-shaped clusters. Do not eat any onionlike bulb unless it has an onion's characteristic odor: the bulb of the poisonous death camas is almost odorless, but looks like an onion.

The ***blazing star*** (Liatris), *also known as the button snakeroot, was once believed to cure snakebites. Among the 30 species of blazing star in North America, two thrive on the Canadian Prairies. They grow to about 20 inches and often have conspicuous resinous dots on the leaves. Their rose-purple flowers grow in dense, spiky clusters.*

Where Plants Endure Drought and Torrential Rain

*The **golden bean** (*Thermopsis rhombifolia*) is also called golden pea or false lupine. This 6-to-12-inch plant flourishes along roadsides and on sunny, sandy prairie slopes. It bears fragrant yellow blossoms in the spring.*

Only the most drought-and-wind-resistant plants survive in Canada's erosion-scarred badlands. Rainfall, scarce but usually torrential, washes away the loose granular surface rock and scant vegetation. Most plants of arid and semiarid regions store water in their roots and fleshy stems.

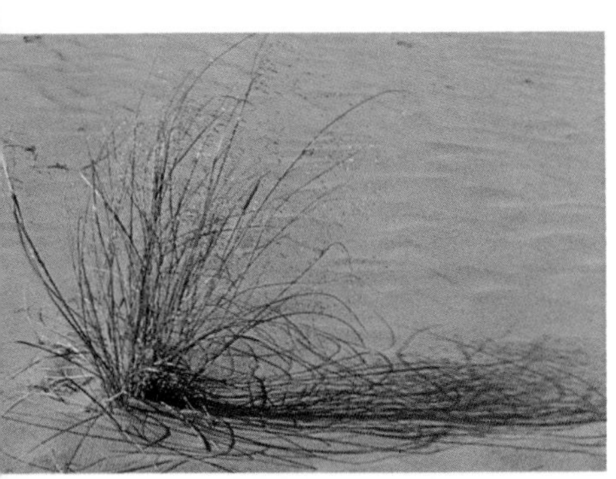

***Indian rice grass** or **Indian millet** (*Oryzopsis hymenoides*) is a tufted, pale-green bunchgrass of sand dunes, dry banks and rocky slopes. The slender leaves curl inward to help the plant conserve moisture in dry, windy weather. The stiff but flexible stems are wind-resistant. Livestock and wild animals eat its seeds and leaves. Indians ground its seeds for flour.*

*The **stinking rabbit brush** (*Chrysothamnus nauseosus*) contains a rubbery resin from which Indians made chewing gum, cough medicine and yellow dye. Despite its nauseous odor, the rabbit brush is eaten by rabbits, deer and mountain sheep. This one-to-two-foot shrub, with pale grayish green leaves and yellow flowers, grows in the poor soil of badlands and eroded hillsides.*

*The flowers of the **yellow umbrella plant** (*Erigonum flavum*) have a pungent odor that attracts pollinating insects. This plant, also called the sulphur flower, blooms in June on prairie hillsides and in dry, eroded areas. Its paddle-shaped leaves are green above, white below.*

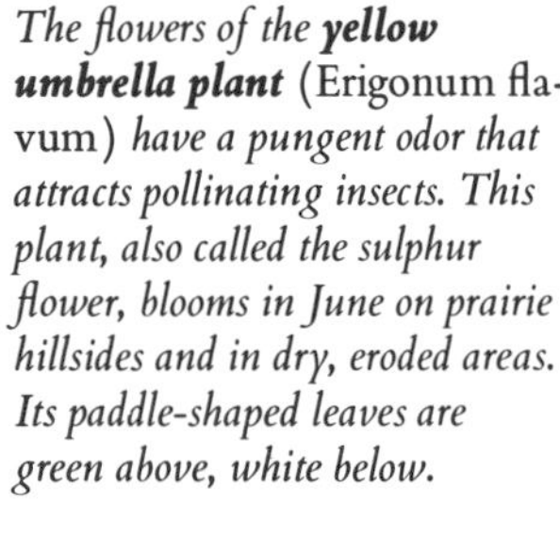

*Roots that grow 20 feet deep enable the **skeleton weed** (*Lygodesmia juncea*) to thrive in dry prairie soil and to withstand severe drought. In spring its almost leafless stems bear small, pink flower heads—hence the name prairie pink. The skeleton weed grows to 18 inches.*

*The **plains prickly pear*** (Opuntia polyacantha) *reproduces prolifically because rabbits and rodents eat its pearlike fruit and consequently scatter its seeds. In times of drought its pink, prickly fruit is the main food of some animals. The fruit is safe for human consumption; it can be peeled and eaten raw or cooked, or used to make jam, candy, liquor or perfume. The yellow, waxy flowers bloom in June and July.*

*The sweet, juicy, brown berries of the **pincushion** or **purple cactus*** (Mamillaria vivipara) *can be used to make jam. The berries ripen in the fall. This round prickly cactus grows one to three inches high, often in clusters. In June and July it bears purple or dark-red, daisylike flowers. Like all cacti, it is able to withstand drought: moisture is readily absorbed by its surface roots and stored in its fleshy stems. It grows in southern regions of the Prairies on hillsides and open fields, usually in stony soil.*

*As night presses against the badlands, the fragrant flowers of the **sand lily** or **evening star*** (Mentzelia decapetala) *open, yielding nectar to foraging insects. This large-petaled wild flower grows in the rocky or sandy soil of dry, eroded hillsides and banks. Its stout, buff-colored stem grows to about two feet. Its creamy white flowers bloom in late summer.*

*The **smooth blue beardtongue*** (Penstemon nitidus) *of southern Saskatchewan and Alberta grows on dry slopes and in eroded areas. In May clusters of deep-blue, purplish or pinkish flowers bloom along the upper part of its smooth, stout stem. This wild flower has a woody rootstock and grows to 12 inches. The scientific name* Penstemon, *a Greek word, refers to the four fertile and one sterile stamens (male pollen-bearing structures) within each of this plant's flowers.*

Food From the Wild

The starchy, tuberous rootstocks of **Indian breadroot** *(Psoralea esculenta)* have a sweet, turnip-like flavor. They can be peeled and eaten raw, roasted or boiled. The plant's hairy leaves consist of five oval leaflets. Its small blue flowers bloom in dense spikes in spring and later develop into tiny seed pods.

Where Grasslands Give Way to Forests

In the Prairie Provinces, parklands of aspen groves, meadows and thinly wooded slopes occur between the grasslands and boreal forest. In the Rocky Mountain foothills, open forests of lodgepole pine, trembling aspen and balsam poplar mark the transition between boreal and subalpine forests.

Lupines, named after the Latin word for wolf, were once thought to rob the soil of minerals. Indians used lupines as food and as a treatment for rheumatism. ***Silvery lupine*** (Lupinus argenteus) *grows on prairies and in foothill meadows. Its radiant flowers, violet to nearly white, bloom in early July. White, silky hairs cover its stems, leaves and seed pods.*

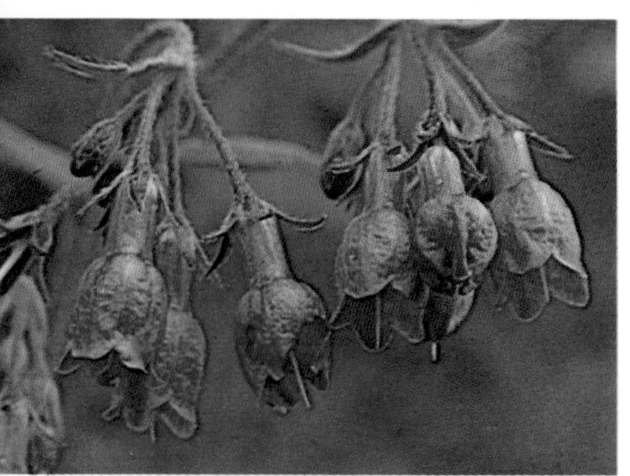

In midsummer, the ***tall lungwort*** *or* ***bluebell*** (Mertensia paniculata) *brightens shady woods and stream edges with its bell-shaped flowers. These are pink at first and become blue or lilac when fully open. This rough-stemmed, two-to-three-foot wild flower also grows in damp willow and alder thickets in the Rocky Mountains. Its fruit is a wrinkled, four-cornered nutlet.*

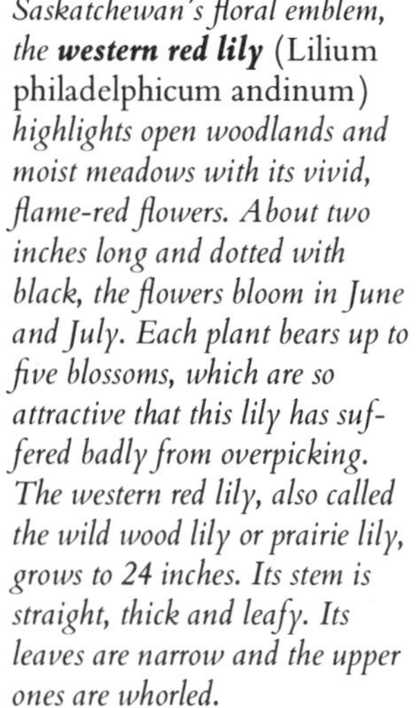

Saskatchewan's floral emblem, the ***western red lily*** (Lilium philadelphicum andinum) *highlights open woodlands and moist meadows with its vivid, flame-red flowers. About two inches long and dotted with black, the flowers bloom in June and July. Each plant bears up to five blossoms, which are so attractive that this lily has suffered badly from overpicking. The western red lily, also called the wild wood lily or prairie lily, grows to 24 inches. Its stem is straight, thick and leafy. Its leaves are narrow and the upper ones are whorled.*

Red Indian paintbrush (Castilleja miniata) *is named for the orange and scarlet petal-like bracts that partially hide its green, tubular flowers. This 18-to-24-inch plant grows in clusters in woodlands and meadows and on well-drained slopes. Its colors are brightest at high altitudes.*

The ***black-eyed Susan*** (Rudbeckia hirta), *also known as the yellow daisy, grows abundantly in fields and parklands and on prairies. This one-to-three-foot plant of the composite family blooms from June to October. Its flower heads, two to three inches wide, are composed of dark brown disks surrounded by 10 to 20 orangish yellow rays. Its stems and long, narrow leaves are rough and hairy.*

Shooting stars are showy, pinkish purple flowers with solitary, leafless stems. Of the 20 species in Canada, the colorful ***saline shooting star*** *or* ***Indian chief*** (Dodecatheon pauciflorum) *is among the most beautiful. Its purplish flowers, each with a pointed maroon and yellow "nose," resemble an Indian chief's headdress. This plant blooms in late May and early June in wet meadows, often beside slow-moving streams.*

Indians called the ***trembling aspen*** (Populus tremuloides) *noisy leaf because the slightest breeze sends it into a panic of whispers. Trembling aspen, probably the most widely distributed tree in North America, grows to 60 feet in moist, sandy or gravelly soil. Like many other poplars, it grows quickly on fire-swept land. Its round, long-stalked leaves turn brilliant gold in fall. Its pale, greenish white bark, although extremely bitter, is a favorite of beavers. Moose eat its leaves. Lumbermen often call this tree the popple. Its soft, moderately light wood is used mainly for pulp.*

Food From the Wild

The plump, sweet, blueberrylike fruits of the **saskatoon** *(Amelanchier alnifolia)* make excellent sauces, preserves and pies. The reddish fruits turn dark purple as they ripen in midsummer. Saskatoon grows as a large shrub.

Witches in the Middle Ages used cinquefoils for casting and breaking spells. Seventeenth-century physicians used them to treat epidemics, toothache, jaundice and other diseases. ***Shrubby cinquefoil*** (Potentilla fruticosa), *a one-to-four-foot shrub, blooms in the summer. Its five-petaled flowers are bright yellow, its leaves grayish green. It grows in meadows and moist foothill grasslands.*

The root of the ***Seneca snakeroot*** (Polygala senega), *used by Indians to cure snakebite, is dug commercially for use in medicine. In June and July this plant bears a spike of greenish white blossoms. Its leaves are lance-shaped. Seneca snakeroot grows in meadows and aspen groves.*

From early summer until the first frost, the ***Western Canada violet*** (Viola rugulosa) *blooms at the edges of bluffs and in shady woodlands. Its white petals are veined with pinks and purples. The Western Canada violet is extremely hardy and is easily transplanted to gardens.*

A Harsh, Treeless Land

The Arctic tundra is Canada's second largest vegetative zone (after the boreal forest). This vast, mostly flat region above the tree line has poor soil and drainage, little precipitation, a long bitter winter and an extremely short growing season. Sometimes called The Barrens, because it is treeless, the tundra is permanently frozen—to depths of hundreds of feet in some areas. The ecology of this permafrost region is so delicate that, once damaged, the land often takes decades to repair itself. Yet, despite its harsh climate and fragile landscape, the tundra

supports an abundance of mosses, lichens, shrubs and wild flowers.

Tundra vegetation flourishes because it has adapted to conserve heat and moisture. Many plants grow in low dense clumps that hug the earth. Large, colorful blossoms catch the sun's warming rays and fuzzy stems provide insulation. Long spreading roots seek out moisture, leathery leaves retain it. Most plants of the tundra are perennial (able to grow after long periods of dormancy).

Seasonal changes are dramatic on the tundra, the seemingly endless white of winter giving way to the browns and greens of spring and summer, and they to the fleeting scarlets and golds of autumn. Some plants even begin to grow before the snow is gone.

Tundra also occurs above the tree line in mountainous regions. In this alpine tundra, hardy plants withstand extremes of temperature—from scorching heat at midday to chilling nighttime frost.

The resinous ***arctic white heather*** (Cassiope tetragona) *makes a good campfire fuel. This dwarf evergreen shrub thrives on the tundra but in the High Arctic it grows only where snow is deep enough to protect its foliage from biting winds.*

Mountain avens (Dryas integrifolia), *one of the commonest flowering plants of the Arctic, is the floral emblem of the Northwest Territories. Leaves preserved in peat bogs reveal that this dwarf shrub, of the rose family, ranged far south of the tree line during the Ice Age. Today it grows on limestone and gravelly barrens north of the tree line. This shrub forms dense clumps with short, horizontal branches that take root freely. Small leathery leaves help retain moisture during drought. Creamy white, saucer-shaped flowers bloom in June or July, each on a fuzzy black stalk two to six inches long. The blossoms develop into tiny, single-seeded fruits with feathery tails. The ripe fruits are easily scattered by the wind. They usually mature within a month but in unfavorable weather they may not ripen at all.*

Long, Sunless Winters; Short, Lush Summers

In the almost one million square miles of Canada's Arctic tundra, north of the boreal forest, winter is up to 10 months long. The northern Arctic may be sunless for most of the winter. During the short summer, abundant vegetation develops rapidly and blankets much of the tundra.

Gnarled mats of ***Lapland rosebay*** (Rhododendron lapponicum) *grow in dry, stony soil and on rocky slopes. Rarely taller than 12 inches, this evergreen shrub has thick, leathery leaves. There are tiny, rust-colored scales on its branches and leaves. Its purple flowers bloom in early summer.*

Cushionlike tufts of ***purple saxifrage*** (Saxifraga oppositifolia), *one of the most northerly plants in the world, hug damp rocks, cliffs and exposed ridges in the Arctic. Its lilac, purple or white flowers bloom in June. Its scalelike evergreen leaves have bristly hairs.*

Like some arctic mosses, ***woolly fringe moss*** (Rhacomitrium lanuginosum) *can withstand being buried under snow and ice for a long time. It flourishes in sunny sites on the tundra. Eskimos of northeastern Labrador make lamp wicks from this grayish green moss.*

The ***arctic poppy*** (Papaver radicatum), *one of Canada's hardiest plants, flourishes throughout the frozen North. Like many arctic plants it conserves heat by growing a rosette of hairy leaves at its base. Old leaves remain on the arctic poppy during the long winter, providing insulation for the growing part of the plant. In spring the buds usually open before the bristly haired flowering stalks lengthen. This delayed growth of the stalks keeps the flowers close to the earth where they are protected from strong winds.*

Woolly lousewort (Pedicularis lanata) *grows rapidly in early spring, as soon as the snow melts. The fleshy taproot of this herb stores food—if it did not, rapid growth would be delayed until the plant developed photosynthetic (food-making) tissue. A thick, woolly covering protects the stems and flowering spikes from the cold and from drying wind. The sweet-smelling pink flowers produce sweet nectar savored by Eskimo children. The lemon-yellow roots and the young flowering stems of woolly lousewort can be eaten raw or boiled.*

Rock tripe *looks like dark, leathery lettuce leaves. Early Arctic explorers used it as an emergency food. The plant is anchored to rocks by a short, strong cord that grows from the center of the plant—hence the scientific name* Umbilicaria.

Dwarf fireweed (Epilobium latifolium), *also called broad-leaved willowherb, is one of the first flowering plants to grow in the North on burned or cleared land. Cooked, its purple flowers and fleshy, green leaves taste like spinach.*

Where the Season Is Short, the Soil Poor

Altitude influences mountain plant life. There are parklands in the foothills, forests and open forests on mountain slopes, stunted growth at the tree line. Alpine tundra lies above the tree line where the growing season is short, daily temperature variations are extreme and the soil is poor.

Dense cushions of ***moss campion*** (Silene acaulis), *also called* moss pink, *form in alpine meadows and on rocky slopes. This plant is not a true moss, but a member of the phlox family. From June to August its tightly matted branches and leaves are arrayed with tiny pink, lilac or white flowers. The seeds of other plants sometimes lodge in moss campion and grow as if part of the moss campion itself.*

The ***alpine forget-me-not*** (Myosotis alpestris) *dots meadows and rocky slopes high above the tree line. It grows in small, low clumps; its tiny, bright blue flowers, with yellow centers, are tightly clustered. This alpine wild flower blooms in summer.*

The ***hawk's-beard*** (Crepis nana), *right, is a dense ball of smooth, fleshy, blue-green or purplish leaves and tiny, yellow flower heads. It grows to three inches on rocky, gravelly or sandy slopes. A similar species* (Crepis elegans), *not shown, grows to 12 inches in foothills.*

The smallest willow, the ***snow willow*** (Salix nivalis), *left, is found in scrub forests and on moist alpine slopes. In spring it bears flowering catkins that become hairy seed pods—similar to those of the* ***pussy willow*** (Salix discolor), *not shown.*

Sitka valerian (Valeriana sitchensis) *takes its name from the Latin* valere, *to be strong. Its rootstocks have a strong, unpleasant odor. Its fragrant flowers—small, white or pinkish and star-shaped—are borne in a cluster at the top of a one-to-three-foot stem. Sitka valerian blooms in July and August in shady areas along the edges of streams and woods. It often blankets alpine meadows in white and grows to the tree line. Indians ate its roots and used them in medicines.*

The ***false hellebore*** (Veratrum eschscholtzii) *causes a deformity known as monkey face in newborn animals, especially in sheep, if females eat the plant shortly after they have conceived. This lily is poisonous, sometimes deadly, to humans. It grows in moist meadows and clearings.*

The ***harebell*** *or* ***bluebell*** (Campanula rotundifolia), *one of Canada's commonest wild flowers, is most often found in sheltered places at high elevations, but it will grow almost anywhere. Its delicate bell-shaped blossoms, ranging from purplish to bright blue, appear from June to August and may be in bloom as late as September. The harebell grows to about 18 inches. At its base are heart-shaped leaves that wither and drop off as the plant matures. The narrow leaves along its stems are arranged alternately. The seeds are borne in pod-like fruits. When the pods are buffeted by the wind the seeds spill out through pores as though shaken from a salt shaker.*

The ***red monkey flower*** (Mimulus lewisii), *which resembles a snapdragon, stands about two feet high and has rose-red, crimson or purplish blossoms. It grows in clumps beside mountain lakes and streams. This bright, showy wild flower is also called the Lewis monkey flower in honor of the explorer Meriwether Lewis.*

When bruised or crushed, the fleshy rootstock of ***roseroot*** (Sedum rosea) *has a roselike fragrance. Its young stems and leaves, a source of vitamin C, are delicious raw or cooked. Northern adventurers ate the plant to prevent scurvy. Roseroot's leafy stems are each topped by a cluster of purple (female) or yellow (male) blossoms.*

Food From the Wild

The kidney-shaped leaves of the **mountain sorrel** *(Oxyria digyna)* are rich in vitamin C and taste like rhubarb. They can be eaten raw in salads, cooked as a green vegetable, or pureed for soup.

Rugged ***mountain heather*** (Phyllodoce empetriformis), *a sprawling shrub that carpets meadows and thinly forested slopes near the tree line, bears red, pink or purplish bell-shaped flowers. They bloom from June to July in dense drooping clusters.*

Man and the Forest

When a farmer abandons a cultivated field that was once wooded, the land gradually returns to forest. Grasses, weeds and wild flowers first invade the field. Shrubs, perhaps raspberries or dogwoods, appear soon after, only to be crowded out a few years later by tree saplings. About 10 years after being abandoned, the field will support many of the tree species that once grew in that location.

Such is the forest's capacity for rebirth on land that has been cultivated or logged with care. But where the land has been repeatedly stripped of all vegetation, the soil may be washed away. Barren roadsides and eroded hills are examples of land abuse. On such derelict sites, forest renewal takes much longer or is only partial.

Fire, usually the destructive result of man's carelessness, can also help keep a forest region healthy. Fire creates excellent conditions for growth by destroying debris on the forest floor, exposing the ground to sunlight and enriching the soil with nutrients. Ashes and charred vegetation contain large amounts of calcium, potash, phosphate and other minerals essential to plants.

The yellow-flowered ***dandelion*** (Taraxacum officinale) *blooms from early spring to August—everywhere, it seems. Its tiny seeds, attached to hairy parachutes, are carried far and wide by the wind. Although regarded as a weed, it is a valuable wild flower. For centuries its leaves have been used in salads, its flowers in wine. Pioneers used its roots as a laxative; today the dried roots are used as a coffee substitute. Grouse, partridge, moose and bear forage on this plant. The dandelion takes its name from the French expression* dents de lion *because its leaves are shaped like lions' teeth.*

Shepherd's purse (Capsella bursa-pastoris), *common throughout Canada, is so named because its seed pods resemble an old-fashioned change purse. This plant, up to three feet high, blooms from early spring to late fall in grainfields and gardens and along roadsides. It has small clusters of white flowers and long ragged leaves.*

Weeds: They Follow Man Everywhere

Man constantly disturbs natural vegetation to build roads, to raise crops, to obtain timber. Native plants are seldom able to grow in the resultant habitats. But weeds can grow almost anywhere. And so weeds, the hardy adaptable plants man most wants to eliminate, thrive wherever he goes.

A vitamin-rich tea can be brewed from the leaves of the ***broad-leaved plantain*** (Plantago major), *a weed common in meadows and cultivated fields and along roadsides. From June to October it bears spikes of minute, greenish flowers.*

Prickly lettuce (Lactuca scariola) *is called the compass plant because its leaves point north or south. This edible, one-to-six-foot plant grows in fields and along roadsides across mainland Canada. It is rare in the Maritime provinces.*

The ***field chickweed*** (Cerastium arvense) *grows to eight inches in dry fields and meadows. Its white, star-shaped flowers bloom from May to July. Unlike other chickweeds, its petals are much longer than the sepals.*

The ***shaggy mane*** (Coprinus comatus) *grows in clusters. Brownish scales cover its fleshy, white cap. Only young specimens, picked before their gills have turned black, are edible.*

The breezes of spring and early summer are often laden with the sweet fragrance of ***red clover*** (Trifolium pratense), *a plant that carpets Canada's meadows and woodlands. It is used to make wine, vinegar and tea and is forage for wild and domestic animals.*

Quack grass (Agropyron repens)*—also called couch grass and quick grass—is one of the most difficult weeds in the world to eradicate. It grows abundantly and tenaciously in gardens, cultivated fields and pastures and along roadsides. Its rootstocks can be eaten raw or ground for flour. Quack grass blooms in late June.*

Wild buckwheat (Polygonum convolvulus), *introduced from Europe, grows throughout Canada but is most abundant on the Prairies. This ground plant is also called black bindweed.*

Quebec's floral emblem, the ***Madonna lily*** (Lilium candidum), *is the only provincial flower not native to Canada. This lily, of Europe and Asia, grows to four feet and bears up to 20 fragrant flowers.*

Many of Canada's Weeds Are "Invaders" From Europe

Toadflax (Linaria vulgaris) *is also called butter-and-eggs for its yellow and orange blossoms. Resembling snapdragons, the flowers bloom throughout the summer. Its slender stem grows to about two feet. Toadflax spreads by winged seeds and by underground stems.*

Many common weeds of farms, fields, roadsides and lawns are hardy plants whose seeds were unintentionally brought to North America by European settlers. Land cleared for farming encouraged the growth and spread of such imported species as chicory, mullein, yarrow and the Canada thistle.

In the summer twilight, ***yellow evening-primrose*** (Oenothera biennis) *unfolds its yellow, four-petaled blossoms. Fragrant and up to two inches wide, they attract night-flying moths. After pollination, the petals wither and fall off. The hairy, inch-long pods that follow contain reddish brown seeds. Yellow evening-primrose grows to six feet. During its first year, when the plant does not bloom, its stout, branching taproot can be eaten.*

Prehistoric relatives of horsetails grew to 100 feet but today these plants rarely exceed four feet. The ***field horsetail*** (Equisetum arvense), *a common weed throughout Canada, is poisonous—especially to young horses. Its light brown, unbranched stems appear in April, then wither. Each stem is topped by a spore-bearing cone. In May green branched stems grow. These resemble pine-tree seedlings and last until frost.*

In Medieval Europe, peasants hung sprigs of ***St. John's-wort*** (Hypericum perforatum) *from doors and windows to ward off evil. It was once believed that medicinal dew collected on the stem of this common roadside weed. Its yellow flowers, with tiny black dots around their edges, bloom in clusters throughout the summer.*

Because its yellow flowers generally close by midday, ***goatsbeard*** (Trapogon) *is sometimes called Johnny-go-to-bed-at-noon. In August, round, puffy seed heads develop at the top of each stem. The young, grasslike leaves and long, fleshy roots are edible.*

In summer, ***ox-eye daisy*** (Chrysanthemum leucanthemum) *blooms in meadows and along roadsides, most abundantly in eastern Canada. Its one-to-three-foot stem supports a single flowering head consisting of a yellow disc surrounded by numerous white rays. The rays drop off after the flower has been pollinated.*

In late summer the ***parasol mushroom*** (Lepiota procera) *appears in meadows and open forests. Its hollow, scaly stalk, no wider than half an inch, grows to 12 inches and is encircled by a thick movable ring. Its umbrella-shaped cap, from four to eight inches across, has a pronounced rise in the center. White spores and a scaly stalk distinguish the edible parasol mushroom from a green-spored, smooth-stemmed, poisonous lookalike.*

Food From the Wild

The young shoots, leaves and flower buds of **milkweed** *(Asclepias)* are delicious boiled. The flowers can be fried in batter; the firm, green seed pods are tasty boiled or baked. Milkweed should be boiled in several changes of water.

The vivid blue flower heads of ***chicory*** (Cichorium intybus) *open in the morning, but shut tight by noon. Its succulent, young leaves are delicious and nutritious whether cooked or raw. Its long, fleshy taproot is used commercially as a coffee additive. Chicory's hairy stem, containing a bitter milky juice, grows to about five feet.*

Next to the dandelion, ***yarrow*** (Achillea millefolium) *may be the most common weed in Canada.* Millefolium, *meaning a thousand leaves, refers to the yarrow's abundant, feathery foliage. Yarrow is hard to eradicate because it spreads by underground stems and by seed. Its white, flat-topped flower heads bloom all summer long.*

Contrary to popular opinion, ***goldenrod*** (Solidago) *is not a major cause of hay fever because its pollen is too heavy and sticky to be blown by the wind. Nearly all 120 species grow in North America. Some reach five or six feet. Masses of tiny yellow flowers begin to bloom in July.*

Vast colonies of the ***Canada thistle*** (Cirsium arvense) *invade gardens, fields and open areas across Canada. Its prickly leaves discourage foraging animals. Its rose-purple or white flower heads bloom from June to October. It spreads rapidly by underground stems and by seed.*

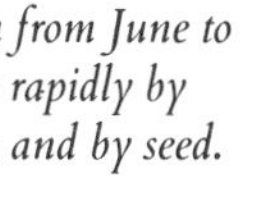

After Fire, Logging or Disease, a Forest Heals Itself

Following fire, logging, disease, insect infestation or some other disturbance, a forest quickly begins to heal itself. Poplars, birches, jack pines, lodgepole pines and Douglas firs are among the first trees to grow. Eventually a relatively stable climax forest, dominated by a few species, develops.

Like most poplars, the ***trembling aspen*** (Populus tremuloides) *spreads by windblown seeds and by suckers—shoots that grow from roots near the surface. When mature poplars are destroyed by fire or cut by loggers, suckers develop rapidly. Poplars thrive in sunlight.*

The foul smell of the ***stinkhorn*** (Phallus) *attracts flies that help to scatter its sticky spores. This spongy, yellowish fungus grows among rotting wood.*

The ***wild sarsaparilla*** (Aralia nudicaulis), *of the ginseng family, has long, sturdy rootstocks that can withstand fire. The aromatic rootstocks have been used as a tonic and as a flavoring in medicines.*

Soon after fire devastates a forest, ***fireweed*** (Epilobium angustifolium) *sprouts and within weeks it grows to five or six feet. Its purplish or magenta flowers bloom throughout the summer. The lower blossoms open first and flowering continues slowly up the spike—the bottom of the spike may bear seed pods while the top is still in bud. The leaves of fireweed, floral emblem of the Yukon Territory, turn bright red in fall. The inner pith of mature stalks can be eaten raw. Boiled, its young shoots taste like asparagus. Fireweed is one of the most widespread plants in the world.*

The ***white birch*** (Betula papyrifera) *has thin, flammable bark and is easily destroyed by fire. However, its charred stumps sprout new shoots and the wind scatters its light, winged seeds over burned areas. White birch saplings are often abundant on burned land but as shade-tolerant trees take over, the white birch survives only in sunny clearings.*

Fire is the only process by which some pine trees, such as the ***lodgepole pine*** (Pinus contorta), *regenerate. The cones of the lodgepole pine, held tightly closed by resin, only open and release their seeds at 40° C. (112° F.) or more—temperatures that occur naturally in the forest only during a fire. The seeds germinate within days and the seedlings develop rapidly on the mineral-rich, fire-prepared ground.*

The ***chokecherry*** (Prunus virginiana), *named for its tart crimson fruit, is Canada's commonest wild cherry. Its leaves and twigs are poisonous but its fruit makes excellent jelly and wine. The chokecherry usually grows as a large shrub on cleared land.*

Mosslike liverworts are the simplest of all green land plants. They reproduce by spores and cling to damp soil or rocks by thin rootlike fibers called rhizoids. Unlike mosses, liverworts rarely cover large areas. Marchantia polymorpha, *a branching ribbonlike* ***liverwort,*** *is common on recently burned land. Liverworts were once thought to cure liver ailments.*

Food From the Wild

About 25 species of **blueberry** *(Vaccinium)* grow in North America. All have small, glossy green leaves, and no prickles. The berries, varying from reddish purple to bluish black, are among the few fruits harvested commercially from the wild.

The ***wild red raspberry*** (Rubus strigosus) *is one of many shrubs that flourish after fire. Its prickly stems (called canes) bear flowers and fruits in their second year, then die. The small five-petaled flowers are white. The sweet fruits are not true berries, but tight clusters of juicy seed cells called drupes. Raspberries turn from white to red as they ripen in July and August.*

Outdoors: The Weather

Weather influences what we do and how we feel. Winter storms keep us indoors; spring sunshine raises our spirits; summer warmth encourages activity outdoors; rain interrupts a baseball game—or ruins a holiday.

Our seasons change because the earth is tilted on its axis. The Northern and Southern Hemispheres receive solar rays at varying angles as the earth orbits the sun—the higher the sun in the sky, the higher the temperature. The belt around the earth's middle is hot; the polar caps are cold; the temperate zones between have distinct seasonal changes. Air movements often override seasonal patterns: warm air from the south can bring mild spells in winter; cool air from the north can bring frost in summer.

All weather occurs inside a layer of atmosphere close to the earth. This layer is about 13 miles thick at the equator, 5 miles at the poles and 5 to 8 miles over Canada. The sun warms the ground, which in turn warms the air. Winds are caused as warm air rises and cool air moves in to replace it. (The earth's rotation influences the speed and direction of winds.) The sun causes evaporation from oceans, seas, lakes and rivers. Water vapor is drawn up into the air, condenses to form clouds and eventually falls as rain, hail, sleet or snow.

High- and low-pressure areas (highs and lows) form because cold air is heavier than hot air. A high, which generally produces clear weather with light winds, is an area of sinking air rotating clockwise. A low, which usually brings cloudy unsettled weather, is an area of rising air turning counterclockwise.

At their most savage, weather forces combine to create hurricanes and tornadoes; at their gentlest, they bring calm, sunny summer days.

Environment Canada's meteorological experts track changes in the atmosphere and issue regular weather forecasts based primarily on air temperature and pressure, wind speed and direction, and humidity. These forecasts are invaluable to air traffic, shipping, agriculture and industry. Technology enables forecasters to make remarkably accurate predictions.

A layman can make his own forecasts by noting cloud formations, wind direction and temperature changes. Many cloud forms indicate that fine weather or rain can be expected; others foretell high winds and storms. In these pages are the fundamentals of weather phenomena and practical advice to help you to make accurate weather predictions.

Forked lightning illuminates a wilderness lake.

Weather Patterns

The sun generates the weather. It causes heat, wind, rain, hail, sleet and snow; it helps create the high- and low-pressure areas that shape weather patterns.

The earth is too far from the sun to be warmed directly by it but solar rays are converted to heat when they are absorbed by the earth. Heat radiated from the surface of the earth warms the air above—the sun does not directly warm the air. Winds are created as warmed air rises and heavier cool air moves in to replace it. Evaporation caused by the sun adds moisture to the air. Eventually, this water vapor condenses and returns to the earth as rain or some other form of precipitation.

Temperature Changes in temperature occur according to the angle at which the sun's rays strike the earth, the nature of the earth's surface and the type and amount of cloud. The sun is at its highest in the sky at noon; the effect is most felt between 2 and 3 p.m.—the hottest time of day. Mornings and late afternoons are cooler because the sun is then lower on the horizon.

Dense forests absorb most of the sun's rays and warm rapidly; snow reflects most of the rays back into the atmosphere. Clouds and microscopic dust in the air absorb and reflect solar rays, preventing them from reaching earth. Therefore, cloudy days are cooler than clear days.

The winds are nature's way of regulating temperatures throughout the earth. Without winds, the polar areas would grow colder and the equatorial regions would grow hotter—until all regions of the earth were uninhabitable.

Humidity Temperature governs the relative humidity of the air—the percentage of moisture in the atmosphere in relation to the air's saturation point. (When air is saturated its relative humidity is said to be 100 percent.) The hotter the air, the more moisture it can hold—so summer days are often muggy. The cooler the air, the less moisture it can hold—so winter days are usually dry.

Most of the sun's energy is lost in space. Of what little does reach earth only 43 percent is absorbed and converted into heat.

42% reflected back to space

15% absorbed by atmosphere

43% absorbed by earth's surface

Clouds, water and earth surfaces absorb varying amounts of solar energy (radiation). A dark forest soaks up more than a snow-clad mountain does.

Highs and lows Atmospheric pressure—the weight of air above any point—varies because the earth's surface is heated unequally.

A high-pressure area, one in which air is sinking slowly, can be several thousand miles in diameter. The earth warms the sinking air, increasing its capacity to hold moisture. Clouds in the path of a high-pressure area are often evaporated and skies become clear. In Canada, highs originate over Arctic regions bringing cool, clear weather south to the Prairies and southeast to Hudson Bay and eastern Canada. Highs from the United States bring warm humid air to Canada in winter, hot and very humid air in summer.

Low-pressure areas, massive depressions of rising air sometimes hundreds of miles in diameter, often form between highs. Lows can become storms. As air rises rapidly it expands and cools, lessening its pressure and its capacity to retain moisture. Most of Canada's lows sweep in from the south and move toward the Great Lakes or along the Atlantic coast.

Warm and cold fronts An air mass, often covering hundreds or thousands of square miles, is a body of air throughout which temperature and moisture are much the same. Such a mass takes on the temperature and moisture characteristics of the surface over which it forms. An air mass formed in winter over Canada is very cold and dry.

Fronts form when air masses meet. The colder, heavier air mass usually pushes under and lifts the warmer, lighter mass. A cold front results when cold air displaces warm air; a warm front develops when warm air replaces cold air. In both cases the weather is likely to be unsettled and stormy.

Weather maps indicate weather patterns with contours along which the atmospheric pressure is uniform. High- and low-pressure areas are indicated by an H or an L and their probable directions by arrows.

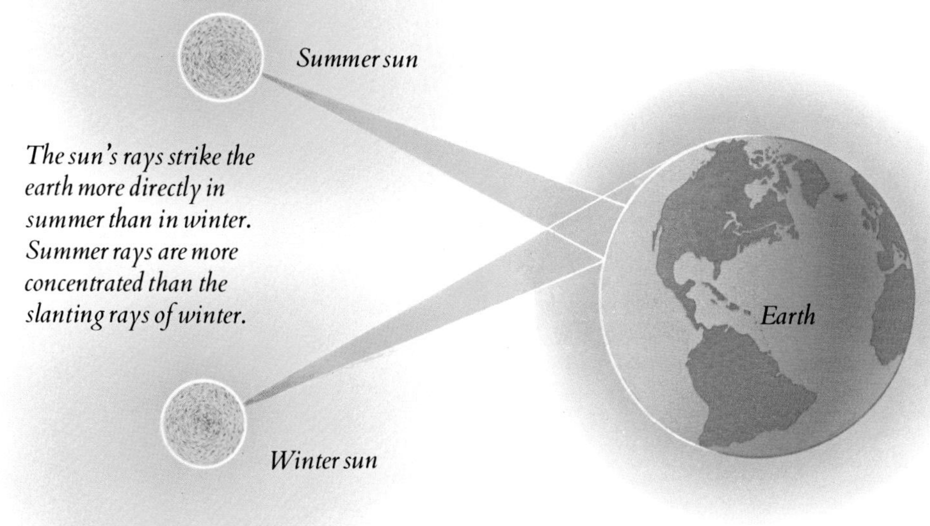

The sun's rays strike the earth more directly in summer than in winter. Summer rays are more concentrated than the slanting rays of winter.

A cold front pushes under a warm front when the two meet. The warm air cools as it rises, causing water vapor in it to condense and fall as precipitation.

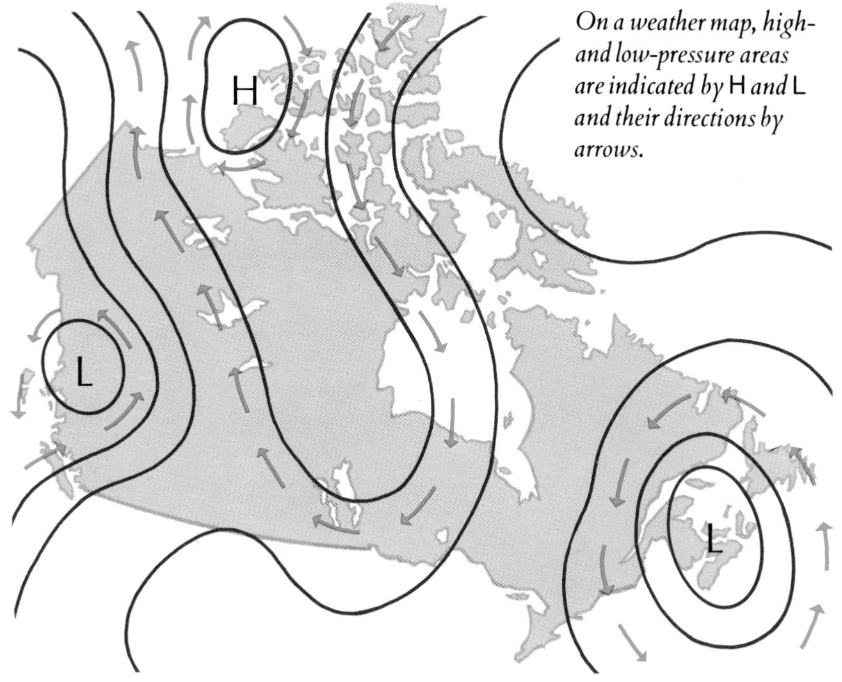

On a weather map, high- and low-pressure areas are indicated by H *and* L *and their directions by arrows.*

Clouds and How They Form

Cumulus clouds (top) are piled up and puffy. Their shapes change constantly in the wind. Stratus clouds (above) are banked in layers, creating a heavy leaden sky.

Cumulonimbus thunderheads tower up to 60,000 feet.

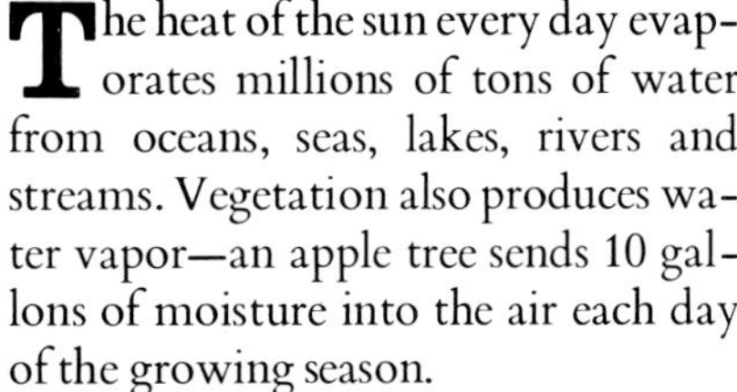

The heat of the sun every day evaporates millions of tons of water from oceans, seas, lakes, rivers and streams. Vegetation also produces water vapor—an apple tree sends 10 gallons of moisture into the air each day of the growing season.

How clouds form Moisture in the air can be invisible or it can cool and condense into clouds—masses of water droplets or ice crystals formed around minute dust or smoke particles. Billions of these particles are constantly present in the atmosphere. As air cools, the droplets or crystals thus created collide and join together. When they are heavy enough they fall as rain, sleet, hail or snow.

The cooling that causes moisture to condense into clouds is usually the result of air being lifted (as when it passes over a warm surface or meets rising ground or a mass of colder air, or when it is blown upward by winds). As it is lifted it is subjected to less atmospheric pressure and expands. Its expansion causes it to cool and this cooling causes water vapor in the air to condense.

Precipitation falling through low-lying warm air can produce clouds. Fog—in substance low clouds—forms when warm, moist air passes over a cool surface.

Cloud classifications The most common clouds are cumulus, which are piled up and puffy, and stratus, which are layered. Clouds are classified as high (or cirrus)—20,000 feet and above; middle (or alto)—between 10,000 and 20,000 feet; and low, with bases at any level up to 8,000 feet. The word nimbus means rain cloud.

High clouds are of three types: cirrus, cirrocumulus and cirrostratus. High clouds consists of ice crystals.

Cirrus clouds are thin, wispy and are often blown into feathery streaks called "mares' tails."

Cirrocumulus clouds form wave-like patterns or thin, patchy shapes like fish scales—the mackerel sky which is often a sign of changing weather.

Cirrostratus clouds look like fine veils or torn, windblown gauze. A halo appears when the sun or the moon is viewed through these clouds.

Middle clouds are either altocumulus or altostratus.

Altocumulus clouds are gray or whitish puffy patches, larger than cirrocumulus and made of water droplets, not ice crystals. When viewed through these clouds, the sun often appears as a pale blue or yellow disc with a reddish edge.

Altostratus clouds are dense, gray veils. The sun and the moon often appear through them as if seen through frosted glass.

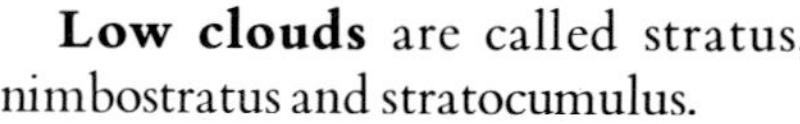

Low clouds are called stratus, nimbostratus and stratocumulus.

The low, uniform sheet of dull gray stratus clouds makes a leaden sky and often produces fine drizzle.

Dark gray and menacing, nimbostratus clouds usually bring a downpour. These low rain clouds develop when altostratus clouds thicken, saturating the air below.

Stratocumulus clouds are irregular masses spread out in rolling or puffy layers over a large area. The sun often shines through thin spots between patches.

Towering clouds are either cumulonimbus thunderheads, which can produce tornadoes and thunderstorms, or massive piles of cumulus clouds associated with fine weather.

Clouds are a good indication of conditions to come, because particular cloud formations are associated with certain types of weather.

They also produce—at all seasons—some of nature's most dramatic and beautiful tapestries.

Cirrocumulus

Cirrostratus

Cirrus

Altocumulus

Altostratus

Nimbostratus

Stratocumulus

Hurricanes and Hailstones

Weather creates the raindrop, the snowflake and the exquisite pattern that frosts a window. It unleashes thunder and lightning and the awesome destructive forces of hurricanes and tornadoes. It is hailstones and rainbows and dew....

Here are descriptions of phenomena that reflect the power and changeability of weather.

Hurricanes Canada seldom takes the brunt of the hurricane—a mass of air swirling at more than 70 miles an hour over a diameter of 400 miles or more. A hurricane is born at sea in hot, moist air near the equator. Winds are deflected by the earth's rotation. Moisture pulled into the growing storm condenses as it is lifted. Eventually it falls as torrential rain.

The eye of a hurricane is a calm area at its center, averaging 20 miles in diameter. The wheeling motion of the winds prevents them from penetrating the eye, which acts like the axle of a turning wheel. A hurricane passes north at about 10 miles an hour. The area beneath is thrashed by east-west winds, then undergoes a period of calm as the eye passes, and finally is buffeted by west-east winds. A hurricane is slowed by friction with land but still may leave a trail of damage hundreds of miles long.

Canada sometimes suffers the last hours of a hurricane. In October 1954 southern Ontario was deluged with 7.15 inches of rain in 24 hours before Hurricane Hazel died. (Hurricanes are given girls' names by the U.S. Weather Bureau; the first hurricane of the year has a name beginning with A, and so on, alphabetically.)

Tornadoes The tornado, nature's most powerful and destructive storm, averages about 200 yards in diameter. It is a funnel of air rotating at up to 300 miles an hour or more and traveling at 20 to 40 miles an hour. In the center is an area of such low pressure that buildings over which it passes often explode. A tornado can drive a piece of straw into a tree and carry an automobile hundreds of feet through the air. Scientists have not determined the cause of tornadoes but know that they often form during thunderstorms when the air temperature is 27°C. (80°F.) or more.

Thunderstorms Lightning is an immensely powerful flash of electricity between heavily charged clouds, or between a cloud and the ground. The heat of a lightning bolt can evaporate the sap in a tree; an electric storm can create more energy than an atom bomb. Lightning is attracted to tall objects, such as buildings and trees.

During a thunderstorm, get indoors as soon as possible. Don't stay under or near isolated trees or structures. If in a small boat, head for land—fast. Avoid hilltops, open spaces, wire fences and exposed sheds. A car offers good protection from lightning.

Thunder is the sound of the shock waves caused when lightning flashes.

Hailstones Hail forms when snow pellets become covered with ice. The hail is flung about by violent air disturbances within a cloud, accumulating new layers of ice. The cross section of a hailstone shows the perimeter of each successive ice layer, similar to the rings which show on a tree stump. Hailstorms in Canada are most common over Alberta.

A snowflake is crystallized water vapor, formed at temperatures below freezing.

A rainbow is the result of sunlight being broken up by raindrops into bands of red, orange, yellow, green, blue, indigo and violet.

When water vapor touches cooler earth surfaces, such as grass, it condenses to form dew; if the temperature of the surface is below freezing, frost forms. The frost patterns on a window are caused by repeated melting and crystallizing of moisture as temperatures fluctuate around freezing.

A tornado twists savagely to the ground. Although the most violent of all winds, a tornado seldom lasts longer than an hour.

Frost on a windowpane... one of nature's most delicate tapestries.

The symmetry of a snowflake (above) is revealed by a microscope. A cross section of a hailstone (below) shows that it formed in layers as it rose and fell in turbulent air.

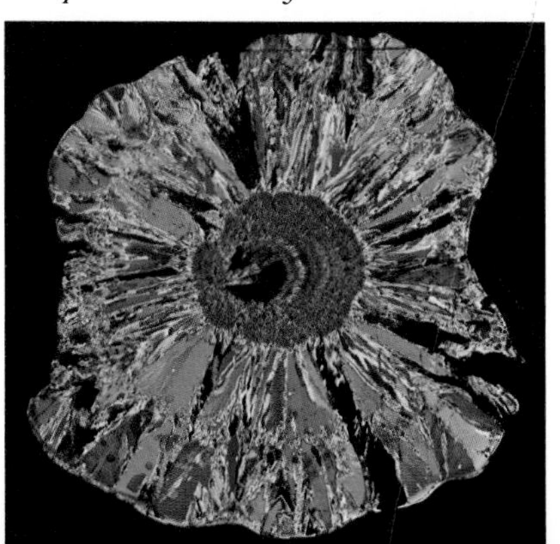

Hurricane Gladys was stalled in the Gulf of Mexico when this photo was taken in 1968 from Apollo 7. The highest winds, near the storm's center, were about 75 miles an hour.

How to Predict the Weather

Anyone can forecast the weather with reasonable accuracy by learning to interpret the many clues in cloud patterns, wind directions and the sunset.

Frequent changes in cloud patterns often precede a storm. Feathery cirrus clouds warn of rain within 48 hours. Soon dense layers of clouds (altostratus) will sweep in front of the sun. The clouds will darken shortly before rain falls. Small puffy clouds indicate a continuing fine spell.

A westerly wind usually brings clear, cool weather; an easterly wind generally indicates rain; a northerly wind often brings clear, cold weather; a southerly wind brings warmth and sudden showers.

You can judge wind direction by noting the drift of low clouds, smoke, dust or snow, or the swaying of long grass or tree branches.

Because most weather patterns drift from west to east in the northern hemisphere, the sunset gives a hint of conditions to be expected the following day. If clouds hide the sun, anticipate cloudy weather; if a luminous circle appears around the setting sun, rain clouds are on the way; if the sunset is bright and red, a clear day is likely to follow.

A barometer is a useful aid to the amateur meteorologist, but those "fair" and "rain" markings are unreliable. Changes in barometric pressure are more significant. Generally, if the barometer is falling, the weather will worsen; if the barometer is rising, better conditions are on the way.

The following weather conditions can be expected after any of the clues indicated:

Cloudy, unsettled

- The barometer falls
- Overnight temperature is higher than normal
- Cloud movement is erratic
- High layers of wispy clouds produce a ring around the sun or the moon
- Clouds darken, hiding the sun

High, thin cirrus clouds refract light to produce this halo around the sun. Soon the clouds will thicken and the weather will become stormy.

Expect a sunny day when morning fog clears rapidly.

Showers
- Dark clouds accompany a west wind
- Thick, puffy clouds (cumulus) develop rapidly

Steady rain, hail, sleet or snow
- A southeast or northeast wind accompanies signs of unsettled weather
- Low dark clouds cover the sky

Clear
- The barometer rises
- The wind becomes northwesterly
- The temperature falls
- Low clouds give way to blue patches in the morning

The following seasonal weather conditions can be expected after any of the clues indicated:

Warmer in summer
- Morning skies are clear

Warmer in winter
- The barometer falls rapidly

Colder in summer
- The barometer falls and clear skies become cloudy

Colder in winter
- Morning skies are clearing while the barometer is rising

There is truth in the ancient rhyme, "Red sky at night, sailors' delight." A picturesque red sky at night usually means fine weather the following day.

Mock suns, or sun dogs (above), tell of precipitation to come. Cumulus clouds in the morning (below) usually mean showers are on the way.

Continuing bright, sunny
- The barometer is high and steady or rising
- The setting sun is like a ball of fire
- Sunset skies are red
- Clouds thin in the late afternoon
- Morning fog clears within two hours of sunrise
- A light, northwest breeze blows

Colder
- A southwest wind becomes westerly, or a west wind becomes northwesterly
- The barometer is low and falling rapidly while the wind is east to northeast, shifting to north or northwest
- Snow accompanies a west or northwest wind

The following cloud formations are generally associated with the weather conditions indicated:
Cirrus—Storm on the way
Cirrostratus—If the sun or the moon is surrounded by a luminous circle, a storm is imminent
Altostratus—Rain, hail, sleet or snow. A small circle may surround the sun or the moon
Altocumulus—Colder
Nimbostratus—Heavy precipitation
Cumulonimbus—Thunderstorms

Outdoors: How to Cope

A campfire crackles. A peaceful lake sparkles in the sunset. A father and his son prepare supper at the end of a satisfying day in the Canadian outdoors.

For many people, camping is an economical way to enjoy the sights, sounds and beauty of nature. For experienced outdoorsmen, camping offers the challenges of exploring the wilderness and living off the land. For the inexperienced, camping provides opportunities to learn new skills and to develop self-reliance.

Camping can provide a peaceful and fulfilling vacation whether you carry a minimum of equipment on your back or enjoy the luxury of a motor home. Campers go everywhere. Some seek the rugged adventure of the wilderness—far from roads, camping neighbors and signs of man. Others enjoy the comfort, convenience and natural attractions of Canada's hundreds of national and provincial parks. Whatever style suits you, your experience will be richer if you choose equipment carefully and learn basic outdoor skills before you set off.

A great variety of equipment is available to modern campers. In these pages you will discover the advantages and disadvantages of different styles of tents and camping vehicles. Lights, lanterns, heaters and coolers, among the most popular accessories, are dealt with. You will learn how to choose and care for sleeping bags and air mattresses, how to make camping gear at home, how to dress comfortably for all kinds of weather.

This section discusses various kinds of camping—with the emphasis on tenting and backpacking. Here you will find a handy checklist to help you plan your outing. You will learn about the pleasures and pitfalls of picnicking, which is really a special kind of camping—day camping.

Other subjects include how to use an ax and a knife, how to tie and use knots and lashings, how to set up a comfortable campsite, how to handle camp sanitation when public facilities are not available, how to recognize poisonous plants and snakes and how to survive if lost or stranded.

If getting off the beaten track in midwinter appeals to you, consider tramping the wilderness with a pack on your back, or tenting. Backpacking basics and equipment are featured, as is advice on how to enjoy camping in the snow.

For the parents of young children, this section offers a variety of activities and safety tips to help make camping enjoyable for the whole family.

The joys of camping: a shimmering sunset, a placid lake, a roaring fire...

What Kind of Camping?

Backpackers trek along a trail through the breathtaking Tonquin Valley in Jasper National Park. The snow-cloaked mountains tower above the placid Amethyst Lakes.

From coast to coast Canada offers abundant opportunities for outdoor vacationing. Accommodation is reasonably priced in thousands of national, provincial and private parks. Many have showers, laundry facilities and electrical outlets. At some, instruction is provided in arts and crafts, nature study and folklore.

You can take advantage of these facilities or you can rough it. You can cook on a portable stove or start a fire with flint and steel or a magnifying glass. You can enjoy the neighborliness and convenience of a campground or the solitude and simplicity of the wild. The choice is yours.

Roughing it Backpacking is inexpensive, arduous and an experience that many regard as the truest and most rewarding form of camping.

Tenting is for the outdoorsman who wants a little more protection from the weather and who travels to a campground by car. Modern tents are designed for easy pitching and packing, and a variety of rugged, practical equipment can make tenting as comfortable as cottage living.

Good tents store easily and last for years. The drawbacks of tents are that they require smooth ground for pitching, they have to be set up and taken down, they are easily damaged and they can be uncomfortable in prolonged wet spells.

Camping vehicles Campers who prefer more comfort than a tent provides can choose from among tent and travel trailers and motor homes. The more luxurious trailers and motor homes have a bath, separate sleeping and living quarters, and connections for electricity and running water. Some persons feel such luxury is contrary to the philosophy of camping. Others find that extra comfort adds to their enjoyment of the outdoors. Again, your choice.

Travel trailers and motor homes are expensive to purchase and to operate. Tent trailers are much less so. Lighter, more compact and easier to tow than trailer homes, they provide such amenities as sleeping berths, a dining table and plenty of storage space for camping gear.

Once you have considered these styles of camping—each is presented in detail in the following pages—the next

This recreational vehicle has sleeping quarters for four adults and a child. The roof can be raised to provide headroom.

Why not rent a canoe—or take your own? This camper is preparing to shoot rapids in Ontario's Quetico Provincial Park.

A tent trailer is easy to erect. It provides a comfortable home for up to six people.

step is to decide where you will vacation. The map section of this volume is designed to help you discover the parks, trails and wilderness areas of Canada from the comfort of your living room.

Before buying a tent, travel trailer or motor home, consider whether it meets your needs. Is it suitable for the terrain and climate where you will camp? Will it accommodate your party comfortably? Will it provide your kind of vacation?

Save on equipment When you are sure you have made the right choice, rent similar equipment for a trial run on a weekend camping trip. This experience can help you assess what you need so that you avoid buying unnecessary gear. You can save also by shopping for used equipment. Secondhand camping vehicles and supplies are readily available—often because many a camper sets off on his first trip without planning as thoroughly as you will have done.

From a lush alpine meadow in Yoho National Park, these campers have a fine view of the Wiwaxy Peaks.

Planning the Trip

Adequate planning, much of it months before your vacation, can overcome many problems that might mar a camping experience. If it's to be a summer vacation, winter is the time to think about where you will go, how you will travel and what equipment you will need.

Camping books and magazines describe popular and unusual places to visit. The map section of this book deals with many national and provincial parks in Canada. Friends may recommend camping areas. Choose several areas that appeal to you and get details by writing to government tourist offices. Check the location and accessibility of parks, campgrounds, beaches, canoe routes, hiking trails, scenic and historic sites.

Talk with those who will share the vacation. Will some want to fish, ride horses, play golf, go shopping? Which areas offer the best opportunities for these activities?

Next, list the equipment you will need. Then visit a camping exhibition or camping store to familiarize yourself with the variety and cost of supplies. Revise your list as you wish, but buy nothing until you consider your budget.

Budgeting Decide what you can afford to spend and estimate what your planned vacation will cost. Calculate the cost of travel, equipment, food, campsite fees and miscellaneous supplies, such as fuel for a stove and lantern and ice for a cooler. Include something for medical emergencies and vehicle repairs.

You can save by making some camping gear, by buying secondhand equipment and by using articles from home—old cutlery, pots, pans and dishes.

Check your camping equipment. Mend tears in tents, sleeping bags and cots. Replace worn tent ropes and damaged pegs. Inflate air mattresses and repair any leaks. Check the operation of camp stoves, lanterns, heaters, coolers and flashlights. Sharpen axes

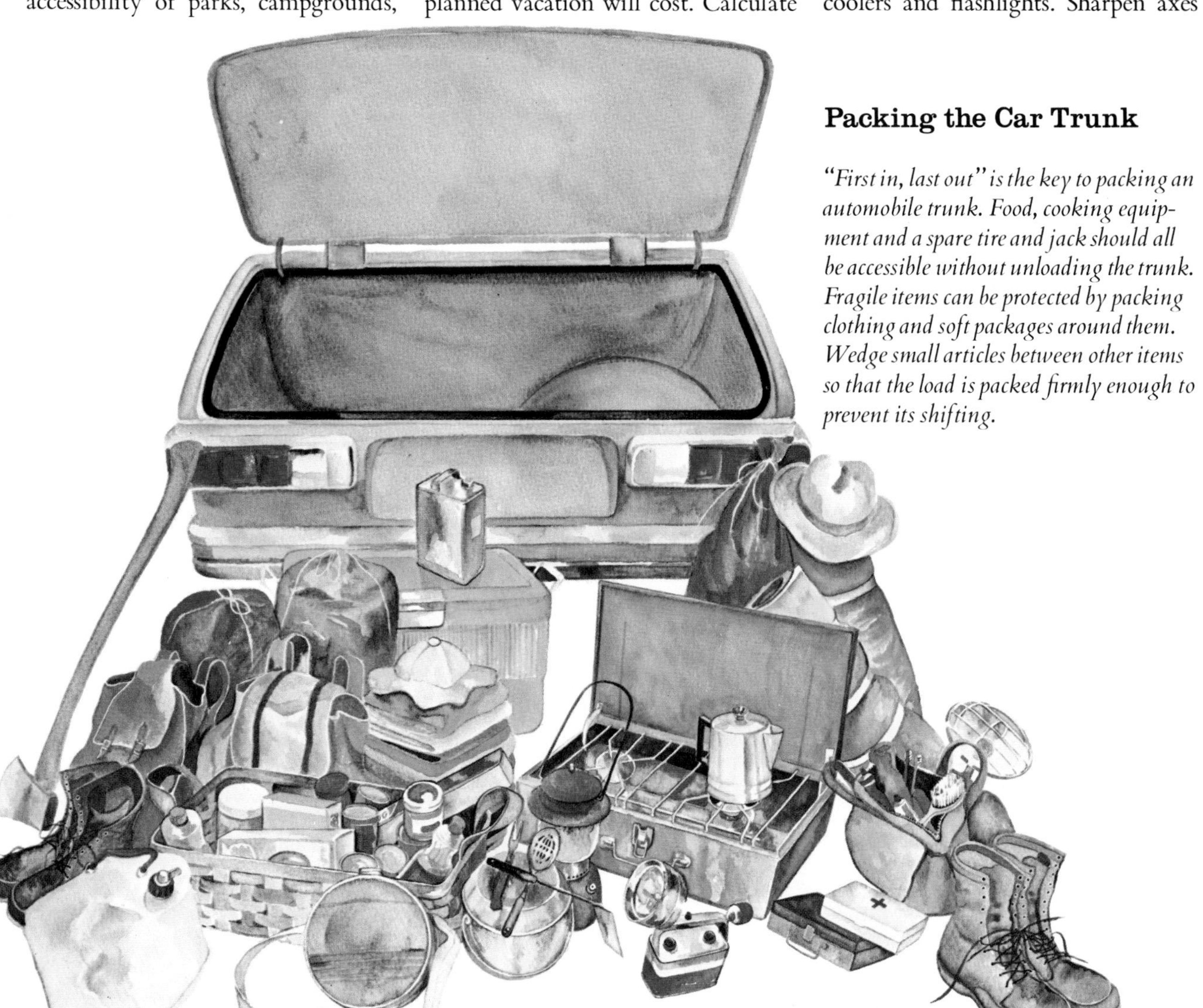

Packing the Car Trunk

"First in, last out" is the key to packing an automobile trunk. Food, cooking equipment and a spare tire and jack should all be accessible without unloading the trunk. Fragile items can be protected by packing clothing and soft packages around them. Wedge small articles between other items so that the load is packed firmly enough to prevent its shifting.

Planning a camping trip can be a time of pleasant anticipation for the entire family. Thorough preparation can help ensure a safe, fun-filled vacation.

and knives. List equipment that needs to be replaced or added.

In late spring or early summer, plan a weekend outing near home. Buy essential equipment and become familiar with it during this short camping venture. If you intend to buy a tent, consider renting a similar one for the weekend. This will help you determine whether your choice is right. Keep a list, adding things you discover you need, deleting items that prove unnecessary. Note what problems develop and plan to avoid similar troubles during your vacation. Is your tent roomy enough? Does it keep out rain and insects? Does it let in enough fresh air? Do you need spare tent pegs, poles or guy lines? Are your sleeping bags warm enough or should you take extra blankets?

About a week before your vacation, have your vehicle serviced. Check brakes, lights, fluid levels, tires (including the spare) and hoses. Buy an extra fan belt and some fuses.

If you are taking a dog or a cat with you, have it vaccinated against rabies and distemper.

Cancel milk, mail and other home deliveries. Give police the dates of your planned departure and return and give them a spare house key.

Packing Load your vehicle a day before the journey. Remember: what goes in first comes out last. Put heavy packages near the center of gravity (low and near the rear of an automobile trunk; on the floor near the center of a trailer). This helps to stabilize your vehicle and puts the least strain on its braking and suspension systems.

If necessary, remove the spare wheel and jack from their usual storage and pack them where they can be easily reached—so you won't have to unpack the trunk to change a tire.

A roof rack is useful for carrying light bulky items, such as sleeping bags and a tent, that would otherwise take up valuable trunk space. Make sure the rack is attached securely and use a tarpaulin as a cover—wind tears thin plastic when the vehicle is moving at highway speeds. Bulging cargo can be secured with elastic cords. Don't overload the rack: a tall load will cause excessive wind resistance, making the vehicle difficult to handle and increasing gas consumption.

Plastic bags containing clothing and linen can be used to protect fragile items and to prevent the load from shifting in a trunk or on a rack. Heavy articles packed loosely can become dangerous projectiles in the event of a sudden stop.

Carry emergency flares, a fire extinguisher and a first-aid kit under the front passenger seat where they are easy to reach but unlikely to roll under the driving pedals.

Finally, turn off lights and appliances, lower thermostats and lock all doors and windows in your home. Give a neighbor or the police a key to your home, an address where you can be reached in an emergency and the date of your return. Check that the car trunk is closed firmly, the trailer hitch is secure and that visibility is good from the driver's seat.

Have a great trip!

Planning Checklist for a Summer Trip

Winter □ Write for maps and travel brochures □ Read camping books and magazines □ Discuss plans with companions □ Prepare budget and equipment list □ Make and repair equipment

Spring □ Visit camping shows □ Revise equipment list and buy essential items □ Plan your travel route □ Make reservations, if needed, at parks and campsites

Week before trip □ Have vehicle serviced and safety checked □ If you are taking a dog or cat, have it vaccinated against rabies and distemper □ Air sleeping bags □ Buy traveler's checks □ Begin packing equipment □ Cancel milk, newspaper and other home deliveries □ Notify police of absence

Day before trip □ Load your vehicle

Day of trip □ Check that all equipment has been packed □ Close your home; check lights, appliances, thermostats, doors and windows □ Leave a house key with the police

Camping Vehicles and Cottages

If you want more comfort than backpacking or tenting gives, you may be tempted by a recreational vehicle—from the collapsible tent on wheels to the luxurious trailer home—or by a cottage.

Self-propelled recreational vehicles, easier to maneuver than trailers, include the camper that fits on the bed of a pickup truck, the converted bus or panel truck and the motorized home. Passengers may travel in the living quarters of these vehicles; the law prohibits this in trailers.

Trailer homes can create problems for the driver—but can be unhooked, allowing normal use of the towing vehicle.

Outer structures of recreational vehicles are of metal, fiberglass, plywood, or a combination of all three.

Tent trailers vary in width from 4 to 6 feet and in length from 7 to 14 feet. When closed for traveling, they are between 3 feet and 4 feet high. Jacks provide support when the tent is opened.

Fabric walls need to be of a robust material, such as army duck, to withstand repeated folding along the same creases. Steel or aluminum makes a durable framework. Check that the structure and hinges are sturdy by pushing gently at a top corner when the tent is up.

Mattresses should be insulated from contact with wood, metal and fiberglass so they don't absorb moisture.

Most large recreational vehicles offer a separate bathroom, kitchen and living room and connections for campground power, water and sewage. Built-in heaters and air conditioners are available for most models.

A gentle push against an outside wall will indicate the outline of the framework, and you can judge the thickness of the walls by a glance at door and window frames. A look inside a drawer or cabinet will reveal the quality of workmanship. Examine the undercarriage of several camping vehicles to help you assess their comparative soundness.

Check that seams are well sealed. Panels should be attached by screws or rivets—nails will work loose—and two layers of plywood make a stronger floor than one.

Sealed windows may look attractive, but most people prefer windows that can be opened in hot weather.

A refrigerator must be level and have an adequate flow of air through floor and wall vents. The quality of furniture and fittings can vary significantly, so examine them carefully.

Ensure that you can move freely in the living quarters.

Towing tips If you choose a trailer, ask dealers and users of similar trailers about the most suitable hitch.

Generally, a loaded trailer should not weigh more than half the total weight of the towing vehicle—including driver, passengers and luggage.

Before towing for the first time, practice backing the trailer on a parking lot. Remember the trailer and the rear of the car go in opposite directions. Turn the steering wheel clockwise to back the trailer to the left and turn it counterclockwise to back the trailer to the right.

To make a forward turn, drive slightly beyond the point where you would normally begin a turn. Take extra care to avoid curbs and soft shoulders. Start and stop smoothly. Shift to a low gear on steep hills.

For each 10 miles an hour showing on the speedometer, stay the equivalent of the combined length of your car and trailer behind the vehicle ahead.

Apart from a jack, spare wheel and tire for your trailer, always carry adjustable wrenches, screwdrivers, pliers, electrical wire, insulating tape and caulking compound. This equipment

A spacious trailer home. The sofas convert to beds. A bathroom is behind the door on the far side.

Home away from home . . . a vacation cottage is an investment in family togetherness and in many cases it is a sound financial investment as well.

Smallest of the self-propelled motor homes, a van like this provides a kitchenette and several berths.

A tent trailer opened for camping. Some models have a stove and sink and sleep eight persons.

The motorized home—a holiday home for all seasons—usually has separate bathroom, kitchen and living area.

This removable camper body fits on a pickup truck. An intercom can keep driver and passengers in touch.

will help you make minor repairs on most trailers.

A wing mirror on each side of your car is required by law if the trailer obscures the view from your interior mirror. Buy the biggest and most secure sideview mirrors available.

Water tanks in a camper or trailer should be drained regularly, cleaned with hot water and baking soda, and flushed out. In winter, water should be removed from tanks and waste traps.

Owning a cottage The prospective cottage owner must consider whether he will be happy to visit the same area time and time again. If so, a vacation home away from home can be a pleasurable investment.

Summer is the logical time to visit a cottage you are tempted to buy. Is the water nearby safe for swimming? Is it deep enough for boating? How high did the worst known flood reach? Don't let a picturesque setting distract you from possible structural defects in the building. Will rain leak in?

If you plan to use the cottage in winter, consider how easy access will be in snow. How effective is the building's insulation?

Find out how much land and water taxes will be, and estimate the cost of heat, light and insurance.

Check water, fishing and hunting rights and local building plans and restrictions.

How far is the cottage from a doctor? Is it served by a fire department? Is vandalism a problem?

A cottage, like any home, requires considerable maintenance. Water and power should be turned off and windows shuttered when your cottage is not in use. Rooms and linen should be aired periodically and the garden will need tending.

Though facing many chores, the owner of a well-chosen cottage enjoys a special consolation—the knowledge that his vacation home will likely be worth at least what he paid for it should he decide to sell.

Choosing the Right Tent

So many kinds of tents are available that choosing the right one can be a bewildering experience. To make a wise choice pay particular attention to size and weight, design, fabrics, frames and ventilation.

Crawl-in tents, intended strictly for sleeping, are light enough for backpacking. Medium-weight tents (about 20 pounds) can be carried easily when you are horsepacking or canoeing. Large wall tents have to be carried by car. A tent to be used during the day should provide about 27 square feet of floor space for each person. A tent 9 feet square (81 square feet overall) provides roomy shelter for three campers and their gear.

Basic features Design is largely a matter of taste, but remember that awnings and extra rooms add weight. The roof of a well-designed tent slopes steeply enough for rain to run off quickly. If there is sufficient headroom in the center of the tent, low walls need not be considered a disadvantage. Cots, chairs and other equipment can be placed alongside the walls beneath the lowest portions of the tent roof. Roll-up flaps over the doorway and windows give protection in stormy weather. Check that they open and close securely and easily. A fly sheet above the tent roof gives added protection in a storm. Air trapped between the fly and the roof also insulates, helping to keep the tent cool in hot weather and warm in cold spells.

A sewn-in floor should be larger than the floor area it will cover so that it will fit over bumps and hollows without stretching. A tent without a floor needs a groundsheet to protect against dampness and insects.

Fabrics Cotton and synthetic fabrics are commonly used for tents. The roof and walls should be water-repellent but not waterproof. Condensation will be excessive unless the fabric "breathes," allowing moist air to escape. Floors should be waterproof.

Cotton, which breathes better than synthetic fabric, makes good tent walls and roofs. It resists stretching when guy lines are tied too tightly, or when puddles form on sagging roof surfaces.

Frames Tubular aluminum frames are sturdy and rustproof and are lighter than those of steel or wood. Wooden frames are likely to warp or splinter.

A tent with an outside frame is usually easier to put up than one with an inside frame, and an outside frame generally provides stronger support. An inside frame can also damage fabric that is stretched over it.

For adequate ventilation, a tent 9 feet square should have at least one window, preferably opposite the doorway, to allow air to pass through the tent. The door should be large enough to allow easy passage to and from the tent and effective airing of the tent's interior.

Fiberglass and nylon make effective, long-wearing screening. Cotton screening is easily torn.

A compact tent such as this, easy to pack and to carry, provides adequate sleeping accommodation for three persons.

Tents for Special Uses

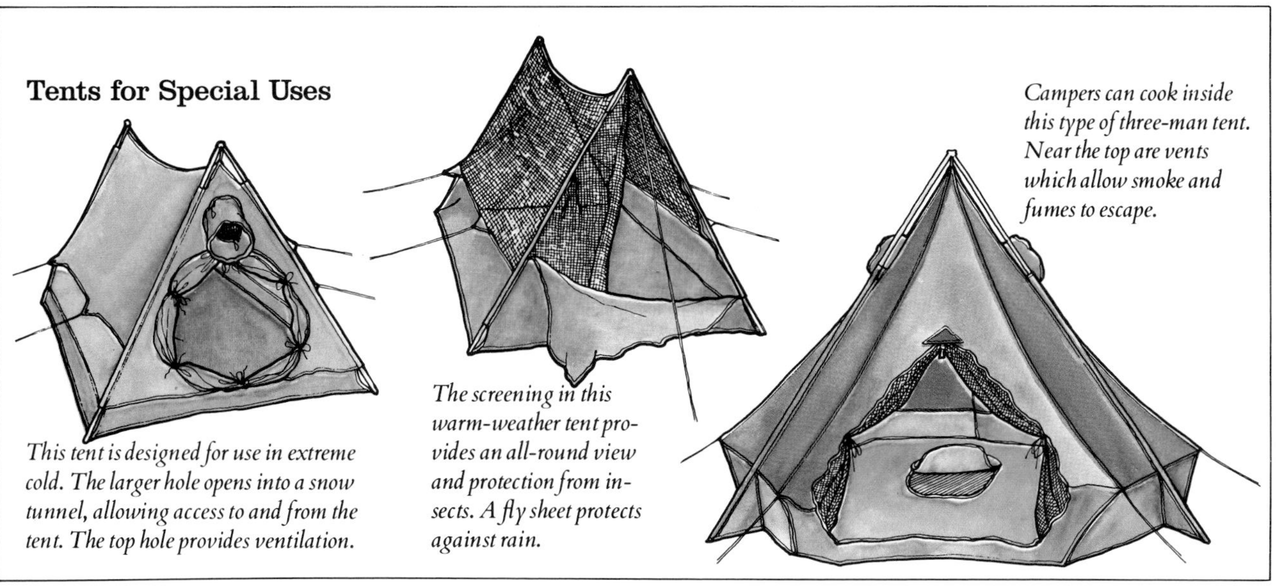

This tent is designed for use in extreme cold. The larger hole opens into a snow tunnel, allowing access to and from the tent. The top hole provides ventilation.

The screening in this warm-weather tent provides an all-round view and protection from insects. A fly sheet protects against rain.

Campers can cook inside this type of three-man tent. Near the top are vents which allow smoke and fumes to escape.

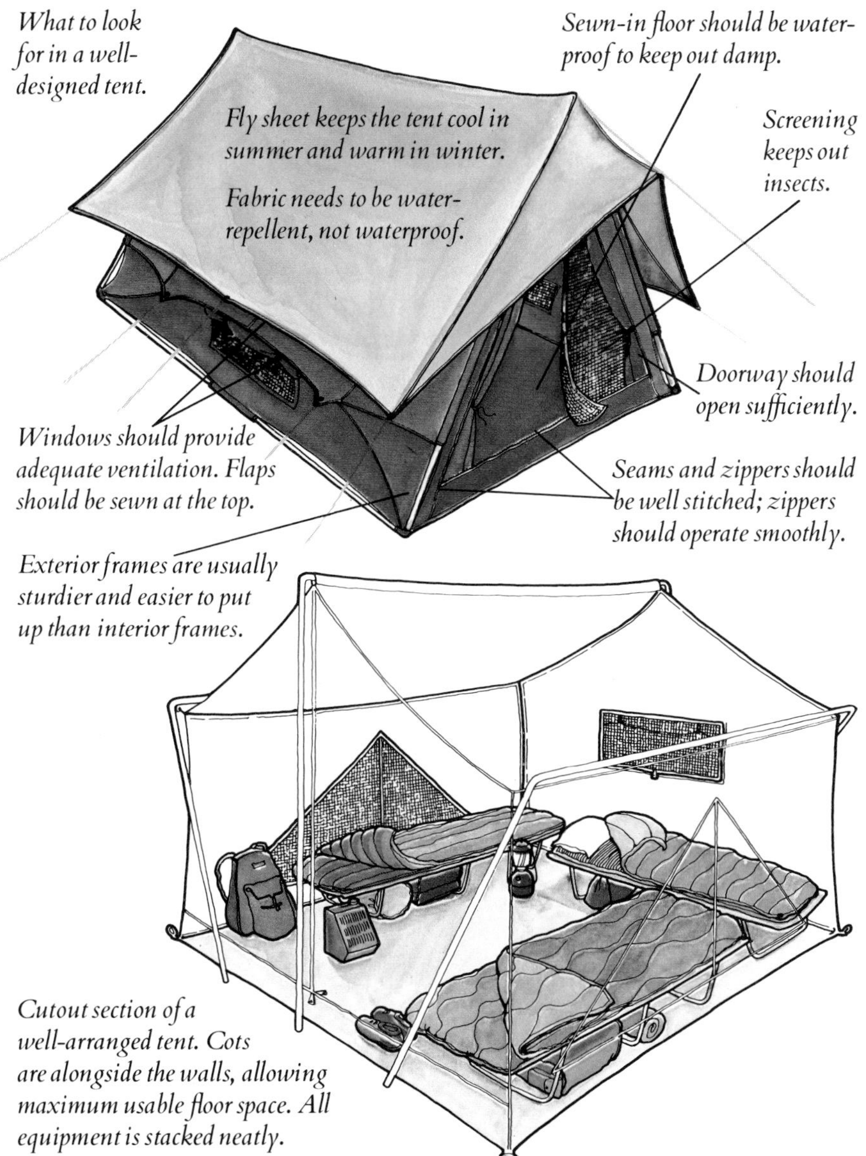

What to look for in a well-designed tent.

Cutout section of a well-arranged tent. Cots are alongside the walls, allowing maximum usable floor space. All equipment is stacked neatly.

The Tepee: A Tent With a Smoke Hole

The conical tepee traditionally used by Indians consisted of animal skins stretched over a framework of wooden poles. A typical tepee, about 20 feet high and 15 feet in diameter, weighed about 300 pounds. It consisted of a covering, an inner lining and poles. A "tepee" tent (illustration at top right, this page) is the only modern tent in which an open fire can be used safely. Smoke escapes through vents near the top. Adjustable flaps enable the vents to be closed in bad weather.

Tents and Tarpaulins

The three basic types of tents are the A-tent, umbrella tent and wall tent.

A-tents include the pup tent, explorer and lean-to. The familiar pup tent is inexpensive and just big enough for two people. It can have an extension at the rear for storing gear, a sewn-in groundsheet and screening to protect against insects. (A small A-tent can be set up without poles by tying the ends to trees.) The explorer is a large pup tent supported inside either by two poles or a T-shaped pole. It is easy to set up and take down and some models are light enough for backpacking. Suitable for winter camping, its wide door lets in plenty of heat from an outside fire. The lean-to shelter is a variation of the A-tent with an open front and a roof that slopes to the ground. It is readily warmed by a fire built in front of it.

Umbrella tents The umbrella tent, with upright walls, provides more headroom that an A-tent, but is bulkier when packed. If secured by an exterior frame, it can usually be set up by one person. Umbrella tents are made in a variety of shapes and sizes—some with awnings, several rooms and large windows. The pop-tent, a small umbrella tent, rivals the pup tent in popularity. Shaped like an igloo, it literally pops up as poles are slid into outer sleeves.

Wall tents The wall tent, which can be as large as a summer cottage, is the roomiest style of tent. It is also often heavy, bulky and difficult to set up. Its interior frame usually has to be held in place by one or more campers while another secures the guy ropes. It offers a large floor area and often has separate sleeping and living quarters. On some models the walls can be

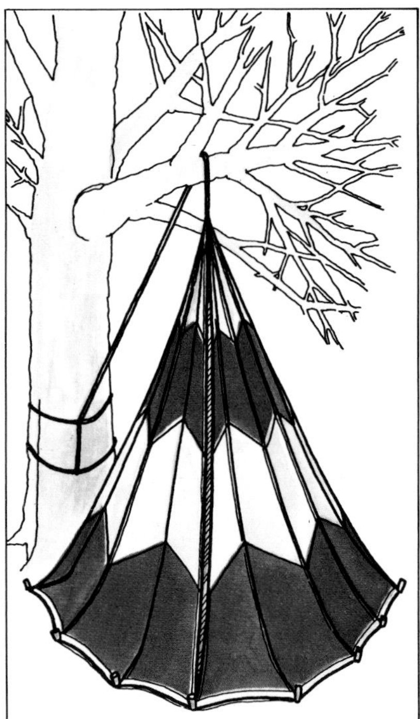

Parachute Tent

A used parachute can be turned into a roomy, rainproof "tepee." Spread the parachute on the ground. Fold it in half and fasten the middle of the folded edge to a limb about 15 feet high. Secure the bottom edge with stones or with tent pegs. Cut a vertical slit for a doorway. This tent will comfortably accommodate three persons. Its lightweight fabric folds into a compact bundle. Used parachutes are available in some camping and surplus stores.

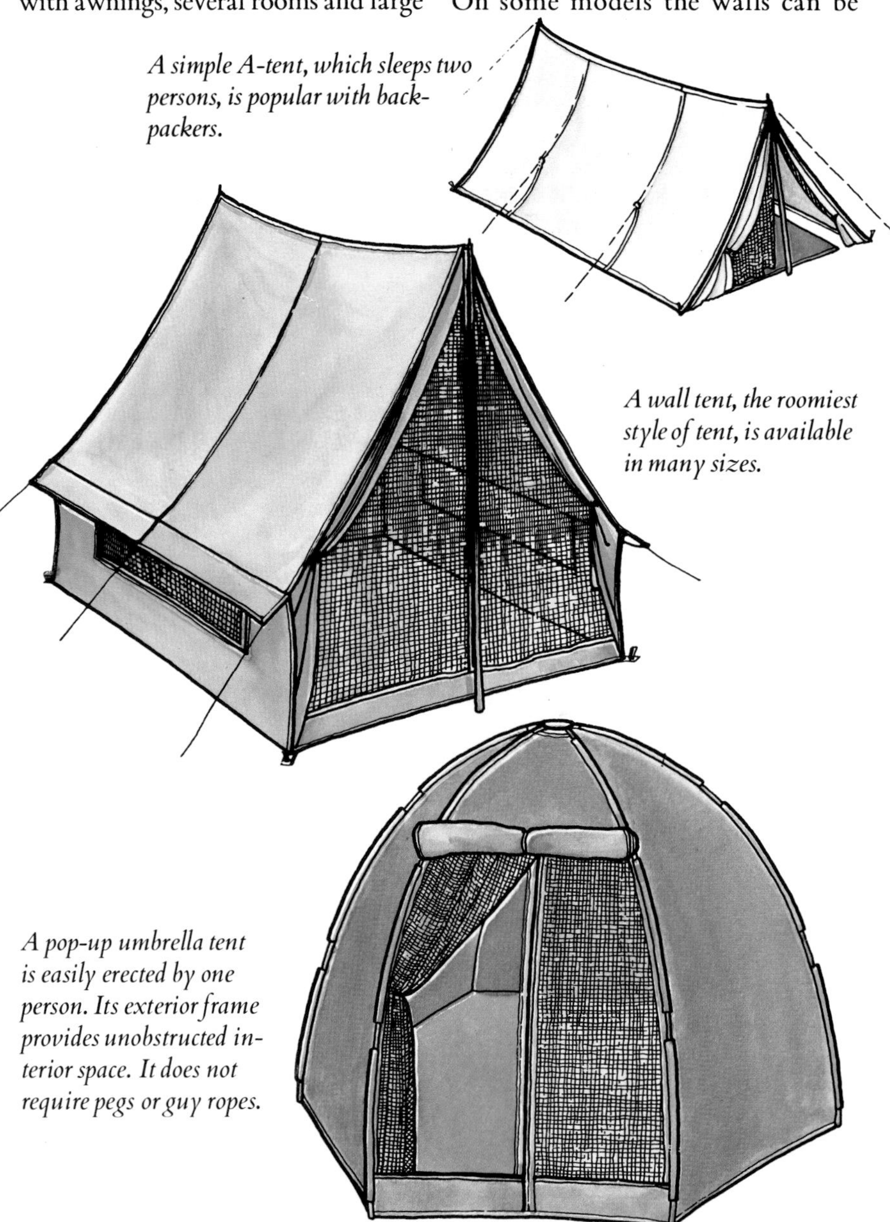

A simple A-tent, which sleeps two persons, is popular with backpackers.

A wall tent, the roomiest style of tent, is available in many sizes.

A pop-up umbrella tent is easily erected by one person. Its exterior frame provides unobstructed interior space. It does not require pegs or guy ropes.

Tarp Shelters

A tarpaulin is invaluable in camp. It can be used as a groundsheet, an awning over a dining or cooking area, a fly over a tent, a windbreak, or a lean-to shelter.

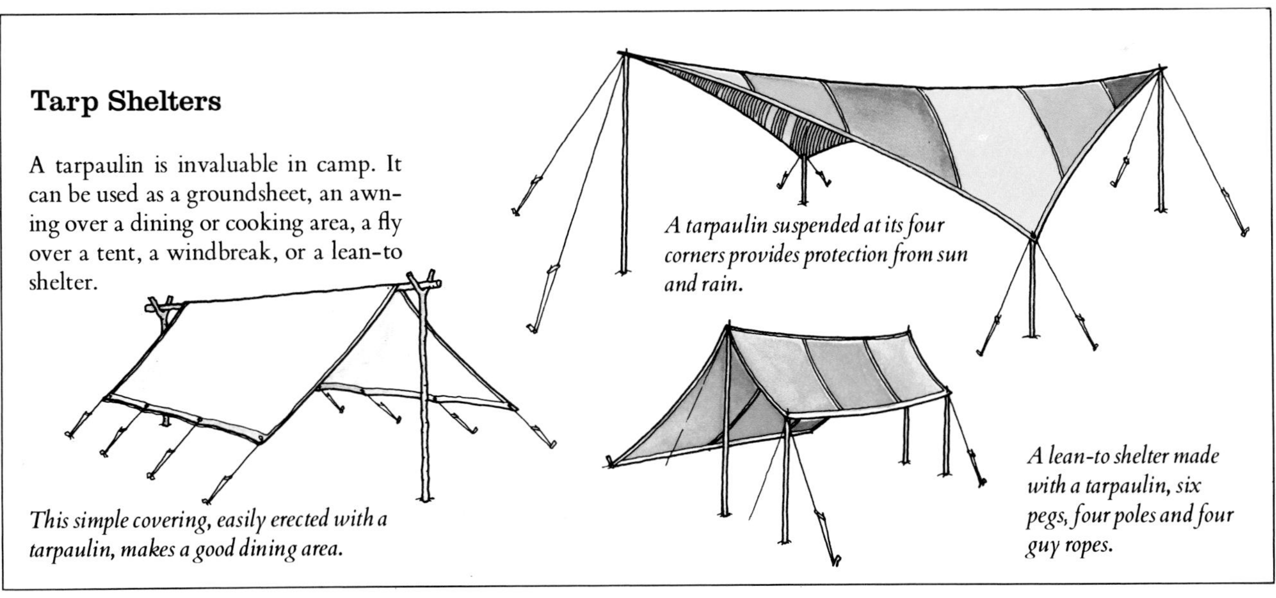

A tarpaulin suspended at its four corners provides protection from sun and rain.

This simple covering, easily erected with a tarpaulin, makes a good dining area.

A lean-to shelter made with a tarpaulin, six pegs, four poles and four guy ropes.

rolled up to improve air circulation.

Some families prefer two or more small tents rather than a large one. This choice provides privacy and plenty of room without the problems of pitching a large, cumbersome tent.

Consider the kind of weather you expect to encounter when camping. In hot weather a tent must have good ventilation; in cold weather you will get maximum benefit from a reflector fire if the front of the tent opens completely. A long tent will not heat well. A tent that is too small will be uncomfortable in a long wet spell. A tent which does not close completely can let in rain in a storm.

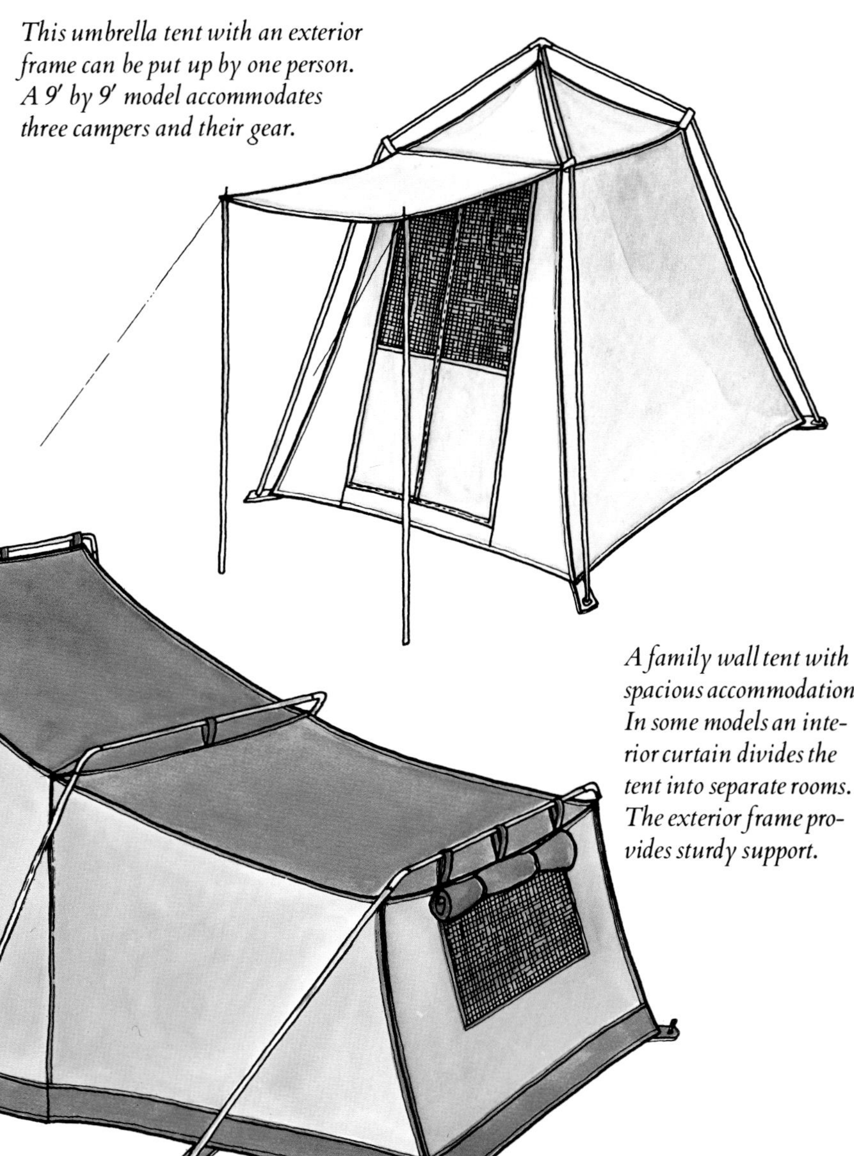

This umbrella tent with an exterior frame can be put up by one person. A 9′ by 9′ model accommodates three campers and their gear.

A family wall tent with spacious accommodation. In some models an interior curtain divides the tent into separate rooms. The exterior frame provides sturdy support.

Tent Care

To put up a tent with a sewn-in floor, first spread the tent on the ground and peg all four corners.

Next, put up a supporting pole and secure it with a guy rope.

Secure other poles, ropes and pegs.

Roll up ventilation flaps.

Proper care can add years to the life of a tent. If your tent is new, read the assembly instructions carefully. Check that all poles, ropes and pegs were included in the package, then set up the tent in your backyard or at a suitable spot in your neighborhood. Don't be dismayed if the task the maker said would take five minutes requires an hour. With practice you'll set up more quickly.

Unless it rains while the tent is up this first time, spray it thoroughly with water. Slacken guy ropes before they get wet (unless they are nylon)—shrinkage can cause them to pull up pegs or even tear the tent. The fabric will also shrink, eliminating the mist that will seep through at first.

Leave the tent up for three or four days, allowing the fabric to adjust to the tensions of the frame, pegs and guy ropes.

Make sure that seams, windows and zippers are properly sewn.

Don't repack the tent until it is dry. Roll it loosely to prevent cracking and chafing—don't fold it flat. Pack the rolled tent in a cloth bag or wrap it in a groundsheet. Pack poles and pegs in a separate bag so their sharp tips will not tear the tent.

Used tents If your tent has been used for several seasons, it is important that you set it up prior to your vacation. Spray it as with a new tent and check carefully for leaks—particularly around seams, windows and zippers. Check the fabric for tears and weak seams. Make repairs with a large needle and heavy, waxed thread. All repaired areas should be painted inside and out with a waterproofing solution. Remember that weakness in one seam could mean others will soon need repair. You may save time and trouble by having an expert resew all seams in an old tent.

Make sure zippers work smoothly. Replace broken ones and rub paraffin wax—a candle will do—on zippers that don't slide smoothly. Check also for frayed guy ropes and lost or damaged tent pegs.

At the campsite, clear the ground of stones, pebbles, twigs and other objects that could tear the tent floor or groundsheet. Air the tent daily, even on rainy days. Prop up the floor for airing if the tent remains in one spot for more than three days.

Guy ropes should be slackened every evening to avoid damage from shrinkage caused by humidity. Rugs of woven grass placed in the aisles between cots and other equipment will reduce wear on the floor. Remove muddy boots before entering the tent.

Protecting fabric In strong wind, ropes should be tightened moderately to stop billowing which can damage tent seams. Constant wind from one direction will cause some tents to lean, stretching the fabric out of shape, perhaps permanently. This can be prevented by attaching ropes from each corner of the frame to outside stakes or nearby trees.

Even exterior frames, though sturdier than interior frames, may require guy lines in strong wind. Don't take literally a manufacturer's claim that "no guy ropes are required."

Tent cleaning Remove leaves and blossoms from the tent—the sap can destroy waterproofing. Bird droppings should also be brushed off.

To plug a leak temporarily at the campsite, rub a "wax stick," which is impregnated with a waterproofing chemical, over the leaky spot—but only after the tent has dried. Never store a wet tent, or mildew will result.

Back home, pitch the tent for thorough cleaning and drying. The inside can be vacuum-cleaned and washed gently with cold water. Detergent, soap and cleaning fluid can damage the fabric and waterproofing. A dirty tent is preferable to a leaky one.

The tent should be stored in a cool dry area. An attic is usually ideal, a damp basement is not.

Patching Near Seams

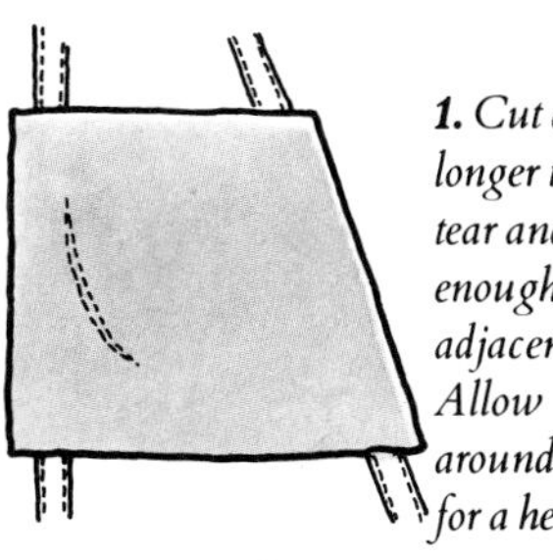

1. Cut a patch longer than the tear and wide enough to cover adjacent seams. Allow ¼" around the patch for a hem.

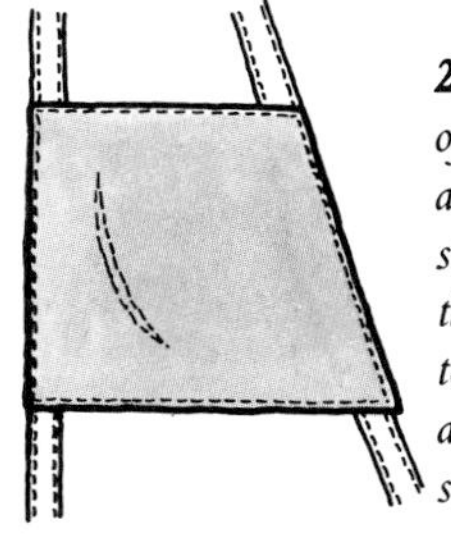

2. Fold the edges of the patch under and hem them; stitch the patch to the outside of the tent, over the tear and along the seams.

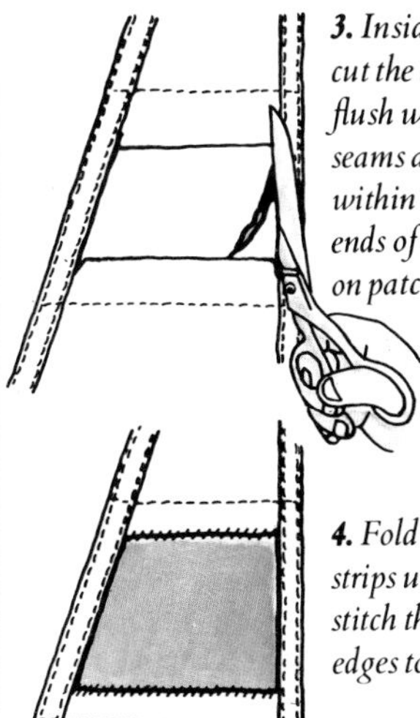

3. Inside the tent, cut the torn cloth flush with the seams and to within 1" of the ends of the sewn-on patch.

4. Fold the 1" strips under and stitch the folded edges to the patch.

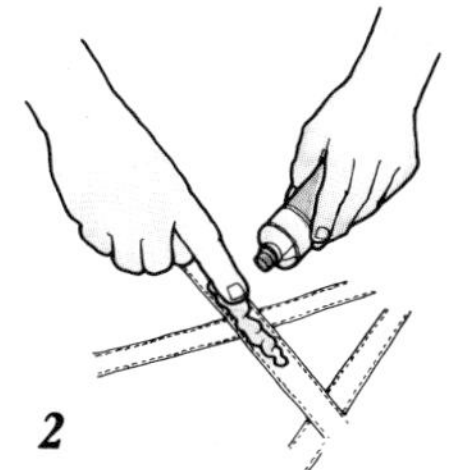

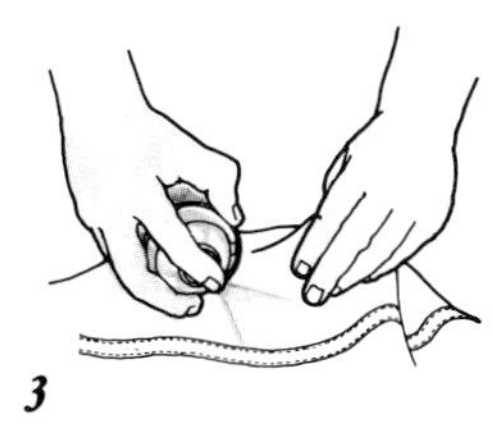

1 2 3

Waterproofing a Tent

The waterproofing in tent cloth should be renewed about every three years.

1. Lay the cloth flat and with firm strokes brush on plenty of waterproofing liquid.

2. When the liquid has dried, work wax sealer into all seams from the outside.

3. If the tent later develops leaks, spray a commercial waterproofing agent on the outside of the leaking areas. It is wise to treat seams once a year with wax sealer.

Removing Mold

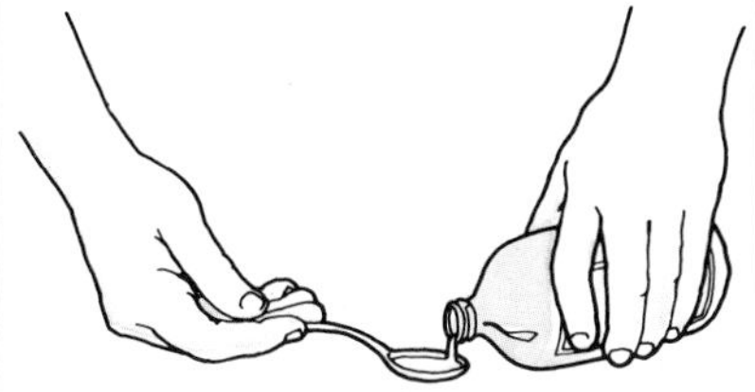

1. Mix 1 ounce of sodium hypochlorite—obtainable from most drugstores—with 20 ounces of warm water.

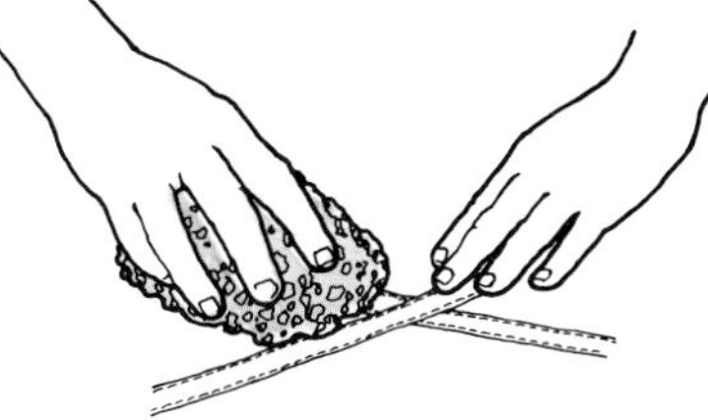

2. Sponge the solution on the moldy area. Let the treated cloth dry, then rinse it with clean water.

Mending a Tear

To make a temporary patch, cut a piece of canvas larger than the tear. Align the edges of the tear and glue the patch to the inside of the tent cloth with adhesive.

Repairing a Long Tear

1. On the inside of the tent, sew a water-repellent cloth patch over the tear.

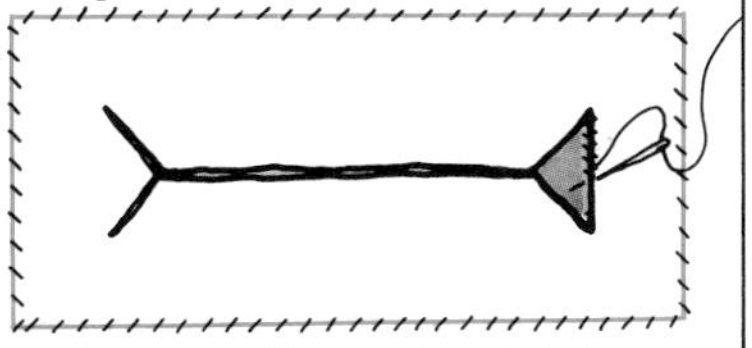

2. Cut diagonally at each end of the tear. The cuts form four flaps. Turn the flaps under and sew their folded edges to the patch.

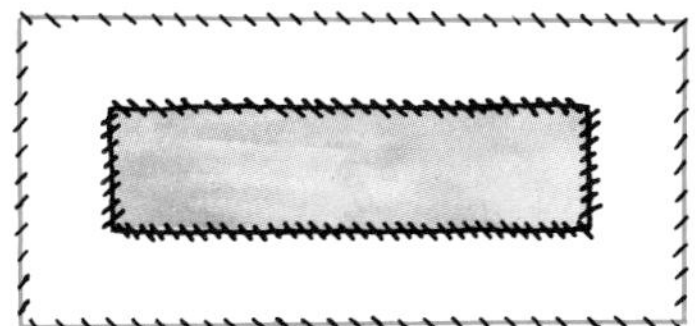

3. Wax the stitching.

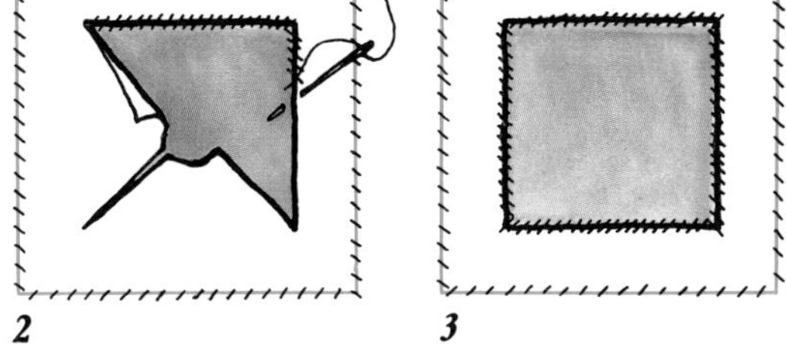

1 2 3

Repairing a Hole

1. On the inside of the tent, sew a water-repellent cloth patch over the hole. Outside, make four diagonal cuts around the hole.

2. The cuts form four flaps. Turn them under, leaving a ½" hem. Sew the folded edges to the cloth patch.

3. Wax the stitching.

Sleeping Bags, Mattresses and Cots

You will spend about a third of your camping vacation asleep. So it pays to be careful when choosing a sleeping bag and air mattress or cot.

A sleeping bag does not produce warmth; it merely helps preserve body heat. How well it does this depends on the covering, filling, lining and fastening.

The covering should be of poplin, duck, sail silk or a synthetic fabric such as nylon. It should be water-repellent but porous enough to let perspiration escape. A waterproof sleeping bag will become cold and clammy as dampness accumulates.

A well-insulated sleeping bag and a cot or air mattress make a comfortable bed. The familiar rectangular bag is available in single, double and child-size models.

Insulating materials Fillings of waterfowl down, polyester, wool, kapok or raw cotton are available. Any filling should be fluffy, to trap insulating pockets of air.

Down, the most expensive, retains the most heat in relation to its weight, but is needed only in cold weather.

Polyester, bulkier than down, is almost as effective. This moth- and mildew-proof synthetic material is used in many medium-priced bags. Unless the bag is labeled "virgin polyester fiberfill," the filling may have been used previously and have lost some of its fluffiness.

Wool costs less and works well but it is heavy and liable to shrink. It also retains odors.

Kapok and cotton, the cheapest fillings, are adequate for warm nights. Both tend to become lumpy and badly distributed. Some canoeists favor kapok-filled bags because they float and can be used as emergency life jackets.

Quilting prevents the filling from shifting, but stitches should be sewn loosely. Tight seams contain few air spaces and little filling so cold spots occur along them. A removable lining of cotton or synthetic fabric simplifies the task of airing and cleaning the bag. Ties or snap fasteners hold the lining to permit easy body movement inside. A lining can be made from a sheet: fold it in half and cut it to fit the inside of the bag. Attach ties or snap fasteners about 12 inches apart along the bottom and the open edge.

Brass, aluminum or nylon zippers provide secure fastening. Those that run down one side and across the bottom enable a bag to be opened for airing. The zipper should be easy to operate from inside and outside. Flaps on both sides of the zipper help prevent heat loss and snagging.

Sizes and styles A sleeping bag should be about 10 inches longer than you are, and wide enough for comfort and adequate air circulation. (Manufacturers' dimensions usually do not allow for length lost when hems and seams are sewn.)

The familiar, rectangular bag is available in a double model. Some single models can be zipped together to make a double bag.

The mummy bag has a fitted hood and is trimmed to body shape. With drawstrings tightened, only the sleeper's face is exposed. Intended for cold-weather camping, it is often filled with down and therefore expensive. Though snug, the mummy bag tends to turn with the sleeper—this can be disturbing until you acquire the trick of maneuvering inside.

Most types of sleeping bags are available in children's sizes.

You should air your sleeping bag daily. Before you go to bed, shake the bag to spread the filling evenly and to fluff up the material.

A label on most bags indicates whether they should be hand-washed, machine-washed or dry-cleaned. Air a bag thoroughly after it has been dry-cleaned—some cleaning solvents produce noxious fumes that can become trapped inside.

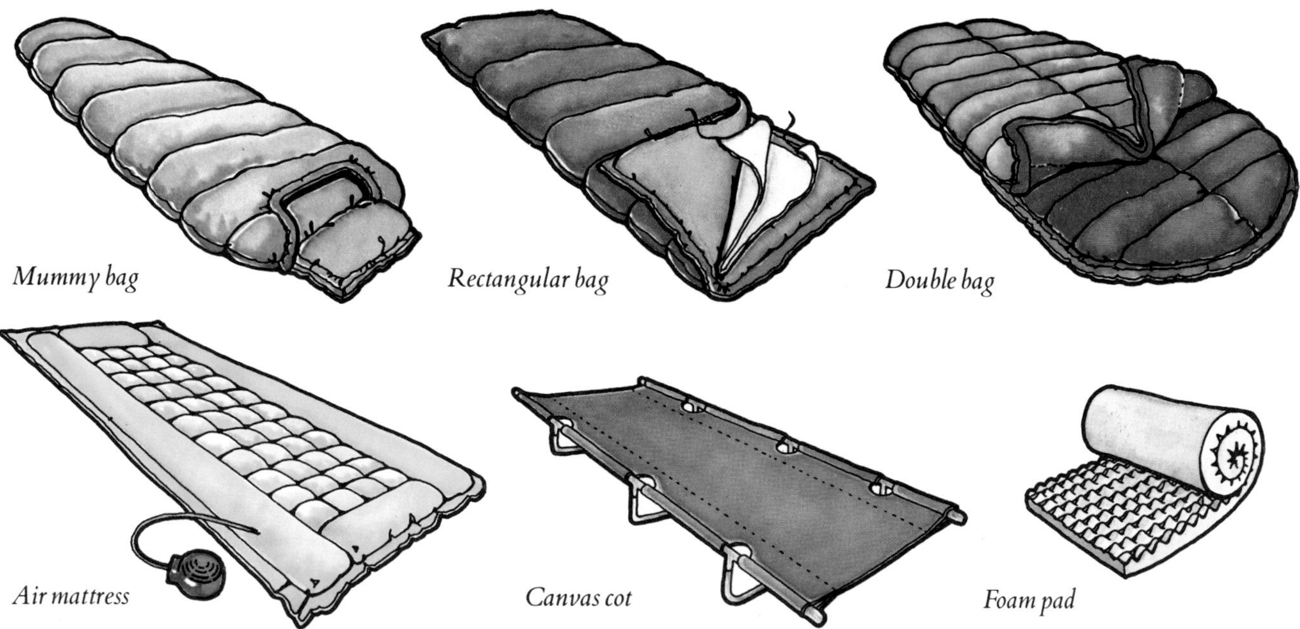

When storing a bag, hang it fully opened or roll it loosely. Rolling it tightly will crush the filling and make the bag more susceptible to mildew.

Groundsheets A good waterproof groundsheet gives added protection against cold and damp, discourages insects and helps to keep the sleeping bag clean. Check the ground for stones, twigs and bumps before spreading the groundsheet.

For a soft, comfortable base, lay several folded blankets on top of a groundsheet or use an air mattress, foam pad or camp cot.

Making a Blanket Bag

A fair-weather sleeping bag can be improvised with two blankets.

Air mattresses An air mattress should be tough and waterproof, preferably of rubberized canvas. The tubular or quilted type will help prevent you from rolling off.

A puncture repair kit is a must, and a hand- or foot-operated pump will ease the chore of inflating the mattress. Electric pumps powered by a car's cigarette lighter outlet are available. Beware of pumps made of inferior plastic—rubber or metal ones are worth the extra cost.

Check the softness or firmness of an inflated mattress by lying on it. Pressing on the center with a fist applies too much pressure over too small an area.

Foam pads and cots A foam pad, lighter and less springy than an air mattress, does not need to be inflated. Since a pad is as large as a sleeping bag, you cannot roll it into a small package as you can a deflated air mattress.

If you use a canvas camp cot you need extra insulation underneath your sleeping bag because cold air circulates under the bed. Some folding camp beds have sewn-in insulation. If yours doesn't, put a couple of blankets beneath your sleeping bag.

Wooden camp beds are the cheapest, but those with steel or aluminum frames are lighter and more stable.

Heaters, Lanterns and Coolers

The comfort and convenience provided by portable heaters, lanterns and coolers make these appliances indispensable to many campers. A tent heater keeps campers comfortable in the chilly days of spring and fall although it may not be needed in summer. A lantern provides warmth as well as light. An inexpensive ice chest enables food to be stored for several days and can be a help in planning nutritious meals.

To avoid the expense and bother of buying and storing different fuels, carry a heater and lantern that burn the same fuel as your stove. With bottled-gas equipment, several units can usually be connected simultaneously to the same fuel container. If a single tank will meet all your needs, you can save by buying fuel in bulk. With only one fuel in camp, you will avoid using the wrong fuel in an appliance. Some heaters will function only with catalytic fuel marketed by the manufacturer of the appliances.

Heaters Catalytic heaters, fueled by vaporized white gasoline, naphtha or propane, absorb fuel in a porous wick and have no open flame. If tipped over, they are unlikely to spill fuel. Catalytic heaters need to be primed—usually with alcohol—and take about 15 minutes to heat up.

An infrared radiant heater, which usually burns propane, produces its maximum warmth in 15 seconds but beams heat only over a narrow area. Parts of the tent not in front of the beam will be warmed slowly, if at all.

A naphtha or alcohol space heater diffuses its warmth in a tent or trailer better than a radiant heater does. Temperature is usually controlled by raising and lowering a wick.

For the camper concerned about fumes, a wood-burning stove may be the answer—but it will need a stovepipe and can be awkward to set up.

Lanterns Bottled-gas lanterns are lightweight and compact, but expensive to operate if disposable containers are used—refillable containers are considerably more economical. Propane lanterns give less light as the gas cylinder empties. Similarly, they are dimmer in cold weather because the gas contracts, reducing the pressure in the cylinder.

Low temperatures have no effect on gasoline- and kerosene-fueled lanterns but these appliances need frequent pumping to maintain pressure in their fuel tanks. Also, the generator of a kerosene lantern must be preheated, usually with alcohol. Some models can be preheated with kerosene but require even more pumping. Vaporized fuel is burned in a small fabric-mesh pouch called a mantle. The mantle, which turns to fragile ash when first used, is easily broken if the lantern is handled roughly.

Never hang lanterns or heaters near a canvas roof or wall. They are safest on a fireproof surface away from combustible material. Check your lantern frequently for leaks and polish it to prevent rust.

For safety and economy, use your fuel-burning lanterns sparingly—a flashlight is safer and often adequate. Remember that heaters and lanterns gulp oxygen, so use them only in a well-ventilated tent. Don't leave a heater or lantern lit all night. Ventilation is particularly important in wet weather. Rain will shrink tent fabric and restrict the normal flow of air.

Take spare batteries, bulbs, mantles and a lantern globe on vacation. Carry an adequate supply of fuel.

Fluorescent lights for camping can be battery operated or plugged into a car's cigarette lighter. An emergency power source can be provided by attaching wires with spring clips to the

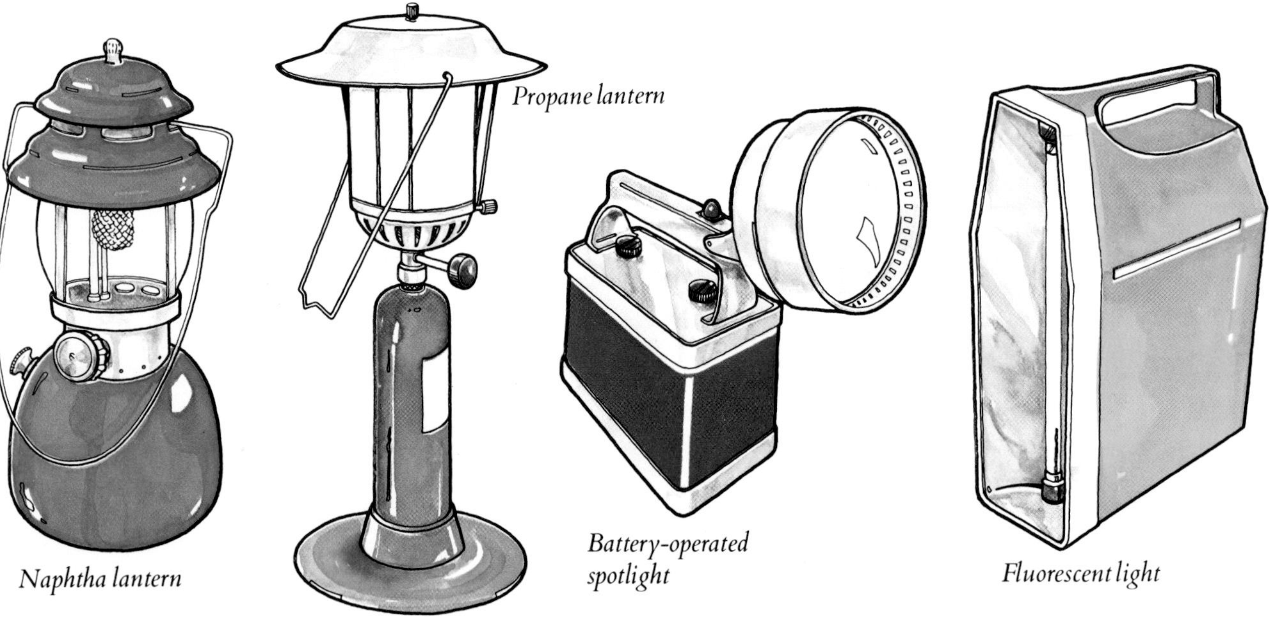

Naphtha lantern

Propane lantern

Battery-operated spotlight

Fluorescent light

A lantern provides light and heat. It can warm a tent sufficiently on all but the chilliest summer nights. When using a lantern in a tent, make sure the tent is well ventilated.

Catalytic heater, fueled by propane

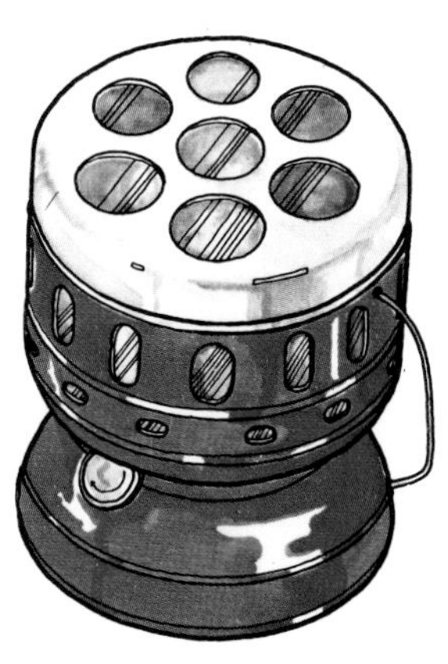

Naphtha-burning catalytic heater

Infrared radiant heater—it warms up quickly

battery of a car or recreational vehicle.

A standard flashlight with two size "D" batteries is sufficient for most campers. A model with the bulb set at right angles to the handle will direct a horizontal beam when set upright on a flat surface or clipped to a belt. Waterproof and shockproof models are available.

A boxlike lamp with a spotlight is powerful and compact. Its far-reaching beam can be a nuisance to other campers if not used with care.

Alkaline or manganese batteries are expensive but last up to 10 times as long as the carbon-zinc type. Before storing a flashlight at the end of the camping season, remove its batteries; they could leak, causing corrosion. A strip of tape over a flashlight switch can prevent its being turned on accidentally, draining the batteries.

Coolers A variety of coolers is available and most will keep food fresh for at least 24 hours. Airtight styrofoam boxes are inexpensive and lightweight but easily chipped or cracked. If your budget allows, choose a cooler with a drain cock, sturdy side handles, rounded corners and a metal shelf that rests above the ice. Even expensive metal coolers eventually rust. Fiberglass is more durable.

Dry ice or ice in closed containers such as milk cartons makes a cooler easy to keep clean and dry. You will need gloves for handling dry ice—it is so cold it can damage the skin.

For best results from a cooler, always replace ice before it melts completely. Pack the fastest-spoiling foods in the bottom of the cooler, keep it away from heat and open it as seldom as possible. After meals, let cooked leftovers cool before putting them in the cooler.

Heaters, lanterns, flashlights and coolers need not be expensive to be effective. Equipment that is chosen carefully and maintained properly can provide some of the comforts of home through many summers of camping.

Clothing and Personal Gear

Whether tenting, backpacking, bird-watching, picnicking or mountain climbing, you should wear comfortable, durable and lightweight clothing. It should keep you dry in the rain, cool in the heat and warm in the cold. It should protect you from sunburn, windburn, insects, prickly underbrush, rocky terrain.

Perspiration and blood circulation help your body maintain its normal temperature. Proper clothing can assist those natural functions so that you stay comfortable and conserve energy—even in extreme weather.

Fabrics and colors Natural fabrics such as wool and cotton absorb moisture and permit air to circulate more effectively than do nylon, rayon and other synthetics. However, most synthetic fabrics resist wind better and wear better than wool and cotton. It makes good sense to wear natural fabrics next to your skin and synthetic outer garments. If wool irritates your skin, wear thin cotton clothing under woolens.

Light, loose-fitting clothes protect you from sunburn and allow circulating air to carry away excess body heat. Light-colored clothes reflect heat so are cooler than dark-colored, heat-absorbent clothes.

However, for bird-watching or photographing wildlife, fabrics in dark greens and browns will help camouflage you. Wear a fluorescent orange or yellow jacket when in the woods during a hunting season. Fluorescent colors warn hunters of your presence but do not seem to disturb most wildlife.

In cold weather, several layers of lightweight clothing will keep you warmer than a single, heavy garment. Air trapped between the layers helps retain body heat but there is enough circulation to evaporate perspiration. As the temperature or your level of activity changes, remove an article of clothing when you become hot or add one when you become cold.

Cold-weather campers need warm mitts or gloves. Thin, silk inner gloves will keep your hands warm for a short time when you remove your mitts to light a fire or take a photograph.

Long pants, preferably without cuffs, protect your legs from sunburn, scratches, insects and poison ivy. Cuffs catch dirt and sand and can trip you if they snag on rocks or branches.

Wise campers carry some kind of headgear even if only a baseball cap or toque that can be rolled up and tucked in a pack or pocket. A felt hat with a wide brim and a high crown provides good protection from sun, rain and wind—although it can be cumbersome in the woods. A large scarf or bandanna can serve as a hat, handkerchief, pot holder, towel, washcloth and carrying bag.

Pajamas are all you need to wear in a sleeping bag in warm weather—but on cool nights add socks and a warm hat or wear a hooded sweat suit.

Rainwear and boots The poncho, a popular type of camping rainwear, is a waterproof sheet with a hood in the middle, snap fasteners along the edges, and grommets at each corner. If the wearer sits with knees drawn up, it can cover him completely. It can be used as a groundsheet, a temporary shelter or a pack. Ponchos of waterproof nylon or heavy, rubberized fabric are more durable than plastic ones.

Soft, low-cut shoes or sneakers may be fine on city streets and country roads but they have no place in the woods. Your feet need the protection and support of sturdy, comfortable boots.

Leather is an excellent boot material. It is pliable and durable, and can be made water-resistant with neat's-foot oil or silicone dressing. Boots should have rubber or composition soles and heels, both with molded treads. Leather soles and heels are not waterproof and are slippery on most surfaces. Leather boots will give long service if kept clean, dry and well oiled. They should be dried slowly. Wet boots left too near a fire or heater will shrink, harden and crack.

Insulated rubber boots are warm and waterproof, but are less durable and provide less support than leather boots. Leather-topped rubber boots, commonly worn by lumberjacks, are practical in winter. Unlike leather,

When in the woods during a hunting season, wear a fluorescent red or yellow jacket to warn hunters of your presence. These bright colors do not seem to disturb wildlife.

A basic first-aid kit contains adhesive tape and bandages, gauze, antiseptic, sunburn ointment, headache tablets and first-aid instructions.

rubber is not porous so your feet will become hot and sweaty when you wear rubber boots in summer. If you do wear rubber boots in hot weather, lace them loosely.

Boots should fit snugly—never tightly—over two pairs of woolen socks. Woolen socks cushion your feet, allow air to circulate and are warm and comfortable even when wet. Tight boots hamper blood circulation to the feet and eliminate the air spaces that provide insulation. Boots are too tight if you can't wiggle your toes freely in them.

Personal gear The kind and amount of personal gear you take on an outdoors trip should depend on how you plan to travel and what you plan to do. Whether traveling by car or on foot, you are wise to travel light.

For most camping trips, take these essential items: medical, tool and sewing kits, ax, sheath knife, whetstone, waterproof matches, insect repellent, canteen, flashlight with spare batteries and bulbs, candles, emergency fishing tackle and compass.

Each camper should also take a towel, metal mirror, toothbrush and toothpaste and soap. You may also wish to take shaving equipment or makeup, and writing materials.

When insects are especially bothersome, head nets or cheesecloth give surer protection than insect repellent or smudge fires.

A great variety of portable equipment is available for your comfort, convenience and recreation. But before you pack tables and chairs, collapsible water jugs, a portable toilet or a television set, ask yourself whether you really need all the comforts of home. Experience is probably the surest guide to the clothing and personal gear that is best for you. Inexperienced campers who take more than they need often spend their time packing, unpacking, setting up and taking down equipment—when they would rather be fishing, swimming or relaxing.

Useful tools and repair equipment are pliers, a screwdriver, a file, a small folding saw, oil, copper wire, rubber bands, nails, safety pins, plastic tape and quick-drying waterproof glue.

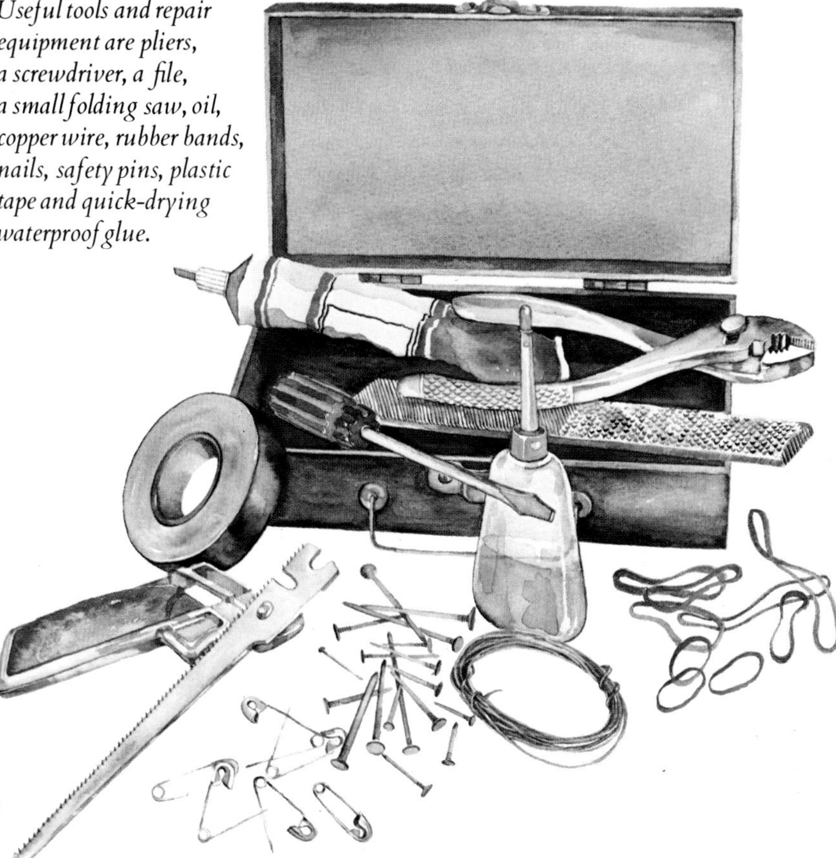

Camping Gear You Can Make

Most of the camping gear you will ever need—from tent pegs to a fully equipped travel trailer—can be made at home. Ambitious projects such as homemade trailers and tents require considerable time, expense and skill. Plans for these can be obtained from camping and handyman publications. But the projects described here can be completed by most persons in an evening.

Cooler

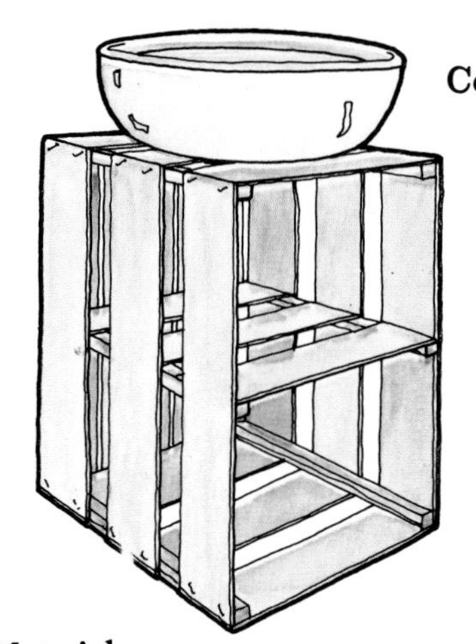

Materials

- Wooden box, such as an orange crate, with one or more partitions
- Burlap sack
- Shallow pan or bowl

Instructions

Place the box on end.

Fill the pan or bowl with water and place it on top of the crate.

Cover the pan and crate with the sack. Put a stone on top to hold the material in the water. The water will gradually wet most of the sack and evaporation will keep the food cool. Hang the cooler in the shade and out of the reach of animals. Keep the pan filled with water so that the burlap sack never dries out.

Canvas Bag

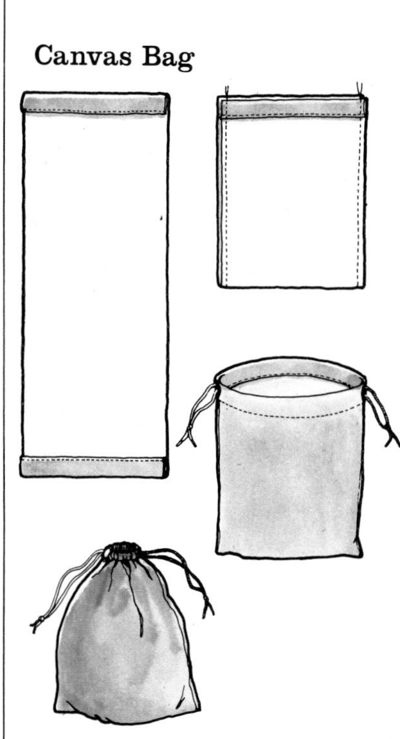

Materials

- Canvas, a bed sheet or a strong cotton or synthetic fabric of suitable size
- Thin rope or heavy cotton cord
- Needle and thread

Instructions

Cut a piece of material about 1″ wider than you want the bag to be—and twice as long.

Hem each end wide enough for a cord to pass through.

Fold the material end to end and sew the sides.

Turn it inside out to hide seams.

Thread the cord through the hems and knot the ends of the cord.

Water Bag

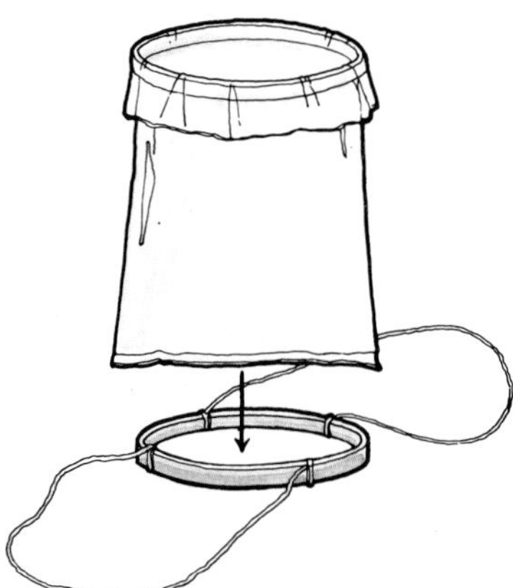

Materials

- Two 10″ by 14″ plastic bags
- One set of 7″ diameter embroidery hoops (a set includes an outer hoop and a smaller inner hoop)
- Two 24″ lengths of heavy twine
- Beeswax

Instructions

Wax both embroidery hoops to make them waterproof.

Wax the twine.

Place one bag inside the other.

Draw their open ends through the center of the larger hoop and stretch the edges carefully over the hoop so that about three inches of plastic overhang.

Make handles by tying the twine to the smaller hoop at four points.

Slide the smaller hoop over the bottom of the bags and over the overhanging plastic until the two hoops meet.

Collapsible basins, without handles, can be made with larger hoops and shorter bags.

Reflector Oven

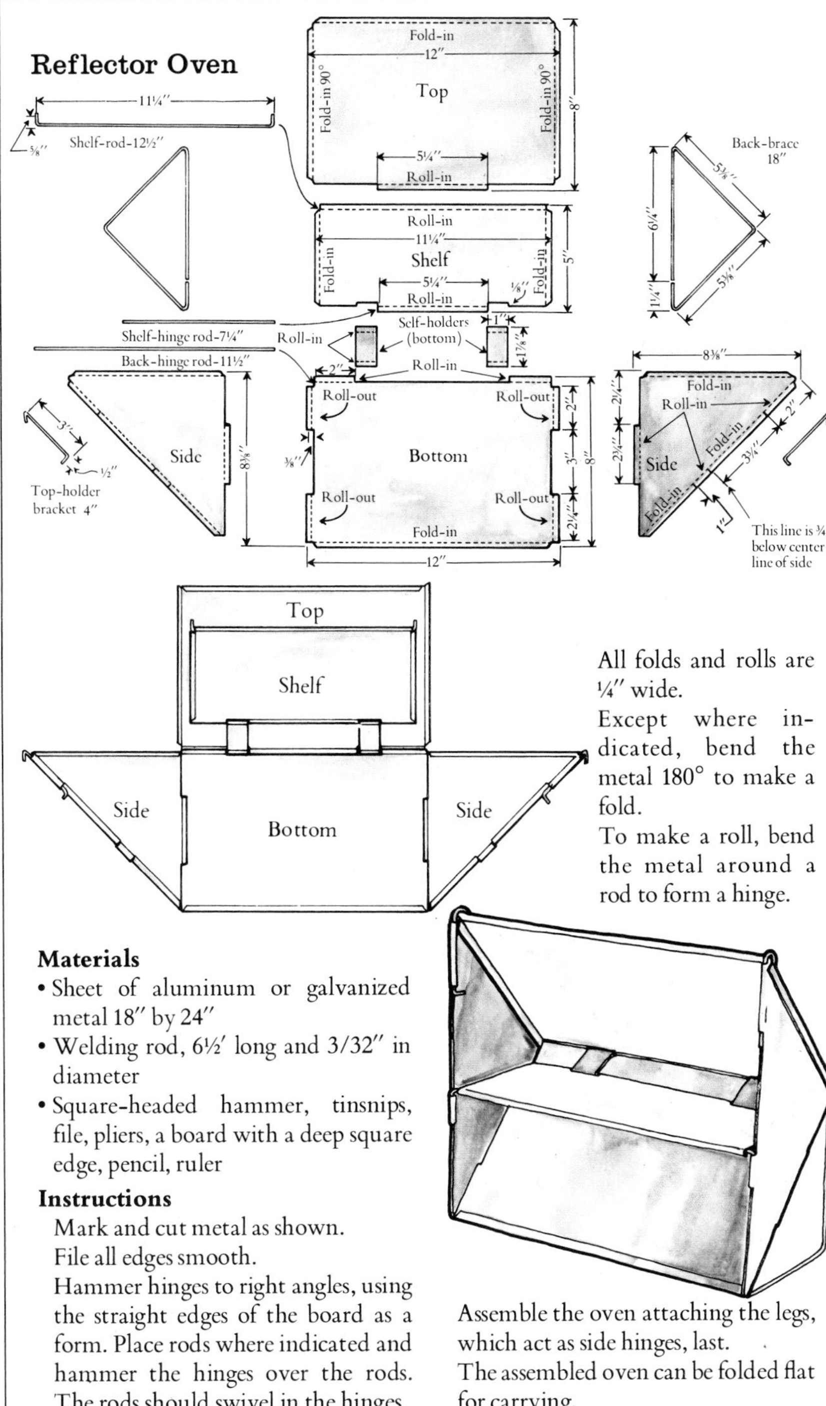

All folds and rolls are ¼″ wide.

Except where indicated, bend the metal 180° to make a fold.

To make a roll, bend the metal around a rod to form a hinge.

Materials

- Sheet of aluminum or galvanized metal 18″ by 24″
- Welding rod, 6½′ long and 3/32″ in diameter
- Square-headed hammer, tinsnips, file, pliers, a board with a deep square edge, pencil, ruler

Instructions

Mark and cut metal as shown.

File all edges smooth.

Hammer hinges to right angles, using the straight edges of the board as a form. Place rods where indicated and hammer the hinges over the rods. The rods should swivel in the hinges.

Assemble the oven attaching the legs, which act as side hinges, last.

The assembled oven can be folded flat for carrying.

Tent Pegs

Use a 10″ length of hardwood, angle iron or aluminum corner molding for each peg. With a knife, saw or file, cut each peg to a point. At the other end, cut a notch. A wooden peg should be notched 2″ from the end. A metal peg can be notched about 1″ from the end. File all edges smooth.

Tin Can Stove

Materials

- One-gallon can
- Short salmon tin
- 6′ strip of corrugated cardboard, as wide as the salmon tin is deep
- Two cakes of paraffin wax
- Tinsnips and a can opener

Instructions

Cut out one end of the one-gallon can with a can opener.

On the side and at the same end, cut an opening slightly larger than the salmon tin.

Punch two smoke holes near the sealed end of the large can.

Cut one end out of the small salmon tin.

To make the fuel cartridge, roll the corrugated cardboard and fit it snugly into the salmon tin. Trim the cardboard flush with the top of the tin.

Melt the wax in a double boiler.

Carefully fill the salmon tin with hot wax and wait until the cardboard has soaked up much of it. Then refill the tin to the top and leave it to cool.

To use the stove, set the open end of the large can on the ground, light the fuel cartridge and slide it under the large can. The wax and cardboard fuel will burn for about 90 minutes.

Axes and Knives

Axes are made in hundreds of shapes, weights and lengths. A popular choice among campers is a light-to-medium-weight poleax with a 2½-to-3-pound head and a 24-to-30-inch handle. The tapered head is good for chopping down dead trees and for splitting firewood. The flat butt, or pole, can be used as a hammer.

Types of axes Although some outdoorsmen carry a large poleax even when backpacking, smaller, lighter axes are available. A hatchet, the smallest kind of ax, has a 1-to-1½-pound head and a 12-to-16-inch handle. A hatchet is easy to carry and pack but difficult to use safely and effectively. The short handle can be grasped with one hand but the axman usually must kneel at his work. A one-handed grasp sacrifices control and a kneeling position endangers the axman's knees and free hand. Because of its lightweight head, a hatchet is suitable only for chores such as pounding in tent pegs and chopping wood for kindling.

If neither a hatchet nor a full-size poleax suits you, consider a hunter's or woodsman's ax—both are shaped like a poleax—or a Hudson Bay ax. Hunter's and woodsman's axes have 1½-to-2¼-pound heads and 14-to-28-inch handles. The Hudson Bay ax usually has a 24-inch handle and a wide cutting edge that tapers sharply to lessen weight. The head weighs about 1¾ pounds.

Large double-bit axes, with two cutting edges and heads weighing up to 5 pounds, are preferred by lumberjacks and loggers. Considerable strength and skill are required to wield them properly and safely. They do not belong on camping trips.

Most ax handles are made of straight-grained hickory, ash or birch. For maximum strength the grain should run the length of the handle and be free of knots and other imperfections of the grain.

Types of knives A jackknife with a 3½-inch folding blade, or a sheath knife with a 4-to-5-inch blade, is as useful as an ax around camp. Both knives are suitable for preparing food, cutting rope and whittling. Sheath knives, generally heftier than jackknives, are well suited for heavy carving or cutting. Some jackknives are versatile tool kits—complete with blades, can and bottle openers, corkscrew, screwdriver, leather punch, even scissors.

Choose carbon tool steel for a general-purpose knife, stainless steel for one to be used near salt water.

The Parts of an Ax

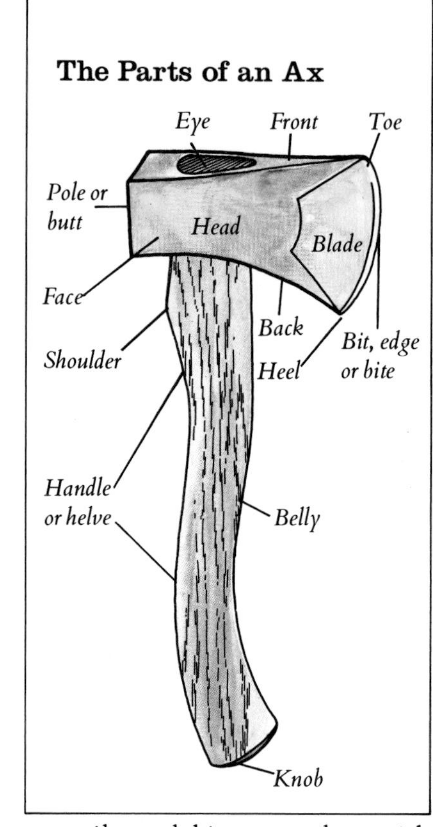

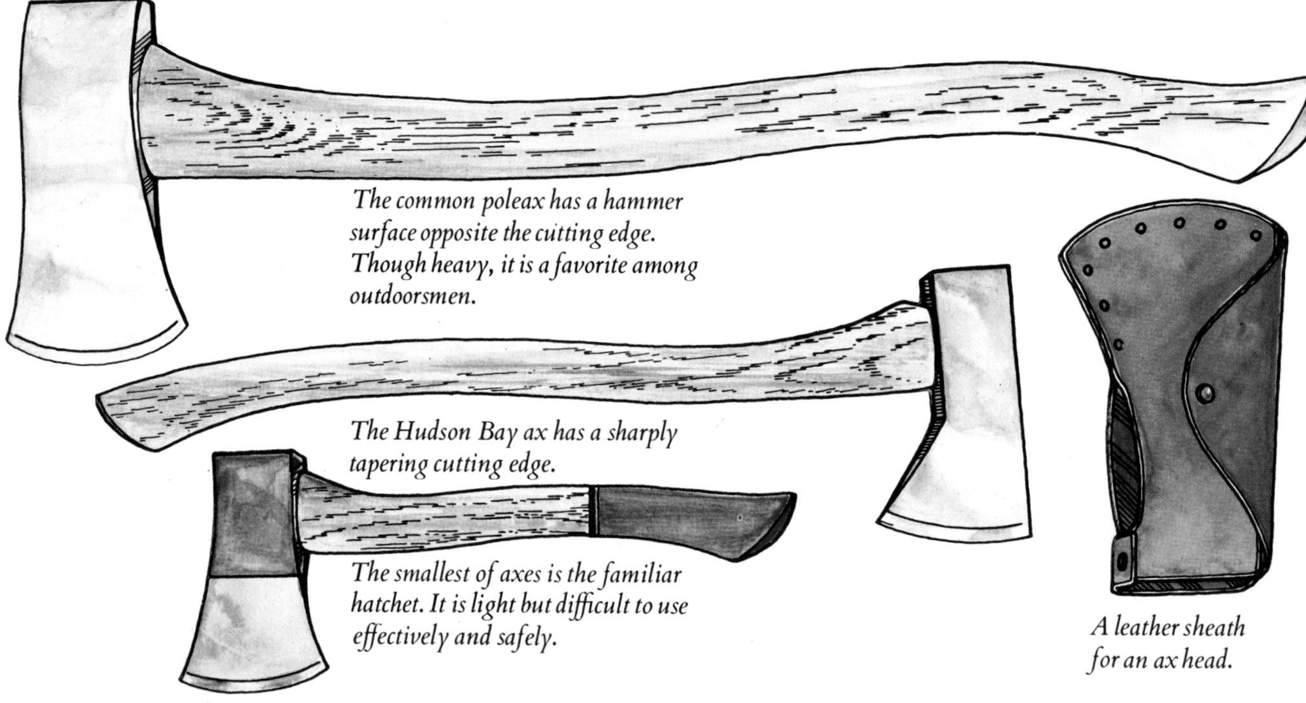

The common poleax has a hammer surface opposite the cutting edge. Though heavy, it is a favorite among outdoorsmen.

The Hudson Bay ax has a sharply tapering cutting edge.

The smallest of axes is the familiar hatchet. It is light but difficult to use effectively and safely.

A leather sheath for an ax head.

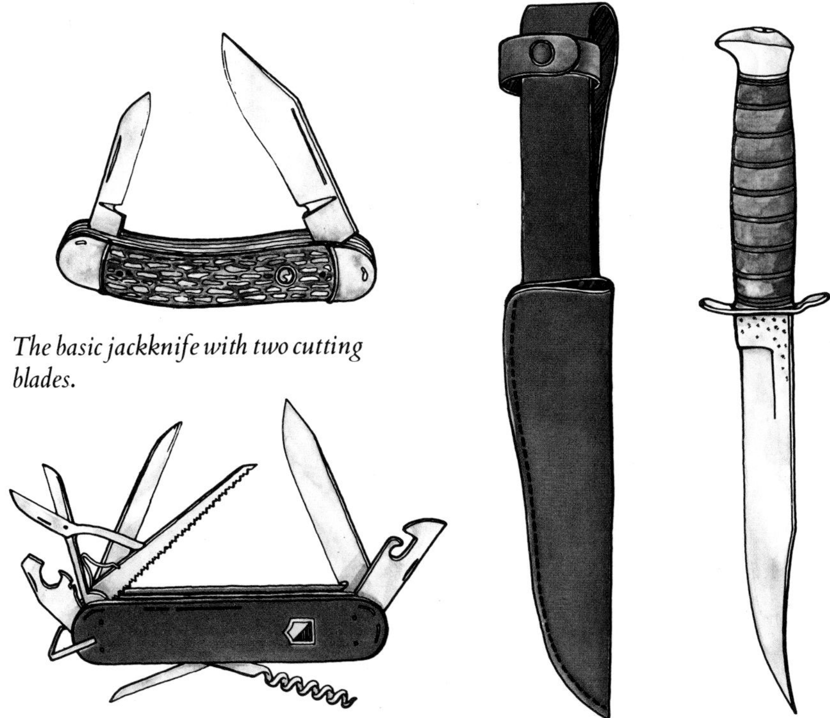

The basic jackknife with two cutting blades.

A jackknife with a strong cutting blade and a variety of tools.

A sheath and knife—easy to carry and a handy tool for the camper.

Safety and maintenance A blade should be hard enough to hold an edge but not so hard that it is difficult to sharpen or so brittle that it is easily nicked or broken.

A sharp ax or knife is safer than a dull one. A blunt ax will glance off wood instead of biting cleanly into it. A dull knife will slip uncontrollably instead of cutting keenly.

Never use an ax that has a loose handle. Check periodically that the handle fits securely into the ax head. Repair a loose handle by hammering a wooden or metal wedge into the eye of the handle.

To avoid accidents and to prevent dulling or nicking a cutting edge, never put an ax or a knife on the ground. Don't leave it embedded in a log or stump or put it into a fire. Never use an ax or the blade of a knife as a screwdriver or can opener. Keep axes and knives out of the reach of children at all times.

When an ax or a knife is not in use, its proper place is in a sheath. A jackknife should be folded and tucked in a pocket or pack. A sheathed knife carried on a belt should be worn over a hip pocket where it is less likely to stab the wearer if he falls.

Knives and axes should be kept clean, dry and lightly oiled to protect them from rust. A brightly colored handle can be a help in finding a mislaid knife.

A broken ax handle can be inexpensively and easily replaced. A knife with a broken handle is a danger and should be discarded.

If chosen carefully, used correctly and maintained properly, good quality axes and knives can make light work of many camp chores—and last through many years of hard use.

How to Sharpen Your Ax and Knife

Most new axes and knives need to be sharpened before being used. Follow these steps in sharpening a new ax or knife or one with a nicked or otherwise damaged edge. (If your ax or knife is dull but the cutting edge is in good shape, follow steps 3 to 5.)

1. Roughly shape the bevel or sharpened edge with a flat or mill file or with a hand grindstone. A power grindstone is likely to overheat the edge and destroy its temper. Extend the bevel back about ⅛″. If thinned too far, the edge will be nicked easily. If left too rounded it will be dull.

2. Moisten the coarse side of a whetstone with water or oil. Place the stone on the blade at a 20-degree angle, with the cutting edge of the blade facing away from you. Push the stone away from you with a curving motion so all, or most, of the edge touches the stone. Then turn the blade over and push the stone across it with the same curving motion and at the same 20-degree angle. Continue stroking one side of the blade then the other until the cutting edge is sharp. Keep the stone wet to avoid overheating the edge of the blade by friction.

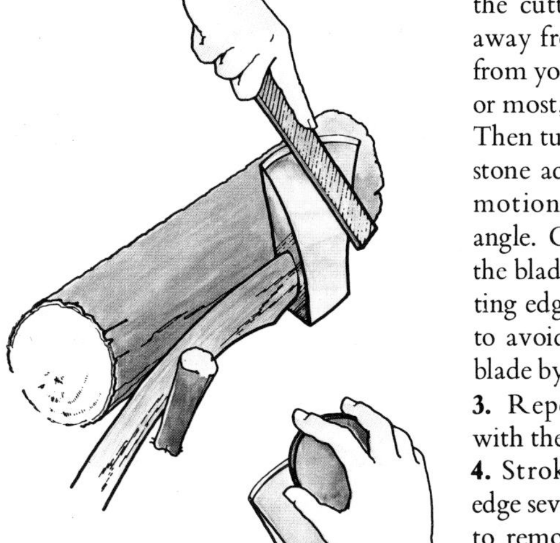

3. Repeat the stroking procedure with the fine side of the whetstone.

4. Stroke both sides of the cutting edge several times on a piece of leather to remove any roughness left by the stone.

5. Test the ax or knife for sharpness. It should easily slit a piece of loosely held paper without tearing it.

Axmanship

An ax can be a dangerous weapon. It will always be so in the hands of a careless person, however experienced, but it need not be so in the hands of an unskilled person determined to be a good axman. He can avoid serious accidents and injuries by having proper equipment and by using commonsense rules. Soon he will be both careful and experienced.

Most novice axmen use brute force at the risk of tiring themselves, losing control of the ax or breaking its handle. The skilled axman has a relaxed, rhythmic swing. His back, shoulders and legs provide power. He lets the momentum and angle of his swing, the weight of the ax head and the sharpness of its cutting edge do most of the work for him. He rests when necessary, knowing that an ax blow is ineffective and often dangerous when he is too tired to direct it accurately. By bending his knees and back with a downward ax stroke, the axman causes the ax head to drop straight instead of in an arc—virtually eliminating the danger of the ax swinging into his feet or shins.

Safety An ax head becomes a missile if it flies off the handle, so no axman worthy of the name wields an ax with a loose handle. Check your ax before using it. If the handle is loose, replace or hammer the wedge firmly into the ax-head eye. Soaking a loose handle in water can be a temporary—but only temporary—remedy. As the handle dries it will shrink and become loose again. The handle of an ax left in the hot sun may also shrink and loosen.

Choose an ax you can wield comfortably. An ax with a long handle may be difficult to aim accurately; one with a short handle may be awkward to use with two hands—and you might strike your legs if you miss the wood you are chopping. A heavy ax may tire you quickly; a light one may not cut effectively.

Carry an ax at your side, holding it just below the head with the blade pointed down and away from you. Don't wear restrictive clothing or slippery gloves when using an ax.

Before chopping, clear branches, brush and other obstacles that might catch the ax. Make sure no person is closer to you than 10 feet. Be certain your footing is firm.

Always split firewood on a wooden chopping block—a stump or log will do. Earth and stones will damage an ax if you chop wood on the ground.

Except when splitting wood, chop across the grain with the ax head tilted at about 45 degrees to the wood. An ax can rebound dangerously and is quickly dulled if you try to cut directly across the grain.

The contact method is effective for

An experienced axman never relies solely on his strength. His relaxed, rhythmic swing lets the ax do most of the work for him.

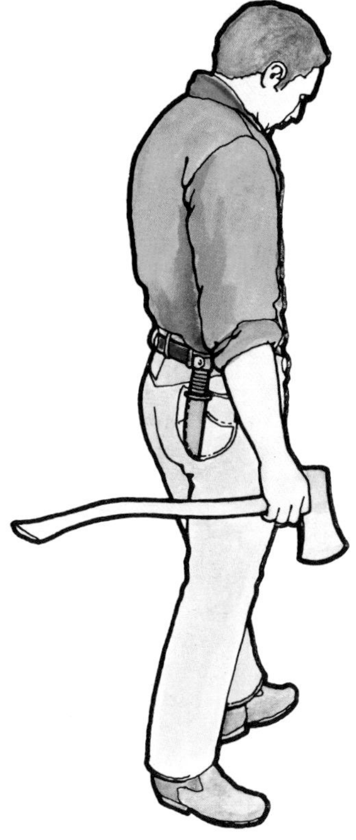

Carry an ax just below the head, with the blade pointed down and away from you.

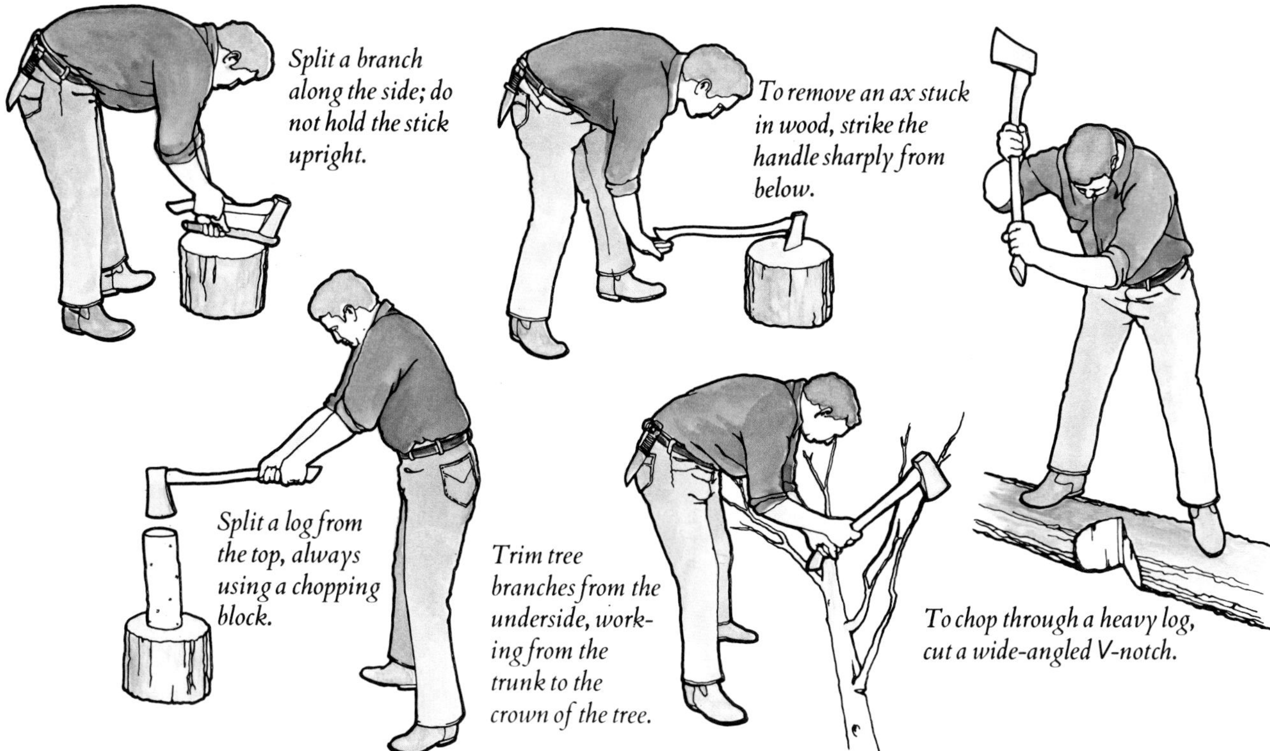

Split a branch along the side; do not hold the stick upright.

To remove an ax stuck in wood, strike the handle sharply from below.

Split a log from the top, always using a chopping block.

Trim tree branches from the underside, working from the trunk to the crown of the tree.

To chop through a heavy log, cut a wide-angled V-notch.

cutting sticks for kindling. Place the edge of the ax against the end of the wood. Raise the wood and ax and bring them down together so the wood strikes the block solidly. Never hold a stick upright with one hand and bring the ax down on the end—you run too great a risk of striking your hand. Never use your feet to steady a piece of wood for an ax swing.

If an ax becomes stuck in wood, loosen it by striking the handle sharply from below—don't wrestle with it.

Chopping a log To chop through a heavy log, cut a V-notch at least as wide as the diameter of the log. Chop alternately right and left to keep the chips flying. If the log is more than six inches in diameter, cut two notches opposite each other and meeting at the center of the log, or roll the log and notch it all around.

Felling a tree is rarely justified, is illegal in most parks, and requires permission on private property. If you cannot find enough wood on the ground, look for a dead tree. Decide where it should drop by observing its natural lean, the force and direction of the wind and whether there are trees on which it might get caught.

Cut a kerf (notch) close to the ground and facing the direction the tree should fall. The kerf should be cut to the center of the trunk and be about as wide at the mouth as the tree's diameter at the cut. Chop the upper part of the kerf at a 45-degree angle and the bottom part nearly horizontal. This will leave an almost flat stump.

Cut a second kerf opposite the first and about four inches higher. The tree should topple as the second cut reaches the center of the trunk. The uncut wood between the two kerfs acts as a hinge to direct the falling tree and to keep its butt from kicking backward.

When the tree begins to fall, move quickly to the side and yell "Timber!" to alert others.

To trim branches from a fallen tree, work from the trunk to the crown. Stand on one side of the tree—don't straddle it. Chop the underside of each branch. An ax will rebound dangerously if you swing it at the springy crutch of a branch.

Felling a Tree

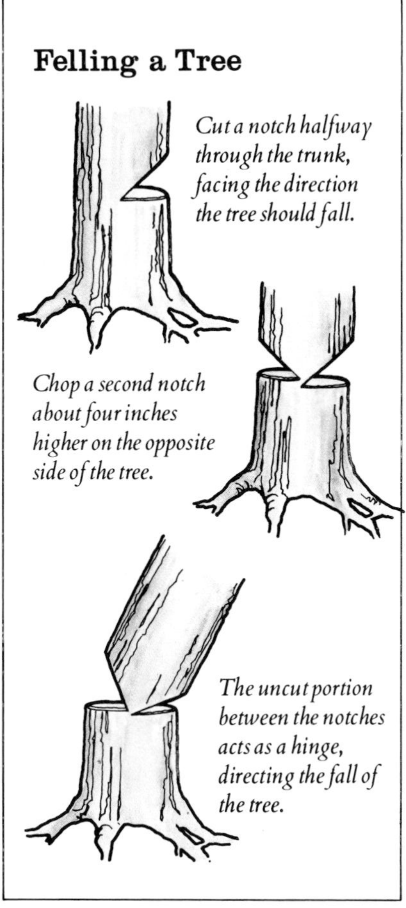

Cut a notch halfway through the trunk, facing the direction the tree should fall.

Chop a second notch about four inches higher on the opposite side of the tree.

The uncut portion between the notches acts as a hinge, directing the fall of the tree.

Knots and Lashings

Knots are invaluable to campers. The right knot for the right task will hold securely and unfasten easily; the wrong knot may come apart under stress, or it may jam, making it difficult to untie.

In these pages you can learn how to whip a rope, secure a guy rope and moor a boat.

Use a six-foot length of rope to practice knot-tying. String is so thin and limp that it will make most of these knots seem more difficult to tie than they actually are.

Parts of a rope These terms are used in knot-tying.

Standing part *Overhand loop* *Underhand loop*

Slipknot Used for tying cord around a package.

Make an underhand loop. Draw the standing part under and through the loop as shown.

How to whip a rope "Whipping" is the term used for binding the ends of a rope with twine to keep them from unraveling.

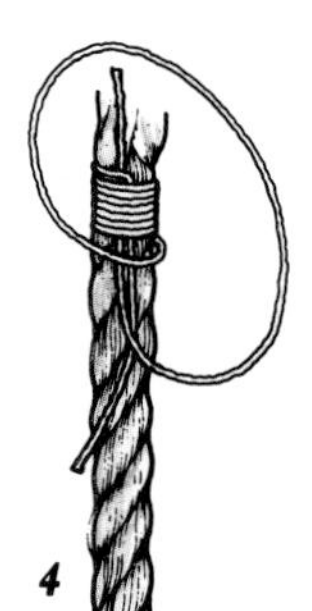

***1.** Loop a 3' length of twine as shown. **2.-3.** Bind the twine around the rope, working from the top of the loop toward the bottom. **4.-5.** Continue until binding is as deep as the rope is thick. Pull the ends of the twine tightly until the loop disappears under the wrapped twine. Trim the ends of the twine.*

Round turn and two half hitches Used to tie a guy rope to a peg, pole or tree.

Pass the running end twice around the pole. Twice bring the running end under and over the standing part until two underhand loops are formed as shown. Tighten by pushing the loops toward the pole.

Taut-line hitch Used for securing guy ropes to tent pegs.

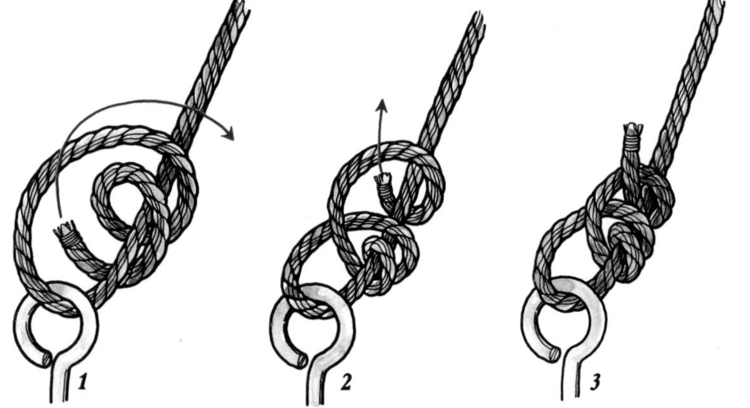

***1.** Pass the running end around the tent peg or through its eye and make two turns around the standing part of the rope, working toward the peg. **2.** Pull the running end through the larger loop and make another loop higher up. **3.** Pull the running end tight. The rope can be made taut by sliding the knot up the standing part of the rope and made slack by pushing the knot down.*

Figure-eight knot Used to prevent a rope from slipping through a hole.

***1.** Make an underhand loop, then pass the running end over the standing part. **2.** Carry the running end through the loop from behind and pull the knot tight.*

Reef knot Used for joining two ropes of the same thickness.

1. Make an over and under crossing. 2. Bring the ends back and cross them as shown. 3. To tighten, simultaneously pull both ends and standing parts.

Sheet bend Used for joining two ropes of different thickness.

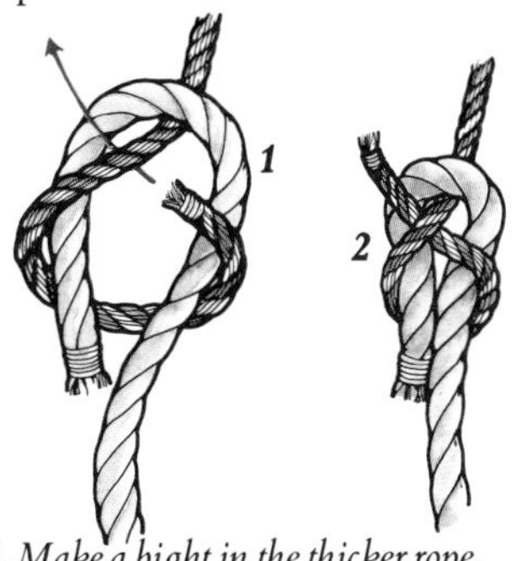

1. Make a bight in the thicker rope. Run the thinner rope down through the bight, then around behind both the running end and standing part of the thicker rope. 2. Draw the running end of the thinner rope under its own standing part and over the thicker rope's bight. To tighten, simultaneously pull both ends and standing parts.

Clove hitch Used to secure a rope to a pole or tree.

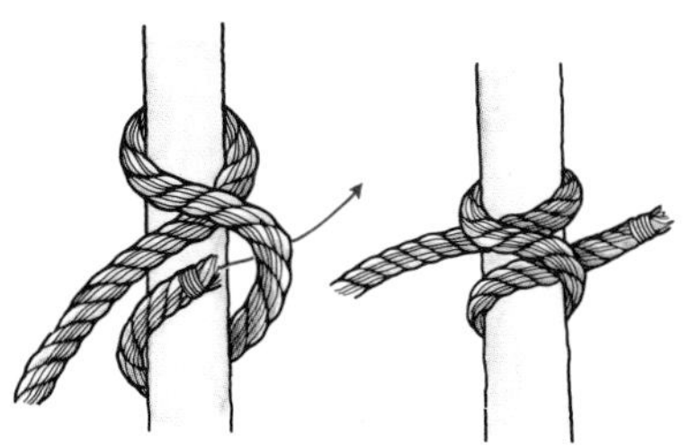

Loop as shown and pull both ends.

Bowline Forms a loop that won't slip. Used for mooring a boat.

1. Make a small overhand loop and bring the running end up through the loop, leaving enough slack to produce a loop of the size you want. 2. Bring the running end behind the standing part and down again through the small loop. 3. Tighten around the standing part.

Sheepshank Used to shorten a rope or by-pass a weak spot.

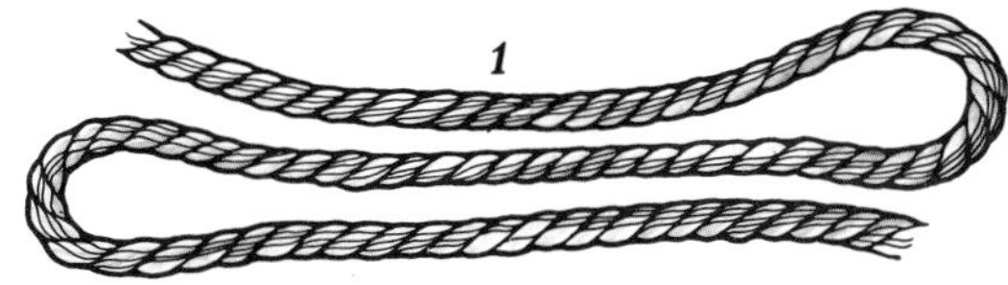

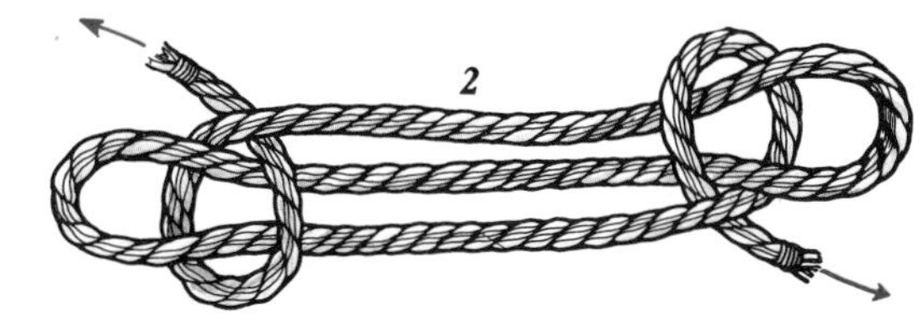

1. Fold to desired length as shown. 2. Make an underhand loop at each end. Tighten.

How to make a washstand

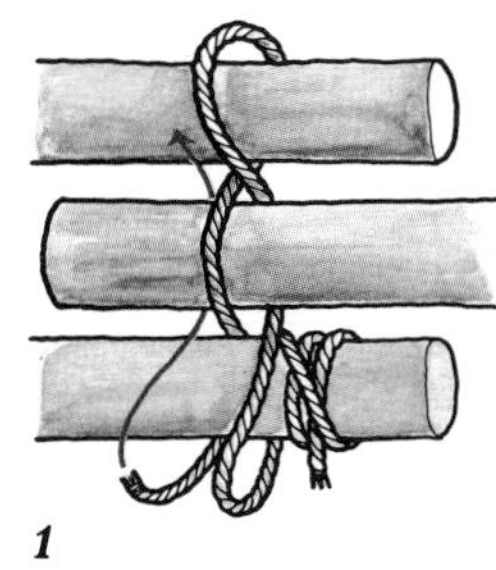

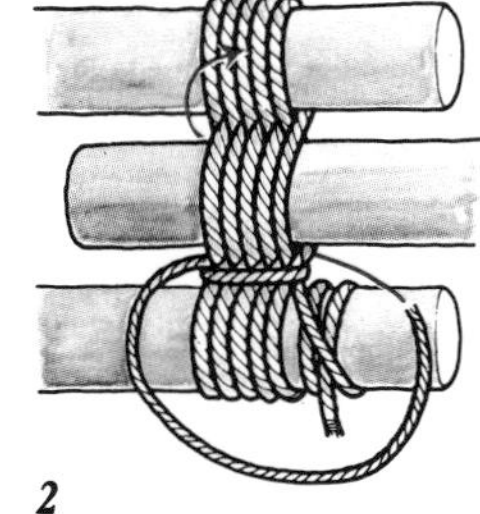

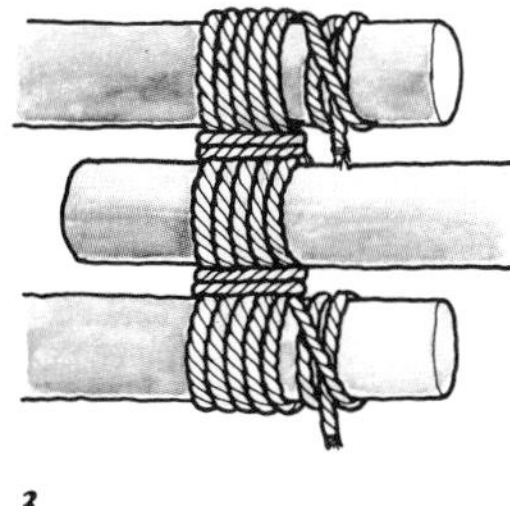

1. Select three straight sticks, each about 3′ long. Lay them on the ground as shown and tie a clove hitch to one of them. Weave over the first stick, under the second, around the third, over the second, and so on. 2. Continue weaving until you have made five turns around the third stick, then make two tight turns between the sticks with the running end. 3. Secure to the third stick with a clove hitch.

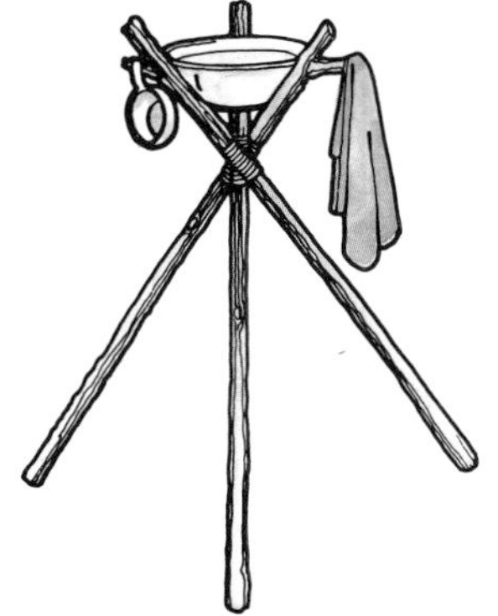

Setting Up Camp

Choose a campsite several hours before sunset. This will enable you to explore the surroundings and pitch your tent in daylight. Setting up camp in darkness is troublesome even for experienced campers—and you might discover in the morning that you are next to a garbage dump.

After the evening chores are done, the intimacy of conversation or singing around a campfire is one of camping's special pleasures.

Choosing a site Look for a level site on gently sloping high ground at the edge of a woods or in a clearing, and close to a water supply. The ground should allow rainwater to run off and be firm enough to hold tent pegs. Sand is a poor camping surface. Trees can provide shelter from prevailing winds and supply fallen twigs for fuel. If possible, place your tent where it will be shaded during midday, but don't pitch it beneath overhanging branches. Falling leaves, blossoms and branches can damage a tent. The edge of a lake, river or stream, though often picturesque, is likely to attract insects as well as other campers.

Face the back of your tent into the prevailing wind—if you know its direction. If not, face the tent door to the north and you will avoid the brunt of most storms.

Never pitch a tent in a dry riverbed or ravine or on a sandbar. A flash flood could swamp the campsite.

Pitching the tent Once you have chosen a site, park your car out of the way of the tent, equipment and guy ropes. Clear the site of stones, twigs and other sharp objects that could puncture the tent fabric or injure a camper.

Two persons can pitch most tents. Other campers can set up the stove, gather firewood, fetch drinking water and unpack the car. Choose a cooking area downwind of the tent and at least 10 feet from it to avoid damage from sparks. Place wood and other fuel upwind and a safe distance from the fire pit. Twigs, brush and other combustible material should be cleared within a radius of 10 feet of the stove or fire. Keep a bucket of water handy.

Most tents are pitched by first spreading the tent floor and pegging the corners. Then poles are raised and guy ropes are tied. Drive pegs into the ground firmly enough to secure guy ropes, but not so deeply that they cannot be pulled out later.

When setting up a tent, use simple knots such as clove hitches, half hitches and reef knots. Rope shrinks when wet making knots difficult to untie, so insert a small stick in each knot you tie in guy ropes. When you untie the knots, remove the sticks. The resulting slack makes the knots easy to undo—even if the ropes are soaking wet.

To help prevent accidents, mark clotheslines and guy ropes with bits of white cloth or reflector tape. When possible place clotheslines and other such accessories above head height.

All equipment kept inside the tent should have its own place and be re-

A Well-Planned Campsite

The tent is in the shade, but not too close to large trees. The fire is a safe distance away. Fuel and equipment are neatly stacked. A sack of food hangs out of reach of animals. A container in the stream keeps food and drink cool.

Picnic Planning

Ants, mosquitoes, hornets and wasps can take the fun out of picnicking. To discourage these insect pests, choose a site away from marsh and dense brush. Use insect repellent liberally. Cover boxes and jars of food when they are not in use.

Picnic supplies are easily carried in a portable cooler, a hamper, a knapsack, or even a cardboard carton. Pack carefully to avoid crushing food. Put heavy, solid items at the bottom of the picnic container and light, fragile foods on top. Double-wrap tomatoes and foods that might leak. Some sandwiches can be frozen the night before a picnic. They will stay fresh for many hours the following day, if packed in insulated bags or wrapped in layers of newspaper.

Take a tablecloth to protect food on the journey and at the picnic site. Pack a minimum of cutlery. Not everyone will need a knife if food is cut into small portions when prepared. Use paper plates and cups. Puncture a hole in the cup lids and insert a straw to prevent drinks being spilled.

A fire or barbecue adds zest to a picnic, making it seem more like a camping trip. Light a fire about 30 minutes before cooking over it. This allows time for the formation of hot coals that provide safe, uniform, nearly smokeless heat.

Keep a container of water near the fire. Make certain the fire is out and the picnic site is tidy before you leave—even if the area was littered when you arrived. If refuse cannot be burned and if no trash receptacle is nearby, put litter in a plastic bag and dispose of it at home.

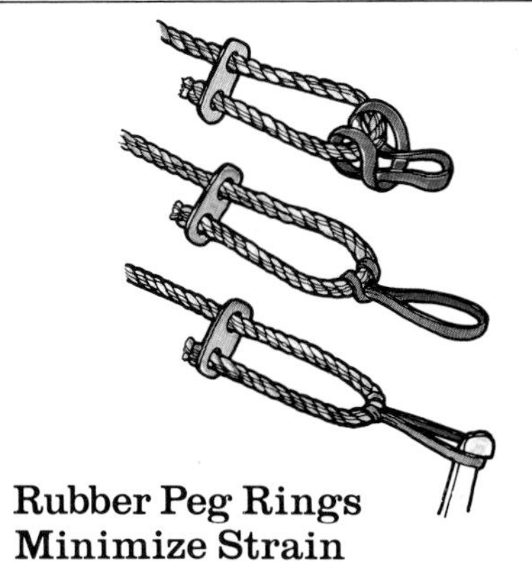

Rubber Peg Rings Minimize Strain

On some tents, the strain from buffeting by wind can be minimized with rubber peg rings. Check the rings regularly and replace worn ones. To fit a new rubber ring, loop it as shown.

turned immediately after use. Each camper should have a bag or case for personal gear. Choose a handy spot for the first-aid kit and flashlights. Cots and other furniture should be arranged so that campers can move freely. Place cots and sleeping bags as level as possible. If they must be on a slight slant, face the foot of camp beds downhill. Campers will sleep poorly if their heads are lower than their feet.

Storing food safely Food and garbage, unless well protected, will attract wildlife. If you don't have a secure metal or wooden box, store provisions in a bag or box and hang it out of reach of wild animals. Nonperishables can be kept in a car trunk. Don't leave food in the passenger compartment of a car if you suspect there are bears near your camp. Bears have been known to smash windows to steal food left inside automobiles.

If you don't have a refrigerator or ice box, keep perishables in a waterproof container immersed in a lake, river or stream. Secure the container with a rope tied to a nearby tree or with heavy stones placed around and on top of it.

If latrines or garbage pits are needed, dig them at least 50 yards downwind of the camp and at least 25 yards from any water.

Decide daily who is to collect firewood and water, cook meals, wash dishes and clothes and tidy the tent. Work fairly shared makes for a happy camp—and a safe, healthy one.

Camping Etiquette

Care, cleanliness and courtesy are fundamental to camping. By being careful you reduce the hazards and discomforts of outdoor living. By keeping your camp clean you discourage the presence of insect and animal pests. By being courteous you allow others to enjoy themselves.

Taking care means, for example, sheathing axes and knives and keeping them out of the reach of children. It means having a flashlight handy at night and keeping your campsite clear of things anyone could trip over.

Fire safety Be especially careful with fire and fuel. Put out a campfire by dousing it with water. Stir the wet ashes until all sparks are extinguished, then cover the ashes with earth.

Don't carry wooden matches loose in a pocket—if you fall or slide on them they could ignite. Better still, use safety matches. Store fuel containers in the shade and keep them away from flames. Always extinguish a stove or lantern before disconnecting or refilling its fuel tank.

Cleanliness is an extension of care. A holiday can be marred by food poisoning or intestinal upset if good hygiene is not practiced. Cover food and dispose of scraps before ants, flies and rodents are attracted. A campsite can become a breeding ground for pests and disease unless sanitation is a part of the camp routine.

Drinking water Take no chances with your water supply. Drink only water that you know is safe. Don't swim in or wash dishes in polluted water. Water from most sources can be made safe for drinking by boiling it for 10 minutes or by adding a chemical purifier. The flat taste of boiled water can be eliminated by pouring the water back and forth between containers to restore its oxygen content. Halazone tablets eliminate the need for boiling. Alternatively, add four drops of iodine to a quart of water, or two drops of laundry bleach to a gallon. Allow the water to stand for 30 minutes before use. Keep treated water in a covered container.

It is not true that the addition of an alcoholic beverage makes impure water safe to drink.

Garbage disposal The best location for a latrine and a garbage pit is a sheltered spot about 50 yards downwind from the tent.

Grease and soap from dishwashing contribute to water pollution. Don't wash dishes in a stream or lake. Use a dishpan and dump the dirty water in a bough-covered trench.

Greasy dishwater attracts insects as surely as other wastes do. It should be dumped in a bough-covered trench. Replace the boughs occasionally and burn the used ones.

Most garbage can be burned. Put nonburnable garbage, such as metal and glass, in a plastic bag and carry it with you until you are able to dump it in a garbage container. If you must dispose of your refuse in the woods, bury it in a pit. Tin cans should be opened at both ends, burned and flattened before being buried. Apart from causing injury, broken glass discarded carelessly in the outdoors can start a fire by concentrating the sun's rays. Dig a garbage pit only as a last resort. Increasing use of the wilderness makes such pits more of a danger to man and wildlife than they once were.

A courteous camper does as little damage to the environment as possible and leaves his campsite cleaner than he found it. Standing trees, even dead ones, should not be cut down or scarred. Don't pound nails into trees. Use only fallen wood for fires and camp projects.

Respect the rights and privacy of others. Observe fishing laws and limits. Ask permission before entering private land. Don't hike across cultivated fields. By practicing care, cleanliness and courtesy you can help preserve the

Be cautious about the water you drink. Unless you know that the water from a natural source is safe, boil it or treat it with a chemical purifier.

Canadian outdoors for yourself and others to enjoy.

Food preparation On picnics and camping trips, unsanitary preparation of food and the difficulty of refrigerating it greatly increase the risks of food poisoning.

Some 400,000 Canadians get food poisoning every year. Common symptoms are stomach cramps, nausea, vomiting and diarrhea. Symptoms of deadly botulism poisoning can include blurred vision and/or difficulty in swallowing, speaking and breathing. If you suffer any of these get medical attention quickly. Some food poisoning causes paralysis or coma and even death if not treated promptly.

The bacteria that cause such illnesses occur naturally in most foods. High cooking temperatures kill them and refrigeration prevents them from multiplying. But on warm moist food they can double their number every 20 minutes. One hundred bacteria can multiply to 1.6 billion in eight hours.

Food that is moldy (with the exception of some cheeses) or has a bad odor or is taken from a damaged or bulging can is likely to contain deadly botulism toxin.

To avoid food poisoning, keep hot foods hot—above 60°C. (140°F.)—and cold foods cold—below 4°C. (40°F.)—until they are served.

Many foods that can be stored safely at room temperature are suitable for outdoor meals: bread, jam,

Before leaving a campsite, douse the fire with water and stir the ashes.

honey, nuts, dry cereal, fruit, raw vegetables, cheese, milk powder and canned goods.

Foods that go bad fast (meat, poultry, fish, milk products) should never be left at room temperature for more than two hours. If you prepare food the day before a picnic, refrigerate it overnight and transport it in a cooler. Cook meat thoroughly and use a meat thermometer to test the internal temperature.

Snakes and Other Dangers

Caution and common sense are the camper's best means of avoiding attack by snakes and animals and infection from insects and plants.

Three species of poisonous snakes are known to inhabit Canada: the small **eastern massasauga** *(Sistrurus catenatus catenatus)*, which lives in swamps around Lake Huron and Lake Erie; the larger **prairie rattlesnake** *(Crotalus viridis viridis)* and the **northern Pacific rattlesnake** *(Crotalus viridis oreganus)*, also found on the prairies.

Most snakes will slither away at the sight or sound of man but will attack if surprised, provoked or otherwise threatened. You can avoid danger by treading warily but noisily. Many nonpoisonous snakes can inflict painful bites. Such wounds are not serious if treated promptly to prevent infection—clean the wound, apply a mild antiseptic, and cover with a dressing.

Poisonous snake bites Symptoms of a venomous bite are pain, swelling and discoloration of the skin, numbness, nausea, and sometimes vomiting and shock. Children may suffer convulsions and paralysis.

First-aid treatment should be started immediately, before the venom spreads. Medical aid should be sought as soon as possible.

Meanwhile, lay the victim down to slow his circulation. Do not administer stimulants. If a limb has been bitten, bind a cord or strip of cloth above the wound, tightly enough to hinder the spread of venom without stopping circulation. Loosen the band for about 90 seconds every 10 minutes. Also loosen it briefly if the limb becomes numb. Move the band higher if the swelling spreads.

With a sterilized razor blade or knife, make X-shaped cuts about ¼ inch long and ⅛ inch deep through each fang mark. Draw out blood and venom with the suction cup provided in a snake-bite kit. If you have no kit, apply suction with your mouth and spit out the venom. *Unless you have a cut or open sore on your lips or in your mouth,* the venom will not harm you.

If swelling spreads away from the fang marks, repeat the cut-and-suck procedure at the newly swollen area. Apply suction frequently.

Wild animals are more likely to prey on man's food than on man himself. Bears are particularly determined raiders. They will barge into almost any camp where food is accessible, devastating equipment in their path. They may flee if you make loud noises. However, the behavior of bears (and other wild animals) is unpredictable, so a safer course is to retreat quietly to a shelter and wait for the intruders to leave.

Porcupines are attracted by salty food and will chew sweaty ax handles, canoe paddles and gunstocks. Porcupines and skunks are easily frightened away, but don't get too close to either creature. A porcupine's barbed quills can be painful weapons. A skunk can spray its foul-smelling musk as far as 10 feet and the odor is evident 400 yards away. The musk can cause temporary blindness.

A northern Pacific rattlesnake guards a mouse it has killed. Like other rattlesnakes, the Pacific avoids humans and is dangerous only if disturbed suddenly.

The dull-colored prairie rattlesnake (above) is poised ready to strike. The eastern massasauga rattlesnake (left) is found around Lake Huron and Lake Erie.

Poisonous plants Mushrooms and berries are another source of danger. Unless you know with certainty that a plant is edible, leave it alone. Learn to recognize common poisonous plants.

Poison ivy *(Rhus radicans)* is easily recognized by its three leaves, which are sometimes shiny. Its berries are greenish yellow in summer and dull white in fall. Poison ivy generally grows as a short, upright plant, or a creeping vine. Contact with the plant can cause discomfort ranging from a mild rash to severe blisters, fever and a general feeling of illness. Calamine lotion or a paste of baking soda and water will soothe infected skin but a doctor should also be consulted. Even inhaling smoke from burning poison ivy can cause illness.

Poison oak *(Rhus diversiloba)*, found on the coast of British Columbia, is similar to poison ivy in its appearance and effect on man.

Poison sumac *(Rhus vernix)*, another menace to the unwary camper, grows as a shrub or as a tree up to 25 feet high. It is rare in Canada and is found mainly in swamps. Its smooth oval leaves grow in pairs, usually with a single leaf at the top of the stem. Its white or greenish berries hang in long clusters.

Insect pests Insects are the most difficult of all outdoor hazards to avoid. Wasps, hornets and bees are best ignored—they usually sting only in self-defense. Stay away from places where they congregate. A nest may be nearby. Wasps often nest in the ground. Hornets and bees nest in trees or other sheltered spots.

Unlike the wasp and hornet, the bee leaves its stinger in the victim's skin. The stinger should be scraped out gently. An ice pack or a paste of baking soda and cold cream applied to a sting will relieve the pain and itching.

Blackflies and mosquitoes are familiar insect pests in Canada. Blackflies breed in running water, mosquitoes in stagnant pools; blackflies prefer daylight and bush country, mosquitoes darkness and undergrowth. Both breed throughout the country, hatch during spring and summer and are particularly numerous in the North.

Most flies transmit disease and should be kept off camp food. Keep a flyswatter handy.

Ticks and chiggers attach themselves to passing animals and people and bite into the skin. Ticks, about ¼ inch long, cause swelling. If you find a tick on your body do not swat it. Its beak may be left embedded beneath your skin to cause infection. Instead, apply alcohol, gasoline, kerosene or a hot match head to make the tick relax its jaws. Chiggers are young mites that live in tall grass. They inject a substance which liquefies skin tissue causing irritation, swelling and blistering. Hot, soapy water or a paste of baking soda will relieve the condition.

Many insect repellents are effective but none works against all insect pests. It is worthwhile experimenting to find an effective brand, but in the battle against insects, good luck is likely to be your most powerful ally.

Poison sumac, with long clusters of white or greenish berries, is rare in Canada.

Poison ivy, with clusters of three leaves, grows as a plant and as a vine.

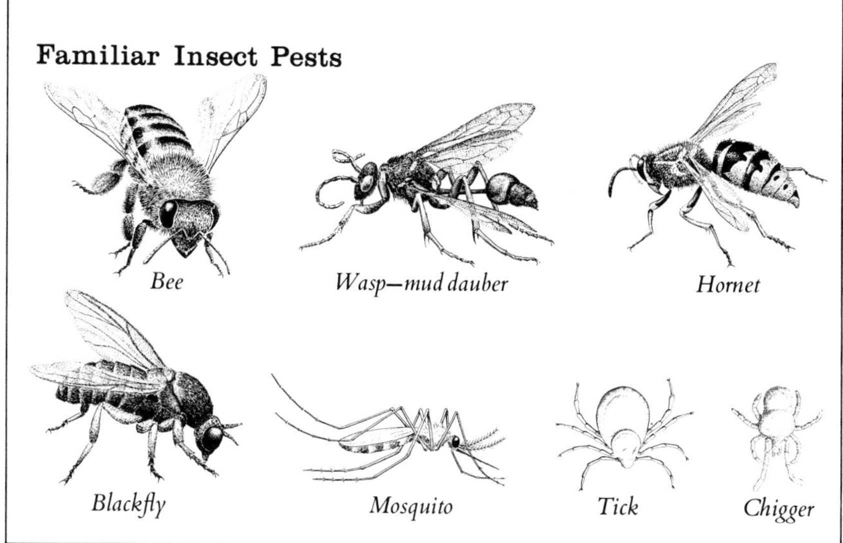

Tips on Good Camping

Years of camping have taught experienced outdoorsmen numerous skills and procedures that increase the fun, comfort and safety of any outing. On these pages are some of those time-tested tips and techniques. By studying them, you will learn how to determine direction without a compass; how to estimate time without a watch; how to light a fire without matches; how to cook food without utensils—and much more.

Travel tips

To use your watch as an emergency compass, point the hour hand toward the sun. South will lie in the middle of the angle formed by the hour hand and the numeral 12 on the watch face.

Even without a watch you can estimate when the sun will set. Extend your arms toward the sun with your palms toward your face, the edge of one hand placed on top of the other. Line the lowest finger with the horizon. Each finger between the horizon and the bottom tip of the sun represents about 15 minutes of daylight.

A car bogged in soft earth can be freed by jacking up the rear wheels and filling the holes under them with brush or gravel. Drive off smoothly and gently.

When hiking in the woods, stay far enough behind the preceding hiker to avoid being hit by branches that might snap back when he brushes by them.

Fire tips

Collect enough wood before lighting a fire. It is a common mistake to return from wood gathering to find the few sticks you lit are burned out.

Stack firewood according to size so that tinder, kindling and logs are each handy.

Tightly rolled newspapers can substitute for logs.

Squaw-wood—dead, dry lower branches—provides good kindling wood even in a downpour.

Bark from a dead birch tree will burn furiously even when wet.

Fairly dry wood can usually be found in the middle of a thick log, even when other fuel is wet. Make kindling from it by feathering small pieces with a knife.

Waxed cartons or candle stubs make good fuel in wet weather.

To make a fire starter, tightly wrap a few feet of thick string around six or seven matches and dip the bundle in melted paraffin wax. This device will blaze for more than five minutes, even in the rain.

You can waterproof matches by dipping them in paraffin or nail polish.

A plastic container with a tight-fitting lid makes an inexpensive waterproof matchbox.

Never leave a fire unattended.

Cooking tips

A long, narrow bed of coals is best for cooking. Logs or rocks placed on both sides of the fire will support cooking utensils over the heat.

Use a flat stone to fry eggs. Bury the stone in coals until it is hot then sweep the coals off, grease the stone and crack an egg onto it.

You can bake bread without a pan by wrapping a strip of thick dough around a green stick.

Bury potatoes under coals and they will bake in 45 to 60 minutes.

A stick with two sharpened prongs can be used to broil meat or fish.

Many foods can be cooked easily in

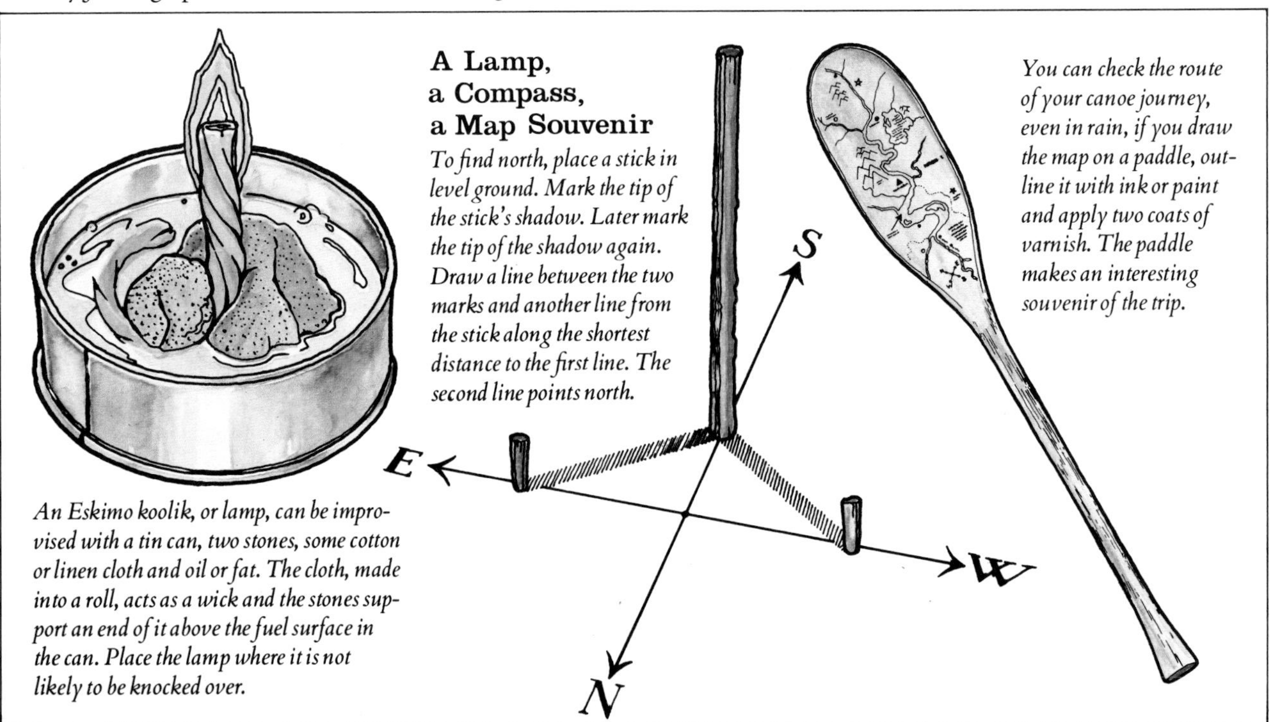

A Lamp, a Compass, a Map Souvenir

To find north, place a stick in level ground. Mark the tip of the stick's shadow. Later mark the tip of the shadow again. Draw a line between the two marks and another line from the stick along the shortest distance to the first line. The second line points north.

You can check the route of your canoe journey, even in rain, if you draw the map on a paddle, outline it with ink or paint and apply two coats of varnish. The paddle makes an interesting souvenir of the trip.

An Eskimo koolik, or lamp, can be improvised with a tin can, two stones, some cotton or linen cloth and oil or fat. The cloth, made into a roll, acts as a wick and the stones support an end of it above the fuel surface in the can. Place the lamp where it is not likely to be knocked over.

Backpackers should travel in groups of at least three. If a hiker is injured, one companion can go for help while the other remains with the victim.

A magnifying glass held so that it concentrates the sun's rays in a tiny spot on dry tinder will quickly produce a flame.

A steak can be fried on a piece of foil fashioned into the shape of a pan (above). Egg-in-the-hole (below) is fried on a hot stone. A hole in a slice of bread holds the egg.

aluminum foil. Double-wrap the food to form an airtight package and bury the package in a bed of coals.

Eating utensils can be fashioned from bone, wood or metal.

Water for dishwashing should be heated while a meal is being cooked. Since warm water boils faster than cold water, leave a covered container of water outside your tent to warm in the sun.

Before using pots and pans over an open fire, smear the outsides of them with a paste of soap and water. They will be easier to clean later.

Equipment tips

A tent warmer can be made with three or four large stones heated for several hours in a campfire. Place the hot stones in a bucket and set it on a fire-resistant surface—not directly on a groundsheet or tent floor.

In camp, tie your pack to a tree at waist height. It will be off damp ground, more convenient to sort through and beyond the reach of inquisitive animals.

Do not cut rope or string unless you must. It may be needed later in its original length.

Don't take glass containers to camp. They are easily broken and often weigh more than the food inside.

An automobile hubcap makes a good emergency shovel.

A paddle or an ax can be used as a measuring stick when inches are marked or notched on the handle.

Pine or spruce pitch is a good temporary cement. It can be used to repair a fishing-rod guide or to patch an air mattress.

Bits of brightly colored cloth or shiny aluminum foil can be tied to a fish hook to provide an emergency lure. Look under rocks for live bait.

Rubber bands worn snugly around trouser cuffs will keep out insects.

Aluminum foil can easily be formed into a hat. It also provides good insulation against cold when wrapped around the body (under clothing) with the foil's shiny side next to the skin.

To keep your feet dry in leaky boots or in shoes that are not waterproof, wear plastic bags over socks.

Camping With Children

A family camping trip can provide some of a child's most rewarding and memorable experiences. The skills he acquires and the appreciation of nature he gains will last a lifetime.

Countless discoveries await the curious child at camp. Even small children enjoy spotting wild flowers and learning to identify trees by their shape, bark, leaves and seeds.

A stump provides adults an opportunity to show a child how to tell a tree's age by counting its annual growth rings.

Bird-watching adds enjoyment to a hike, especially in the early morning when birds are hungry and active. Children soon learn to move quietly and to "freeze" and point, instead of shouting, when they spot a new bird.

Some national and provincial parks provide lists of common birds. With these lists and a guidebook even the novice can easily identify many birds.

Stars are always brighter away from city lights, and children enjoy identifying constellations on star maps.

Clouds too can be identified and a child can learn about the relationship of clouds to the weather.

A night trip to a pond, stream or shallow lake can be fascinating for everyone. Fish that lurk in deep water during the day often come close to the surface at night and are attracted to light. Birds and animals such as owls and raccoons usually forage at night.

Field trips can provide mementos and craft materials that will keep children occupied for hours in a tent or camper on rainy days.

Freshly fallen leaves can be collected and pressed or waxed for later mounting on cardboard or in a souvenir album.

Leaf-pressing The easiest method is to press leaves for about 10 days between newspaper pages, under a heavy weight. For better preservation and a glossy finish, dip leaves in melted paraffin or press them at home between sheets of waxed paper with a hot iron. Always melt paraffin in a double boiler.

The insect hunter can collect interesting specimens at night by shining a bright light on a white cloth suspended between two trees, then brushing the specimens attracted by the light into a jar.

Pebbles and small stones can be gathered on field trips, identified and polished later. Wrap a few in cloth and crack them on rocks to discover how different the insides can be from the dull outer surfaces.

A gnarled root can make an attractive mantel decoration, with a little trimming and polishing, and there are decorative possibilities in pine cones, acorns, leaves, feathers and other woodland treasures. Beaches offer interesting shells, stones and pieces of driftwood.

With a sieve, or with a dip net improvised from cheesecloth, a child can catch tadpoles, minnows and aquatic insects.

The outdoors provides fascinating discoveries for a child. With adult guidance, he will learn to appreciate and protect wildlife.

Attractive shells can be collected and turned into jewelry. Some children love this kind of activity and will work at it diligently.

The key to successful projects of this kind, and to happy camping in good or bad weather, is preparedness. Adults should list and pack items they are likely to need to keep children busy—glue, transparent tape for mounting, crayons, string, scissors, coat-hanger wire and cheesecloth for making dip nets.

Each child should have his own knapsack for the things he is bound to collect during a camping trip.

Handy items Insect repellent and sun lotion are essential, and a waterproof tarpaulin is one of the most useful items families can pack, regardless of the type of shelter they are using. In hot weather it can be rigged to provide

Children often spend hours collecting shells, stones, driftwood and other "treasures." Many of these can be turned into attractive jewelry and decorations.

shade, in stormy conditions it provides a windbreak and in a downpour it can be stretched above a picnic table. It can also cover camping gear that has to be left outdoors.

Maps and first-aid supplies should be kept handy, in the glove compartment of a car or under the front seat.

The floor of the back seat is a good spot for a small carton of field guides, games and toys that will help children while away the hours on the road. Older children can keep track of mileage and help with map reading.

Once a campsite has been selected, adults should inspect the area and warn children of special hazards such as a well or a cliff. But in general, a well-chosen campsite offers children more fun with less risk than many homes.

Safety rules The chance of accident can be minimized by following a few basic rules.

Children should not be allowed to run near a fire. Axes and knives should be kept out of their reach. They should be taught to recognize poisonous plants such as poison ivy. They should be warned against eating mushrooms and unfamiliar berries and other fruit.

Children—and adults too—should wear life jackets when boating, even on a calm day.

A pocket knife should be kept closed and a hunting knife in its sheath when not being used.

A playpen or similar enclosure is a necessity for toddlers.

A baby should not be exposed to direct sunlight for more than two or three minutes for his first sunbath. The time can be increased over several days to a maximum of 15 minutes.

A backpack carrier makes it easier to take a baby—properly protected against the elements—on his first short hikes.

Older children should be encouraged to report back to the campsite frequently. If they become lost, they should know what to do—stay put, and keep signaling for help.

One good way to maintain contact is to equip children with whistles, and agree on a few signals. Three whistles —like three smoky fires or three gunshots—is the internationally recognized signal for "help" or "I'm lost." Families can decide on other signals to indicate mealtime or a return to camp.

Animal Track Molds

This project call for five pounds of plaster of paris, a large can for mixing, a few salmon or tuna tins with tops and bottoms removed and a few shallow, slightly larger tins with just the tops removed.

Look for tracks on game trails and along shorelines. Bait, such as stale bread and peanut butter, will attract small animals to a desirable spot.

Tin surrounds the print.

Grease the inside of the ring made from the salmon or tuna tin and press it gently into the ground, surrounding the desired print.

First cast about to be pressed into tin containing fresh plaster.

Pour in plaster, mixed to the consistency of toothpaste, to a depth of one inch and let it harden for five or six hours.

Slip the hardened cast out gently and use a soft brush to remove any earth clinging to it.

Then pour an inch of plaster into a larger greased tin. Let the plaster begin to harden. Then grease the first cast and press it gently, print downward, into the plaster in the larger tin.

The finished print.

Let the plaster harden for about six hours. Then remove it in one piece and pry the casts apart gently.

Winter Camping

Camping amid the splendor of snow-covered landscapes can be an exhilarating experience. The swamps, lakes, rivers and streams of summer become winter's wilderness trails—free of crowds and bugs.

For your first winter camping venture team up with an experienced companion. You should be in top physical condition. Build up your strength and stamina with regular exercise, frequent hikes and a balanced diet. Proper clothing is a must. Be prepared for the worst possible weather.

Winter clothing Your coat or parka, like an Eskimo parka of animal skins, should fit loosely—to trap insulating air pockets—and be wind- and water-resistant. Your winter outfit should also include long thermal underwear, a woolen turtleneck sweater, a flannelette shirt, woolen or insulated trousers and a woolen jacket. Wear two pairs of woolen socks or, if wool irritates your skin, a cotton pair under a woolen pair. Mitts are warmer than gloves; wear woolen mitts under a water-repellent pair.

Boots should be waterproofed. Shoepacs, larrigans and mukluks are lighter than leather hiking boots. In most conditions, rubber boots can be worn comfortably over moccasins or running shoes.

Although you can travel faster through snow on cross-country skis, snowshoes are better for crossing brush-covered terrain. Snow goggles are essential—snow glare can cause eye strain and temporary blindness.

Keep inner clothing dry. Damp clothing insulates poorly and moisture can freeze next to the skin. Avoid excessive perspiration by removing a layer or two of clothing before you exercise strenuously. Remove your parka and jacket, for example, before chopping wood. Clothing and bedding should be aired daily. Never sleep in damp clothing or bedding.

Frostbite Cheeks, nose and ears are particularly vulnerable to frostbite, caused when extreme cold restricts blood circulation. The onset of frostbite is not necessarily painful, so companions should watch each other for telltale white spots. "Making faces" as you move about will stimulate circulation. Always keep ears covered and wear a face mask in below-freezing weather.

To treat frostbite, slowly warm the affected area by holding a warm, bare hand against it. Keep moving, seek a warm shelter or build a fire—but don't sit too close to the fire: rapid thawing of frostbite can cause inflammation and even gangrene. Rubbing frostbitten flesh may damage frozen tissues. Never rub snow on frostbite. With proper treatment, the whiteness, stiffness and numbness that accompany frostbite should gradually diminish. However, if the flesh turns black or the skin peels—or if a whole limb is frozen—do not attempt first aid but get medical attention as soon as possible.

A hot beverage will help restore blood circulation to an affected area. Don't drink alcoholic beverages: alco-

A fire pit dug out of banked snow provides a well-shielded and cosy cooking area.

A winter camping outfit should include all these items. Clothing should be loose-fitting to trap insulating pockets of air between layers. Check that you can wiggle your toes when wearing your boots—tight-fitting footwear increases the risk of frostbite.

hol restricts blood circulation. To treat chilblains—an inflammation of fingers, toes, nose, ears and sometimes cheeks, caused by exposure to cold—soak the affected area in diluted alcohol or alum water and paint it with iodine. If the inflammation becomes an open sore, seek medical attention.

Setting up in snow A winter campsite should be well protected from wind—choose a spot on the leeward side of a hill or in a clump of evergreens. Make camp several hours before sunset and work at a leisurely pace. Clear loose snow and tramp an area large enough for your tent. A layer of evergreen boughs, covered with a sheet of foam rubber, will insulate the tent floor.

To build a fire pit, dig to the earth if possible, or clear away loose snow and tramp the area. Build the fire on a floor of stout sticks or rocks to prevent melting snow from dousing the flames. Burn hardwood if you can find it. Use waterproof matches and have fire starters and twigs in your kit in case dry kindling is scarce.

Pack plenty of energy foods such as chocolate, nuts, raisins and sugar. Avoid foods that are damaged by freezing.

Winter Camping Tips

- Tents should have steep roofs to shed snow.
- Place evergreen branches against the sides of the tent to trap falling snow. The snow-covered branches will provide insulation.
- A hooded sweatshirt or a parka hood stops heat loss from the head and neck.
- Flannelette pajamas, a good choice for winter camping, can also be used as underwear.
- Dress and undress in the sleeping bag to retain body heat.
- Most food for a trip can be frozen at home. In camp, pack the food in snow to keep it frozen.
- Avoid taking food that can be damaged by freezing.
- Protect water from freezing by carrying it next to your body, hanging it near the campfire and keeping it in a sleeping bag at night.
- Pack an ice chisel and a kitchen strainer—to cut a water hole and to skim ice from it.
- Fresh snow can be melted for drinking water, but eating snow can cause cramps.
- Don't use ice to quench your thirst—ice is only as pure as the water from which it froze.

Wind Chill Chart

- Comfortable: wear a wool sweater and jacket or topcoat.
- Uncomfortable: wear a parka. Skiers typically face these conditions.
- Caution: extra clothing, warm boots and a hood are needed.
- Danger: extra clothing is vital; watch for frostbite.
- More dangerous: add a face mask.
- Extreme danger: don't travel or work outdoors alone.
- **Stay indoors**

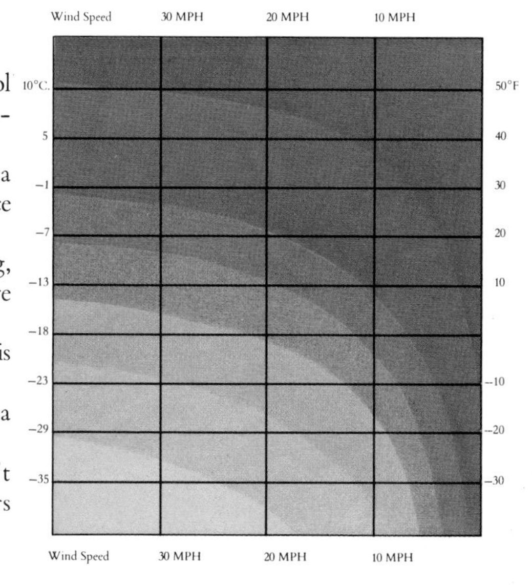

Securing Guy Ropes

In deep snow, guy ropes can be tied to foot-long sticks lashed together to form an X. Bury the sticks deep and pack snow over them. Ropes can also be tied to a rock or log that is then buried. Either method will hold the guy ropes securely.

Metal tent pegs or spikes are easier to drive into frozen ground than wooden pegs are.

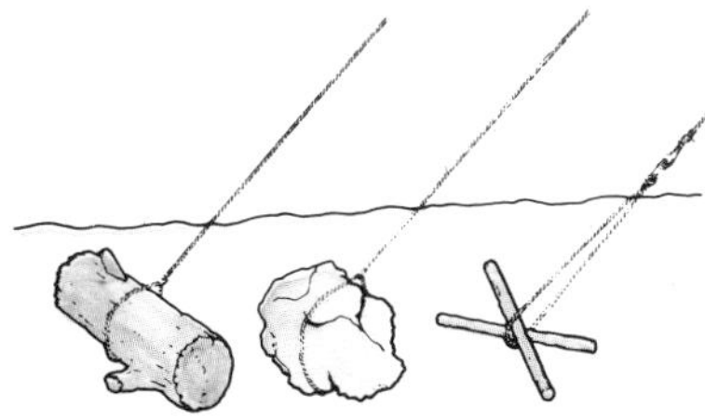

Backpacking—Choice and Care of Equipment

The successful backpacker is self-sufficient, limited only by his stamina and experience and by how much he can carry. Given the right equipment and food, and careful planning, the backpacker can live outdoors in comfort for weeks all the while enjoying great personal freedom. The key to his success is what he carries.

Types of packs There are four basic types of packs: the knapsack (or rucksack), the packsack, with or without a rigid frame, the backpack and the pack basket.

The knapsack, a small leather or canvas bag with shoulder straps, is useful for short hikes and rambles. The other three packs should be considered for serious backpacking.

The packsack is a medium to large pack, often with a rigid frame that distributes the load and allows air to circulate between the pack and the body, helping to keep the backpacker cool.

The backpack, designed for heavy loads, is mounted on a light wood or metal frame webbed with canvas or nylon and contoured so that only the fabric touches the wearer's back.

The pack basket, usually of woven ash or willow strips, is a rigid carrier with shoulder straps. It is useful for carrying breakables, tools, canned goods and other hard objects that, if carried in a cloth pack, might dig into the hiker's body.

Many backpackers prefer a rigid-frame packsack. It allows them to carry up to 35 pounds in comfort.

Choosing a pack Bulk and weight are important considerations in preparing for backpacking. Loads of 30 pounds or more will require a rigid-frame packsack or a backpack.

Choose a pack of lightweight, durable, waterproof fabric such as treated canvas or nylon. Plenty of outside pockets on a pack are practical. They should have flaps large enough to keep the contents dry in case of rain. Detachable pockets are handy for stowing personal gear.

Wide shoulder straps with thick shoulder pads are recommended. Look for a wide waist belt that can be buckled tightly to transfer weight from the shoulders to the hips. All straps should be well-padded and fully adjustable.

A backpack frame should be light and sturdy, with rounded corners and canvas or nylon webbing.

Backpacking boots Footwear is important in successful backpacking. The more weight you plan to carry, the heavier your boots should be. Light boots might be comfortable initially but they provide less protection for the feet and ankles than do heavy sturdy boots. Thin leather may not prevent your toes from pushing into the ends of the boot, especially when you are going downhill.

A good fit is essential. If boots are too large, blisters will result; boots that are too small will cause blisters, cramps and aching feet. Look for boots with the fewest possible seams, and make sure the seams are double-stitched. Consider padded insoles and flexible lug soles. Boots with tension eyelets can be laced with varying degrees of pressure on the ankle and toes. Avoid leather soles; they are slippery when wet.

Many experts recommend two pairs of socks—a light pair under a heavy pair—to prevent abrasions from the rough material of thick socks. Although special hiking socks are available, thick woolen ones are adequate and probably cheaper.

The right clothing is essential. When hiking, you will rarely need to bundle up to stay warm, even in snow. Mesh underwear allows perspiration to evaporate quickly. A long-sleeved shirt is handy when insects become

The knapsack, used for light loads, has a large flap over the bag to protect the contents from rain.

The packsack's outside pockets allow easy access to needed equipment.

The pack basket, inexpensive and lightweight, is an excellent storage box in camp.

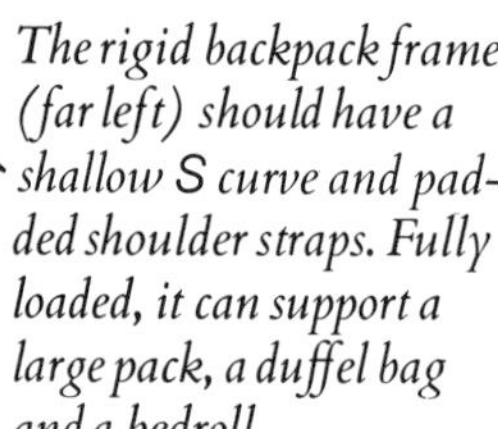

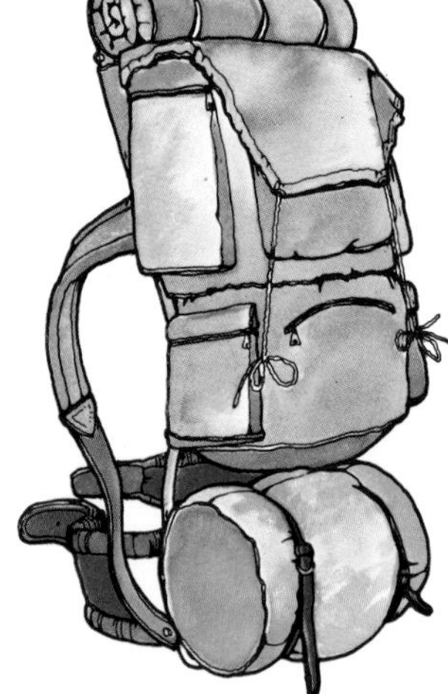

The rigid backpack frame (far left) should have a shallow S curve and padded shoulder straps. Fully loaded, it can support a large pack, a duffel bag and a bedroll.

Basic backpacking equipment, weighing less than 35 pounds, can be carried easily by a healthy adult and sustain him for a week or two. By adding fishing tackle, more food and fuel, an experienced backpacker could live comfortably for a month or more.

bothersome. A waterproof poncho can double as a groundsheet. A cowboy hat protects against the sun and is useful for carrying water or fanning a fire. Take sunglasses, especially if you will be traveling in snow.

Essential equipment What goes into the pack should be selected as carefully as the pack itself. When choosing equipment, ask yourself: "Is it necessary? Is it lightweight? Is it durable? Is it compact?"

The sleeping bag that you select should be warm, lightweight and not too bulky. To a great extent, warmth depends on the thickness of the insulation. Get the smallest bag you will be comfortable in; otherwise you will have to warm up extra space before you are cozy. The "mummy" bag, which hugs the body, is more practical than a larger rectangular bag.

A tent will keep you dry and afford some privacy but will add weight and cost to your adventure.

The backpacker should consider a tent weighing less than five pounds. Alpine tents give good protection against wind and snow. A thin plastic tube tent is cheaper and lighter.

When choosing a portable stove, consider its weight and bulk. A portable gas stove is compact and efficient, a butane stove is clean-burning, easy to use and safer to operate.

Unless you plan to "live off the land"—often an impractical idea—you will have to carry food. Freeze-dried and dehydrated foods are good for backpacking. They are easy to prepare, nutritious and lightweight. These factors usually outweigh the disadvantages of extra cost and occasional lack of flavor. Include some snack foods to eat on the move.

Equipment Checklist

1. tent **2.** a wide-brimmed hat **3.** backpack and frame **4.** hatchet **5.** boots **6.** mess kit—including two pots, a frying pan, a plate and a cup **7.** freeze-dried food **8.** stove **9.** extra gas **10.** aluminum containers **11.** poncho **12.** foam pad **13.** sleeping bag **14.** clothing—socks, wool shirt, long underwear, T-shirt **15.** utensils and can opener **16.** first-aid kit **17.** matches **18.** soap and toothbrush **19.** compass **20.** file **21.** sheath knife **22.** whetstone **23.** flashlight

Backpacking Basics

An experienced backpacker takes everything necessary for a safe, comfortable trip without carrying more than 35 pounds.

For success in backpacking, strike a balance between traveling as light as possible and taking everything necessary for a safe, comfortable trip.

An adult male of average build can hike comfortably with a 35-pound load. An inexperienced backpacker or a person of small build should restrict his load to 25 pounds.

Weigh your equipment. If it exceeds 35 pounds, reconsider your need for each item. Cameras, fishing equipment, guns, saws—even tents are not generally essential. But do not leave behind first-aid and emergency equipment. On trips of up to 10 days, you will need no extra clothing other than socks and underwear. The weight and nuisance of dirty laundry is seldom justified.

Water for your freeze-dried or dehydrated food should be obtainable at your campsite, so usually you need carry only a one-pint canteen of drinking water. Extra water should be carried only when you travel in dry or desert areas—water weighs about one pound per pint.

By arranging equipment properly in your pack, you will avoid problems later on. Place the pack flat and lay groundsheet and clothes on the bottom to shield the body from hard objects. Distribute heavy items (food, pots, stove) in the next layer. This is important for good balance. Cover these items with another layer of soft materials.

Determine in what order you will use your equipment, so you won't have to rummage through the pack. Place small items (flashlight, pocket knife, first-aid kit, sunglasses, toothbrush and waterproof matches) in the side pockets of your pack.

A tent and sleeping bag can be tied outside the pack, one above the pack, the other below. Experiment to find the most comfortable position for them. If the pack does not feel balanced, redistribute heavy items.

Before leaving for the wilderness, plan a menu for each meal. This will enable you to prepare an adequate food list. Among your dehydrated foodstuffs, include some that can be eaten cold in case rain makes cooking impractical. Avoid meals that require special utensils; if possible use only a pot and a skillet.

Long-lasting protein and high-calorie foods are more important on the trail than balanced nutrition. If hot weather is expected, plan to take salt tablets or extra salt with meals. The symptoms of salt deficiency are headache, nausea, leg cramps and weakness.

Hiking skills Novices should tone up muscles with trial hikes before their first major venture. Soak new boots in water and walk in them until they are dry to make them supple and conform to the shape of your feet.

Never embark on a backpacking trip in a hurry. Backpacking is not an endurance race. Unless you are a seasoned hiker, limit yourself to five or six hours of hiking the first day. You will gradually find your best pace. Keep the pace steady. Carefully step over, not on, logs and rocks to conserve energy and to avoid tripping. Have slower members of your group hike ahead while the others break camp. Meeting places can be established along the trail.

Rest is vital: up to six minutes every hour. But stops of more than six minutes will likely be wasted. Studies have shown that beyond six minutes the increased benefit to the body is slight.

Take care of your feet; blisters can ruin a day's hiking or spoil an entire trip. At the first sign of a tender spot on your foot or toe, apply a moleskin patch or plain adhesive tape. Change socks daily.

Hiking safety Don't be a constant sky-watcher. Holes, loose stones and tree stumps can be hazardous especially when you are carrying a full pack. Hikers should keep a safe distance apart to avoid injury from dislodged rocks and springy branches.

Up to six minutes of rest every hour takes the strain out of backpacking. Studies have shown that the body gains little from a longer break.

Before wading a stream or river, test the flow and temperature with your hand. Any stream more than a foot deep is hazardous, and cold water can reduce sensation in the feet and legs, increasing the risk of a fall. Remove your socks to keep them dry but put your boots on to minimize injury from sharp rocks.

While crossing, probe with a stick for boulders or sudden changes in depth. Ford a stream or river at a wide shallow point, where the flow is slower than through a narrow passage.

In cases of particular risk, use a rope. Tie one end around your waist and loop the other around a tree or rock so that a second person can play it out from the bank. Unbelt the pack and slip one arm out of its strap before entering the water so that the pack can be released quickly if necessary.

Before hiking on an unfamiliar trail, learn as much as possible about checkpoints and prominent landmarks from someone who has used the trail. Inquire about those places where you are likely to take a wrong turn. Don't rely too much on the map you spread out at home. Keep a record of checkpoints or prominent features and the time of day you pass them. Fix in your mind the approximate time you should reach the next checkpoint.

As soon as you return home, clean your equipment and store it in a way that will reduce the preparation needed for your next trek.

Equipment Checklist

Cooking □ Food and menus □ Stove □ Extra gas □ Waterproof matches □ Mess kit □ Canteen □ Scouring pads □ Tea towel □ Can opener □ Sheath knife

Sleeping □ Sleeping bag and liner □ Foam pad or air mattress □ Groundsheet □ Tent □ Tent pegs, poles and ropes

Pack and clothing □ Packboard or rigid-frame backpack □ Boots □ Camp shoes □ Socks □ Long underwear □ Fishnet underwear □ Long pants □ Short pants □ T-shirt □ Cotton shirt □ Wool shirt and sweater □ Jacket □ Poncho □ Hat with brim □ Sunglasses

Survival □ Extra food and water □ Water purifying kit □ Extra clothing □ Waterproof matches □ Fire starter □ Map and compass □ First-aid kit □ Pocket knife □ Flashlight and extra batteries

Miscellaneous and personal gear □ Ax and whetstone □ Fishing tackle □ Watch □ Toothbrush □ Toothpaste □ Comb □ Soap □ Toilet tissue □ Sun lotion □ Insect repellent □ Notebook and pen □ Camera and film □ Tool kit

For Specific Trips

LIST 1 Essentials for All Trips □ First-aid kit □ Map and compass □ Food and water □ Extra clothing □ Matches □ Fire starter □ Pocket knife □ Flashlight □ Toilet tissue □ Insect repellent □ Hat

LIST 2 One-Day Hike (Add to List 1) □ Knapsack □ Parka or jacket □ Boots □ Sunglasses

LIST 3 Overnight Trips (Add to Lists 1 and 2) □ Packsack (instead of knapsack) □ Sleeping bag □ Foam pad or air mattress □ Groundsheet □ Tent

LIST 4 Mountain Climbing (Add to Lists 1 and 3)

For snow: □ Winter clothing □ Goggles □ Snowshoes □ Ice ax □ Crampons □ Stove □ Sun lotion

For rock: □ Rock-climbing boots □ Pitons □ Piton hammer □ Carabiners □ Ropes □ Slings

Survival in the Wilderness

Campers and hikers frequently become lost in the Canadian outdoors but seldom do they require more than water, shelter and common sense to see them through the experience unscathed.

If you are lost, food is the least important of your needs. A healthy adult can survive for two or three weeks without food. But water and protection from extremes of heat and cold are essential. So is a calm approach to your predicament.

Water is the only remedy for dehydration—which can be fatal. Fast-running water in isolated areas is likely to be safe to drink. Water may also be found by digging into low-lying, moist ground. Clues to the nearness of water in rocky areas include clumps of lush vegetation, dark stains on rock walls and seepages in cracks and caves.

Other sources of water are rain, dew on plants and, in spring, the sap of birch and maple trees. Water can be wrung from wet moss and from some green vegetation.

Purifying water To be sure water is pure, boil it for at least five minutes. To restore oxygen, shake the water in a closed container, or pour it back and forth from one vessel to another.

A person needs at least two quarts of water every day—more in hot, dry weather—to maintain a stable body temperature. Dehydration is insidious. A man who loses 2½ percent of his body weight through dehydration loses about 25 percent of his physical ability. Loss of 15 percent of body weight is usually fatal.

Dehydration symptoms include loss of appetite, sleepiness, nausea, dizziness, headache, impaired speech and inability to walk.

In virtually every part of Canada, every day of the year, the human body needs some protection from the sun, wind, rain or cold. Sun can raise body temperature faster than the body can dissipate the heat. Wind and rain can rob the body of heat faster than the body can replace it. Extreme cold can cause frostbite, and even death.

Shelter is essential when any of these dangers threatens.

In wind and rain the experienced woodsman does as animals do—he shelters in a burrow or among protective foliage.

In forested areas it is better to put up a small shelter quickly, using fallen branches and foliage, than to waste energy and body heat by building an elaborate structure. A fallen tree in a well-drained area offers effective shelter. Hollow out a space under a log and enclose it with whatever is handy—slabs of bark, boughs or pieces of rotten logs. Plug all holes with foliage and keep the living area small, to reduce heat loss. Cover the floor with boughs to insulate the body from the cold ground.

In snow, dig out a shelter below the surface or in a snowbank.

A cave dug out of snow provides a safe and cozy shelter. Food can be cooked on a stove immediately outside. The stove will also provide warmth.

A small space may be warmed by body heat alone, but it is more comfortable physically and psychologically with a small fire at the entrance. Fire, apart from keeping the body warm and dry, is valuable for signaling, cooking, and purifying water by boiling.

There are several different ways to start a fire if you become lost or stranded without a lighter or waterproof matches.

The friction method, using a bow and drill, will produce a fire for a trained person but should be a last resort for the inexperienced. The technique takes practice and requires considerable energy.

An easier method involves the scraping together of flint (or a hard rock) and steel to direct sparks onto dry tinder. Stones that scar or break when struck are useless. Hard rock grated briskly against the back of a knife with a downward scraping motion will direct sparks onto tinder—finely shredded dry bark or fine wood dust produced by insects, often found under the bark of dead trees. When the tinder smolders, blow or fan it into flames.

A spark from a car battery can also be used to ignite tinder.

A convex lens, as in a magnifying glass, a camera or binoculars, can be used on a sunny day to concentrate the sun's rays to a pinpoint on tinder.

After you have found water and shelter, prepare signals to attract rescuers. Most wilderness areas of Canada are patrolled from the air by rangers who are trained to spot unusual signs or movements.

Internationally recognized distress signals are based on threes—three gunshots at five-second intervals, three whistle blasts, flares or three fires set about 100 feet apart in a triangle. Dark smoke can be produced by burning oil, plastic or rubber.

Signal fires should be built tepee fashion, protected from rain and kept ready to light as soon as an aircraft or search party is heard.

Emergency Shelter

A lean-to shelter can be made in minutes. Place boughs as shown.

Foliage on top will provide protection against wind, rain and snow.

The letters SOS or the word HELP, tramped in snow or formed in grass from contrasting stones, dirt or brush, have saved many lives.

In low brush far from an open space, tramp down a large area into a shape likely to arouse curiosity if seen from the air—such as a triangle or a square.

A mirror, a piece of polished metal or a sheet of foil can be used to reflect sunlight toward an aircraft. A hole punched in a sheet of metal or in the bottom of a tin can enables the signal to be aimed toward a potential rescuer.

In most areas food is readily available. All Canadian birds and animals—with the exception of some toads and shellfish—are edible. Although many plants are edible, many are also poisonous; animal food is safer, more nourishing and usually easier to obtain. Often the nourishment gained from plants is less than the energy expended to find and gather them.

Lizards, frogs, snakes and turtles are all tasty, boiled or fried. Grasshoppers, considered a delicacy in some countries, can be toasted on a stick after wings and legs have been removed.

Small game such as rabbits, squirrels and mice can be captured without a gun. Improvised snares, traps, nets and fishing lines will work night and day to feed a person lost in the wilds.

Beaver and muskrat can be snared on well-worn paths. When cut off from the safety of the water, they can be clubbed. The slow-moving porcupine, found in most forested areas, can be killed with a club or spear but requires care in handling. Slit the skin along the belly and peel it back, working from the inside of the skin to avoid contact with the quills.

Partridge or grouse found roosting in thickets can be snared easily with a wire noose attached to a long pole.

Fruits and plants Eat only plants that you know are safe. Blue and black berries not in clusters are usually safe. White berries should always be shunned. Eat only familiar red ones such as strawberries.

Edible plant greens, which provide roughage and vitamins, include dandelion leaves, bracken fronds (fiddleheads), young green milkweed and water lily pods, pigweed and the lower inner 12 inches of cattail or bulrush stalks. They can be boiled to make a tasty soup.

Edible roots, which provide starch and protein, include those of the cattail, bracken, tiger lily and lady's slipper. They can be eaten raw or boiled.

Outdoors: Camp Cookery

Among the pleasures of camping is eating a meal that has been cooked to perfection over an open fire. Successful outdoor cooking starts with taking the right foods on a camping trip. Campers need a well-balanced diet to provide the energy for vigorous outdoor activity. Campers who plan to travel far off the beaten track will also need a supply of nourishing survival food. Well-chosen food and equipment make the time spent in the open easier and more enjoyable. And a knowledge of camp cooking skills can transform the simplest fare into a memorable outdoor feast.

A camp stove is an asset on any camping trip—especially in rainy weather. Some small stoves can be tucked into a backpack. Larger twin-and-triple-burner stoves, too heavy to carry long distances, are ideal for car camping. Designed for safety, portable stoves are available in a wide range of sizes, prices and styles. Various types of camp stoves and ovens are featured in this section.

Open fire cooking is slow and hard work but it imparts the sharp, lingering tang of wood smoke to food. On the following pages you will learn how to build and use a campfire safely. You will discover several types of fires for different cooking needs. For example, the easy-to-build wigwam fire is good for brewing coffee quickly on the trail, but for a hearty breakfast or substantial dinner, a trench fire or a hunter-trapper fire works well. Stick cooking and barbecuing and cooking with clay are discussed and numerous outdoor cookery tips are offered. For a taste of old-time woodsmen's fare, there are recipes for sourdough, bannock, hardtack, jerky and pemmican.

You will learn commonsense ways of reducing the weight and bulk of your rations, without sacrificing nutritional value. For example, dehydrated, freeze-dried and vacuum-dried foods are lightweight and nourishing. You will find out how to pack compactly. And you will discover how to prevent food spoilage by using nature's own refrigerator—a cold, bubbling brook.

If you travel by car, you may want to take a cooler, an ice chest or several hot-and-cold packs, all of which are described in this section. There are also instructions for building an inexpensive portable kitchen that holds enough food and utensils for a sumptuous outdoor spread for an entire family.

Enlivened by outdoor activity, campers relish food cooked over a crackling fire.

Camp Cooking the Portable, Practical Way

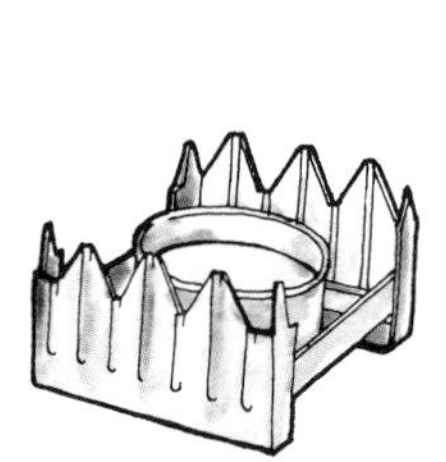

Solid fuel stove

European stove

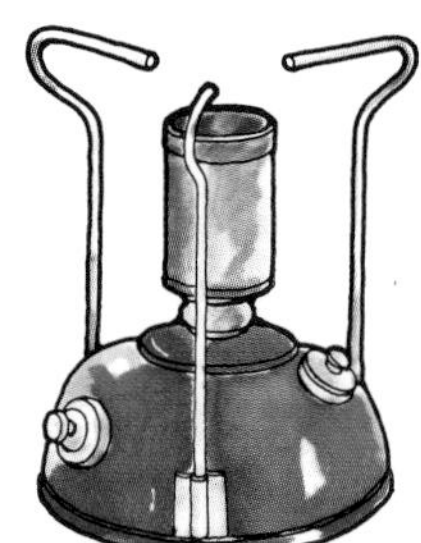

Kerosene stove

White gas stove

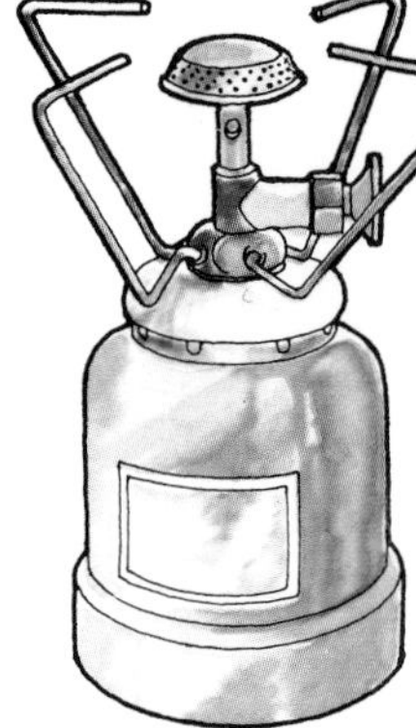

Propane stove

Few campers would deny that the smell of wood smoke and sizzling bacon is one of the special joys of camping. But when it's pouring rain or when firewood is scarce, even the most dedicated campfire cook lights a portable stove. Many campers use portable stoves exclusively for, unlike a campfire, camp stoves are quick and easy to use; they provide predictable heat; and perhaps most importantly, they don't blacken pots and pans.

Most portable stoves on the market are lightweight, easy-to-use and reasonably priced. But don't rush out and buy. Consider carefully the pros and cons of the various types—there is probably one suited to your particular needs.

No matter what type of stove you choose, be sure that the top is wide enough to hold as many large pots or pans as there are burners. This is especially important when considering triple-burner stoves.

What type of fuel? Of the five main camp stove fuels, *kerosene* is the cheapest. Although it produces soot and odor, it won't explode under normal conditions. A single-burner kerosene stove is fine for one-pot meals.

White (naphtha) gas A clean fuel, white gas is reasonably priced and it ignites readily and burns efficiently. A single-burner gas stove is good for fishing or hiking trips. Larger models, because of their size and weight, are best used in standing camps. For multicourse meals, a triple-burner model is practical.

Butane and propane These compressed gases are expensive but convenient. They require no priming and the risk of explosion is low. However, they liquefy in freezing weather, limiting their usefulness in cold weather. Butane and propane are fed to burners through a pressure regulator.

The butane single-burner ignites instantly and its heat can be easily regulated. It can be used for short outings.

The single-burner propane stove, light and compact, is widely used by backpackers to prepare hot drinks and quick meals. The burner and the tank form a single unit. Double- and triple-burner models have tanks separate from the burners so that other appliances, such as heaters and lanterns, can be operated from a single tank. Because of their bulk and weight, multiburner models are best used in trailers, houseboats and standing camps.

Solid fuel Although inexpensive, solid fuel is used infrequently because its heat output is low. Single-burner models are light and compact. Some fold flat, and all are adequate for hiking. The double-burner, also light and compact, is favored by some backpackers.

Alcohol Also low priced, alcohol produces a low heat (it takes almost six minutes to boil a pint of water) so it is used infrequently. But it is adequate for lightweight camping, and it doesn't explode.

The most popular of these stoves is the double-burner, white (naphtha) gas stove. It is compact and inexpensive to buy and operate. Its fuel (naphtha or unleaded gas) is readily available. Its main drawbacks—pumping and refilling—are minimal. Flare-ups often frighten people, so fill a plastic detergent bottle with bicarbonate of soda and keep it handy. If a flare-up occurs, simply sprinkle the area lightly to control the flame.

A close second in popularity is the propane stove. Although expensive to buy, it is inexpensive to operate. A 20-pound capacity fuel tank will often last an average family all summer. Smaller tanks (4½ and 9 pounds) are available.

European stoves Popular, well-made, and generally smaller than domestic makes, European stoves usually burn white gas or alcohol. They are noisy but they resist the wind well. However, they cannot be interchanged with North American equipment without an adapter.

Baking To vary your outdoor menu you may want to do some baking, and that requires an oven. The three basic types of portable ovens are the reflector oven, the Dutch oven and the box oven.

The *reflector oven* is a folding, metal structure that reflects the heat of an

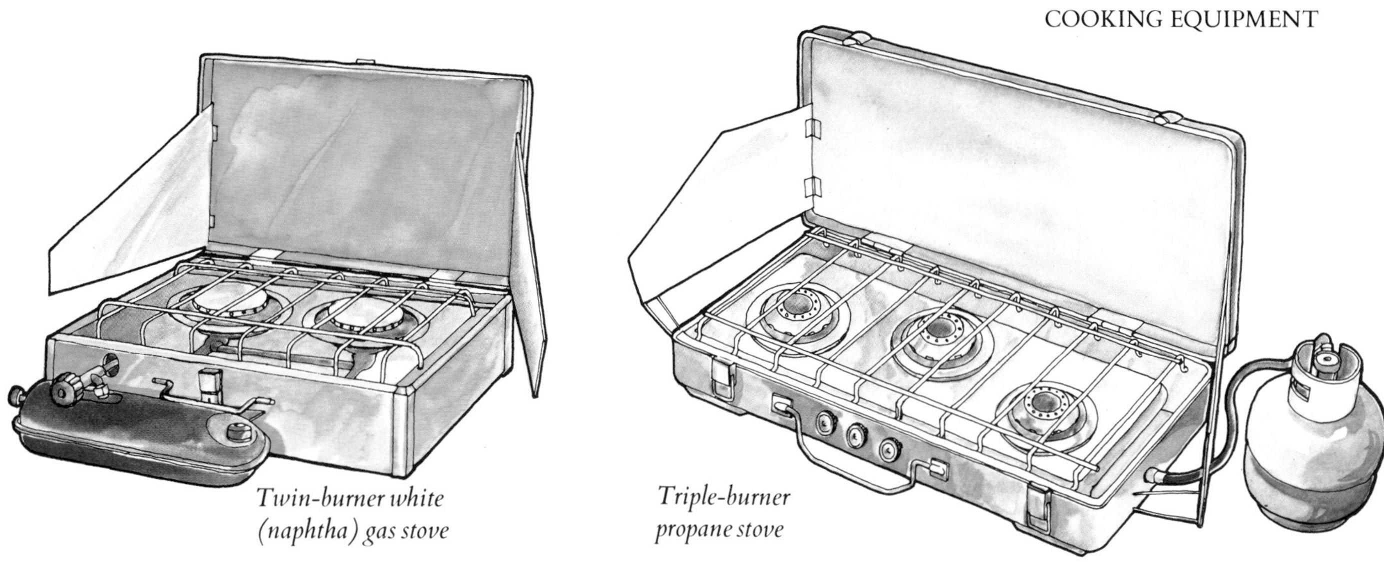

Twin-burner white (naphtha) gas stove

Triple-burner propane stove

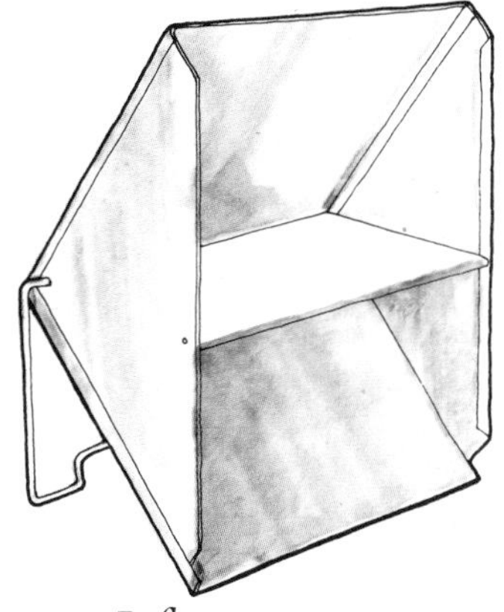

Reflector oven

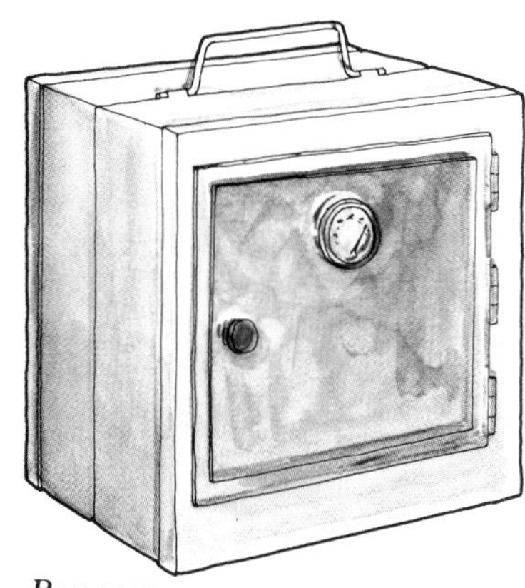

Box oven

open fire. To regulate its temperature, move the oven closer to or farther from the fire.

The *Dutch oven* is handy but heavy. It consists of a pot with a sunken lid, both of cast iron. The pot is placed over hot coals and more coals are heaped in the lid. When using the Dutch oven for baking, support pastry on a small fretwork of sticks at the bottom of the pot. To cook meat, simply add a little water.

A makeshift Dutch oven can be made from a large cooking pot. Set the pot (on four stones) above hot coals, cover it with a frying pan and fill the frying pan with hot coals.

The *box oven* is a collapsible unit, designed for use with white gasoline (naphtha) stoves. It is equipped with a thermometer and has about the same capacity as the Dutch oven. A box oven is lighter than a Dutch oven and can be folded into a compact bundle.

For high-altitude camping, a lightweight, aluminum *pressure cooker* is almost indispensable. Dividers, for cooking several foods at the same time, are available for most models.

For those who like to experiment, two types of *solar stoves* are available. One uses a fresnel lens to concentrate the sun's rays, the other uses a parabolic reflector. Although light, they are bulky and fragile and have only one burner.

Each burner of a white (naphtha) gas stove can be regulated individually for different cooking jobs.

Campfires for All Kinds of Cooking

It is wise (often mandatory) to use the fireplaces provided in many of Canada's national and provincial parks. They have been constructed to reduce the risk of forest fires as well as for the convenience of campers. But when you are off the beaten path, you will have to decide where you can safely build a campfire.

Select an open, level area away from trees, dry brush and other fire hazards. If possible, build your fire close to water and on rock, sand or loose soil. Rake away leaves, sticks and other burnable debris that are within 10 feet of the fire site. Some campers clear all vegetation, and even lift sod, within six feet of the fire site—this is not only unnecessary but it mars the landscape and can encourage soil erosion.

Gather dead wood for your fire—never damage or cut down living trees—and stack firewood upwind of and well away from the fire site. Build and tend your fire carefully. Remember: most forest fires are caused by human negligence.

There are several common types of cooking fires—each suited to different needs.

Wigwam fire This is the simplest of the cooking fires. First, collect tinder such as birch or cedar bark. Tiny evergreen twigs, cellophane paper—anything that burns quickly—may also be used. Next, find some softwood sticks and, with a sharp knife, pare them gently so that the shavings curl. These are called fuzz sticks. Arrange them in a pyramid shape around the tinder. Then add more sticks, leaving spaces for the fire to breathe. Ideally, the kindling should be no more than six inches high, the fire less than a foot. The smaller the fire, the easier it is to work with. As soon as the match touches the tinder, you will have a good, efficient flame. Add more sticks as needed.

The wigwam fire is good for quick stopovers when you want to boil water or make a one-pot meal.

Hunter-trapper fire Perhaps the most popular of all cooking fires, the hunter-trapper fire is ideal for large meals. Two logs laid side by side, closer together at the downwind end, form the initial structure. The logs, about six inches thick and three feet long, should be placed close enough to support a variety of pots and pans. Build a wigwam fire between the logs. Above this, using larger sticks, make a crisscross arrangement on top of the logs. Once the fire is burning and the crisscrossed sticks are ready to drop, knock them into the gap and scatter them throughout the length of the two logs. Add more wood and the fire should burn well. A damper effect can be achieved by placing a small block of wood under one of the logs, at the downwind end. If the wind becomes too gusty, the entrance can be blocked with stones.

Stone hunter-trapper fire This is simply a stone variation of the hunter-trapper fire. In place of logs, use large stones to create the open V formation. The stones should be about five inches in diameter—gaps between them can be sealed with smaller stones. The stones *must* be dry—not taken from streams or damp areas. Damp rocks often crack or even explode when heated. Although logs provide a better support for cooking utensils, stones retain heat. It's an easy matter to suspend pots and pans from a makeshift crane over the fire. For a quick meal, arrange three stones in a triangle and make a wigwam fire in the center.

Trench fire Although this fire is more difficult to build than hunter-trapper fires are, it uses firewood efficiently and it retains and reflects heat well. Because it floods easily, it is impractical in rainy areas.

Dig a sloping trench from ground level to about a foot deep and long enough to accommodate the pots and pans you plan to use. Make the trench about six inches wide at the deep end,

A hearty stew bubbles over a crackling fire framed by a Yukon rainbow.

To make "fuzz sticks," pare the wood into strips that remain on the stick.

One of the simplest cooking fires is the hunter-trapper fire.

A wigwam fire is easiest to work with if no higher than one foot.

A trench fire takes a little time to build but burns more efficiently than most fires.

twice as wide at the shallow end. The wide, shallow end should face the prevailing wind. In sandy ground, line the walls of the trench with small stones. Build a wigwam fire in the trench. When the fire is blazing, scatter it along the trench. Place a grill across the wide end of the trench to hold small pots.

Reflector fire This fire is good for baking, for roasting and for spreading warmth on cold evenings. It consists of a fire bank—a wall of logs resting on two stakes—facing the prevailing wind. The logs should be green and covered with a layer of dirt, so they won't burn. If no logs are available, use large stones. Build a wigwam fire against the fire bank. Then place a reflector oven opposite the fire. You can bake biscuits in a skillet or muffin tin by tilting it upright in front of the fire. The skillet or muffin tin should be heated over hot coals first so that the biscuits will brown on the bottom. In all cases, baking is normally done before a fire of blazing softwood—but hardwood embers may also be used.

Estimating temperatures Often it is handy to be able to estimate fire temperatures for grilling. This can be done by holding your hand, palm down, two inches above the grill. If you have to move your hand away in less than three seconds, the fire is about 205°C. (400°F.). If you can hold your hand above the grill for four or five seconds, the temperature is about 177°C. (350°F.).

Firewood Softwoods, such as pine, cedar and fir, are good for starting a fire and for boiling water. Hardwoods are better for broiling, roasting and baking: they yield more coals and a longer, more even heat. Gather wood from the ground or break off dry dead branches from trees. Don't take live wood from trees—this damages the vegetation and usually results in a poor fire. Store firewood in a dry place.

Starting fires Although it is possible to make fire by rubbing two sticks together, this procedure is laborious, time consuming and rarely successful. Use wooden matches—safety matches are hopeless in the outdoors—and make sure you pack plenty. Pack them separately to keep them dry. Matches can be waterproofed by dipping them in melted paraffin wax.

Some campers use gasoline to start their fires in the rain. This is a bad practice. If flammable liquids are to be used, kerosene should be your choice. Better still, make trench candles. Roll newspaper into a one-inch-thick bundle. Tie the roll with string at three-inch intervals, then cut the roll between the strings. Dip each section several times in paraffin wax—and you will have a guaranteed fire-lighter. Put the trench candle on the end of a stick, light it and then hold it under the firewood until the wood ignites. A length of rubber tubing is a handy device for reviving a fire. Point one end at the base of the fire and blow through the other end. This creates a bellows effect, and embers burst into flame.

Putting out the fire When the time comes to put out your fire, make sure no partially burned sticks or coals remain. These don't disappear and so they make the landscape unsightly. Douse the ashes well with water, stir them, and douse them again. Feel them to make sure they're cool. If you have built your fireplace with rocks, wait until they are cool and then return them to where you found them. Similarly, scatter unused firewood. When you leave, there should be no trace of your visit. A good camper leaves nothing behind but his thanks.

Fire Tips

- Make sure you are in an area where fires are allowed. Follow regulations.
- Build your fire on noncombustible material—rock, sand or wet earth.
- Always build your fire at least 10 feet away from the nearest brush and trees.
- Never leave a fire unattended.
- Avoid building fires on dry, windy days.
- Make sure your fire is out—dead out—when you leave.

Planning, Packing and Preserving Camp Foods

The weight and bulk of food supplies and cooking equipment is more important to hikers than it is to car campers. Yet in both cases proper organization can help make mealtime enjoyable. Before you even begin to pack, make a list of all the food and cooking equipment you intend to use. Read the list and eliminate unessential food and equipment. Wherever possible, substitute light, compact items for heavy, bulky ones. Finally, refer to the list as you pack so that you don't forget anything.

The smell of campfire cooking often attracts bears, raccoons and other wild animals. Don't invite trouble—keep food out of their reach.

Weight and storage A loaded backpack should weigh about 35 pounds; 20 pounds of this may reasonably consist of food. There are several ways of minimizing weight and storage problems when you pack food.

Before packing meat, remove bone and excess fat.

A fresh egg is 11% waste, unless the shell is used. Powdered egg has almost the same nutritional value as a fresh egg—and is easier to store. Similarly, powdered milk is more convenient than liquid milk.

When transporting whole eggs, use a noncrush egg case and arrange the eggs with their large ends up—to keep the yolks centered.

Eggs broken into a jar can be used later to make scrambled eggs or omelet.

Single eggs can be carried by burying them in a can of oatmeal.

Pack food in plastic containers and bags, not glass jars. Ice-cream containers and airtight tobacco tins are particularly useful. Waxed paper and aluminum foil are convenient for resealing partially used foods.

Combine spices in advance. Salt and pepper can be mixed in a three-to-one ratio. Ketchups, jams, jellies and other condiments are available in small plastic envelopes.

Dry foods—such as flour, cereal and sugar—should be wrapped in waterproof bags. Strong-smelling food, such as onion and garlic, should be sealed in plastic. Always keep detergents separate.

For safety, sharp knives should be tipped with cork. A cutting board—always useful around a campsite—can be fitted into the food box.

Make sure all cans are well marked. If possible, invest in a set of nesting aluminum pots which are specially designed for camping. Similarly, nesting cups and plates will facilitate packing.

A wire basket submerged in a cool stream or lake makes a handy cooler. Be sure to anchor the basket.

Perishable food Although not nearly as efficient as a refrigerator, a covered cooler containing ice maintains a temperature of about 5°C. (41°F.). At this temperature fresh fish and hamburger are safe for only 24 hours. Large cuts of meat keep for three or four days. Bacon, smoked meat, ham, eggs, butter, cheese, vegetables, fruit and milk are safe for several days.

A cooler, though too bulky and usually too heavy for backpacking, is good for carrying fresh food in an automobile. If you don't expect the cooler to be roughly used, an inexpensive styrofoam model may be

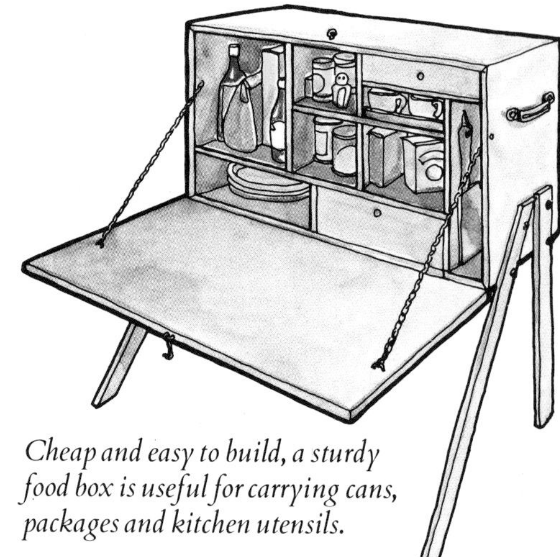

Cheap and easy to build, a sturdy food box is useful for carrying cans, packages and kitchen utensils.

How to Fillet a Fish

1. You need a fish of about three pounds and a razor-sharp knife for filleting. Cut to the backbone behind the gills and just ahead of the tail.

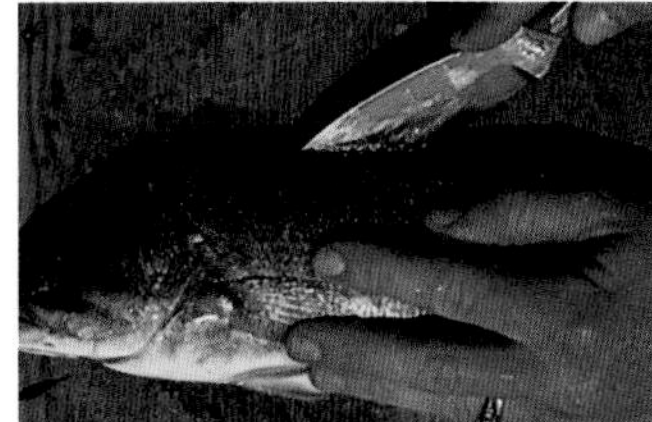

2. Cut off the dorsal fin, then cut along the spine.

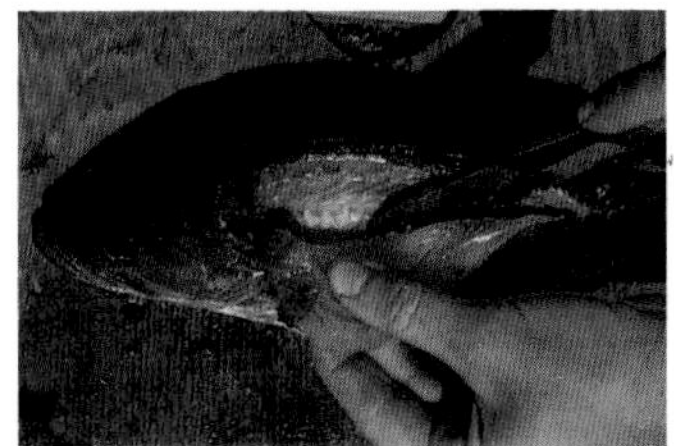

3. Insert the knife in the tail and separate the flesh from the vertebrae and ribs.

4. Slip knife between the flesh and the skin at the tail. Slice forward.

5. The skinless, mostly boneless fillet can be baked in butter or fried in batter.

right for you. Sturdier, more expensive models—with metal exteriors—are also available.

Handier and neater than ice are hot-and-cold packs made of tough plastic and filled with a gelatinous substance. Freeze them at home for 6 to 10 hours, then put them on top of food in your cooler. They will keep the contents of the cooler as cold as ice would, but once thawed they can be thrown into a duffel bag for later use. After being heated in boiling water for 5 to 10 minutes, they can be used to keep things warm—including your feet on a chilly night.

Always store the cooler in the shade—beneath a tree or in the trunk of a car—but not in a tent. Tents are usually warm, and—in bear country—there is always the danger of attracting an unwanted visitor.

Another method of keeping food frozen for the first day is to wrap it in several layers of newspaper. Place it in a plastic bag—in case of leakage.

If you are traveling by car, or staying in a public campground, you will probably be able to buy perishables—such as meat and fish—as you need them. If you intend to spend several weeks in the wilds, take canned, dried, dehydrated or concentrated food that will not spoil.

A useful addition to camping equipment are nesting aluminum pots. The large pot acts as a container for the rest of the set.

Portable camp kitchen For the car camper, this piece of gear is well worth its weight in convenience. Also called a food box, it is expensive to buy, but cheap and easy to build.

Use exterior plywood to build the box. Assess the number of compartments you will need and draw up a plan. There should be room for a bread box, a long narrow compartment for storing utensils and a place for tall packages and cans. A sliding drawer that holds cups snugly is also handy.

At camp, legs can be bolted to the box, or the unit can be placed on a picnic table. The front of the box should be hinged so that it folds down to provide extra working space.

Paint the outside of the box to protect it from the weather. You can attach such items as a bottle opener, a can opener, a towel rack and plastic-coated cup hooks to the outside of the box.

At the campsite There is truth in the proverb that too many cooks spoil the broth; when cooking, make the camp kitchen a restricted area.

Lightweight Foods for the Trail

Normally, a 150-pound man needs about 2,250 calories daily. Yet, in the outdoors, he will likely need 4,000 calories a day in summer, and as many as 6,000 in winter.

Since fat is high in calories, foods such as butter, margarine, lard, and bacon drippings should be used regularly at the campsite. And be sure to take along more sugar than you would normally use at home. Sugar, honey, syrup and chocolate provide quick energy. But avoid sugar substitutes—except for dietary reasons; substitutes contain much less fuel than the real thing.

As a rule, campers should get at least 20 calories per day per pound of body weight. To determine the exact caloric value of different foods, use an inexpensive caloric counter.

Nutrition Although calories provide a good indication of the body's energy requirements, it is inadvisable to select foods on this basis alone. Vitamins, minerals, proteins and carbohydrates are equally essential to proper nutrition. A well-balanced daily diet should include food from each of the following four groups (quantities will differ with activity levels and preferences):

Milk group Adult campers should receive 1½ to 2 cups of such foods as cream soup, cheese and pudding. Adolescents should receive four or more cups.

Meat group This group includes meat, poultry, fish, eggs, dry beans, peanut butter and cheese (although cheese is a milk product it can be a meat substitute). Each camper should receive two or more servings.

Vegetable/Fruit group One dark green (or yellow) vegetable and one citrus fruit should be served daily to each camper.

Bread/Cereal group This consists of such foods as whole-grain enriched bread, cereal, macaroni and rice. Four or more servings should be consumed by each camper. (A "serving" is a slice of bread or an ounce of cereal.)

Also, a variety of dried peas, beans and lentils could be included on the menu if you're stopping long enough to cook them. These foods are rich in carbohydrates—which yield energy—and they contain B vitamins. Split peas and lentils can be cooked without soaking, but beans and whole peas should be soaked overnight.

Scurvy If you are in the wilderness for a month or more, you must eat some fresh fish, meat, fruit or vegetables, or supplement your diet with vitamin-C tablets, in order to avoid scurvy—a disease caused by a lack of vitamin C. All fresh foods contain this vitamin.

Roughage Many trail foods—hard candy, nuts, raisins—supply quick energy, but have no indigestible fibers. This can result in digestive problems. To provide your body with roughage, eat such items as bran, corn and raw leafy vegetables.

Dehydrated foods Dehydration removes the water from food. Food prepared in this way is light and compact and will keep for a long time. Jerky and pemmican were among the earliest types of dehydrated foods. Today, a much wider variety of foods—including fruit, onions, potatoes, soups, milk and eggs—are available in dehydrated form.

Although supermarkets stock dehydrated foods, it should be remembered that many meats labeled "instant" or "dried," are not necessarily dehydrated. Your local sports or camping store may be a better place to stock up on dehydrated foods.

Most foods can be dehydrated at home if your oven will maintain a steady temperature between 43° and 63°C. (109° and 145°F.). The ideal temperature for drying meat is 66°C. (150°F.). Salt meat before drying it.

This Kit Could Save Your Life

No one should venture into the wilderness without a survival kit. You can make your own kit, or buy one at a camping store. Your survival kit should include emergency food (bouillon cubes, sugar, chocolate or malted milk tablets), waterproofed matches, a compass, a razor blade, a knife, fishing line, hooks and lures, 5 to 10 feet of wire for making snares, a whistle and a mirror for signaling, a pencil and paper for leaving messages, adhesive tape and bandages, water purification tablets, and aluminum foil for making cooking and drinking utensils.

Milk, cheese, cottage cheese, ice cream, yogurt and butter are especially important in the diets of growing children.

To meet the demands of strenuous outdoor sports, such as cross-country skiing, the camper must eat a well-balanced diet that will provide reserves of energy.

Slice foods thin and remove any inedible parts. Most vegetables take about three hours to become properly dehydrated; fruit takes about five hours. Apricots and plums should be boiled for about 20 minutes before they are dehydrated.

Properly dehydrated food should feel dry and pliant. Place the dried food in a plastic bag and seal the bag with a warm iron. Make sure there is as little air as possible in the bag and that the seal is airtight.

Some dehydrated fruits can be eaten raw but most dehydrated foods should be boiled to restore their water.

Freeze-dried food Like dehydrated food, freeze-dried has been processed to remove most of its moisture. This is accomplished by quick-freezing the food and then placing it in a vacuum chamber for dehydration. The process, which takes about 12 hours, is expensive and too difficult for the do-it-yourselfer.

Although expensive, freeze-dried foods are light and compact and need only be soaked in water for 10 to 30 minutes before mealtime.

Vacuum-dried food Although similar to freeze-drying, vacuum-drying is usually limited to the processing of fruit. Moisture is evaporated in a vacuum chamber.

Vacuum-dried fruit looks like gravel, but don't be deceived by its appearance; it is tasty. Like freeze-dried food, it is light and compact, and keeps indefinitely.

The cells in food remain intact throughout freeze-drying and vacuum-drying, so the food's taste and texture are retained. Since food processed by either of these methods is also odorless (until its water is replaced), insects are not attracted to it.

Radiation-preserved food A modern process, used to preserve food for spaceflights, keeps food fresh and nutritious without refrigeration. Although not yet commercially available, radiation-preserved food could become popular with campers.

Foods rich in protein and fat include meat, fish, eggs, peanut butter, cheese and dried beans.

Campers should eat green vegetables and one citrus fruit daily. Many foods in this group will keep in a cool place for several days or weeks.

Whole-grain bread and cereal are excellent sources of roughage. The daily requirement for a camper is four slices of bread or four ounces of dry cereal.

Simple, Mouth-Watering Outdoor Meals

For campers who have worked up hearty appetites from a day of activity in the sunshine and fresh air, nothing beats the appeal of juicy steaks or fresh-caught fish sizzling over an open fire. Even the simplest camp meals can be mouth-watering and fun to prepare. On these pages are tips and techniques that will help you cook delicious campfire meals.

Cooking with clay This is an old practice, employed for centuries by Indians. Birds, small animals and a variety of vegetables can be cooked in this manner. It is also a good way to bake fish, particularly for breakfast.

In the evening, take a fish and clean it. Pack a layer of clay or mud, at least a half-inch thick, around the fish and bury it in a solid bed of coals. Heap coals over the clay-encrusted fish, then leave it overnight.

In the morning the clay shell will be baked hard. Give it a sharp rap and peel the pieces away from the fish. The scales of the fish stick to the clay and the fish is ready for eating.

Fowl or poultry cooked in this way should be cleaned first, but skin and feathers can be left on.

Aluminum foil—neater, and usually more accessible than clay—is a good substitute. Wrap heavy-duty foil (or double-wrap ordinary foil) around the food to form an airtight package. Bury the package in a bed of coals.

Many vegetables—such as potatoes and onions—can be cooked in their skins, without foil or clay. Oysters can be baked in their shells, and eggs pierced at both ends (to allow steam to escape) can be baked near the fire.

Stick cooking A sharpened stick can be used to cook wieners, shish kebab and a variety of medium-sized foods. A cooking stick should be green and sweet-tasting; you can test this by biting the tip. Hickory, sugar maple and birch can be used, but willow and resinous woods have an unpleasant flavor. A bed of glowing coals is necessary for good results.

To cook large steaks, construct a tennis-racquet broiler. Take a long forked stick and twist together the ends of both prongs. Interlace the space with several thin sticks—or pieces of wire—to create a loose mesh. The steak can then be worked between the crisscrossed sticks.

A block of wood or a split log can also be used for cooking. Heat the block in front of the fire and then pin a split-open fish, skin side down, to its surface. Place the block at the windward side of the fire and tilt it so that the fish faces the flames. Cook the fish reflector style; across the fire, opposite the fish, erect a reflector wall, of logs or

An outdoor treat: chicken on a spit, potatoes baked in aluminum foil.

Even easy-to-cook foods become special when cooked over an open fire.

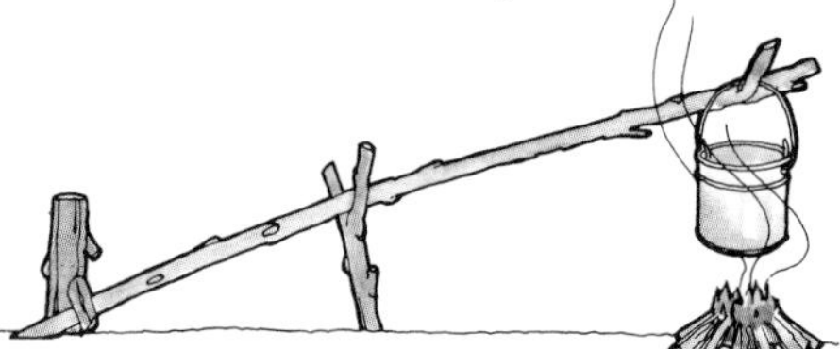

A green pole and two forked sticks make a good pot holder.

Wire grill barbecuing is quick and easy.

Try spit barbecuing for poultry and roasts.

This device will hold several pots at a time.

stones. Make sure the fire is blazing. Baste the fish regularly with butter.

Barbecuing Meat and poultry are quick and easy to barbecue—and the results are delicious. The secret of successful barbecuing is to start with a solid bed of hot coals. Lay a fire with hardwood or charcoal briquets and let it burn for about 20 minutes before cooking over it.

Spit barbecuing Build a fire in a shallow trench. The spit can be made from a peeled green stick, although a metal skewer will distribute heat to the inside of the meat. Impale the meat or poultry on the skewer so that all sides will be well exposed to the fire. Pin back any wings and flaps so they won't burn. Rest the skewer on a pair of forked sticks and rotate it regularly. Baste every 10 minutes with bacon fat or shortening to keep the food moist and tender.

Wire grill barbecuing Let a hardwood fire burn down to coals, and then—with sticks—draw a grill over the coals and support it on two parallel logs. When barbecuing meat, turn it over regularly with a long forked stick, but do not pierce it. Piercing meat allows juices to escape. Wieners, chops and steaks can be cooked this way.

Never use an old refrigerator grill for barbecuing: many were made of cadmium which may contaminate food and gives off poisonous vapors when heated.

Barbecues

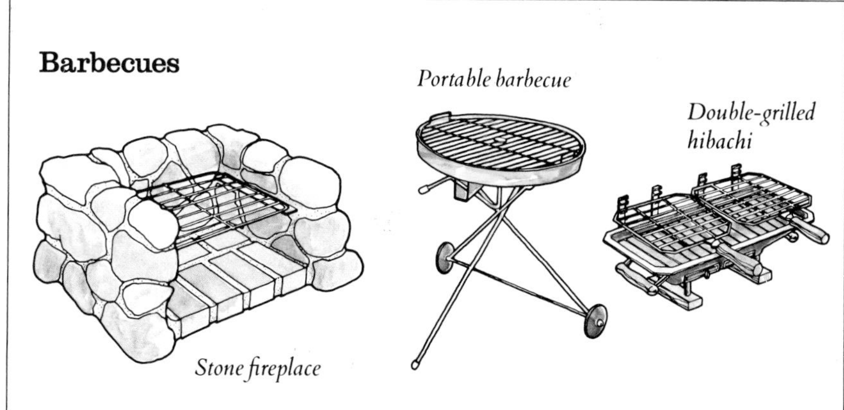

Pit barbecuing This is a rather elaborate process, but one which yields excellent results. Dig a hole two or three times larger than the food to be cooked. Line the sides and bottom with rocks, and build a good hardwood fire in the pit. When the fire has burned down to coals, and the rocks are hot, remove some of the rocks and place the food in the pit.

Ideally, the food should be contained in a preheated Dutch oven or similar cast-iron pot. Lacking this, the food can be wrapped in damp paper towels, leaves or grass.

Replace the coals and rocks and pack them around and over the food. Cover with about six inches of dirt and make sure that no steam escapes. The barbecue can now be left unattended.

A large animal takes about 20 hours to cook in this manner; a chicken takes 3 or 4 hours. A pit barbecue is excellent for cooking corn, onions, potatoes, clams, hams and many other foods.

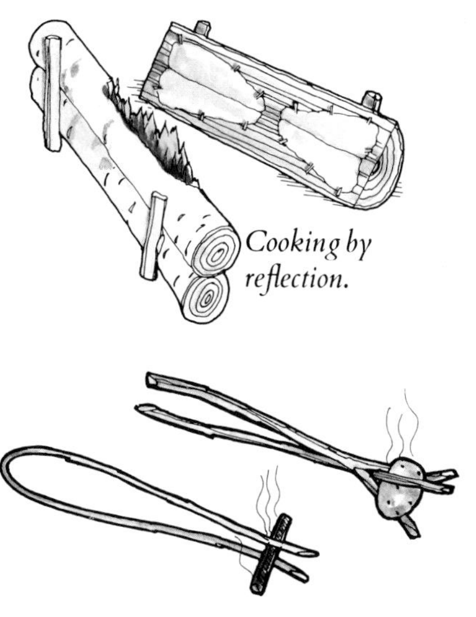

Cooking by reflection.

Fire tongs made from sturdy saplings.

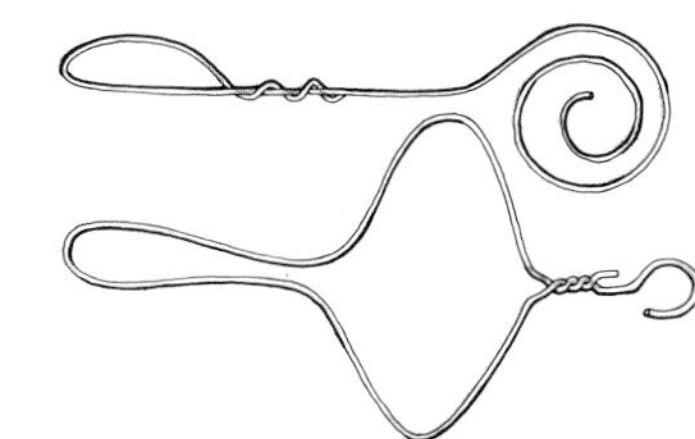

Wire coat hangers can be twisted into handy toasters.

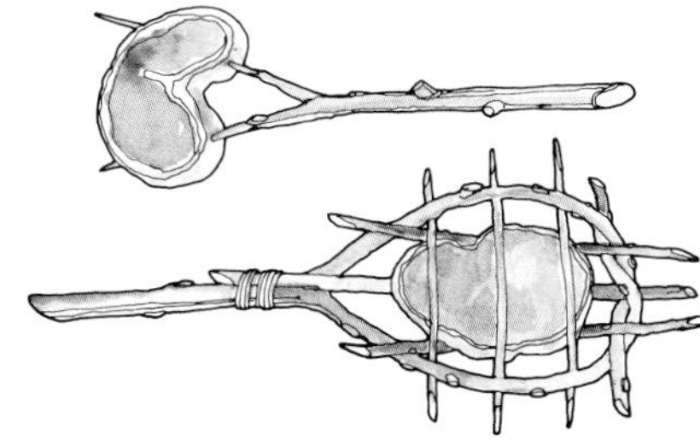

Forked sticks can be used to broil meat.

General cooking tips A pot can be suspended over a fire on a long green pole that is anchored at one end and supported in the middle by forked sticks.

A sturdier structure—for holding two and three pots at once—can be made from two forked sticks and a strong, green pole. Sharpen the ends of the sticks and drive them into the ground on both sides of the campfire. Rest the pole in the forks of the two upright sticks. Pots can then be suspended from the pole.

Pot hooks can be fashioned from coat-hanger wire or forked sticks.

Fire tongs can be made by bending a sturdy sapling into a V shape. The sapling will bend without splitting if you shave away some of the middle and warm that section over a fire. Bind the tongs with cord.

Hearty, Traditional Fare of Old-Time Woodsmen

Old-time woodsmen and prospectors maintained that no bread could beat the flavor of sourdough. (In fact, old-timers in the Yukon and Alaska were called "sourdoughs.") To make your own sourdough starter—a leavening and flavoring agent that can be used in any bread recipe—shake a packet of dry granular yeast or one yeast cake with 2 cups of flour and 2 cups of warm water in a covered crock or glass jar. (Never use a metal container or leave a spoon in the starter.) Cover the starter loosely with a light cloth and let it stand overnight in a warm, draft-free spot. By morning the mixture is bubbly and called a sponge. Take ½ cup of sponge and store it in a clean covered jar in a cool place as a new starter. The remaining dough can be used immediately.

To sustain your stock of sourdough, for every cupful removed add a cup of water and flour mixture of the same consistency as the sourdough. Prolonged fermentation produces a flavor that quick-leavening agents cannot match. If the sourdough loses its clean, sour-milk odor, throw it out and start anew.

Sourdough flapjacks, bannock and hardtack are among the old-time recipes you can prepare to enliven outdoor meals.

Sourdough bread

4 cups sifted flour
2 tablespoons sugar
1 teaspoon salt
2 tablespoons melted shortening
2 cups sourdough sponge

1. Mix the flour, sugar and salt in a bowl. Make a well in the center of the mixture.
2. Pour the melted shortening into the well, then add the sourdough sponge. Blend with flour mixture to form a soft dough.
3. Knead with firm strokes for 10 to 15 minutes on a lightly floured surface. Do not knead too long or gas will escape and the bread will not rise fully.
4. Cut the dough to fit the pan or pans. Put it in a warm place to rise for about 2 hours. When the loaves have doubled in size, bake 50 to 60 minutes in a reflector oven that is hottest in the first 15 minutes. The loaves should double in size again. Test with a sharp knife—if it comes out clean the bread is baked.

Sourdough flapjacks

2 cups sourdough sponge
2 eggs (fresh or reconstituted)
½ teaspoon salt
1 tablespoon sugar
1 teaspoon baking soda
2 tablespoons melted shortening

1. Mix eggs, salt and sugar.
2. Dissolve baking soda in 1 teaspoon warm water.
3. Stir egg mixture, dissolved soda and melted shortening into the sourdough sponge. If the batter is too thick to pour, add milk.
4. Lightly grease a hot skillet. Pour batter into the skillet. Flip when it starts to bubble; the second side will cook in half the time.

Hot, fresh bread is the outdoorsman's specialty. Bannock, sourdough and hardtack are more practical and nutritious than bulky, air-filled bakery bread—which spoils quickly. Steaming bannock, an old favorite, is simple to make.

Fresh-picked huckleberries make a tasty addition to bannock.

Bannock

For one serving:
1 cup white flour
¼ teaspoon salt
1 teaspoon baking powder
About ⅓ cup cold water

For enriched bannock, add any or all of the following for each serving:

1 tablespoon dry powdered egg (or ½ fresh egg)
2 tablespoons skim milk powder (enough to make ½ cup milk)
1 tablespoon melted butter, margarine, commercial lard, hydrogenated vegetable oil, or bacon drippings

1. Mix dry ingredients thoroughly in a bowl.

2. Add water and melted fat. Stir until the mixture forms a thick dough. (The dough should be firm enough that it doesn't flow, yet not so thick that it can be kneaded. The proper texture can be achieved with experience.) If it is too thin, add more flour; if it is too thick, add more water. Fruits such as raisins, huckleberries and blueberries may be added.

3. Spread a one-inch layer of dough over the bottom of a greased frying pan. Prop the pan about 6 to 8 inches from a flaming fire and bake the bannock in the reflected heat. Turn the bannock over until it is golden brown on both sides.

Hardtack

Hardtack is a dry, unleavened bread. Combine 1 cup flour for each person and enough water to make a stiff dough. (A sprinkling of sugar and ¼ teaspoon of salt can be added if desired.) Roll the dough into a flat cake and bake it in a skillet until the hardtack is dry.

Jerky and pemmican

A day on the trail consumes huge amounts of calories. Jerky and pemmican, the original dehydrated foods carried by outdoorsmen, are high in fats and carbohydrates and provide excellent trail nutrition.

Jerky is lean meat divided into wide strips about ½ inch thick and hung to dry in the sun. A small, smoky fire under the meat keeps flies away. When ready, the jerky will be hard and black. It can be eaten uncooked or cut into thin strips and boiled—or added to a milk sauce and served on biscuits.

Pemmican, made from jerky, contains all the elements of nutrition except vitamin C.

To make pemmican, chop a pound of jerky into small pieces. Cut a pound or more of animal fat into lumps and fry it over a moderate heat until the grease leaves the lumps. Discard the lumps. Pour the grease over the shredded jerky, mixing until you have a sausagelike consistency. Ideally, the pemmican should be half fat and half meat by weight.

Frequently such trail foods as chocolate bars, nuts, cereals and fruits are more appealing than traditional fare. And don't overlook the delicious and vitamin-packed fresh fruits and greens along the trail.

Baked beans

1 pound dried navy or pea beans
¼ to ½ pound diced salt pork
½ tablespoon salt
2 tablespoons brown sugar

Wash the beans, then cover with water and leave them to soak overnight. In the morning, add salt and simmer the beans until they are tender. Drain the beans, saving the liquid. Layer them with salt pork in a Dutch oven, sprinkle the sugar on top. The following ingredients may be added to improve the flavor of the beans:

1 onion, whole or sliced
2 to 4 tablespoons molasses
1 teaspoon dry mustard
pepper
¼ cup vinegar
¼ cup maple syrup
dash of Worcestershire sauce

Line a shallow pit with coals. Put the covered Dutch oven in the pit for 6 to 8 hours. Add some of the saved liquid whenever the beans become too dry.

Clambake! A Seafood Feast That's Fun

You've probably heard of clambakes, but have you ever sampled food prepared this fun way? The menu for each person can include a lobster, a dozen clams, a few ears of corn, a potato, an onion, shrimps, scallops or fish fillets. Allow a pound of melted butter for every 10 people.

Plenty of kindling and an eighth of a cord of wood (2 feet wide, 2 feet high and 4 feet long) are needed for a clambake. Start with the kindling, then pile on about 2 bushels of dry, fist-sized rocks (see illustration). Light the fire. When it is well ablaze, stack the cordwood on and around the fire. With the fire going well, prepare the food: scrub the clams clean of sand; husk the corn. Put the butter in covered cans or pots so that it can be melted. The lobsters can be split and stuffed. Now it's time to build the bake. Quickly rake out the embers (steam does the job, not smoke) and level out the rocks. Cover them with eight bushels of wet seaweed or wet corn husks. Save some for the top layer. Lay cheesecloth over the seaweed. Put the ingredients on top of the cheesecloth in layers: first the potatoes, then the lobsters, then the corn, then the clams. Don't forget the cans of butter. Throw a canvas tarp over everything and weigh down the edges. If steam escapes from any spot, close it off with sand. In about 90 minutes, lift a corner of the tarp and test a potato. If it's done, so is your meal.

Pile dry rocks on kindling, then cover with cordwood.

Place food on seaweed and rocks. Cover with canvas and leave to cook.

Outdoors: Just for Fun

Canada is a vast playground where the outdoorsman can enjoy sailing, canoeing, kayaking, swimming, fishing, hiking, climbing, skiing, snowshoeing and many other invigorating activities. Or he can spend a lazy afternoon on the beach, take a scenic drive, or share a roadside picnic with family and friends.

Energy, as well as enthusiasm, is often needed for outdoor adventure. In the following pages you are advised to begin strenuous or unfamiliar activities cautiously and to build up your endurance. Canoeing or kayaking is best learned on a placid lake or a quiet stream. Novice hikers should begin with easy strolls along well-marked paths before undertaking a muscle-stretching trek over high mountains.

In this section you'll learn how to make a long hike easier, how to tackle a cliff face, and what gear to take on a camping, hiking or climbing trip. You'll discover how to avoid accidents while exploring the dark, intriguing world of caves. You'll learn much of the lore of the backwoodsman: how to read topographical maps, how to use a compass, how to find your way in the wilderness by using the sun or the stars, and how to find North by interpreting Nature's signs.

You'll find tips on swimming, lifesaving, drownproofing, canoeing and kayaking. For fishermen there is information on tackle, casting, popular freshwater game fish, and reading a river, lake or seashore for the best fishing spots.

Sailing or powerboating is an exciting way to explore coastal regions and inland waterways. And some boats can be both transportation and a home away from home. This section discusses how to choose a boat and what regulations must be observed when operating it.

By following the advice on photography, you can take better pictures of scenery and wildlife. With the star map in this section, you can find and identify major stars and constellations of the Northern Hemisphere. On other pages you will discover how to make camping as much fun in winter as it is in summer. There is also information about snowshoeing and cross-country skiing—among the best ways to appreciate the beauty of a snow-covered landscape.

Hike, climb, swim, canoe, fish, ski—whatever you do outdoors, your pleasure will be increased if you master the proper techniques, choose the right equipment and observe safety rules.

High above rolling hills, a skier glides past ice-laden evergreens and drifting snow.

Swimming Is for All Ages

Swimming can be enjoyed from childhood to old age at almost no cost. It develops lung capacity, strengthens muscles and exercises the body without overheating it. Yet, despite its benefits, swimming has dangers too.

Knowledge and caution are increasingly important as more and more persons participate in water sports. You can minimize the risk of accident if your attitude is always "safety first." Learn to read the weather, the beach, the water. Above all, learn to swim well.

Flotation equipment Rings, inner tubes and inflatable toys tend to handicap rather than help the beginning swimmer. Worse, flotation gear may lure a nonswimmer or a poor swimmer beyond his depth by imparting a false sense of security. Use such equipment only if you swim well enough to cope without it.

The lifesavers Next to a life jacket the most effective lifesaver is the ability to tread water. Even a nonswimmer can learn to tread water—a simple skill that could mean the difference between life and drowning. Swimming itself involves little risk of injury but carelessness and risk-taking cause many fatal accidents. So:

- Whenever possible, swim where there is a lifeguard.
- Do not swim alone.
- Do not swim at night.
- Be sure your group includes at least one adult knowledgeable in lifesaving and first aid.
- Discourage long-distance swimming by persons not in top physical condition—and make sure that a long-distance swimmer is accompanied by at least one other accomplished swimmer in a boat.
- Be wary of whirlpools, swift currents, rocks, stumps, entangling water plants and deep holes in lakes, ponds and rivers.
- Never dive without first ascertaining the depth of the water and the condition of the bottom.
- Remember: if you're cold and tired, you're susceptible to cramps.
- In salt water be alert to the dangers of heavy surf, undertow and ocean currents.
- Beach conditions may be altered drastically and dangerously by changing winds, currents and tides. An offshore sandbar that is easily accessible at ebb tide, for instance, may not be so at flood tide.
- Only experienced swimmers dare venture beyond supervised surf-bathing areas—and why should even they do so?

Undertow The return flow of water from waves breaking on the shore is stronger on a short, steep beach than on one with a gentle slope. The undertow may topple you from your feet and carry you out to deeper water, but its action is reversed with the surface force of each new wave. To escape from an undertow, brace your feet and work diagonally toward shore, using your hands as paddles. If beyond your depth, swim away from that part of the beach, then approach the shore diagonally.

Currents Perhaps the most startling of currents for swimmers is the runout, which flows seaward at as much as six miles an hour. It generally occurs when water, which has built up behind a temporary sandbar, suddenly flows outward through a weak spot in the bar. Easily spotted from the beach, a runout looks different from the surrounding sea: the waves are small, choppy, jumbled; the water may appear dark or sandy.

Rip currents are similar to runouts but narrower; they are mushroom-shaped and occur 15 to 30 yards from shore, usually along irregular beaches. If caught in a runout or rip current, don't panic. Swim parallel to shore until you are free of the current.

The Kiss of Life

Speed and know-how are crucial in saving a drowning person's life. Make sure the air passages are open and air is entering the lungs.

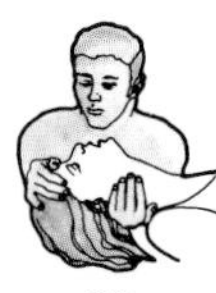

1. Tilt the head back and lift the neck.

2. Pinch the nostrils closed. Open the mouth.

3. Blow into the victim's lungs (12 times a minute for an adult, 20 for a child).

4. Remove your mouth, release the nostrils; let the victim exhale. As the chest falls, repeat procedure.

Drownproofing

This easy-to-learn method of treading water can help you avoid panic and exhaustion in the water.
1. With lungs full, relax, float face down, rest 3 seconds. 2. Exhale slowly through your nose while extending your arms and moving your legs as if pedaling a bicycle. 3-4. Lift head, push down with hands, and inhale. 5. Lungs full, drop head, push down and back. 6. Hold your breath, relax, repeat sequence. Maintain a pace that gives you a feeling of comfort and safety in the water.

One of the greatest joys of summer—the first pell-mell dash into the cool, clear water of your favorite vacation lake.

Drift or set currents run roughly parallel to shore. They are caused by surf coming across a sandbar and hitting the beach at an angle.

Cramps In spring and early summer many an overeager swimmer plunges into chill waters, inviting cramps—or even a heart attack. A swimmer is most susceptible to cramps when cold and tired. This painful knotting of muscles is usually in the foot, calf or hand, and occasionally in the thigh. The afflicted swimmer should inhale deeply, roll face down in the water and grasp the cramped muscle firmly. A few seconds of pressure should relieve the cramps but vigorous kneading may be necessary.

Stomach cramps, sometimes caused by swimming too soon after eating, are more serious. Excruciating pain makes breathing difficult and may cause the body to jackknife, forcing the victim's head underwater. A swimmer with stomach cramps is likely to drown unless rescued quickly. After a full meal, don't swim for two hours.

Children Youngsters should always be attended by a competent adult swimmer. Inflatable toys belong on the beach, not in the water. Play involving mock distress calls should be forbidden. Temperature, weather and individual tolerance tell experienced swimmers when to leave the water but children may want to stay in longer than is wise. Watch for goose pimples, shivering and bluish lips.

Lifesaving Swimming rescues are beyond most inexperienced swimmers. Call for help. Use a boat if possible, and haul in the victim at the stern. Attempt a swimming rescue only if other methods are impractical and you are an accomplished swimmer trained in lifesaving. If no other means of rescue are possible and you must directly contact a swimmer in distress, approach him from the rear and seize him by the hair or chin or around the chest.

Call a doctor. If the rescued person has stopped breathing, remove any foreign material from his mouth and start artificial respiration (see The Kiss of Life, previous page).

From Snorkeling . . .

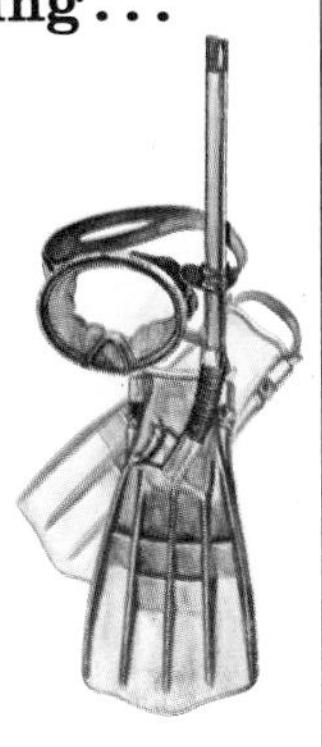

Snorkeling (skin diving) originated in the Mediterranean. It requires a mask, fins and a snorkel (breathing tube): the curved end is in the mouth; the other protrudes from the water as the diver floats face down.

. . . to Scuba Diving

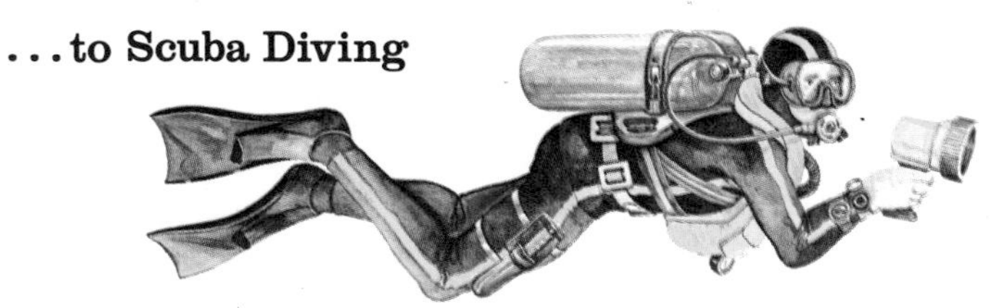

From the relatively unsophisticated sport of skin diving pioneered before World War II has evolved scuba diving, which employs tanks of pressurized air (Scuba stands for Self-Contained Underwater Breathing Apparatus). A valved mouthpiece automatically increases the flow of air as the diver descends and decreases it as he ascends. A single tank usually lasts about an hour under normal diving conditions.

Boating . . . the Right Way

Boating is many things to many people. It is racing, cruising, fishing, waterskiing. It is a placid backwater under a lazy summer sun. It is the exhilarating response of a sensitive craft in a strong wind and a following sea. It is a dinghy, a powerful motorboat, a tall-masted sailboat . . . Small wonder that more than a million Canadians take to their boats every year in confident pursuit of sheer fun—and perhaps a little adventure.

Choosing a boat Prices vary widely, even among models of similar design. If you select a secondhand craft, be particularly choosy if it is a wooden boat: watch for rotten planks and rusty fittings. If possible, have the boat examined by a marine surveyor before you buy. A fiberglass boat is durable, requires little maintenance and will not rot.

If sailing is your thing, with an emphasis on racing, select a model adopted by a local club. But make sure your boat will be suitable for the waters you intend to sail—a deep-keeled craft can't be sailed in a too shallow lake.

Many sailors prefer a boat that fits into the racing-cruising category—fun for both the racer and his family. Models generally range between 16 feet and 24 feet.

Sailboats are more stable and more comfortable than powerboats on long voyages over open water. But they require much time and preparation; sails must be hoisted and lines rigged before you even cast off. Powerboats, on the other hand, can be started within 5 to 10 minutes after a blower has cleared the bilge of fumes.

Small powerboats are light enough to trail behind a car and fast enough to tow a water-skier. Big ones, some with as many as 12 berths and most of the comforts of home, are extremely expensive. Some have radar, an automatic pilot and a ship-to-shore radiotelephone.

When buying, whether a dinghy or an expensive cruiser, it is wise to discuss your needs with dealers and experienced sailors. From a builder get a warranty covering construction and parts. When buying any boat, insist on a trial run in average (not perfect) weather conditions.

Once you have chosen a boat, you should enroll in a boating course. Canadian Power Squadrons offers a beginners' course in power boating, and sailing instruction is available from the Canadian Yachting Association and from many yachting schools.

Licensing Every pleasure craft up to 20 registered tons and equipped with an engine of 10 horsepower or more must be licensed under the Small Vessels Regulations. Licenses are free from Canada Customs offices. Charts, sailing directions and tide tables for all the navigable waters of Canada can be bought from the Hydrographic Service, Marine Sciences Branch, Department of Energy, Mines and Resources, Ottawa.

Regulations The Small Vessels Regulations govern most traffic. Pleasure skippers who venture into wide waters must also obey the rules of the road for the Great Lakes and even the International Regulations for the

Powerful outboard engines make power boating a fast, exciting sport.

Inflatable boats can be rowed, sailed or powered, and are easily transported.

A cruising powerboat offers sleeping berths, a galley complete with sink and stove, and ample seating for a family that wants to travel on water.

There is a special thrill to sailing before a brisk breeze.

Prevention of Collisions at Sea. The federal Ministry of Transport will provide a free Boating Safety Guide listing up-to-date regulations.

The law demands that you proceed with due care and attention. In general, power-driven vessels are required to keep out of the way of sailboats, rowboats and canoes. An exception to the tradition that power gives way to sail is when an unpowered boat is overtaking a motorboat. The right of way on water always rests with the craft being overtaken.

Vessels leaving docks, piers or landing stages have no right of way until they are clear of all traffic in nearby waterways. Fishing boats are not permitted to fish in traffic channels or to obstruct normal navigation.

There are regulations covering danger to other boats or swimmers, waterskiing without due care, maximum speed areas, whistle and flag signals, the carrying of fire extinguishers and lifesaving equipment, and maximum-load plaques.

All vessels must carry lights between sunset and sunrise. It is wise (and mandatory in vessels 26 feet long or longer) to carry a buoyant heaving line, flares, smoke devices for daytime signaling, and a handbell or horn for signaling in fog.

In bad weather, make sure everyone is seated and wearing a life jacket. If it can be done safely, head for port.

Make sure your boat is properly moored when alongside. When refueling, put passengers ashore and do not smoke, strike matches or switch on electrical equipment.

The Life You Save...

A life jacket is for saving a life, maybe yours. So use only the best. Acceptable jackets are approved by the federal Ministry of Transport. Test yours: wade into chest-deep water and bend your knees; the jacket should support you in a backward position with your mouth and nose clear of the water. Fighting to "climb out" of the water tends to nullify a jacket's floating capabilities. Replace kapok jackets if the vinyl inserts become torn or the fibers matted. Unicellular foam jackets are more durable but careless treatment and exposure to sunlight will damage them.

Expect plenty of spills if you're sailing a high-performance sailboat.

The DOs and DON'Ts of Boating Safety

Do • Learn and practice the Rules of the Road • Keep bilges aired and free of gas and oil • Respect your boat and know its limitations • Carry fire-extinguishing, lifesaving gear • Give fishermen and swimmers a wide berth • Carry two oars or two paddles • Slow when making sharp turns

Don't • Mix liquor and boating • Use a leaky or poorly built craft • Leave a steering wheel or tiller unattended • Blow your horn unnecessarily • Stand or change seats in a small boat • Attempt to swim ashore if swamped • Create dangerous swells near other boats.

How to Choose and Equip a Canoe

Canoeing provides a spectacular opportunity to explore many remote areas of Canada that cannot normally be reached on foot or approached by car. Although the initial outlay may be high, the rewards can be enormous—and a good canoe will last for years. Choosing the right one is extremely important.

The canoe originated in North America and is generally called the "Canadian canoe." While racing canoes are highly specialized craft that come in a wide variety of models, recreational canoes are divided into three basic designs:

The standard recreational canoe has a slightly rounded bottom and a small keel.

The white water model is fast, less stable than the standard model, and has no keel.

The flat-bottomed canoe is designed for carrying heavy loads.

Material An aluminum canoe is a good choice for beginners. Aluminum canoes are light, durable, and require little maintenance. They are also unsinkable—unless, of course, an air chamber is punctured.

Aluminum canoes do reflect light; to overcome this, they can be painted. Unless specially treated, aluminum canoes should never be used in salt water, which corrodes aluminum.

When purchasing an aluminum canoe, check that the construction is stretch form—that is, made of two sheets of aluminum stretched in a mold and welded. Stretch-form canoes are lighter and faster than cut-form canoes. Avoid aluminum that is less than 62/1,000-inch thick. Thinner aluminum will be too easily dented.

Fiberglass canoes, canoes made of wood and canvas, birchbark canoes and plywood canoes are generally more aesthetic and quieter than aluminum models. They are also more easily damaged.

Design Ideally, your canoe should be 16 feet long (17 feet if intended for regular use in rough water) and 12 to 14 inches high amidships. The beam should be at least 30 inches. A good canoe should carry 12 times its weight and still have 6 inches of freeboard.

The shape of a canoe determines its performance. Flat-bottomed canoes are very stable, but round-bottomed canoes glide more efficiently. A compromise between the two types—with a slightly curved bottom that provides stability without sluggishness—is recommended for campers.

When selecting a keel, remember that a straight, deep keel holds its course well but makes maneuvering

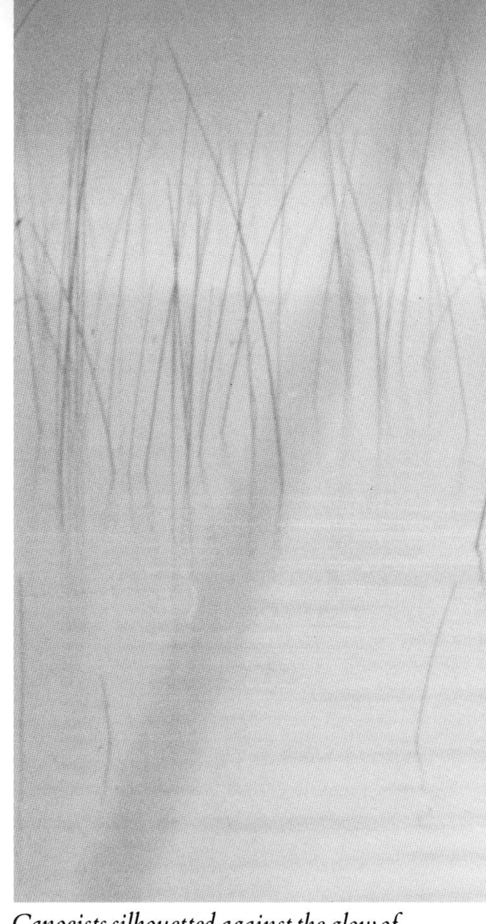

Canoeists silhouetted against the glow of a wilderness sunrise.

Life jackets are essential.

Nylon cord is useful as a mooring rope.

A plastic container serves as a bailing bucket.

A spare paddle for each canoeist.

Foam pads wrapped in waterproof material cushion the knees.

difficult. A small center keel provides both stability and maneuverability.

Equipment A paddle should reach from the ground to your chin. The blade (unless for racing) should be no wider than seven inches, and the edge should be about ⅛-inch thick. Good woods for paddles are white ash, white spruce and white maple. Always stow an extra paddle in your gear. Have it within easy reach, in case of emergency.

Life jackets are essential for swimmers and nonswimmers. Make sure the jackets you purchase are of a type approved by the federal Ministry of Transport. Vest-type jackets are usually the most convenient for canoeists.

A painter or mooring line should be purchased. About 25 feet of ¼-inch nylon cord is recommended. For bailing use a large household sponge or a plastic container. Metal containers tend to rust.

Kneeling pads can be fashioned by covering six-inch squares of foam with waterproof material. For greater comfort line the seats of the canoe with foam, or sew squares of cork into the canvas.

Reading a River

Even the most experienced canoeist takes nothing for granted—he exercises caution on all waterways. This rule should apply equally to novices. By learning to read a river—to recognize details that indicate the nature of your chosen course—your trip will be smoother and safer.

If you plan on returning by the same route, take note of any hazards you encounter. Never let your canoe be swept broadside into a stationary object. Obstacles deflect the current, creating dangerous situations. Fallen trees, large rocks—these may cause the canoe to capsize.

Remember that many river forks lead to dead ends. Check the underwater vegetation. If the weeds are vertical, this usually suggests a dead-end tributary. If they are bent, you are probably on a main stream. A pileup of debris—logs and branches—also suggests a main stream.

Techniques for Confident Canoeing

Even on the calm waters of a stream or lake canoeists should wear life jackets and observe the rules of safe canoeing in case unexpected hazards arise.

You can canoe with greater confidence and pleasure once you have learned the essentials of safe canoeing and have mastered the basic paddle strokes.

Loading It is usually best to place any load near the middle of the canoe. When you expect to be traveling with the wind place the load near the stern. When traveling into the wind put the load near the bow.

If you anticipate rough water, cover the load with a tarpaulin tied down with strong rope. Packs should be tied to the thwarts.

Entering To enter from a dock, make sure the canoe is fully afloat and parallel to the dock. The sternman enters first, stepping into the middle of the canoe while the bowman steadies the craft. Once seated, the sternman holds the canoe steady against the dock while the bowman enters. Both bowman and sternman should stay as low as possible.

Portaging–When Walking Is Wiser

It is often more practical and usually safer for canoeists to bypass hazardous stretches of river by portaging—carrying a canoe and any gear to calmer water. If the distance is only a few yards, one person can carry the canoe. You can portage a canoe while wearing a backpack but it is best to leave your gear and come back for it. When portaging, put some padding on your neck and shoulders to cushion the weight of the canoe. A horseshoe-shaped yoke made of foam rubber works well.

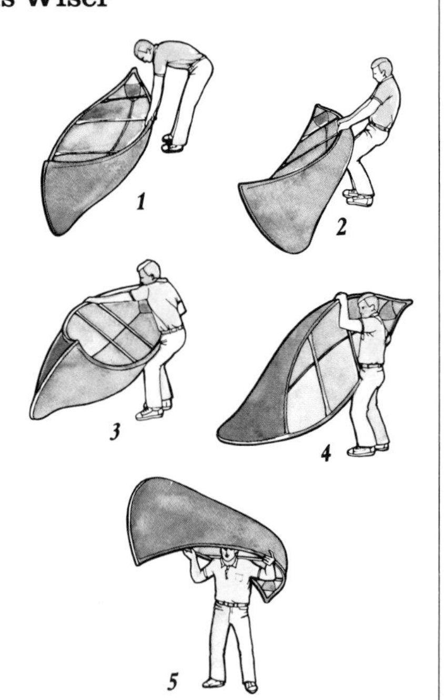

1. *To lift a canoe, stand at its port (left) side and grasp the near gunwale with both hands.* **2.** *Pull the canoe on to your knees.* **3.** *Reach across and grasp the other gunwale with your left hand.* **4.** *Lift the canoe so that you are facing the bow.* **5.** *Move to the center of the canoe and balance it on your hands and shoulders.*

To enter from shore, make sure that the canoe is fully afloat. The sternman steadies while the bowman places his paddle across the gunwales and steps into the canoe, using the paddle to balance. Again, the body should be kept low.

Lining It is often wise to avoid navigating rapids, especially in unfamiliar territory. If a bank alongside rapids is not too rugged, you can line your canoe to calmer waters.

To line a canoe, attach a rope to the stern seat and another to the bow seat. Make sure the bow of the canoe points upstream.

Stand on the bank, hold the stern line taut, and push the bow into the current. Play out the stern line until the canoe is parallel to the shore and the bow and stern lines are both taut. Tow the canoe in the direction you wish to travel. Steer with the bow rope, increasing and decreasing the rope's tautness as necessary. Always keep a firm grip on the ropes—if you lose control, the current may flip the craft.

Lining is best done by two persons, one holding the bow rope, the other the stern rope.

In very rough water remove all gear from the canoe before lining.

Poling Occasionally canoeists can walk their canoes through shallow rapids, but in deeper water poling is advisable.

Poling requires two persons, each equipped with a slender pole—cut from a shoreline forest—about 12 feet long. Never use paddles: they break easily.

Kneel in the canoe, plant the pole in the river bottom and push down on the pole to move the canoe forward. When traveling downstream in rapids, the sternman uses the pole to guide the canoe around rocks and other dangerous obstacles while the bowman paddles.

Swamping and capsizing If a swamped or capsized canoe is still afloat don't abandon it—a canoe is often your best life preserver.

When your canoe swamps close to shore stay seated and paddle slowly to the nearest bank. In deep water begin bailing immediately. It is often best to get out of the canoe and rock it back and forth. This will throw much of the water out of the craft—and make bailing easier.

If an unloaded canoe is sinking, lash paddles to a thwart or wedge them in the bow or stern. Then capsize the canoe. Air trapped underneath will keep the craft afloat.

To right the canoe, grip the nearest gunwale, rock the canoe to gain momentum, then flip it over. Board the canoe from the bow or stern and bail out the remaining water.

If your canoe is loaded when it swamps, jettison your gear. (A float attached to your equipment will keep it from sinking.)

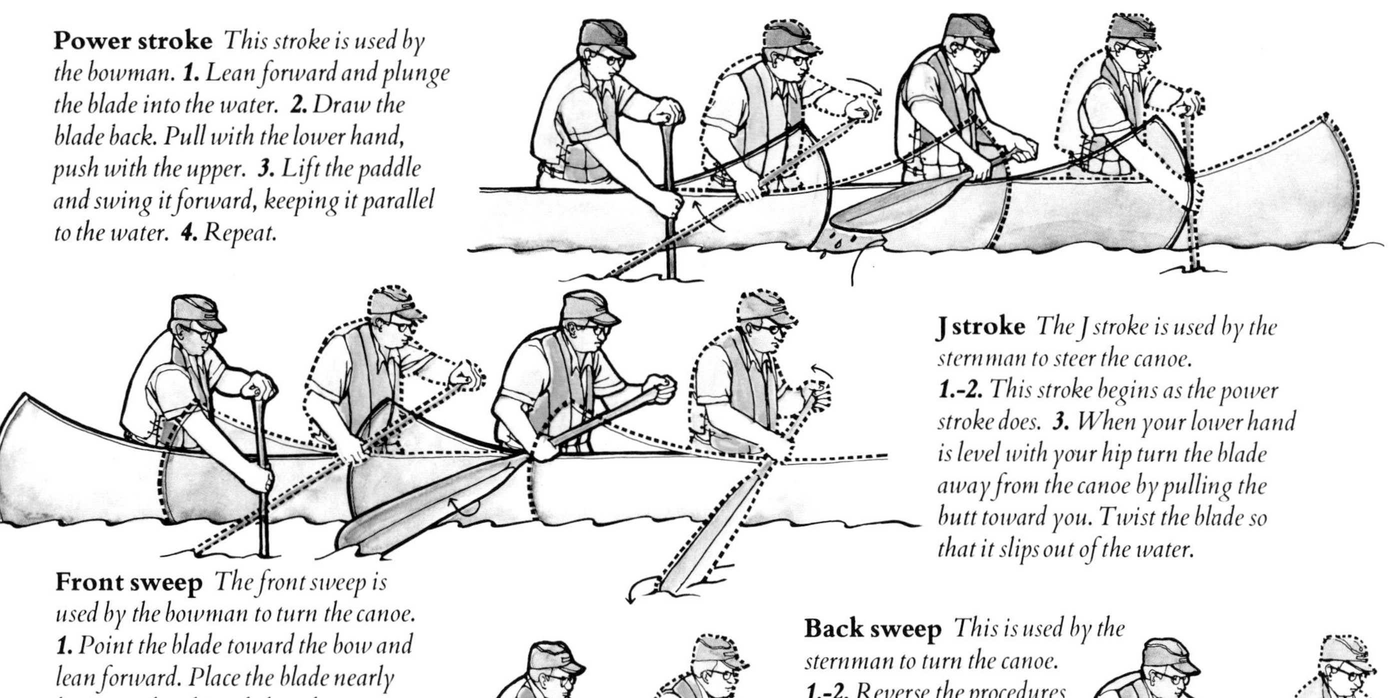

Power stroke *This stroke is used by the bowman.* ***1.*** *Lean forward and plunge the blade into the water.* ***2.*** *Draw the blade back. Pull with the lower hand, push with the upper.* ***3.*** *Lift the paddle and swing it forward, keeping it parallel to the water.* ***4.*** *Repeat.*

J stroke *The J stroke is used by the sternman to steer the canoe.* ***1.-2.*** *This stroke begins as the power stroke does.* ***3.*** *When your lower hand is level with your hip turn the blade away from the canoe by pulling the butt toward you. Twist the blade so that it slips out of the water.*

Front sweep *The front sweep is used by the bowman to turn the canoe.* ***1.*** *Point the blade toward the bow and lean forward. Place the blade nearly horizontal and just below the water surface.* ***2.*** *Sweep the blade in a semicircle ending alongside your hip. Lift the blade, swing it forward and repeat the stroke.*

Back sweep *This is used by the sternman to turn the canoe.* ***1.-2.*** *Reverse the procedures of the front sweep.*

Kayaks for Camping, Cruising and White-Water Fun

The paddler becomes one with his kayak as he twists and plunges through rapids, propelled by racing water, guided by quick thrusts of his double-bladed paddle.

First developed by Eskimos for hunting, the kayak has changed little over the centuries. It is a low, sleek vessel—faster than the Canadian canoe—with covered decks. It is light, seaworthy and highly maneuverable.

Yet for campers it has one major disadvantage: its covered decks limit storage space and make loading, which must be done through the cockpit, awkward and time-consuming. However, the covered decks help to keep stores dry.

Eskimo kayaks are still covered with sealskin. Modern commercial kayaks for recreation and racing are usually made of fiberglass. Folding, fabric-covered models are recommended for cruising and camping. When buying a cruising kayak, you should make sure that the hull is rubberized. Avoid kayaks with too many nuts and bolts as hardware is easily lost. Folding models that interlock are easy to portage and are probably the most practical for campers.

A 16-to-17-foot double kayak is generally recommended for campers. If you intend to use the kayak for recreation instead of for transportation, an 18-foot model might be better. It will accommodate two children and two adults. Cruising kayaks should have a beam of 28 to 32 inches. But allow a few more inches in the beam if you buy a model with an inflatable gunwale, which prevents the kayak from tipping.

A single-seater kayak should be about 14 feet long. Avoid racing models unless you want to race. Racing kayaks are unstable and have almost no storage space.

Paddles Double-bladed paddles are used to propel kayaks. Fiberglass spoon-bladed paddles are very efficient. The length of the shaft should be about twice the beam of the kayak, and the blade should be no wider than eight inches. If you are five feet six inches tall, use a seven-foot paddle. For every inch you are shorter than five-six, use a paddle a half inch shorter; for every inch over five-six, use a paddle a half inch longer. A plastic guard over the tip of a paddle blade will reduce wear.

Jointed paddles are easy to store and good as spares, but one-piece paddles are stronger. A jointed paddle can also be used as a single-bladed paddle. Jointed paddles should be soaked at the joint overnight at the beginning of the season and for a half hour before setting off on any trip.

Other gear should include a mooring line, life jacket and bailing bucket.

A wide range of optional kayak equipment is also available.

Hip board This is useful if a kayak

does not already have a built-in bucket seat. The hip board, used to increase control over a kayak, can be made from a high (fiberglass) bucket seat attached to the regular kayak seat. If the seat is oversized, pad it with foam. Fiberglass molded exactly to your shape is much better.

Padded knee braces These should be located under the front of the cockpit. In many kayaks you can simply brace your knees against the inside of the deck.

Footrests Fitted to the floor of the kayak, footrests make paddling more comfortable. They should be adjustable if more than one person will use the kayak.

Spray cover This waterproof fabric attaches to the cockpit coaming and helps to keep a kayaker dry.

Loading and entering One person enters the kayak while another steadies from the dock. Loads are passed to the person aboard and stowed under the decks. If the kayak has a canvas hull make sure that nothing presses against it, as this could cause a leak. After supplies are loaded, the second person enters the kayak while the first person steadies it.

Paddling the kayak Set the paddle shafts parallel to the surface of the water. Keep the blade close to the side of the kayak and use your wrists (in a pedaling motion) to propel the kayak.

A turn is accomplished by using a single blade and paddling in short, close sweeps. To make a wider turn without reducing speed, paddle wide on the outside and close on the inside.

The back stroke (or back sweep) and the J-stroke are the same as those used for the Canadian canoe (see previous pages).

In a double kayak, both occupants should use the same stroke and paddle in rhythm.

Tip a Kayak . . . and Roll Right Back

The Eskimo roll is an effective way of recovering after capsizing, but it is a tricky maneuver and it requires practice.

1. Rest the paddle along the starboard (right) gunwale, with one blade near your hip, the other toward the bow. Lean forward and to starboard. Reach across the foredeck with your left arm, grasping the middle of the paddle with your left hand. Take a deep breath, then throw your weight to starboard to capsize the kayak.

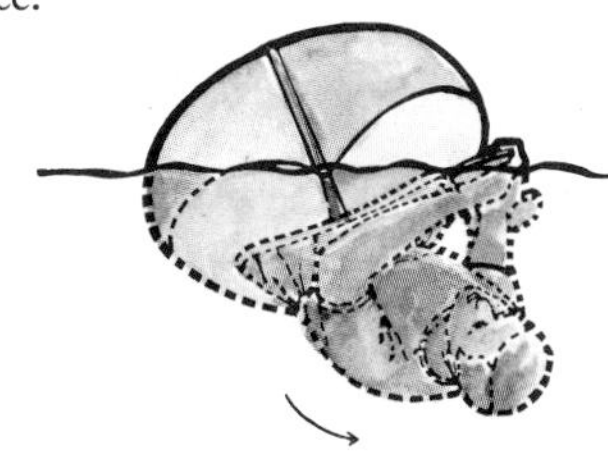

2. Use your hips and torso to increase momentum.

3. To complete the roll, sweep the forward blade out in an exaggerated arc, and pull down with the left hand, up with the right.

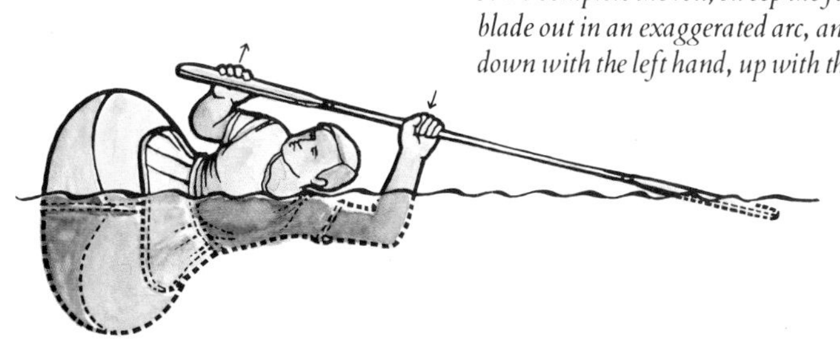

To avoid capsizing, three strokes can be used:

Forward brace On the side toward which the kayak is starting to roll, turn the paddle blade parallel to and close to the surface of the water. Press the blade down sharply.

Sculling Tilt the paddle blade slightly and make short, back-and-forth sweeps on the capsizing side.

Sweeping Tilt the blade and trace a large arc through the water.

Rescuing If a capsized paddler is unable to right his craft, you can assist him by maneuvering the bow of your craft to within his reach. By using your craft for support, he can push himself upright. To steady your kayak during this procedure, place your paddle across both crafts and grasp the stern of the upturned kayak with one hand.

Safety Tips for Kayakers and Canoeists

- Be able to swim
- Wear a life jacket at all times
- Don't stand up or move around quickly in a kayak or a canoe
- If your canoe tips, or if you are thrown from your kayak, hang on to the craft and use it for support as you swim to shore
- Where possible, follow the shoreline on any journey. Avoid crossing open water
- Don't wear heavy boots in a kayak or a canoe
- Don't overexert yourself
- Be alert for a sudden increase in current—this may mean rapids ahead. Paddle to shore and investigate. Beginners should never run rapids
- Stay clear of power craft
- Use a bow light at night
- Watch for weather changes and head for shore if a storm threatens

Good Fishing Requires More Than Good Luck

When the seasoned angler returns home time and again with prize catches of fish, you can be certain that luck has only a little to do with it. The successful fisherman relies on good equipment, knowing how to use it, and some knowledge of the fish species he is after.

There are four basic methods of casting: bait casting, spinning, spin casting and fly casting.

Bait casting The equipment used to cast live and preserved bait (as well as artificial lures) is adaptable to most freshwater and saltwater angling.

The bait-casting reel has a large spool that is geared to turn four times faster than the reel handle as it pays out and retrieves up to 100 yards of line and more. Line tension is adjusted by applying pressure to the spool with the thumb of the casting hand.

The average length of a bait-casting rod is between 5 and 6 feet. The experts' rule of thumb is that the lighter the bait and line, the longer the rod should be. Most rods are made of hollow or solid fiberglass, although some are still made of split bamboo and metal alloys.

Spinning The spool of a spinning reel does not revolve. During the cast, line is pulled from the end of the spool by the weight of the lure (usually less than ⅝ of an ounce). Since there are no revolving parts, there is little friction and so good distance casting is possible with the lightest of equipment. Spinning rods are usually about 6½ feet long and made of hollow fiberglass.

Spin casting Spin-casting equipment is also noted for its versatility. It combines the best features of bait casting and spinning. If it is of the "fast-taper" variety, the spin-casting rod can be used with a bait-casting reel, providing a versatile piece of equipment that can handle lures weighing from a few grams to an ounce.

As in bait casting, the spin-casting reel is on top of the rod and line control is maintained with the thumb of the casting hand (on a spin-casting reel, by depressing and releasing a "push-button"). Like the spinning reel, the storage spool remains motionless, allowing for almost resistance-free casting.

Fly casting The fly fisherman tries to fool fish into thinking that what is being offered—lightweight imitations of insects, larvae and minnows—is the real thing. These imitations are called "flies," and a fly fisherman usually has a good assortment of both "wet" and "dry" flies in his tackle box. Wet flies sink below the surface, appearing to be dead insects, insect larvae or tiny minnows. Dry flies float on the surface, looking like surface-walking insects or insects that have fallen into the water. The experienced fisherman often uses a combination of wet and dry flies on a single cast, on the chance of hooking a surface-feeding fish or a bottom feeder. If he is very lucky, he may even

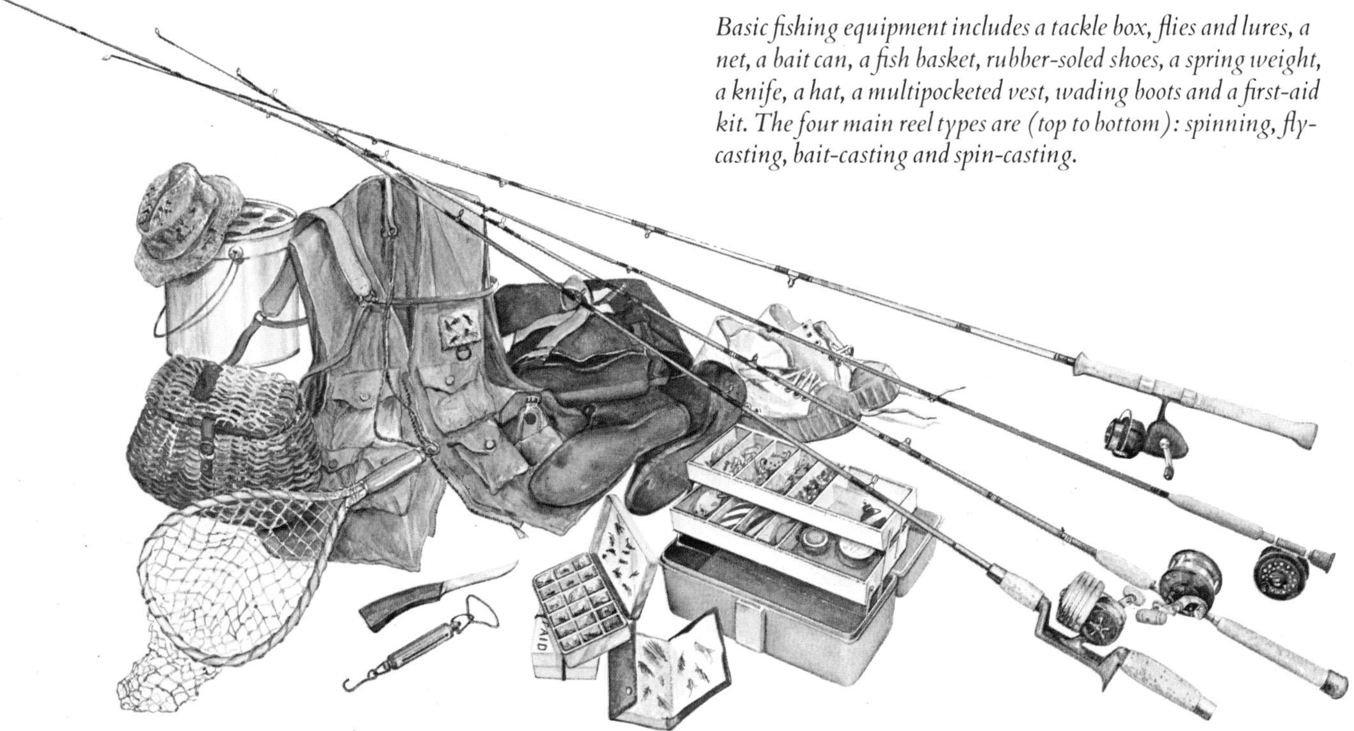

Basic fishing equipment includes a tackle box, flies and lures, a net, a bait can, a fish basket, rubber-soled shoes, a spring weight, a knife, a hat, a multipocketed vest, wading boots and a first-aid kit. The four main reel types are (top to bottom): spinning, fly-casting, bait-casting and spin-casting.

It's a whopper! Good fishing is the angler's reward for using the right bait or lure in the right place at the right time.

hook one of each at the same time!

The fly-casting reel, unlike previously mentioned reels, does not play an active role during the cast. Whereas other reels are constantly brought into play to cast, retrieve and adjust the tension on a line, the fly reel is simply a storage spool for unneeded line. The line is "stripped" from the reel by hand. It is this slack line that is "picked up" by the fly rod to cast the featherweight lures. (Some fly reels feature an automatic spring-loaded return device that rewinds "stripped" line.)

The average fly rod is about 7½ or 8 feet long and weighs about 4 ounces. Some are as long as 17 feet! But experts favor the shorter variety, especially for stream and river fishing where trees and shrubs might obstruct casting.

When choosing a fly rod for the first time, ask an experienced fly fisherman to accompany you. He can advise you on the best rod for the type of fishing you want to do and the amount of money you have to spend. Be sure to use the kind of line recommended by the rod manufacturer. Many a fly fisherman's difficulties stem from using the wrong line.

Freshwater Fishes

There are some 180 species of fishes in Canada's lakes, rivers and streams. These are nine of the most popular and common freshwater game fishes:

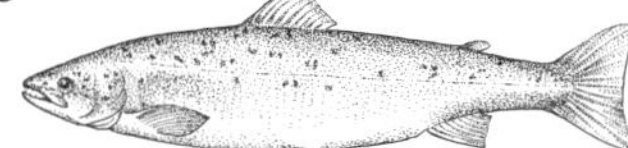

Ouananiche (landlocked salmon)

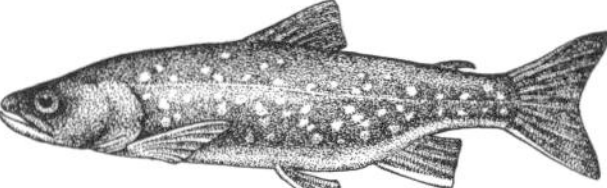

Arctic char

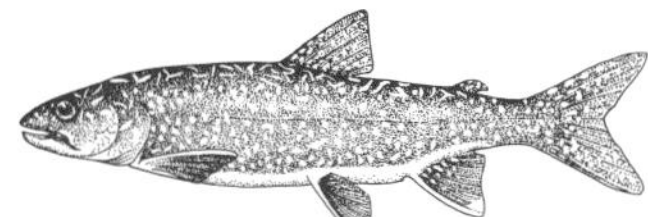

Lake trout

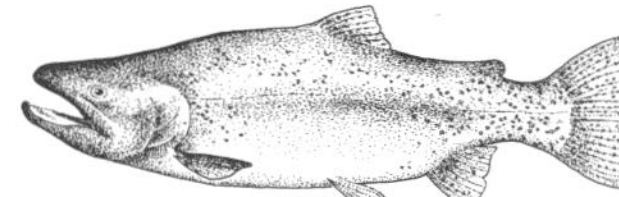

Rainbow trout

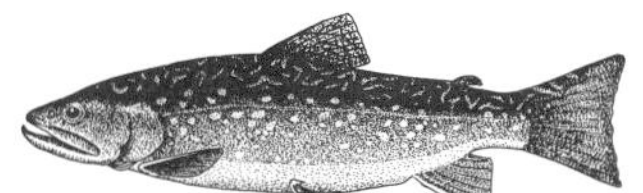

Brook trout (speckled trout)

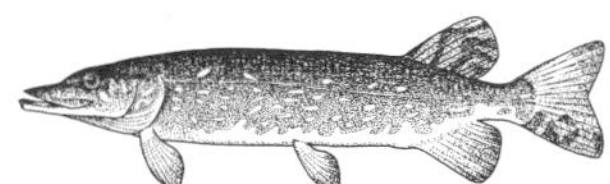

Northern pike

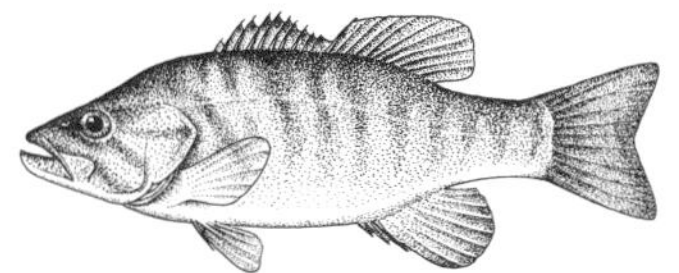

Smallmouth bass

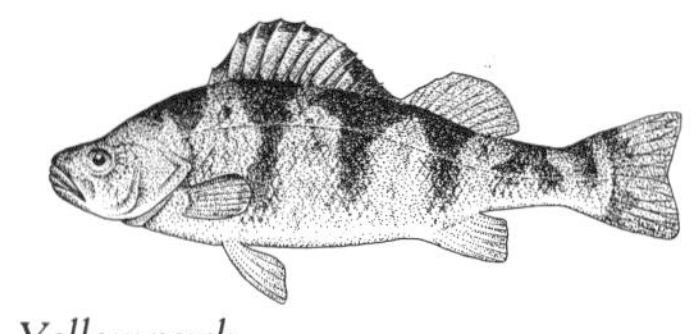

Yellow perch

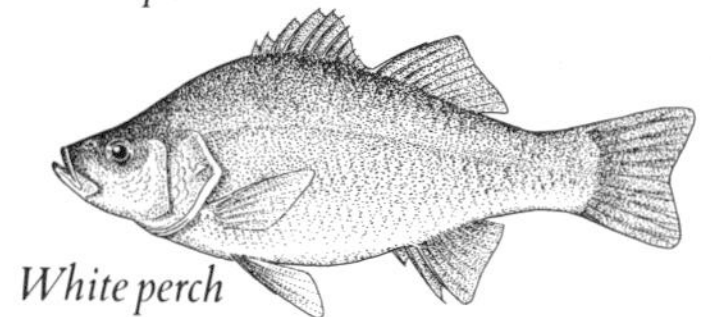

White perch

Read the Water to Hook the Big Ones

Just as a sailor reads the sky for signs of changing weather, so the successful fisherman reads the water for clues as to how and where to fish. And he does his reading even before opening his tackle box. He makes a new study of conditions from one fishing trip to the next, for he knows that the underwater world is forever changing as sand and silt are deposited, currents create new channels and pools, and insects and underwater plants flourish and die. Here is a seven-point list for reading a lake:

Vegetation Scan the shoreline for plant growth. Insects and minnows abound in weedy shallows, providing food for many game fishes.

Steelhead! This wary, sea-run rainbow trout fights like fury.

Drop-offs These underwater ridges, where the bottom of a waterway drops off sharply, appear as dark lines in contrast to the lighter tints of shallower water. Drop-offs are good hatching grounds for aquatic insects and other marine life. If the fish are biting, a few casts along a drop-off should yield good results.

Obstructions Submerged rocks and logs provide cover for a variety of game fishes. For best results present a weedless lure—one with a wire guard that prevents the hook from snagging.

Surf fishing is tangy ocean air, crashing breakers and the thrill of catching mackerel, cod, rockfish or striped bass.

The fly fisherman's delight: a clear, sun-sparkled pool where trophy-size trout may lurk.

Cast the lure over obstructions into open water.

Gravel bars These relatively smooth bottoms are favorite feeding grounds for game fish. Best results in deep water are obtained by trolling the full length of the bar with deep-diving plugs. In shallower water, cast beyond the bar with lighter plugs and retrieve slowly.

Springs Fish congregate in oxygen-rich waters around springs and falls. When you fish in such areas, expect lively action.

Tributaries The mouths of streams and creeks are rich sources of food. From a boat, allow your line to drift naturally toward the shore.

Wind direction Check the direction of the wind periodically. Always cast with the wind into choppy water. Not only will you avoid a sharp hook blowing back at you, but the choppy water will reduce the chance of a fish spotting you or your boat.

Reading a stream A stream fisherman must also learn to read his stream if he is to fish it successfully.

In slow streams, try the outside of curves first; the current is swiftest there and so carves deep holes where fish like to lie.

Rainbow trout enjoy fast water and position themselves ahead of rocks where the current splits on either side.

Brook trout prefer the shelter of calmer waters behind rocks, where they can feed in the crosscurrent.

Some fishes enjoy the shelter of rocks below fast, choppy, shallow water.

Fish are usually livelier along the edges of fast water where food and oxygen are plentiful.

Game fish like to wait at the mouths of creeks for forage fish. The mouths of tidal streams are particularly good during outgoing tides.

Just below a waterfall is a natural spot for fishing. Let flies drift over the falls; cast heavier lures and spinners into deep pools.

Water temperature The temperature in a lake or stream affects fish activity. Largemouth bass, for instance, are most active when the water is between 18° and 24°C. (65° and 75°F.). When fishing deep lakes, some fishermen use thermometers to check the temperature at various depths. They can then use the right lure at the right depth to catch the fish they want. Generally, game fish lie in deep water at midday and move to the shallower water in the cool of evening.

Surf casting Contrary to what many believe, surf casting can be done with virtually any kind of fishing tackle, from a homemade bamboo pole with line and bait to expensive rods and reels.

If you plan to fish from shore, use a well-made surf-casting rod that is at least 8 to 10 feet long. Shorter rods seldom provide the casting distance needed to reach the first line of breakers where game fish feed.

The successful surf caster reads the seashore in the same way his freshwater counterpart checks his fishing grounds. He studies the shoreline at low tide to spot areas that would make good feeding grounds at high tide. Underwater obstructions, deep holes, drop-offs, tributaries and vegetation form an essential part of the surf caster's reading list. He also consults tide tables, and when possible he fishes during an incoming tide.

Deep-sea fishing This can be costly. Expensive equipment is needed to land very large fish and it is usually necessary to charter a good boat.

You can reduce your deep-sea-fishing costs by sharing a charter boat with other anglers. Charter boats usually provide everything needed, from bait and tackle to afternoon tea.

To Net a Fish

Netting a fish is easy if you have learned the right technique. But if you don't net your fish properly you could lose a prize that took hours to hook.

Whether you are fishing from shore or from a boat, once you have decided to land your catch, brace yourself. With one hand, lower the net so that it is half underwater. Then carefully maneuver the fish so that it swims head-first into the net. Lower the tip of your fishing rod just enough to provide slack for a deft scooping motion.

For larger fish such as pike, use a gaff to land your catch. Gaff the fish in the gills or under the jaw.

Sturdy Boots and a Healthy Respect for the Wild

To some persons, a hike is nothing more than an easy stroll along a well-marked trail; to others it is a muscle-stretching trek along a high mountain path. To the photographer or artist, a hike is an outing to capture nature on film or canvas. To a rock-hound or other collector, a hike is a chance to seek a new specimen.

Whatever hiking is to you, all you need to enjoy the sport is a sturdy pair of boots and a healthy respect for the wilderness. Hiking can be a time of pleasant camaraderie outdoors if common sense is used.

Light walking boots or ankle-high sneakers with heavy soles are good for hiking along clearly marked trails in summer or autumn. Heavier boots are needed to protect feet and support ankles when you hike over rough terrain or carry a heavy load. Make sure your boots fit comfortably over two pairs of socks. Laced footwear is recommended. Leather soles can be slippery when wet; treaded rubber or synthetic soles are safer. Don't try to break in new boots on a hiking trip—you'll end up with sore feet.

Study a guide map of the area you have decided to hike. Consult hikers who are familiar with the conditions you'll encounter, and participate in any nature interpretation programs that are available. As you hike, follow trail markers and take note of major landmarks. It is wise to allow more time than you estimate you will need to arrive at your destination well before dusk.

A fast start usually means a poor finish. Start slowly and build up to a steady pace. Strive for rhythm, not speed. When traveling in a group, don't drop out at erratic intervals. This disrupts pace and rhythm. Take a six-minute break each hour, and let the slow hikers walk up front so that the group stays together. Lack of oxygen at high altitudes may make you light-headed and nauseous. If this occurs, lie on your back and prop your feet up on a rock.

To walk, point your toes straight ahead, and lean from the hips. Swing your legs forward in a slow, easy arc and bend your knees just enough to let your feet clear the ground. To increase

One of the joys of autumn: hiking through leafy woods where the air is crisp, the brilliant foliage unforgettable.

On a vertical rock face a climber needs to be able to trust his equipment.

Glaciers are a challenge for the experienced climber. Specialized equipment is required for this strenuous sport.

Spelunking

Cave exploring—also called spelunking or caving—takes you into a dark, intriguing world underground.

There should be at least four persons in any cave-exploring party, and at least one should be experienced. If a caver is injured, a companion should stay behind while the others go for help.

A detailed plan of the explorers' route should be left with a responsible person, with instructions to summon help if your group doesn't return on schedule. Should you become separated from your group, stay where you are until help arrives.

Experienced spelunkers carry a compass and a reliable source of light, such as a carbide lamp. (If you're using a flashlight, be sure to carry spare batteries and bulbs.) They pay close attention to landmarks and the shapes of passages as they pass through. Reflective tape can be used to mark your route into the cave, and it should be removed when you leave.

Most caves are damp and cool, so warm clothing is a must, as is a helmet. Leather gloves prevent cuts from sharp rocks; hiking boots are good protection against snakes. Carry first-aid and snakebite kits.

speed, lengthen your stride, don't hurry it.

When descending a hill, flex your knees and lean slightly back. Shorten your stride and take many small steps across the slope if you want to reduce your speed.

Rock climbing After you have acquired hiking experience you might try the more challenging sport of rock climbing. This demands precise and smooth movement, agility, rhythm, timing and coordination. The risk of injury is minimal if you use common sense and proper techniques.

Never climb alone. The novice should learn the fundamentals in a climbing party whose leader is an experienced climber.

You can begin with bouldering—free climbing on boulders no higher than 30 feet. Free climbing means that any aids are used solely for protection or safety. Shoes—such as tennis shoes—with narrow welts and rubber soles are appropriate for sampling this sport. Climbing boots, which fit tightly around the foot, are recommended for more advanced participants. The narrow toe of the climbing boot is designed to fit into crevices. Belaying—securing a climber at the end of a rope—is an effective safety method that can be used in bouldering. One person takes an easy, safe route to the top and anchors a rope to which the climber at the bottom is attached. As the climber scales the boulder, the person at the top takes up the slack to keep the rope taut. If the climber slips or falls, he can swing back to where he lost his footing or he can be lowered to the ground.

A swami belt is useful here. This is an inch-wide strip of webbing that is wrapped around the waist several times. The belt cushions falls by distributing the climber's weight.

Direct-aid climbing This sport requires a variety of hardware that is actually used to ascend a rock face, as well as to provide protection.

Chocks and pitons anchor ropes to a rock face. Chocks are used more frequently than pitons because pitons tend to disfigure a rock face.

In this type of climbing it is essential to plan all movements so that you climb easily and are not caught in an awkward position. Climb as you would climb a ladder: use your legs to climb and your hands to balance. Maintain an upright posture so that your weight is centered over your feet and legs. This creates greater stability. Clinging close to the rock face will only obscure your view of handholds and push your feet away from the rock.

Safety depends on good footholds rather than on hanging on by your hands. Test each foothold. Do not shift a foot when your weight comes down on it. If your footing is unsteady, adjust your position by placing your heel or the side of your feet on the hold for a moment. When the rock is wet or slippery, the hold must be taken carefully.

Always maintain three points of contact with the rock so that you will have two points of support if one of your holds gives way.

When descending, face outward or sideways. Face inward only if the rock face is very steep. Descending blind is difficult because you are forced to look through your arms and legs for holds.

Basics of Bicycling

Even if it is used only moderately, a bicycle is a sound investment. Whether it is for touring or commuting, a bicycle provides exercise, cheap transportation and pleasure. Consider buying your bicycle from a reputable dealer—preferably one with a mechanic on staff. Department stores may offer discount prices, but a good cycle shop offers service and experience—both indispensable to the amateur cyclist.

The type of bicycle you choose depends on how much you want to spend and how far you intend to travel. A basic (heavy) bicycle without gears may be functional in the city, but it is extremely impractical for touring. A tourist should opt for a 10-speed model. Although a 3-speed bicycle has its merits (the gears seldom require maintenance), a 10-speed, derailleur-type bicycle is usually lighter and faster and the gear ratios have a wider range. This last factor is extremely important for travelling over hills.

Design Double-butted tubing is reinforced internally at stress points. Conventional tubing is cheaper but heavier. All quality frames are double-butted.

Lugged joints These are joints reinforced with an overlay of metal, making a frame stronger. A frame that has been lugged and brazed, rather than welded, is recommended. Light alloy steel is an excellent material for the frame. On road and touring bicycles, the frame is normally 72° parallel. This means that the angle formed by the top tube against the seat and head tubes is 72°. On faster bicycles, for sprinting and coursing, this angle is sometimes increased to 73° or 74°.

There are two ways to determine the best size of frame for yourself: measure the distance from your crotch to the floor when you're standing in stocking feet, and substract nine inches, or divide your height by three. The frame is measured from the seat lug to the center of the bottom bracket.

Wheel rims Most wheel rims are made of aluminum alloy or steel. Alloy rims are lighter but slightly weaker than steel rims. Knurled rims—which increase braking power—are available in both materials.

Quick-release hubs Slightly more expensive than those with conventional nuts, quick-release hubs will allow you to remove a wheel in seconds without a wrench. Although they are extremely practical, quick-release hubs increase the possibility of your wheels being stolen. When leaving your bicycle unattended, remove the front wheel and chain it to the rear wheel.

The Parts of a Bicycle

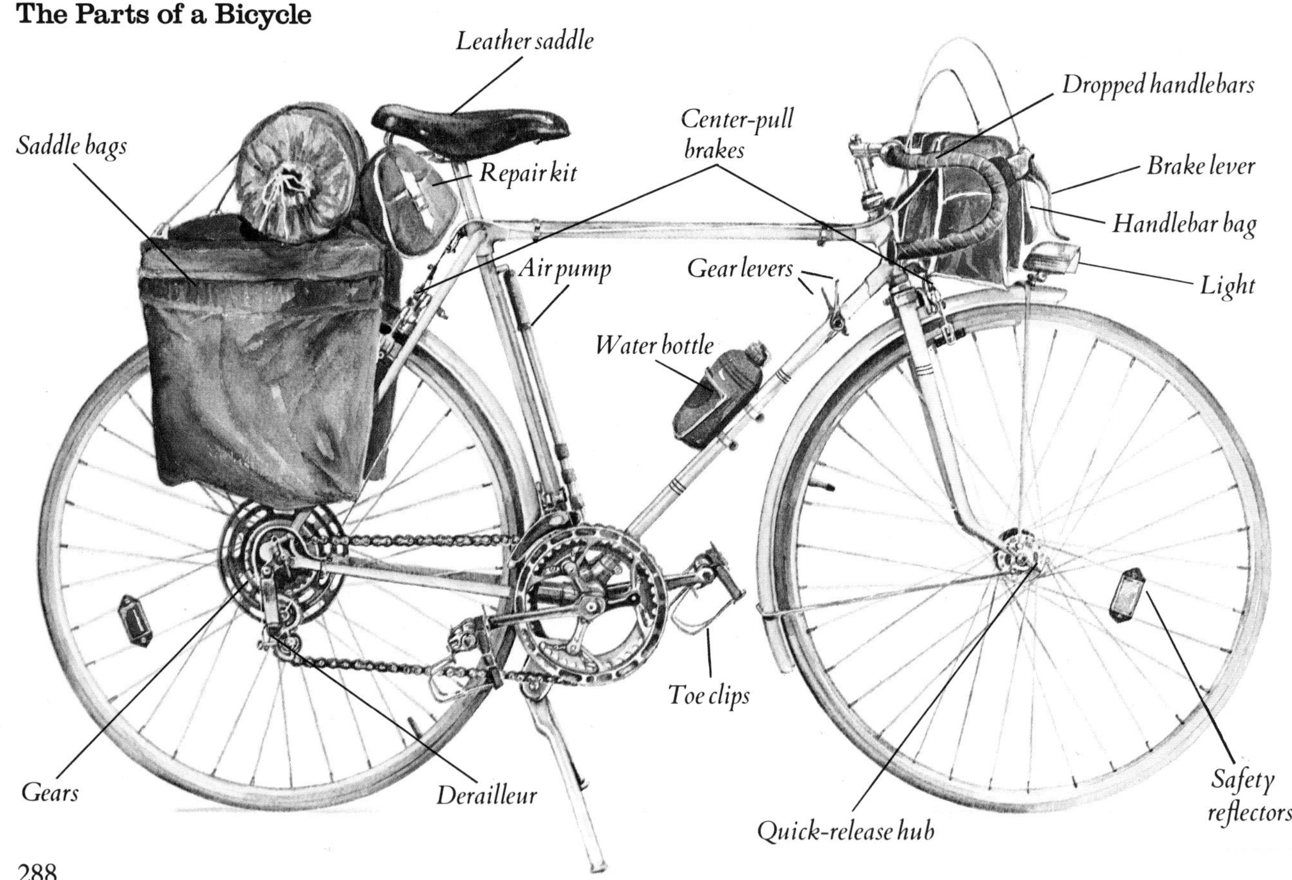

Using efficient, lightweight racing bicycles, competitive cyclists often exceed 40 miles an hour.

Tires There are two types of tires, tubular and clincher. Tubular tires are lighter and generally smoother rolling than clinchers. But they cost more, are more easily punctured, and are difficult to repair. If you intend to use tubulars, it is a good idea to invest in a pair of tire savers. These small gadgets, mounted over the tires, automatically brush stones, broken glass and other road debris from the tires. It is also advisable to carry a spare tire. These tires weigh as little as four ounces.

Clinchers These tires, reinforced with wire, are often preferred by touring cyclists because of their durability and the ease with which they can be repaired. Many cyclists prefer to sacrifice weight for the convenience of these tires. For city cycling, clinchers are recommended.

Handlebars and saddle Dropped handlebars are, in all ways, more efficient than flat bars. They allow for better distribution of weight, a greater variety of body positions, and—in the long run—they are more comfortable.

A good leather saddle is essential. It may be uncomfortable at first, but you will soon get used to it. Avoid plastic saddles. There is a simple way to determine the correct saddle height when seated: with your heel on the pedal at its lowest point, your leg should be straight; with the ball of your foot on the pedal at its lowest point, your leg should be slightly bent.

Brakes Two types of caliper brakes are featured on bicycles: center-pull and side-pull. Center-pull brakes are almost standard equipment on a good bicycle. Their advantage over side-pull brakes is that they distribute pressure more evenly to the wheel rim, thus increasing braking power.

Gears This is a complex subject. Basically, the range of your gears determines the ease and speed with which you will be able to pedal. Numerous sprocket combinations are available. With experience you will be able to decide for yourself which range of gears is best suited to your needs. A recommended combination is: a rear sprocket set of 14-16-19-23-28 and a front sprocket set of 40-52. If you are using a triple front sprocket set—for 15 gears—a good combination is 36-45-52.

Accessories A great variety of bicycle accessories is available. Some, such as an air pump and a tire repair kit, are essential for country touring.

Lights If you travel at night, lights are essential. Dynamo and battery-operated lights are available. Dynamos are heavy, require more pedaling effort and are alight only when the bicycle is moving. Battery-operated models are lighter and more convenient.

Carriers A light aluminum bracket over the rear wheel is good for city cycling. For long trips, use panniers, handlebar bags and saddle bags.

Cycling technique Pedal with the ball of the foot, not the heel or arch.

Never shift gears on a 10-speed unless you are pedaling. Shift just before the gear is needed, as when you are nearing the bottom of a hill. In this way speed is maintained. When downshifting on a 3-speed bicycle, backpedal slightly. To shift to a higher gear, ease the pressure off the pedals and move the selector.

Braking should be kept to a minimum.

General maintenance Keep tires inflated to pressure shown on sidewalls • Check valves for leaks and tighten dust cap • Tighten loose spokes • Replace worn brake shoes • Lubricate and adjust fork bearings • Lubricate and tighten wheel bearings and locknut • Clean and lubricate the chain • Check for worn links • Lubricate and adjust pivot points on brakes

Snowshoeing for Travel, "Tramps"—and Snowmobiles

Snowshoeing is one of the easiest, most reliable ways of traveling through deep snow, and sometimes it is the *only* way. Safe and inexpensive, snowshoeing is a simple, wonderful way of seeing the winter countryside.

Snowshoes, probably first used by the nomadic tribes of central Asia nearly 6,000 years ago, were brought to North America when the ancestors of Indians and Eskimos migrated across the Bering Strait.

Indians had held snowshoe races long before the first settlers arrived, but the newcomers were quick to adopt the sport, especially in Quebec. The Montreal Snowshoe Club, founded in 1840, is one of the oldest athletic clubs in North America.

At the beginning of the 20th century, snowshoeing was still a popular sport. Annual international snowshoe races had an avid following. Clubs across Canada held both competitive events and "tramps"—simply outings for their members.

In the 1930s participation in the sport declined, but in recent years there has been a renewal of interest in snowshoeing. Recently, too, snowshoes have become an emergency item on snowmobiles, as indispensable as life jackets are in boats.

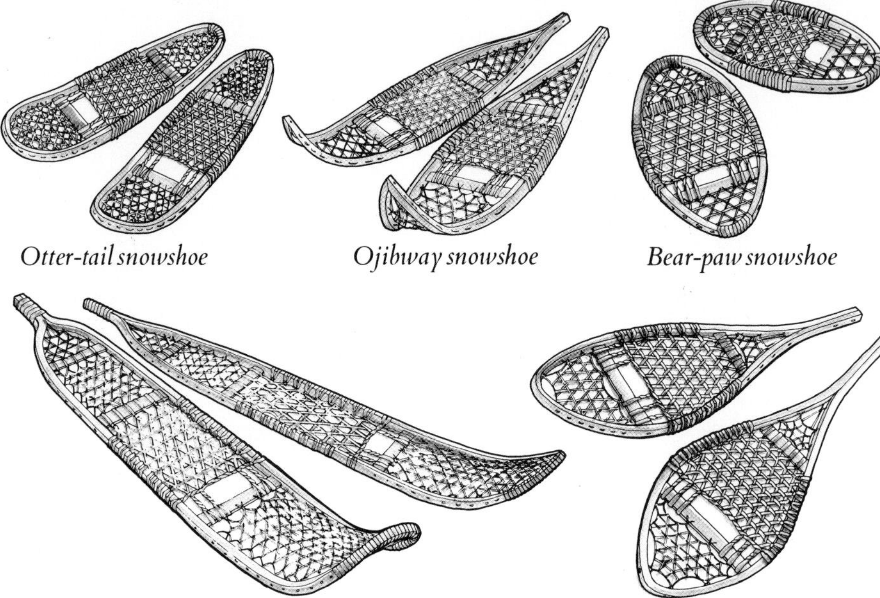

Otter-tail snowshoe *Ojibway snowshoe* *Bear-paw snowshoe*

Algonkian snowshoe *Beaver-tail snowshoe*

Designs Snowshoes were probably designed by the earliest makers to resemble nature's own model—the wide, fringed paws of the snowshoe hare.

There are several kinds of snowshoes, made of a variety of materials and for use under different conditions.

Traditionally, frames are of wood, particularly white ash. Wood-frame snowshoes are expensive because they are entirely handmade. Frames are also manufactured of plastic, tubular aluminum and magnesium. Plastic framed snowshoes are relatively inexpensive but are not recommended for long distances. Metal frames are durable but they lack the resilience of wooden frames.

Webbing The traditional *babiche* or webbing material is caribou hide. Some snowshoe makers use the hides of moose, horses or cows. Neoprene-coated nylon, the best webbing, is water-repellent and strong, and it sheds snow better than animal hide does. Nylon webbing won't decay, or stretch when wet, and animals don't gnaw it.

A snowshoe's webbing should be tight, and fairly coarse in the middle third of the snowshoe, which carries most of a user's weight. For travel in eastern Canada, where the snow is wet and heavy, a thick open webbing should be used. In the light, fluffy snow of western Canada, a thin close mesh is preferable.

Harnesses A good commercially available snowshoe harness is of leather and consists of toe, instep, and heel straps that buckle individually. In some harnesses, the heel strap ties around the ankles. A length of lamp wick (loosely twisted or woven cotton cord), crisscrossed over the toe and around the heel, usually served as a harness for hunters and trappers. An effective homemade harness can be cut from a tire inner tube. It is important to be able to slip out of harnesses easily, especially in hazardous situations.

The oldest and simplest type of snowshoe, called a bear-paw because of its shape, is easy to handle over rough trails and in thick forests. It can be turned quickly but it is too wide for use in hilly country. A modified bear-paw, longer and narrower and with a slight upturn at the front, is called an otter-tail. Otter-tails are best on hills and mountains.

The most popular snowshoe is the Algonkian. Its teardrop shape with a long tail helps it to track in a straight line. It is well balanced and suited to forest, bush and trail.

Ojibway snowshoes, also long and narrow, are made of two pieces of wood instead of one. Their upturned, pointed tips cut through snow without filling up.

Footwear Soft boots without heels, high Indian moccasins or rubber overshoes are good footwear for snowshoeing. Snowmobile boots with felt liners, suitable for short trips, should be large enough to be worn with two or three pairs of socks.

Rope, tape and a pocketknife should be carried for emergency re-

Snowshoeing is fine exercise, a reliable means of travel—and an exhilarating way to explore the outdoors.

pairs. Spiked iron plates, called crampons, can be attached to snowshoes for traction on icy, crusty hills. A long-handled ice ax is also useful.

Technique Walking on snowshoes is easy to learn and requires no special training. Beginners should carry staffs (such as ski poles) for better balance on hills. Lift one foot, move it over the edge of the other snowshoe, and put it down in front. Your feet need not be abnormally far apart. Move in a sliding gait and do not lift your feet quite as high as in regular walking. It only takes a few minutes to perfect a comfortable stride.

To slide downhill, lean back, putting pressure on the snowshoe tails. If the hill is steep, put one snowshoe behind the other, sit on the rear one and slide.

Occasionally, a snowshoer suffers an attack of what the coureur de bois called *mal de raquette,* or snowshoe sickness. It is a severe cramp of the muscles of the leg and instep which, in the days when novices traveled long distances, could be disabling for days.

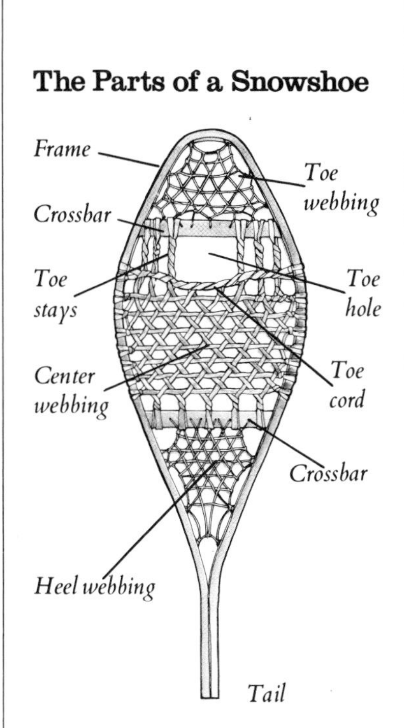

Muscles seldom used in ordinary walking are strained in snowshoeing. To avoid cramps, use a smooth hip stride with the knees slightly bent.

There are a few other hazards to watch out for when snowshoeing. Never cross ice which is less than two inches thick. When traveling alone on ice, carry a long branch or sapling to support you should the ice give way. In mountains, avalanches can be triggered by a sudden change in temperature, a heavy snowfall or vibrations caused by loud noises. It is best to snowshoe in areas away from avalanche danger.

Maintenance Aluminum and plastic snowshoes require little attention, but wooden ones should be allowed to dry thoroughly after use, away from direct heat that could cause warping. Snowshoes with rawhide webbing should be hung out of reach of rodents, which like to chew the rawhide. Clear shellac will waterproof rawhide webbing and prevent it from becoming too brittle. Varnish wooden frames once a year, or whenever the finish looks worn. With care, wooden snowshoes with rawhide lacing will last many years.

Cross-Country Skiing Is as Easy as Walking

Cross-country skiing can be a competitive and exhausting sport but for most people it is simply an invigorating way of touring the winter countryside. Today, enthusiasts combine skiing with camping and exploration—taking full advantage of the heavy snowfall and varied terrain that is typical of so much of Canada.

Virtually anyone who can walk can learn to ski cross-country. Beginners can practice on old logging roads, golf courses (if it is allowed) and in public parks. A few basic lessons can help you master the combination of walking, skating, sliding and shuffling that is cross-country skiing.

Equipment for cross-country skiing need not be expensive: look for lightness and simplicity of design. If possible, buy your equipment from a well-stocked ski shop where the sales staff can advise you on brand names.

Standard-weight touring skis with a thick hickory base and lightweight birch and beech laminations are ideal for beginners. Steel edges improve control on icy surfaces. But they are heavy and really needed only in mountain country.

To determine the correct length of ski for you, extend your hand above your head. Place a ski vertically alongside your body. Its tip should reach the wrist or the palm of your extended hand.

Choose ski poles that reach your armpits when you are standing in normal shoes and your arms are extended. The poles should have sharp metal tips, which may be curved forward to prevent their sticking in the snow. Bamboo poles are best for beginners. Although not as light or as durable as aluminum and fiberglass models, they are less expensive. Poles should have adjustable handle loops to enable the skier to take a firm grip.

Boots should be light, flexible and ankle high. The squared-off soles should project beyond the toe of the leather uppers. When the foot is bent, the toes should not touch the front of the boots. Always use good, strong laces.

The two main types of ski-tour bindings—cable and toe—differ from downhill bindings, for they allow a full bend of the foot when you take a stride.

A rucksack is generally adequate for carrying extra clothing, a small first-

Here is how to determine what ski and pole lengths are best for you.

This creek in Jasper National Park is only a minor obstacle—but cross-country skiers should always be ready to tackle the unexpected.

Even skis don't always prevent you from sinking into snowdrifts!

Cross-country skiers and snowshoers can explore the winter wilderness in its billowy cloak of fresh-fallen snow.

Waxing Your Skis

Before waxing skis, coat them with a thin layer of pine tar to seal them against water and provide a base for the wax. In the beginning it is best to choose one good brand of cross-country waxes and learn how to use them properly. Two types of any particular make are usually adequate: red for wet snow (above 0°C.), blue for dry (under 0°C.). It is often wise to consult experienced skiers on this subject.

aid kit, food, a spare ski tip—in case of breakage—and waxes. A roll of electrical tape is also useful—you can repair a broken tip by taping it back in place. Clothing should be worn in layers so that some can be removed and stowed in the rucksack during a vigorous workout. All clothing should be comfortable and allow freedom of movement. Woolen socks, mitts and flannel or woolen shirts are basic items. It is also wise to wear a hat or ear band.

Corduroy knee-britches are excellent for cross-country skiing. A windproof ski jacket is generally too warm for touring; a close-woven cloth jacket is better.

Waxes are applied to cross-country skis to increase traction for ascents, sliding power for descents.

Technique Skiing on the flat is very similar to walking. A strong downward kick, usually supplemented by poling, propels the skier. In simple poling, arms and legs work together as in walking. In double poling, used to increase speed, the skier pushes with both poles at the same time.

Step-turning This is the usual way of changing direction. One ski is placed obliquely in front of the other. The diagonal position of the back ski is used for thrust. After pushing against the back ski, the weight of the body is transferred to the forward ski. The back ski is brought forward and placed at an oblique angle. The action is repeated in a series of short, quick steps.

To climb a steep slope, position the skis horizontally across the slope. Keep the feet together, the knees bent, and step sideways. Move the poles in unison with each step.

When falling, try to fall backward and sideway with the feet and knees together. Let the body go limp. When rising, use one or both poles for support and keep the skis horizontal to the slope.

More advanced techniques can be employed in cross-country skiing, but these can only be learned with time and experience. There are cross-country ski clubs in most areas of Canada.

Stargazing: Looking Deep Into the Distant Past

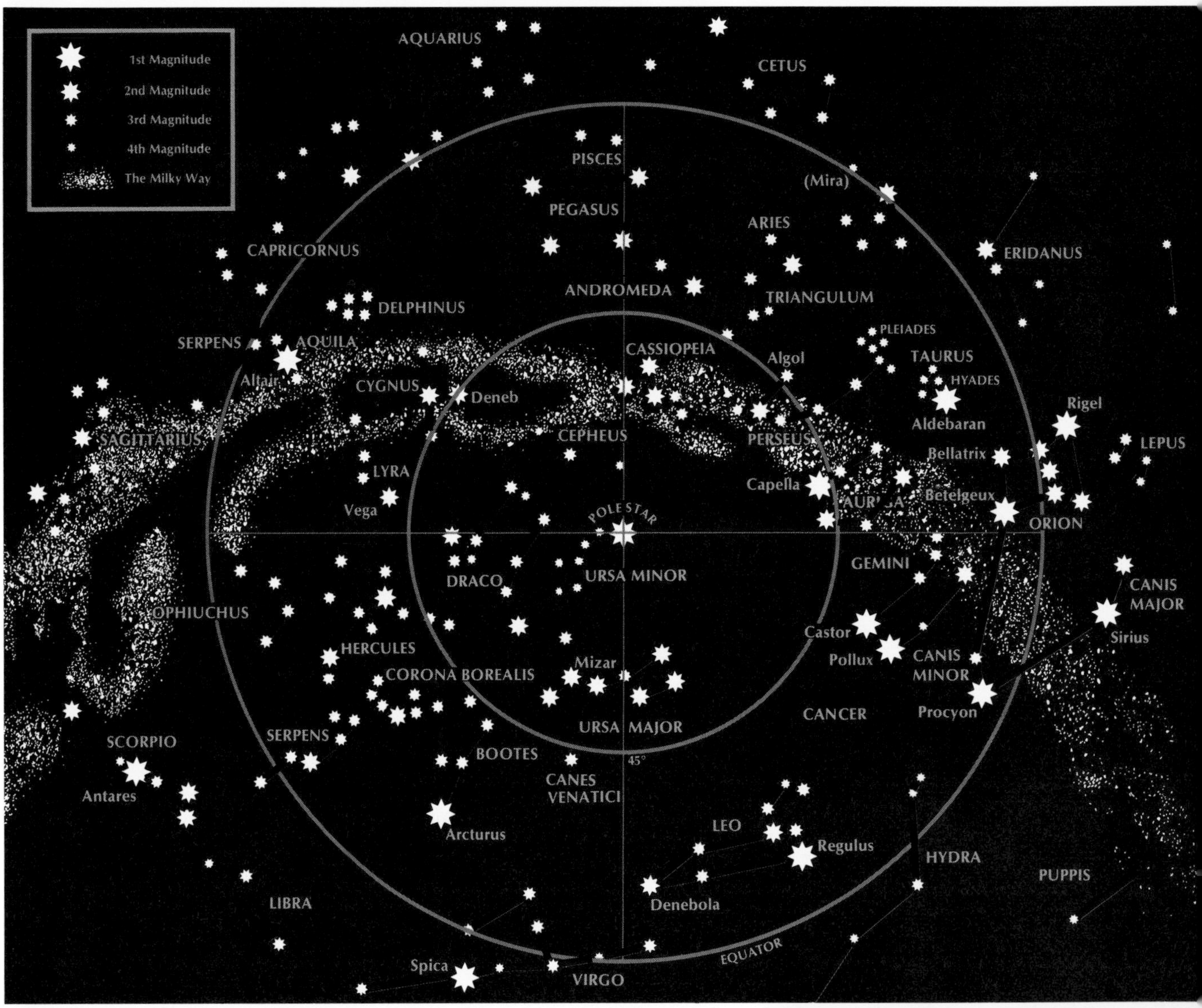

This map of the night sky can help you identify some of the stars and constellations of the Northern Hemisphere. Hold the map above your head and turn the map until the polestar and Ursa Major (the Big Dipper) correspond to their location in the heavens. The other constellations and stars will then be in the same position on the map as they are in the sky.

For centuries man has looked to the sky for navigational guidance and for clues to his past and future. The vastness of the universe—even of our galaxy—has always intrigued stargazers. Of the more than 100 billion stars in the galaxy, about 6,000 are likely to be visible on a clear evening, and no more than 2,500 can be seen from any one place on earth.

A warm summer evening is best for comfortable stargazing. Good locations are open fields, and hilltops and rooftops—any place that offers an unobstructed view of the heavens, with little or no interference from lights.

Only the brightest stars can be seen in full moonlight or just after sunset. On dark, moonless nights, fainter constellations are visible. Although thousands of stars are visible to the naked eye, binoculars or a telescope greatly

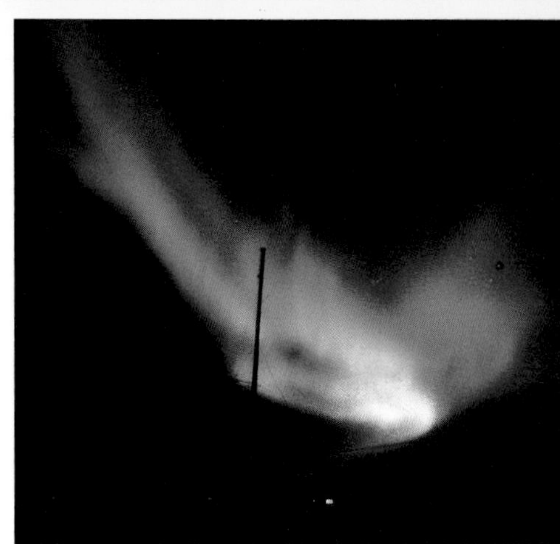

The shifting, shimmering northern lights are brightest in arctic skies.

Jupiter's bands and several of its moons can be seen with binoculars.

Bright, reddish Mars, our smallest planet, is best seen at midnight.

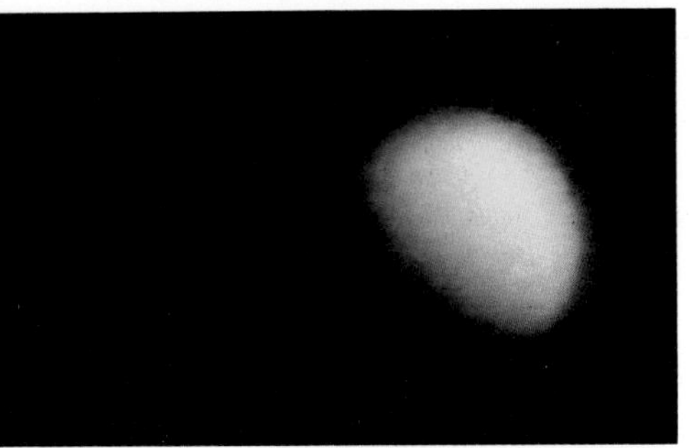

Brilliant Venus is located in the East at sunrise, in the West at sunset.

increases the number of stars and constellations you can spot.

Five of the planets in our solar system can be seen with the unaided eye: Mercury, Venus, Mars, Jupiter and Saturn. The others are Uranus, Neptune, Pluto and the Earth itself.

Unlike stars, the planets constantly change positions in the sky as they rotate about the sun. Generally, if a heavenly body twinkles, it's a star; if its light is steady, it's a planet. Stars generate their own light, but planets reflect the light of the sun.

When we look at a star we actually look into the past—light from the stars takes as little as a few minutes or as much as several thousand years to reach earth. It takes eight minutes for light to travel the 93 million miles from the sun to earth. Light from Proxima Centauri, the nearest star, takes four light-years to reach us. (A light-year is the distance that light travels in a year at 186,000 miles a second.)

The brightest star is Sirius, the dog star, in the constellation Canis Major. In galactic terms, Sirius is close to our planet—a mere 8.7 light-years away.

Roughly midway between the polestar and the constellation Orion, and 3,400 light-years away from the earth is the largest known star, Epsilon Aurigae, 2,700 times the size of our 864,900-mile-wide sun.

Our nearest celestial neighbor, and our only satellite, is the moon, roughly 239,000 miles away. Even without binoculars or a telescope, the moon's craters, jagged peaks and broad, dry plains are visible on a clear night. Occasionally, you may see a hazy ring around the moon. The ring, actually within the earth's atmosphere, results from the refraction of moonlight by ice crystals 25,000 to 30,000 feet above the earth.

On any cloudless night you are almost certain to spot shooting stars (meteors) as they blaze across the sky. These fragments of comets or planets burst into flames when they encounter the friction of the earth's atmosphere. Most of the more than 15,000 shooting stars that enter the atmosphere each day burn up and never reach earth.

Clear, moonless nights are best for watching the Milky Way, thought by astronomers to be near the edge of our galaxy. Stretching across the sky, the Milky Way is a twinkling haze containing myriad clusters of faint stars.

One of the most spectacular sights in the night sky is aurora borealis—the northern lights. The shifting, ethereal patterns of the lights occur whenever a storm on the sun's surface increases the flow of electrically charged particles toward earth. The 4,000-mile-thick magnetic field that surrounds the earth deflects most of these particles. But above the magnetic poles, where the magnetic field is weakest, some particles break through into the atmosphere, where they strike and excite molecules, causing them to glow. The hauntingly beautiful aurora borealis often lasts for hours, and frequently all night. It is best observed in northern Canada.

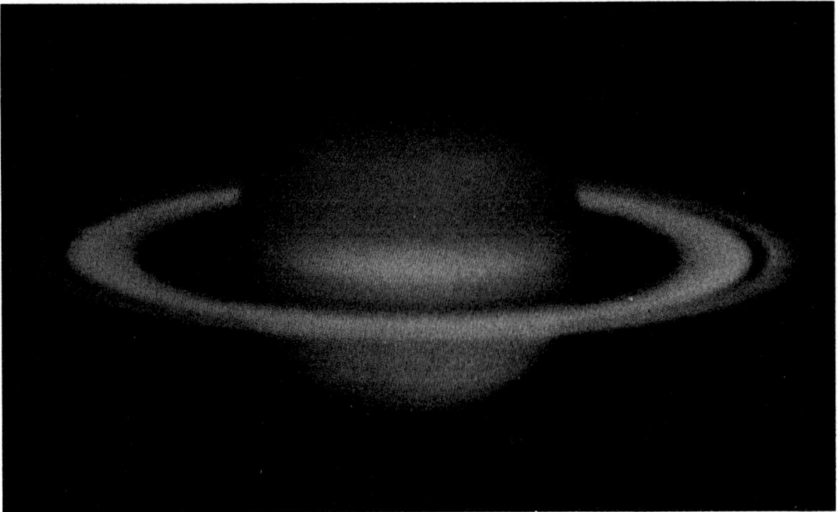

Saturn is bright to the naked eye, but its rings can only be seen through a telescope. Four of this planet's nine moons are outside the rings.

Light: The Secret of Spectacular Scenics

Glorious landscapes, superb to behold on your trip, have a disconcerting habit of losing their grandeur in photographs. Majestic mountain peaks are reduced to puny pimples, a sublime seascape turns out as an endless expanse of dull water. The reason for this is that the human eye and the camera "see" the same scene differently. The eye sees it selectively and in three dimensions, the camera records it nonselectively and in two dimensions. To overcome this, the photographer has to create the illusion of space and depth.

This is best done by making picture "planes of vision"—foreground, middleground and background. Include boats or birds in the foreground and your picture of the seashore instantly gains interest and depth. Or include a portion of the shore, wave-sculptured rocks or wind-bent trees. The slanting light of morning and late afternoon brings out texture and relief.

Wait and watch for "moody" light—before or just after a thunderstorm the sky looks dark and ominous. There is a feeling of violence and power that matches the ocean's mood. In such a scene the sky should occupy more than half of the picture.

The combination of fog and early morning sunlight creates a soft, mysterious, tranquil mood: some trees in the foreground, a quiet cove and, perhaps, some boats in the distance, just barely visible through the romantic mist. It is often a good idea to select a scenic composition, and then return to the spot when the light is right to give it that special atmosphere, when, for instance, the rays of the evening sun glint golden upon the water. Expose for highlights, to get color saturation, and always use skylight filters to eliminate excess blue and to protect the lens.

While the grand view is impressive, evocative detail should not be neglected.

Near the ocean, include subjects that will "speak" of the sea: wave-washed pebbles, seaweed draped over glistening rocks, limpets or mussels clinging to stones, sea urchins in a tidal pool. A wide-angle lens with its great depth of field is best for such pictures.

Perspective and depth are essential to good mountain pictures. The "scenic lookout points" along highways usually offer superb views but rarely good picture possibilities because a foreground is lacking. A good mountain picture might consist of treetops in the foreground, a lake in the middle of the picture, and a majestic background of snow-covered peaks. Or a mountain meadow, aglow with flowers, fills the foreground and middle of the picture, and the mountains rise beyond. Take this with a small *f*-stop for maximum depth of field and at a low angle to enlarge and accentuate the flowers in the foreground.

Learn to "see" light and the possibilities it provides. Shadows create depth in photographs. Avoid taking pictures at noon when shadows are shortest. A picture taken on a clear, sunny day, as most pictures are, is pleasing but often trite. Mood is created by light: the "soft" light of morning and evening; the "dramatic" light of a mountain storm; the gray "gentle" light of an overcast day; the bright "flamboyant" light of a sunset. It is possible to photograph "moonlight" scenes near water in early morning or

A telephoto lens magnifies the sun behind an Eskimo inukshuk *marker. Below: refracted by the camera lens, the sun flares dramatically. Light reflected from the water reveals the boat.*

The sidelight of early evening and slight underexposure bring out the texture of wind-sculpted snow.

Sidelight and a foreground of leafy branches add depth and beauty to this waterfall photo taken near Trois-Pistoles, Que.

Gulls, bright against a blue sea, lend interest to this shot of a cove.

late afternoon. Shoot toward the sun and deliberately underexpose. The reflection of sunlight on water will give the illusion of moonlight.

The predominant feeling of the Prairies is one of nearly infinite space. This can be visually emphasized by letting the sky dominate the photo. The sky should occupy at least two-thirds of the image area. And the foreground? Something that says: "this is the Prairies"—a lone farm, vast fields of golden grain, or a green-rimmed slough. Prairie rivers are lovely; their high bluffs provide excellent vantage points for a photographer. And the patterns of the Prairies, the checkerboard of black and yellow in fall when some fields are plowed and others in stubble, provide beautiful picture possibilities.

To photograph in forests is difficult because all those trees are in the way. The coastal forests of British Columbia have marvelous primeval-looking trees festooned with trailing mosses and lichens. It is best to be at the edge of the forest where one can shoot "out" toward the light. The contorted, moss-draped limbs of the trees will then be partly silhouetted, the colors deep and saturated.

The coniferous forest of the Canadian Shield looks somber, but beautiful when its trees are reflected in a lake or river. Silvery birches or aspen growing in a clearing look superb against a backdrop of dark pines or firs, especially in spring when birch and aspen leaves are a bright, translucent green. A fast-flowing brook winding its way through the forest is best photographed at low shutter speeds, at ½ or ¼ of a second; the rippling water will be blurred in the picture, and look swift and smooth.

For beautiful snow scenes, slanting light is essential. It brings out the texture of snow and the contours of drifted snow. Slight underexposure will darken the sky deep blue, snow and shadow areas light blue, but leave highlights pure white. A skylight or UV (ultraviolet) filter is essential; without it snow is often too bluish.

For really spectacular pictures, shoot directly into the sun. Exposure should be for the sun (be careful not to snap the needle off the meter); it may be as low as *f*/11 at 1/250 second, with a 25 ASA film. The sun will flare; sky and snow will be deep blue. Anything dark in this picture, such as trees, will be completely underexposed, and will show in silhouette against the sky.

In the weak and oblique rays of the setting sun, snow has a reddish glow and shadows are deep violet. With a telephoto lens the sun can be magnified so that it shimmers above the horizon like a great ball of fire.

Shooting Animals in the Wild–With a Camera

It is the dream of most photographers to produce beautiful animal pictures. For you to realize that dream, you need adequate camera equipment, some knowledge of animal behavior, a lot of patience and a bit of luck.

Any camera accepting interchangeable lenses is suitable for animal photography. Most professional wildlife photographers use the 35mm single-lens reflex (SLR). It is compact, light, versatile, sturdy and dependable. A wide range of lenses and accessories is available for most models. Both viewing and focusing is done through the lens; the position and size of the image seen in the viewfinder just before the shutter clicks is identical to what appears on the film.

Animals are everywhere but they are not all equally easy to approach and photograph. Canada geese are notoriously wary, but at the Jack Miner Bird Sanctuary near Kingsville, Ont., where they receive protection and food, they are trusting and can be photographed at close range.

Greater snow geese breed on remote Bylot Island in the Arctic. During their migration in spring and fall, they rest and feed for a few weeks on the tidal flats of the St. Lawrence River near Quebec City. As the tide rises, the geese come closer and closer to shore. The photographer who sits on shore and waits can get beautiful pictures.

Polar bears congregate in late fall near Churchill, Man., and often come so close to roads, one can photograph them from the safety of a car. And the place to get pictures of the now extremely rare prairie dog is Frenchman Creek Valley near the South Saskatchewan town of Val Marie. Many photographers collect such information and, by being at the right place at the right time, are able to photograph with ease animals that elsewhere might be nearly impossible to approach.

National and provincial parks are the haven of many animals. Animals are creatures of habit, many following unvarying daily routines. Birds have favorite perches, bison favorite wallows, elk favorite meadows, seals favorite beaches. Park wardens can often predict with amazing accuracy where animals in their region will be at any given time of day.

In Jasper National Park, moose feed on aquatic plants near the edge of a lake, not far from a road. They come nearly every morning and remain until about one hour after sunrise, when the light is marvelous: soft, oblique, warm, a bit hazy in the distance.

The picture possibilities of such a moment are nearly infinite. But in practice they fall into two broad categories: the close-up, taken with a telephoto lens, and the more panoramic picture taken with a shorter focal length lens, showing the animal in its environment. It is often possible to take both, by changing lenses or by using two cameras, each equipped with a lens of the appropriate focal length.

All animals should be approached slowly, with patience and caution. When an animal appears apprehensive, keep a low profile: sit or kneel quietly for a while. Mammals, because of their acute sense of smell, must be stalked from downwind.

Light should also be kept in mind. Frontal lighting is fine, but tends to be rather flat. Backlighting, especially by the slanting rays of a low sun, is dramatic. It shows the animal in silhouette, its fur outlined by an aureole of light. Sidelighting brings out fur texture, and provides a beautiful interplay of highlights and shadows.

Exposures for back-lighted and side-lighted pictures tend to be tricky. Generally, one should expose for highlights to achieve color saturation. When in doubt, bracket—take one or more pictures at the exposure indicated by the light meter, and additional pictures at ½ *f* stops above and below that setting. The correct exposure is likely to be within this range, giving the assurance of some pictures with perfect exposure.

To capture that fleeting moment

Focus on Nature

Close-up nature photography opens to enthusiasts a new, yet accessible, world. A 35mm single-lens reflex camera is particularly well suited for close-up photography. For extreme close-ups, extension tubes or bellows units are required. Subjects of postage-stamp size and larger are most easily photographed with versatile "macro" lenses, which can be focused all the way down to a life-size image.

The disadvantage of "macro" lenses is that with them one has to be very close to one's subject.

The secret of successful close-up photography is simplicity achieved through careful composition. A single flower, full frame, is more impressive than a cluster of flowers, most of them out of focus, since the depth of field in close-up pictures, even at small *f* stops, is very shallow. Nothing should intrude between lens and subject—dry leaves, withered stalks or grass blades must be carefully removed.

The rich hues of wild flowers come out best on a bright but slightly overcast day. On a sunny day, eliminate harsh shadows by using a flash or a reflector to throw light into shade areas.

Birds in flight are difficult to photograph but patience and preparedness often pay off—as with this picture of a kestrel.

A ground squirrel eyes the camera—operated by remote control.

Back light from a setting sun adds drama to this shot of a polar bear.

when an animal looks its best—a bull moose with his antlered head held high and turned slightly toward the camera, a deer looking shyly out from a frame of foliage, a bighorn ram in majestic stance on a mountain ridge—requires patience and preparedness. Keep the animal in focus at all times to capture that perfect instant. Occasionally it helps to make odd noises, such as a squeak or trill. Many animals respond to this by adopting an alert, impressive pose. They will look toward the camera. A few, intrigued and curious, may even approach. Never wave or shout. This will only frighten the animal. It will flee and a rear view is rarely rewarding.

Pictures of animals in action, of a flying bird or a running deer, are thrilling but difficult to take. For a good picture, the animal must be in focus and as close to full-frame as possible. Through knowledge of animal behavior, action can often be anticipated and the prepared photographer is the one most likely to get that memorable shot.

By following a running animal with the camera and tripping the shutter during this "panning" motion, the animal's image will be sharp, even at relatively slow shutter speeds, while the background is blurred, creating the visual impression of movement and speed.

Some seabirds "ride" the air currents and follow quite predictable flight paths, making it fairly easy to get good pictures. Predominantly white birds, such as gulls or gannets, should not be photographed against a cloudy sky, since the color of their plumage blends with that of the clouds. But they are superb against a deep blue sky (the "deep blue" is achieved by slight underexposure), or with a backdrop of dark water.

Animals that are shy (or those that should not be disturbed, such as birds at their nest) are best photographed from a blind, or with the help of an air-pressure shutter release. This is a long, thin plastic tube, with a squeeze bulb at one end and a shutter release at the other.

The camera, tripod mounted and with its shutter cocked, is set up and focused (and camouflaged if necessary) on the spot where the animal is most likely to be—the entrance to a ground squirrel burrow, for instance. The photographer hides at a discreet distance and, when the animal appears at the predetermined spot, he trips the shutter by squeezing the bulb. The advantage of the air-pressure release is that it is small and light. But unless a camera is motor driven, the photographer has to emerge from hiding after each picture to advance the film and cock the shutter, and this obviously scares his subject away.

A blind offers greater possibilities to observe and photograph animals without frightening them. It is best to set up a blind near a nest or den and leave it alone for a few days, to allow the animal to get accustomed to its presence.

Maps and How to Read Them

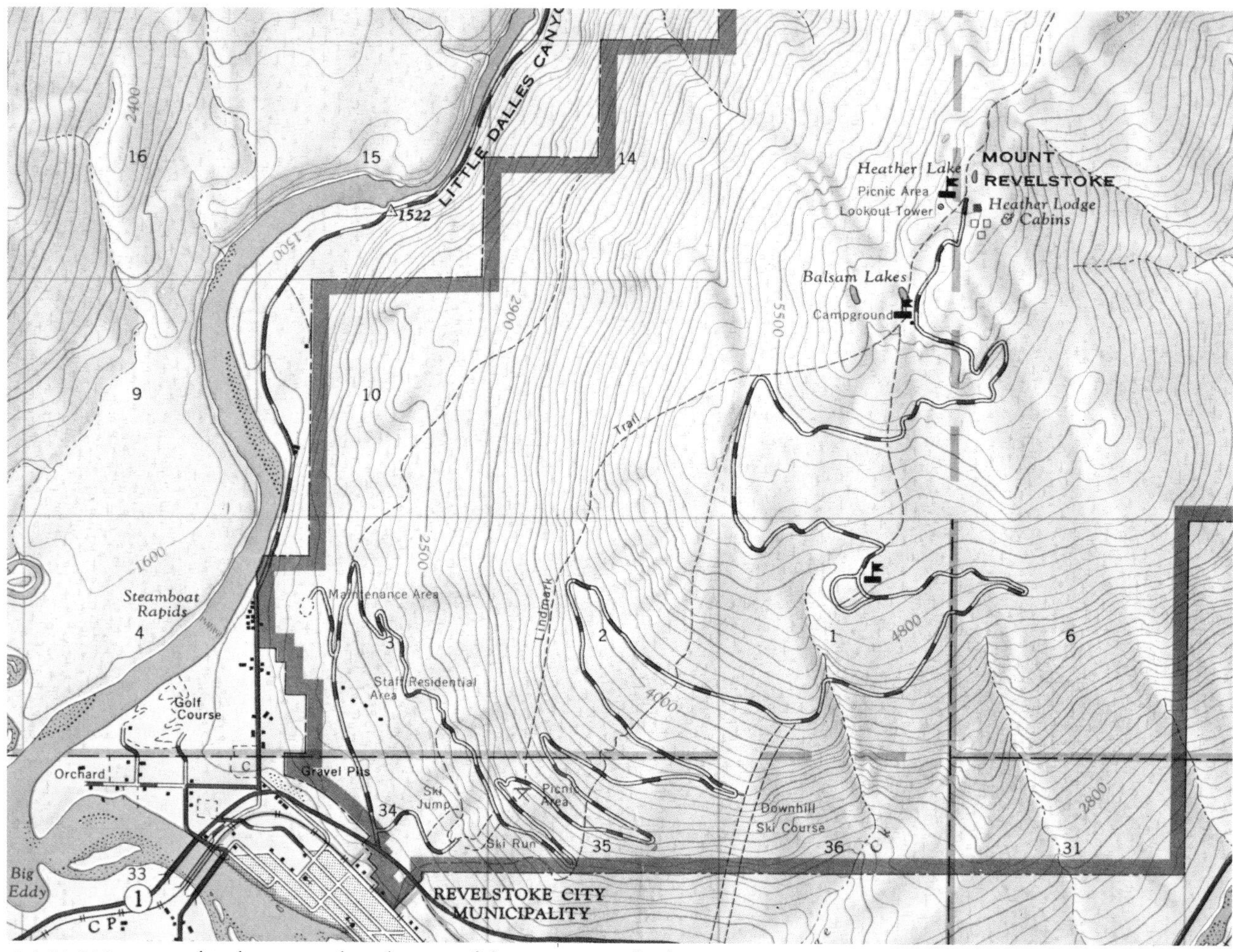

A 1:50,000 topographical map—such as this map of the Mount Revelstoke area in B.C.—has a detailed legend and is ideal for most hiking trips.

Of the several types of maps in use today, the most useful to campers is the topographical map. It gives the nature of the terrain, the heights of major elevations, and the presence of waterways, roadways and utilities. All of these features are important to anyone traveling through unfamiliar countryside.

A legend, containing a group of symbols (at right), is usually found in a bottom corner of a map. In addition, an arrow (usually in the margin of a map) shows where true north lies. Also shown is the angle of declination—the variation between true north and magnetic north in the region of the map. The variation must be allowed for when taking a compass reading.

Scale is usually depicted in inches to the mile, or as a proportion. Most modern maps express scale as a proportion (e.g. 1:250,000 means that 1 inch on the map equals 250,000 inches on the ground).

Scales currently being used on Canadian topographical maps are:
1:25,000 (about 2½ inches to the mile)
1:50,000 (about 1¼ inches to the mile)
1:125,000 (about ½ inch to the mile)
1:250,000 (about ¼ inch to the mile).

In Canada, topographical maps at a scale of 1:50,000 are generally regarded as best for hiking.

When reading a map, it is extremely important to take into account the contours that lie between you and your destination. Although a

Legend

- Hard surface roads, all weather
- Loose surface roads, all weather
- Trail
- Railway
- Picnic area
- Warden's cabin with telephone
- Buildings
- Other buildings with telephone
- Other buildings without telephone
- Barn
- Cemetery
- School
- Church
- National park boundary
- Horizontal control point, with elevation
- Contours (2000)
- Foreshore flats
- Gravel pits
- River with bridge
- Stream, intermittent or dry

straight line is the shortest distance between two points, it is not necessarily the best route when traveling in the wilderness. Often a detour around a mountain or a valley or stream may prove wiser.

Estimating distances In the outdoors it is often helpful to be able to glance at an object and assess its height, width or its distance from you. This skill is particularly useful when selecting a route, or making a map of your own. A few simple tips are worth remembering:

Estimate distance by dividing the distance into lengths familiar to you—100 yards, one yard, a foot. Use familiar distances, such as the length of a football field or the width of a hockey rink.

Finally, before you set off, measure your height, your normal stride, the length of your foot, the length of your forearm. This will help you make accurate estimates.

Always carry a detailed map of the area in which you are traveling. Maps can be waterproofed by applying several coats of clear shellac or acrylic spray to both sides.

How High Is It?

To estimate the height of an object, have a friend stand at its base. Hold a ruler vertically and sight along its bottom end. Step back until your friend appears to be half an inch high. Now sight the top of the object and note where it intersects the ruler. Count the number of half inches between that point and the bottom of the ruler. Multiply that number by the height of your friend. The result is the height of the object.

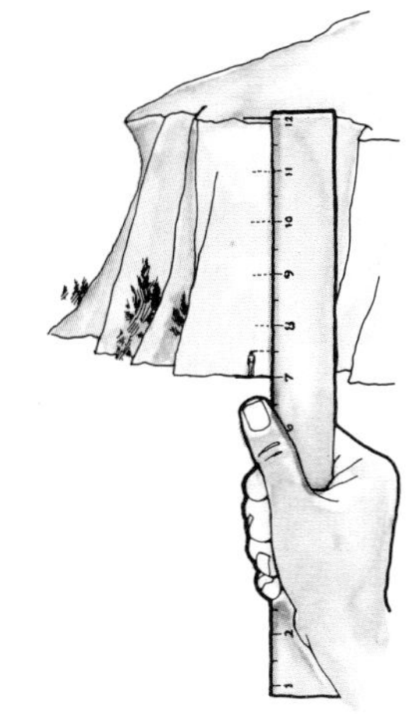

How Wide Is It?

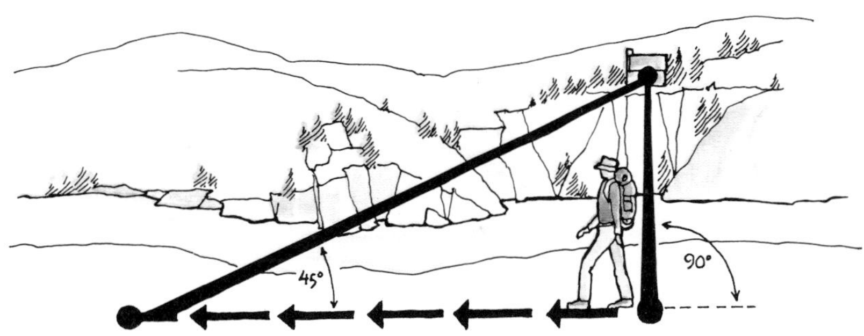

To estimate the width of a river, select a house or other landmark on the opposite bank. Mark the spot where you are standing with a rock, an article of clothing, or a piece of camping equipment, and walk along the riverbank until you are at a 45° angle to the house or landmark on the opposite bank. The distance you have walked is approximately the width of the river.

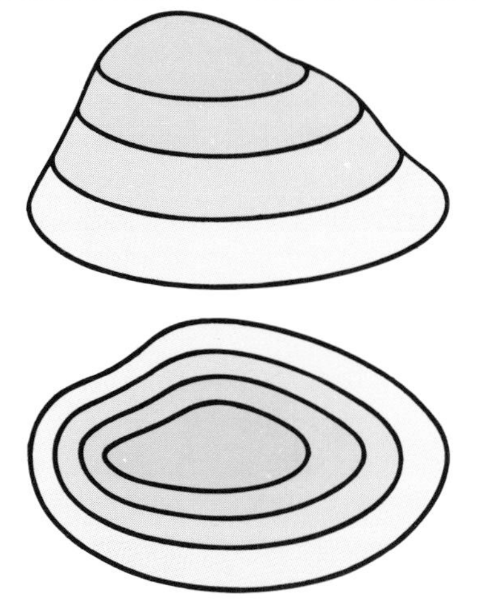

Reading Contours

A contour shows the outline of a hill at one elevation. Widely spaced lines indicate a gentle slope. Closely spaced lines indicate a steeper slope.

How to Find a Map Reference

Grids and coordinates are vertical and horizontal parallels that divide a topographical map into sections. Each section carries an address, given in latitudinal and longitudinal degrees, and each section can be subdivided into 100 smaller units. With this system any feature can be found easily on a topographical map.

To determine the position of ⚑:

1. Find the number of the coordinate west of ⚑. This is 80. Now count off in tenths from 80 east to ⚑. This is found to be 2. Write down the reference as 802. This is called *easting*.

2. Find the number of the coordinate south of ⚑. This is 71. Count off in tenths from 71 north to ⚑. This is found to be 8. Write down the reference as 718. This is called *northing*. Combining the two figures, the final reference is 802718.

Always find the easting first, then the northing.

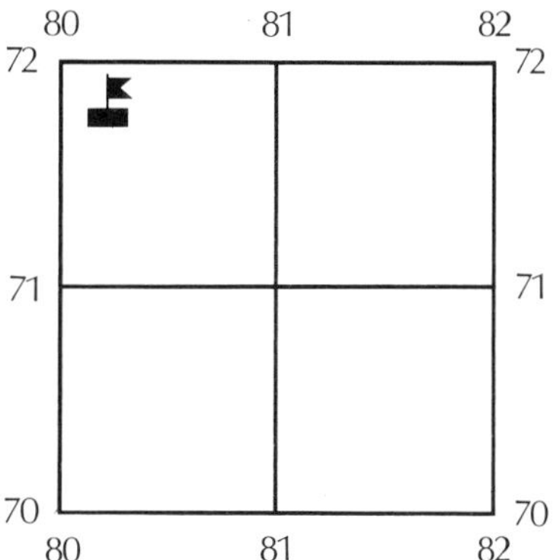

Finding Your Way in the Wilderness

Before setting off into the wilderness, always tell someone where you are going and when you intend to return. Be specific. Point out your route and destination on a map, and make it clear that any delay after a certain time means trouble.

Seek expert advice about the area you wish to explore. Get the best maps and a good compass.

On the map, select landmarks, such as mountains and lakes, that will serve as checkpoints. Check the slope of the land and the direction in which streams are running. Take note of prominent or unusual landforms.

If there is snow on the ground it is wise to stay close to roads, trails and waterways. Unless you are experienced, do not travel alone and do not travel at night. By following these guidelines, your chances of getting lost will be greatly reduced. *If you do lose track of where you are, stop and take stock of the situation:*

- Don't panic.
- Depending on the arrangements you have made, it may be wisest to sit tight and wait for searchers to find you. If so, build a shelter and make a fire.
- Assume that the point at which you realize you are lost is also the point closest to your original course. Make this your home base.
- If you move from your home base, blaze a trail. Use strips of colored cloth (which should be removed on the way back) or small piles of stones to mark your route.
- Don't wander in the dark. When night falls, check your position with the North Star.
- Distress signals given at regular intervals will help searchers find you. Three blasts of a whistle, three rifle shots, three shouts or three small fires—these are standard distress signals.

The compass The most practical way to determine direction is by means of a compass. Compasses—for the most part—are foolproof and reliable. They rarely require maintenance and they are usually simple to operate. Buy the best model for hiking that your budget will allow. Avoid toys and compasses that are combined with something else, or that are elaborately designed for military or survey use.

A good compass should be sensitive, accurate and sturdily made. It should have a stop mechanism, and the needle should rest on a heavy, tempered steel point. A Scout compass—with a clear plastic base plate to facilitate map reading—is a good buy. Compasses with floating dials are also worth considering.

No matter how efficient your compass, it will be affected by the presence of metal in the nearby surroundings. Take care that a belt buckle, a knife or a similar metal object does not create an improper reading.

How to use a compass A compass dial has from 4 to 32 points, each indicating a major direction. More important are the 360 degrees on the compass dial. These degrees permit greater accuracy when determining direction. For example, when referring to south in terms of degrees (or bearings), we can say that south is exactly 180 degrees from north. Similarly, any location can be pinpointed to within a single degree on the map.

To determine true north A compass needle always points to magnetic north, an area about 1,400 miles south of the true north pole. Because of this, there could be a difference (depending on your location) between true north (also called map north) and north indicated by a compass needle. In eastern Canada, a magnetic needle points to the west of true north; in western Canada, the opposite applies. To determine true north, you must know the compass variation for the area in which you are traveling. For example, in Ottawa the compass variation is 12 degrees 54 minutes (12°54′) west of true north. Thus, to establish true north, simply add 12 degrees 54 minutes to the east of the compass reading. In western Canada subtract the variation from the compass reading.

Navigating by Stars and Sun

If you are facing the North Star you are facing true north—give or take a degree. The simplest way to find the North Star is to look for the Big Dipper. Follow the outer edge of the Dipper with your eyes: the solitary bright star in line with the edge is the North Star.

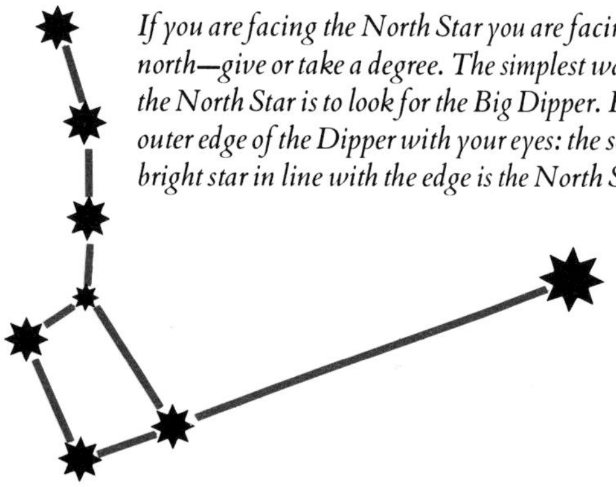

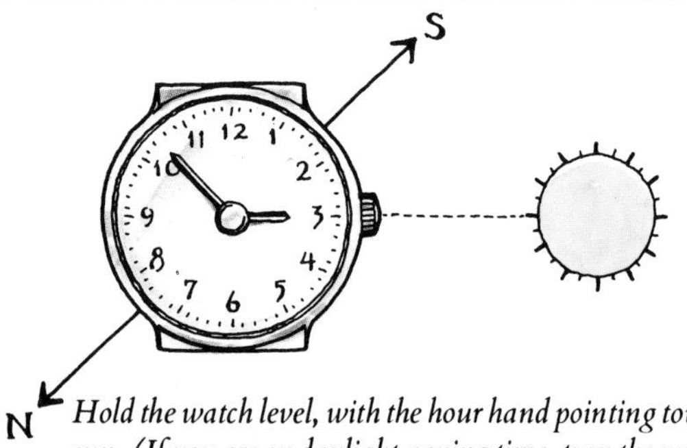

Hold the watch level, with the hour hand pointing toward the sun. (If you are on daylight-saving time, turn the watch back an hour to standard time.) A halfway line between the hour hand and 12 will point to south. In the morning, count counterclockwise from 12; in the afternoon, count clockwise. By reversing the procedure, you can use a compass to set your watch.

The ability to read maps is essential to trouble-free travel. When camping or hiking, carry a detailed topographical map and consult it frequently.

The Parts of a Compass

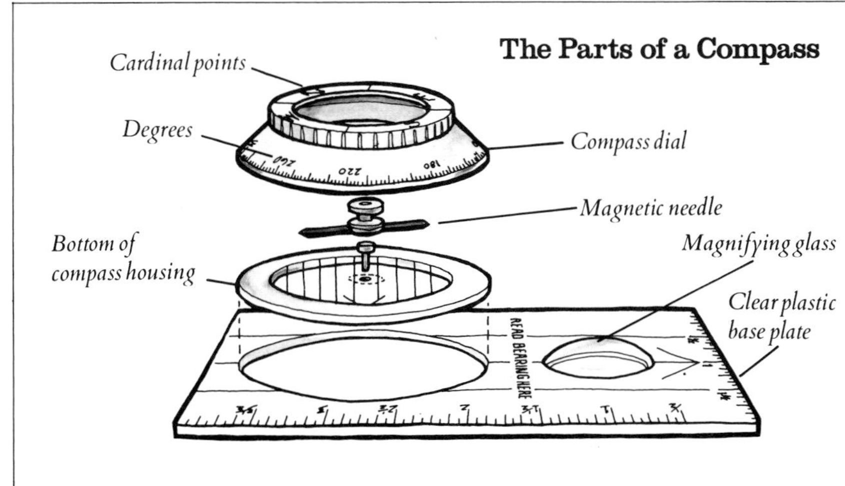

Using a compass and a map The most practical type of compass for map reading is fitted with a base plate. Place the edge of the base plate along the map route you wish to travel, with the arrow on the plate pointing in the direction of travel. Now turn the compass housing until the north arrow on the dial is pointing to map north. Lift the compass, hold it level, and turn your body slowly until the needle and the north arrow on the dial are aligned. The arrow on the base plate will now point in the direction you must travel. *Remember, at this time, to make allowance for the magnetic variation.*

To find a bearing Face the direction in which you wish to travel. The direction arrow on the base plate should also point this way. Turn the compass housing until the north part of the needle aligns with north on the dial. Now read the degree number at the point where the direction arrow and the edge of the housing coincide.

To follow a bearing Given the bearing, set the compass housing at this number of degrees so that it aligns with the direction arrow on the plate. Hold the compass level, and slowly turn your body until needle north and north on the dial are aligned. Now select a landmark at which the direction arrow is pointing and walk toward it.

Nature's Compasses

Since the accuracy of the following methods is questionable, they should be used only as a last resort. • Woodpeckers generally peck holes in the northeast side of trees • Spiders usually spin webs on the south side • The tips of pines and hemlocks usually lean eastward • The north side of a hill is moist and mossy; the south side has twigs and dry leaves • Growth rings are widely spaced and the bark is thickest on the north sides of trees.

BAYE DE BAFFIN
TERRES
James Lancaster
I.Woman
Hope Sanderson
DET. DE DAVIS
Waygat
James-Island
C.Bedfort
I.Bisko
Spiering
GROENLAND
C.Grace a Dieu
C.Walsingham
Mideton en 1742
Baye de Repulse
Wagers
Warwick Forcland
C.de la Reine Marie
C. Confort
Milles Isles
Pte. Shark
R.de l'ours Blanc
Pte de la Reine Anne
B.de Bonne fortune
Delfshaven
Elizabeth
Whit I.
C.Christian
Désolation I.
C.Discorde
Det.de Forbisher
C.Farwel
Côtes découvertes par
Nottingam I.
DETROIT D'HUDSON
C.Charles
Salvages
C.Elisabeth
I.de Résolution
C.Southampton
Mansfelt I.
Dormeur du Nord
BAYE D'HUDSON
I.du Foin
I.Buttons
I.Baston
R.de la Mine
R.de Buttons
Isles du Dormeur
I.Cardinales
du Loup Marin
R.de Munck
F. et C.Churchil
R.Bourbon
P.Bourbon ou Yorck
la 12me du Boulanger
R.Ste. Therese
Roche Noire
F.de Niew Savane
BRETAGNE
TERRE DE LABRADOR
ou ESTOTILAND
Steyl Pte.
I.Sadal
Havre S.Pierre
Ance Ste.Anne
B.Hollandoise
Grande B. des Esquimaux
R. de Niew Savane
C.Henriette Marie
Lac des Dechargeurs
Christinaux
NOUVELLE
B. de James
Pitchiboucouni
Nitchik Irimiouetchs
F.S.Germain
R. Albani
F.Ste.Anne
L.des Mistassins
L.Peretibe
L.Achouarupi
ESQUIMAUX
Bell'isle
I.du Quirpon
D.de Bell'isle
P.Blanche
I.d'Aves
C.Boñeviste
B.de la Trinité
L.Alemipigon
R. Pere
F.Rupert
MISTASSINS
Papinachois
I.St.Laurent
Port a Port
ISLE DE T.NEUVE
L. des Abitibis
Pie-kouagamiens
Tadoussack
Gaspesie
C.des Rosiers
B.S.George
Plaisance
C.de Raye
Michipicoton
Ance aux Sables
Attikamegues
L.Caouinagamie
B.des Chaleurs
G. de St. Laurent
I.Royale
Lac Superieur
CANADA
I.Beauharnois
I.S.Jean
I.Royale
L.Nipissing
Quebec
Algonquins
les 3 Rivieres
I.d'Orleans
Freneuse
C.Tourmentin
Louisbourg
de l'Est
Ste.Marie
Monreal
R.des Outaouais
Sorel
Chambli
ETECHEMINS
Chedabouctou
C.Canceau
Gr.Banquereau
I.Manitoualin
L.Huron
I.Taronto
L.Quentio
Acadie
L.Michigan
Renards
les Sakis
Lac Ontario
I.des Monts déserts
C.Negre
C.de Sable
B.des Marsouins
Hurons
Iroquois
Boston
Plimouth
C.Cod
Miamis
L.Erie
Pensylvanie
Philadelphie
I.Longue
Elsimbourg
B.de Lawaré
I.Bermudes ou Sommers
Maryland
Chaouanons
Somerset
VIRGINIE
B.de Chesapeack
Albemarle
Koanok I.
Bath
CHERAQUIS
Upha
Quanese

Outdoors: Where It Is

More Canadians than ever before are escaping from cities and towns to enjoy the great Canadian outdoors—for an afternoon, a week, a month, a summer. The modern outdoorsman may canoe and camp and climb where not long ago explorers trod, voyageurs raced their birchbarks, other men sought gold—and the buffalo roamed.

The voyageurs are gone but much of Canada remains as it was, blessed with pristine lakes and wild rivers in a still unspoiled wilderness. The outdoors is a gift often overlooked, a national resource to be cherished and conserved, to be used too—but wisely.

The maps in this section are designed to help Canadians explore their outdoors. They are a guide for the weekend traveler and the summer camper, the fisherman, hiker, canoeist—for every kind of outdoorsman.

On these pages you learn where to use many of the techniques discussed elsewhere in this book—and where to see Canada's wildlife.

Scores of hiking trails and canoe routes, 28 national parks (covering some 50,000 square miles), more than 300 provincial parks and numerous wildlife preserves and wilderness and conservation areas are highlighted in this section. The maps direct you to campgrounds and spectacular scenic attractions, to areas you know well and many others you have not seen.

Here are the Bay of Fundy's 50-foot tides; Mount Edziza, a dormant volcano in British Columbia; the wave-lashed shores of the Atlantic Provinces; northern Saskatchewan's mosaic of lakes and rivers; British Columbia's 1,248-foot Takakkaw Falls, Canada's highest waterfall; the weird shapes of the Red Deer Badlands in southern Alberta; Canada's loftiest peak, 19,524-foot Mount Logan in the Yukon; and the exotic plant and animal life where Point Pelee juts into Lake Erie.

Canada's outdoor recreation opportunities are almost unlimited. You can dip into an icy mountain stream or tramp in the shadow of jagged mountains; pause to observe a pageant of migrating wildfowl; sit by a glassy lake steaming with morning mist; challenge the rage of a rapid-strewn river, or sleep under a canopy of stars and evergreen boughs.

These maps will help you know Canada better. They will serve as an invaluable aid to discovery and they will enrich your awareness and appreciation of Canada's outdoors.

This detail from a map by Robert de Vaugondy shows eastern Canada and the northeastern United States as they were thought to be in 1750.

How to Read the Maps

On the following pages are 49 regional maps and numerous descriptions of outstanding outdoor recreation areas from Vancouver Island to Newfoundland's Avalon Peninsula to Baffin Island. Maps and text locate and describe national and provincial parks; conservation, recreation and wilderness areas; provincial forests; canoe routes, hiking trails and bird and game sanctuaries. The text also lists the outdoor activities available to campers and travelers. On page 308 is a map of Canada with red circles locating the regional maps, and numbers indicating the pages on which the regional maps are found.

Maps

On each regional map is a miniature map of Canada; a red dot indicates the location of the map area.

A number adjoining a name means that the attraction is described in accompanying text bearing the same number.

Large provincial parks with camping, or parks of special interest without camping are tinted green (small parks are represented by a green symbol). "Special interest" parks contain features of scenic, geological or archeological significance, Quebec has two park classifications; the text indicates whether a Quebec park is a provincial park or a fish and game preserve.

The 28 **national parks**—from Pacific Rim National Park on Vancouver Island to Auyuittuq National Park on Baffin Island—are tinted brown.

Recreation and wilderness areas are tinted light brown (small areas are represented by a light brown symbol). These include: **conservation areas** and **provincial recreation areas** that permit camping; **provincial forest areas** set aside for recreation and offering camping; **conservancy areas** (wildlife preserves in several of British Columbia's larger provincial parks); **wilderness areas;** and federal and provincial **bird sanctuaries** and **game preserves** including nature refuges, wildlife management areas, Crown game preserves and national wildlife areas.

This symbolizes a **game preserve.**

This represents a **bird sanctuary.**

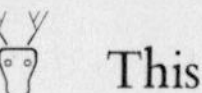

A series of brown dots indicates a **hiking trail** established and maintained by a private or government organization. The trail name appears if space permits.

A line of black dots represents a **canoe route.** Most routes are suitable for novices; some, however—especially those in remote areas—should be attempted only by experienced canoeists. Two types of routes are shown. Official names are used for routes charted and maintained by private and government organizations. For example:

Grand River Canoe Route

Routes selected by the editors are shown thus:

Canoe Route (Brandon to Spruce Woods Park)

▪ A **point of interest** symbol represents a feature mentioned in the text.

∧ This indicates that federal or provincial authorities operate developed campgrounds—areas set aside for camping and usually offering sanitary facilities, picnic tables, a safe water supply and barbecues or wood stoves. Many campsites have electrical hookups for trailers. A small fee is usually charged for camping.

A camping symbol inside an area or partially superimposed on a park or recreation area symbol indicates the availability of developed camping facilities.

Text

The name of each recreation area is followed by a number; the same number locates that attraction on the accompanying map. Each entry notes which facilities and activities are offered at that recreation area. Size is shown in italics; areas of more than 1,000 acres are given in square miles. These are the terms used:

Fish and game preserve This provincial park classification is used only in Quebec. Such areas have controlled hunting and fishing and limited recreational facilities.

Camping Developed camping is available.

Wilderness camping Developed camping is not available. Camping is permitted either at random or only at undeveloped sites (usually clearings with primitive cooking areas).

Climbing Rock climbing is permitted.

Supervised swimming Swimming is supervised by qualified personnel.

Cross-country skiing Cross-country ski trails are usually clearly marked. Some trails are used in summer for hiking.

Alpine skiing Downhill ski slopes are maintained; facilities may include T-bars, chair lifts or cable cars.

Hiking Trails are blazed and maintained.

Fishing Fishing is permitted; the species caught are indicated in parentheses. Visitors should check whether licenses are required.

Canoeing Canoe routes exist and trip maps may be available.

Horseback riding Horseback trails, usually blazed. Horses perhaps can be rented.

Self-guiding nature trail Hikers are guided by signposts or descriptive text explaining natural features along the trails.

Nature house A building in which are displayed such things as plant and animal specimens, features of geological interest or perhaps archeological artifacts.

372
373
314
315
374
314
324
325
328
317
323
336
330
311
312
320
319
321
326
332
333
336
339
335
322
327
334

Where to Find the Maps

The numbers on this map are the numbers of the map section pages. They indicate that, for instance, the Gaspé Peninsula is mapped and described on page 360, and that information on the Cypress Hills of Alberta and Saskatchewan is on page 327.

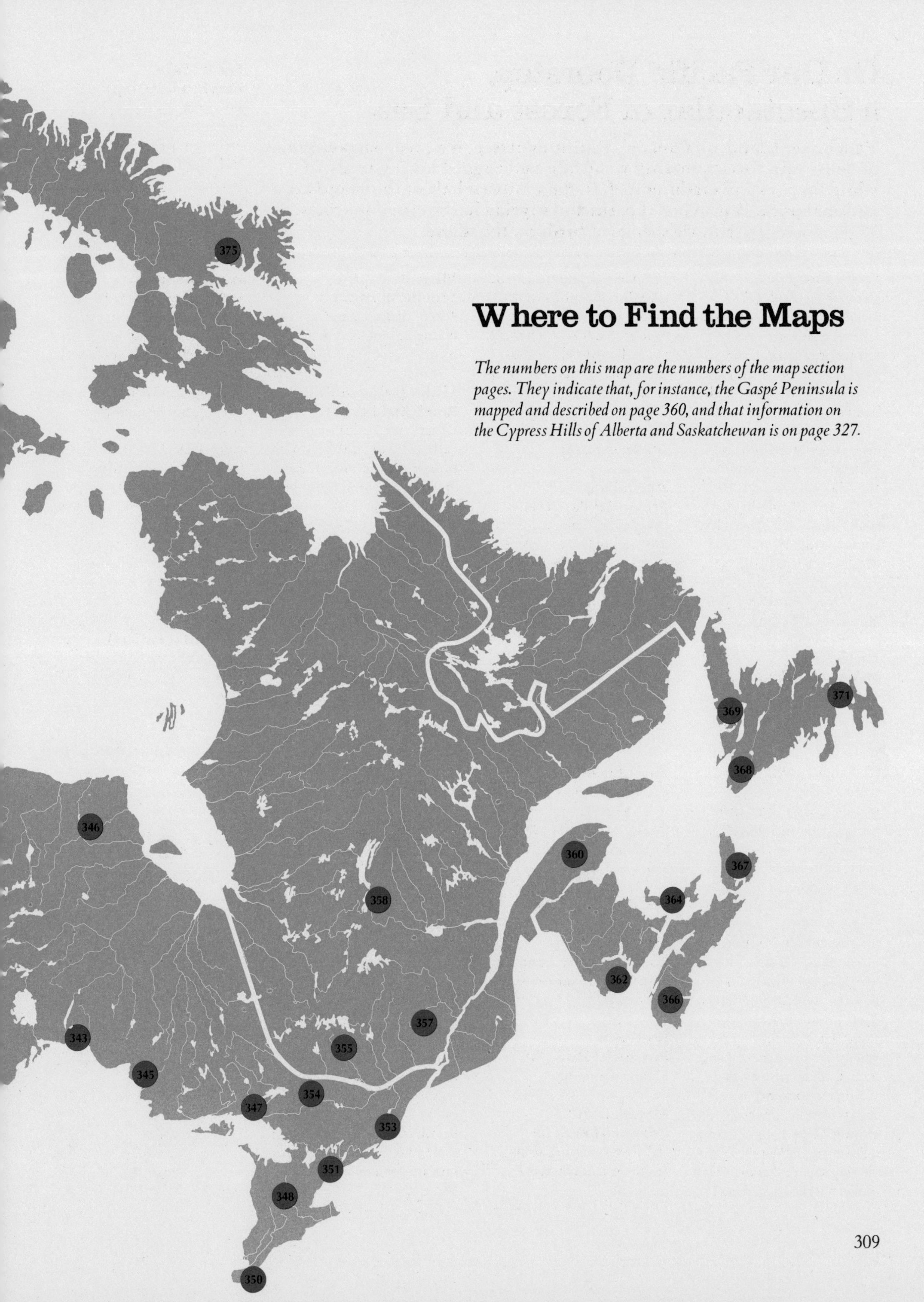

On Our Pacific Doorstep, a Spectacular of Forest and Sea

Vancouver Island, on Canada's Pacific doorstep, is a great extravaganza of dense rain forests, roaring waterfalls and rugged hiking trails, of white beaches and crashing surf. In the southern half of the island are a national park, 19 provincial parks and myriad harbors and marinas. There are more than 150 species of birds on the island.

Strathcona Provincial Park (1)
Della Falls, the highest waterfall in Canada, plunges 1,443 feet to Della Lake in the southern section of the park. To the northwest is Forbidden Plateau where, according to Indian legend, evil spirits devoured women and children. In the park's center is the 7,219-foot Golden Hinde, Vancouver Island's highest peak. One of the island's last elk herds roams Strathcona. *877 square miles.* Camping, climbing, alpine skiing, hiking, fishing (cutthroat, Dolly Varden and rainbow trout).

Pacific Rim National Park (6)
In Barkley Sound are the Broken Group Islands, the "Graveyard of the Pacific" that has claimed an estimated 50 ships since 1803. Black oyster catchers, Leach's storm-petrels, pelagic cormorants and more than 170 pairs of bald eagles nest on the islands. Squads of killer whales occasionally cruise through island channels. Pacific gray whales dive offshore for plankton and shrimp, and mammoth Steller's sea lions, weighing as much as 2,200 pounds, are frequent visitors. To the north is seven-mile Long Beach, backed by the 4,000-foot Mackenzie Range. Rough trails crisscross past weathered rock arches and water-blasted blowholes. The 45-mile West Coast Trail was a lifesaving trail established to aid shipwrecked sailors. It is a difficult trek—rugged near Logan Creek and treacherous near Port Renfrew—and should be attempted only by experienced hikers. The trail passes Tsusiat Falls, a 100-foot-wide cataract that drops 50 feet to a small pool. *250 square miles.* Camping, supervised swimming, fishing (steelhead trout).

Macmillan Provincial Park (11)
Douglas firs, some more than 800 years old, tower 200 feet and more in Cathedral Grove. The tallest, 244 feet high, is 30 feet in circumference. *337 acres.*

Stamp Falls Provincial Park (7)
583 acres. Camping, hiking, fishing (steelhead and cutthroat trout).

Englishman River Falls Provincial Park (14)
A wooden footbridge offers a dramatic view of 120-foot Englishman River Falls. *240 acres.* Camping.

Marshall-Stevenson Migratory Bird Sanctuary (13)
The brant—an arctic goose—winters in the sanctuary. *73 acres.*

Ivy Green Provincial Park (18)
62 acres. Camping.

Morton Lake Provincial Park (2)
165 acres. Camping, fishing (rainbow and cutthroat trout).

Elk Falls Provincial Park (3)
4 square miles. Camping, hiking, fishing (steelhead trout).

Little Qualicum Falls Provincial Park (12)
Picturesque Little Qualicum Falls, plunging 200 feet down three giant steps, is at the end of a one-mile trail from the park entrance. *1.5 square miles.* Camping.

Newcastle Island Provincial Park (16)
Cars are not permitted on the island, which is reached by ferry from Nanaimo. There are mooring facilities on the island's south shore. *760 acres.* Camping, supervised swimming.

McDonald Provincial Park (19)
49 acres. Camping.

Mitlenatch Island Provincial Park (4)
The island is a haven for glaucous-winged gulls, pelagic cormorants and black oyster catchers. Offshore are purple and orange starfish, northern abalones and single-shelled mollusks. Harbor seals and sea lions are occasionally seen wallowing near kelp beds or sunning on ledges. In June, prickly pear cactus blooms on Mitlenatch—the only cactus on the B.C. coast. The island can be reached by boat from the mainland—a crossing that is often stormy. Docking facilities are not available. *382 acres.*

Sproat Lake Provincial Park (9)
Five Indian petroglyphs, figures carved in rock, have been preserved here on a limestone rock face 100 feet wide and 15 feet high. *98 acres.* Camping, supervised swimming, fishing (cutthroat trout).

Horne Lake Caves Provincial Park (10)
Visitors descend to an eerie underground world of stalactites (iciclelike calcium deposits), stalagmites (inverted stalactites) and helictites (twiglike calcium deposits that protrude from the cave walls). Horne Lake Main and Horne Lake Lower caves are open to the public. The Riverbend and Euclataws caves are open only to experienced cavers who have obtained permission from the British Columbia Parks Branch. *71 acres.*

Fillongley Provincial Park (8)
The park is reached by car ferry from the mainland. *57 acres.* Camping.

Lovely Englishman River Falls.

Gordon Bay Provincial Park (17)
The densest stands of fir on Vancouver Island are in this park.
122 acres. Camping, supervised swimming, fishing (salmon, rainbow and cutthroat trout).

John Dean Provincial Park (21)
Dominated by 950-foot Mount Newton, one of the highest peaks on the Saanich Peninsula, the park offers spectacular views of the Gulf Islands.
382 acres. Wilderness camping.

Goldstream Provincial Park (20)
Gold was discovered here in 1885 and old mining shafts and tunnels remain. Dotted throughout the park are Douglas firs, some almost 600 years old. Canada's only broad-leafed evergreen, the arbutus, grows along the two-mile Arbutus Ridge Trail.
828 acres. Camping, hiking.

Rathtrevor Beach Provincial Park (15)
A mile-long sand beach, the longest on Vancouver Island, skirts the park's eastern edge. At low tide almost 500 acres of flats are exposed, dotted with clams and oysters. Among the 42 species of birds found here is the black brant, an endangered member of the Canada goose family.
859 acres. Camping, supervised swimming.

Miracle Beach Provincial Park (5)
Killer whales occasionally surface offshore in deep water. Almost 160 bird species are found here, including the great blue heron, bald eagle, cormorant and pileated woodpecker.
334 acres. Camping, supervised swimming, hiking, nature house.

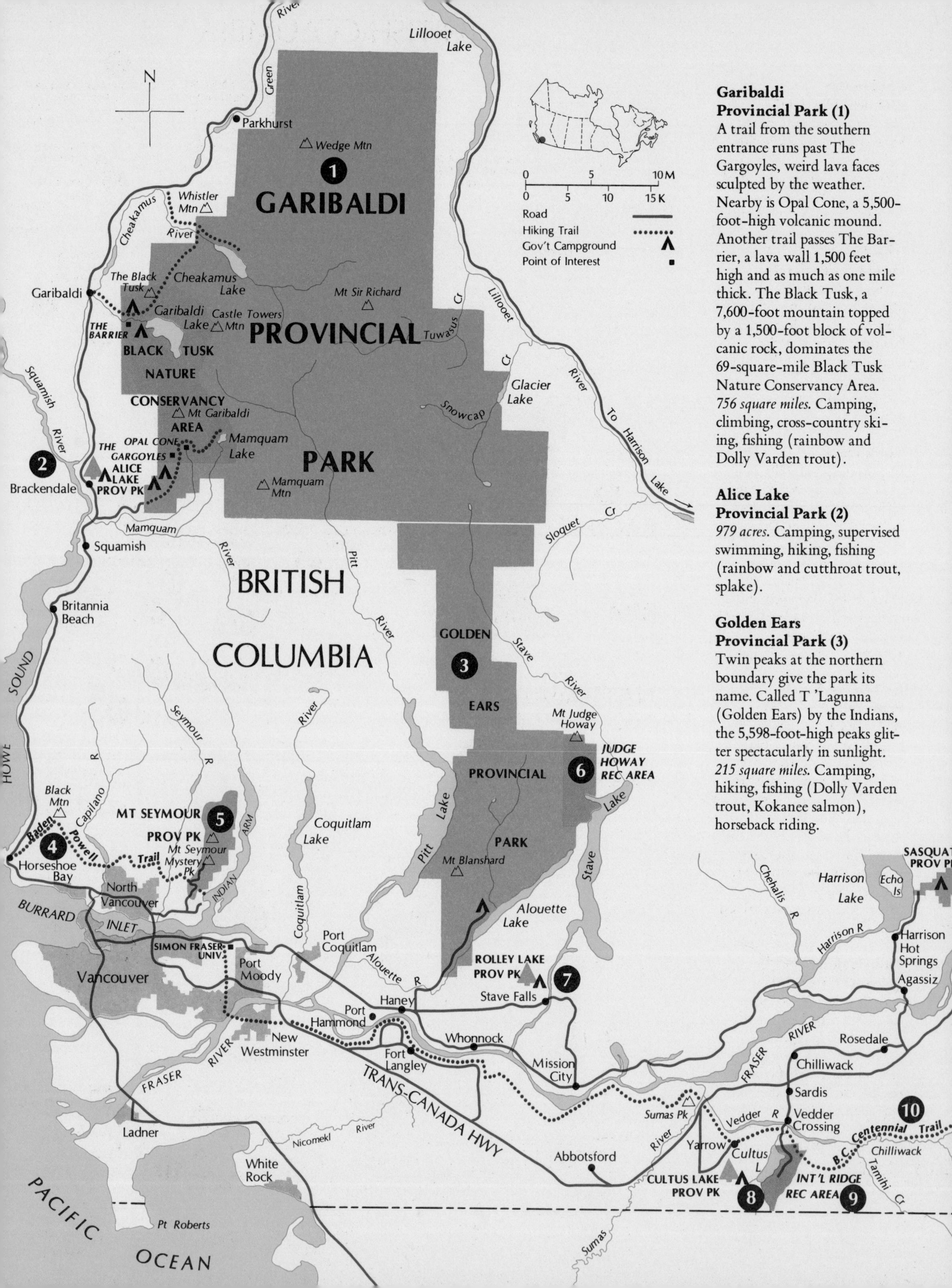

Garibaldi Provincial Park (1)
A trail from the southern entrance runs past The Gargoyles, weird lava faces sculpted by the weather. Nearby is Opal Cone, a 5,500-foot-high volcanic mound. Another trail passes The Barrier, a lava wall 1,500 feet high and as much as one mile thick. The Black Tusk, a 7,600-foot mountain topped by a 1,500-foot block of volcanic rock, dominates the 69-square-mile Black Tusk Nature Conservancy Area. *756 square miles.* Camping, climbing, cross-country skiing, fishing (rainbow and Dolly Varden trout).

Alice Lake Provincial Park (2)
979 acres. Camping, supervised swimming, hiking, fishing (rainbow and cutthroat trout, splake).

Golden Ears Provincial Park (3)
Twin peaks at the northern boundary give the park its name. Called T 'Lagunna (Golden Ears) by the Indians, the 5,598-foot-high peaks glitter spectacularly in sunlight. *215 square miles.* Camping, hiking, fishing (Dolly Varden trout, Kokanee salmon), horseback riding.

Wilderness and Scenic Beauty in the Southwest Mainland of B.C.

Garibaldi Provincial Park dominates the southwest corner of the British Columbia mainland. In this area are remote wilderness, countless lakes, fields of mountain flowers, strange volcanic landforms and superb recreation facilities. South of Garibaldi are hundreds of miles of hiking trails linking the fjords of Howe Sound and Indian Arm with Manning and Cathedral provincial parks.

Baden-Powell Centennial Trail (4)
Well blazed with orange markers, it crosses 3,992-foot Black Mountain. *25 miles.*

Mount Seymour Provincial Park (5)
Mount Seymour (4,766 feet) is a favorite among mountain climbers.
13.5 square miles. Alpine and cross-country skiing, hiking.

Judge Howay Recreation Area (6)
24 square miles. Wilderness camping.

Rolley Lake Provincial Park (7)
285 acres. Camping.

Cultus Lake Provincial Park (8)
2.5 square miles. Camping, supervised swimming, hiking, fishing (steelhead trout, coho salmon).

International Ridge Recreation Area (9)
80 square miles. Wilderness camping, climbing, hiking.

British Columbia Centennial Trail (10)
From Simon Fraser University in Burnaby this trail crosses the Skagit River and Manning Provincial Park and follows a former packhorse route to Cathedral Provincial Park. *200 miles.*

Sasquatch Provincial Park (11)
The park is on a plateau 500 feet above Harrison Lake. Near the south end of Trout Lake a creek plunges 150 feet into a bed of boulders.
4.5 square miles. Camping, hiking, fishing (rainbow trout), canoeing.

Manning Provincial Park (12)
Near the west entrance is one of the few areas in British Columbia where native rhododendrons flower. Near the timberline, the Frosty Mountain Loop Trail passes stands of rare alpine larch. The 200-mile British Columbia Centennial Trail crosses the park. Other trails join the Pacific Crest Trail, which stretches 2,400 miles between the park's southern boundary and Mexico. In spring, the 14-mile Heather Trail snakes through a dense carpet of mountain flowers more than 15 miles long and up to 3 miles wide.
276 square miles. Camping, alpine and cross-country skiing, fishing (rainbow trout).

Cathedral Provincial Park (13)
Near Smoky the Bear, a 45-foot eroded granite formation, is Giant Cleft, an eight-foot-wide gap in the rock face through which can be seen a valley floor 600 feet below. A trail links both attractions with Stone City, a 1½-mile-long jumble of boulders that resembles a small city.
28.5 square miles. Camping, climbing, fishing (Kamloops and cutthroat trout).

The Bigfoot That Walks Like a Man

Two-legged, apelike (or manlike) creatures have been reported seen scores of times in remote parts of British Columbia and the northwestern United States. This beast of the wilderness—if it is a beast—is called Sasquatch in Canada, Bigfoot in the United States. It is usually described as more than seven feet tall and walking erect, with a flattened nose, a sloping forehead and unusually long arms. Its footprints are said to be up to 17 inches long.

There is no conclusive evidence that Sasquatch/Bigfoot exists, but the most persuasive documentation is 24 feet of 16-mm color film taken by Roger Patterson near Yakima, Wash., in 1967. The blurred film, shot from a distance, shows a large hairy creature loping across a clearing. Scientists disagree as to whether the film is authentic.

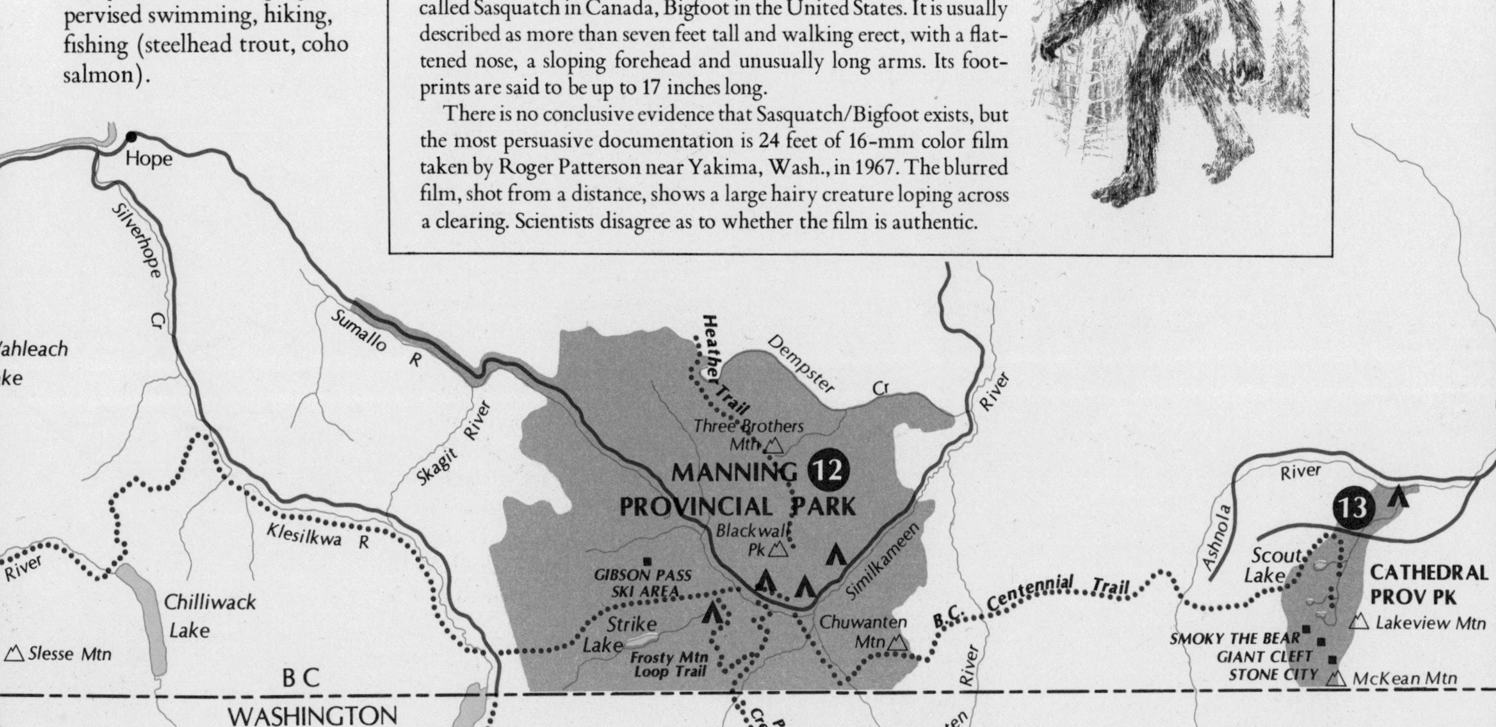

Hunlen Falls and Trumpeter Swans, a Dormant Volcano, a Giant Ice Field

In central and northern British Columbia are some of the province's most spectacular parks. In the biggest, Tweedsmuir Park, are such attractions as Hunlen Falls and the trumpeter swans of Lonesome Lake. One park, Mount Edziza, is named for a dormant volcano. Farther north, in the region of the Alaska Highway, are Kwadacha's ice field and the Liard River Hotsprings.

Tweedsmuir Provincial Park (1)
Hunlen Falls on the Atnarko River tumbles 1,150 feet and is third in Canada only to Vancouver Island's 1,443-foot Della Falls and 1,248-foot Takakkaw Falls in Yoho National Park. Nearby Lonesome Lake attracts some 400 trumpeter swans between November and March, an estimated 20 percent of the world population of that rare bird. Tsitsutl Peak (8,172 feet) in bright sunlight is an array of violet, lavender, yellow and red.
3,788 square miles. Camping, hiking, fishing (rainbow, Dolly Varden and cutthroat trout, Rocky Mountain whitefish), canoeing, horseback riding.

Sir Alexander Mackenzie Provincial Park (2)
Visitors see Mackenzie's Rock on which are the words of the explorer's famed inscription: *Alexander Mackenzie, from Canada, by land, the 22nd of July, one thousand seven hundred and ninety-three.* Mackenzie's was the first crossing of northern North America by a European. The park is reached by boat from Bella Coola.
6 acres. Wilderness camping.

Mount Edziza Provincial Park (3)
Mount Edziza, a 9,143-foot dormant volcano, last erupted 1,400 years ago, but evidence suggests it has been active since then. Eve Cone, one of 30 cinder cones surrounding the volcano, is 500 feet high and 1,300 feet across the crater. South of Mount Edziza is the 6,000-foot Spectrum Range with its red, yellow and purple rock strata. Along the park's northern boundary the Stikine River flows between rock walls almost 600 feet high. The canyon of the Stikine is littered with sandstone chimneys—columns shaped by erosion—and huge boulders. Shoreline cliffs are colored green and pink. The river is impassable by canoe because of whirlpools, rapids and falls. Experienced hikers can enter the park by taking the Telegraph Trail from the Stewart-Cassiar Road.
900 square miles. Wilderness camping, fishing (rainbow trout).

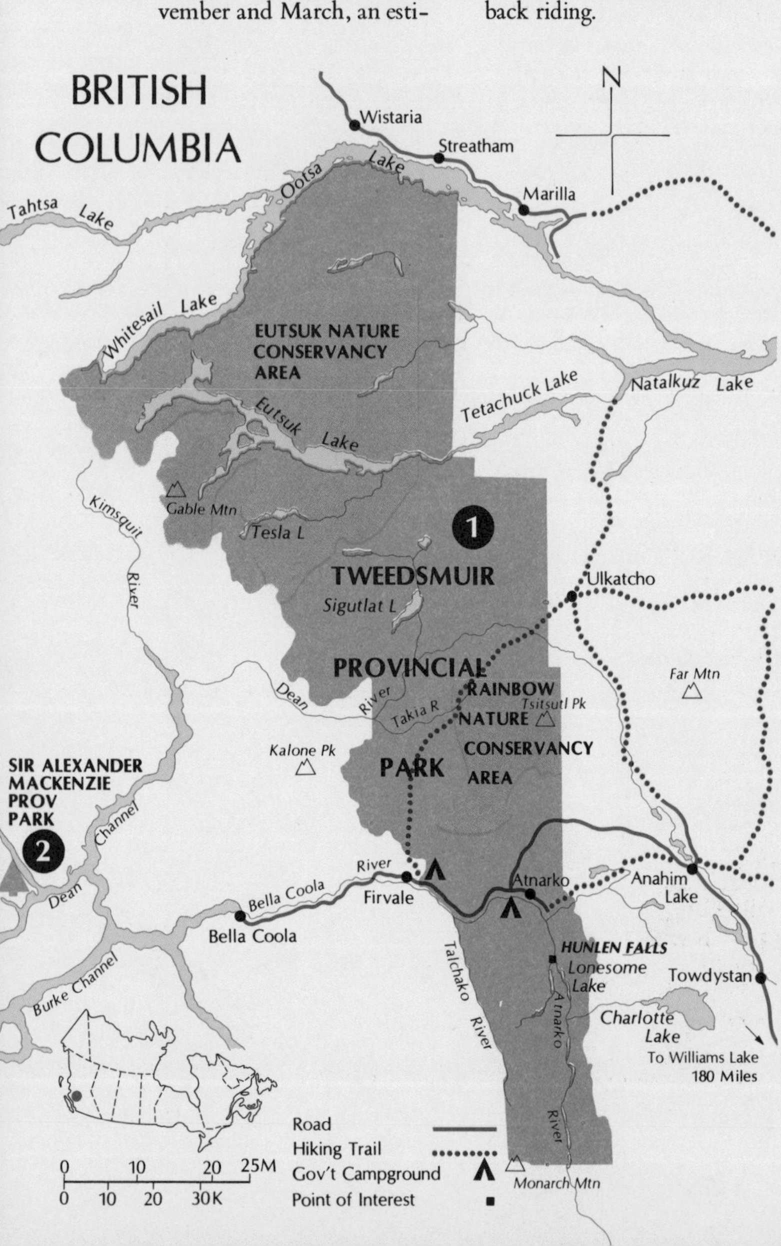

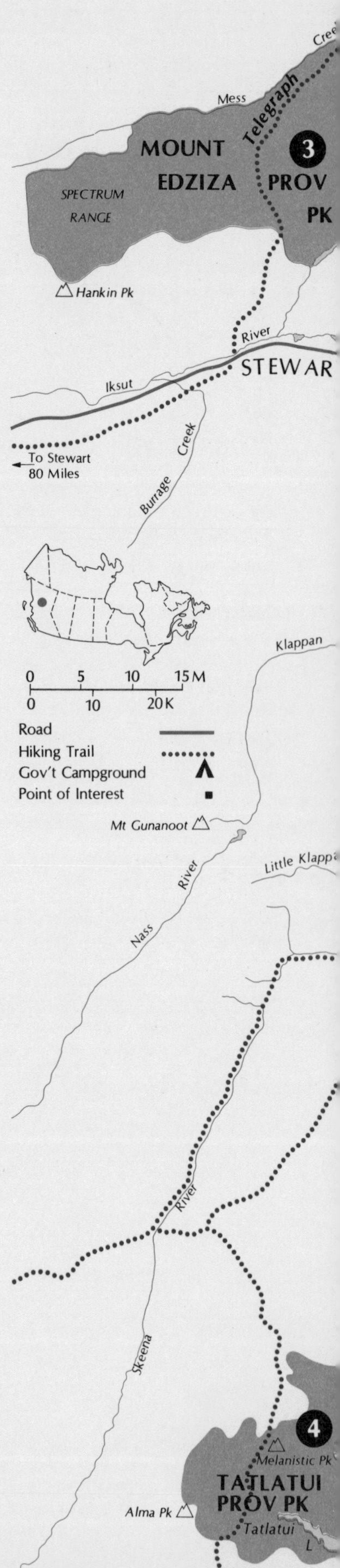

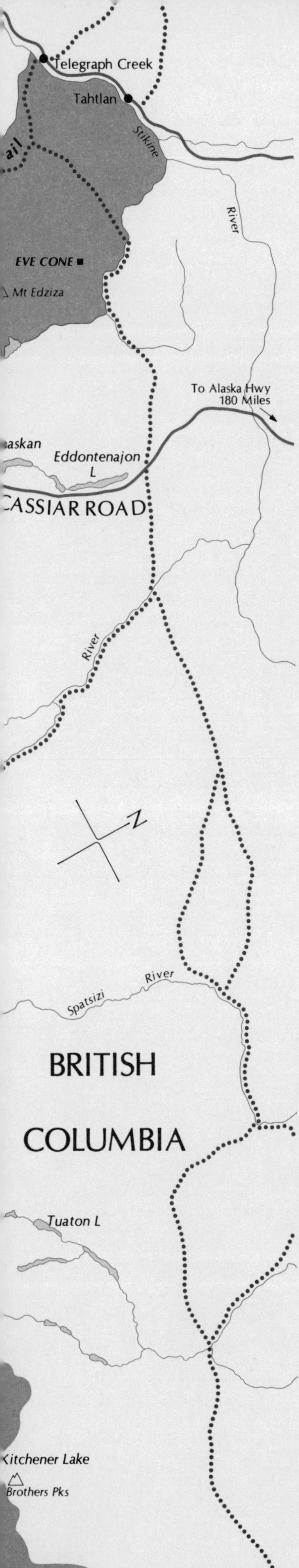

Tatlatui
Provincial Park (4)
This park is accessible only by seaplane. Near Kitchener Lake are Bohemian waxwings and Bonaparte gulls.
409 square miles. Wilderness camping, fishing (rainbow trout).

Kwadacha
Provincial Park (9)
The Lloyd George Icefield, the largest accumulation of ice in the northern Rockies, spills down 9,570-foot Mount Lloyd George. An 18-mile hiking trail cuts through 4,500-foot-high Bedaux Pass.
647 square miles. Wilderness camping, fishing (arctic grayling, Rocky Mountain whitefish, rainbow trout).

Liard River Hotsprings
Provincial Park (5)
The two spring-fed pools reach 46°C. (115°F.)
2.5 square miles. Camping.

Stone Mountain
Provincial Park (8)
Eroded pillars of sand and gravel—some 60 feet high—stand near 4,218-foot-high Summit Pass, highest point on the Alaska Highway.
100 square miles. Wilderness camping, fishing (Rocky Mountain whitefish).

Racing River Wayside
Provincial Park (7)
176 acres. Camping.

Muncho Lake
Provincial Park (6)
Stone's sheep and caribou, licking at minerals in the rock, have hollowed out large holes in cliffs and pillars here.
341 square miles. Wilderness camping, fishing (lake trout, arctic grayling), canoeing.

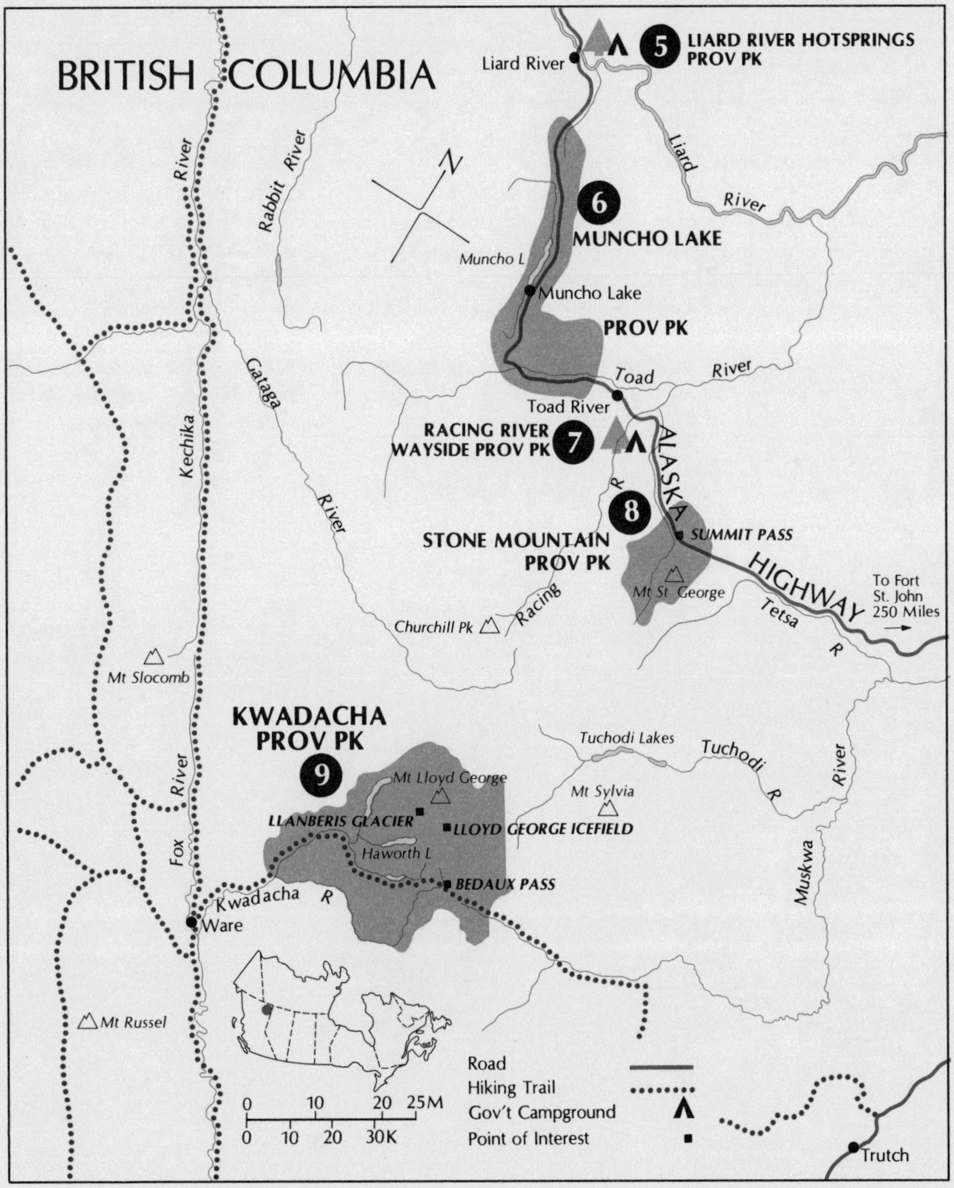

A Panorama of Snowcapped Peaks and Icy Emerald Lakes

Along the Continental Divide is a magnificent sprawl of towering mountains and awesome glaciers, icy emerald lakes and fragrant fields of alpine flowers. From the challenging canoe route of Bowron Lake Park to the wild slopes of Mount Robson and the waterfalls of Wells Gray Park, this is a world of breathtaking beauty.

Jasper National Park (9)
The Columbia Icefield feeds three great river systems: the Athabasca, which flows to the Arctic Ocean; the Saskatchewan, which drains to Hudson Bay; and the Columbia, which empties into the Pacific Ocean. The 110-square-mile ice field, the largest in the Rockies, is visible from the Icefields Parkway. The park has more than 400 miles of hiking trails, many in the picturesque Tonquin Valley on the eastern flank of The Ramparts, a craggy rock wall on the Continental Divide. Rushing between limestone walls, the Maligne River has carved a 160-foot-deep gorge. Near Medicine Lake the bubbling of underground waterfalls can be heard. At Miette Hotsprings temperatures of 54°-58°C. (129°-136°F.) make this the hottest spring water in the Canadian Rockies. Jasper's 200 species of birds include the golden eagle, great blue heron, Canada jay and bald eagle.
4,200 square miles. Camping, climbing, alpine skiing, fishing (Rocky Mountain whitefish, rainbow, cutthroat, Dolly Varden and eastern brook trout), horseback riding, self-guiding nature trails.

Wells Gray Provincial Park (3)
Among a dozen waterfalls in the park are 450-foot Helmcken Falls, and Dawson Falls, 300 feet wide and 60 feet high. In the Murtle River is The Mush Bowl, a series of riverbed craters carved by the raging waters. An 800-foot-high extinct volcano rises from the north shore of Kostal Lake. On the rim of its cone, 5,000 feet above sea level, is a stand of Douglas fir, a tree which normally grows at lower elevations. A round-trip canoe route runs 64 miles between the Clearwater Lake campground and Azure Lake. Canoeists can fish for rainbow trout downstream from 80-foot-high Rainbow Falls. There are more than 100 icy mineral springs in the park. Golden eagles and rufous hummingbirds are occasionally seen here—particularly at Ray Farm, an abandoned homestead.
2,035 square miles. Camping, hiking.

Bowron Lake Provincial Park (1)
The park's rough rectangle of lakes and rivers lies amid the peaks of the Cariboo Mountains. The 73-mile route around the perimeter is a favorite of experienced canoeists.
475 square miles. Camping, fishing (Rocky Mountain whitefish, Kokanee salmon, Kamloops, Dolly Varden and lake trout).

Spahats Creek Provincial Park (6)
Spahats Creek has carved through layers of lava, forming a 400-foot-deep gorge in the park. The 200-foot Spahats Creek Falls links the creek and the Clearwater River.
755 acres. Camping, fishing (rainbow, Dolly Varden and Kamloops trout, Rocky Mountain whitefish, Chinook and coho salmon).

Willmore Wilderness Park (2)
A rugged hiking trail from Rock Lake leads to this wilderness park.
1,700 square miles. Wilderness camping, hiking, fishing (Dolly Varden trout, Rocky Mountain whitefish, arctic grayling).

Maligne Lake nestles at the foot of snowcrowned peaks in Jasper National Park.

Mount Robson Provincial Park (8)
The 12,972-foot mountain for which the park is named is the highest in the Canadian Rockies. Also in the park is the 14-mile Berg Lake Trail, where some 15 glaciers can be seen, among them the Berg Glacier, 6,000 feet thick and half a mile wide. Berg Lake is often cluttered with ice slabs that have broken away from the glacier. In the Valley of a Thousand Falls, spring runoff creates a series of rapids and falls which drop 1,500 feet in three miles.
848.5 square miles. Camping, climbing, fishing (Dolly Varden and rainbow trout, Kokanee salmon), self-guiding nature trails, nature house.

Hamber Provincial Park (11)
This wilderness park can be reached only by a 14-mile hiking trail from Sunwapta Falls in Jasper National Park. Six-mile-long Fortress Lake is noted for its abundance of eastern brook trout.
94.5 square miles. Wilderness camping.

William A. Switzer Provincial Park (10)
Five lakes, linked by Jarvis Creek, make up a 20-mile canoe route in the park.
10.5 square miles. Camping, fishing (rainbow trout, northern pike, yellow perch, whitefish).

Shuswap Lake Provincial Park (7)
285 acres. Camping, fishing (Kokanee salmon, Dolly Varden, rainbow and lake trout).

Canim Beach Provincial Park (4)
13 acres. Camping, fishing (rainbow and Kamloops trout).

North Thompson River Provincial Park (5)
317 acres. Camping.

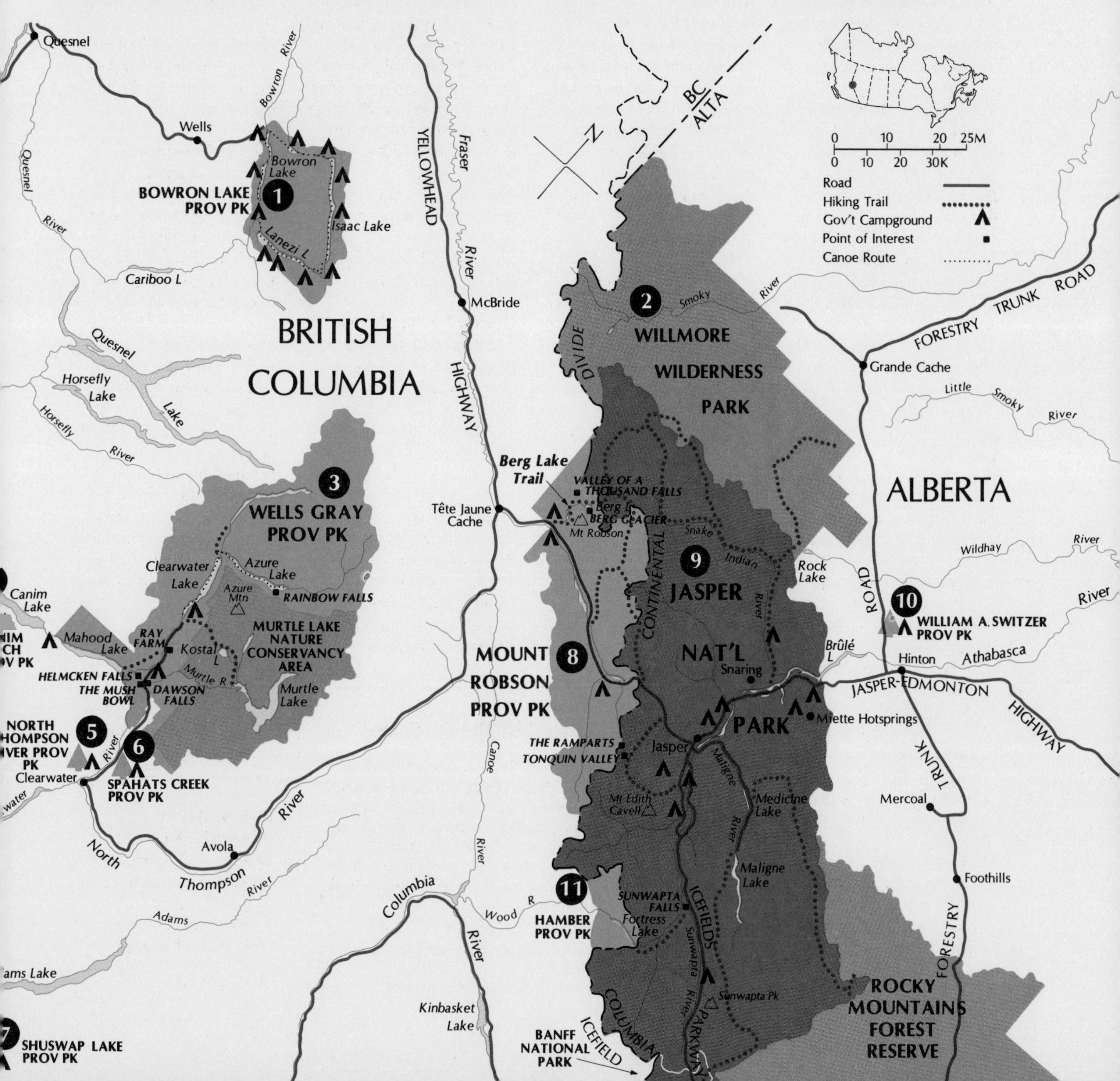

A Splendor of Ice Fields, Hot Springs and Glaciers Along the Great Divide

Banff, Kootenay, Yoho, Glacier, Revelstoke, Assiniboine . . . these are some of the colorful names in Canada's great chain of Rocky Mountain parks. Here too are Lake Louise, Takakkaw Falls, Radium Hot Springs, the Paint Pots, the Valley of the Ten Peaks, Marble Canyon and a mountain called the Tower of Babel. Serving this part of southern British Columbia and Alberta are three scenic major roads—the Trans-Canada Highway and the Banff-Windermere and Icefields parkways—and a vast network of hiking trails and campgrounds.

Banff National Park (5)
More than 700 miles of hiking and nature trails meander through the immense grandeur of Canada's oldest national park. They snake past rockslides, hanging valleys and hoodoos (weathered pillars of rock). At the base of 11,365-foot Mount Victoria lies Lake Louise, which is fed by the Victoria Glacier. In the Valley of the Ten Peaks is Lake Agnes, gouged out by glacial ice, and Moraine Lake, dammed by rockslides from the Tower of Babel, a 7,590-foot mountain. The Bow Glacier, an extension of the Wapta Icefield and source of the Bow River, can be seen from the 142-mile Icefields Parkway which extends into Jasper Park. Bow Pass (6,787 feet) is the highest point on the route. On the northeast slope of lofty Sulphur Mountain, the Upper, Kidney, Middle and Cave and Basin hot springs rise to the surface at temperatures of 29°-46°C. (85°-115°F.). Swimming is permitted at the Cave and Basin and Upper hot springs. A 2,300-foot gondola trip up Sulphur Mountain provides a view of the Bow River. Sixty species of mammals and 225 species of birds inhabit the park.
2,564 square miles. Camping, climbing, alpine and cross-country skiing, fishing (rainbow and cutthroat trout), self-guiding nature trails.

Kootenay National Park (6)
Marble Canyon, its gray walls streaked with white marble, is accessible by a half-mile trail from the Banff-Windermere Parkway. The canyon contains a 70-foot waterfall and a rock bridge. Also along the trail are the Paint Pots, three ponds stained red, yellow and orange by mineral-bearing springs. At the foot of Redstreak Mountain, water from Radium Hot Springs is sometimes 45°C. (113°F.).
543 square miles. Camping, climbing, supervised swimming, cross-country skiing, fishing (Dolly Varden, rainbow and eastern brook trout).

Yoho National Park (4)
Glacier-fed Takakkaw Falls, the third highest uninterrupted waterfall in North America, drops 1,248 feet into the Yoho River. West of Field a road leads to the Natural Bridge on the Kicking Horse River. Nearby are the dark green waters of Emerald Lake. On the Kicking Horse River, Wapta Falls plunges 90 feet in a 200-foot-wide sheet of water. More than 28 peaks in the park exceed 10,000 feet; the highest is 11,750-foot Mount Goodsir.
507 square miles. Camping, cross-country skiing, fishing (cutthroat, brook and lake trout), horseback riding, self-guiding nature trails.

Glacier National Park (2)
The park has more than 100 glaciers and an average annual snowfall of more than 400 inches. The Illecillewaet and Asulkan glaciers, cloaking the slopes of 10,818-foot Mount Sir Donald, are reached by hiking trails from the Illecillewaet campground. The one-mile Abandoned Rails Nature Trail crosses the summit of 4,354-foot-high Rogers Pass. Caribou, wapiti, grizzly bears and mountain goats roam the park.

A Walk on the Roof of the Rockies

When the 280-mile Great Divide Trail is completed, perhaps by 1985, it will extend 350 miles from Mount Assiniboine Provincial Park through Banff, Kootenay and Yoho national parks to Jasper townsite. The divide for which it is named is the watershed from which some rivers flow to the Pacific, others to the Arctic Ocean or Hudson Bay. The highest point on the trail is 8,747-foot Duchesnay Pass. Hikers must cope with dense underbrush, rock-strewn slopes, rushing streams and, even in summer, below-freezing night temperatures and sometimes blizzards.

521 square miles. Camping, climbing, fishing (Dolly Varden, cutthroat and eastern brook trout, whitefish).

Mount Revelstoke National Park (1)
More than 40 miles of hiking trails cross this Selkirk Mountains park. Among alpine flowers growing here are white valerian and blue lupine. Near the summit of 6,300-foot Mount Revelstoke is "the icebox," a cool shaded crevice that retains snow all year.
100 square miles. Climbing, fishing (eastern brook and cutthroat trout), self-guiding nature trails.

Mount Assiniboine Provincial Park (7)
The park is dominated by 11,870-foot Mount Assiniboine, resembling Switzerland's Matterhorn. Access to the park, which has more than 20 peaks exceeding 9,000 feet, is by four hiking trails. One leads from the junction of the Simpson and Vermilion rivers near the Banff-Windermere Parkway to 1½-mile-long Lake Magog, largest lake in the park. Shelters have been built on the lake's east side. Above the timberline there are stands of 500-year-old alpine larch.
150 square miles. Camping (trailers prohibited), cross-country skiing.

Rocky Mountains Forest Reserve (3)
8,000 square miles. Camping, hiking, fishing (Dolly Varden, eastern brook, rainbow and cutthroat trout, Rocky Mountain whitefish).

Bow Valley Provincial Park (8)
Boulders and debris deposited by Ice Age glaciers litter the park landscape.
3 square miles. Camping, cross-country skiing.

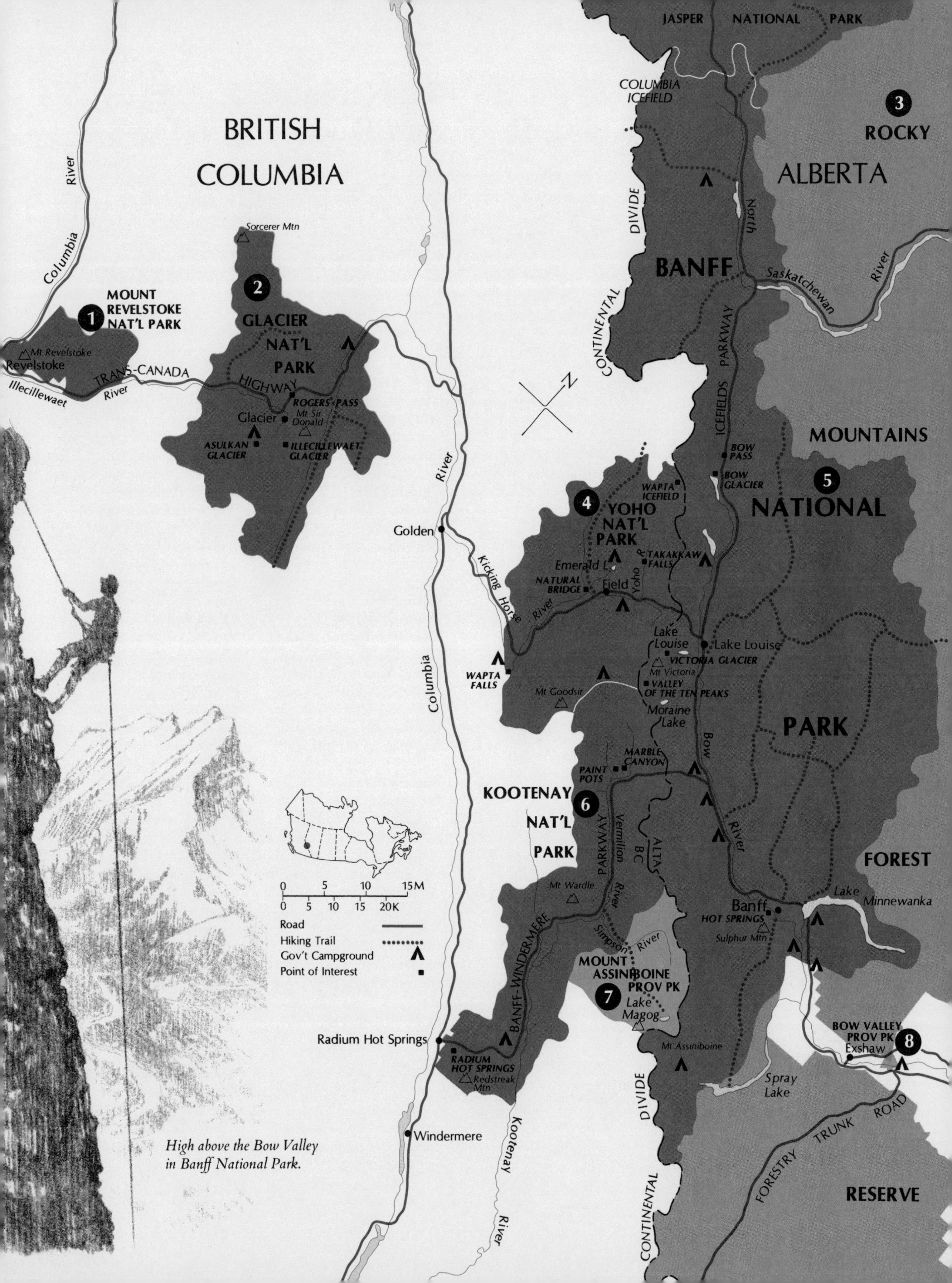

High above the Bow Valley in Banff National Park.

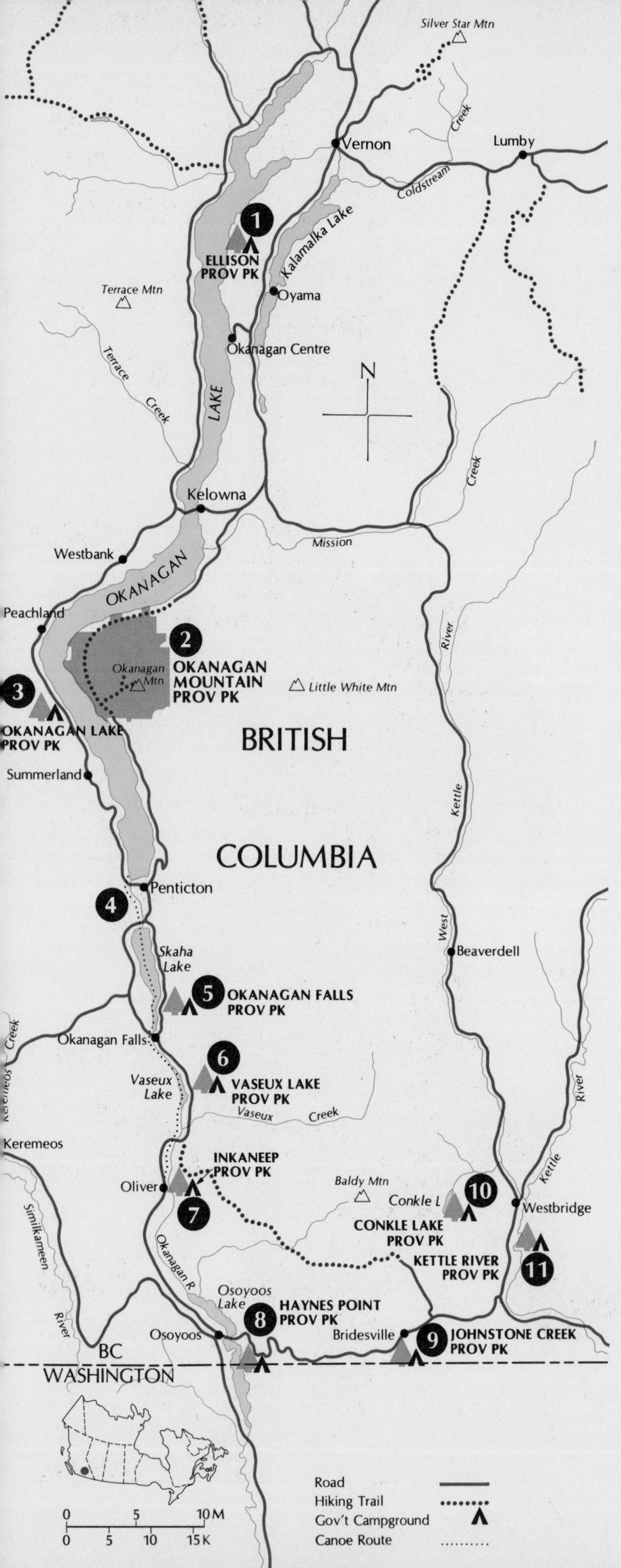

The Great Okanagan and Kootenay Valleys

The Okanagan Valley, famous for its apples, apricots and cherries, is a richly endowed resort area. To the east is the lovely Kootenay Valley, with more than a dozen provincial parks and recreation areas and the great Creston Valley Wildlife Management Area.

Okanagan Lake Provincial Park (3)
Irrigation has turned the park, once a semidesert, into a lush forest of Russian olive, Siberian elm and weeping willow. *198 acres.* Camping, fishing (lake and Kamloops trout, Kokanee salmon, whitefish).

Conkle Lake Provincial Park (10)
2 square miles. Camping, fishing (rainbow and cutthroat trout).

Ellison Provincial Park (1)
Three bays, fringed by a 2,000-foot-long sand beach, lie within the park. *495 acres.* Camping, hiking, fishing (carp, whitefish, Kokanee salmon, lake and Kamloops trout), canoeing.

Haynes Point Provincial Park (8)
This park, on a sandspit jutting into Osoyoos Lake, is dotted with beachfront campsites. Cactus and sagebrush are abundant. *13 acres.*

Vaseux Lake Provincial Park (6)
Rare California bighorn sheep graze on Vaseux Lake's eastern shores. Western spadefoot (a burrowing toad), black-nosed bats, Lord pocket mice and pygmy horned toads also inhabit the park. Now a migratory bird sanctuary, the lake is a refuge for chukar partridges, white-headed woodpeckers, canyon wrens and trumpeter swans. *14 acres.* Camping, hiking, fishing (largemouth bass).

Okanagan Falls Provincial Park (5)
6 acres. Camping.

Okanagan Mountain Provincial Park (2)
The park is reached by hiking trails from Kelowna or by boat across Okanagan Lake. *40 square miles.* Wilderness camping, fishing (Kamloops and cutthroat trout), canoeing.

Kettle River Provincial Park (11)
Bluffs 250 feet high give a fine view of the spruce-fringed Kettle River. *346 acres.* Camping, fishing (rainbow and cutthroat trout).

Johnstone Creek Provincial Park (9)
93 acres. Camping, hiking.

Inkaneep Provincial Park (7)
28 acres. Camping.

Canoe Route (Penticton to Oliver) (4)
This route, backed by wooded mountains, winds alongside sandy beaches on Skaha and Vaseux lakes. *30 miles.*

Wasa Provincial Park (23)
347 acres. Camping.

Fry Creek Canyon Recreation Area (12)
A six-mile trail winds along

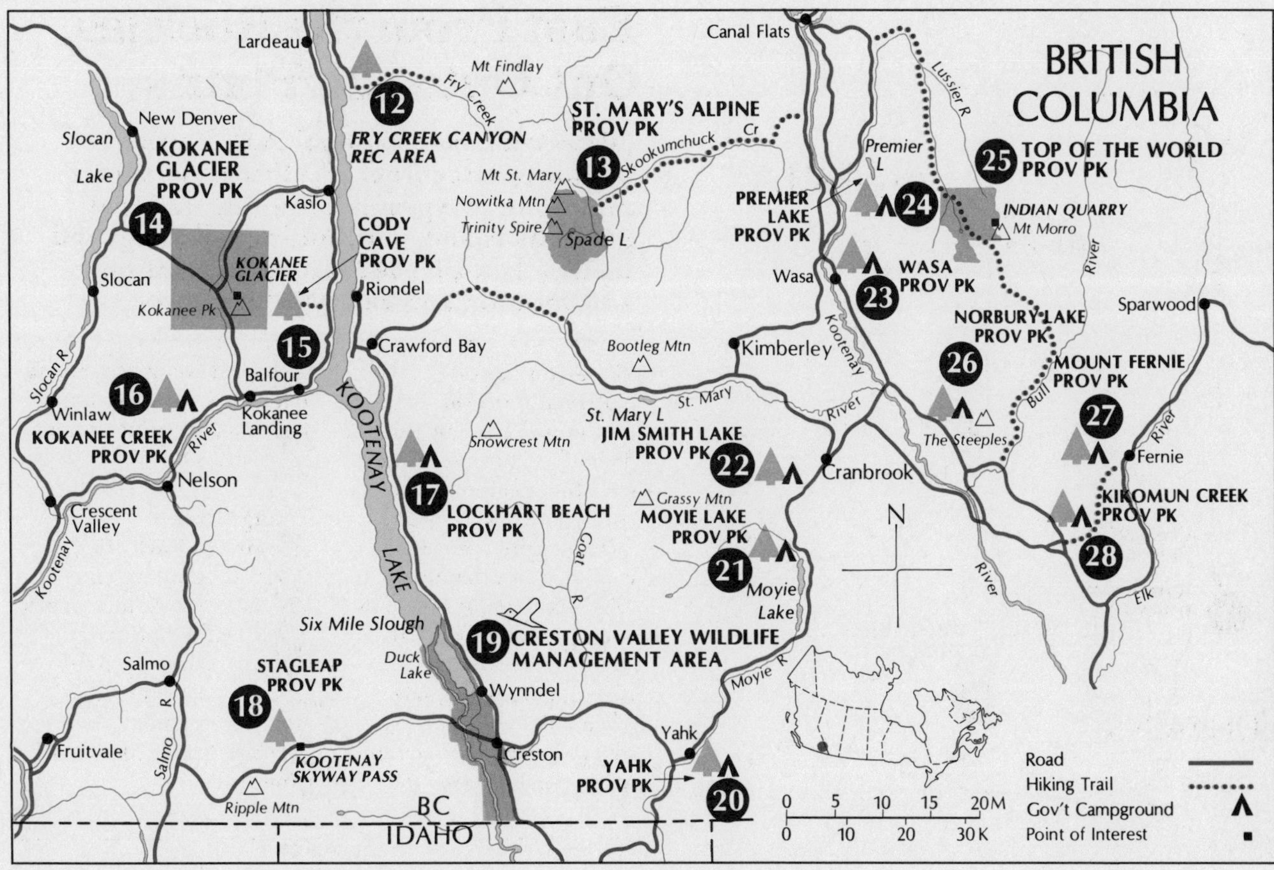

the lip of 100-foot-deep Fry Creek Canyon.
2 square miles. Wilderness camping.

St. Mary's Alpine Provincial Park (13)
The park can be reached by a 17-mile hiking trail along Skookumchuck Creek. Eight waterfalls prevent fish from entering all but one of the park's 32 lakes. Spade Lake's cutthroat trout are the only fish found.
35 square miles. Wilderness camping.

Moyie Lake Provincial Park (21)
153 acres. Camping, fishing (rainbow and cutthroat trout).

Jim Smith Lake Provincial Park (22)
29 acres. Camping, fishing (rainbow and cutthroat trout).

Cody Cave Provincial Park (15)
The park's underground tunnels and chambers, gouged out by Cody Creek, were discovered by prospector Henry Cody in the 1880s. The largest chamber is the Throne Room, a 428-square-foot limestone gallery of "soda straws" (hollow fingers of calcium), stalactites and stalagmites. *155 acres.*

Stagleap Provincial Park (18)
The park borders 5,800-foot Kootenay Skyway Pass, the highest all-weather pass in Canada.
4.5 square miles. Hiking.

Yahk Provincial Park (20)
18 acres. Camping, fishing (Dolly Varden and cutthroat trout).

Creston Valley Wildlife Management Area (19)
More than 200 bird species, including the blue-winged teal, great blue heron, snow goose and whistling swan, can be seen here in one of Canada's largest waterfowl protection areas. *25 square miles.*

Mount Fernie Provincial Park (27)
640 acres. Camping, fishing (cutthroat trout).

Kokanee Glacier Provincial Park (14)
Kokanee Glacier, which spills down 9,100-foot Kokanee Peak, is one of three glaciers in the park.
100 square miles. Wilderness camping, hiking, fishing (Kokanee salmon, cutthroat trout).

Top of the World Provincial Park (25)
Piles of chert chips used for arrowheads can be seen in an ancient Indian quarry here.
31 square miles. Wilderness camping, fishing (Dolly Varden and cutthroat trout).

Kikomun Creek Provincial Park (28)
2 square miles. Camping, fishing (rainbow trout).

Kokanee Creek Provincial Park (16)
The park is famous for its Kokanee salmon, which feed on the shrimp in Kootenay Lake.
643 acres. Camping, canoeing.

Premier Lake Provincial Park (24)
165 acres. Camping, fishing (rainbow trout), canoeing.

Lockhart Beach Provincial Park (17)
7 acres. Camping, fishing (rainbow trout).

Norbury Lake Provincial Park (26)
240 acres. Camping, fishing (rainbow trout).

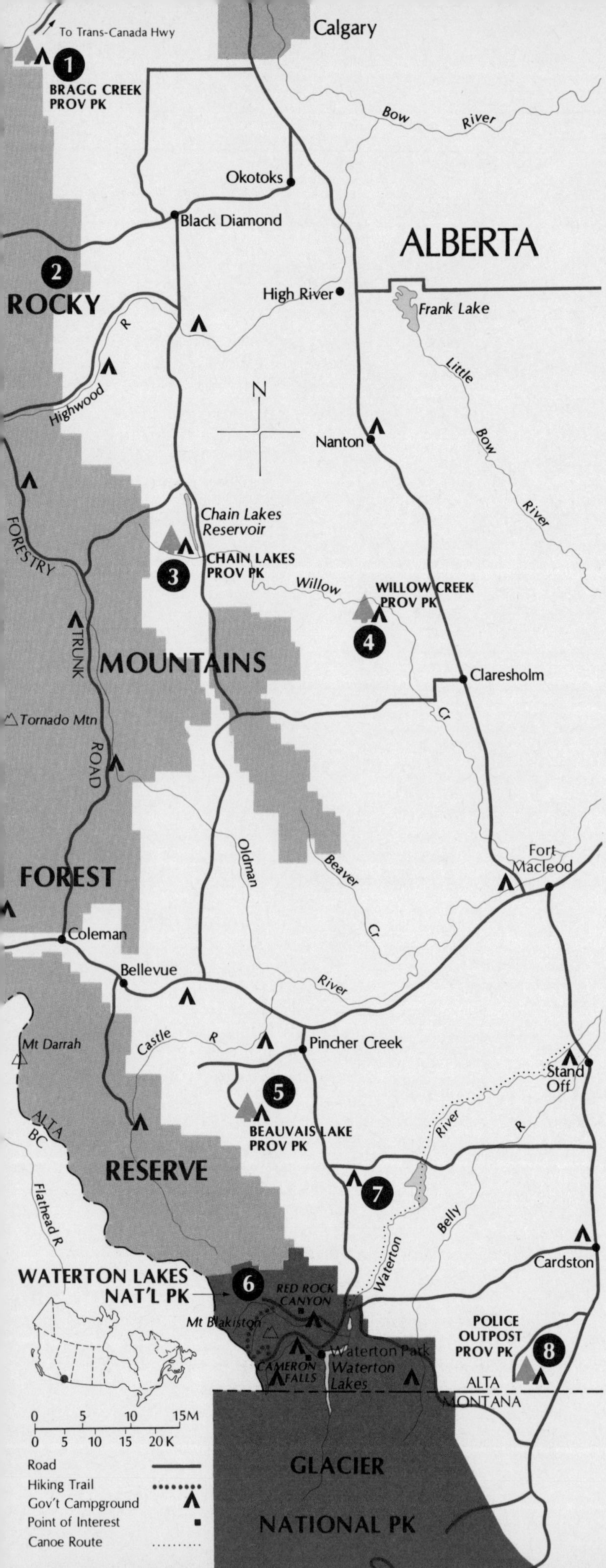

East From the Rockies, Out Onto the Plains

Waterton Lakes National Park, nestled in the southwest corner of Alberta, is a superb mountain playground. Another national park, Elk Island, with rolling hills, bogs and shallow lakes, is the heart of a recreation and vacation area east of Edmonton.

Waterton Lakes National Park (6)
This upland area was once the floor of an immense inland sea. Movements of the earth's crust uplifted layers of sediment, creating a mountainous landscape now dominated by 9,600-foot Mount Blakiston. Subsequent glaciation carved valleys, cirques (steep-sided basins) and hanging valleys. Chemicals in the rock have streaked many of Waterton's mountains red, green and purple. An unusual blend of flora exists in the park: silverberry and chokecherry, common prairie species, give way to mountain stands of Engelmann spruce and alpine fir. More than 100 miles of hiking trails meander through the park, linking such features as Red Rock Canyon and 45-foot Cameron Falls. Waterton Park adjoins Montana's Glacier National Park to form Waterton-Glacier International Peace Park.
203 square miles. Camping, supervised swimming, hiking, fishing (rainbow, cutthroat, lake and eastern brook trout), canoeing.

Bragg Creek Provincial Park (1)
There are kayaking and canoeing on a 10-mile stretch of the swift Elbow River.
303 acres. Camping, cross-country skiing, hiking, fishing (rainbow trout, arctic grayling, Rocky Mountain whitefish).

Chain Lakes Provincial Park (3)
Rainbow trout are abundant in 6½-mile-long Chain Lakes Reservoir.
1.5 square miles. Camping.

Beauvais Lake Provincial Park (5)
2 square miles. Camping, hiking, fishing (rainbow trout).

Canoe Route (Waterton River) (7)
Pronghorn antelopes can be seen along this route. *54 miles.*

An "International" Game Farm

The world's only captive breeding herd of Rocky Mountain goats roams a miniature man-made mountain in the two-square-mile Alberta Game Farm at Ardrossan, east of Edmonton. Père David's deer, white rhinoceroses and Przewalski's horses—rare horses that closely resemble their prehistoric ancestors—are among more than 4,000 animals at the farm. Flamingos, red-breasted geese from Siberia and Bewick's swans from the U.S.S.R. are found on 1½-mile-long Lost Lake. The farm was established with less than 200 animals by zoologist-explorer Al Oeming in 1958. He returned from the Arctic in 1970 with two Peary caribou, the first ever taken into captivity.

Willow Creek Provincial Park (4)
Tepee rings—circles of rock once used to anchor tepees—have been found in the park, a former Indian campground.
156 acres. Camping.

Rocky Mountains Forest Reserve (2)
8,000 square miles. Camping, hiking, fishing (Dolly Varden, eastern brook, rainbow and cutthroat trout).

Police Outpost Provincial Park (8)
The park is the site of an early North West Mounted Police post.
361 acres. Camping, hiking, fishing (rainbow trout).

The Waskahegan Trail (12)
This circular route is scheduled to be completed by 1980. Much of the Waskahegan Trail crosses private farmland. In Elk Island and Miquelon Lake parks, the Waskahegan links existing paths. Great blue herons occasionally nest on a small pond near Ministik Lake. Sections of the trail near the lake are used by cross-country skiers. Shelters offer overnight accommodation.
260 miles.

Elk Island National Park (11)
Some 100 rare wood bison inhabit an isolated area in the south of the park. The park was named for the large herds of wapiti (elk)—now greatly reduced—that once roamed the region. Throughout the park are ridges, kettles (small depressions), bogs and shallow lakes, all formed by retreating glaciers. The park's largest body of water, 2½-mile-long Astotin Lake, only 21 feet at its deepest point, is dotted with 21 islands. More than 200 bird species have been spotted in the park, including great horned owls, downy woodpeckers and black-capped chickadees. Wilderness camping is prohibited.
75 square miles. Camping, supervised swimming, hiking, self-guiding nature trails.

Canoe Route (Edmonton to Elk Point) (9)
This North Saskatchewan River route is free of white water and portages. Riverside slopes are suitable for wilderness camping. *150 miles.*

Miquelon Lake Migratory Bird Sanctuary (13)
This sanctuary, linked by trail to Miquelon Lake Provincial Park, is a migration stopover for golden eagles, American bitterns, red-necked grebes, rough grouse, Canada geese and 10 species of ducks.
6.5 square miles.

Miquelon Lake Provincial Park (14)
A ¾-mile-long sand beach borders the southeast shore of the largest of the three Miquelon Lakes.
1.5 square miles. Camping, hiking, self-guiding nature trails.

The Vermilion Provincial Park (15)
792 acres. Camping, fishing (walleye, yellow perch, northern pike).

Garner Lake Provincial Park (10)
183 acres. Camping, fishing (northern pike, yellow perch).

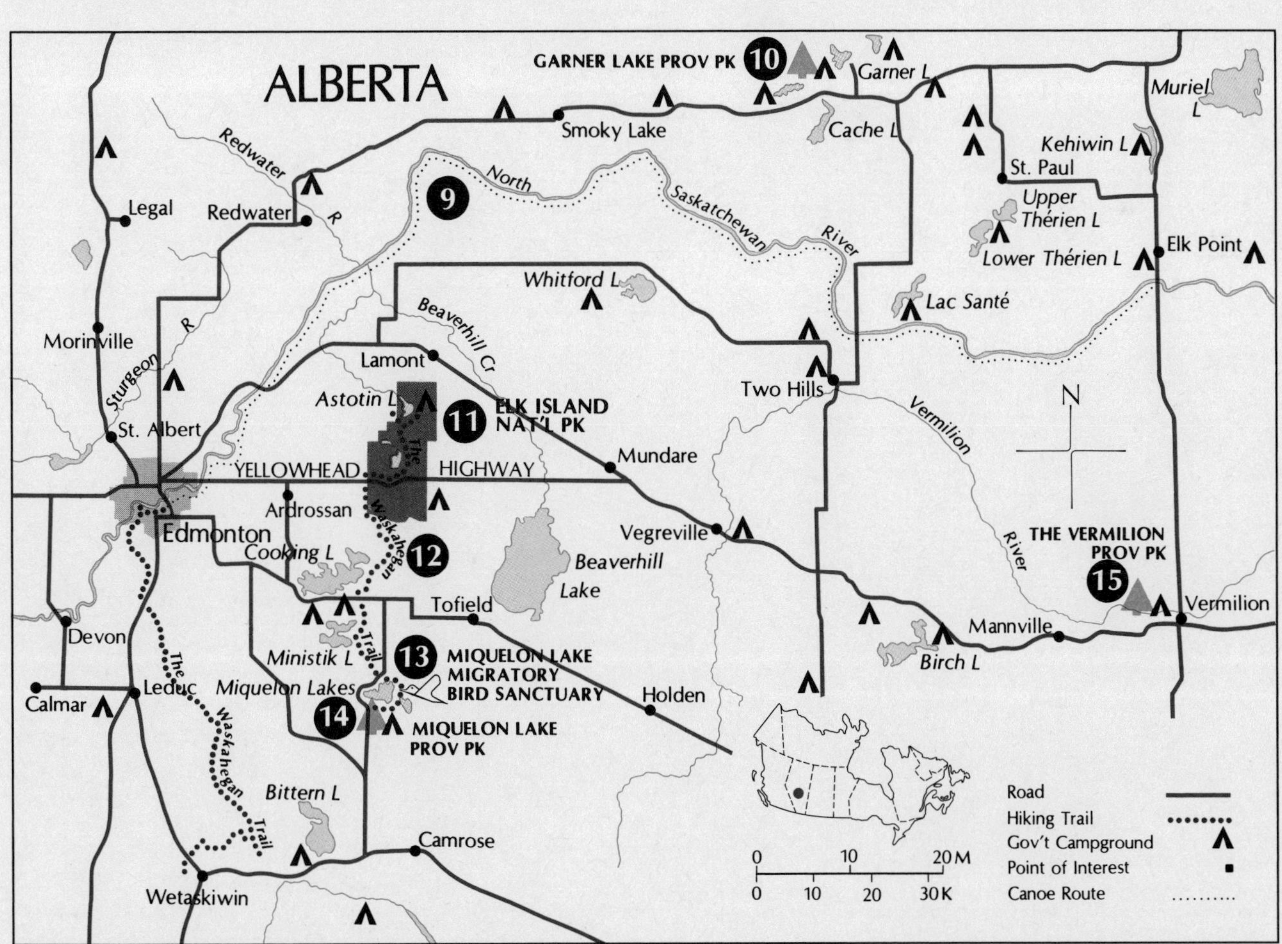

The Mighty Athabasca: Great Canoe Routes Along a Wild River

Like some great snake, the mighty Athabasca River slithers through a land of mountain, forest and muskeg, journeying 756 miles from the ice fields of the Rockies to Lake Athabasca. Two stretches of the river are shown here. Below: it runs east from near Windfall to about Fort Assiniboine, then north to Smith. The river then swings south and east to Athabasca (map opposite), then winds north through the Athabasca Tar Sands to Fort McMurray.

A grizzly bear stands guard in the rugged Swan Hills.

Canoe Route (Whitecourt to Smith) (4)
Five Mile Island in the Athabasca River is a favorite wilderness camping area for canoeists. Along the route is Fort Assiniboine, at the northern end of an old Hudson's Bay Company link between Edmonton and the Athabasca River. *150 miles.*

Thunder Lake Provincial Park (5)
As many as 12 blue herons nest on islands in Thunder Lake.
514 acres. Camping.

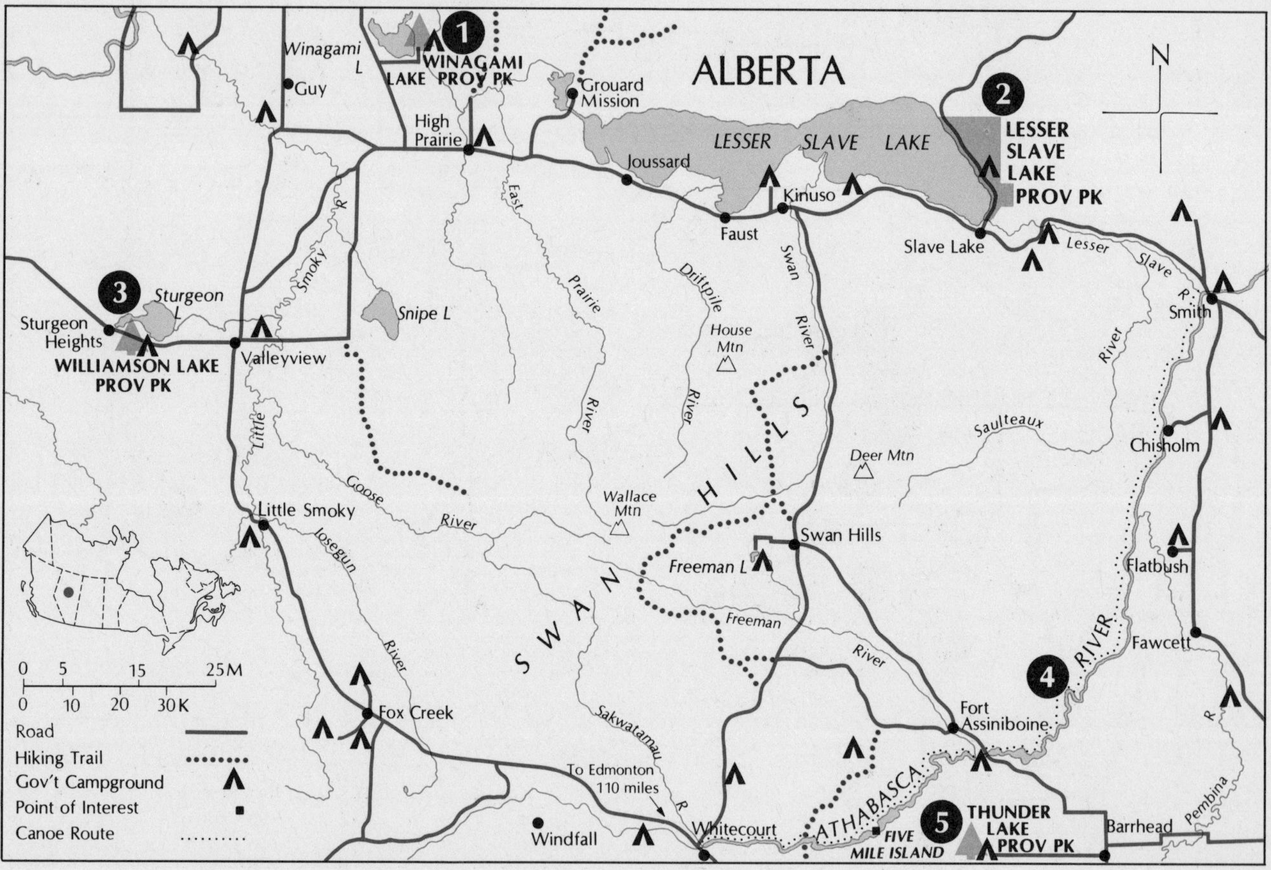

Winagami Lake Provincial Park (1)
4.5 square miles. Camping, fishing (northern pike, yellow perch).

Lesser Slave Lake Provincial Park (2)
There is a three-mile-long belt of sand dunes at the southern end of 461-square-mile Lesser Slave Lake.
28 square miles. Camping, hiking, fishing (walleye, northern pike), canoeing.

Williamson Lake Provincial Park (3)
43 acres. Camping, fishing (yellow perch, northern pike), canoeing.

Cross Lake Provincial Park (9)
6.5 square miles. Camping, fishing (northern pike, yellow perch), canoeing.

Canoe Route (Athabasca to Fort McMurray) (7)
On this challenging route are the Grand Rapids, which drop 30 feet in less than a half mile and are audible almost three miles upstream. Canoeists must portage 1½ miles around the rapids. Natural gas bubbles to the surface near Brule Rapids. Cliffs up to 150 feet high, studded by boulders, border the Athabasca here. South of Fort McMurray the river cuts through the Athabasca Tar Sands and its banks are blackened with oil. Bald eagles, pelicans and great blue herons inhabit riverside forests. Bears, wolves, deer and, occasionally, moose and lynx can be seen along the route. *231 miles.*

Sir Winston Churchill Provincial Park (8)
This island park in Lac La Biche is reached by a 1½-mile causeway. The lake has five sandy beaches.
591 acres. Camping, hiking, fishing (yellow perch, walleye, northern pike), canoeing.

Gregoire Lake Provincial Park (6)
2.5 square miles. Camping, hiking, fishing (yellow perch, northern pike, walleye).

Insects and How to Beat Them

To reduce insect bother, know your enemy. Blackflies, worst in late spring and early summer, are particularly active in wooded areas by day. In open areas they bite most often at dawn and dusk. Mosquitoes are fiercest at night. Deerflies prefer hot days. To help protect yourself:

- Choose light-colored clothing. Blackflies, deerflies and mosquitoes are attracted by dark colors and are easily spotted on a light background.
- Wear close-fitting garments and tuck long pants into socks or boots. Long-sleeved shirts should fit snuggly at the neck and wrists to keep out insects.
- Wear a hat to prevent insects from crawling into your hair.
- Use insect repellent on exposed skin, paying special attention to areas around cuffs and collars and avoiding lips, eyes and nose. Liquid repellents containing diethyltoluamide are most effective. For temporary protection, rub orange or lemon peel on your skin.
- Apply repellent frequently during strenuous activity; perspiration reduces a repellent's effectiveness.
- Avoid colognes and scented soaps—they attract insects.
- Don't camp near dense brush or a marshy area.

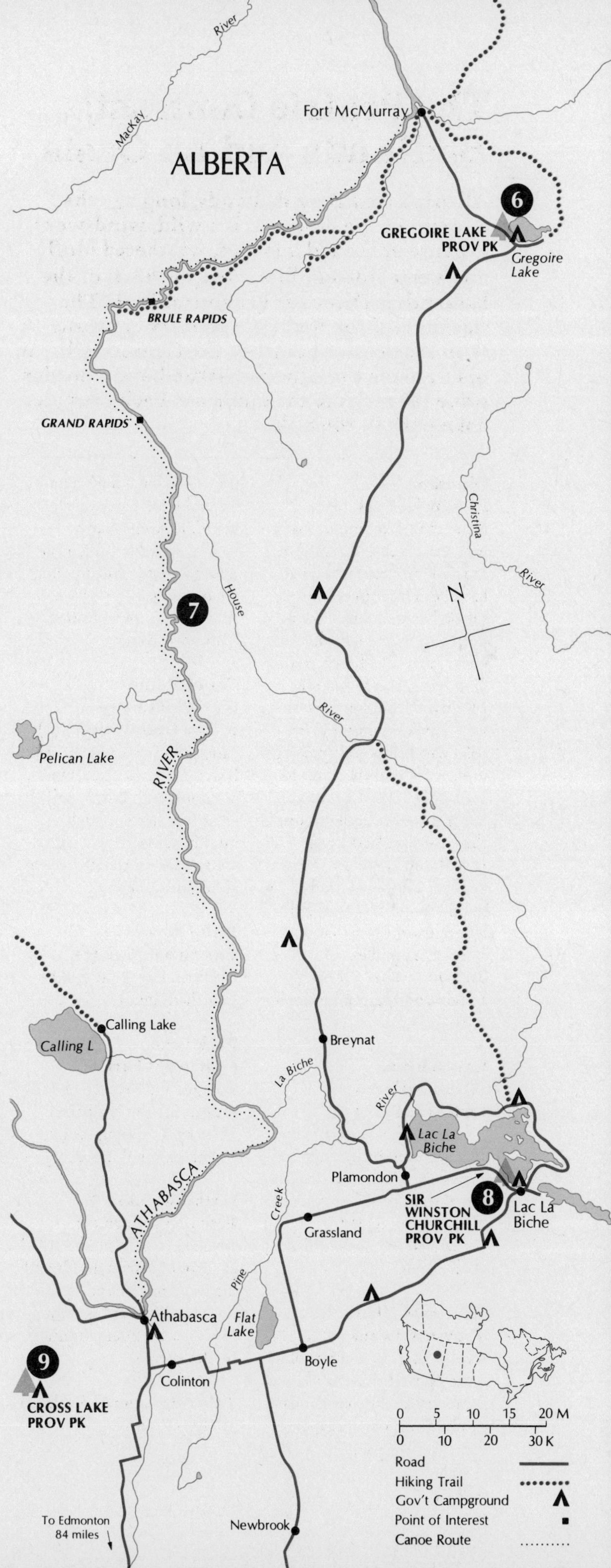

The Prairie Contrast: Badlands and an Oasis

Alberta's Red Deer Badlands, long ago the domain of the dinosaur, is a wild, windswept expanse of eroded hoodoos, weathered bluffs and steep-sided gullies. Near the heart of the badlands is Dinosaur Provincial Park. The starkness of the Red Deer country contrasts with the gentler beauty of the Cypress Hills, an oasis astride the Alberta-Saskatchewan border some 100 miles to the southeast. Each province has a park in the hills.

Dinosaur Provincial Park (3)
More than 125 dinosaur skeletons have been unearthed in the park and protective huts have been built over four of the skeletal remains. Pronghorn antelopes roam the park and a great blue heron colony nests here. Also found are McCown's longspurs, Swainson's hawks and prairie falcons. Sagebrush and creeping juniper cling to the parched soil—only 12½ inches of rain fall annually. A lookout on the 1½-mile Dead Lodge Canyon Nature Trail provides a view of weathered bluffs, hoodoos—pillars of eroded clay and sandstone—and steep-sided gullies.
34.5 square miles. Camping, fishing (northern pike, goldeye).

Canoe Route (Drumheller to Dinosaur Park) (2)
This section of the Red Deer River meanders through the badlands. Fossils and dinosaur bones have been discovered along the route. Petrified wood is found in solidified lava. *85 miles.*

Kinbrook Island Provincial Park (4)
This park in 10½-mile-long Lake Newell, Alberta's largest man-made lake, has stands of plum, apricot and apple trees. There is a nine-acre natural prairie area on the island. Pelicans, marsh hawks, western tanagers and double-crested cormorants are often seen.
95 acres. Camping, fishing (rainbow trout).

Canoe Route (Crowfoot Ferry to The Grand Forks) (5)
Along this stretch of the Bow River are hawks, sandpipers, pheasants and, occasionally, great blue herons. High, muddy banks restrict camping to a provincial site south of Scandia. *111 miles.*

Little Bow Provincial Park (6)
272 acres. Camping, fishing (northern pike).

Park Lake Provincial Park (7)
Coyotes, red foxes, deer and badgers inhabit the park.
557 acres. Camping, fishing (northern pike), canoeing.

Little Fish Lake Provincial Park (1)
The lake was an Indian fishing ground. Arrowheads and the stone remains of tepee rings can be found nearby.
151 acres. Camping, fishing (yellow perch).

Taber Provincial Park (8)
125 acres. Camping.

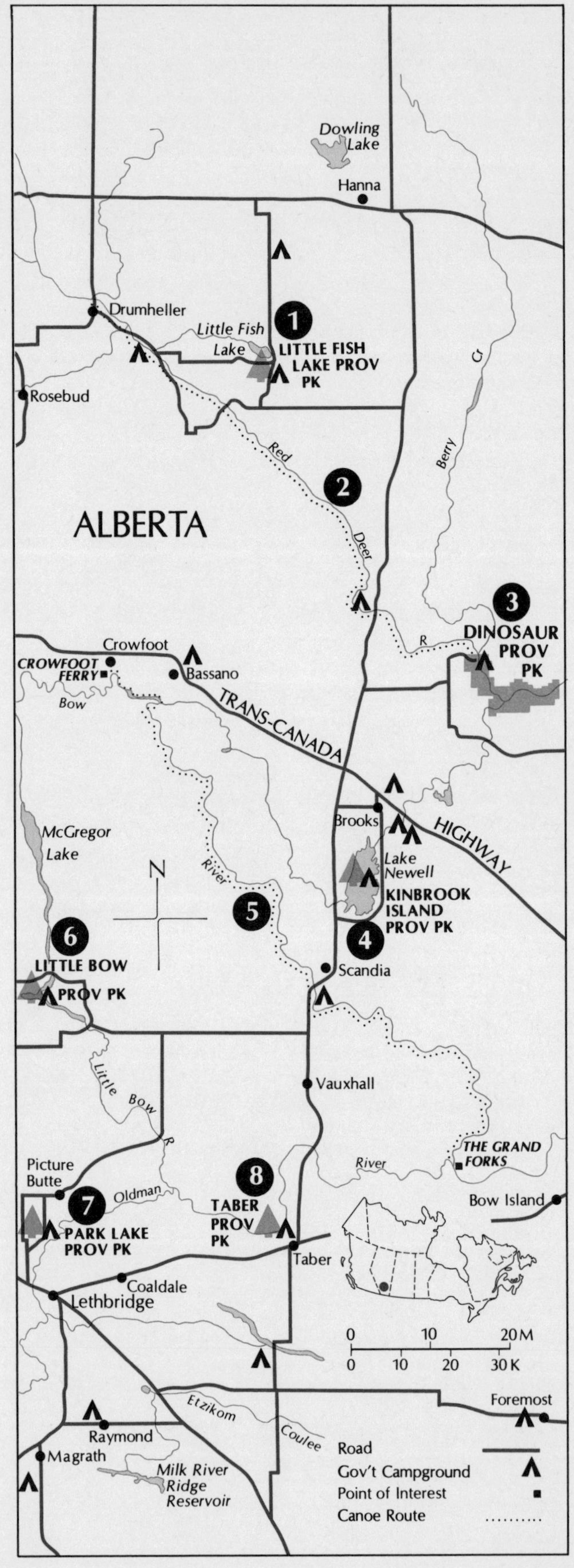

Water's Work in the Badlands

Some 10,000 years of erosion have shaped the ruggedly beautiful badlands along the Red Deer River in Alberta. And water is erosion's main instrument.

Rain is scarce in this semi-arid region but it is sometimes torrential, stripping the land of soil and vegetation and exposing the underlying rock.

The badlands are composed mainly of shale and sandstone; both are soft and easily eroded but they wear away at different rates. Soft shale, when wet, turns to mud and is washed away. Sandstone, grains of sand bonded by a natural cement (usually bentonitic clay), absorbs water and is slightly more resistant.

Water eats into soft rock and carves gullies and canyons. Eventually the canyons are widened into valleys containing isolated masses of resistant rock—buttes, hoodoos and sandstone ridges.

Cypress Hills

The Cypress Hills are 1,000 square miles of gently undulating forests, lakes and rivers surrounded by semi-arid plains. Temperatures here are 6° to 8°C. (10° to 15°F.) cooler than in the surrounding prairies, almost 2,000 feet below. An annual rainfall of 18 inches—only 7 inches fall on the plains—feeds fescue grasslands and stands of lodgepole pine. Silvery lupine, shooting star and bunchberry —common alpine flowers— grow here. Thirteen orchid species have been recorded, including calypso, green-flowered bog orchid and the rare round-leafed orchid. Seventy-six butterfly species recorded here include tiger swallowtails and giant sulphurs. Among 207 bird species sighted in the hills are red-breasted nuthatches, trumpeter swans, Audubon and MacGillivray's warblers and wild turkeys. Also found are the nests of Townsend's solitaire, the first discovered outside the mountains of southwest Alberta. The hills are dominated by 4,810-foot Head of the Mountain, the highest elevation between Labrador and the Rocky Mountains.

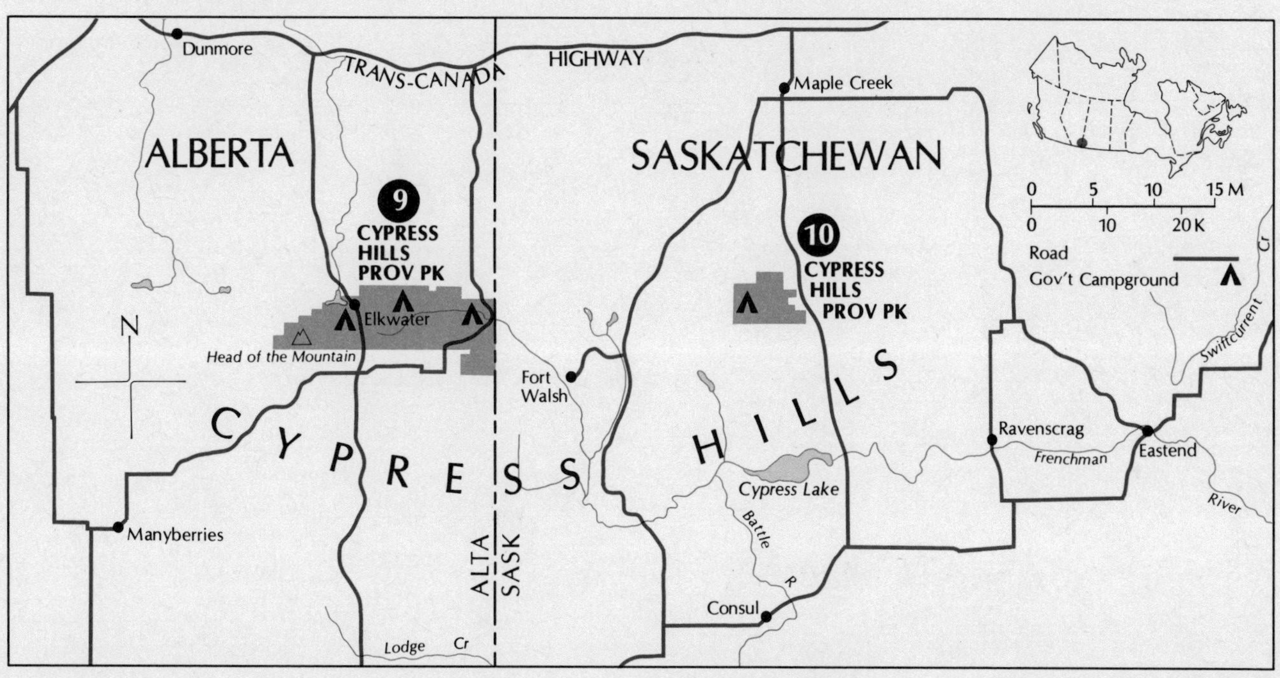

Hoodoos shaped by wind and water have a resistant cap of hard rock that shields the soft strata underneath.

Cypress Hills Provincial Park (Alta.) (9)

78 square miles. Camping, fishing (northern pike, rainbow and brook trout), self-guiding nature trails.

Cypress Hills Provincial Park (Sask.) (10)

18 square miles. Camping, supervised swimming, alpine skiing, fishing (brook trout), canoeing, horseback riding.

Saskatchewan's Majestic Northland

Along the mighty Churchill River as it cuts across northern Saskatchewan are raging white water, craggy gorges, treacherous rapids and a maze of lakes and islands. This is wild country, little changed since penetrated by explorers and fur traders during the 1700s. Some 147 miles north of Prince Albert is Lac La Ronge Provincial Park, renowned for its challenging canoe routes and superb fishing. At Stanley Mission is Saskatchewan's oldest Anglican church (1856) and on the Rapid River is scenic Nistowiak Falls.

Meadow Lake Provincial Park (1)
A boardwalk on the two-mile White Birch Nature Trail spans a bog where tamarack, club moss and insect-eating sundew grow. Clusters of kames—mounds of sand and gravel deposited by glacial meltwater—can be seen on the east shore of Flotten Lake. A half-mile northeast of the Waterhen River is an esker—a narrow ridge of glacial deposit—20 feet high and 150 feet wide at the base. Canoe instructors—and free use of canoes within the park—are available. The 22-mile Pierce Lake-Lac des Iles Canoe Route has few rapids and no portages. A more challenging trip is the Waterhen River-Beaver River Canoe Route—70 miles of rapids, islands, twisting channels and high sandbanks. Naturalists conduct guided hikes in the park. *596 square miles.* Camping, supervised swimming, fishing (rainbow and lake trout, arctic grayling, northern pike, yellow perch, walleye).

Islands dot vast Lac La Ronge.

Canoe Route (Ile-à-la-Crosse to Otter Lake) (2)
Ile-à-la-Crosse was once the site of a Hudson's Bay Company post, one of the centers of the local fur trade with the Indians. Indian paintings can be seen on cliffs in Black Bear Island Lake. Along the route are outcrops of pink granite and black basalt formed some two billion years ago. Moose, caribou, lynx, wolves and black bears inhabit shoreline forests. Many of the route's 19 rapids and falls must be portaged. *240 miles.*

Canoe Route (Otter Lake to Sandy Bay) (4)
Ducks and geese abound and ospreys and bald and golden eagles can be seen. Forests of spruce and pine cloak low-lying hills. At Frog Portage, canoeists can veer south onto a chain of lakes that joins the Sturgeon-weir River, part of the historic fur-trade route that linked the Churchill and Saskatchewan rivers. *140 miles.*

Lac La Ronge Provincial Park (3)
This rugged park—almost a third of it water—is noted for outstanding northern pike, walleye and rainbow trout fishing. The Rapid River, emptying Lac La Ronge, ends at Nistowiak Falls which drops 40 feet into the Churchill River. Saskatchewan's first Anglican church, completed in 1856, is at Stanley Mission. Eight canoe routes—ranging from 22 to 126 miles—begin and end in the park. Two are suitable for novices, but white water and long portages restrict the others to skilled canoeists. *600 square miles.* Camping.

Modern Voyageurs and Canoe Safety

A program to provide canoeing information and to promote canoe safety was started in 1974 by the Saskatchewan Department of Tourism and Renewable Resources. Canoeists choose from among 50 charted routes in the northern part of the province. Each person who participates in the program completes a voyageur permit—giving his name, address, proposed route and expected date of completion of the trip—at one of 17 registration offices in northern Saskatchewan. At the end of the trip canoeists check in at the nearest registration office and later each receives a voyageur certificate by mail.

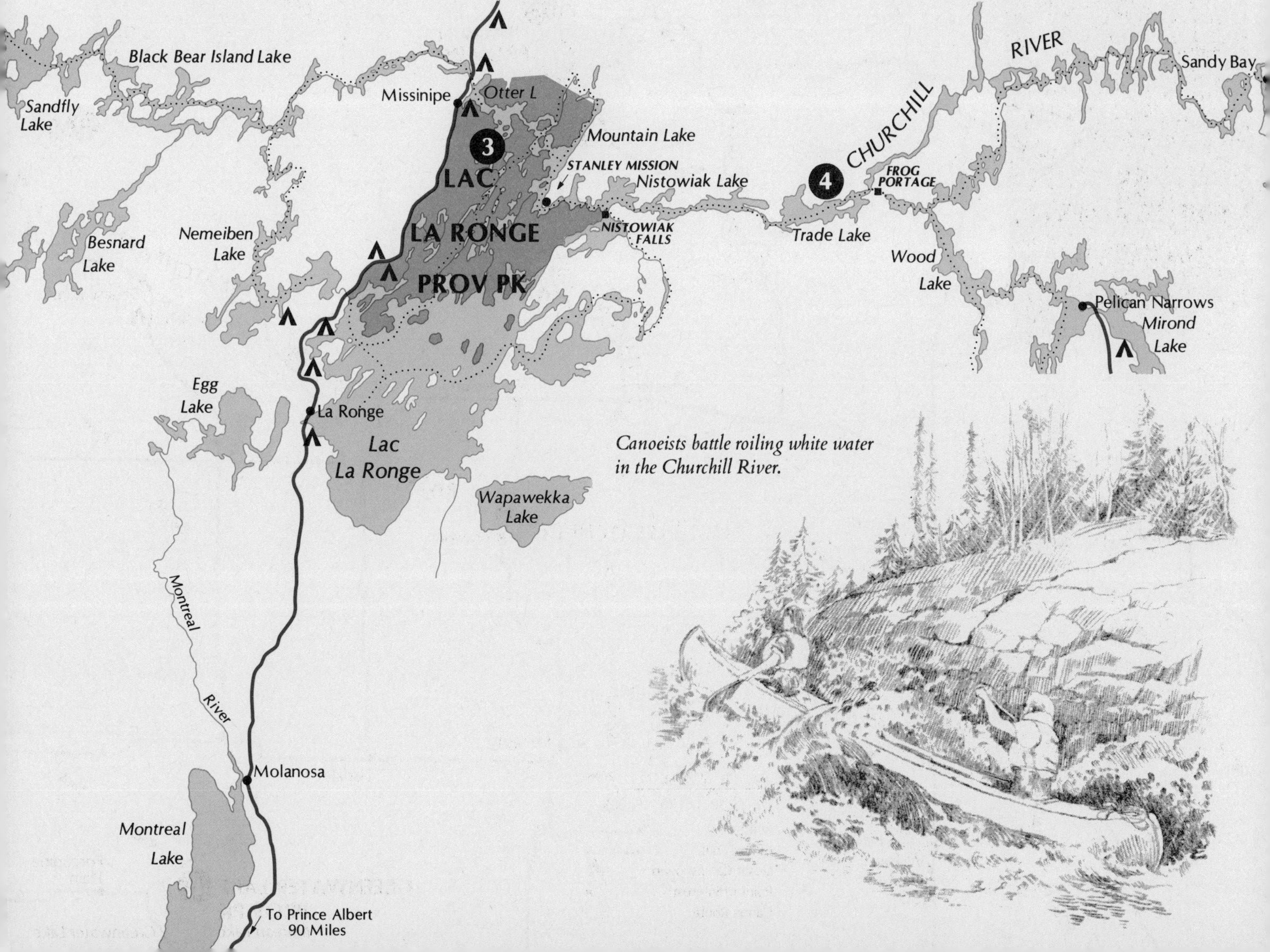

Black Bear Island Lake
Sandfly Lake
Missinipe
Otter L
Mountain Lake
3
LAC LA RONGE PROV PK
STANLEY MISSION
Nistowiak Lake
NISTOWIAK FALLS
CHURCHILL RIVER
4
FROG PORTAGE
Trade Lake
Sandy Bay
Wood Lake
Pelican Narrows
Mirond Lake
Besnard Lake
Nemeiben Lake
Egg Lake
La Ronge
Lac La Ronge
Wapawekka Lake
Montreal River
Molanosa
Montreal Lake
To Prince Albert 90 Miles

Canoeists battle roiling white water in the Churchill River.

Prairie, Parkland and Boreal Forest

In Prince Albert National Park prairie grassland gives way to aspen parkland and it, in turn, gives way to boreal forest. The park was once the hunting and fishing ground of Cree and Chipewyan Indians; wapiti, badgers, caribou, bears and wolves still roam here. Cougars are found to the east in the Pasquia Hills. Cumberland House, which dates from 1774, is Saskatchewan's oldest settlement.

Prince Albert National Park (1)
Lobsticks—trees from which Indians and trappers lopped branches when blazing trails—mark some of the park's 150 miles of hiking paths. Along the one-mile Boundary Bog Nature Trail are pitcher plants, muskeg and kettles (small hollows formed in sand and gravel by glaciers). Prince Albert has three distinct vegetation zones. Badgers inhabit a prairie region typified by such flowers as meadow rue and woolly yarrow. Wapiti roam aspen parkland—an area abundant with red osier dogwood and wild sarsaparilla—and gray wolves range boreal forests of white spruce and tamarack. Among 200 bird species here are white pelicans (there is a rookery on Lavallée Lake), herring gulls, bald eagles, ospreys, belted kingfishers and great blue herons. The 15-mile Bagwa Canoe Route passes several beaver lodges. Permission is required for wilderness camping.
1,496 square miles. Camping, supervised swimming, fishing (northern pike, walleye, yellow perch, whitefish), horseback riding.

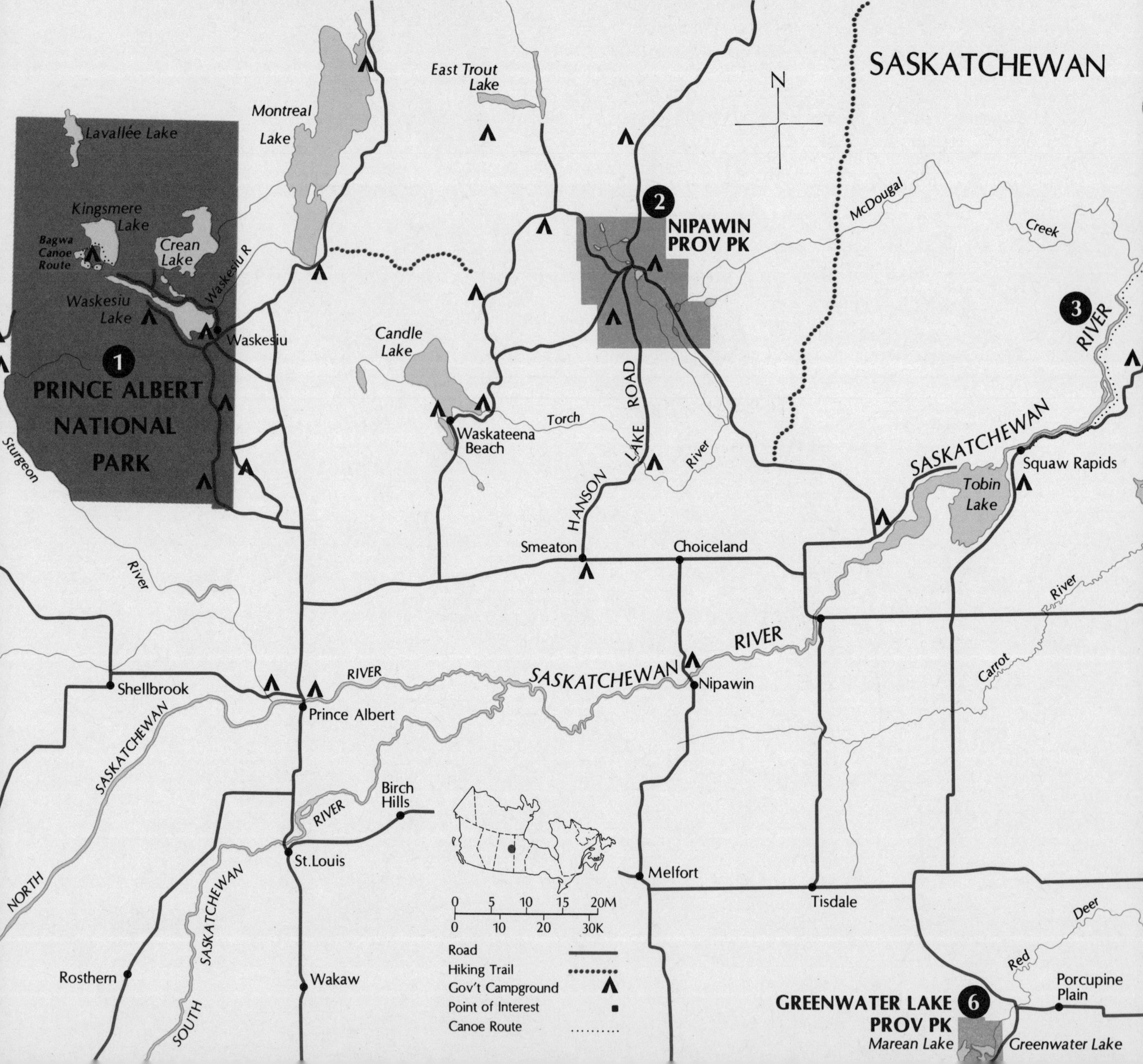

Canoe Route (Squaw Rapids to The Pas) (3)
Seventy miles downstream from Squaw Rapids is Cumberland House, the oldest settlement in Saskatchewan. It was there, in 1774, that Samuel Hearne established the first inland trading post of the Hudson's Bay Company. West of Cumberland House, canoeists pass through lowlands cloaked with marsh grass and alive with the sounds of ducks and geese. A herd of some 75 wapiti can be seen near Squaw Rapids. Rapids at the Pemmican Portage ferry crossing can be avoided by a portage. *153 miles.*

Canoe Route (Amisk Lake to Cumberland House) (4)
Limestone outcrops and craggy granite walls line this route. *54 miles.*

Nipawin Provincial Park (2)
A ridge of sand and gravel—the Narrow Hills esker—runs through the park. Following old wagon trails to the summit, hikers gain an impressive view of lakes, forests and rolling hills. Several lakes in the park are stocked with coho and Kokanee salmon, brook and rainbow trout—fishes not native to the area.
360 square miles. Camping, canoeing.

Wildcat Hill Wilderness Area (5)
This area is in the Pasquia Hills, the western shoreline of ancient Lake Agassiz, which once covered 110,000 square miles. Cougars, thought to be extinct here, have been spotted recently. Wildcat Hill can be reached by hiking from the Otosquen Road.
70 square miles. Wilderness camping, fishing (northern pike).

Greenwater Lake Provincial Park (6)
Pelicans inhabit the northeast tip of Greenwater Lake and great blue herons nest on an island in Marean Lake.
72 square miles. Camping, supervised swimming, fishing (northern pike, walleye, yellow perch), nature house.

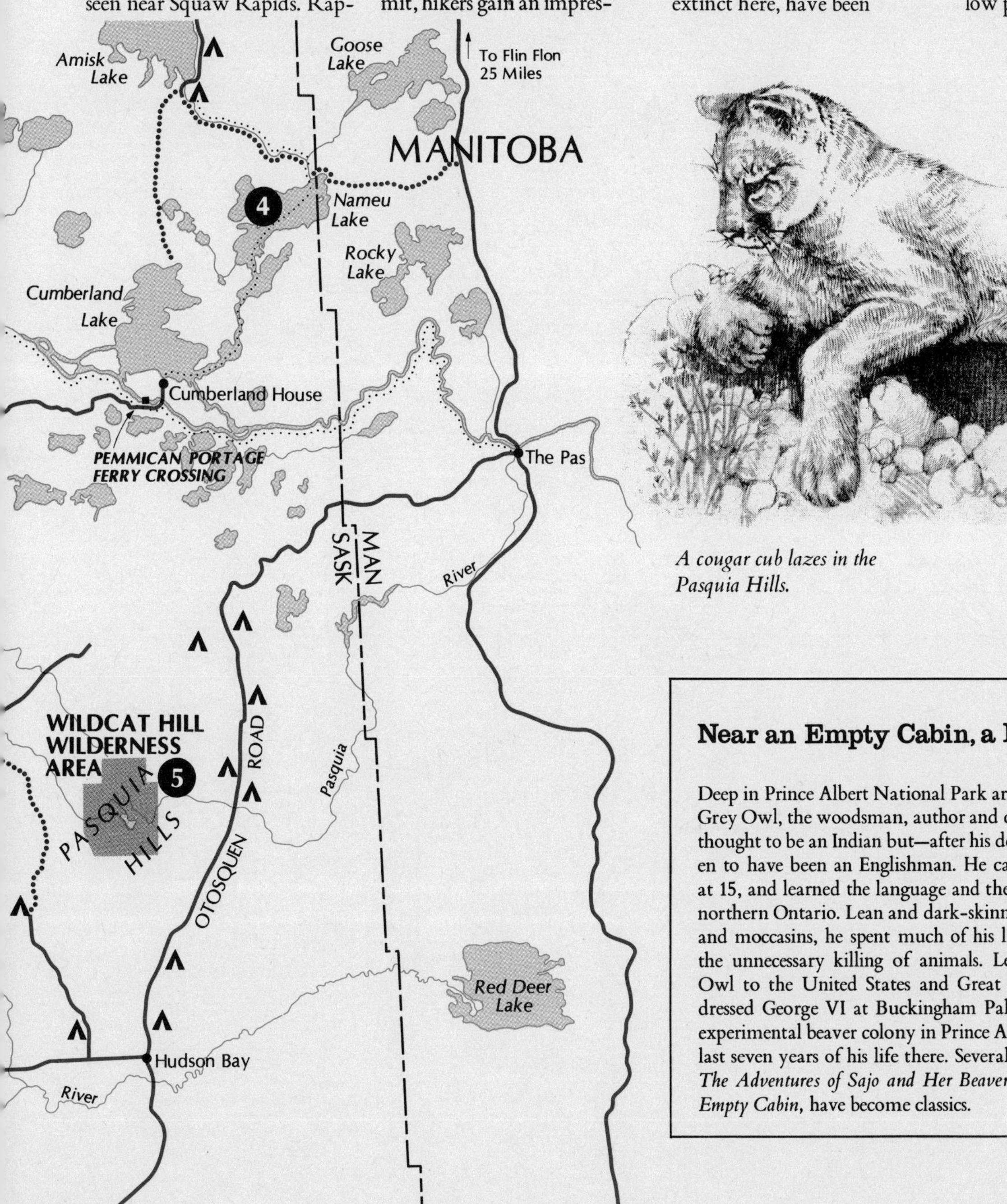

A cougar cub lazes in the Pasquia Hills.

Near an Empty Cabin, a Lonely Grave

Deep in Prince Albert National Park are the cabin and grave of Grey Owl, the woodsman, author and conservationist who was thought to be an Indian but—after his death in 1938—was proven to have been an Englishman. He came to Canada in 1903, at 15, and learned the language and the lore of the Ojibway in northern Ontario. Lean and dark-skinned, dressed in buckskins and moccasins, he spent much of his life campaigning against the unnecessary killing of animals. Lecture tours took Grey Owl to the United States and Great Britain (where he addressed George VI at Buckingham Palace). He established an experimental beaver colony in Prince Albert Park and spent the last seven years of his life there. Several of his books, including *The Adventures of Sajo and Her Beaver People* and *Tales of an Empty Cabin,* have become classics.

A Huge Dam, a Man-Made Lake—and the Lovely Qu'Appelle Valley

One of the major features of the southwestern Saskatchewan landscape is man-made Lake Diefenbaker on the South Saskatchewan River. It stretches for 140 miles behind the Gardiner Dam, Canada's biggest earth-fill dam, which is 65 miles south of Saskatoon. North of Regina in southeastern Saskatchewan is the Qu'Appelle Valley, a great slash in the prairie, 250 miles from east to west and up to 1½ miles wide. On the shores of Lake Diefenbaker and in the Qu'Appelle Valley are numerous provincial parks and other recreation areas. At the north end of Last Mountain Lake is North America's oldest bird sanctuary.

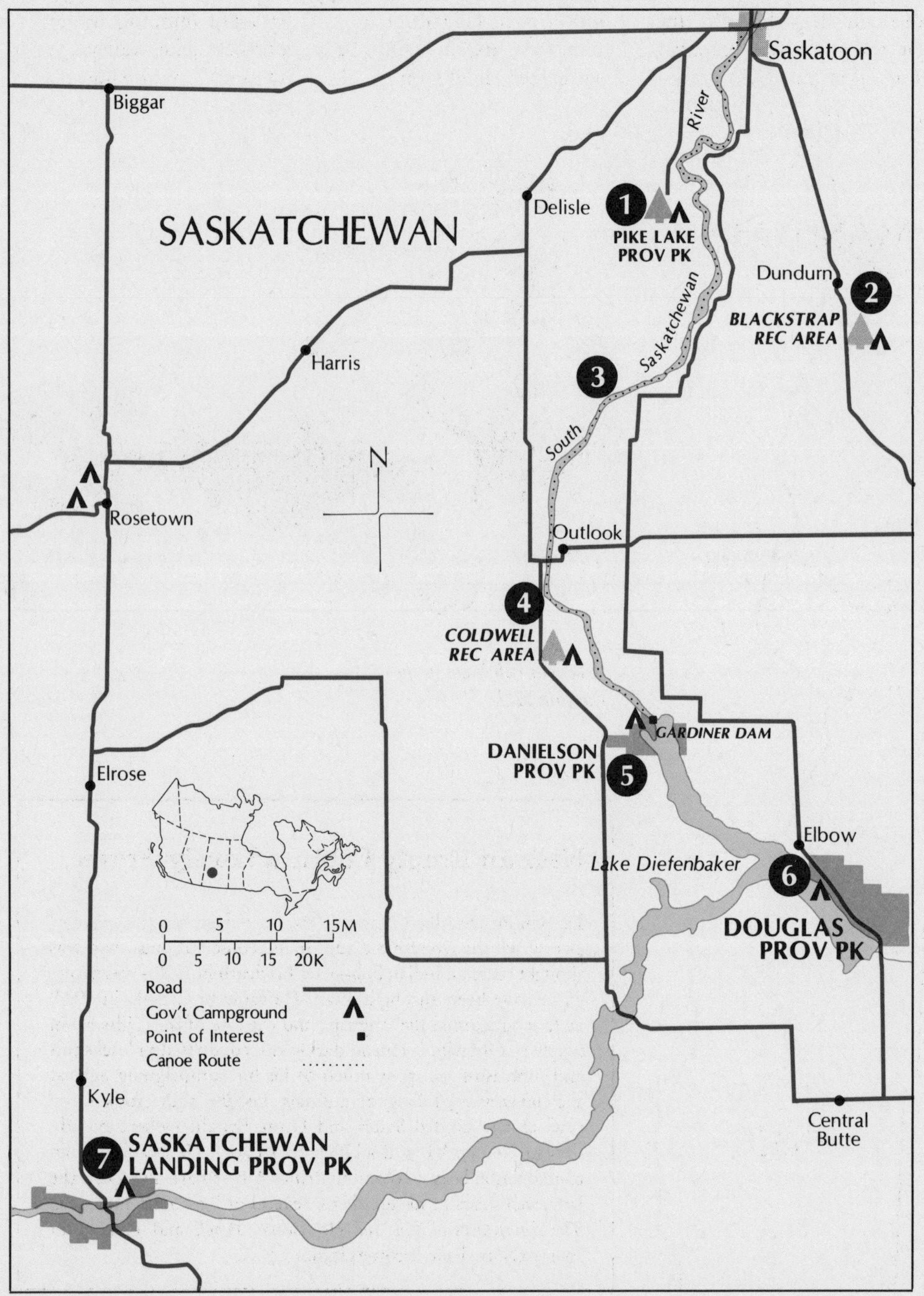

Saskatchewan Landing Provincial Park (7)
Burial rings—circles of rock used to anchor tepees during Indian funeral rites—can be seen in the park. Terraces along the 1½-mile Cougar Track Trail are slump lines formed by the slippage of waterlogged earth. Underground springs feed a small stream near the trail.
21.5 square miles. Camping, supervised swimming, fishing (walleye, northern pike, sauger, sturgeon).

Danielson Provincial Park (5)
Petrified wood, agates and Indian arrowheads have been discovered along the shores of Lake Diefenbaker. Nanking cherry trees have been planted as food for pheasants and songbirds. Deer, antelope, coyotes and badgers inhabit the park.
12 square miles. Camping, supervised swimming, fishing (sturgeon, sauger, walleye, northern pike, lake and rainbow trout).

Douglas Provincial Park (6)
The park has some 1½ square miles of shifting sand dunes.
15 square miles. Camping, supervised swimming, fishing (northern pike, lake trout, sturgeon, whitefish).

Canoe Route (Gardiner Dam to Saskatoon) (3)
There is wilderness camping on sandy islands along the South Saskatchewan River. In places the river meanders past 200-foot-high cliffs. *50 miles.*

Pike Lake Provincial Park (1)
A 1½-mile self-guiding nature trail skirts muskeg, grasslands and 80-foot-high poplar trees. Sand dunes fringe the western shores of Pike Lake.
2 square miles. Camping (trailers prohibited), supervised

swimming, cross-country skiing, fishing (northern pike).

Blackstrap Recreation Area (2)
2 square miles. Camping, climbing, supervised swimming, alpine and cross-country skiing, fishing (walleye), canoeing.

Coldwell Recreation Area (4)
30 acres. Camping.

Last Mountain Lake Bird Sanctuary (9)
Established in 1887, this preserve at the north end of Last Mountain Lake is the oldest bird sanctuary in North America. In mid-September it attracts as many as 10,000 double-crested cormorants and 20,000 sandhill cranes. Migrating Ross's geese and whooping cranes stop here. White pelicans and white-winged scoters nest on islands in the lake. *4 square miles.*

Rowan's Ravine Provincial Park (11)
The ravine for which the park is named is 20 feet deep and more than a mile long.
720 acres. Camping, supervised swimming.

Buffalo Pound Provincial Park (12)
A small herd of bison roams a 265-acre compound at the east end of the park. Along the Big Valley Nature Trail is a ravine where sagebrush and cactus grow.
4 square miles. Camping, supervised swimming, alpine and cross-country skiing, fishing (northern pike, walleye, yellow perch), canoeing.

Wascana Migratory Bird Sanctuary (14)
Birds in this sanctuary, a part of Regina's Wascana Waterfowl Park, include spotted sandpipers, blue-winged teals, marbled godwits, whistling swans and sora rails. The wastewater from a power plant warms a one-acre section of Wascana Lake and food is plentiful, so many birds winter here. *360 acres.*

Echo Valley Provincial Park (16)
Two nature trails climb a 200-foot hill and enter ravines forested with maple, poplar, elm and birch.
1.5 square miles. Camping, supervised swimming, fishing (northern pike, walleye, yellow perch).

Stalwart National Wildlife Area (10)
Great blue herons, Canada geese, black-crowned night herons and American bitterns are seen in the area's 1½-square-mile marsh. *2 square miles.*

Etter's Beach Recreation Area (8)
360 acres. Camping, fishing (walleye, yellow perch, northern pike).

Valley Center Recreation Area (17)
200 acres. Camping.

Condie Nature Refuge (13)
In autumn, hundreds of ducks and geese visit this preserve on Condie Reservoir. The Fred Bard Nature Center houses mounted bird specimens. Indian stone effigies—animal shapes outlined on the ground with rocks—have been moved from the nearby prairies and reassembled in the refuge. *320 acres.*

Canoe Route (The Fishing Lakes) (15)
Four lakes linked by the Qu'Appelle River make up the route. There is a portage around the Echo Lake Dam. *30 miles.*

Katepwa Provincial Park (18)
13 acres. Supervised swimming, fishing (yellow perch, northern pike, walleye).

The Great Geese at Project Nisk'u

The Saskatchewan government and Ducks Unlimited, an organization of sportsmen dedicated to the preservation of waterfowl throughout Canada and the United States, work together to maintain a breeding flock of 900 Canada geese in Project Nisk'u. Nisk'u (Cree for big goose) was founded in 1969, at the east end of marshy Eyebrow Lake, some 25 miles southeast of Elbow. By 1985 close to 15,000 goslings will have been raised in the 35-square-mile reserve and distributed to other Saskatchewan lakes. Project Nisk'u has created an ideal habitat for wildfowl, planting grain for feed and building islands for nesting. Many ducks are caught in baited cages, tagged and set free, helping scientists to monitor the migration of birds. Among more than 160 species in the reserve are whistling swans, golden eagles, ospreys, burrowing owls and ruby-throated hummingbirds. Motorists tour the area on a network of dikes.

Rare Cactus, Shifting Dunes of Sand, a Baffling Butterfly—and the Skink

In the rolling plains of southwest Manitoba are shifting sand dunes, rare pincushion cactus and lakes and marshes teeming with birdlife. Cree and Assiniboine Indians and Métis crisscrossed this area in pursuit of huge herds of bison. Rising above a patchwork of farm fields and grasslands east of the Saskatchewan border is Riding Mountain. Many wapiti, a few bison and hundreds of unusual satyrid butterflies are to be seen in Riding Mountain National Park.

Spruce Woods Provincial Natural Park (9)
The 1½-mile Spirit Hills Interpretive Trail crosses the Bald Head Hills, four square miles of shifting sand dunes, small springs and 100-year-old white and black spruce trees. Pincushion cactus—rare in Manitoba—and the prairie skink, a lizard, are found in the dunes. Along the Assiniboine River are several oxbow lakes (once U-shaped bends in the river, now separated from the main channel).
90 square miles. Camping, supervised swimming, cross-country skiing, fishing (northern pike), canoeing.

Canoe Route (Souris River) (4)
Indians once stampeded buffalo over 70-foot-high cliffs that border the northern banks of the Souris River south of Wawanesa.
165 miles.

Moose Mountain Provincial Park (1)
Moose Mountain's aspen forests contrast with the rolling grasslands of the prairies 500 feet below. Hundreds of small lakes and marshes attract blue-winged teals, ring-necked ducks and the occasional turkey vulture.
154 square miles. Camping, supervised swimming, fishing (northern pike, walleye, yellow perch), horseback riding, self-guiding nature trails.

Rivers Provincial Recreational Area (2)
20 acres. Camping, supervised swimming, fishing (walleye, yellow perch), canoeing.

William Lake Provincial Recreational Area (6)
293 acres. Camping, hiking, fishing (rainbow trout), canoeing.

Turtle Mountain Provincial Park (5)
Scattered throughout the park are kettles—depressions formed in the ground by melting glacial ice.
73.5 square miles. Camping, supervised swimming, fishing (walleye, yellow perch), canoeing.

Rock Lake Provincial Recreational Area (7)
8 acres. Camping, fishing (northern pike, yellow perch), canoeing.

Oak Lake Provincial Recreational Area (3)
30 acres. Camping, fishing (northern pike, walleye, yellow perch), canoeing.

Canoe Route (Brandon to Spruce Woods Park) (8)
One-hundred-foot-high sand cliffs border the river 10 miles east of Brandon and extend downstream to Spruce Woods Park. The Assiniboine flows through rolling grasslands, but pockets of boreal forest have survived along the river's edge in punch bowls—deep hollows formed by the collapse of sand. *65 miles.*

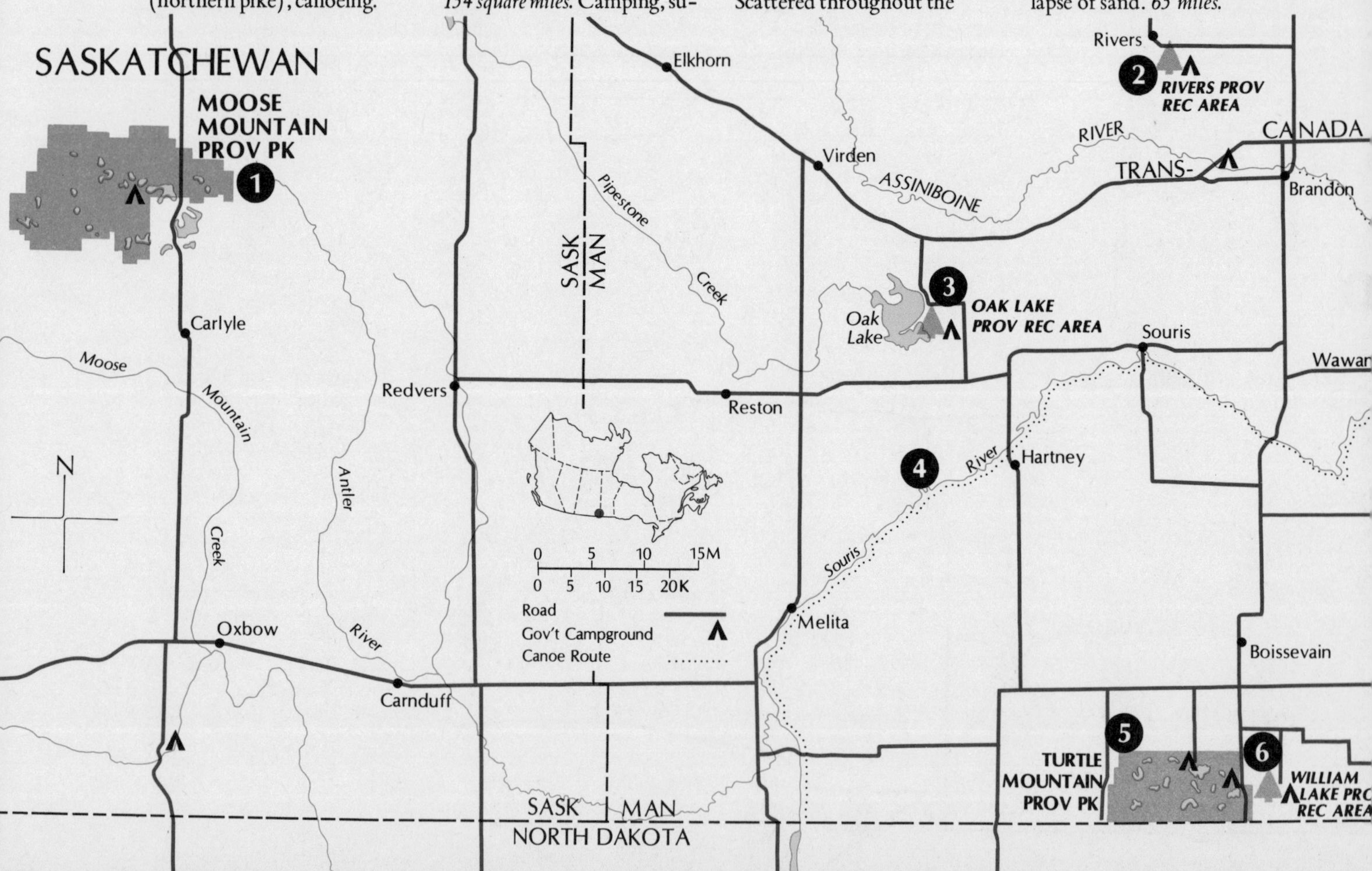

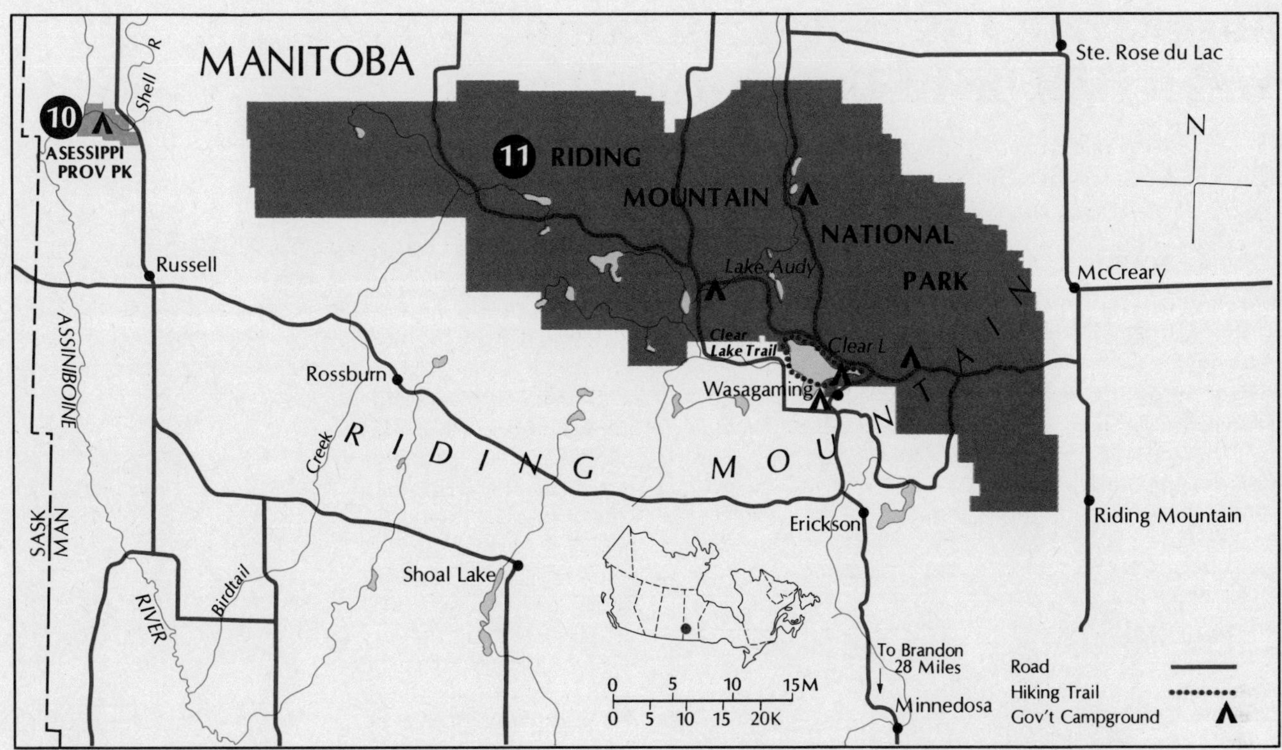

Asessippi Provincial Park (10)
The Shell River cuts through an esker (a narrow ridge of sand and gravel deposited by a subglacial stream). *8 square miles.* Camping, supervised swimming, fishing (northern pike, walleye), canoeing.

Riding Mountain National Park (11)
The park has one of Canada's largest herds of wapiti and some 40 bison roam near Lake Audy. Riding Mountain is on three major migratory routes and among 233 species of birds sighted are black-backed three-toed woodpeckers, ospreys, bald eagles, golden eagles and turkey vultures. The varied terrain supports an unusual range of plant life—almost 500 species—including vines and ferns, fields of wild flowers, groves of trembling aspen, and evergreen forests of tamarack, pine, black spruce and balsam fir. The 15-mile Clear Lake Trail passes a terminal moraine (a gravel ridge, once the forward edge of a glacier, left when the ice retreated). Riding Mountain is believed to be the dividing line of the satyrid butterfly's range. In even-numbered years these creatures are seen only east of the park, but in odd-numbered years they occur only west of here—a phenomenon not understood. *1,150 square miles.* Camping, supervised swimming, cross-country skiing, fishing (northern pike, whitefish, walleye, brook, lake and rainbow trout), horseback riding, self-guiding nature trails.

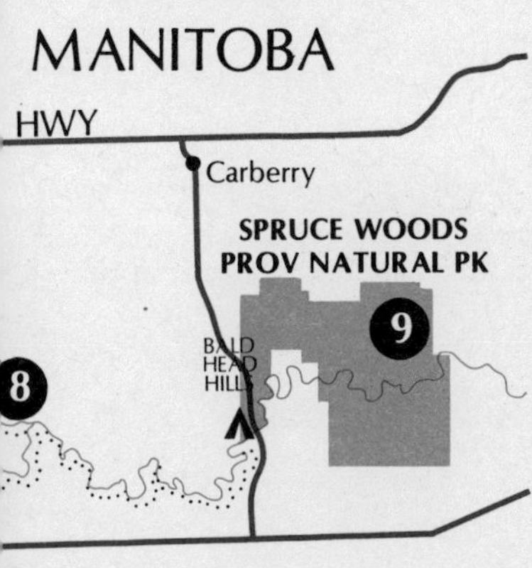

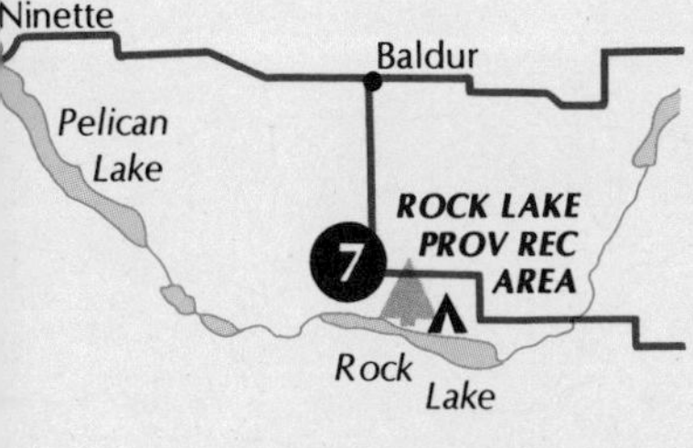

Rippling sand, swaying marram grass, a lone spruce . . . the Bald Head Hills of Manitoba.

Manitoba's Highest Mountains and a Ribbon of Lakes and Rivers

Provincial parks near the Manitoba-Saskatchewan border are the home of great blue herons, horned owls and turkey vultures. In one park is Baldy Mountain, the highest point in Manitoba. Myriad waterways north of The Pas wind through virgin forests and limestone hill country.

Young great blue herons roost in treetop nests in Manitoba's Duck Mountain Provincial Park.

Duck Mountain Provincial Park (Sask.) (2)

One of Canada's few flocks of turkey vultures is here.
100 square miles. Camping, supervised swimming, cross-country skiing, fishing (northern pike, yellow perch), self-guiding nature trails.

Porcupine Provincial Forest (1)

A road leads to the base of 2,700-foot Hart Mountain, the second highest point in Manitoba.
807 square miles. Camping, fishing (walleye, northern pike, rainbow and brook trout), canoeing.

Duck Mountain Provincial Park (Man.) (3)

The park is dominated by 2,727-foot Baldy Mountain, the highest elevation in Manitoba. More than 150 great blue heron nesting sites have been counted here. Other birds seen are double-crested cormorants, pelicans and great horned owls. Elk and mule deer roam the slopes of the Duck Mountains. The park is in 1,451-square-mile Duck Mountain Provincial Forest.
492 square miles. Camping, fishing (rainbow and lake trout, Kokanee salmon, northern pike).

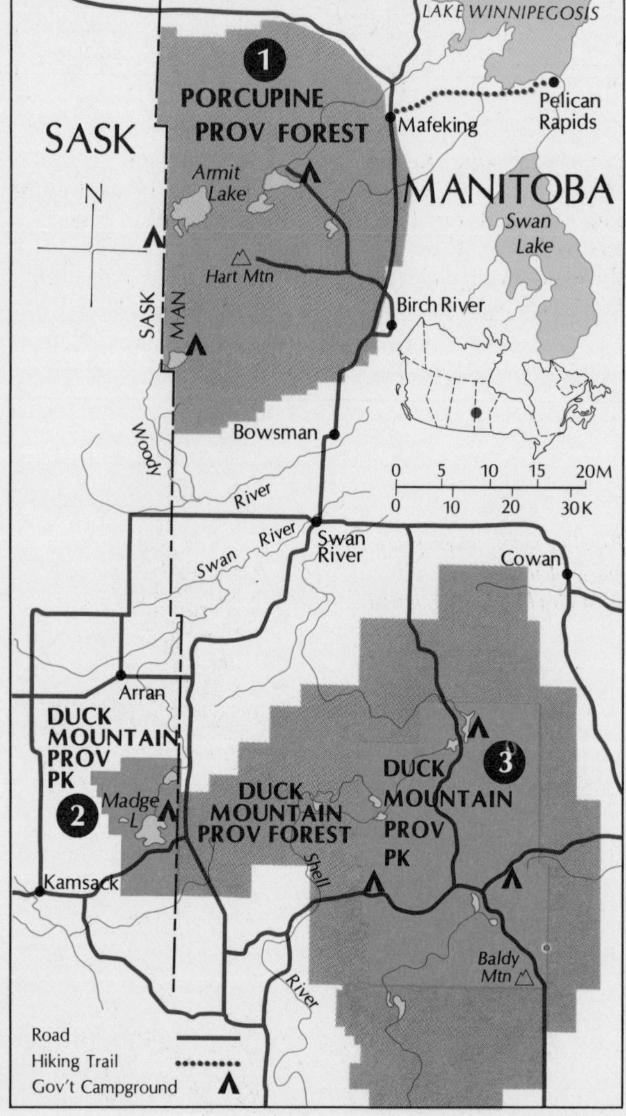

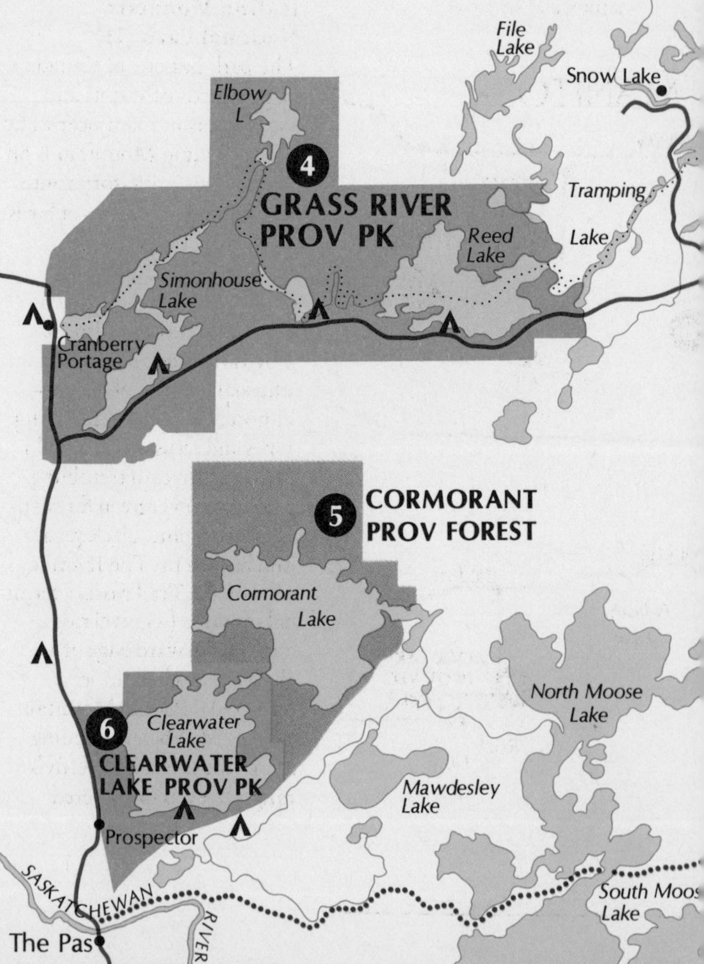

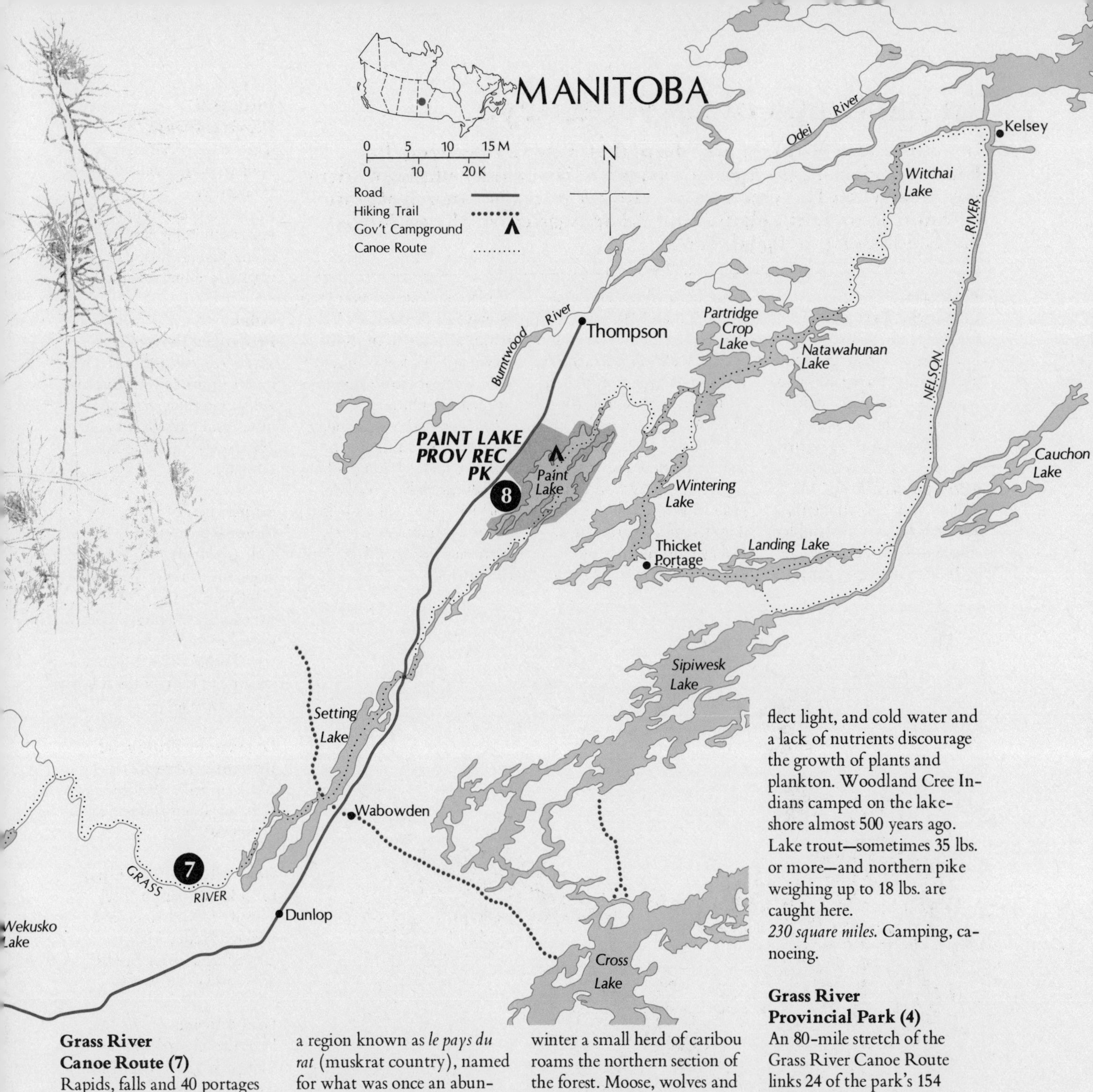

Grass River Canoe Route (7)
Rapids, falls and 40 portages are scattered along the route, which follows the Grass and Nelson rivers. Steep limestone cliffs—some are 200 feet high—line the Nelson. Kettles—holes eroded in rock by water-suspended pebbles—can be seen in the riverbanks. At places are 150-year-old ever-greens with only six-inch-thick trunks. This route, traveled by explorer Samuel Hearne in 1774, cuts through a region known as *le pays du rat* (muskrat country), named for what was once an abundance of muskrats. A chimney at Setting Lake may be a remnant of a fur-trading post. Some of Manitoba's best preserved Indian paintings are on outcrops on the north shore of Tramping Lake. *450 miles.*

Cormorant Provincial Forest (5)
Bald eagles nest here and pelicans, ospreys and great horned owls have been sighted. In winter a small herd of caribou roams the northern section of the forest. Moose, wolves and black bears are common but heavy snows limit the deer population.
575 square miles. Wilderness camping, fishing (northern pike, walleye), canoeing.

Clearwater Lake Provincial Park (6)
Spring-fed Clearwater Lake is noted for its remarkably clear blue water. Dissolved limestone particles in the lake reflect light, and cold water and a lack of nutrients discourage the growth of plants and plankton. Woodland Cree Indians camped on the lakeshore almost 500 years ago. Lake trout—sometimes 35 lbs. or more—and northern pike weighing up to 18 lbs. are caught here.
230 square miles. Camping, canoeing.

Grass River Provincial Park (4)
An 80-mile stretch of the Grass River Canoe Route links 24 of the park's 154 lakes.
884 square miles. Camping, fishing (northern pike, lake trout, walleye).

Paint Lake Provincial Recreational Park (8)
In 42½-square-mile Paint Lake are more than 150 islands.
87.5 square miles. Wilderness camping, supervised swimming, fishing (walleye, northern pike), canoeing.

In the Steps of La Vérendrye

In southeastern Manitoba are a deep lake formed by a meteor, the beaches of glacial Lake Agassiz, ancient Indian boulder effigies, wilderness areas where La Vérendrye traveled 250 years ago, a march of grain elevators across fertile plains—and Belair, Agassiz, Northwest Angle and Sandilands provincial forests.

Whiteshell Provincial Park (12)
Bordering the Winnipeg River are rock outcrops and strata thought to be 2½ billion years old—among the oldest rocks on earth. The bed of West Hawk Lake, up to 365 feet deep, was formed by a meteorite an estimated 150 million years ago. Along the Whiteshell River are boulder effigies—stone outlines made by Indians—of birds, turtles, fishes and snakes. Some may be more than 1,000 years old. The park is on the eastern flyway, one of North America's major bird migration routes. At the 3¾-square-mile Alf Hole Wild Goose Sanctuary as many as a thousand Canada, lesser snow and other geese gather at a time. Other birds in Whiteshell include double-crested cormorants, turkey vultures and bald eagles. The circular 105-mile Whiteshell Canoe Route, part of explorer Pierre de La Vérendrye's route to the Red River in 1733, leaves the park only where it crosses Boundary Lake in Ontario.
1,058 square miles. Camping, supervised swimming, cross-country skiing, hiking, fishing (smallmouth bass, walleye, northern pike, whitefish, lake, brook and rainbow trout), horseback riding, self-guiding nature trails.

Riders pause beside a lake in Whiteshell Provincial Park.

Birds Hill Provincial Park (8)
The park is on an esker, a sand and gravel ridge formed by a glacier.
3 square miles. Camping, supervised swimming, cross-country skiing, hiking, horseback riding, self-guiding nature trails.

Belair Provincial Forest (5)
The 17-mile North Star Trail leads to a fire tower that provides a sweeping view of spruce and pine forests.
289 square miles. Wilderness camping.

Kautunigan Canoe Route (1)
Indian pictographs can be seen along the banks of Sasaginnigak Creek and near Big Moose Falls. Kettles—hollows carved in rock by water-tossed pebbles—are exposed at the base of Kettle Falls at low water. *300 miles.*

Grindstone Provincial Recreation Area (2)
100 square miles. Wilderness camping, fishing (walleye, silver bass).

Canoe Route (Winnipeg to Lake Winnipeg) (7)
This Red River route cuts through Netley Marsh, a major nesting area for hawks, ducks and geese. *40 miles.*

Grand Beach Provincial Park (4)
This park on Elk Island and the southeast shore of Lake Winnipeg has a 1½-mile-long beach and is visited by pelicans and great blue herons.
92 square miles. Camping, supervised swimming, cross-country skiing, fishing (northern pike), canoeing.

Northwest Angle Provincial Forest (13)
Eastern white cedar and red and white pine, trees normally found farther south,

grow on the south shore of Moose Lake. Granite outcrops up to 30 feet high rise above black spruce bogs in the north of the forest.
280 square miles. Camping, cross-country skiing, hiking, fishing (yellow perch, northern pike), canoeing.

Hecla Provincial Park (3)
This island park supports red pines, unusual in northern Manitoba. Great blue herons and bald eagles nest on Hecla Island. The park and the mainland are linked by a one-mile causeway.
333 square miles. Camping, cross-country skiing, hiking, fishing (walleye, silver bass), canoeing, self-guiding nature trails.

Rivière aux Rats Canoe Route (9)
South of St. Malo, turbulent white water washes over ledges that once formed part of the beaches of Lake Agassiz, a glacial lake that covered this area more than two million years ago. *140 miles.*

Agassiz Provincial Forest (10)
275 square miles. Wilderness camping, cross-country skiing, hiking, fishing (northern pike, walleye, brook trout).

Sandilands Provincial Forest (11)
584 square miles. Wilderness camping, cross-country skiing, hiking, fishing (northern pike, walleye).

Oak Hammock Marsh Wildlife Management Area (6)
Each spring and fall some 250,000 snow, Canada and blue geese visit these uplands, marshes and grainfields—all within 10 miles of Winnipeg. Fourteen miles of dikes, used to control water levels, and 58 nesting islands have been built. *13 square miles.*

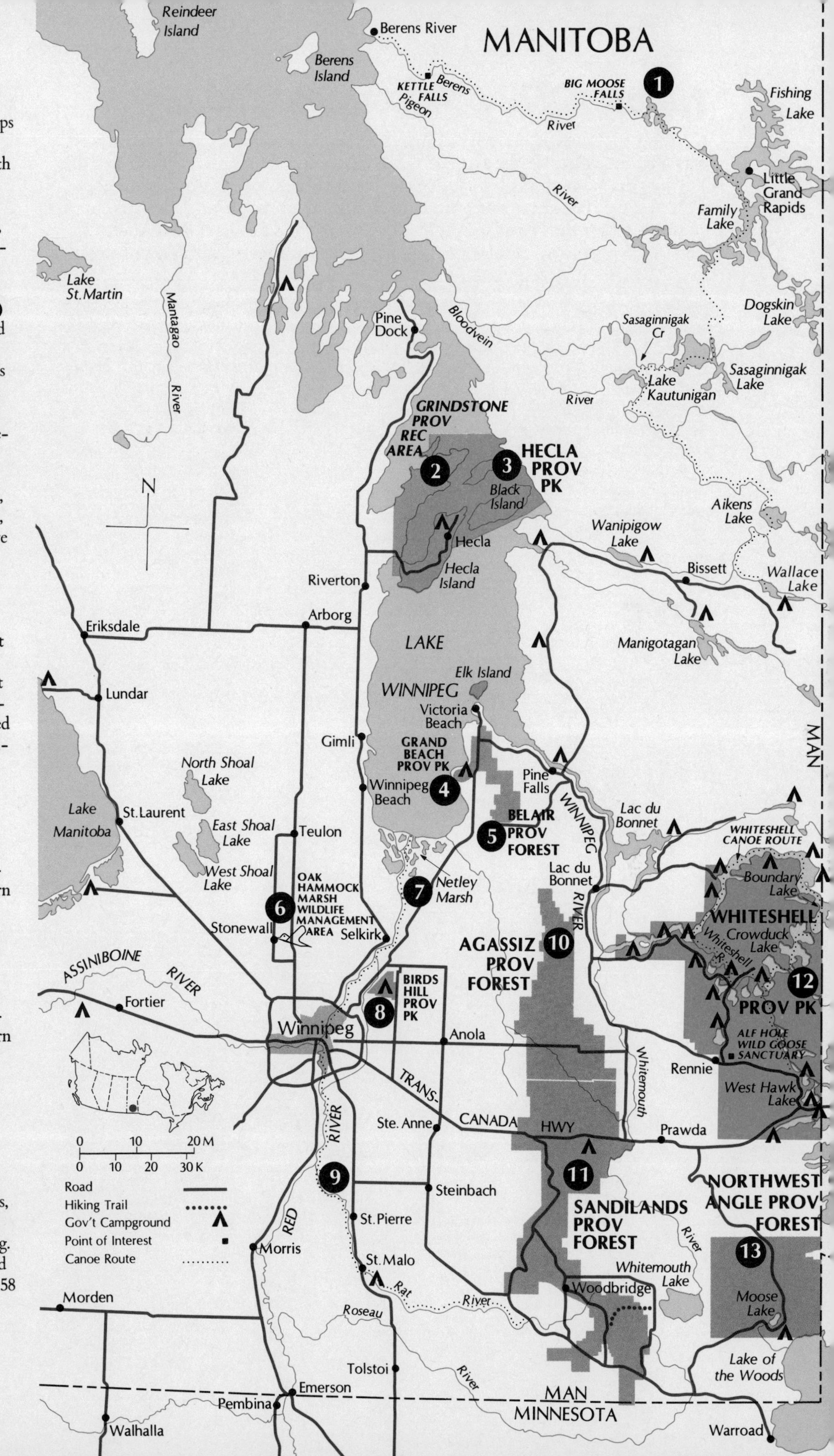

Along a Wild Watery Boundary

A string of lakes and rivers along the Canadian-American boundary was a main route to the furs of the Northwest from about 1780 to 1840. Today this watery highway evokes the wildness of its voyageur heritage. Along its course are bald eagles, burial mounds and the spectacular beauty of Quetico Provincial Park. Also in this area are Kakabeka's roaring waters and one of Ontario's most northerly pelican colonies.

Quetico Provincial Park (7)
Indian rock paintings of animals, canoes and tepees—some more than 2,000 years old—are on cliffs at 28 shoreline sites. Most of these paintings, 8 to 12 inches high, are 5 feet above the water (probably because the painters stood in canoes). Dams, locks and wagon roads along Quetico's Dawson Trail (completed in 1870) were used by troops sent to quell the Riel Rebellion in Manitoba. Among 61 bird species nesting in the park are bald eagles, great blue herons and ospreys. Twelve canoe routes range in length from 40 to 126 miles.
1,794 square miles. Camping, hiking, fishing (sturgeon, smallmouth bass, lake trout, northern pike), self-guiding nature trails, nature house.

Rushing River Provincial Park (1)
395 acres. Camping, cross-country skiing, fishing (walleye, northern pike), self-guiding nature trails.

Inwood Provincial Park (8)
81 acres. Camping, fishing (rainbow trout).

Boundary Waters Fur Trade Canoe Route (6)
Canoeists face 43 portages on this chain of lakes and rivers running through Canadian and U.S. territory. Sandy beaches and towering granite walls are found along the route. (A 600-foot-high cliff overlooks North Fowl and South Fowl lakes.) Near Grand Portage is 70-foot-high Partridge Falls and along Cherry Portage is a swamp where weirdly twisted white

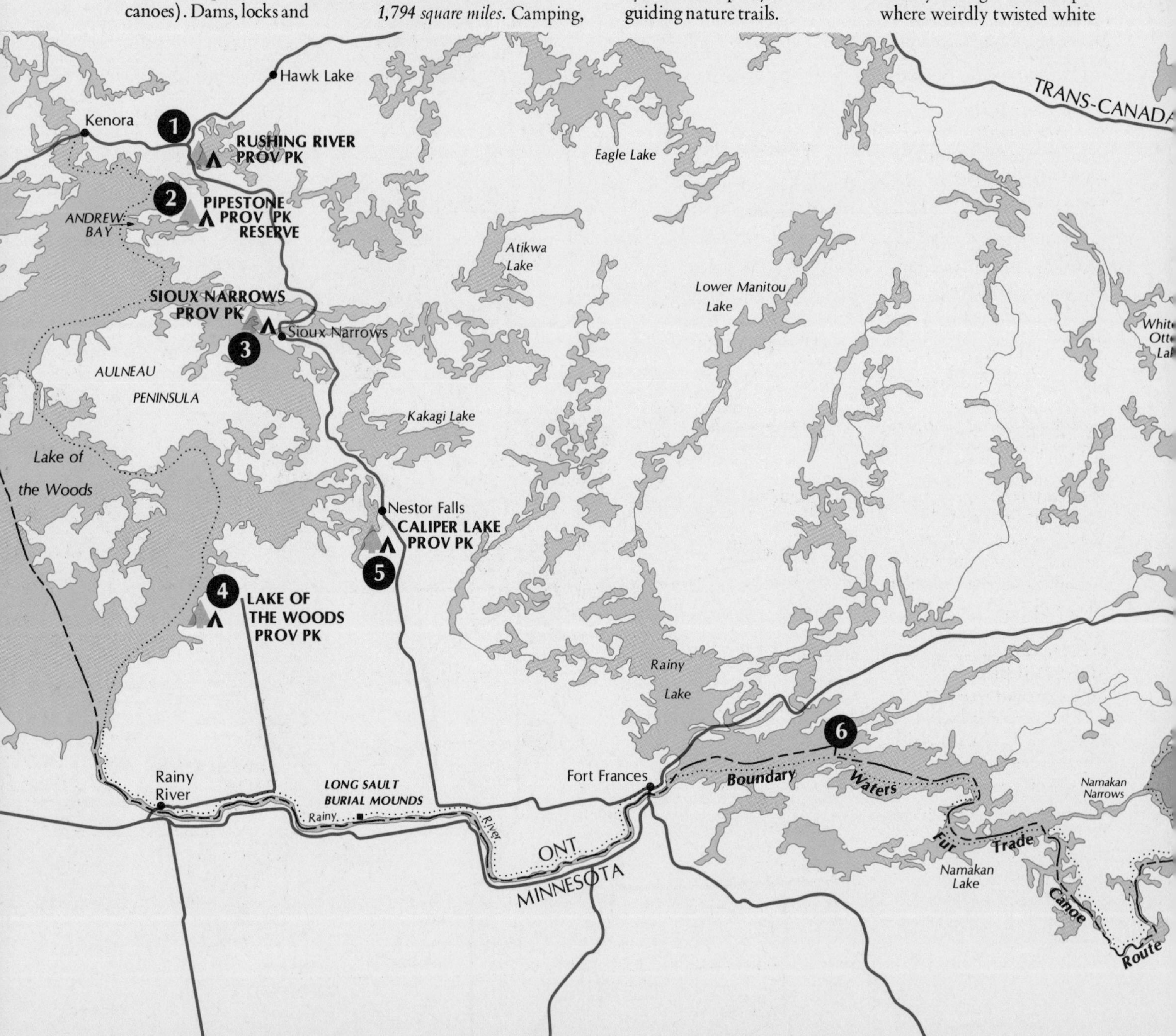

cedars grow. Faded Indian rock paintings can be seen in Namakan Narrows and 35 miles west of Fort Frances are the Long Sault burial mounds, the ancient graveyard of an Indian tribe that lived here for more than 1,000 years. Along the route is one of the last bald eagle breeding grounds in North America outside of Alaska. *325 miles.*

Sioux Narrows Provincial Park (3)
Nearby is Sioux Narrows, named after a massacre of Sioux Indians by Ojibway. *322 acres.* Camping, fishing (northern pike, walleye), self-guiding nature trails.

Pipestone Provincial Park Reserve (2)
This area of forest and steep outcrops can be reached by boating into Andrew Bay. *5.5 square miles.* Wilderness camping, fishing (northern pike, walleye, lake trout).

Lake of the Woods Provincial Park (4)
One of Ontario's most northerly pelican colonies nests on a small island in the park. Because of the warming influence of Lake of the Woods, stands of elm, poplar and basswood grow in an area normally dominated by coniferous forest. A high rock outcrop overlooks Lake of the Woods and many of its 14,632 islands. *4 square miles.* Camping, hiking, fishing (muskellunge, northern pike), canoeing, self-guiding nature trails.

Kakabeka Falls Provincial Park (9)
The Kaministikwia River roars through a steep-walled gorge after plummeting 108 feet over 326-foot-wide Kakabeka Falls. About 1,000 feet below the falls, the winds howl through the Cave of the Winds, making eerie noises that Indians believed were spirits of the wind. In the rock banks above the falls are fossils 2½ billion years old—among the oldest in the world. *1.5 square miles.* Camping, supervised swimming, cross-country skiing, fishing (walleye), canoeing, self-guiding nature trails.

Caliper Lake Provincial Park (5)
246 acres. Camping, fishing (walleye, northern pike), canoeing.

Middle Falls Provincial Park (10)
The Pigeon River drops over 150-foot High Falls, then races through a series of rapids. *3 square miles.* Camping, hiking, fishing (walleye, northern pike), canoeing.

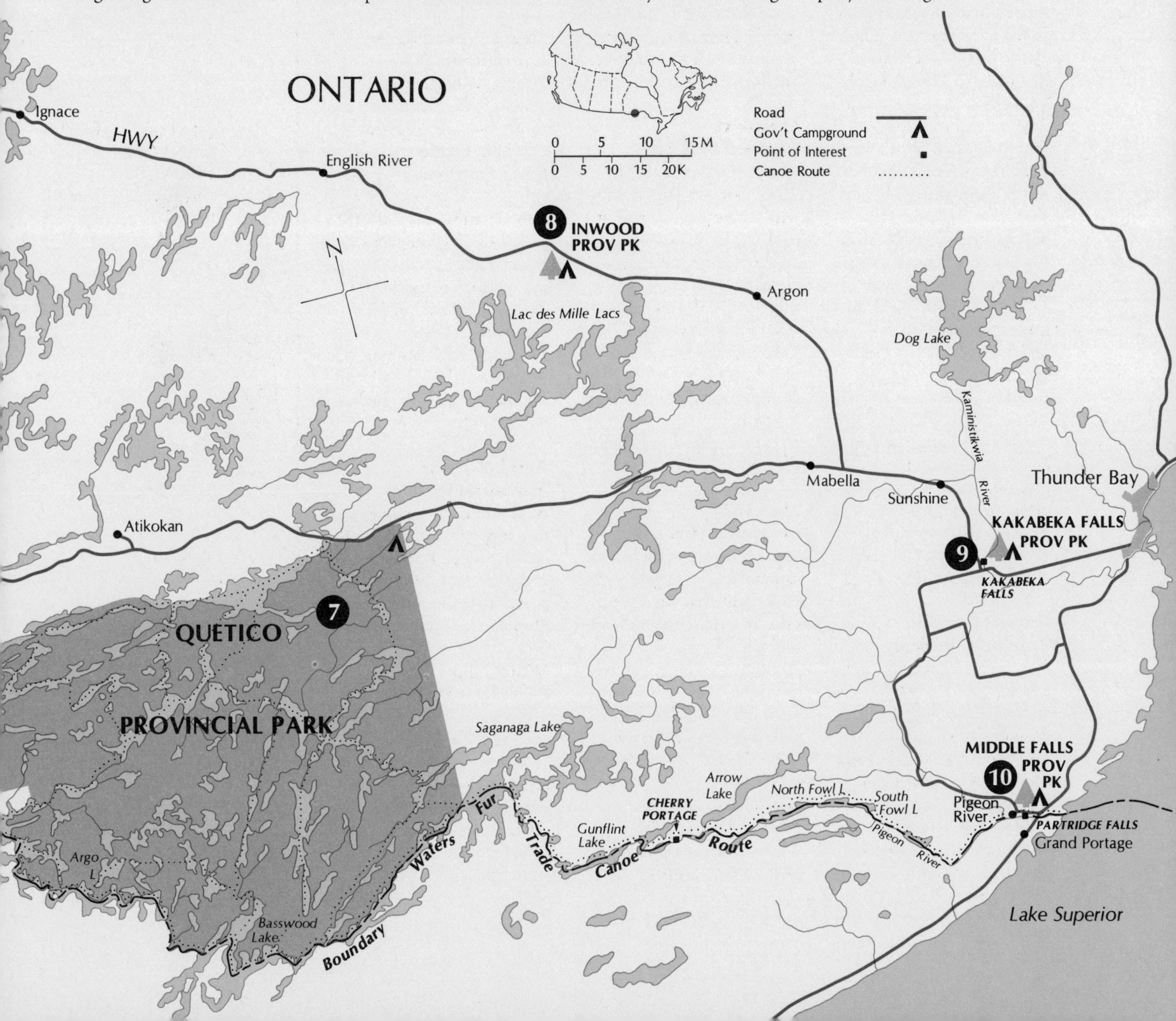

Towering Cliffs and a Great Trench Near the Shores of Lake Superior

Ontario's highest cliffs and The Sleeping Giant rear above the waters of Thunder Bay. Arctic plants thrive in remote Pukaskwa National Park and along the floor of Ouimet Canyon, a great trench carved by thousands of years of erosion. To the north are Lake Nipigon's 1,000 islands. Woodland caribou are seen in Neys Provincial Park and on nearby Pic Island. Near Thunder Cape is Silver Islet, site of a silver discovery in 1868.

Sibley Provincial Park (1)
The highest cliffs in Ontario—up to 800 feet high—are north of The Sleeping Giant, a hill that, when viewed from the city of Thunder Bay, resembles a prone man. Ravines in the park support green adder's mouth and yellow lady's-slipper, orchids not common to the area. The two-mile Piney Wood Hills Nature Trail, one of 12 trails in Sibley, ends at Joe Lake, a watering ground for moose. The four-mile Giant Fire Tower Trail rises 1,100 feet to a fire tower overlooking Thunder Bay. Near Thunder Cape is Silver Islet, a rocky island 80 feet across, where silver was discovered in 1868. More than $3 million worth of ore was mined before the shaft—which was 1,230 feet deep—filled with water and was closed in 1884. Some 200 bird species have been sighted in the park, including mourning doves, peregrine falcons, mockingbirds, spotted sandpipers and 14 duck species.
94 square miles. Camping, climbing, fishing (northern pike, brook trout).

Ouimet Canyon Provincial Park (2)
Rare arctic plants grow in this canyon, which is 500 feet wide and two miles long. Because the gorge's 350-foot-high walls block the sun, shallow depressions in the canyon floor provide a cooler growing habitat than normally found at this latitude. A carpet of moss is strewn with arctic wintergreen and several species of northern liverwort. Stunted cedar and birch trees cling to piles of eroded rock along the canyon bottom. Gnarled jackpine and spruce protrude from the canyon's rim. On the west wall is the Indian Head, a high rock pinnacle that resembles a human profile. The park is a nature preserve and has no camping facilities. *3 square miles.*

Pukaskwa National Park (10)
The park is dominated by 2,099-foot Tip Top Mountain. Arctic plants thrive in cool microclimates—small areas of localized climate—along the park's 50-mile shoreline. A 5½-mile hiking trail that skirts the shore of Lake Superior is accessible only by boat. A herd of up to 20 woodland caribou inhabits the park.
725 square miles. Camping, canoeing.

MacLeod Provincial Park (5)
Rock hounds still find an occasional nugget of gold in the park, located in what was once an important gold-mining area.
200 acres. Camping, supervised swimming, fishing (walleye, northern pike, whitefish and yellow perch), self-guiding nature trails.

Black Sand Provincial Park (3)
A two-mile trail leads to a lookout near 1,870-square-mile Lake Nipigon, Ontario's fifth largest lake. An Indian cemetery and the remains of a tribal village are in the park.
5 square miles. Camping, supervised swimming, fishing (walleye, northern pike, whitefish, lake and brook trout).

Steel Lake and River Canoe Route (7)
Fishing for northern pike and walleye is excellent along this route, and lake trout can be caught in Cairngorm and Steel lakes. *96 miles.*

Neys Provincial Park (8)
A mile-long white sand beach fringes Lake Superior. Woodland caribou roam the park and a small herd inhabits nearby Pic Island.
13 square miles. Camping, hiking, fishing (lake, brook and rainbow trout), self-guiding nature trails.

Rainbow Falls Provincial Park (4)
A one-mile self-guiding nature trail crosses a bridge over 300-foot-high Rainbow Falls.
2 square miles. Camping, supervised swimming, fishing (brook trout), canoeing.

White Lake Provincial Park (9)
6 square miles. Camping, supervised swimming, canoeing.

Klotz Lake Provincial Park (6)
210 acres. Camping, fishing (northern pike, walleye, whitefish).

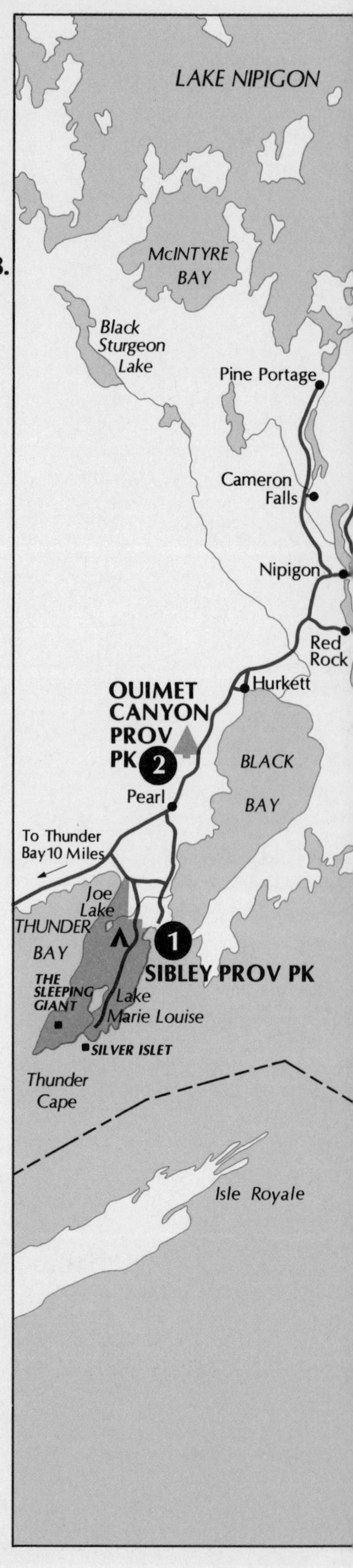

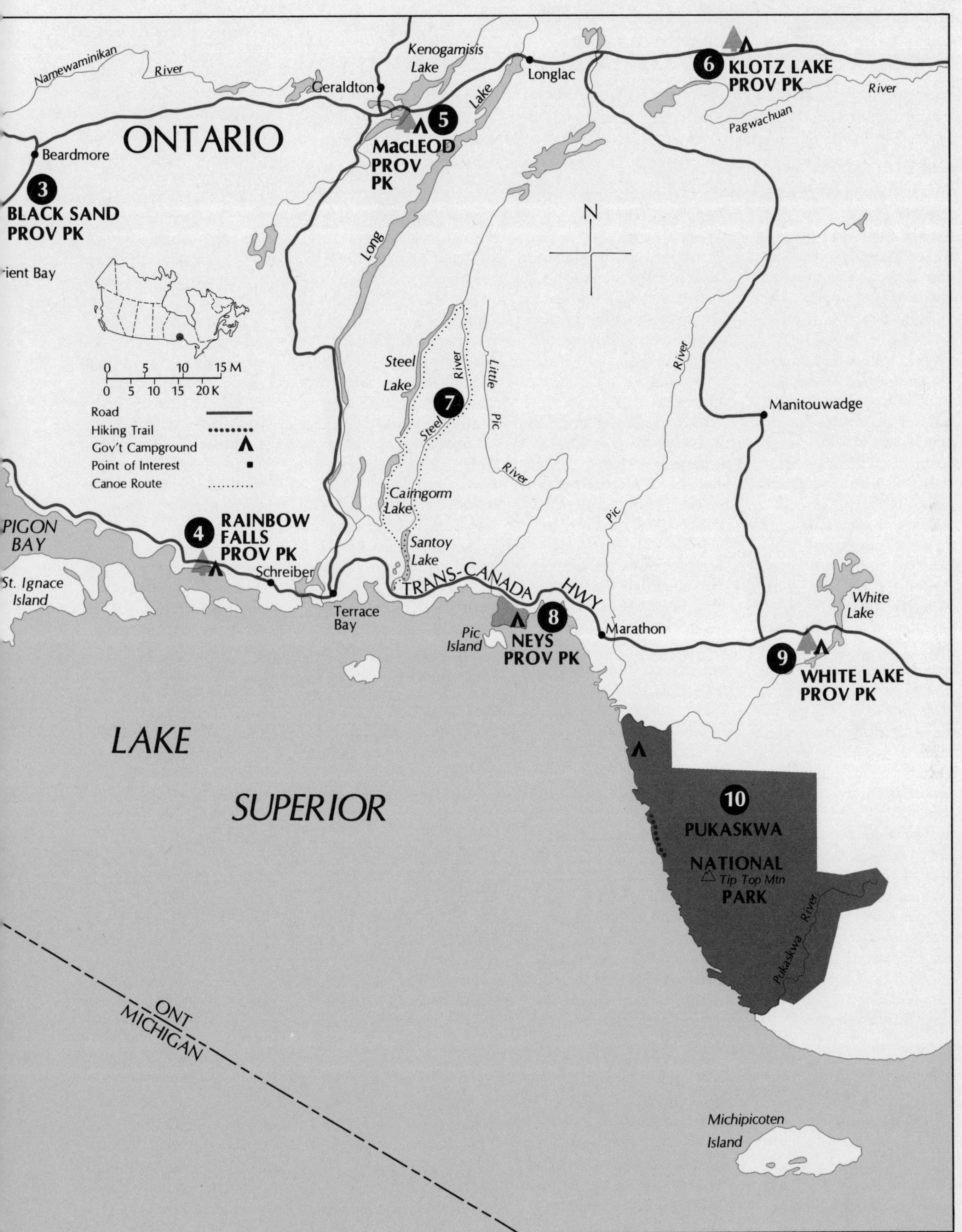

ONTARIO
Namewaminikan
River
Kenogamisis
Lake
Geraldton
Longlac
6 KLOTZ LAKE PROV PK
River
Pagwachuan
5 MacLEOD PROV PK
Lake
Long
Beardmore
3 BLACK SAND PROV PK
rient Bay
N
0 5 10 15 M
0 5 10 15 20 K
Road
Hiking Trail
Gov't Campground
Point of Interest
Canoe Route
Steel Lake
River
Steel
7
Little Pic River
River
Pic
Manitouwadge
Cairngorm Lake
Santoy Lake
PIGON BAY
4 RAINBOW FALLS PROV PK
Schreiber
St. Ignace Island
Terrace Bay
TRANS-CANADA HWY
Pic Island
8 NEYS PROV PK
Marathon
White Lake
9 WHITE LAKE PROV PK
LAKE
SUPERIOR
10
PUKASKWA NATIONAL PARK
Tip Top Mtn
Pukaskwa River
ONT
MICHIGAN
Michipicoten Island

A Land of Splendid Scenery and Abundant Wildlife

Indian rock paintings can be seen in Lake Superior's Agawa Bay and on Fairy Point in Missinaibi Lake. On the Mississagi River are forbidding Hellgate Rapids and picturesque Aubrey Falls. Wapiti roam the Brunswick Wilderness Area in Missinaibi Lake Provincial Park.

Lake Superior Provincial Park (7)
A crested serpent and a horned panther are among 37 Indian rock paintings—thought to be more than 200 years old—found on overhanging cliffs on Agawa Bay. Shoreline terraces, some more than 200 feet high, are the remains of ancient beaches raised by upward shifts in the earth's crust. Dunes, sandspits and water-blasted caves are common along the shore. Kames (mounds of stratified gravel left by glaciers) and eskers (sand and gravel ridges) are found in the park. More than 160 bird species have been sighted in deciduous forests and boreal woodlands here. Southern species such as scarlet tanagers and bobolinks share the forests with purple finches, pine siskins and northern three-toed woodpeckers—all northern birds. The 35½-mile Sand River Canoe Route drops 600 feet along a course that includes Calwin and Lady Evelyn falls (each about 30 feet high) and a rapid- and boulder-strewn gorge.
601 square miles. Camping, hiking, fishing (northern pike, brook and lake trout), self-guiding nature trails.

Chapleau Crown Game Preserve (1)
Moose, bears, lynx, mink and otters are among the animals that roam here in one of North America's largest game preserves.
2,840 square miles. Camping, fishing (northern pike, walleye, whitefish, brook, lake and rainbow trout).

Mississagi River Canoe Route (11)
At Aubrey Falls the Mississagi River tumbles more than 100 feet in three steps. South of Snowshoe Creek the river enters a narrow gorge some 300 feet deep. *90 miles.*

Mississagi Provincial Park and Park Reserve (15)
Rippled rock—solidified sand shaped by waves millions of years ago—is seen along the half-mile Flack Lake Nature Trail. Some of the 200 lakes in the park reserve are visible from the Wilkie Fire Tower, 1,850 feet above sea level. Between Mount and Flack lakes the 35-mile Boland River Canoe Route cuts through virgin forests and black spruce swamps. Bitterns, herons, grebes and sandpipers nest along the route.
158 square miles. Camping, fishing (yellow perch, whitefish, lake and rainbow trout), self-guiding nature trails.

Missinaibi Lake Provincial Park (3)
One of Ontario's few herds of wapiti roams the nine-acre Brunswick Wilderness Area, once the site of New Brunswick House, a Hudson's Bay Company post established in 1879. On Fairy Point, a 250-foot cliff bordering Missinaibi Lake, are Indian paintings of animals and a setting sun. The lake has a 130-mile shoreline of granite outcrops and sandy beaches. Whitefish Falls drops 60 feet in 100 yards on the Little Missinaibi River.
176 square miles. Camping, fishing (northern pike, yellow perch, brook stickleback, whitefish, lake trout, smallmouth bass).

The Shoals Provincial Park (6)
A five-mile ridge crosses the park and fans out into a delta of smaller ridges at Little Wawa Lake. Nearby are kettle holes—deep hollows formed in rock by melting glacial ice. The half-mile Black Spruce Trail leads to a bog in which insect-eating pitcher plants and round-leaved sundews grow. The 25-mile Shoals Loop Canoe Route has 13 portages, none longer than 300 yards.
68 square miles. Camping, fishing (walleye, northern pike).

Obatanga Provincial Park (2)
Red-tailed hawks, ruffed grouse and 15 duck species are seen on marshy lakes here. Pink lady's-slipper grows in forests and bogs.
36 square miles. Camping, fishing (northern pike, walleye), canoeing.

Wakami Lake Provincial Park (13)
34 square miles. Camping, hiking, fishing (northern pike, walleye, whitefish, brook trout), self-guiding nature trails.

Pancake Bay Provincial Park (9)
A two-mile-long sand beach borders Lake Superior.
1.5 square miles. Camping, hiking, fishing (rainbow trout, coho salmon, yellow perch).

Chapleau-Nemegosenda River Provincial Park (4)
This canoe route and its shores were established as a provincial park to preserve the natural splendor of this rugged chain of lakes and rivers—dotted with waterfalls, rapids and granite cliffs. Spring-fed Emerald Lake is noted for its clear blue-green waters. Wilderness camping is permitted within the park's boundaries—400 feet back from the banks of the route.
145 miles. Fishing (northern pike, walleye).

Five Mile Lake Provincial Park (12)
1.5 square miles. Camping, fishing (walleye, northern pike, brook trout), canoeing, self-guiding nature trails.

Goulais River Canoe Route (10)
The Goulais River rushes through 1,200 feet of rapids before dropping 40 feet at Twin Falls. *40 miles.*

Batchawana River Canoe Route (8)
Sheer cliff faces from 200 to 500 feet high border the north shore of the Batchawana River along the first four miles of the route.
30 miles.

Mississagi Wild River Provincial Park (14)
The Mississagi River is now preserved as a provincial park between Rocky Island and Biscotasi lakes. Hellgate Rapids tumbles through a narrow, steep-walled gorge.
76 square miles. Wilderness camping, fishing (northern pike, walleye).

Ivanhoe Lake Provincial Park (5)
4.5 square miles. Camping, fishing (walleye, northern pike, brook trout), canoeing, self-guiding nature trails.

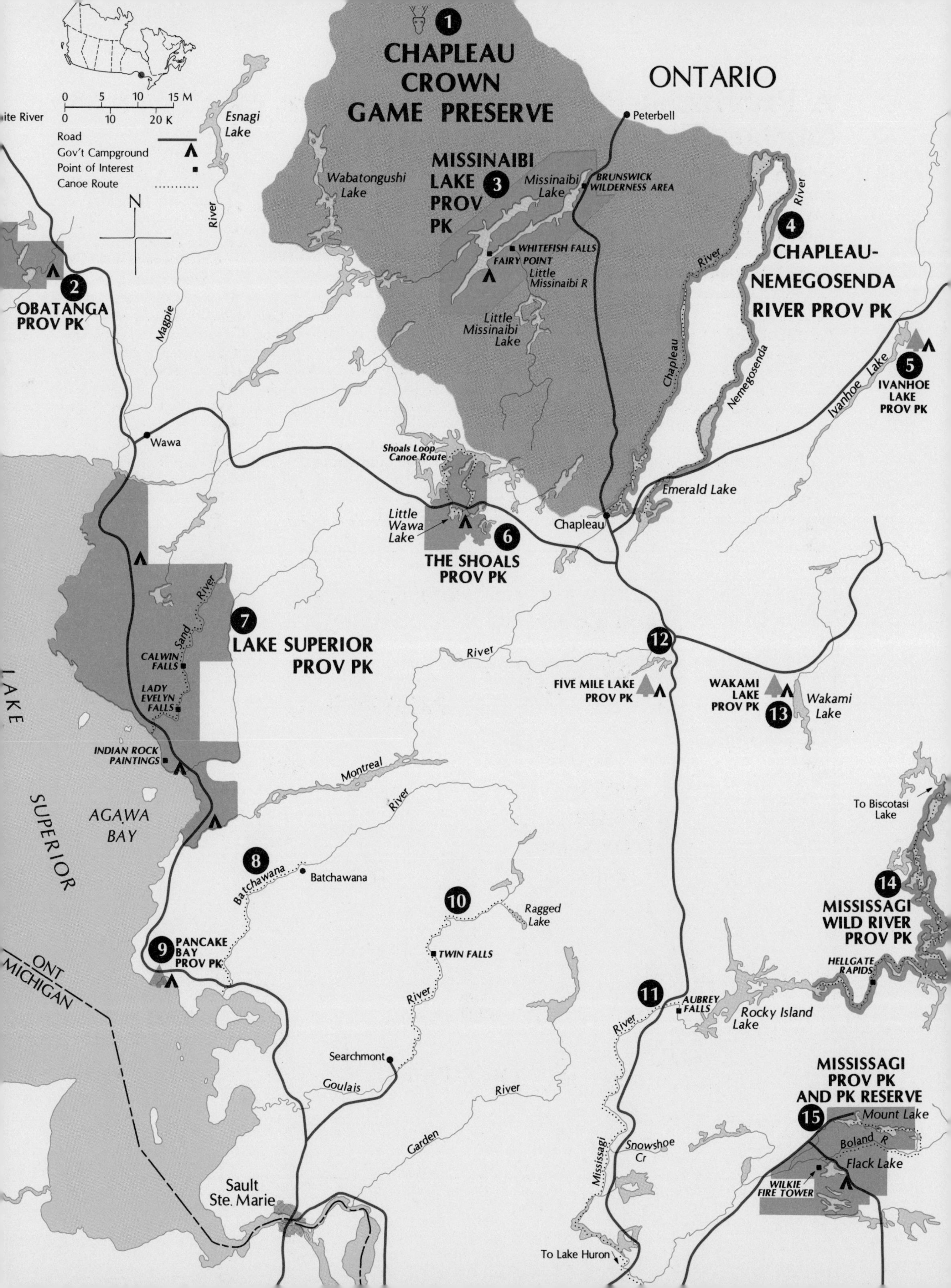

1
CHAPLEAU CROWN GAME PRESERVE
ONTARIO
0 5 10 15 M
0 10 20 K
Road
Gov't Campground
Point of Interest
Canoe Route
N
ite River
Esnagi Lake
Peterbell
MISSINAIBI LAKE PROV PK
3
Wabatongushi Lake
Missinaibi Lake
BRUNSWICK WILDERNESS AREA
River
4
CHAPLEAU-NEMEGOSENDA RIVER PROV PK
WHITEFISH FALLS
FAIRY POINT
Little Missinaibi R
Little Missinaibi Lake
River
2
OBATANGA PROV PK
Magpie
Chapleau
Nemegosenda
Ivanhoe Lake
5
IVANHOE LAKE PROV PK
Wawa
Shoals Loop Canoe Route
Emerald Lake
Little Wawa Lake
6
THE SHOALS PROV PK
Chapleau
7
LAKE SUPERIOR PROV PK
Sand
River
CALWIN FALLS
LADY EVELYN FALLS
River
12
FIVE MILE LAKE PROV PK
WAKAMI LAKE PROV PK
13
Wakami Lake
LAKE
SUPERIOR
INDIAN ROCK PAINTINGS
Montreal
River
AGAWA BAY
To Biscotasi Lake
8
Batchawana
Batchawana
10
Ragged Lake
14
MISSISSAGI WILD RIVER PROV PK
9
PANCAKE BAY PROV PK
TWIN FALLS
HELLGATE RAPIDS
ONT
MICHIGAN
River
11
AUBREY FALLS
Rocky Island Lake
River
Searchmont
Goulais
River
MISSISSAGI PROV PK AND PK RESERVE
15
Mount Lake
Garden
Snowshoe Cr
Boland R
Flack Lake
Mississagi
Sault Ste. Marie
WILKIE FIRE TOWER
To Lake Huron

A Provincial Park With Polar Bears, Caribou, Whales, Walrus and Seals

Polar bears and beluga whales inhabit Polar Bear Provincial Park, a remote expanse of arctic tundra and limestone ridges where Hudson Bay and James Bay meet. Winding eastward from Lansdowne House is a challenging canoe route on the Attawapiskat River. Some 350 miles to the south, near Georgian Bay's northeastern shore, are Killarney Provincial Park and an historic canoe route on the French River.

Polar Bear Provincial Park (1)
On eight-mile-long Cape Henrietta Maria, at the northeast corner of the park (where Hudson Bay and James Bay meet), is one of the world's most southerly extensions of arctic tundra. The cape is dotted with shallow lakes, most less than two feet deep, and lined with limestone ridges. Trees are few but hardy plants such as cloudberry, milk vetch and rock cranberry thrive. Mud flats are exposed along the cape at low tide. Ice drifts offshore as late as August. Polar bears, arctic foxes and caribou roam the park; beluga whales, walrus and bearded seals are seen in adjacent waters; golden eagles nest on cliffs up to 100 feet high along the Winisk River. Access to Polar Bear Park is by boat or by plane from Moosonee.
9,300 square miles. Wilderness camping, fishing (whitefish, brook trout), canoeing.

Winisk River Provincial Park (2)
The heart of the park is a 238-mile canoe route through a wild and remote land populated by polar bears, caribou and arctic foxes. The route leaves the park and continues 32 miles to Winisk.
649 square miles. Wilderness camping, fishing (brook trout).

Canoe Route (Lansdowne House to Attawapiskat) (3)
Fossilized corals and sponges more than 225 million years old are embedded in vertical cliffs along the Attawapiskat River. Pillarlike islands up to 20 feet high rise above the river's channels. In September thousands of ducks and geese visit grassy marshes at the mouth of the river. Lansdowne House is accessible by seaplane from Moosonee.
320 miles.

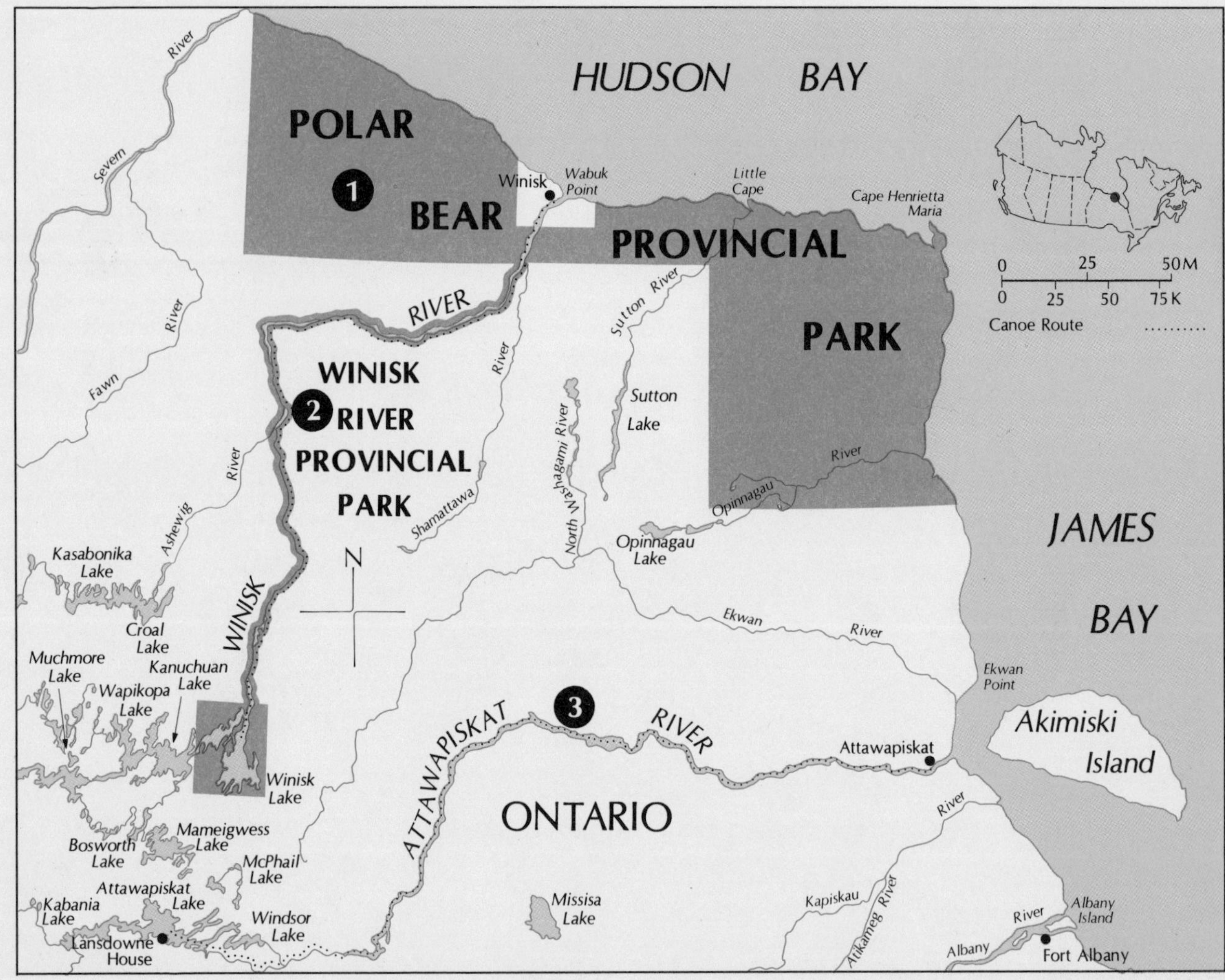

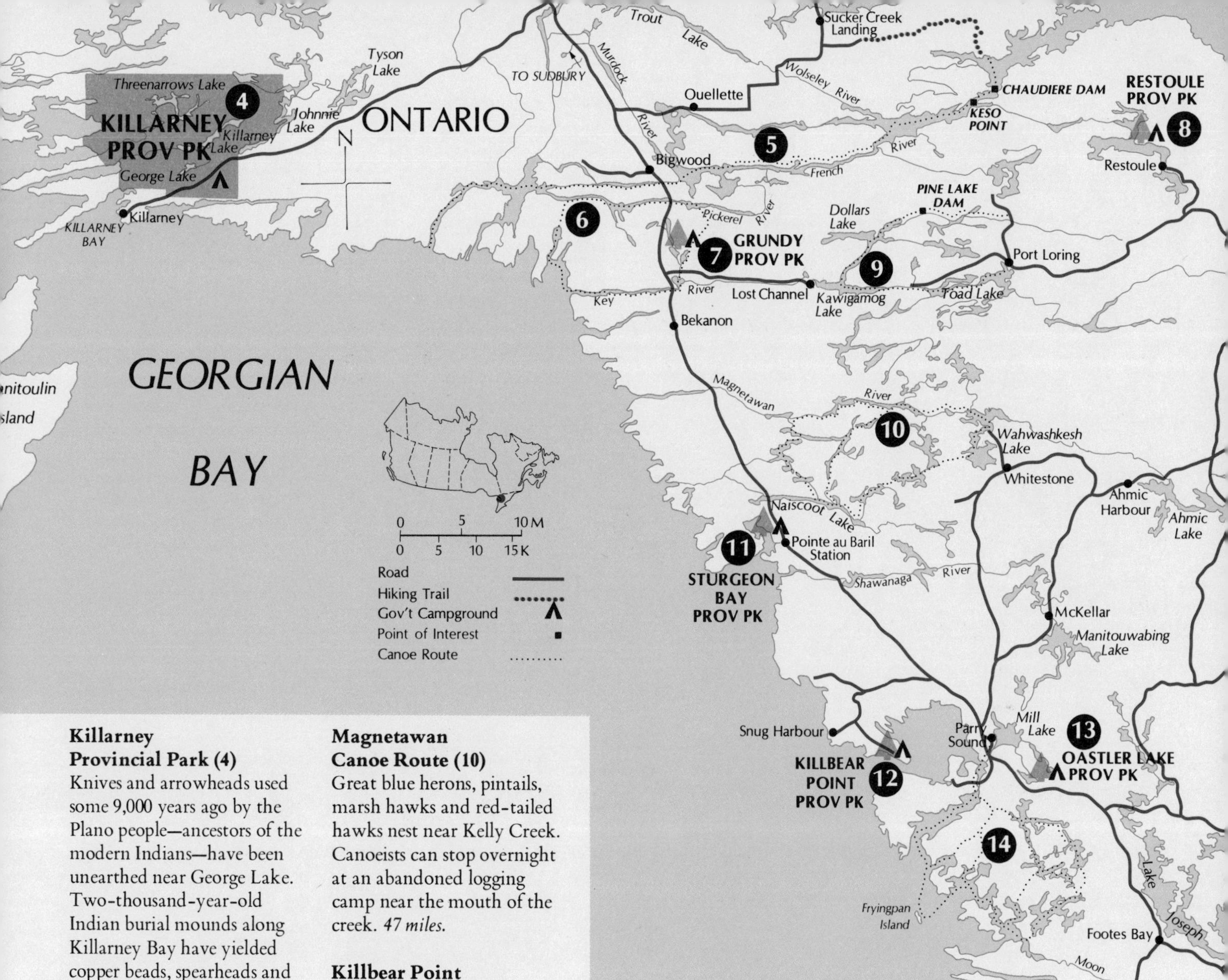

Killarney Provincial Park (4)
Knives and arrowheads used some 9,000 years ago by the Plano people—ancestors of the modern Indians—have been unearthed near George Lake. Two-thousand-year-old Indian burial mounds along Killarney Bay have yielded copper beads, spearheads and the remains of woven baskets. White quartzite outcrops contrast with the pink and gray granite common in the region.
133 square miles. Camping, climbing, cross-country skiing, hiking, canoeing, self-guiding nature trails.

French River Canoe Route (5)
The French River, part of an old voyageur route linking Montreal and Lake Superior, is a maze of channels, secluded bays and countless rapids and falls. Kettles—waterworn holes in rock—can be seen near Chaudiere Dam. There are Indian rock paintings on granite outcrops near Keso Point. *60 miles.*

Magnetawan Canoe Route (10)
Great blue herons, pintails, marsh hawks and red-tailed hawks nest near Kelly Creek. Canoeists can stop overnight at an abandoned logging camp near the mouth of the creek. *47 miles.*

Killbear Point Provincial Park (12)
Some 2½ miles of sand beach (unusually long on Georgian Bay) and three rocky headlands are in the park. In winter, up to 300 deer gather here in deeryards (areas sheltered from snow by overhanging branches).
4.5 square miles. Camping, hiking, fishing (smallmouth bass, northern pike), canoeing, self-guiding nature trails.

Sturgeon Bay Provincial Park (11)
The massasauga rattlesnake, an endangered species and the only venomous snake in eastern Canada, is found here.
20 acres. Camping, fishing (northern pike, smallmouth bass, walleye), canoeing.

Smoked Pickerel Canoe Route (14)
A stone cross on Fryingpan Island commemorates Champlain's first journey through this area some 350 years ago. *49 miles.*

Pickerel River Canoe Route (6)
Pine trees bent by westerly winds can be seen along Georgian Bay. Granite cliffs up to 100 feet high border the Key and Pickerel rivers. *36 miles.*

Oastler Lake Provincial Park (13)
49 acres. Camping, fishing (smallmouth bass), canoeing.

Restoule Provincial Park (8)
3.5 square miles. Camping, fishing (lake trout, yellow perch, smallmouth bass, walleye), canoeing, self-guiding nature trails.

Grundy Provincial Park (7)
10 square miles. Camping, supervised swimming, hiking, fishing (northern pike, walleye, yellow perch), canoeing, self-guiding nature trails.

Wolf and Pickerel Canoe Route (9)
A spring bubbles to the surface near Pine Lake Dam. *32 miles.*

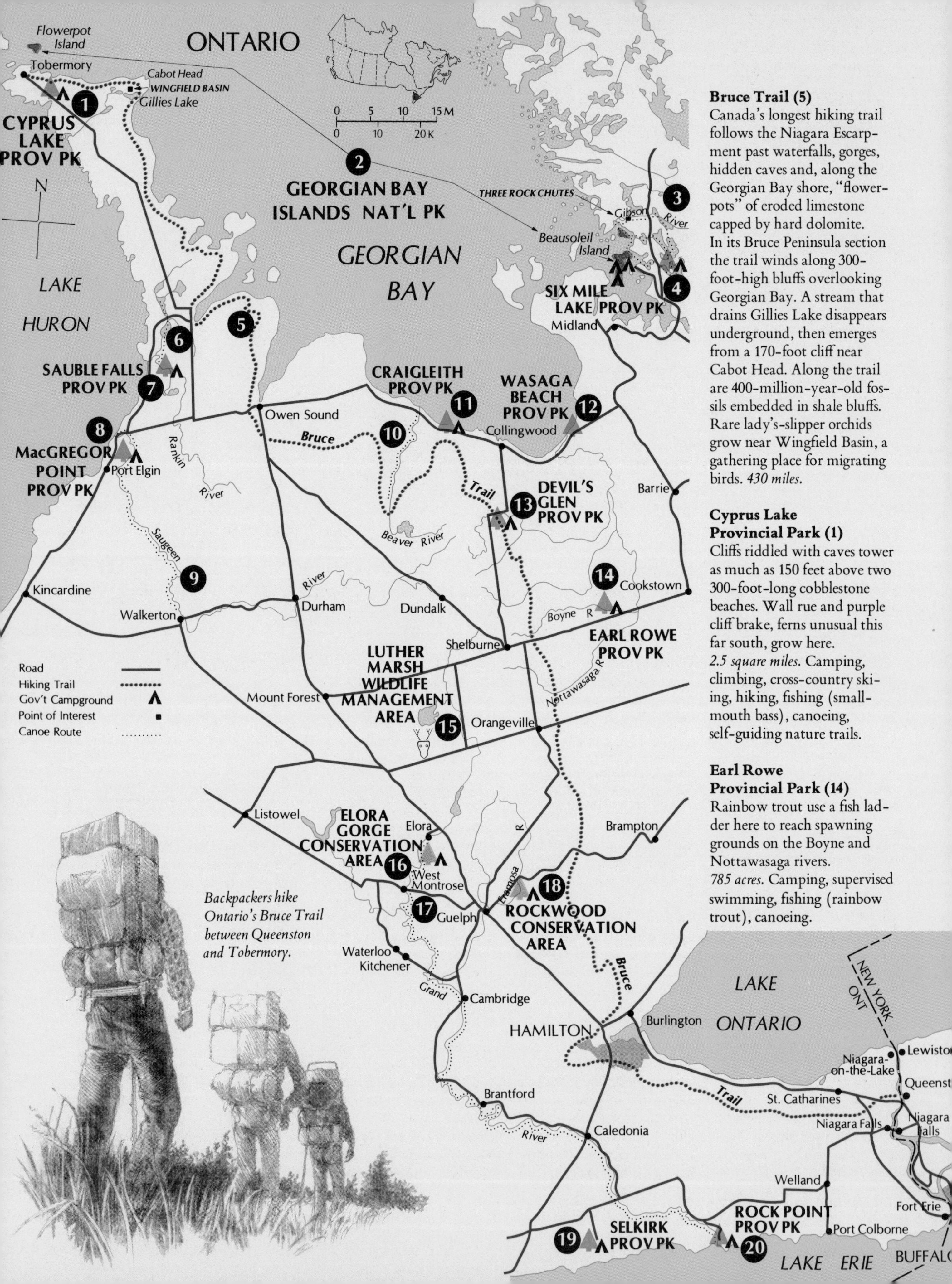

Backpackers hike Ontario's Bruce Trail between Queenston and Tobermory.

Bruce Trail (5)
Canada's longest hiking trail follows the Niagara Escarpment past waterfalls, gorges, hidden caves and, along the Georgian Bay shore, "flowerpots" of eroded limestone capped by hard dolomite. In its Bruce Peninsula section the trail winds along 300-foot-high bluffs overlooking Georgian Bay. A stream that drains Gillies Lake disappears underground, then emerges from a 170-foot cliff near Cabot Head. Along the trail are 400-million-year-old fossils embedded in shale bluffs. Rare lady's-slipper orchids grow near Wingfield Basin, a gathering place for migrating birds. *430 miles.*

Cyprus Lake Provincial Park (1)
Cliffs riddled with caves tower as much as 150 feet above two 300-foot-long cobblestone beaches. Wall rue and purple cliff brake, ferns unusual this far south, grow here. *2.5 square miles.* Camping, climbing, cross-country skiing, hiking, fishing (smallmouth bass), canoeing, self-guiding nature trails.

Earl Rowe Provincial Park (14)
Rainbow trout use a fish ladder here to reach spawning grounds on the Boyne and Nottawasaga rivers. *785 acres.* Camping, supervised swimming, fishing (rainbow trout), canoeing.

Flowerpot Island, 'Hole-in-the-Rock' and Canada's Longest Hiking Trail

The Bruce Trail, Canada's longest hiking trail, links Queenston (near Niagara Falls) and Tobermory at the tip of the Bruce Peninsula. The trail crosses southwestern Ontario's heartland, an area rich in provincial parks and conservation areas. Here are the pillars of Flowerpot Island, Elora Gorge's Hole-in-the-Rock, Georgian Bay Islands National Park and, at West Montrose, Ontario's only covered bridge.

Saugeen River Canoe Route (9)
The Saugeen River originates near Dundalk, one of the highest points in southwestern Ontario, and flows between forested banks to Lake Huron. *62 miles.*

Georgian Bay Islands National Park (2)
Endangered massasauga rattlesnakes inhabit swamps on Beausoleil Island, one of 50 islands in the park. On Flowerpot Island, 100 miles northwest of the others, waves have shaped two rock pillars, 50 and 35 feet high. Caves, some more than 60 feet deep, and sheer limestone cliffs can be seen on the island.
5.5 square miles. Camping, hiking, fishing (northern pike, muskellunge, yellow perch, sturgeon, brook, brown and lake trout), canoeing, self-guiding nature trails.

Sauble Falls Provincial Park (7)
43 acres. Camping, fishing (Chinook salmon, smallmouth bass, rainbow trout), canoeing.

Wasaga Beach Provincial Park (12)
Sand dunes up to 150 feet high support plants rare in Canada, among them green-leaved rattlesnake plantain and ram's-head and fairy slipper orchids.
350 acres. Supervised swimming, cross-country skiing, fishing (walleye, smallmouth bass, northern pike), canoeing, self-guiding nature trails.

MacGregor Point Provincial Park (8)
4 square miles. Camping, hiking, fishing (smallmouth bass, yellow perch), self-guiding nature trails.

Six Mile Lake Provincial Park (4)
177 acres. Camping, fishing (smallmouth and largemouth bass, northern pike, muskellunge, walleye), canoeing.

Six Mile Lake Canoe Route (3)
The Gibson River splits into three 20-foot-high waterfalls at Three Rock Chutes. Buttonbush, a shrub seldom found this far north, grows along the route. *35 miles.*

Devil's Glen Provincial Park (13)
A lookout provides a view of Devil's Glen, a gorge some 2,500 feet wide and 500 feet deep.
28 acres. Camping, hiking, fishing (Chinook salmon, smallmouth bass).

Rankin River Canoe Route (6)
The Rankin River meanders past forested sand dunes and fields of wild rice. *11 miles.*

Beaver River Canoe Route (10)
Only experienced canoeists should attempt this route, which is dotted with rapids, limestone cliffs and flooded forests. *18 miles.*

Elora Gorge Conservation Area (16)
Islet Rock, 50 feet high, stands in the middle of swift rapids in the Grand River. Hikers on the south side of the river pass through Hole-in-the-Rock, a small cave, and follow paths and steps to the bottom of the gorge.
300 acres. Camping, supervised swimming, hiking, fishing (yellow perch, smallmouth bass), canoeing.

Craigleith Provincial Park (11)
Hundreds of limestone terraces, each an inch or two higher than the one before, stretch back 50 feet from the Georgian Bay shore. They contain fossils of marine creatures that inhabited a sea which covered this region 375 million years ago.
27 acres. Camping, hiking, fishing (rainbow trout, yellow perch).

Rockwood Conservation Area (18)
Along the Eramosa River are some 200 potholes up to 40 feet deep and 20 feet across, formed by the grinding of stones caught in the eddies of glacial meltwater streams.
197 acres. Camping, supervised swimming, cross-country skiing, fishing (largemouth and smallmouth bass), self-guiding nature trails.

Luther Marsh Wildlife Management Area (15)
More than 15,000 ducks and geese visit man-made Luther Marsh each fall. Among the birds found here are great blue herons, black-crowned night herons, hooded mergansers and blue-winged teal.
27 square miles.

Rock Point Provincial Park (20)
Fossilized corals up to 400 million years old are embedded in a limestone shelf at the base of 40-foot-high cliffs.
273 acres. Camping, fishing (yellow perch).

Selkirk Provincial Park (19)
180 acres. Camping, cross-country skiing, fishing (northern pike, yellow perch), canoeing, self-guiding nature trails.

Grand River Canoe Route (17)
At West Montrose, on the Grand River, is Ontario's only covered bridge, a 200-footer. *116 miles.*

Birds Get Surgery, X-Ray, Heat Lamp

Canada has a unique "hospital" for birds of prey: the 1½-acre Owl Rehabilitation Research Foundation operating since 1969 near Vineland, Ont. Each year the center cares for some 95 owls, hawks and falcons—crippled usually by gunshot and trapping wounds or collisions with such objects as towers and cars. Treatment may include surgery, x-ray and heat lamp therapy and antibiotic drugs. Rehabilitated birds readapt to the wild in flight pens that closely resemble an owl's natural habitat. Once recovered, birds are released within their species range, usually near where they were injured. Because birds here are sensitive to outside disturbance, visitors are allowed by appointment only.

Rondeau and Pelee: Showpieces on Canada's Southernmost Shore

Jutting into Lake Erie at the southernmost tip of the Canadian mainland is Point Pelee National Park. Pelee's gentle climate nurtures exotic plants and animals and attracts swarms of colorful birds. Nearby is Rondeau Provincial Park, a haven for rare Fowler's toads and hog-nosed snakes. To the east, and north of Lake Ontario, are the Warsaw Caves, Algonkian Indian petroglyphs and strange Serpent Mounds. Hikers can explore Minesing Swamp on the 250-mile Ganaraska Trail.

Point Pelee National Park (1)
The park, at the same latitude as Rome and northern California, lies on an 11-mile-long sand spit at the southernmost tip of the Canadian mainland. The mild climate and Lake Erie's warming influence—the shallow lake moderates temperature changes—give Point Pelee one of the longest frost-free growing seasons in Canada. Among 600 plant species here are white sassafras, hop tree, spicebush and fragrant sumac—plants found nowhere else in Ontario. Prickly-pear cactus, found mostly in semi-arid regions, and pink swamp rose mallow, Canada's only wild hibiscus, also occur. Mammals rare at this latitude include Baird's white-footed mice, evening bats and eastern moles. Two migratory flyways overlap in the park and more than 300 bird species have been recorded, including Lapland longspurs, short-billed dowitchers, parasitic jaegers and chuck-will's-widows. Ruby-throated hummingbirds, Carolina wrens, blue-gray gnatcatchers and Louisiana water thrushes are among roughly 100 species which nest here.
6 square miles. Camping, fishing (northern pike, yellow perch, largemouth bass), self-guiding nature trails.

Rondeau Provincial Park (3)
Of 15 parasitic wasp species identified here in 1972, 5 were previously unknown and 10 had never been reported in Canada. Nesting here are Acadian flycatchers, prothonotary warblers and white-eyed vireos, birds found nowhere else in Canada. Opossums and gray foxes—animals usually seen farther south—roam here. Rare hog-nosed snakes and Fowler's toads, both nearly extinct in Ontario, are among the park's 32 species of reptiles and amphibians. The endangered soft-shelled turtle can be seen along the five-mile Marsh Nature Trail. One of the province's few Carolinian forests (made up of sassafras, shagbark hickory and black, tulip and chestnut oak) grows here.
18 square miles. Camping, supervised swimming, fishing (bluegill, yellow perch), horseback riding, nature house.

Wheatley Provincial Park (2)
Black gum trees and flowering dogwood, both rare in Ontario, grow here.
600 acres. Camping, supervised swimming, fishing (yellow perch, carp).

Iroquois Beach Provincial Park (4)
Green alder, a plant seldom found this far south, thrives alongside pink swamp rose mallow (a flower native to Florida) in a swamp at the base of 65-foot bluffs.
640 acres. Camping, supervised swimming, fishing (yellow perch).

Ganaraska Trail (14)
The trail skirts 20,000-acre Minesing Swamp, home of snapping turtles, star-nosed moles, muskrats and, in summer, some 160 species of birds. Southern Ontario's largest stands of tamarack grow in the swamp. Two-thirds of the trail is blazed; it is incomplete between Emily Provincial Park and Orillia. *250 miles.*

Warsaw Caves Conservation Area (12)
Ten thousand years ago the Indian River percolated through limestone to create an intricate network of subterranean caves and passages here. In 280-foot-long Glacière Cave year-round temperatures rarely exceed 0°C. (32°F.). Above ground the river flows between 100-foot-high walls, then passes hills filled with kettles (holes eroded by boulders caught in swirling water). The largest kettle, 15 feet deep, narrows from 7 feet at the top to 3 feet at the bottom. A 15-foot-high waterfall in the river vanishes underground at low water, exposing a rock bridge. Near-

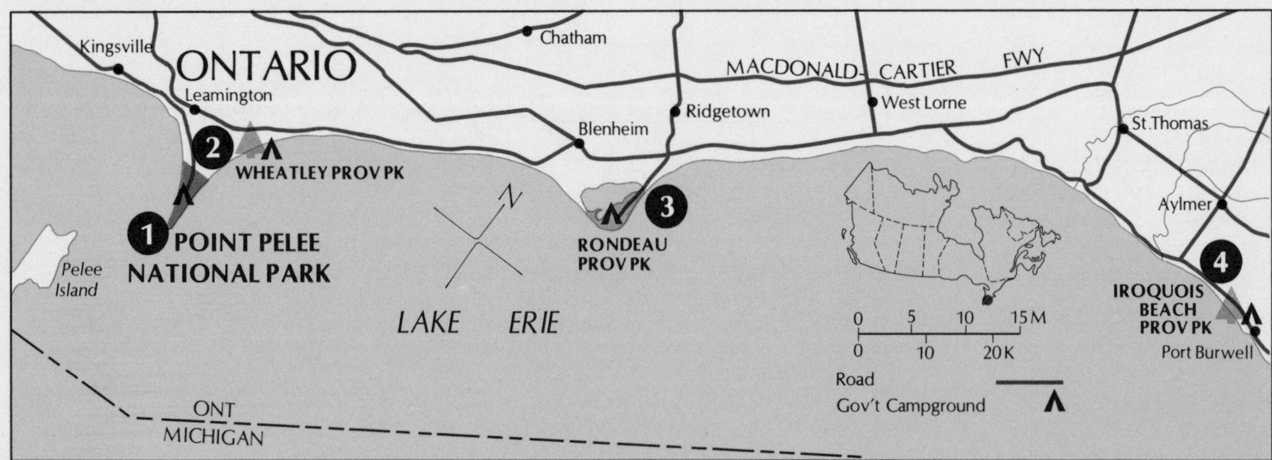

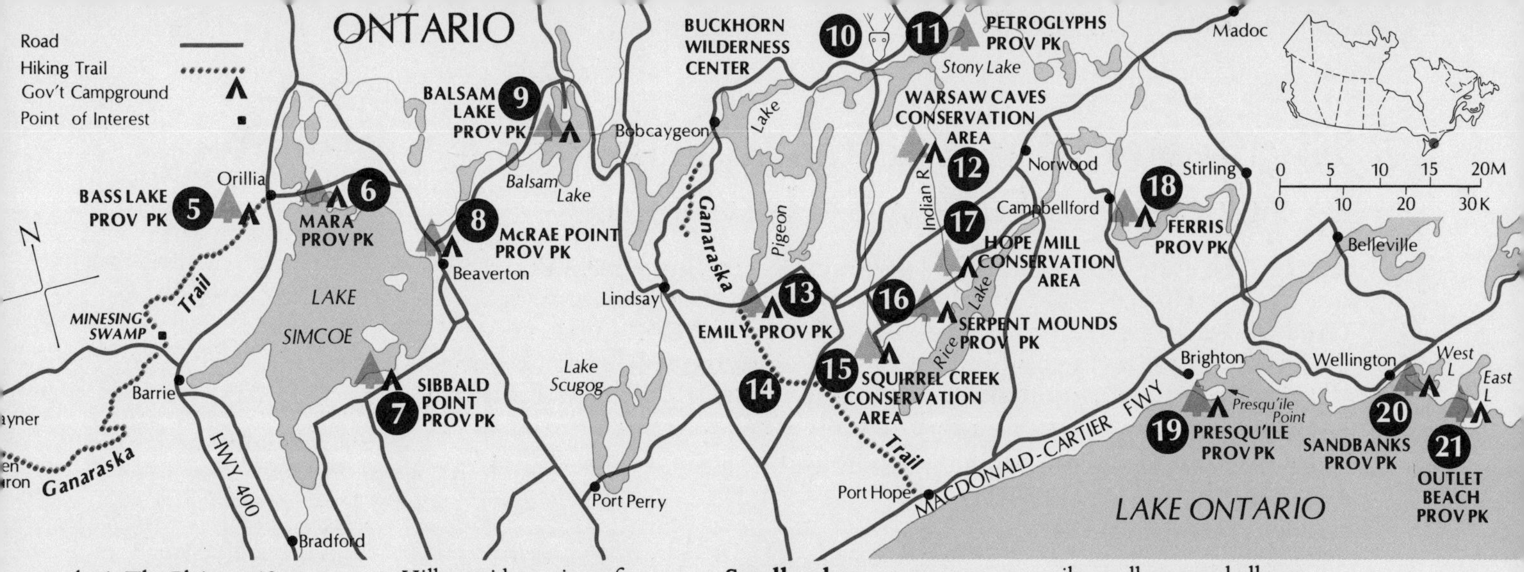

by is The Plains, a 10-acre slab of fractured limestone.
675 acres. Camping, cross-country skiing, fishing (largemouth bass), canoeing, self-guiding nature trails.

Sibbald Point Provincial Park (7)
495 acres. Camping, cross-country skiing, fishing (lake trout, walleye, whitefish), self-guiding nature trails.

Squirrel Creek Conservation Area (15)
275 acres. Camping, hiking, canoeing.

Bass Lake Provincial Park (5)
190 acres. Camping, fishing (smallmouth bass), canoeing, self-guiding nature trails.

Balsam Lake Provincial Park (9)
A 20-foot tower on Lookout Hill provides a view of Balsam Lake and the surrounding brushland.
1.5 square miles. Camping, cross-country skiing, fishing (muskellunge, smallmouth and largemouth bass), canoeing, self-guiding nature trails.

Petroglyphs Provincial Park (11)
The two-mile Petroglyph Hiking Trail leads to more than 900 petroglyphs (figures carved in rock) that cover a limestone surface here. The carvings of canoes, animals and humans were probably made by Algonkian Indians between 500 and 1,000 years ago. Some are up to one inch deep and five feet high.
42 square miles. Canoeing.

Mara Provincial Park (6)
99 acres. Camping, fishing (lake trout, yellow perch, whitefish), canoeing.

Sandbanks Provincial Park (20)
A five-mile sandbar here is said to be longer than any other at the mouth of any freshwater bay in the world. It sweeps across the mouth of West Lake, almost separating it from Lake Ontario.
2 square miles. Camping, supervised swimming, fishing (northern pike, walleye, muskellunge, smallmouth and largemouth bass), canoeing.

McRae Point Provincial Park (8)
170 acres. Camping, fishing (smallmouth bass), self-guiding nature trails.

Presqu'ile Provincial Park (19)
As many as 10,000 terns and ring-billed gulls breed in summer on a small offshore island. More than 225 species of birds have been sighted; 110 nest in the park.
3 square miles. Camping, supervised swimming, cross-country skiing, fishing (walleye, yellow perch, smallmouth and largemouth bass), canoeing, self-guiding nature trails, nature house.

Outlet Beach Provincial Park (21)
A two-mile sandbar shaped by Lake Ontario currents has dammed the mouth of a small bay to form East Lake.
675 acres. Camping, supervised swimming, fishing (northern pike, walleye, muskellunge, smallmouth and largemouth bass), canoeing, self-guiding nature trails, nature house.

Hope Mill Conservation Area (17)
40 acres. Camping, fishing (largemouth bass, walleye), canoeing.

Serpent Mounds Provincial Park (16)
Canada's only serpent-shaped burial mound encloses the remains of some 200 members of an Indian society that lived here 2,000 years ago. The 200-foot-long mound is surrounded by eight small oval mounds.
70 acres. Camping, fishing (walleye, smallmouth and largemouth bass), canoeing.

Ferris Provincial Park (18)
500 acres. Camping, cross-country skiing, hiking, fishing (yellow perch, northern pike, largemouth bass), canoeing.

Emily Provincial Park (13)
167 acres. Camping, fishing (muskellunge, walleye, smallmouth and largemouth bass), canoeing.

Buckhorn Wilderness Center (10)
Eighteen miles of hiking trails crisscross this rugged expanse of forests, lakes and marshes.
1.5 square miles. Wilderness camping, canoeing.

Banding at Jack Miner's Sanctuary

One day in 1909, curious about bird migration, naturalist Jack Miner stamped "Box 48, Kingsville, Ont." on an aluminum band and attached it to the leg of a black duck. A month later the bird was shot in Anderson, S.C., and the band was returned. That was the start of a banding program that continues to this day at the 300-acre Jack Miner Bird Sanctuary near Kingsville. Up to 20,000 birds, mainly mallards and Canada geese, visit the sanctuary during spring and fall. Each November and December some 2,500 birds are trapped in a wire cage baited with grain. Before being set free they are tagged with bands bearing biblical quotations—Miner was a deeply religious man—as well as the sanctuary's name and address.

Eighteen of the Thousand Islands Form a Park in the St. Lawrence

Bordered by the Ottawa and St. Lawrence rivers, this southeastern corner of Ontario is one of Canada's most popular vacation areas. Scattered in the St. Lawrence between Gananoque and Brockville are the Thousand Islands (18 of which make up St. Lawrence Islands National Park). Between Kingston and Ottawa is the 200-mile Rideau Trail and at Lake Mazinaw is towering Bon Echo Rock. Each year thousands of Canada geese gather at Carillon Provincial Park and at the Upper Canada Migratory Bird Sanctuary.

Bon Echo Provincial Park (1)
The High Pines Trail leads to a view of 375-foot-high Bon Echo Rock, a granite cliff bearing 135 Indian paintings. *25.5 square miles.* Camping, climbing, cross-country skiing, fishing (northern pike, walleye, smallmouth and largemouth bass), self-guiding nature trails.

Col. Roscoe Vanderwater Conservation Area (3)
623 acres. Camping, cross-country skiing, hiking, fishing (northern pike, muskellunge).

Second Depot Lake Conservation Area (5)
12 acres. Camping, fishing (walleye, largemouth bass), self-guiding nature trails.

Moira River Canoe Route (4)
South of Huff's Corners are some 20 craters formed by the collapse of cave roofs. They are up to 50 feet across and 30 feet deep. Nearby is a 1,000-foot-long cave, part of a network of limestone caverns and tunnels. *47 miles.*

Rideau Trail (15)
Spy Rock, 100 feet above Upper Rideau Lake, offers a spectacular view of forests and lakes. White pines near Westport are 150 feet high and 3 feet across. Insect-eating pitcher plants thrive in a sphagnum bog west of Merrickville. *200 miles.*

St. Lawrence Islands National Park (17)
The park supports a rich diversity of flora and fauna, much of it usually found in more southerly latitudes. Among 800 plant species are black oak, mayapple and swamp white oak, Canada's only deerberry and the world's most northerly growth of rue anemone. Rare ebony spleenwort ferns grow on Georgina Island. Some 65 species of birds sighted here include cardinals, Carolina wrens, wild turkeys, bald eagles and great blue herons; 28 species of reptiles and amphibians include eastern ribbon snakes and blue-spotted salamanders. The endangered black rat snake, which grows to eight feet, inhabits open woodland. Bowfins and longnose gars are among 35 species of fish found off the park's 18 islands. *1.5 square miles.* Camping, supervised swimming, hiking, canoeing.

Sharbot Lake Provincial Park (8)
98 acres. Camping, supervised swimming, cross-country skiing, fishing (northern pike, walleye, lake trout, largemouth and smallmouth bass), canoeing, self-guiding nature trails.

Silver Lake Provincial Park (9)
78 acres. Camping, fishing (northern pike, smallmouth and largemouth bass, lake and rainbow trout), self-guiding nature trails.

Tay River Canoe Route (7)
Waterworn holes up to five feet deep and two feet across can be seen in rock along the shore of Bobs Lake. East of Christie Lake the Tay River flows over pink and white granite. Marine fossils more than 10,000 years old are embedded in the riverbank near Port Elmsley. *41 miles.*

Shirleys Bay Crown Game Preserve (13)
Snowy owls, ospreys, hawks and thousands of ducks and geese stop in the preserve each year. Waterfowl nesting islands have been built in a 25-acre pond. *10 square miles.*

Skootamatta River Canoe Route (2)
Near Flinton the river races through a rocky gorge and drops 50 feet at The Chutes, a steep set of rapids. *33 miles.*

Carillon Provincial Park (21)
In spring as many as 2,000 Canada geese visit the park. A one-mile self-guiding nature trail passes a 40-ton boulder carried here by glaciers some 12,000 years ago. *2.5 square miles.* Camping, supervised swimming, cross-country skiing, fishing (northern pike, yellow perch, largemouth bass), canoeing.

Charleston Lake Provincial Park (16)
Near a two-ton boulder of white granite on the 1½-mile Pioneer Hiking Trail is a rock shelter used by Indians some 1,200 years ago.
7 square miles. Camping, cross-country skiing, fishing (northern pike, yellow perch, lake trout, largemouth and smallmouth bass).

Mississippi River Canoe Route (10)
Hundreds of small potholes—craters eroded by water-tossed pebbles—can be seen near Ragged Chute. In Mississippi Lake wild rice grows in beds up to a mile long and a quarter mile wide. *115 miles.*

Buells Creek Conservation Area (18)
Each spring, about 200 migrating Canada geese join a resident flock of 40.
2 square miles. Camping, fishing (northern pike, walleye, yellow perch).

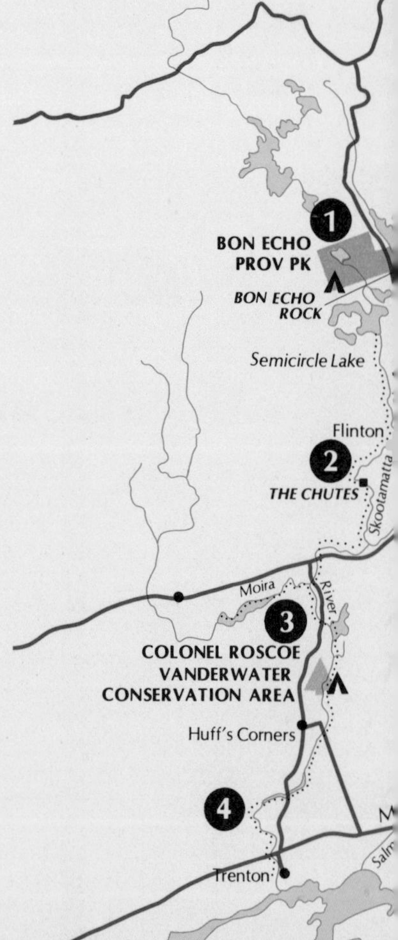

Rideau River Provincial Park (14)
176 acres. Camping, cross-country skiing, fishing (muskellunge, northern pike, walleye, smallmouth and largemouth bass, yellow perch), canoeing.

Gould Lake Conservation Area (6)
Flooded pits in which mica once was mined support luxuriant ferns and water flowers. *1,200 acres.* Camping, supervised swimming, hiking, fishing (lake trout, largemouth bass, walleye, yellow perch)

K and P Trail (11)
Golden eagles are occasionally seen from the trail. Horseback riding is permitted. *22 miles.*

Upper Canada Migratory Bird Sanctuary (19)
As many as 8,000 Canada geese at a time feed in ponds and grainfields here each fall. *5.5 square miles.*

South Nation Provincial Park (20)
13 acres. Camping, fishing (largemouth and smallmouth bass, walleye, northern pike, yellow perch, muskellunge), canoeing.

Fitzroy Provincial Park (12)
435 acres. Camping, cross-country skiing, fishing (northern pike, yellow perch, walleye, smallmouth and largemouth bass), canoeing, self-guiding nature trails.

The five-span Thousand Islands International Bridge crosses the St. Lawrence between Ivy Lea, Ont., and Clayton and Alexandria Bay, N.Y.

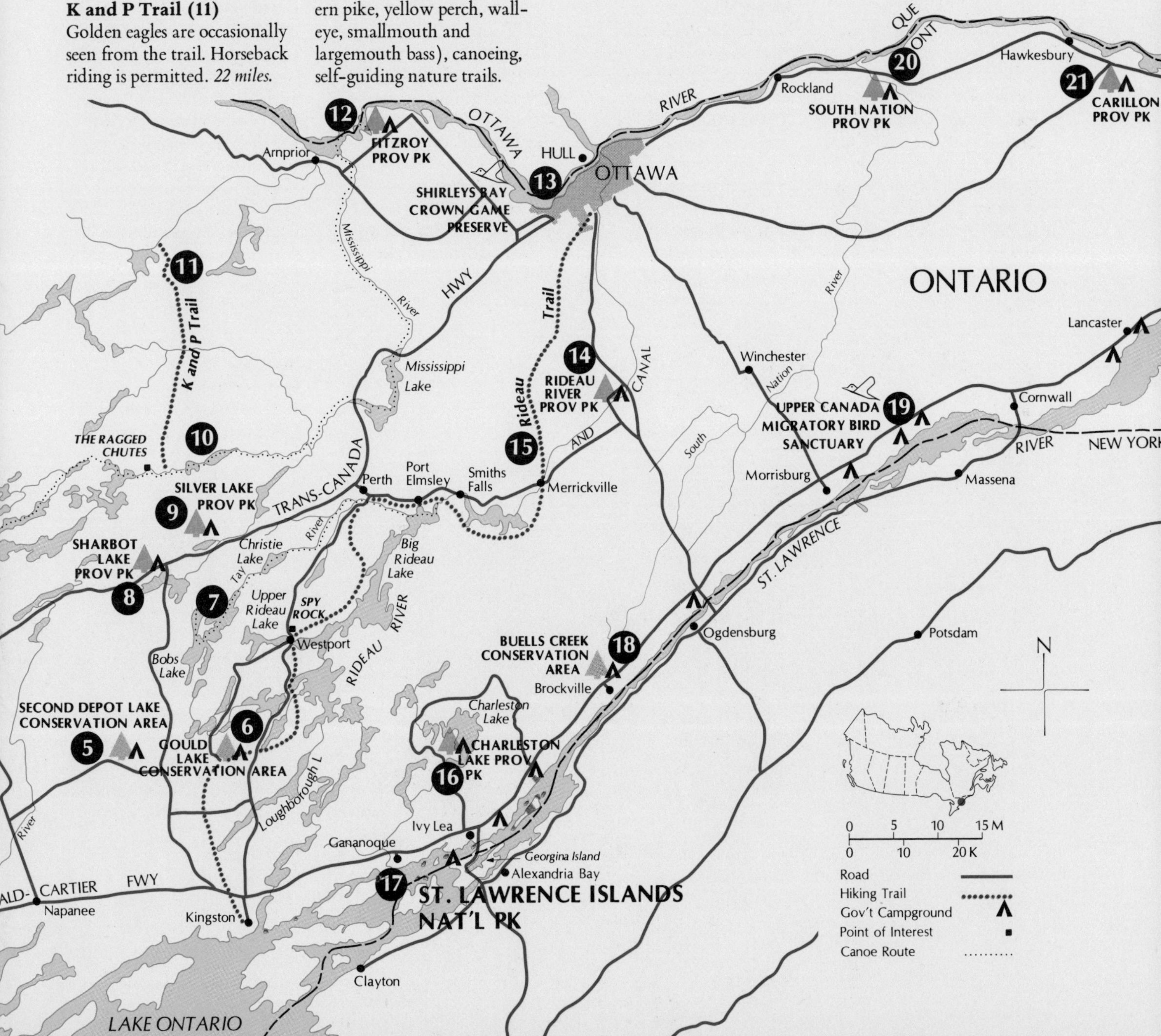

Two Great Provincial Parks: Algonquin and La Vérendrye

In eastern Canada are two of the country's biggest and finest provincial parks—Algonquin in Ontario, La Vérendrye in Quebec—and, on Ottawa's doorstep, Gatineau Park, run by the National Capital Commission. Algonquin and La Vérendrye are seemingly endless lands of lakes and rivers. Together they have more than 2,500 miles of canoe routes. Algonquin also contains 300-foot-deep Barron River Canyon.

Mattawa River Provincial Park (1)
Twenty-five miles of the wild Mattawa River are in the park. At Portage de Talon the river plunges 40 feet between 75-foot-high walls. In the cliff face are weathered rock formations resembling castles. Near Portage de la Cave canoeists enter a steep-walled corridor darkened by an overhang of spruce, cedar and pine trees. On a 100-foot cliff near La Porte de l'Enfer is a seven-foot-high rock formation in the shape of an Indian head.
12.5 square miles. Camping, fishing (walleye, smallmouth bass, northern pike).

Silent Lake Provincial Park (6)
4.5 square miles. Camping, cross-country skiing, hiking, fishing (largemouth and smallmouth bass), canoeing.

Arrowhead Provincial Park (4)
Many oxbow lakes have been formed by the East River.
3.5 square miles. Camping, cross-country skiing, fishing (smallmouth bass, brook and lake trout), canoeing, self-guiding nature trails.

Lake St. Peter Provincial Park (7)
Among 140 species of birds sighted here are ruby-throated hummingbirds, broad-winged hawks, Nashville warblers and Traill's flycatchers.
63 acres. Camping, cross-country skiing, hiking, fishing (rainbow trout), canoeing.

Bonnechere Provincial Park (9)
250 acres. Camping, fishing (smallmouth bass, walleye, northern pike), canoeing.

Carson Lake Provincial Park (8)
15 acres. Camping, fishing (smallmouth bass, lake trout).

Algonquin Provincial Park (5)
Among its more than 1,000 plant species is the Algonquin wood fern, a hybrid thought to be found nowhere else. Unusual arctic plants such as encrusted saxifrage and xanthoria (a lichen) thrive in the calcium-enriched soil of 300-foot-deep Barron River Canyon. Yellow-bellied flycatchers, yellowthroats and northern water thrushes, birds typical of wetlands, inhabit dry, wooded slopes in the canyon. Rare bald and golden eagles are occasionally seen in the park. Some 200 other species of birds include boreal chickadees and spruce grouse, both uncommon this far south. In the northeast is Brent Crater, 500 feet deep and two miles across, formed by a meteorite 450 million years ago. More than 1,000 miles of canoe routes link many of the park's 2,500 lakes, rivers and streams.
2,910 square miles. Camping, hiking, fishing (smallmouth bass, lake and brook trout), self-guiding nature trails.

Mikisew Provincial Park (3)
289 acres. Camping, fishing (brook and lake trout, yellow perch, smallmouth bass, walleye), canoeing.

Samuel de Champlain Provincial Park (2)
The 5½-mile Etienne Trail, named for Etienne Brûlé, one of the first explorers of this part of Ontario—in the 17th century—winds through stands of pine near Long Lake.
9 square miles. Camping, fishing (brook trout, smallmouth bass, walleye, northern pike), canoeing, self-guiding nature trails, nature house.

Driftwood Provincial Park (10)
654 acres. Camping, hiking,

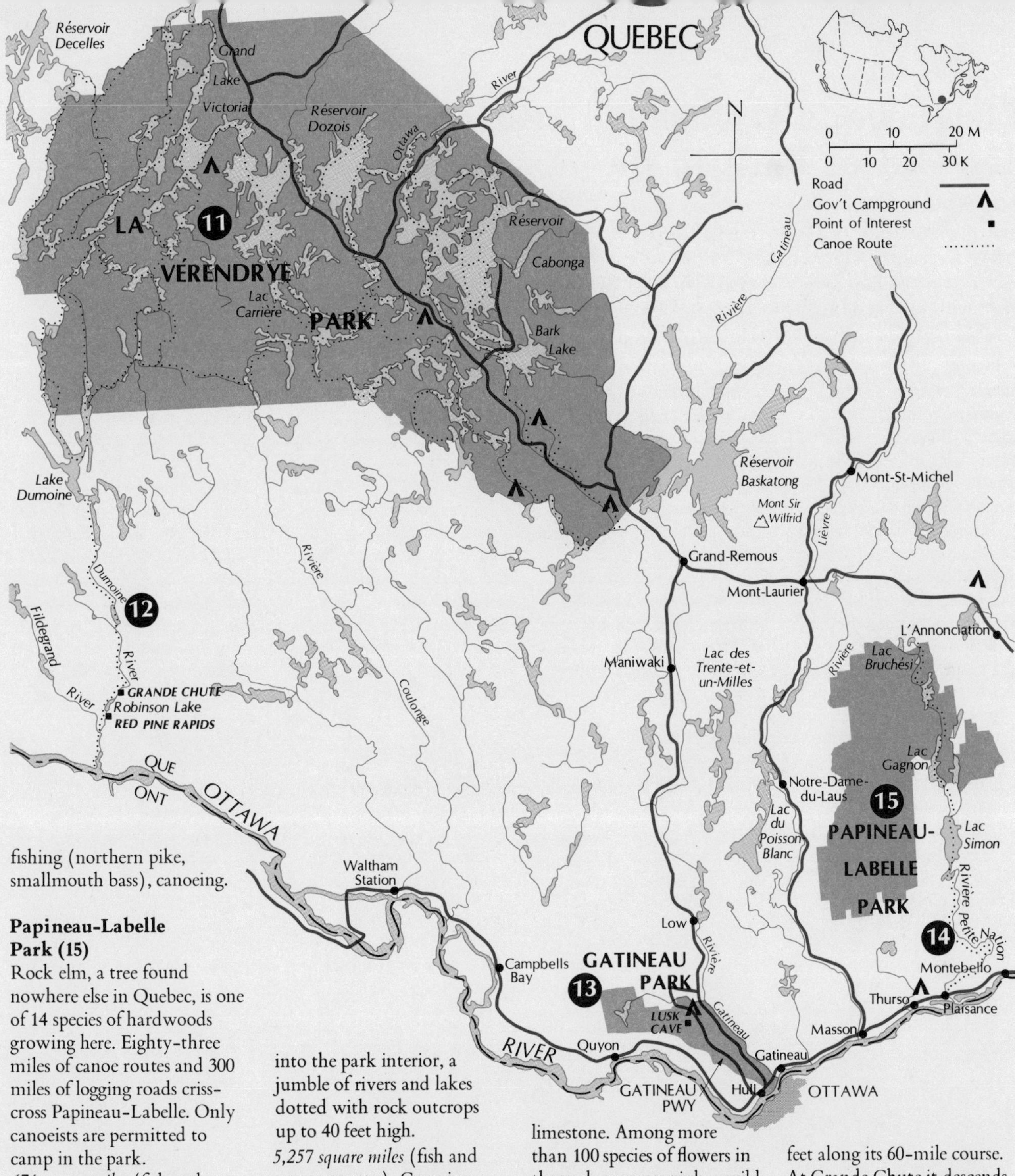

fishing (northern pike, smallmouth bass), canoeing.

Papineau-Labelle Park (15)
Rock elm, a tree found nowhere else in Quebec, is one of 14 species of hardwoods growing here. Eighty-three miles of canoe routes and 300 miles of logging roads criss-cross Papineau-Labelle. Only canoeists are permitted to camp in the park.
671 square miles (fish and game preserve). Fishing (northern pike, walleye, brook trout).

La Vérendrye Park (11)
Some 1,500 miles of canoe routes (600 miles are mapped) wind through Quebec's biggest park, named after explorer Pierre de La Vérendrye. Route possibilities are almost infinite but visitors must register before canoeing into the park interior, a jumble of rivers and lakes dotted with rock outcrops up to 40 feet high.
5,257 square miles (fish and game preserve). Camping, fishing (northern pike, small-mouth bass, lake trout).

Gatineau Park (13)
This federal park, operated by the National Capital Commission, has 60 miles of hiking trails and a five-mile bicycle path that parallels the Gatineau Parkway. In Lusk Cave, a maze of passages and blind alleys, is a 700-foot tunnel of white, pink, green and blue limestone. Among more than 100 species of flowers in the park are grass pink, a wild orchid, and insect-eating sundews and pitcher plants.
137 square miles. Camping, supervised swimming, alpine and cross-country skiing, hiking, fishing (smallmouth bass, northern pike, lake trout), canoeing.

Canoe Route (Lake Dumoine to Ottawa River) (12)
The Dumoine River drops 500 feet along its 60-mile course. At Grande Chute it descends 100 feet in three steps before emptying into Robinson Lake. At the lake's outlet the river runs through Red Pine Rapids then flows 11 miles over rocky shelves. *60 miles.*

Canoe Route (Lac Bruchési to Plaisance) (14)
Canoeists camp on a mile-long sand beach at the south end of Lac Gagnon. *81 miles.*

In Quebec's Lovely Laurentians, the Oldest Park in the Province

On the northern edge of the Laurentian ski country, two hours by car from Montreal, is Mont-Tremblant Provincial Park, Quebec's oldest provincial park (established as a forest reserve in 1894). The park has many rivers and streams and almost 1,000 lakes. To the east is the wild splendor of La Mauricie National Park. To the south of La Mauricie, on the Rivière Maskinongé, is magnificent Sainte-Ursule Falls.

Mont-Tremblant Provincial Park (1)
Some 30 miles of blazed hiking trails crisscross Quebec's oldest provincial park. One trail leads to La Corniche, a 1,575-foot ledge overlooking Lac Monroe. A 60-mile canoe route on the Rivière du Diable begins at Lac aux Herbes and runs outside the park to Saint-Jovite; there is a portage around 60-foot Chute du Diable. Near Lac Lajoie is Chute aux Rats, a 50-foot waterfall that tumbles over a cliff cut like a staircase. Roughly 1,000 moose roam the park, and the black bear, lynx and fox are among 26 other mammal species here. *990 square miles.* Camping, climbing, cross-country skiing, fishing (northern pike, walleye, brook and lake trout), canoeing, self-guiding nature trails.

Canoe Route (Matawin River) (2)
The Matawin River begins its wild descent in Mont-Tremblant Provincial Park, then drops more than 1,000 feet through rapids, waterfalls and whirlpools. At Chute de la Grand-Mère the river plunges 35 feet. *92 miles.*

Canoe Route (Ouareau River) (3)
Near Darwin Falls, 100 feet high and 50 feet wide, is a rock outcrop in the shape of an Indian head. Only experienced canoeists should attempt this rugged route. *74 miles.*

La Mauricie National Park (8)
Indian rock paintings an estimated 2,000 years old can be seen near Lac Wapizagonke. The 10-mile-long lake is flanked by cliffs up to 250 feet high. Knives, axes and arrowheads have been unearthed on a small island. *215 square miles.* Camping, cross-country skiing, hiking, fishing (smallmouth bass, brook and lake trout), canoeing, self-guiding nature trails.

Canoe Route (Lac de L'Assomption to Joliette) (4)
Rivière L'Assomption plummets 100 feet at Montapel Falls before racing through 200 feet of rapids. *78 miles.*

Saint-Maurice Park (9)
Spruce and birch blanket northern hillsides here; southern slopes support stands of maple and yellow birch. *617 square miles* (fish and game preserve). Camping, fishing (brook and lake trout).

Canoe Route (Rivière Maskinongé) (5)
Sainte-Ursule Falls drops 202 feet over rock steps that extend 1,500 feet. *53 miles.*

Mastigouche Park (7)
Set in rolling hills up to 2,000 feet high, the park offers fishing for ouananiche (landlocked salmon) in Shawinigan and Anselme lakes. A 12-mile canoe route on the Rivière du Loup begins at Les Sept Chutes, a series of waterfalls. Only canoeists are permitted to camp in the park. *678 square miles* (fish and game preserve).

Canoe Route (Rivière du Loup) (6)
Canoeists portage around five miles of treacherous white water beginning at Hunterstown. *65 miles.*

Skiers cross a high ridge in Quebec's Mont-Tremblant Provincial Park.

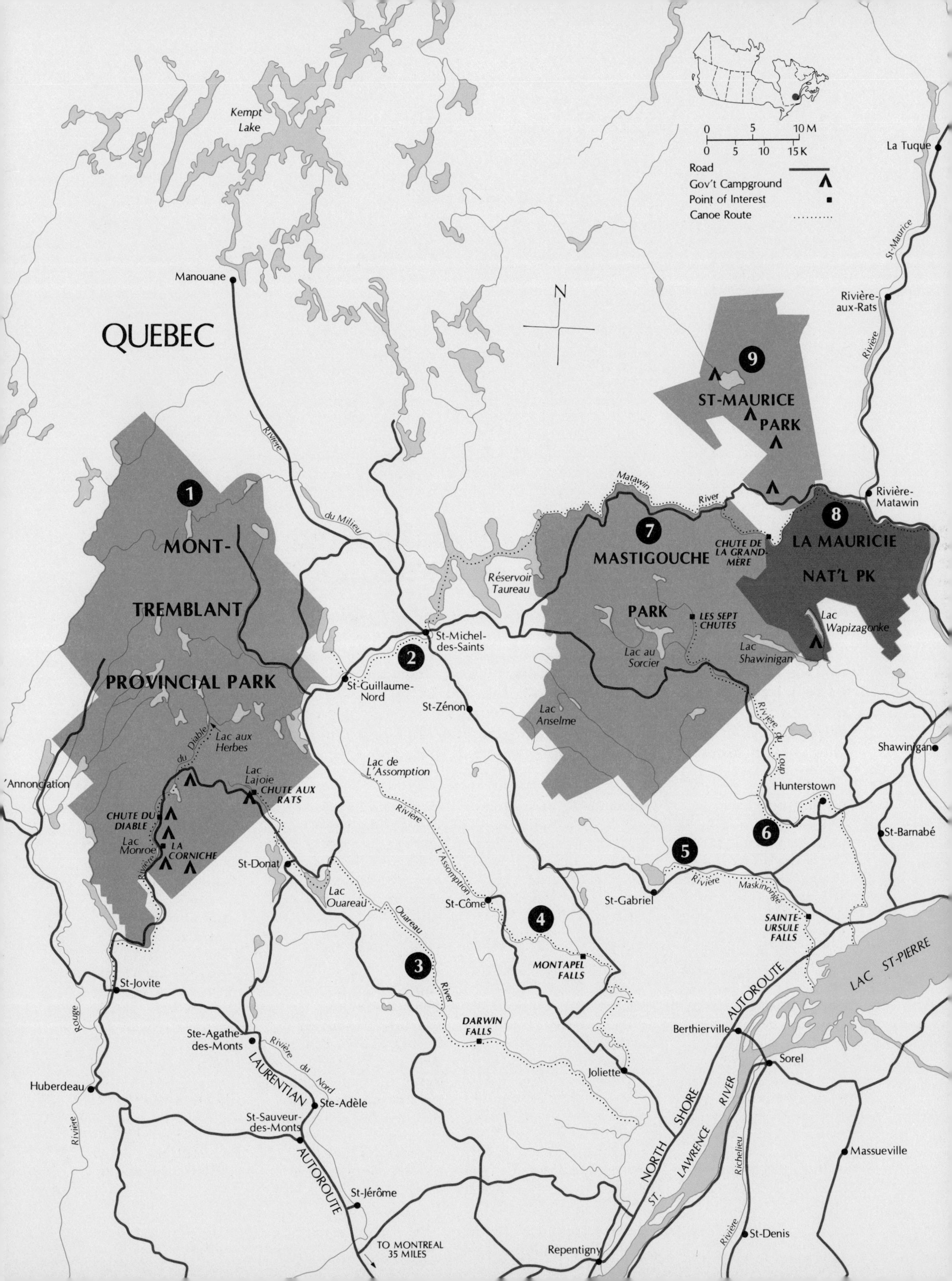

QUEBEC
Kempt Lake
Manouane
0 5 10 M
0 5 10 15 K
Road
Gov't Campground
Point of Interest
Canoe Route
La Tuque
Rivière St-Maurice
Rivière-aux-Rats
9
ST-MAURICE PARK
Matawin River
Rivière-Matawin
8
LA MAURICIE NAT'L PK
7
MASTIGOUCHE PARK
CHUTE DE LA GRAND-MÈRE
LES SEPT CHUTES
Lac Wapizagonke
Lac Shawinigan
Lac au Sorcier
Lac Anselme
Réservoir Taureau
1
MONT-TREMBLANT PROVINCIAL PARK
Rivière du Milieu
St-Michel-des-Saints
2
St-Guillaume-Nord
St-Zénon
Lac aux Herbes
du Diable
Lac Lajoie
CHUTE AUX RATS
CHUTE DU DIABLE
Lac Monroe
LA CORNICHE
Rivière
L'Annonciation
Lac de L'Assomption
Rivière L'Assomption
St-Donat
Lac Ouareau
Ouareau River
3
St-Côme
4
MONTAPEL FALLS
DARWIN FALLS
5
St-Gabriel
Rivière Maskinonge
6
Hunterstown
Rivière du Loup
Shawinigan
St-Barnabé
SAINTE-URSULE FALLS
LAC ST-PIERRE
St-Jovite
Rouge
Ste-Agathe-des-Monts
Rivière du Nord
LAURENTIAN AUTOROUTE
Huberdeau
Rivière
Ste-Adèle
St-Sauveur-des-Monts
St-Jérôme
TO MONTREAL 35 MILES
Joliette
Berthierville
NORTH SHORE AUTOROUTE
Sorel
ST. LAWRENCE RIVER
Richelieu
Rivière
Massueville
St-Denis
Repentigny
N

Untamed and Lonely, a Remote Land of Great Parks, Lakes and Fishing

Most of the vast area between the St. Lawrence River and James Bay is wilderness, an untamed and lonely land laced with racing rivers and thundering waterfalls. But many of its attractions are close to the settled parks of Quebec—or easily accessible. Among them are Chibougamau, Laurentides, Portneuf and Val-Jalbert parks and the ski slopes of Mont Sainte-Anne. There is fishing for huge brook trout and northern pike in Lake Mistassini—Quebec's largest lake—and near Quebec City is Montmorency Falls, the highest waterfall in eastern Canada.

Canoe Route (Baie-du-Poste to Rupert House) (2)
East of Lac Némiscau the Rupert River cuts through a 100-foot-deep gorge, and at Oatmeal Falls it tumbles 75 feet before churning through swift rapids. In places the river passes eskers (ridges formed at the end of the Ice Age) and patches of muskeg dotted with black spruce. *378 miles.*

Mistassini Park (3)
Brook trout grow up to 40 lbs. and northern pike reach 10 lbs. in 840-square-mile Lake Mistassini, Quebec's largest lake. At Chutes à Voir, on the Chalifour Canoe Route, the Chalifour River splits into two waterfalls, both more than 40 feet high.
9,471 square miles (fish and game preserve). Camping, fishing (brook and lake trout, whitefish, northern pike).

Val-Jalbert Provincial Park (6)
At Val-Jalbert Falls the Ouiatchouane River plummets 236 feet onto rocks filled with fossils of trilobites (marine creatures that disappeared some 240 million years ago). Philomène's Cave, a cavern eroded in limestone, is 200 feet long but only the first 50 feet are accessible.
640 acres. Camping.

Boatswain Bay Bird Sanctuary (1)
Canada's most easterly population of sandhill cranes nests on marshy Boatswain Bay in James Bay. Each spring and fall thousands of Canada and lesser snow geese visit the area.
10 square miles.

Canoe Route (Baie-du-Poste to Saint-Félicien) (5)
Between Baie-du-Poste and File Axe Lake canoeists must paddle upstream and portage one mile around six rapids and a waterfall. *206 miles.*

Laurentides Park (7)
Caribou, once scarce here, now range throughout the park. A short trail in the 26-square-mile Montmorency Experimental Forest leads to 91-foot-high Chute de la Rivière Noire.
3,696 square miles (fish and game preserve). Camping, climbing, cross-country skiing, hiking, fishing (brook trout), canoeing.

Mont Sainte-Anne Provincial Park (11)
This winter recreation park has 28 downhill ski runs—on 2,625-foot Mont Sainte-Anne—and 80 miles of cross-country trails.
25 square miles. Hiking.

Montmorency Provincial Park (9)
A suspension bridge overlooks 274-foot Montmorency Falls, eastern Canada's highest waterfall. Spray from the falls forms a winter cone of ice up to 90 feet high.
60 acres. Camping.

Chibougamau Park (4)
The Chamouchouane River drops 107 feet at Chaudière Falls. Black bears, beavers, marmots and wolves are

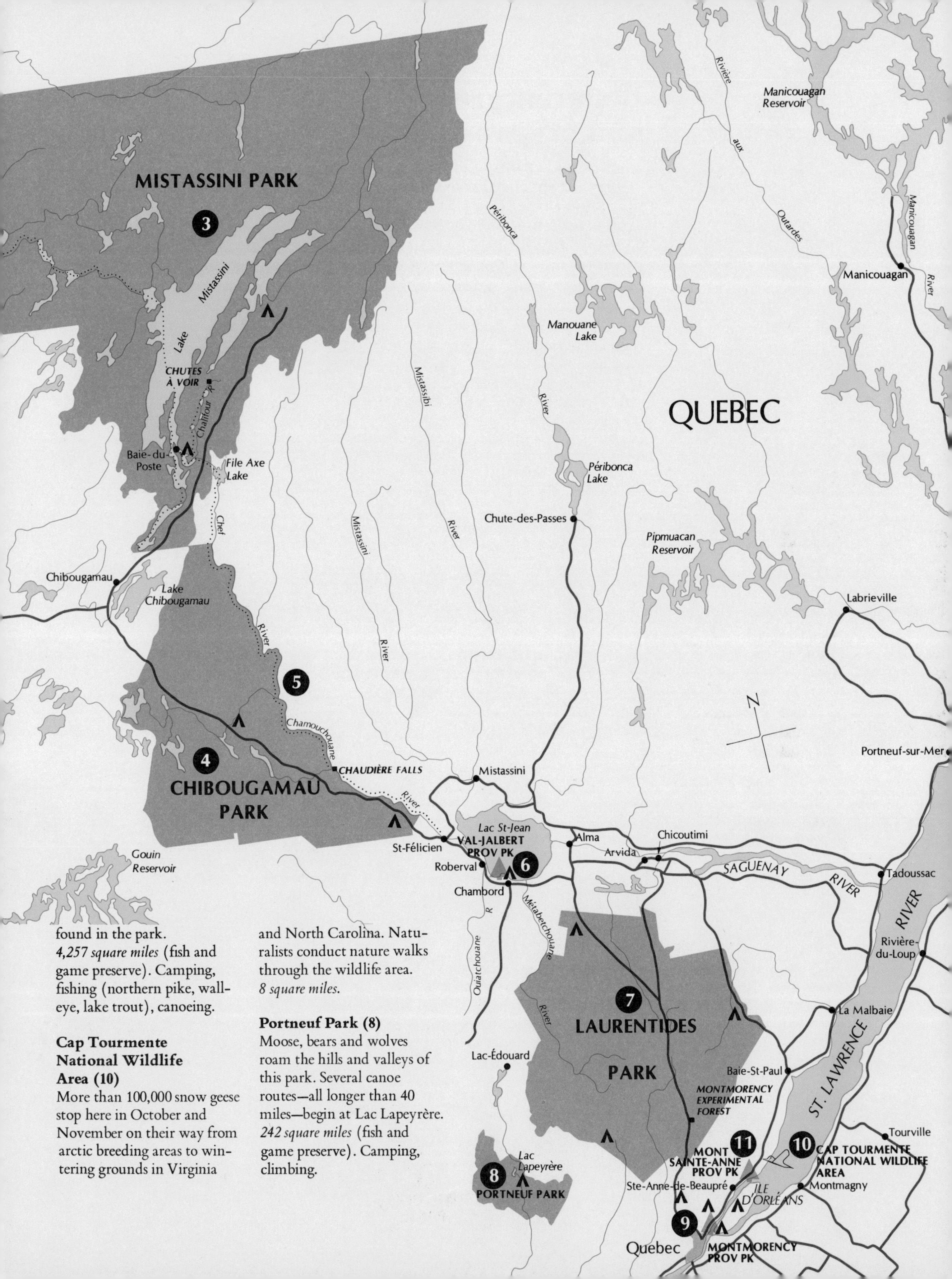

found in the park.
4,257 square miles (fish and game preserve). Camping, fishing (northern pike, walleye, lake trout), canoeing.

Cap Tourmente National Wildlife Area (10)
More than 100,000 snow geese stop here in October and November on their way from arctic breeding areas to wintering grounds in Virginia and North Carolina. Naturalists conduct nature walks through the wildlife area.
8 square miles.

Portneuf Park (8)
Moose, bears and wolves roam the hills and valleys of this park. Several canoe routes—all longer than 40 miles—begin at Lac Lapeyrère.
242 square miles (fish and game preserve). Camping, climbing.

Bonaventure's Great Gannet Colony and a Rare Herd of Woodland Caribou

The Gaspé Peninsula is a world of delightful variety: tiny fishing villages, steep cliffs, rivers abundant with salmon and, in the interior, the rugged Shickshock Mountains. Roads that weave and dip along almost 450 miles of coastline offer breathtaking views of the Baie des Chaleurs and the St. Lawrence River. North America's largest colony of gannets nests on Bonaventure Island and one of the world's last herds of woodland caribou inhabits De la Gaspésie Park.

Forillon National Park (8)
Black spruce and reindeer moss, usually found 500 miles to the north, grow on Penouille, a mile-long peninsula facing the Baie de Gaspé. Some 36 species of lichen thrive in sandy soil on the peninsula. Nearby are sand dunes and salt marshes. Fractured limestone cliffs up to 600 feet high face the Gulf of St. Lawrence. They support herring gulls, black guillemots and double-crested cormorants. The park has some 160 bird species in all. Pilot whales are the most common of 12 whale species in the waters off Forillon. *92 square miles.* Camping, cross-country skiing, hiking, fishing (herring, mackerel), self-guiding nature trails.

Métis Provincial Park (3)
Among 189 plant species here are musk saxifrage, self-heal and beauty bush—not found this far north anywhere else in North America. *85 acres.*

Matane Park (5)
Deer and the occasional caribou roam forests of black spruce and balsam fir in the park. *417 square miles* (fish and

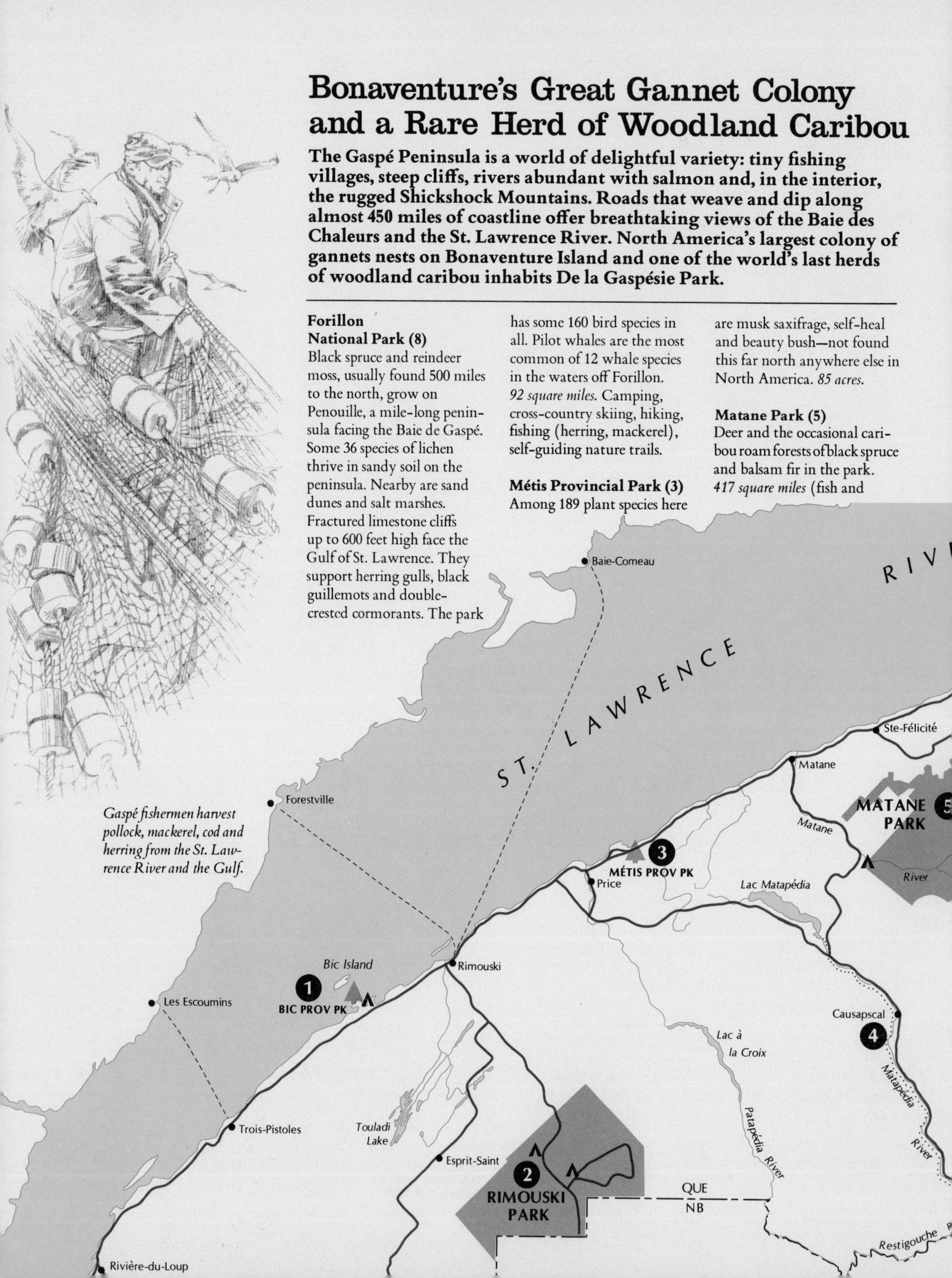

Gaspé fishermen harvest pollock, mackerel, cod and herring from the St. Lawrence River and the Gulf.

game preserve). Camping, cross-country skiing, fishing (brook and lake trout, landlocked salmon).

Canoe Route (Lac Matapédia to Restigouche River) (4)
Loons breed on islands in 12-mile-long Lac Matapédia, the Gaspé's longest lake. In the Matapédia River ("river of 222 rapids") are numerous small chutes and waterfalls flanked by steep mountain slopes. The river offers fine fishing for salmon. *56 miles.*

De la Gaspésie Provincial Park (6)
One of the world's last herds of woodland caribou lives on the slopes of 4,160-foot Mont Jacques-Cartier, highest peak in the Shickshock Mountains. As many as 150 alpine flower species—plants that survived here above the reach of Ice Age glaciers—grow on a 12-square-mile plateau at the summit of Mont Albert. There are more than 150 miles of hiking trails in the park. *498 square miles.* Camping, climbing, cross-country skiing, fishing (brook trout, landlocked salmon), self-guiding nature trails.

Bonaventure Island Provincial Park (10)
North America's largest colony of gannets—up to 35,000 birds—roosts on the island's 300-foot sandstone cliffs. Other birds include black guillemots, kittiwakes and razorbilled auks. The park is accessible by boat from Percé. *1.5 square miles.* Hiking, self-guiding nature trails.

Percé Rock Bird Sanctuary (9)
Herring gulls and double-crested cormorants nest on Percé Rock, 1,420 feet long and up to 288 feet high. The rock, 600 feet offshore, is reached on foot at low tide. *600 acres.*

Bic Provincial Park (1)
As many as 8,000 eider ducks nest on islands in the park; sea otters and harbor and harp seals sun on reefs and rocky shores. Bays and inlets indent eight miles of shoreline here. *7.5 square miles.* Camping, climbing, cross-country skiing, hiking, fishing (cod, mackerel, herring, pollack), self-guiding nature trails.

Rimouski Park (2)
Bears, moose and deer are common in the park's maple and birch forests. *308 square miles* (fish and game preserve). Camping, fishing (brook trout).

Port-Daniel Park (7)
Salmon are plentiful in the Port-Daniel River; 18 lakes in the park are stocked with brook trout. *25 square miles* (fish and game preserve). Camping, cross-country skiing, self-guiding nature trails.

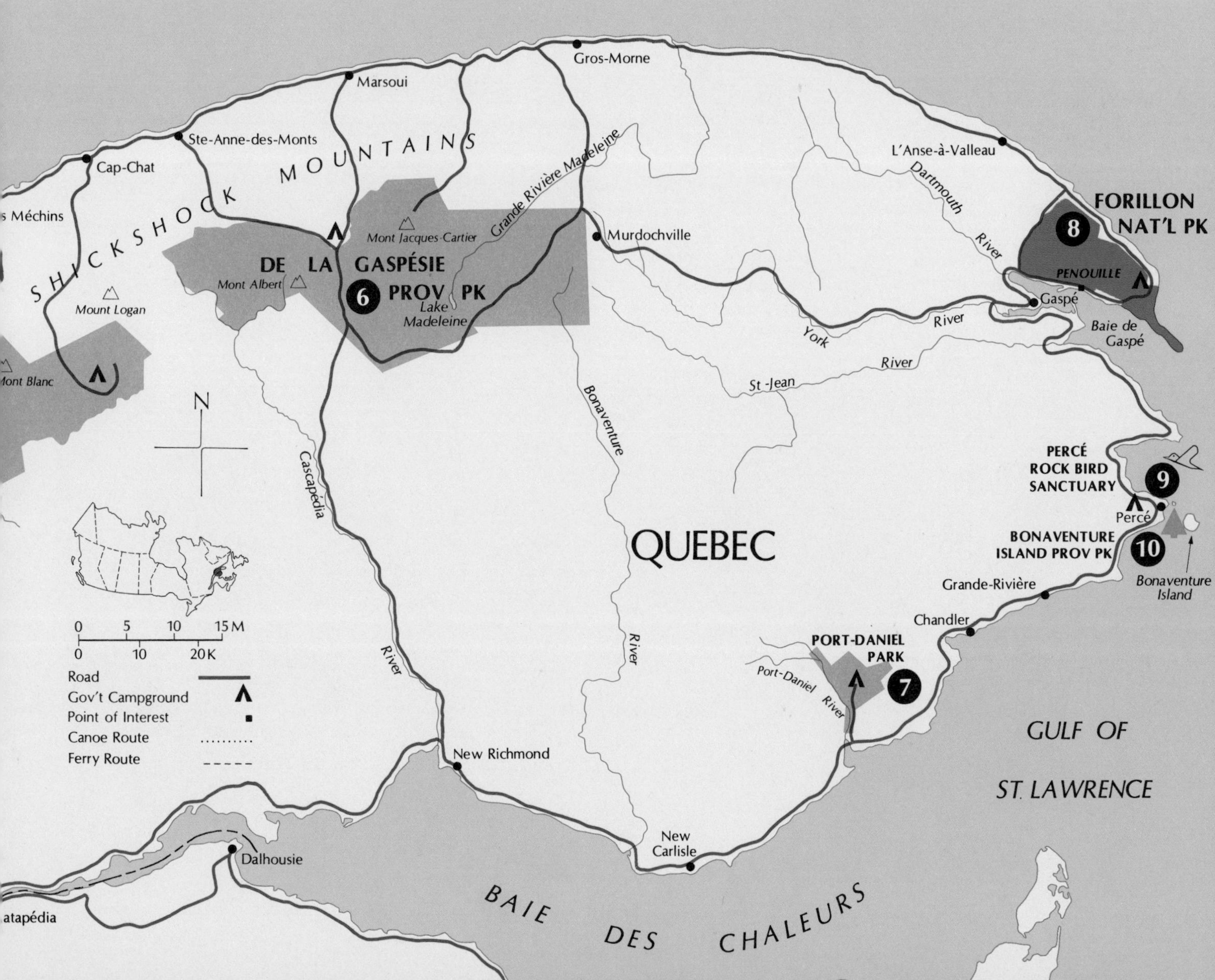

Fundy and Kouchibouguac Are National Parks in N.B.

There are two national parks on the New Brunswick coast: Kouchibouguac faces Northumberland Strait and Fundy fronts on Chignecto Bay. In soft rock at Hopewell Cape are "flowerpot" pillars that become islands at high tide. There are bird sanctuaries on Grand Manan and Machias Seal islands near the mouth of the Bay of Fundy. Powerful Bay of Fundy tides create the unusual Reversing Falls at the mouth of the Saint John River.

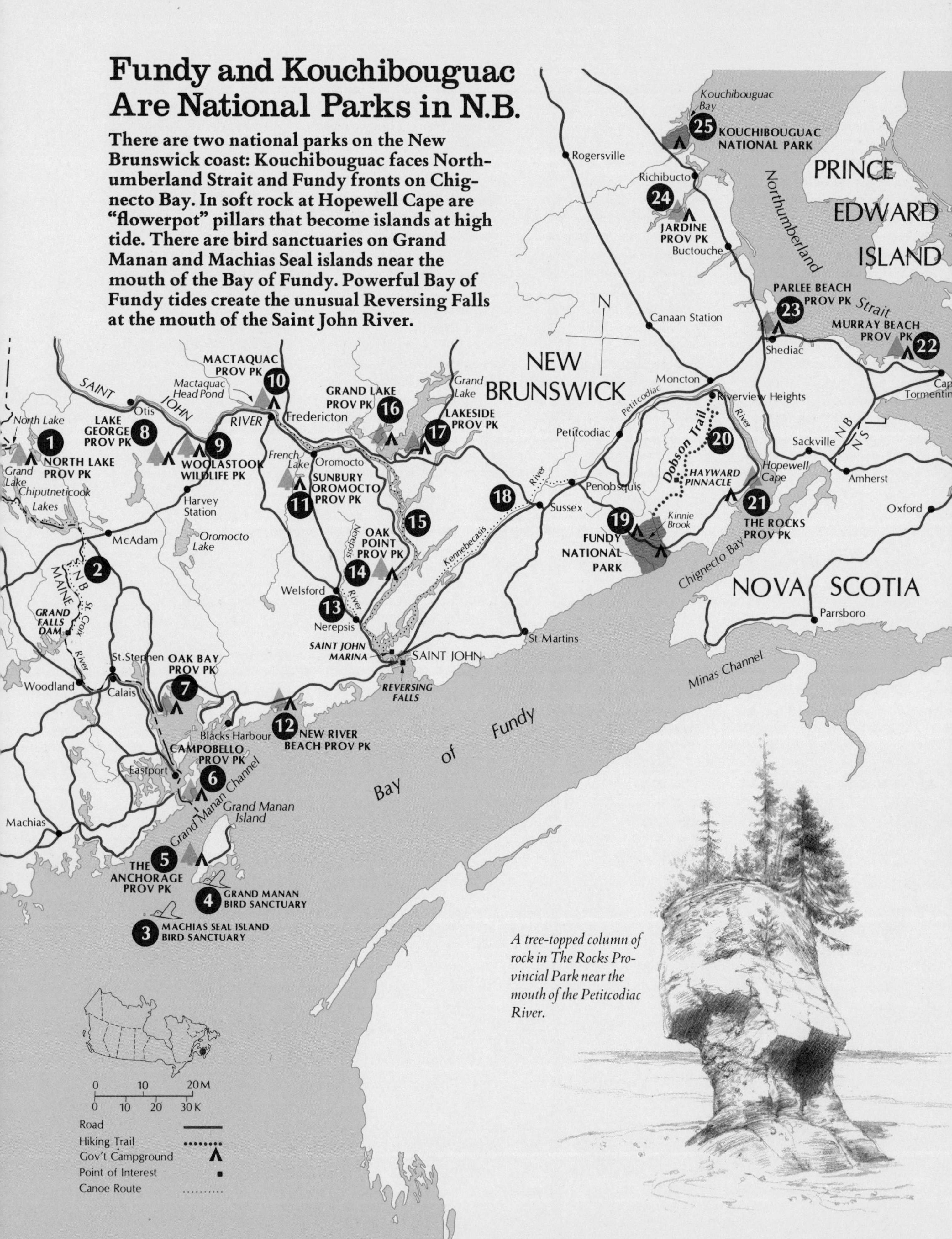

A tree-topped column of rock in The Rocks Provincial Park near the mouth of the Petitcodiac River.

Fundy National Park (19)
Behind the coves and sandstone cliffs of the park's eight-mile shoreline are the Caledonia Highlands, a rolling plateau of beech, yellow birch and maple hills. Growing in bogs along the 2½-mile Caribou Plain Trail (one of five self-guiding nature trails in the park) are insect-eating pitcher plants and 100-year-old tamarack trees. Another trail passes Kinnie Brook, a small stream that disappears underground, then emerges 750 feet away. Among 185 bird species here are the great blue heron, bald eagle, peregrine falcon and osprey.
80 square miles. Camping, supervised swimming, cross-country skiing, hiking, fishing (brook trout, Atlantic salmon), horseback riding.

Oak Point Provincial Park (14)
The park is on a point jutting into the Saint John River.
51 acres. Camping.

Campobello Provincial Park (6)
Campobello Island is reached by ferry from the mainland. (Also on the island is 4½-square-mile Roosevelt-Campobello International Park.)
294 acres. Camping.

Parlee Beach Provincial Park (23)
90 acres. Camping, supervised swimming.

Grand Manan Bird Sanctuary (4)
Some 245 bird species including eider, ring-necked duck, blue- and green-winged teal and merganser have been sighted here. Some of the 2,000 black ducks and 1,200 brants that visit the sanctuary during spring and fall remain to nest on marshes and ponds. Access to Grand Manan Island is by ferry from Blacks Harbour, N.B. *200 acres.*

Oak Bay Provincial Park (7)
Pines grow to 75 feet in the park.
28 acres. Camping.

Kouchibouguac National Park (25)
A 15½-mile curve of offshore sandbars shelters lagoons and salt marshes in Kouchibouguac Bay. Along the shore are peat bogs an estimated 10,000 years old, and sand dunes anchored by marram grass and false heather.
93 square miles. Camping, supervised swimming, cross-country skiing, hiking, fishing (brook trout, striped bass), canoeing.

Dobson Trail (20)
This route, between Riverview Heights and Fundy National Park, winds through grassy meadows and forests of birch, maple and spruce. Hikers gain an impressive view of the Caledonia Highlands from 1,200-foot Hayward Pinnacle. Pools in small streams abound with brook trout. *37 miles.*

The Anchorage Provincial Park (5)
The park is in the Grand Manan Bird Sanctuary.
285 acres. Camping.

North Lake Provincial Park (1)
Dense forests of maple, birch, spruce and pine grow to the edge of North Lake.
115 acres. Camping, fishing (walleye, yellow perch).

Mactaquac Provincial Park (10)
Five guided nature hikes, numerous walking trails and six miles of snowshoe routes wind through the park. In winter there is ice fishing in 65-mile-long Mactaquac Head Pond on the Saint John River. One of the world's largest Atlantic salmon hatcheries is two miles downstream at French Village.
2 square miles. Camping, supervised swimming, cross-country skiing, horseback riding.

Canoe Route (Penobsquis to Saint John) (18)
There is fishing for brook trout and striped bass in the Kennebecasis River. *58 miles.*

Machias Seal Island Bird Sanctuary (3)
In spring and fall rocky Machias Seal Island teems with migrating birdlife: Leach's storm-petrels, arctic terns, puffins and razorbills. Charter boats from Grand Manan Island provide access to the sanctuary. *15 acres.*

Lakeside Provincial Park (17)
105 acres. Camping.

The Rocks Provincial Park (21)
Wind, frost and 35-foot tides have shaped top-heavy columns of soft rock at Hopewell Cape near the mouth of the Petitcodiac River. At high tide these pillars—up to 50 feet high—become small islands.
37 acres. Supervised swimming.

Jardine Provincial Park (24)
12 acres. Camping, supervised swimming.

Canoe Route (Welsford to Nerepsis) (13)
The Nerepsis River passes marshes, farmland and hills forested with spruce, fir, maple and birch. *17 miles.*

Sunbury Oromocto Provincial Park (11)
Goldeneyes, black ducks and blue-winged teal nest on the shores of French Lake.
200 acres. Camping, fishing (walleye).

Canoe Route (Fredericton to Saint John) (15)
Twice daily some of the world's highest tides (up to 50 feet) surge into the Bay of Fundy, forcing water upstream over the Reversing Falls at Saint John on the Saint John River. Canoeists avoid this treacherous white water by landing at the Saint John marina. *97 miles.*

Lake George Provincial Park (8)
29 acres. Camping.

Canoe Route (North Lake Park to Grand Falls Dam) (2)
Landlocked salmon up to 16 lbs. inhabit 24-square-mile Grand Lake. Black bears and moose are occasionally seen and ospreys and bald eagles are common along the St. Croix River. *80 miles.*

Murray Beach Provincial Park (22)
Winter temperatures and salt spray turn shoreline pines a bright red. On a clear day visitors can see Prince Edward Island nine miles to the east.
65 acres. Camping, supervised swimming.

Grand Lake Provincial Park (16)
212 acres. Camping, supervised swimming, fishing (Atlantic salmon, alewife).

New River Beach Provincial Park (12)
A half-mile sand beach nestles at the base of 25-foot-high dunes.
835 acres. Camping, self-guiding nature trails.

Woolastook Wildlife Park (9)
Caribou, black bear, bobcat and panther are among 20 species of animals that roam enclosures in the park.
2.5 square miles. Camping.

In the Smallest Province of All, Beaches That Stretch for Miles

Some of North America's loveliest beaches are along the 1,100-mile coastline of Prince Edward Island. On the north shore is Prince Edward Island National Park where sand dunes rise to 60 feet and sandstone cliffs are up to 100 feet high. Scattered throughout the island are numerous provincial parks, most of which offer camping.

Prince Edward Island National Park (8)
This park, fringed by the Gulf of St. Lawrence, has some of North America's finest beaches. Near Cavendish is sand tinted pink by the erosion of bleached red clay. Between Rustico and Orby Head are more than six miles of red sandstone cliffs up to 100 feet high. At Brackley Beach, wooden walkways pass sand dunes up to 60 feet high. Sweeping to the edge of the dunes is a coastal forest where white spruce thrive, stunted by wind and salt—some are 75 years old and only 2 or 3 feet high. Among 210 species of birds are the northern phalarope, Swainson's thrush, marsh hawk and slate-colored junco. Great blue herons nest on Rustico Island.
7 square miles. Camping, supervised swimming, cross-country skiing, hiking, fishing (brook trout), canoeing, self-guiding nature trails.

Cedar Dunes Provincial Park (4)
Shifting dunes back a 1½-mile-long sand beach.
100 acres. Camping.

Anglo Provincial Park (1)
19 acres. Camping, canoeing.

Green Provincial Park (5)
Two hiking trails wind through forests of poplar, beech and white birch.
158 acres. Camping, fishing (brook trout, cod, mackerel), canoeing.

Linkletter Provincial Park (7)
41 acres. Camping, canoeing.

St. Peters Provincial Park (17)
17 acres. Camping.

Jacques Cartier Provincial Park (2)
22 acres. Camping, supervised swimming.

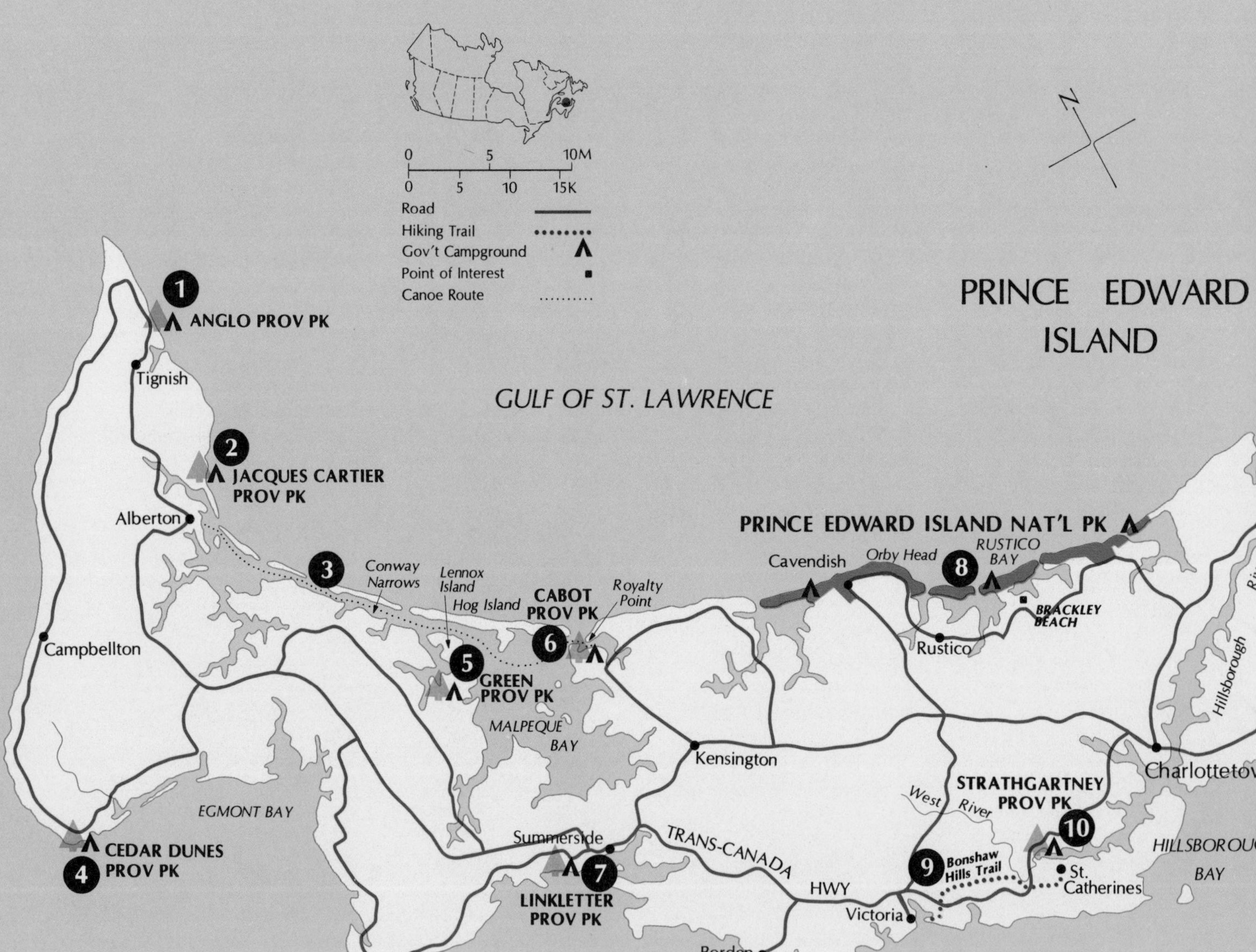

Black Pond Bird Sanctuary (18)
Great blue herons, black ducks, blue-winged teal and American goldeneyes visit ponds and a lagoon in the sanctuary. *2.5 square miles.*

Brudenell Provincial Park (16)
A self-guiding nature trail passes a spruce bog where sheep-laurel, Labrador tea and sphagnum grow.
2 square miles. Camping, supervised swimming, canoeing, horseback riding.

Buffalo Provincial Park (14)
The park is a preserve for a herd of bison and no camping is permitted. *150 acres.*

Lord Selkirk Provincial Park (11)
Clams can be dug along the park's sandy shoreline.
114 acres. Camping, canoeing.

Panmure Island Provincial Park (15)
Sand dunes are up to 20 feet high on a causeway between Smith Point and Panmure Island.
18 acres. Camping, supervised swimming.

Cabot Provincial Park (6)
Flocks of migrating Canada geese visit a salt marsh each spring and fall.
261 acres. Camping, hiking.

Bonshaw Hills Trail (9)
This trail between St. Catherines and Victoria crosses hills and winds through farmfields and hemlock forests. Raccoons, muskrats and minks inhabit the area. *20 miles.*

Northumberland Provincial Park (13)
A half-mile red sand beach lies at the foot of steep cliffs.
75 acres. Camping, supervised swimming, hiking.

Campbells Cove Provincial Park (20)
50 acres. Camping.

Strathgartney Provincial Park (10)
A grassy hill offers a fine view of the meandering West River.
40 acres. Camping, fishing (brook trout), self-guiding nature trails.

Canoe Route (Alberton to Royalty Point) (3)
Most of this route is sheltered from the winds and surf of the Gulf by four offshore sandbars. Canoeists travel through Conway Narrows before entering Malpeque Bay, P.E.I.'s largest bay. Gulls, herons and ducks nest on sandy Hog Island. *25 miles.*

Red Point Provincial Park (19)
5 acres. Camping, supervised swimming.

Sir Andrew Macphail Provincial Park (12)
143 acres. Camping.

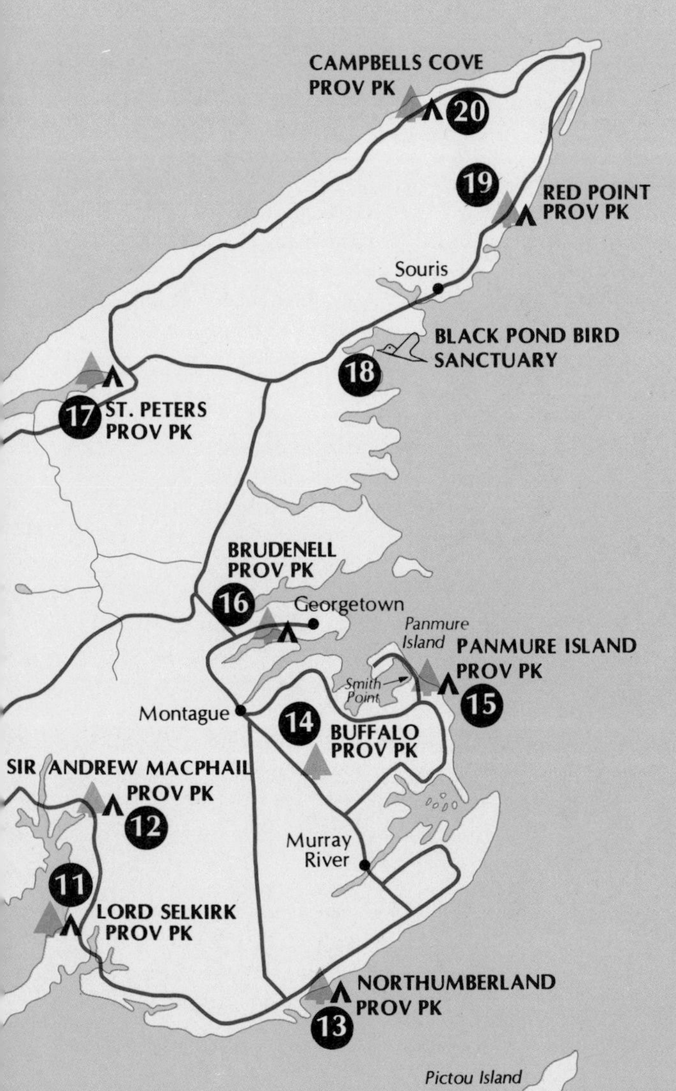

Low tide is best for digging clams—a popular activity along many Prince Edward Island beaches.

Kejimkujik and an Inland Sea– and Cape Breton's Cabot Trail

Nova Scotia offers spectacular variety and contrast: coastal bird sanctuaries and immense game preserves, the lush wilderness of Kejimkujik Park and the fertile beauty of the Annapolis Valley. In Cape Breton Island are desolate highlands, cliffs up to 1,000 feet high, pools teeming with salmon, Bras d'Or Lake—a vast inland sea—and the Cabot Trail, one of North America's finest scenic drives.

Kejimkujik National Park (6)
Near Kejimkujik Lake are petroglyphs carved in slate by Indians some 300 years ago. They depict fishermen, hunters, animals and a four-legged bird encircled by stars (probably an Indian god). Because this region has longer, hotter summers than the rest of Nova Scotia, unusual plants and animals exist here: greenbrier and witch hazel and such birds as the scarlet tanager, great crested flycatcher and wood thrush. The ribbon snake, Blanding's turtle and the southern flying squirrel—species found nowhere else in the Atlantic Provinces—inhabit the park. Kejimkujik has five species of snakes and salamanders, three of turtles and eight of toads and frogs—one of the most varied reptile and amphibian populations in eastern Canada. Several lakes support whitefish, a species common farther west. There are seven canoe routes and more than 70 miles of hiking trails in the park.
145 square miles. Camping, supervised swimming, cross-country skiing, fishing (yellow perch, brook trout), self-guiding nature trails.

Waverley Game Sanctuary (11)
Wildlife here includes bears, moose, hawks and bald eagles.
65 square miles.

Blomidon Provincial Park (14)
A 15-mile trail between Borden Brook and Cape Split begins in the park and runs atop 600-foot cliffs. Lookouts provide sweeping views of the Annapolis Valley, Minas Basin and the Bay of Fundy. Amethysts and agates can be found along the trail.
2 square miles. Camping.

Ellenwood Lake Provincial Park (1)
281 acres. Camping, supervised swimming, fishing (brook trout, yellow perch), canoeing.

Graves Island Provincial Park (9)
Granite boulders polished by wave action litter the shores of Graves Island. The park is linked to the mainland by a causeway.
123 acres. Camping, fishing (mackerel, cod).

Islands Provincial Park (4)
230 acres. Camping, fishing (brook and sea trout, cod, mackerel, pollack), canoeing, horseback riding, self-guiding nature trails.

Sand Pond National Wildlife Area (3)
In September as many as 2,000 black ducks gather on a 200-acre freshwater pond in the sanctuary. *2 square miles.*

Smiley's Provincial Park (13)
101 acres. Camping.

Tobeatic Game Management Area (5)
Bears, moose, muskrats and fishers roam forests of hemlock and yellow birch. Erratics—boulders deposited by Ice Age glaciers—are found here.
190 square miles. Wilderness camping, fishing (brook trout), canoeing.

Rissers Beach Provincial Park (8)
A ¾-mile sand beach is backed by dunes up to 10 feet high.
331 acres. Camping, supervised swimming, self-guiding nature trails.

Valleyview Provincial Park (7)
134 acres. Camping.

Melbourne Lake Waterfowl Sanctuary (2)
Up to 1,500 migrating birds at a time can be seen on shallow Melbourne Lake: Canada geese, greater scaup, black ducks and blue-winged teal. The lake is fed by coastal currents and at low tide becomes a mud flat crisscrossed by silty channels. *200 acres.*

Porter's Lake Provincial Park (10)
200 acres. Camping, fishing (brook trout), canoeing.

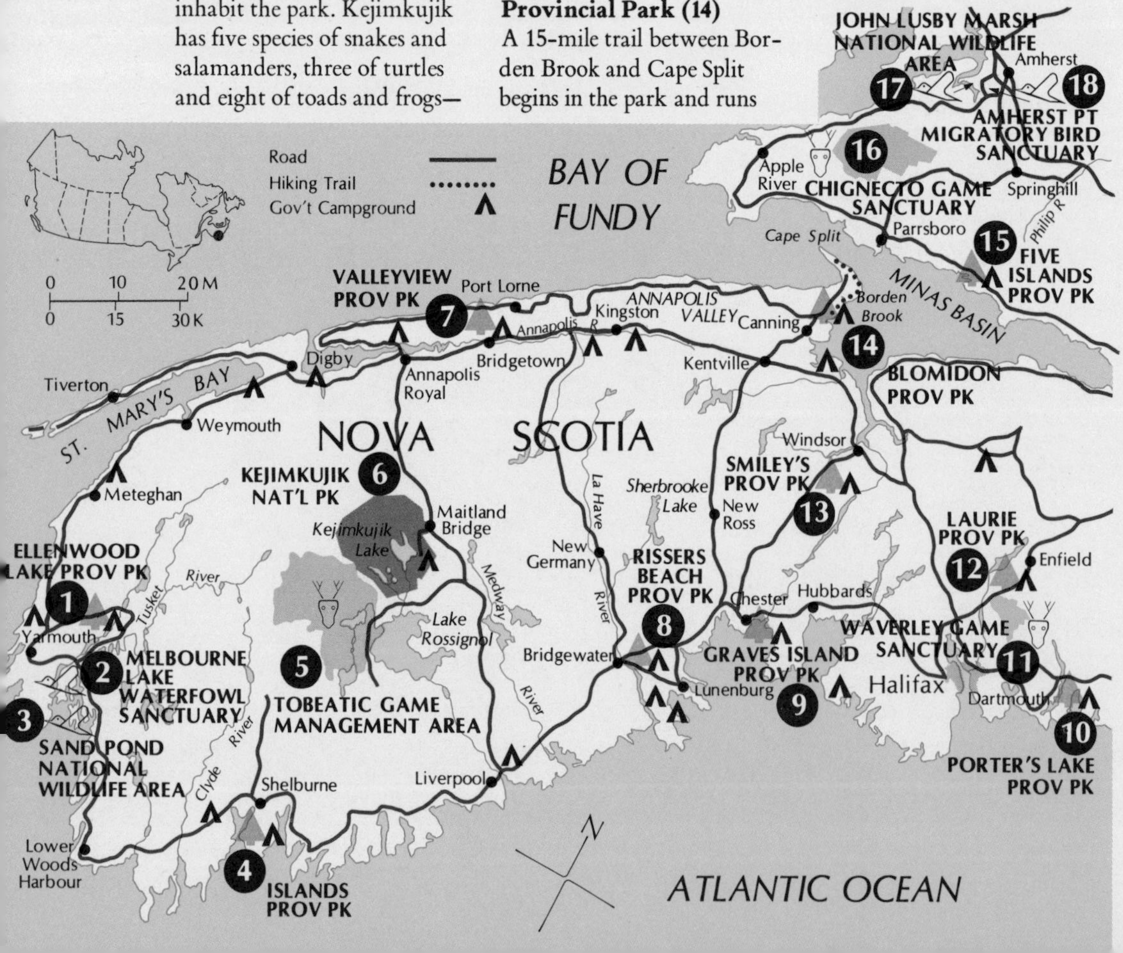

Laurie Provincial Park (12)
65 acres. Camping, fishing (brook trout, grayling, striped bass), canoeing.

Chignecto Game Sanctuary (16)
Moose, deer, wildcats, black bears and fishers inhabit the sanctuary. *85 square miles.*

John Lusby Marsh National Wildlife Area (17)
In late March and early April as many as 6,000 Canada geese visit a 1,200-acre marsh here. *2.5 square miles.*

Five Islands Provincial Park (15)
Tides along the shoreline here are among the highest in the world—up to 50 feet. A 2½-mile hiking trail winds along the crest of 150-foot cliffs facing Minas Basin.
839 acres. Camping, climbing, cross-country skiing, fishing (striped bass, flounder, cod).

Amherst Point Migratory Bird Sanctuary (18)
Two small lakes and a freshwater marsh support American widgeons, pintails and green- and blue-winged teal. *725 acres.*

Whycocomagh Provincial Park (22)
Several lookouts on the southwest slope of 1,000-foot Salt Mountain offer spectacular views of Bras d'Or Lake, a 400-square-mile inland sea that resembles a Scottish loch.
377 acres. Camping, climbing, fishing (Atlantic salmon, rainbow trout), canoeing.

Margaree Island National Wildlife Area (20)
Colonies of black guillemots, common terns, great cormorants and great black-backed gulls roost on pinnacles and ledges along 60-foot cliffs on Margaree Island. Forests of spruce and fir near the island's center support a rookery of great blue herons. *250 acres.*

Cape Breton Highlands National Park (19)
Some 70 miles of the Cabot Trail, a 184-mile highway that is one of North America's most scenic drives, follows the park's eastern, northern and western boundaries. The trail passes sheltered coves and white gypsum bluffs and offers views of near-vertical cliffs up to 1,000 feet high. White Hill, at 1,747 feet Nova Scotia's highest point, dominates the park interior, a desolate tableland of bogs, ponds and heath barrens. Spruce, gnarled by wind, cling to the plateau's thin soil. Subarctic plants such as reindeer moss and sheep-laurel thrive here. The more than 180 bird species in the park include arctic tern, bald eagle, osprey, golden eagle and boreal and snowy owl.
367 square miles. Camping, supervised swimming, fishing (Atlantic salmon), self-guiding nature trails.

Canoe Route (Scotsville to Margaree Harbour) (21)
In the Southwest Margaree River are some of Canada's best salmon pools. *26 miles.*

Mira Provincial Park (23)
166 acres. Camping, hiking, fishing (brook trout, Atlantic salmon), canoeing.

Battery Provincial Park (24)
A steep trail climbs to the forested summit of 200-foot Mount Granville.
144 acres. Camping, fishing (mackerel, Atlantic salmon).

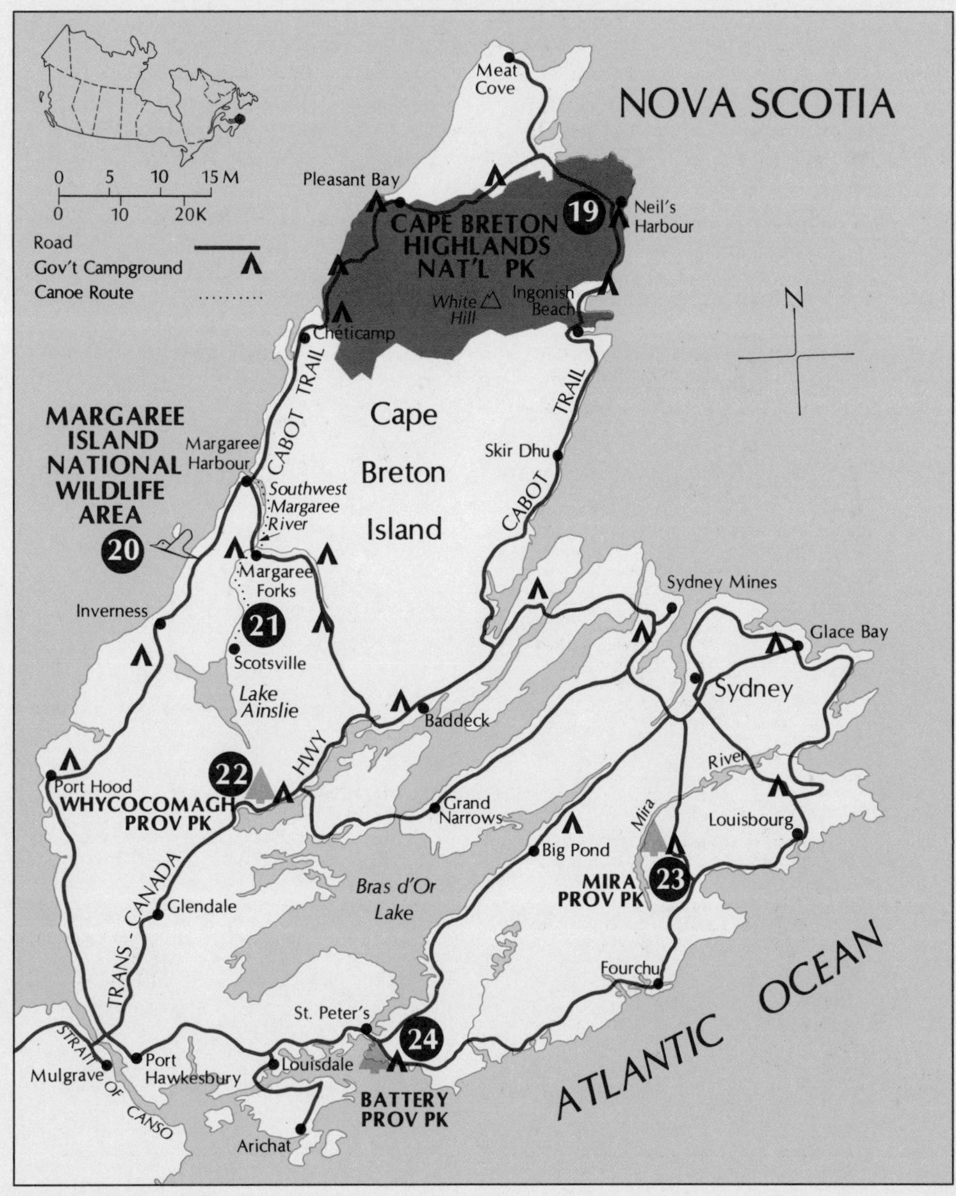

Caribou Country, a Volcanic Plain and a World-Famous Salmon Stream

Much of western Newfoundland is a rugged blend of fjord-like lakes and stark barrens, great sand dunes and dense forests. In Gros Morne National Park is the Serpentine Tableland, a plateau strewn with volcanic rocks. Newfoundland caribou and rare peregrine falcons inhabit the park. East of Gros Morne the headwaters of the Humber River offer some of the world's finest salmon fishing.

Sandbanks Provincial Park (8)
Some 1½ miles of sand beach are backed by dunes up to 30 feet high. To reach the park visitors must hike one mile from Burgeo which is accessible by boat from Channel-Port aux Basques.
700 acres. Camping, hiking, fishing (brook trout).

John T. Cheeseman Provincial Park (6)
A sandbar shelters a saltwater inlet from the thundering surf of the Atlantic. The park is surrounded by the desolate barrens of Cape Ray. Nearby is 2,375-foot Table Mountain.
450 acres. Camping, fishing (cod, flounder, capelin, mackerel, brook trout).

Crabbes River Provincial Park (3)
The Crabbes River abounds with spawning salmon in June and early July.
7 acres. Camping, fishing (Atlantic salmon, brook trout).

Otter Bank Provincial Park (7)
Shrubs no more than two feet high, and yellow, orange and green lichens mantle much of the rolling terrain.
400 acres. Camping, fishing (brook trout).

Mummichog Provincial Park (5)
A lagoon supports the mummichog, a fish found in few other places in Newfoundland. The lagoon is a mixture of fresh water from the Little Codroy River and salt water from the Atlantic. Bacteria have stained the lagoon shores purple. Great blue herons and American woodcocks, birds unusual in Newfoundland, are seen in the park.
204 acres. Camping, hiking, fishing (Atlantic salmon, brook trout), canoeing, self-guiding nature trails.

Barachois Pond Provincial Park (2)
A two-mile hiking trail winds through birch and spruce forests to the summit of 1,000-foot Erin Mountain. Moose, caribou and, occasionally, lynx are spotted.
13.5 square miles. Camping, hiking, fishing (Atlantic salmon, brook trout).

Grand Codroy Provincial Park (4)
As many as 500 migrating Canada geese at a time stop on the banks of the Grand Codroy River. Other birds include black ducks, common goldeneyes and blue- and green-winged teal.
8 acres. Camping, fishing (Atlantic salmon, brook trout), canoeing.

Piccadilly Head Provincial Park (1)
A sand beach backed by 40-foot limestone cliffs fringes the west shore of Piccadilly Bay in the park. In fall, the cliffs offer a fine view of migrating blue- and green-winged teal.
100 acres. Camping, hiking, fishing (cod, mackerel, capelin, brook trout).

River of Ponds Provincial Park (10)
150 acres. Camping, hiking, fishing (Atlantic salmon, brook trout), canoeing.

Sop's Arm River Provincial Park (12)
The horseshoe-shaped park rises some 70 feet above the Main River.

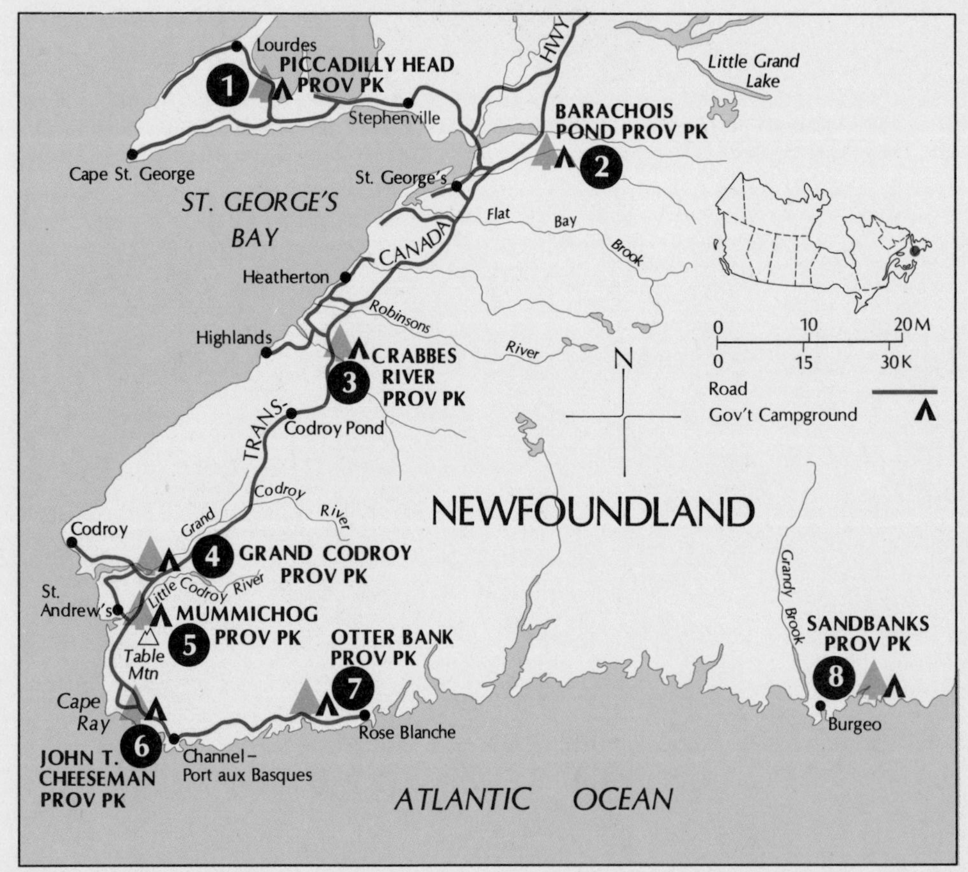

20 acres. Camping, fishing (Atlantic salmon, brook trout, cod, flounder, mackerel).

Flatwater Pond Provincial Park (11)
244 acres. Camping, fishing (brook trout), canoeing.

Gros Morne National Park (13)
The arctic hare, usually found only in the Arctic, and the Newfoundland caribou, one of the world's biggest caribou, inhabit this west-coast Newfoundland park. It is named for 2,644-foot Gros Morne Mountain, part of the Long Range Mountains. Several river valleys deepened by mile-thick ice during the Ice Age cradle spectacular fjord-like lakes (one is Western Brook Pond, more than 500 feet deep). The Long Range Mountains end in a low coastal plain crisscrossed by small rivers and covered with bogs and grassland. Along 45 miles of park coastline are steep cliffs, mud flats and sand dunes up to 40 feet high. Tidal pools along the shore teem with sea urchins, starfish, sponges and sea anemones. South of Bonne Bay is the Serpentine Tableland, an upland plain littered with ocher-brown volcanic boulders that have resisted erosion. Among more than 175 bird species sighted in Gros Morne are the endangered peregrine falcon and the gyrfalcon, American golden plover, osprey and whimbrel.
750 square miles. Camping, climbing, cross-country skiing, hiking, fishing (cod, Atlantic salmon, brook trout, mackerel).

Canoe Route (Grand Lake to Sheffield Lake) (15)
South of Sheffield Lake are The Topsails, granite spires that rise up to 500 feet above low-lying barrens. They were named for the topsails of a square-rigged ship: Gaff Topsail, Mizzen Topsail and Main Topsail. Canoeists must portage between Birchy and Sheffield lakes. *90 miles.*

Pistolet Bay Provincial Park (9)
3 square miles. Camping, fishing (Atlantic salmon, brook trout), canoeing.

Blue Ponds Provincial Park (17)
Two lakes are a deep turquoise; the lakes drain through underground sinkholes.
152 acres. Camping, hiking, fishing (brook trout).

Sir Richard Squires Memorial Park (14)
Spawning salmon use a ladder to bypass 30-foot Big Falls on the Humber River. Fishing near the falls is among the best in Newfoundland.
6 square miles. Camping.

Blow Me Down Provincial Park (18)
Wooden stairs climb a steep rock overhang and lead to a lookout with a fine view of the Bay of Islands.
550 acres. Camping, hiking, fishing (cod, flounder, mackerel, capelin).

Canoe Route (Osmond's Pond to Corner Brook) (16)
The Humber River drops 1,500 feet in 110 miles of lakes, turbulent rapids, waterfalls and forested islands. The upper 16 miles are virgin wilderness; canoeing this section requires extreme caution. In places downriver rounded hills back shoreline forests of spruce and white birch. Below Burnt Hill Pond the river flows between narrow canyon walls up to 300 feet high. The headwaters of the Upper Humber provide some of the best salmon fishing in the world. *110 miles.*

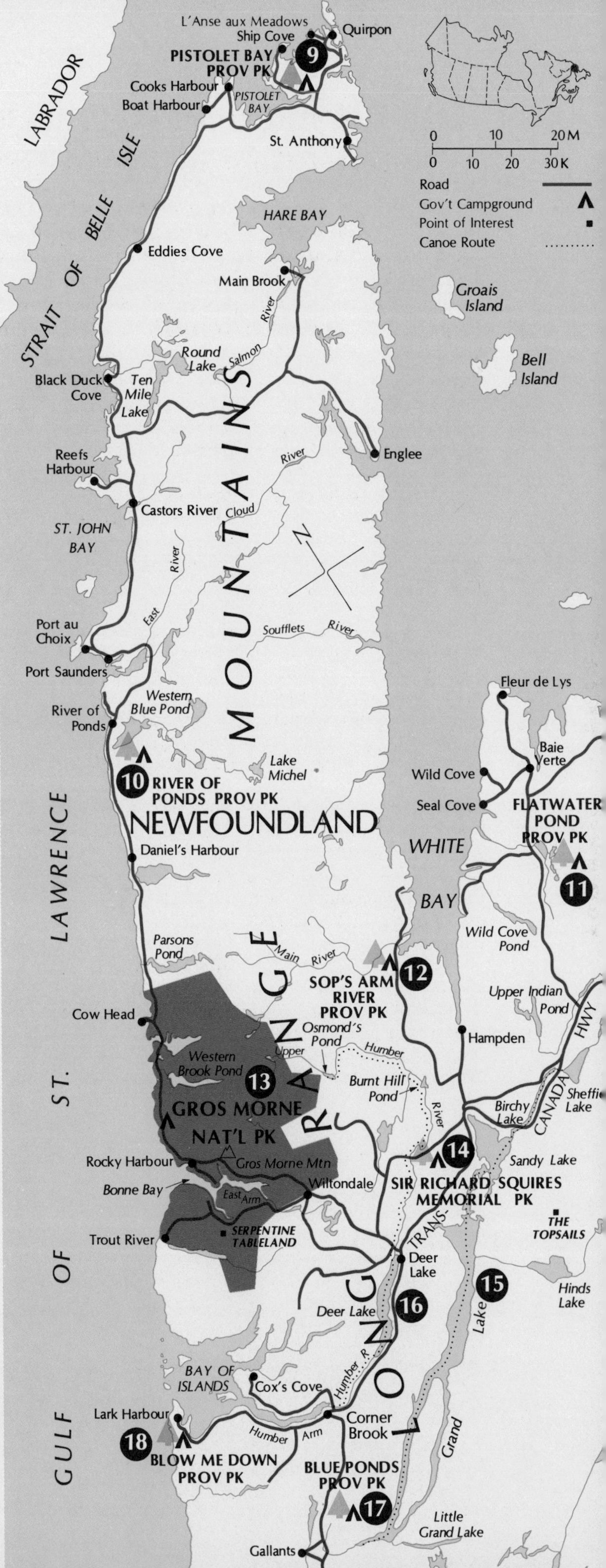

Killer Whales and Giant Squid Where Stately Icebergs Drift

Until midsummer a stately procession of icebergs flows past Terra Nova National Park on Newfoundland's east coast. The waters off the park contain abundant sealife: dolphins, killer whales and giant squid, bay and harp seals and giant bluefin tuna. Huge bird colonies roost in sanctuaries on Funk Island and at Witless Bay. A bird sanctuary at Cape St. Mary's contains North America's second largest gannet colony.

Terra Nova National Park (10)
Long into summer, icebergs carried by the cold Labrador Current drift off Terra Nova's ragged coastline of fjords, headlands and beaches. Bay and harp seals are occasionally seen offshore; dolphins and killer whales cruise in Bonavista Bay. Deep-sea fishing offshore is superb: bluefin tuna up to 700 lbs. have been landed; flounder, cod and mackerel are common. Squid, 20 to 50 feet long, are found in Bonavista Bay. Among the park's 350 plant species are several rare bog orchids including dragon's tongue, broad-lipped twayblade and spotted coral-root.
153 square miles. Camping, supervised swimming, hiking, canoeing, horseback riding, self-guiding nature trails.

La Manche Valley Provincial Park (20)
Downy woodpeckers, Swainson's thrush, boreal chickadees and northern water thrush are among the birds sighted here.
4.5 square miles. Camping, hiking, fishing (brook trout), canoeing.

Lockston Path Provincial Park (11)
600 acres. Camping, hiking, fishing (brook trout).

Northern Bay Sands Provincial Park (12)
12 acres. Camping, fishing (cod, capelin, flounder).

Holyrood Pond Provincial Park (23)
Ocean perch, haddock, skate and several ray species inhabit Holyrood Pond, a saltwater lake 14 miles long and up to 300 feet deep.
1.5 square miles. Camping, canoeing.

Funk Island Bird Sanctuary (1)
More than 1,500,000 murres nest on rocky Funk Island, some 40 miles northeast of Cape Freels. The great auk nested here in great numbers until exterminated by hunters in the early 1800s. The island is accessible by boat from the mainland but rough seas and treacherous reefs make the crossing difficult. *66 acres.*

Square Pond Provincial Park (8)
96 acres. Camping, hiking, fishing (brook trout, arctic char), canoeing.

Windmill Bight Provincial Park (3)
There is a mile-long sand beach here and icebergs are seen offshore as late as July.
182 acres. Camping, fishing (Atlantic salmon, brook trout, cod, mackerel).

Dildo Run Provincial Park (2)
455 acres. Camping, fishing (cod, mackerel).

Butter Pot Provincial Park (18)
The Lookout atop 1,000-foot Butter Pot Hill provides a fine view of Conception Bay, renowned for giant bluefin tuna.
6.5 square miles. Camping, cross-country skiing, hiking, fishing (brook trout), self-guiding nature trails.

David Smallwood Provincial Park (9)
127 acres. Camping, hiking, fishing (Atlantic salmon, brook trout).

Notre Dame Provincial Park (5)
278 acres. Camping, fishing (brook trout).

Fitzgerald's Pond Provincial Park (16)
3 square miles. Camping, hiking, fishing (Atlantic salmon, brook trout), canoeing.

Cape St. Mary's Bird Sanctuary (24)
North America's second largest gannet colony (the largest is on Quebec's Bonaventure Island) crowds ledges and crannies on Bird Rock, a 500-foot-high sea stack. *160 acres.*

Gushue's Pond Provincial Park (17)
205 acres. Camping, fishing (brook trout), canoeing.

Chance Cove Provincial Park (21)
Bay seals often congregate in shallow Chance Cove.
8 square miles. Wilderness camping, fishing (Atlantic salmon, brook trout).

Jacks Pond Provincial Park (13)
A stream meanders between grassy banks then tumbles over a small falls into Jacks Pond.
2 square miles. Camping, fishing (brook trout), canoeing.

Canoe Route (Gambo to Indian Bay) (7)
This string of lakes and rivers offers some of the best brook trout fishing in Newfoundland. *40 miles.*

Even in July great icebergs are seen off Newfoundland's east coast.

Avalon Wilderness Area (22)
A herd of 1,500 caribou feeds on lichens in this preserve on the Avalon Peninsula. Visitors must obtain permits from the Department of Tourism at St. John's before entering the area.
335 square miles. Wilderness camping, hiking, fishing (brook trout), canoeing.

Backside Pond Provincial Park (15)
A short trail through an evergreen forest links a freshwater pond and a coastal beach.
2 square miles. Camping, fishing (brook trout, cod, mackerel).

Jonathan's Pond Provincial Park (6)
1.5 square miles. Camping, fishing (Atlantic salmon, brook trout), canoeing.

Witless Bay Bird Sanctuary (19)
Parts of Gull Island, one of three islands in the sanctuary, are riddled with the burrows of some 1,250,000 Leach's storm-petrels. Black-legged kittiwakes, herring gulls and approximately 200,000 common puffins nest on the island. Green Island supports 100,000 Atlantic murres and Leach's storm-petrels inhabit Great Island. Charter boats circle the islands. *346 acres.*

Bellevue Beach Provincial Park (14)
A small saltwater pond is sheltered from the sea by a barachois (a bar of sand and gravel).
188 acres. Camping, fishing (brook trout, cod, mackerel).

Canoe Route (Gambo to Gander Bay) (4)
Canada geese, green-winged teal and ring-necked ducks nest along this route which winds through forests of white birch and balsam fir.
85 miles.

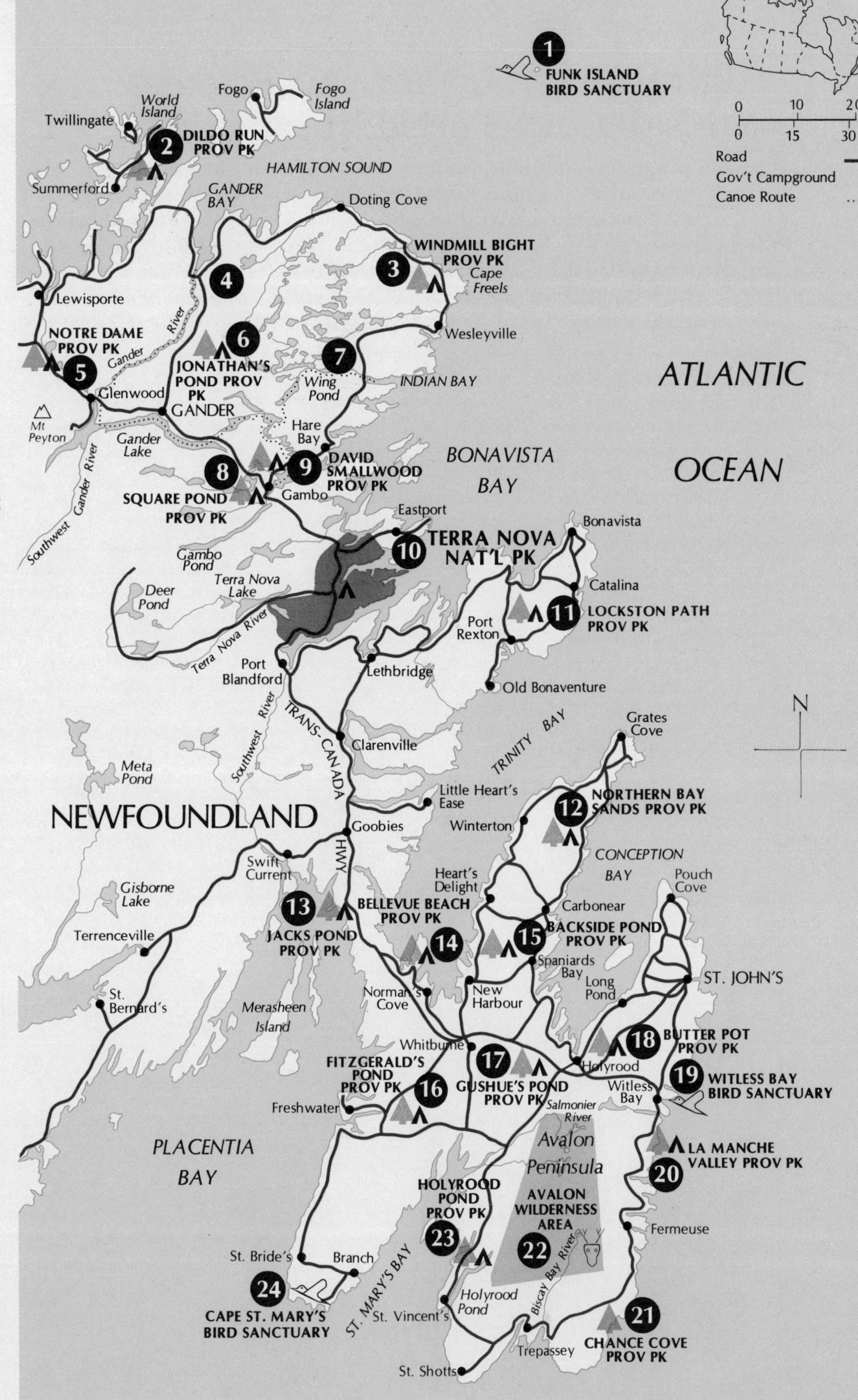

Mighty Mount Logan, Our Highest, and Nahanni's Forbidding Canyons

Canada's highest mountain, the Yukon's 19,524-foot Mount Logan, is the mightiest of the St. Elias range in Kluane National Park. To the east, in the Northwest Territories, are Nahanni National Park's forbidding canyons and stunning Virginia Falls. Southeast of Kluane, crossing the Alaska-British Columbia border, is the Chilkoot Pass Hiking Trail, which dates from the Klondike gold rush of '98. There are canoe routes on the remote Liard, Stewart, Pelly, Teslin and Yukon rivers.

Kluane National Park (6)
Towering above the rest of the St. Elias Mountains (eight peaks are over 15,000 feet) is 19,524-foot Mount Logan, Canada's highest mountain. More than half of Kluane is under ice fields and glaciers. The Steele Glacier, one of more than 2,000 glaciers in the park, moves as much as a half-mile a month. A two-foot layer of white ash spewed from a volcano some 1,400 years ago blankets the Klutlan Glacier, whose ice is almost a mile thick in places. An old packhorse trail from the Slims River bridge passes sand dunes and mud flats and ends at the foot of the Kaskawulsh Glacier. Dall's sheep, caribou, mountain goats and grizzly bears inhabit Kluane—a combination of animals found in no other national park. Spruce grouse, bald eagle, rock ptarmigan and whistling swan are among 170 bird species here. Only experienced hikers should venture into the interior—even in July fierce blizzards are common in the mountains. Climbers and overnight hikers must register at the park headquarters in Haines Junction; visitors who want to climb in the St. Elias Mountains must apply three months in advance.
8,500 square miles. Camping, fishing (Kokanee salmon, whitefish, arctic grayling, lake and Dolly Varden trout).

Canoe Route (Ross River to Fort Selkirk) (3)
Northwest of the Faro bridge the Pelly River meanders past 5,900-foot Rose Mountain; some 40 miles downstream are 7,100-foot Mount Hodder and 6,900-foot Tay Mountain. The river races through three sets of rapids in Granite Canyon, 4 miles long and up to 250 feet deep. Two 20-foot-high outcrops split the river into three channels at Gull Rocks. *249 miles.*

Canoe Route (Hess River to Dawson) (1)
Steep 75-foot-high banks riddled with waterworn holes border Fraser Falls, a series of rapids in the Stewart River that drops 25 feet in a quarter mile. *360 miles.*

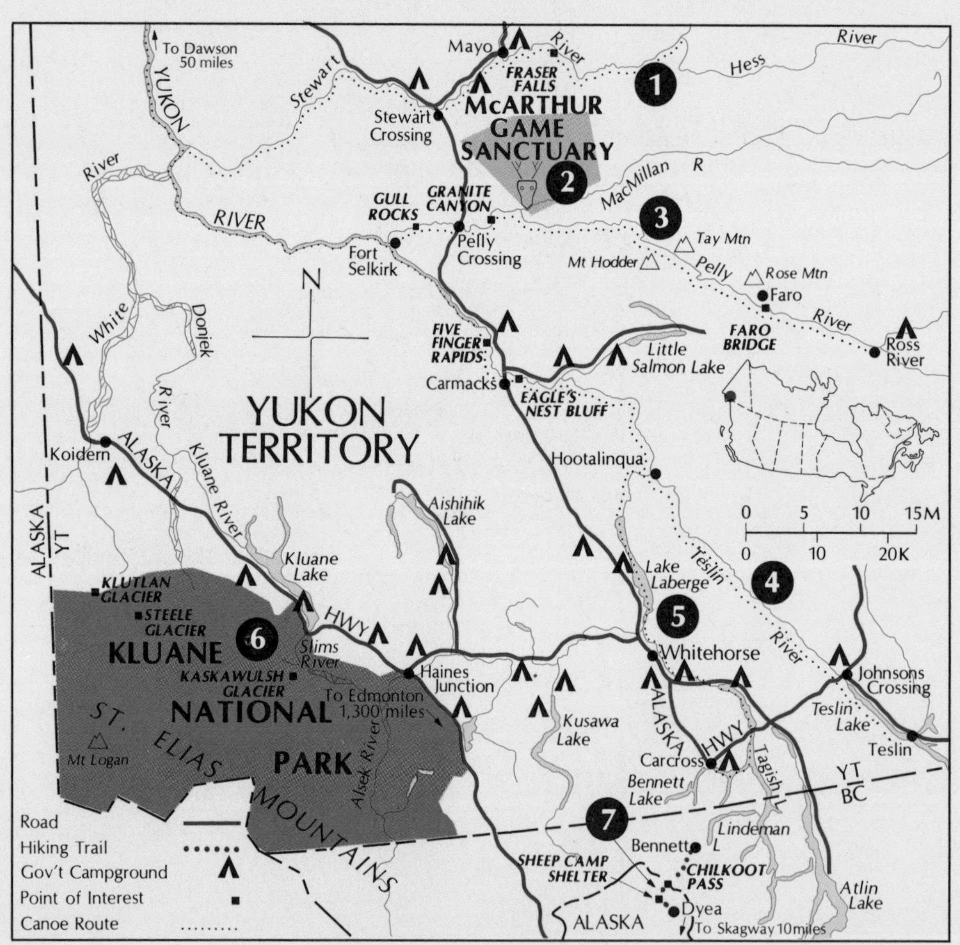

On the Trail of '98

For the thousands of fortune seekers who tramped the treacherous White Pass Trail during the Gold Rush of '98 the completion of the White Pass and Yukon Route—in 1900—came too late. Now it's a tourist attraction, a 110-mile train journey from Skagway, Alaska, to Whitehorse, Y.T., following the old trail through some of the most spectacular scenery in North America. Operating on a narrow-gauge (36-inch) track, the train climbs to 2,916-foot Log Cabin, B.C., the highest point on the route. A bridge near White Pass Summit spans Dead Horse Gulch, named for the nearly 3,000 horses that perished during the gold rush. The railway connects with shipping lines at Skagway and with bus and air service at Whitehorse.

Canoe Route (Teslin to Carmacks) (4)
The Teslin River passes cliffs up to 300 feet high. Wild rice grows in some parts of the river. *260 miles.*

Chilkoot Pass Hiking Trail (7)
This rugged trail was the Chilkoot Pass route to the gold fields of the Yukon. The route begins at Dyea, Alaska, winds for 13 miles along the east bank of the Taya River to Sheep Camp Shelter, then climbs 3 miles to 3,740-foot Chilkoot Pass before descending to Lindeman Lake. Hikers can return by foot or take a White Pass and Yukon Route train to Whitehorse or Skagway, Alaska. *35 miles.*

McArthur Game Sanctuary (2)
The sanctuary was created to protect a small herd of Fannin (saddle-backed) sheep once thought nearing extinction. *204 square miles.*

Canoe Route (Bennett Lake to Dawson) (5)
Between Lake Laberge and Hootalinqua, the Yukon River surges through a winding channel bordered by sand-and-gravel cliffs up to 300 feet high. At Five Finger Rapids four 50-foot-high sandstone columns divide the river into five streams. Near Carmacks is 700-foot-high Eagle's Nest Bluff and north of Fort Selkirk are black basalt cliffs up to 450 feet high. Arctic grayling, whitefish and northern pike are found in the river and its tributaries. Abandoned cabins—many built during the gold rush of 1898—and beaches, sandbars and wooded islands provide excellent campsites. *600 miles.*

Canoe Route (Frances Lake to Fort Simpson) (8)
The Liard River flows through two miles of turbulent white water between 100-foot-high cliffs at Portage Brûlé Rapids, the longest stretch of rapids on the route. Near where the South Nahanni River joins the Liard is Nahanni Butte, a limestone cliff rising 4,580 feet above sea level. Bald eagles, belted kingfishers, hawks, Bohemian waxwings and, occasionally, ospreys are seen along the route. *850 miles.*

Nahanni National Park (9)
One of Canada's great wilderness trips is the 130 miles by boat up the South Nahanni River from Nahanni Butte to Virginia Falls. Travelers pass rock walls up to 3,000 feet high in 17-mile-long First Canyon, then enter Deadmen Valley, where two headless bodies were discovered in 1908. Then come the 4,000-foot ramparts of Second Canyon. In Third Canyon, 21 miles of fast water, the river makes a hairpin turn at the base of a sheer rock wall at The Gate, then passes Pulpit Rock, a 200-foot limestone pinnacle. There is a final 10 miles of white water before Virginia Falls, whose twin chutes tumble 294 feet in a haze of spray. At Rabbitkettle Hotsprings, on the Rabbitkettle River, water up to 41°C. (106°F.) bubbles from the top of a 90-foot mound of porous rock and spills down a series of lime and salt terraces. Species of bulrushes and clover found nowhere else in the North bloom nearby. At The Sand Blowout, wind has created a strange landscape of pillars, arches and hollows. Dall's sheep, moose and grizzly bear are among 31 mammal species in the park. Nahanni Butte, 20 miles southeast of the park border, is accessible by aircraft from Fort Simpson. Visitors must register at the park headquarters before entering Nahanni.
1,840 square miles. Wilderness camping, climbing, fishing (arctic grayling, whitefish, Dolly Varden and lake trout), canoeing.

Norah Willis Michener Territorial Park Game Preserve (10)
Dall's sheep, moose, grizzly bears and wolverines roam the preserve, accessible only by float plane from Fort Simpson or Watson Lake. Birds here include hairy woodpeckers, white-winged crossbills, boreal owls and spruce grouse. *3.5 square miles.*

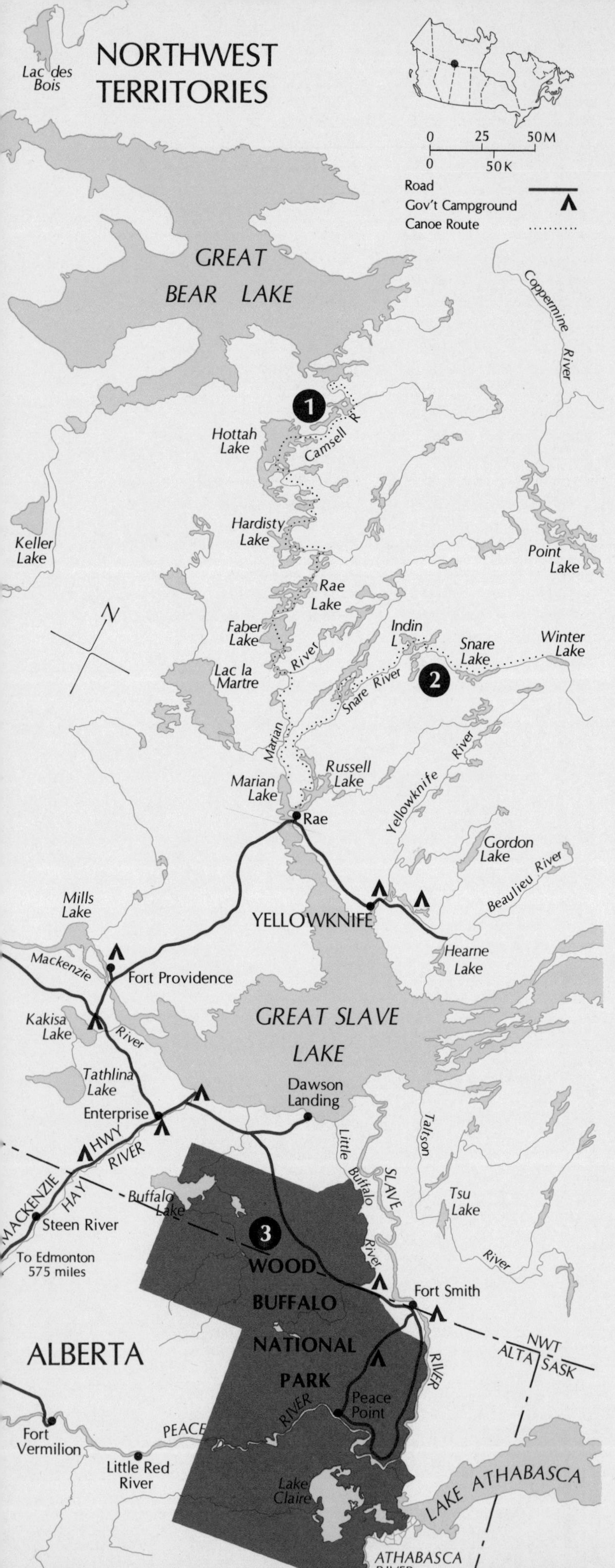

Wood Buffalo Is Biggest, Auyuittuq Farthest North

Wood Buffalo Park, the world's largest national park, straddles the Alberta-Northwest Territories border and contains much of the immense Peace-Athabasca Delta. Some 2,300 miles to the northeast, on Baffin Island, is Auyuittuq Park, Canada's first national park north of the Arctic Circle.

Wood Buffalo National Park (3)
The world's largest national park—eight times the size of Prince Edward Island—was established in 1922 to protect North America's last herd of wood bison, some 1,500 animals. About 6,600 plains bison, a smaller species, were introduced later. Four migratory flyways overlap in the park and there is an abundance of birdlife. Some 37 whooping cranes—more than half the world population of that rare bird—nest in Wood Buffalo. North America's most northerly colony of white pelicans is also found here. The park contains two-thirds of the 2,344-square-mile Peace-Athabasca Delta, an expanse of poorly drained bogs, meandering streams and silty river channels. Near the Slave River are salt plains, an area crisscrossed by salt streams; evaporation has formed salt mounds up to 70 feet across and 3 feet high. Throughout the park are huge sinkholes where subsurface runoff has dissolved underlying soft rock causing the collapse of the surface terrain. One sinkhole is 120 feet across and 80 feet deep. *17,300 square miles.* Camping, fishing (walleye, northern pike, whitefish, lake trout).

Canoe Route (Great Slave Lake to Great Bear Lake) (1)
This often treacherous route (suitable only for experienced canoeists) links numerous lakes and streams. In 12,275-square-mile Great Bear Lake, the world's eighth largest lake, is found the four-horned sculpin, a fish species thought to have migrated south from the Arctic Ocean during the last ice age. *300 miles.*

Canoe Route (Winter Lake to Marian Lake) (2)
Near Marian Lake is North America's northernmost nesting colony of Caspian terns. Lake trout—up to 30 lbs.—thrive along the route. Rapids on the Snare River drop 270 feet in 18 miles above Indin Lake. *200 miles.*

Auyuittuq National Park (5)
This land of icy mountain heights, steep-sided fjords and hardy arctic flowers is Canada's first national park north of the Arctic Circle. Mantling the Cumberland Peninsula highlands is the 2,200-square-mile Penny Ice Cap, second largest continental glacier in the Northern Hemisphere after the Icefield Ranges in the Yukon's St. Elias Mountains. Coronation Glacier, 20 miles long and 2 miles wide, flows from the ice cap and smaller glaciers spill down the slopes of Pangnirtung Pass, an ice-carved trough extending 60 miles across the peninsula. Towering above the pass is 7,050-foot Mount Odin, probably the loftiest peak between the Carolinas and Ellesmere Island. Along the

Cumberland Peninsula are fjords whose walls rise up to 3,000 feet above the sea. Arctic foxes, arctic hares, polar bears, arctic wolves and lemmings inhabit the park. Rare blue and humpback whales occasionally surface among huge icebergs that drift in Davis Strait. In autumn narwhals and walruses migrate along the northeast coast of Baffin Island. Among 38 species of birds in Auyuittuq are the endangered peregrine falcon and whistling swan. Nearby is Cape Searle where more than 200,000 northern fulmars—thought to be the world's largest colony—nest on 1,400-foot cliffs. The park is reached on foot or by canoe from Pangnirtung, which is accessible by air from Montreal. *8,300 square miles.* Wilderness camping, climbing, hiking, fishing (arctic char, stickleback, sculpin), canoeing.

Bylot Island Bird Sanctuary (4)
Some 800,000 thick-billed murres and 100,000 black-legged kittiwakes nest on sheer cliffs along the northeast coast of Bylot Island. A plateau to the southwest supports 15,000 greater snow geese. Polar bears roam the north and east coasts of the island; hooded, ringed and bearded seals can be seen offshore. *4,273 square miles.*

Dewey Soper Bird Sanctuary (6)
In this the world's largest goose colony are one million Canada geese, lesser snow geese and black brants. *3,150 square miles.*

Cape Dorset Bird Sanctuary (7)
Some 6,500 northern eiders nest on rocky islands here. Other birds include Iceland gulls, snow buntings, water pipits, redpolls and king eiders. *100 square miles.*

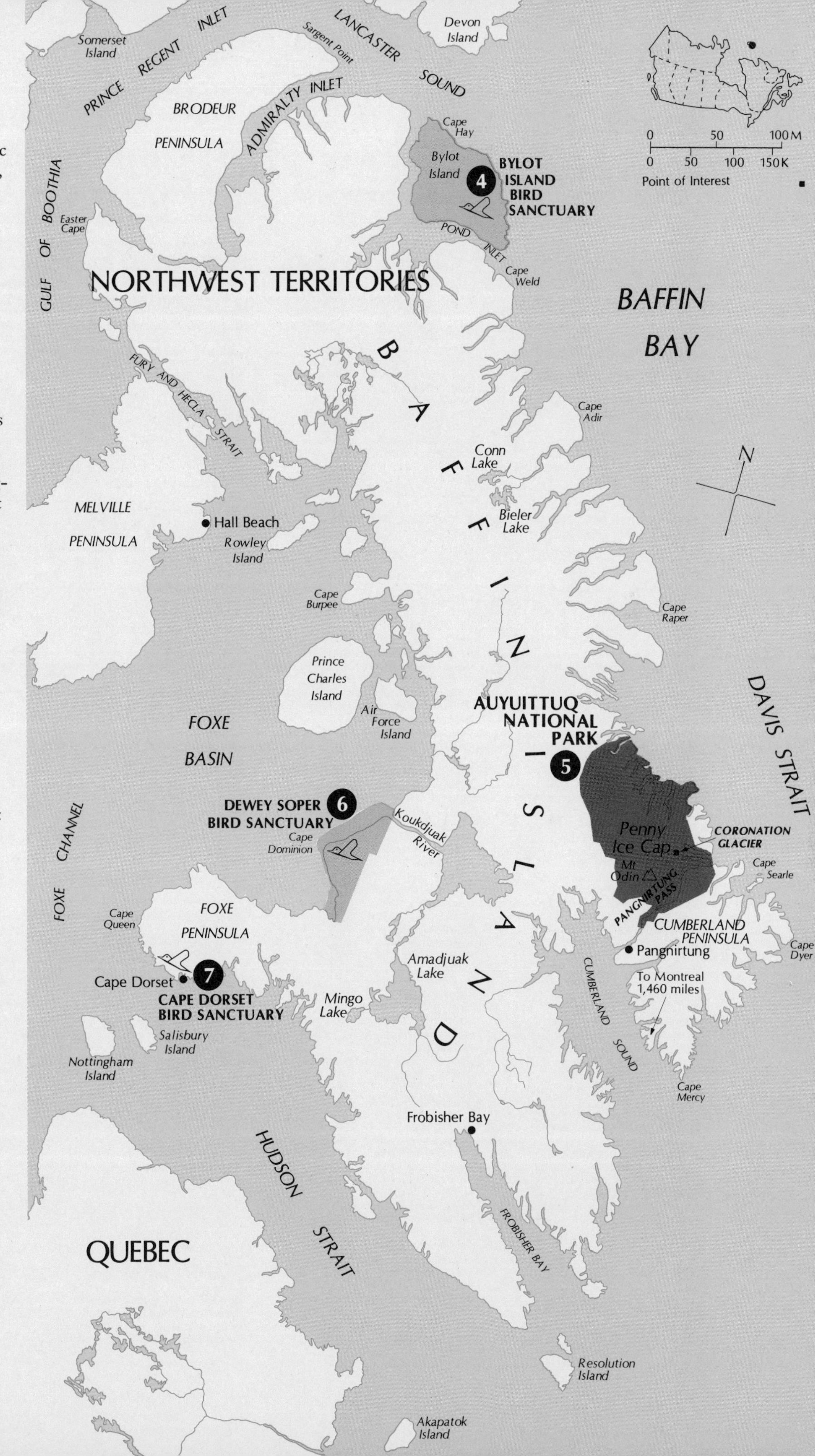

Index

The page numbers in regular type are references to the text, in **boldface** to photos or illustrations. Page numbers followed by the letter m are references to the maps.

A

B

C

D

E

F

G

H

I

J

K

L

M

N

O

P

Q

R

S

bighorn, 40; snow, 40; Stone's 40, **41**, 315

T

U

V

W

Picture Credits

The abbreviations used here are these:

BCI Bruce Coleman, Inc.
BKD Barbara K. Deans
CC Cynthia Chalk
CH Chic Harris
CP Carroll Perkins
DH Dave Hatler
DMc Don McPhee, Chilliwack, B.C.
EK Edi Klopfenstein
FB Fred Bruemmer
GH Grant Heilman
GL Gisèle Lamoureux
HAT Harry A. Thomson
HH Hazel Hudson
HVG Harold V. Green
IBC The Image Bank of Canada
JGW John Gregory Woods
KG Keith Gunnar
LC Lorne Coulson
LLR Leonard Lee Rue III
MD Marjorie Dezell
MF Mary Ferguson
MS Miller Services, Toronto
NCNP National Collection of Nature Photographs
NRL Norman R. Lightfoot
RW Richard Wright
SC Stewart Cassidy
SJK Stephen J. Krasemann
TWH Tom W. Hall
WDS Wilfried D. Schurig

Credits are left to right, top to bottom, with additional information as needed. A single credit means all photographs on that page or pages are from the same source. A dual credit (Doug Long/Super Photo) identifies the photographer first, the agency or photo collection second. Numbers in parentheses (2) indicate more than one photograph on that page or pages are from the same source.

2 David W. Hamilton/IBC; 6 Paul von Baich;
8-9 Allan Harvey;
10 Fernando Levi; 11 Dan Howard;
12-13 CH; 13 GH;
14-15 David Steiner; 15 Kent & Donna Dannen;
16 RW; 16-17 Parks Canada;
18-19 Hale Flygare; 19 SJK, EK;
20 KG; 21 Hans Fuhrer;
22 LC; 22-23 Ulvis Alberts; 23 Richard Charette;
24-25 CP; 25 Bruce Hayes;
26 RW; 27 SC;
28 Gabe Palmer/IBC; 29 Allan Harvey;
30-31 Dr. Ulrich Kretschmar;
32-33 Ellis Roddick;
34 SJK; 34-35 FB;
36-37 SJK;
38 Jerome Knap Photo; 39 David G. Allen, Ithaca, N.Y.;
40-41 J. C. Holroyd/NCNP; 41 SJK;
43 J. M. Burnley/BCI;
44 NRL;
47 SC;
48 FB; 48-49 EK; 49 Jack Templeton;
50 SC; 51 Jack Couffer/BCI;
52 Ralph Connor, SC; 53 Jack Couffer/BCI;
54-55 F. A. Curylo/C.P.S. Productions; 55 Hans Reinhard/BCI;
56 LLR; 57 William W. Bacon III;
58 WDS; 59 William W. Bacon III;
60 NRL; 60-61 HAT;
62-63 Cy Hampson; 63 LLR;
64-65 TWH; 65 SJK (2), TWH;
66 SJK; 67 Jane Burton/BCI, Parks Canada;
68-69 James A. Sullivan;
70 Jane Burton/BCI, Jeff Foott/BCI;
72 R. Barry Ranford, SJK; 72-73 HAT; 73 Richard Fyfe/Canadian Wildlife Service;
74 HAT, NRL; 75 LLR;
76 Peter Tasker/NCNP;
78 The Sea Library; 78-79 Jen & Des Bartlett/BCI; 79 The Sea Library, Norman Owen Tomalin/BCI;
80 Jen & Des Bartlett/BCI, The Sea Library; 81 Gordon Willianson/BCI, Jen & Des Bartlett/BCI;
82 The Sea Library; 83 Neil G. Carey, FB;
84-85 FB;
86 F. A. Curylo/C.P.S. Productions; 86-87 Vince Claerhout;
88-89 G. F. Fairbrother, Ottawa; 89 FB, RW;
90 Jack Templeton, RW; 91 RW, WDS;
92 RW; 93 Ralph Connor;
94-95 Gary R. Jones; 95 Jen & Des Bartlett/BCI, DH;
96 HAT, HVG; 97 Ralph Connor;
98 MD; 99 James Murray, FB;
100 FB, HVG; 101 FB;
102-103 Lorne Scott; 103 LLR, Doug Woods;
104 DH, Marjorie R. Dow; 105 Barry Griffiths;
106 Leonard Zorn; 107 W. Aubrey Crich, BKD;
108 WDS; 109 DMc, NFB Photothèque ONF;
110 WDS, TWH, Cy Hampson, Leonard Zorn; 111 HVG;
112 William W. Bacon III, W. Aubrey Crich, Doug Woods; 113 Dr. George K. Peck;
114 Thase Daniel/BCI (2), R. Barry Ranford; 115 Lorne Scott;
116 Jean-Louis Frund; 117 Ken Carmichael;
118 WDS, Ken Carmichael; 119 HVG;
120 David A. Sprott/NCNP, CP; 121 Dr. George K. Peck;
122 Hans-Ludwig Blohm, Tom Willock; 123 Edgar T. Jones, SJK, Cy Hampson;
124 MD; 125 Ken Carmichael, Joe vanWormer/BCI;
126 Maxime St-Amour/NCNP; 126-127 Hal Harrison/Grant Heilman Photography; 127 Vince Claerhout, Hal Harrison/Grant Heilman Photography;
128 Thase Daniel/BCI, Doug Gilroy (1); 129 WDS;
130-131 Gary N. Corbett; 131 David G. Allen, Ithaca, N.Y.;
132 Wilbur S. Tripp; 133 Gary R. Jones, Gary N. Corbett;
134 SC; 135 Gary W. Seib, Vince Claerhout, TWH;
136 DH, NFB Photothèque ONF; 137 Ken Carmichael, Albert Karvonen;
138 SC, SJK; 139 Bert Hoferichter, MPA;
140 David G. Allen, Ithaca, N.Y., W. Aubrey Crich; 141 Peter Tasker/NCNP;
142 LLR; 142-143 NRL; 143 LLR;
144 J. R. Simon/BCI, Dr. George K. Peck; 145 Dr. E. R. Degginger/BCI;
146 TWH (2), Robert Carr/BCI; 147 NFB Photothèque ONF, NRL;
148 HAT; 149 MF/NCNP, Cy Hampson, Maxime St-Amour;
150 NRL; 151 Valerie J. May;
152 Vince Claerhout; 152-153 MF; 153 CP, SJK;
154 R. Barry Ranford; 154-155 Jane Burton/BCI, NRL, Peter Tasker/NCNP (2); 155 Barry Griffiths, Maria Zorn;
156 CC, William H. Amos/BCI; 156-157 DH; 157 DH, B. B. Jones;
158-159 LC;
160 Ted Gorsline, JGW, BKD (2), Valerie J. May; 161 William E. Ruth/BCI, WDS, Maxime St-Amour, Elaine Edwards, Joy Spurr/BCI;
162 George Zimbel/Island Documentaries Ltd., MF, BKD; 162-163 David Overcash/BCI, Hans Reinhard/BCI, Doug Gilroy; 163 CP, BKD (2), JGW;
164 GH, CP, DMc, HVG, Kenneth C. Alexander, Menno Fieguth, HH; 164-165 Dunkin Bancroft, Harry Rowed; 165 HH, MD;
166 Wm. K. Kirkwood, MD, Joy Spurr/BCI, Gary W. Seib; 166-167 WDS, MD, Lorne Scott; 167 HH, CC, GH;
168 Hans Reinhard/BCI, Betty Greenacre, CC, Kay McGregor; 168-169 GH, Hal Harrison/Grant Heilman Photography; 169 W. A. T. Gilmour/NCNP, GH, Betty Greenacre, Parks Canada/Point Pelee National Park;
170 Manitoba Government Travel, Ted Maginn (2), Betty Greenacre (2), Elaine Edwards, Nancy Anderson; 170-171 R. Barry Ranford; 171 GH, CH;
172 Stephen E. Homer, TWH, Joy Spurr/BCI, Valerie J. May, Robert Carr/BCI, Etgar T. Jones; 172-173 Paul von Baich, HVG, Garnet McPherson; 173 DH, GH, CP;
174 Ross Harris, Arthur Holbrook, J. Ray Baker, TWH; 174-175 Bert Hoferichter, MPA; 175 GH, John Powell, Kay McGregor, Garnet McPherson, MF, David Moore;
176 LC, S. Naiman, Gary N. Corbett, MF, BKD; 176-177 MF; 177 P. M. Light, Menno Fieguth, MD, BKD, HH;
178 LC, BKD, David A. Gray, JSK/IBC, G. K. Bain; 178-179 CC; 179 BKD, CP, TWH, HVG, HAT, Neville Fox-Davies/BCI;
180 Lucette Durand, George Zimbel/Island Documentaries Ltd., Mary Primrose, GL, DMc; 180-181 DMc, Marian C. Goldstrom; 181 DH, Peter D'Angelo;
182 Menno Fieguth, BKD, Lorne Scott, CP; 182-183 J. R. Simon/BCI, J. Y. C. Quong; 183 MF, HH, HVG, GH, Manitoba Government Travel;
184 Marian C. Goldstrom, HH, James Simon/BCI, Etgar T. Jones; 184-185 CC, Doug Gilroy; 185 MF, Dawna H. Newell, Gary W. Seib;
186 K. F. Dudley, William Hackett, Steve R. Cannings, Gary W. Seib, DH, Manitoba Government Travel; 186-187 Fred Lahrman; 187 HH, Fred Lahrman, Gary W. Seib;
188 Sydney G. Cannings, CH, Sig Bradshaw, Don Langford; 188-189 Victor A. Bernyk, Menno Fieguth; 189 Hale Flygare, Harry Rowed, Betty Greenacre, MD, Tom Willock;
190 Dunkin Bancroft; 190-191 SJK; 191 K. W. Fink/BCI, SJK, Albert Karvonen, Dr. Dorothy Swales (2), GL, J. Y. C. Quong, Parks Canada;
192 George Hunter, FB, KG, DH, Mildred McPhee, Etgar T. Jones, Fred Knezevich; 193 MD, P. M. Light, Dunkin Bancroft, Brian Milne;
194 J. A. Kraulis, Robert Carr/BCI, GH; 194-195 Bruce Hayes, CH; 195 GH, SJK, David A. Gray, GL, Gwen Walker, CH, GL;
196 MF, George F. Long, David A. Gray, Eva Hackett, GL, Mary M. Smith; 197 Gilles Ouellette, Elaine Edwards, Mary Primrose, RW, George F. Long, Elaine Edwards;
198 GL, CC, J. A. Kraulis, BKD, Parks Canada; 198-199 DMc; 199 BKD, Doris J. Mowry, Eva Hackett, Garnet McPherson;
200-201 MS;
204 CC, Carole Miklos; 204-205 Ray Atkeson; 205 GH (2), Sig Bradshaw, MF, CC, Teldon of Canada, Jean Isaacs;
206-207 National Oceanic & Atmospheric Association, BKD; 207 MS, NASA, National Center for Atmospheric Research;
208 Ray Atkeson; 209 CH, MF, Ellis Roddick, CC;
210-211 MS;
212 EK, Brian Priest, HAT; 213 J. A. Kraulis, MS;
215 KG/BCI;
217 Jean-Claude Gagnon;
218 MS; 219 RW;
222 Georgia Clarke;
224 Carole Miklos;
227 Brian Priest;
228 Pierre Léveillé;
234 Paul von Baich;
238 Menno Fieguth; 239 EK;
240 LC; 241 KG;
242 TWH, Wayne Tester, Tom Willock; 243 F. A. Curylo/C.P.S. Productions, HAT;
245 KG/BCI, Pierre Léveillé (3);
246 David A. Gray, Wilbur S. Tripp; 246-247 David A. Gray;
248-249 EK;
252 KG; 253 SJK;
254-255 Chris Harris;
256-257 Paul von Baich;
259 JGW;
260-261 John Foster; 261 Ellis Roddick;
262 TWH, CH; 263 JGW;
265 Bill Brooks/BCI;
266 Etta M. Parker; 266-267 Neil G. Carey;
268 LC, Don Beers;
270-271 Malak/MS;
273 Chris Harris;
274 Larry D. Gordon/IBC, Neil G. Carey, MS; 275 T. Rankin/IBC, Alisson Brown/IBC;
276-277 John Foster; 277 Dianne Kretschmar;
278 Patrick H. Davies/BCI;
280 Shorty Wilcox/IBC;
283 Ontario Ministry of Industry and Tourism;
284 Jerome Knap Photo, MD; 285 Clyde H. Smith, Jerome Knap Photo;
286 DMc; 286-287 J. Elder/IBC; 287 KG/BCI, RW;
289 M. Julius Baum/BCI;
291 John Foster;
292 Hans Fuhrer; 292-293 Gilles Ouellette; 293 EK, KG;
294 Bert Hoferichter, MPA; 295 California Institute of Technology and Carnegie Institution of Washington (2); NASA Photographs (2);
296-297 FB;
298 FB; 299 Wilbur S. Tripp, FB (2); 300 map reproduced by permission of the Surveys and Mapping Branch, Department of Energy, Mines and Resources, Ottawa;
302-303 Pierre Léveillé;
304 map reproduced by permission of the Department of Rare Books and Special Collections of the McGill University Libraries.

Color separation: Prolith Incorporated
Typesetting: Fast Typesetters of Canada Limited
Printing: Montreal Lithographing Ltd.
Binding: Volumex Limited
Binding material: Payne-Jones Inc.
Paper: Rolland Paper Company Limited